The Longman Writer

Rhetoric, Reader, Research Guide, and Handbook

TENTH EDITION

Judith Nadell

John Langan

with contributions from

Deborah Coxwell-Teague
Florida State University

New York, NY

VP & Portfolio Manager: Eric Stano
Development Editor: Steven Rigolosi
Marketing Manager: Nick Bolte
Program Manager: Rachel Harbour
Project Manager: Integra
Cover Designer: Pentagram
Cover Illustration: Anuj Shrestha
Manufacturing Buyer: Roy L. Pickering, Jr.
Printer and Binder: LSC Communications
Cover Printer: Lehigh-Phoenix Color/Hagarstown

Acknowledgments of third-party content appear on pages 583–586, which constitute an extension of this copyright page.

Library of Congress Cataloging-in-Publication Data
Names: Nadell, Judith, author. | Langan, John, author. | Coxwell-Teague, Deborah, author.
Title: The Longman writer: rhetoric, reader, research guide, and handbook /
Judith Nadell, John Langan, Deborah Coxwell-Teague.
Description: Tenth edition. | New York, NY: Pearson Education,
[2018] | Includes index.
Identifiers: LCCN 2016047708 | ISBN 9780134407647 (student edition) | ISBN 9780134408453 (brief edition)
Subjects: LCSH: English language—Rhetoric—Handbooks, manuals, etc. | Report
writing—Handbooks, manuals, etc. | College readers.
Classification: LCC PE1408 .N188 2018 | DDC 808/.042—dc23
LC record available at https://lccn.loc.gov/2016047708

2   17

www.pearsonhighered.com

Student Edition ISBN 10:   0-134-40764-4
Student Edition ISBN 13: 978-0-13440764-7
A la Carte ISBN 10:   0-134-40807-1
A la Carte ISBN 13: 978-0-13440807-1

Contents

Preface

*T*he *Longman Writer* brings together equal parts product and process. We describe possible sequences and structures to stress the connection between reading and writing, and we emphasize that these steps and formats should be viewed as strategies, not rigid prescriptions, for helping students discover what works best for them. This flexibility ensures that *The Longman Writer* can fit a wide range of teaching philosophies and learning styles.

The Longman Writer includes everything that students and instructors need in a one- or two-semester, first-year composition course: (1) a comprehensive *rhetoric*, including chapters on each stage of the writing process and discussions of the essay exam and literary paper; (2) a *reader* with *professional selections* and *student essays* integrated into the rhetoric; (3) a *research guide*, with information on writing and properly documenting a research paper in both MLA and APA formats, including up-to-date guidelines based on the 8th edition of the *MLA Handbook* and the 6th edition of the *APA Publication Manual*; and (4) a concise, easy-to-use *handbook*. Throughout the text, we aim for a supportive, conversational tone that inspires students' confidence. Numerous *activities* and *writing assignments*—more than 500 in all—develop awareness of rhetorical choices and encourage students to explore a range of composing strategies.

What's New in the Tenth Edition

The tenth edition of *The Longman Writer* has been fully updated to provide helpful advice on academic writing, critical reading and thinking and the recursive stages of the writing process along with more in-depth coverage of the research process and new examples of student writing throughout.

An increased emphasis on academic writing is integrated into the chapters on the writing process (Part II) and throughout the chapters on the patterns of development and the research essay (Parts III–IV), with more professional selections including MLA and APA in-text references and works cited or reference lists.

The importance of reading and thinking critically is emphasized throughout the text, beginning in Chapter 1, "Becoming a Critical Reader and Thinker." Each chapter teaches students how to think critically during the composing process, including tips for thinking critically about the sources they might integrate in their essays.

A revised section on the writing process (Chapters 2–9) clearly illustrates the recursive stages students will move through as they craft an essay. The eight chapters follow a new student essay through the composing process, showing writers what they need to do during each step—from the time they receive the assignment to the day they submit the final draft.

Revised chapters on the research essay incorporate the guidelines in the *MLA Handbook*, 8th edition.

A revised, more thorough treatment of plagiarism includes discussion of intentional and unintentional plagiarism and "patchwork writing."

More complete coverage on writing the research essay includes an annotated bibliography to accompany a new sample student research essay in both MLA and APA formats.

All new student essays—twelve in all—cover a range of subjects, from academic (review of a piece of art) to personal (relationships) to political (gender equality). Many of the new student essays are written using third-person point of view, integrated sources, and illustrations including photos, charts, and graphs.

New professional selections range from those written by Hillary Rodham Clinton ("Remarks to the United Nations Fourth Conference on Women Plenary Session") to food columnist and TV personality Mark Bittman ("What Causes Weight Gain") to Chinese history professor Jeffrey M. Wasserstrom ("A Mickey Mouse Approach to Globalization").

The Book's Plan

Part I, "The Reading Process," provides guidance in a three-step process for text and images in which students learn the importance of developing critical reading skills.

Part II, "The Writing Process," takes students, step by step, through a multistage composing sequence. Each chapter presents a stage of the writing process and includes:

- Checklists that summarize key concepts and keep students focused on the essentials as they write.
- Diagrams that encapsulate the writing process, providing at-a-glance references as students compose their own essays.
- Activities that reinforce pivotal skills and involve students in writing from the start, showing them how to take their papers through successive stages in the composing process.

Part III, "The Patterns of Development," covers nine patterns: description, narration, illustration, division-classification, process analysis, comparison-contrast, cause-effect, definition, and argumentation-persuasion. Each chapter contains a detailed explanation of the pattern, as well as the following:

- *Checklists* for prewriting and revising summarize key concepts and keep students focused on the essentials as they write.
- *Diagrams* encapsulate the patterns of development, providing at-a-glance references as students compose their own essays.
- *Annotated student essays* clearly illustrate each pattern of development. Commentary following each essay points out the blend of patterns in the paper and identifies both the paper's strengths and areas that need improvement.

- *Prewriting* and *Revising Activities* ask students to generate raw material for an essay, help them to see that the essay may include more than one pattern of development, and allow students to rework and strengthen paragraphs and examine and experiment with rhetorical options.
- *Professional selections* represent not only a specific pattern of development, but also showcase a variety of subjects, tones, and points of view. Extensive apparatus accompanies each professional selection.
  - *Biographical notes* provide background on every professional author and create an interest in each piece of writing.
  - *Pre-Reading Journal Entries* prime students for each professional selection by encouraging them to explore their thoughts about an issue.
  - *Diagrams* outline the structure of professional readings and provide students with an easy reference for identifying each pattern of development.
  - *Questions for Critical Reading* help students to interpret each selection, while *Questions About the Writer's Craft* ask students to analyze a writer's use of patterns.
  - *Writing Assignments* ask students to write essays using the same pattern as in the selection, to write essays that include other patterns, and to conduct research.
- End-of-chapter *General Assignments, Assignments Using Multimedia,* and *Assignments with a Specific Purpose, Audience, and Point of View* provide open-ended topics for students to explore and applications of rhetorical context to real-world settings.

Part IV, "The Research Essay," discusses how to locate, evaluate, analyze, synthesize, integrate, and document electronic and print sources for a research paper and includes the following:

- *Checklists* summarize key concepts and keep students focused on essentials as they select a research topic, evaluate sources, write and revise a research essay, and create their bibliography.

- *Source Samples* provide concrete examples of how students can locate all the necessary components of an MLA citation by presenting the actual source and its corresponding citation.
- *Activities* ensure mastery of key research skills.

Part V, "The Literary Essay and Essay Exam," shows students how to adapt the composing process to fit the requirements of two highly specific writing situations.

Part VI, "A Concise Handbook," provides easy-to-grasp explanations of the most troublesome areas of grammar, punctuation, and spelling that students encounter.

Marginal icons alert students and instructors to unique elements of this book:

- In Part II, student writing in progress is indicated with 🖮.
- In Part III, assignments that are conducive to using the library or Internet are indicated with ✐.
- In Parts II–V, ethical issues are indicated with ⚖.
- In Parts II, III, and V, combined patterns of development are indicated with 🐾.

Supplements

REVEL™

Educational Technology Designed for the Way Today's Students Read, Think, and Learn

When students are engaged deeply, they learn more effectively and perform better in their courses. This simple fact inspired the creation of REVEL: an interactive learning environment designed for the way today's students read, think, and learn.

REVEL enlivens course content with media interactives and assessments—integrated directly within the authors' narrative—that provide opportunities for students to read, practice, and study in one continuous experience. This immersive educational technology replaces the textbook and is designed to measurably boost students' understanding, retention, and preparedness.

Learn more about REVEL

http://www.pearsonhighered.com/revel/

Acknowledgments

Many writing instructors have reviewed *The Longman Writer*, and their practical comments guided our work every step of the way. To the following reviewers we are indeed grateful: Nina Beaver, Crowder College; Ken Bishop, Itawamba Community College; Ann Bukowski, Bluegrass Community and Technical College; Philip Wayne Corbett, South University Columbia; Denise Dube, Hill College; Wynora W. Freeman, Shelton State Community College; Virginia Armiger Grant, Gaston College; Carolyn Horner, South University; Rick Kmetz, South University; Jacquelyn Markham, South University; and Jeannine Morgan, St. Johns River State College.

We are most indebted to Deborah Coxwell-Teague of Florida State University for her significant, conscientious, and expert contributions to the tenth edition, including the selection of new and contemporary readings; new questions and activities; a new emphasis on incorporating visuals and sources; a thoroughly reimagined treatment of the research process with expanded discussion of analyzing, evaluating and synthesizing sources; and even new chapter-opening images.

To both sides of the families of Judy Nadell and John Langan go affectionate thanks for being so supportive of our work. Finally, we're grateful to our students. Their candid reactions to various drafts of the text sharpened our thinking and kept us honest. We're especially indebted to the students whose work is included in this book. Their essays illustrate dramatically the potential and the power of student writing.

Judith Nadell

John Langan

Chapter 1
Becoming a Critical Reader and Thinker

 ## Learning Objectives

1.1 Read, annotate, and critically evaluate texts.

1.2 Read, annotate, and critically evaluate visuals.

Why don't more people delight in reading? After all, most children feel great pleasure and pride when they first learn to read. As children grow older, though, the initially magical world of books is increasingly associated with homework, tests, and grades. Reading can turn into an anxiety-producing chore. No wonder some people end up avoiding it.

Nevertheless, people with this kind of negative experience can still find reading gratifying and enjoyable. The key is to be an active participant as a reader. Even a slick best seller requires the reader to decode and interpret what's on the page. In addition, many readings include visuals—images and graphics—that need to be explored and evaluated. Effective reading takes a little work, but the satisfactions of reading, whether for pleasure or information, more than reward any effort involved.

As a college student, you are expected to think critically about the words and images you read. You need to adopt a questioning attitude and interact with the ideas presented in the text. As you read, make a habit of asking yourself the following questions:

- What is the purpose of the text?
- How is it organized?
- Who is the author, and what are his or her credentials?
- Who is the intended audience?
- How is the text structured?

Asking yourself these questions will help you become an active reader rather than a passive one.

Also keep in mind that you will encounter difficult texts that require more than one reading. Not understanding a text the first time you read it doesn't mean that you're not smart or not a "good reader." Don't give up if you read a passage and don't understand what you've read. That happens to all college students. Texts that present unfamiliar ideas and those that use complex, seemingly convoluted sentence structures quite often require repeated reading. So do texts that use vocabulary you don't understand. Instead of becoming frustrated and giving up when you don't understand a passage, realize that you need to check the meaning of unfamiliar words and read the passage again. When you make a little extra effort, the ideas in the text will begin to make sense to you.

Reading, Annotating, and Critically Evaluating Texts

1.1 Read, annotate, and critically evaluate texts.

The three-stage approach discussed in the following sections will help you get the most out of the readings in this book as well as any other readings, including those with visual aids. See in particular the checklists that follow each stage, and use them each time you read.

Stage 1: Get an Overview of the Selection

Ideally, you should get settled in a quiet place that encourages concentration. If you can focus your attention while sprawled on a bed or curled up in a chair, that's fine. But if you find that being too comfortable is more conducive to daydreaming and dozing off than it is to studying, sit at a desk or table instead. If you're reading on a computer screen, tablet, or e-book reader, make sure you've adjusted the type size, font, and other features so that you're comfortable.

Once you're settled, it's time to read the selection. To ensure a good first reading, try the following hints.

☑ First Reading: A Checklist

☐ Get an overview of the essay and its author. Start by checking out the author's credentials. If a biographical note precedes the selection, as in this book, you'll want to read it for background information that will help you critically evaluate the writer's credibility as well as his or her slant on the subject. For other materials, do a computer search for information on the author and the publication or website where the reading appears.

☐ Consider the title. A good title often expresses the selection's main idea, giving you insight into the selection even before you read it.

☐ Read the selection straight through purely for pleasure. Allow yourself to be drawn into the world the author has created. Because you bring your own experiences and viewpoints to the piece, your reading will be unique.

☐ If a reading has visual aids, ask yourself the following questions, which will help you think critically about what you're seeing: Who created the visual? Is the source reliable? What does the caption say? If the visual is an image (such as a photograph), what general mood, feeling, or other impression does it convey? If it is a graphic (such as a graph or chart), is information clearly labeled and presented?

☐ After this initial reading of the selection, briefly describe the piece and your reaction to it.

Stage 2: Deepen Your Sense of the Selection

At this point, you're ready to move more deeply into the selection and to think more critically about it. A second reading will help you identify the specific features that triggered your initial reaction.

You can use several techniques during this second, more focused reading. Mortimer Adler, a well-known writer and editor, argued passionately for marking up the material we read. The physical act of annotating, he believed, etches the writer's ideas more sharply in the mind, helping readers grasp and remember those ideas more easily. Adler also described various annotation techniques he used when reading. The following checklist presents several of these techniques, adapted somewhat to reflect our critical reading of both print and digital texts.

☑ Second Reading: A Checklist

Using a pen (or pencil) and highlighter for print texts—or digital commenting and highlighting features if you're reading online—you might …

☐ Underline or highlight the selection's main idea, or *thesis*, often found near the beginning or end. If the thesis isn't stated explicitly, write down your own version of the selection's main idea. If you're reading the selection online, you might add a digital sticky note or comment with your version of the thesis.

☐ Locate the main supporting evidence used to develop the thesis. Number the key supporting points by writing in the margin or adding digital sticky notes.

☐ Circle or put an asterisk next to key ideas that are stated more than once.

☐ Take a minute to write "Yes" or "No" or to insert these comments digitally beside points with which you strongly agree or disagree. Your critical reaction to these points often explains your feelings about the selection's key ideas.

☐ Return to any unclear passages you encountered during the first reading. The feeling you now have for the piece as a whole will probably help you make sense of initially confusing spots. You may find yourself able to make *inferences* that you were unable to make during the first reading, making connections and "reading between the lines" in a way that you were not able to do earlier. You may also be able to use *context clues* to determine the meanings of some words you weren't sure you understood the first time you read the passage. As you think critically about the selection, you may also discover that the writer's thinking isn't as clear as it could be.

☐ Use a print or online dictionary to check the meanings of any words of whose meaning you're unsure.

☐ Take some quick notes about any visuals. If you're reading online, you might choose to make digital comments. As you think critically about the visuals, ask yourself the following questions: What is the author's purpose? Do the images tell a story? Do they make assumptions about viewers' beliefs or knowledge? What elements stand out? How do the colors and composition (arrangement of elements) work to convey an impression? Are any graphs and similar visuals adequately discussed in the text? Is the information current and presented without distortion? Is it relevant to the text discussion?

☐ If your initial impression of the selection has changed in any way, try to determine why you reacted differently on this reading.

Stage 3: Critically Evaluate the Selection

Now that you have a good grasp of the selection, you may want to read it a third time, especially if the piece is long or complex. This time, your goal is to make critical judgments about the selection's effectiveness. Keep in mind, though, that you shouldn't evaluate the selection until after you have a strong hold on it. Whether positive or negative, any reaction is valid only if it's based on an accurate reading.

To evaluate the selection, ask yourself the following questions.

☑ **Critically Evaluating a Selection: A Checklist**

☐ *Where does support for the selection's thesis seem logical and sufficient? Where does support seem weak?* Which of the author's supporting facts, arguments, and examples seem pertinent and convincing? Which don't?

☐ *Is the selection unified? If not, why not?* Where are there any unnecessary digressions or detours?

☐ *How does the writer make the selection move smoothly from beginning to end?* Are any parts of the selection abrupt and jarring? Which ones?

☐ *Which stylistic devices are used to good effect in the selection?* How do paragraph development, sentence structure, word choice *(diction)*, and tone contribute to the piece's overall effect? Where does the writer use figures of speech effectively?

☐ *How do any visuals improve the reading and support the writer's main points?* Are the visuals adequately discussed in the text? Are images such as photos thought-provoking without being sensationalistic? Do graphs and similar visual aids provide relevant, persuasive details?

☐ *How does the selection encourage further thought?* What new perspective on an issue does the writer provide? What ideas has the selection prompted you to explore in an essay of your own?

Critically Assessing Visuals in a Reading

1.2 Read, annotate, and critically evaluate visuals.

Writers may use visuals—images and graphics—to help convey their message. You can incorporate your critical "reading" of these visuals into the three-stage process you use for reading a text: In stage 1, *preview* the visuals at the same time that you get an overview of the text. In stage 2, *analyze and interpret* the visuals as a means of deepening your sense of the reading. Finally, in stage 3, *evaluate* the visuals as part of your evaluation of the entire selection.

Some common visual aids you are likely to see are listed in the table below. Following this list are two examples of critical assessment using the three-stage process.

Illustrations

- Photographs, paintings, drawings, and prints — Illustrate a particular scene, time period, activity, event, idea, or person.
- Cartoons and comics — May make a joke, comment on a situation, or tell a story.

Graphics

- Tables — Use columns and rows to present information, especially specific numbers, concisely.
- Bar graphs — Use rectangular bars of different sizes to compare information about two or more items.
- Line graphs — Use horizontal lines moving from point to point to show changes over time.
- Pie charts — Use a circle divided into wedges to show proportions.
- Charts and diagrams — Use different shapes and lines to show flow of information, organization of a group, layouts such as room plans, or assembly instructions.
- Maps — Present information by geographical location.

Photos, paintings, and similar illustrations may appear in webpages, periodicals, books, and advertisements. Graphics regularly appear in academic, technical, and business writing. You can critically evaluate all these visuals just as you would print text.

Critically Assessing an Image: An Example

Suppose a reading aims to persuade readers that the international community must set up an organization that stands ready to implement an immediate and coordinated response to natural disasters, no matter where they occur. The reading includes a photo (shown here) taken in the aftermath of the magnitude 7.5 Hindu Kush earthquake that hit South Asia on October 26, 2015. How can we critically evaluate this image and its effectiveness?

1. **Previewing the photo.** If we saw that the photo was found at *Time* magazine online and was taken by a photographer for the Associated Press (AP), we could assume that both are reliable sources that we could trust. As we preview the photo, we would see that the author of the selection has written a caption that clearly explains the image, and the phrase *Using whatever implements are at their disposal* supports the author's point that an immediate response is needed. We also notice, however, that the caption uses strong language: *catastrophic* and *devastated*. Information in the reading would have to support the use of these terms as it explains the extent of the damage caused by this powerful earthquake. Still, our first response to the photo would be one of sympathy and compassion for the people of South Asia.

2. **Critically analyzing and interpreting the photo.** The photo tells a story of people coming together to help one another in the aftermath of the earthquake. The elements in the photo are arranged so that we first see people in the foreground,

Using whatever implements are at their disposal, individuals search through the rubble that resulted from the catastrophic Hindu Kush earthquake that devastated parts of South Asia on October 26, 2015.

blanketed in dark shadows, and others in the background, standing in sunlight. Then we see piles of rubble from the remains of the crumbled structure and what is left of whitewashed walls, some bathed in sunlight, with blue sky overhead. We realize that this pile of rubble might have been the home of one or more of the individuals we see in the photo, and we wonder if they are searching for missing family members. Now we begin to understand the scope of the devastation. We can see both determination and a sense of disbelief in the people's faces as they cope with the disaster. We sympathize with their plight as they go about the urgent task of finding what might be buried in the rubble.

3. **Critically evaluating the photo.** The photo powerfully illustrates the scale of the work facing South Asia and the probable inadequacy of the people's resources. The contrast between the destroyed building and the determined workers conveys a sense of the hopefulness of the human spirit even in dire situations. Many readers will feel an emotional response to these people, will see that they need help, and will want to help them. The photo and caption together, therefore, successfully support the idea that some countries may not have the means to cope effectively with huge natural disasters. The text of the reading will have to convince the reader that setting up an international organization to coordinate responses to these crises is the right solution.

Critically Assessing a Graph: An Example

Imagine that a reading's purpose is to show how changes in behavior have affected the health of the U.S. population since 1960. The article includes the bar graph in Figure 1.1. How can we approach this graphic element and assess its usefulness to the reader?

1. **Previewing the graph.** We see right away that the authors have created a bar graph that shows the effects on life expectancy of six changes in behavior (smoking, motor vehicle fatalities, heavy drinking, obesity, poisonings, and firearm deaths) from 1960 to 2010. The graph is clearly labeled, and a full caption tells us that the information is from reliable sources—the National Health Interview Survey and the National Health and Nutrition Examination Survey.

2. **Critically analyzing and interpreting the graph.** The source's date tells us that the information is not only reliable but also current. The graph clearly shows that declines in smoking and increases in obesity are the two factors that have had the greatest impact on changes in life expectancy, while decreases in motor vehicle fatalities and increases in poisonings have played less dramatic roles. We also see that slight decreases in heavy drinking and slight increases in firearm deaths have affected life expectancy. What we can't determine from analyzing the graph is the role that various factors played in the increases and decreases shown. For example, we don't know whether the significant decrease in the number of motor vehicle fatalities can be attributed to safer driving habits or to improvements in air bags, safer roads, and enforcement of seat belt laws. We can conclude, however, that

Figure 1.1   The Impact of Behavioral Changes on Life Expectancy, 1960–2010

SOURCE: Figure by Courtney Coile, summarizing research by Susan Stewart and David Cutler. "How Behavioral Changes Have Affected U.S. Population Health Since 1960." National Bureau of Economic Research Bulletin on Aging and Health (1): 1–2.

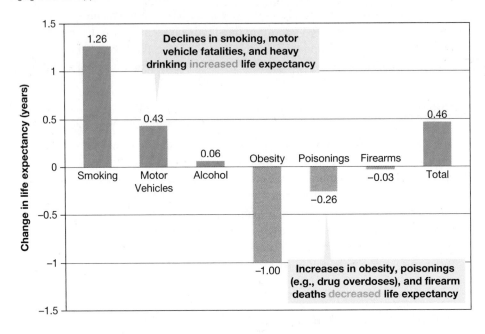

while some changes in Americans' behavior have resulted in longer life expectancies (decreases in smoking, motor vehicle fatalities, and heavy drinking), other behaviors (obesity, poisonings, and firearm deaths) have had the opposite effect, with an overall increase of .046 years in life expectancy between 1960 and 2010.

3. **Critically evaluating the graph.** Without being sensationalistic, the graph is striking. It effectively dramatizes the point that behavior plays a major role in life expectancy. The bar graph shows that while Americans are moving in the right direction with fewer of us smoking, being killed in vehicle accidents, and drinking heavily, an increasing number of us are obese, and more of us are dying from poisonings and being shot by firearms.

A Model Annotated Reading

To illustrate the multi-stage reading process, we've annotated the professional essay that follows: Larry Rosen's "Our Obsessive Relationship with Technology." As you read Rosen's essay, try applying the three-stage sequence. You can measure your ability to dig into the selection by making your own annotations on Rosen's essay and then comparing them with ours. You can also see how well you evaluated the piece by answering the questions in "Critically Evaluating a Selection: A Checklist" on page 5 and then comparing your responses with ours on pages 12–13.

LARRY ROSEN

Professor of Psychology at California State University, Larry Rosen is considered an expert in the psychology of technology. His major areas of research include the impacts of multitasking, social networking, and texting. He has been a commentator on *Good Morning America*, *NPR*, and *CNN*, and he has been quoted widely in a variety of publications including *USA Today*, *The New York Times*, and *Newsweek*.

Pre-Reading Journal Entry

Technology is often blamed for having harmful effects. Do you think this criticism is merited? In what ways does technology in general, or a specific kind of technology that especially interests you, exert a negative influence? In what ways does it exert a positive influence? Take a few minutes to respond to these questions in your journal.

Our Obsessive Relationship with Technology

Using a casual tone, Rosen establishes his credentials and shares his positive view of the overall effects of technology.

I am an inveterate people watcher, which is probably why I started college thinking that I was going to be a math teacher and ended up getting my degrees in psychology. For the past 30+ years, as I have studied the "psychology of technology," I have always taken a strongly positive view about the impact it has on our culture, and all of my writing has been in service of seeing how we can make the most of these marvelous inventions. From the beginnings of the Internet, to the rapid rise of the WWW, laptops, smartphones, tablets and more, we now have the world at our fingertips whenever we want and wherever we might find ourselves.   1

Transition from Rosen's overall positive view of effects of technology to his concerns about our relationships with our smartphones.

Rosen explores the difference between an "obsession" and an "addiction."

Author establishes thesis: We are obsessed with—not addicted to—technology.

Lately, however, I have witnessed something that profoundly troubles me. WE CAN'T SEEM TO KEEP OUR FACES OUT OF OUR SMARTPHONES FOR EVEN A MINUTE OR TWO. Some people call it an addiction. Others call it an obsession. But, there is an important difference between the two. Addiction means that you are trying to get your brain to release neurotransmitters that we have learned signal a pleasurable experience. Obsession also involves neurotransmitters, but those chemicals are associated with symptoms of stress and anxiety. When we are addicted to something, we strive for the pleasure it brings. When we are obsessed with something, we strive to reduce the anxiety molecules in our brain. Personally, I think that our constant obsession with technology—obsession being an anxiety-based disorder—is mostly about reducing anxiety and very little about gaining pleasure. Just as Jack Nicholson kept doing repetitive activities in *As Good As It Gets*, we seem to be doing the same with our smartphones.   2

For example, how many times have you seen someone   3
pat their pocket and smile, having been reassured that their
phone was still safely nestled close at hand? How often have
you experienced "phantom pocket vibrations" where you
felt a tingling near your pocket area—or wherever you keep
your phone—only to discover that rather than the alert or
notification you "thought" you just received, what you felt
was just some neurons near the surface of your skin randomly
firing? A few years ago I would have just reached down and
scratched that itch. Now I am supremely disappointed that it
is only an itch.

Walking around Times Square on vacation, I could not   4
find one person who was not gazing into a phone, even those
who were traveling with others. My friends around the world
tell me that they see the same behaviors. The other day in the
dining room at my campus, I watched a young woman eating
lunch with her supervisor pick up her phone while he was talking and check her email. And the more interesting part is that
he kept on talking to her and didn't seem slighted at all.

Last summer I took a road trip with my youngest daugh-   5
ter and visited some of the most beautiful scenery in the US,
traversing four western national parks. One day we hiked all
the way up to Inspiration Point, only to find that since there
was a cell tower up there, nearly every hiker was looking down
rather than out at the magnificent vista. And those who were
looking were busily snapping pictures instead of simply looking and experiencing the magnificent views. I doubt whether
they can have the same experience of nature through that small
lens. Will those who were taking videos get the same enjoy-
ment by reliving the views rather than experiencing them? Will
they even watch those videos again?

Another interesting and somewhat troubling observation   6
is that many young people, and a lot of older ones too, carry
their phone in their hand. I often ask them why and the answer
is always the same: "So I know immediately when I get a text
or an email or someone posts on social media." I guess taking a
second or two to take that phone out of a pocket or purse is not
soon enough in our tech-rich world.

And I find it amusing (and somewhat disconcerting) that   7
people make excuses to escape whoever they are supposed to
be spending time with so that they can check in with other people who may not even be real-life friends. I like going out to
dinner with friends and am bewildered at how many people
put their phone on the table, and if it vibrates, they interrupt
whatever is going on to tap a few keys and return to the conversation often asking, "What did I miss?" Some people call
this FOMO—Fear of Missing Out—but by choosing to not miss

Brief real-life examples and observations support thesis

More examples, observations, and reflections

Additional personal examples, observations, and reflections that support the thesis

Personal observation and reflection that supports thesis

Additional personal observations and reflections that support the thesis out on their virtual social world they are missing out on their real social world right in front of their face.

8   Another view of our obsession is evident as bedtime nears. People use their phones right up until they turn out the lights, even though all of the research shows that this leads to suppression of melatonin and difficulty sleeping. Three fourths of teens and young adults sleep with their phone next to their bed, either with the sound on or on vibrate, and awaken several times a night to check incoming alerts. This disrupts our sleep cycle, which then impairs the all-important processes that our brain requires for its nightly housekeeping.

9   I am still a believer in the major benefits technology brings to our world, but I sincerely hope that what we are seeing is just another pendulum swing where we become so excited about something new that we want to use it obsessively, and as time passes we become less captivated and use it less often until the next new thing comes into our world and the pendulum swings again. But the observer in me shakes his head and wonders whether the pendulum has reached its apex yet and, if not, what that will do to our relationship with the world and the "real" people who inhabit it. I remain optimistic.

> Rosen makes a general reference to research findings that support his thesis.
>
> Specific source of information?
>
> Author returns to the view of technology shared in first introductory paragraph.
>
> Rosen looks to the future, shares his concerns, and ends on a positive note.

Thesis: After providing background information in the opening paragraph and exploring the difference between the meanings of the words *addiction* and *obsession* in paragraph 2, Rosen states his thesis close to the end of the second paragraph: "Personally, I think that our constant obsession with technology—obsession being an anxiety-based disorder—is mostly about reducing anxiety and very little about gaining pleasure."

First Reading: Rosen provides a quick take on a potentially serious subject to which most readers can relate. His informal tone and use of extensive examples get to the heart of the technology-as-obsession issue.

Second and Third Readings:

1. In addition to including responses from various individuals regarding their use of smartphones, as well as a reference to research that has been conducted, Rosen uses a number of personal examples, observations, and reflections to illustrate our widespread obsessive relationship with smartphones.

2. Rosen uses *illustration* with his extensive use of examples to support his thesis. He also uses both *comparison/contrast* and *definition* in his explanation of the difference between the terms *addiction* and *obsession*, along with description and narration in the various examples he includes.

3. While the essay succeeds overall, Rosen could have made a stronger case for his thesis if he had included references to specific research. In paragraph 8, he refers to "all of the research." What specific research?

4. At first, the ending might seem weak with the closing statement: "I remain optimistic." But after a second reading, it becomes clear that in his conclusion, Rosen is returning to an idea in the introduction regarding his positive view of technology's impact on our culture. He brings his essay to closure by returning to that idea and making clear that

despite his concern with our obsessive relationship with smartphones, he is hopeful that as time passes we will "become less captivated" with our new technology.

The following questions and answers will help crystallize your reaction to Rosen's essay.

1. **Where does support for the selection's thesis seem logical and sufficient? Where does support seem weak?** Rosen begins to provide evidence for his thesis in his description of people keeping their smartphones in their pockets so they can feel them vibrate (paragraph 3). He further buoys his thesis with examples of the crowd in Times Square, all on their phones (4); a young woman on her phone while at lunch with her supervisor (4); and hikers in a national park who are attached to their phones (5). Rosen also uses general examples from others, including his "friends around the world" (4), nameless young and older people he questions (6), friends with whom he goes out to dinner (7), and research in general (8). However, his support would be stronger if he included specific references to research from other reputable sources to support his thesis.

2. **Is the selection unified? If not, why not?** In the first two paragraphs, Rosen provides background information to establish his credentials and state his thesis. However, after stating his thesis near the end of the second paragraph, he includes what could be considered a distracting and puzzling reference to *As Good As It Gets*, a film starring Jack Nicholson. Rosen seems to assume that his audience is familiar with the film and will understand the connection he makes between the film's main character and his thesis. He then provides numerous examples in paragraphs 3–8 to convince his readers that many of us are truly obsessed with technology and that our obsession is " … mostly about reducing anxiety and very little about gaining pleasure" (paragraph 2). In the concluding paragraph, Rosen returns to an idea he stated in the introduction regarding his overall positive view of technology, but he adds that he wonders how our obsession with technology will affect "our relationship with the world and the 'real' people who inhabit it."

3. **How does the writer make the selection move smoothly from beginning to end?** The first two paragraphs of Rosen's essay are clearly connected. The phrase *Lately, however* at the beginning of the second paragraph signals the reader that Rosen is about to contrast the ideas in the preceding paragraph with those to come. While his reference at the end of the second paragraph to a film with which some readers might not be familiar could be distracting, Rosen gets back on course at the beginning of the third paragraph. He uses the phrase *For example* to let readers know he is about to provide evidence to support his thesis. Then at the beginning of paragraphs 6–8, Rosen uses the connecting words *Another* and *And* to move readers smoothly along from one example to another and then to the essay's conclusion.

4. **Which stylistic devices are used to good effect in the selection?** Rosen uses several patterns of development in his essay. The selection as a whole *illustrates* the obsession many individuals have with technology. In the two introductory paragraphs, Rosen *contrasts* his overall positive view of the effects of technology with his concerns about the constant need to have smartphones available at all times. In the second paragraph he *compares* and *contrasts* the terms *addiction* and *obsession*, and he also *defines* each term. Then in paragraphs 3–8, Rosen provides one *example* after another to provide support for his thesis, using both *description* and *narration* in the various examples. In the closing paragraph he *compares* his overall positive view of technology with his concerns about possible negative effects of our obsession. Throughout, Rosen's *informal, conversational tone* draws

readers in as he provides examples to which most readers can relate. These varied stylistic devices help make the essay a quick, easy read. Finally, although Rosen is concerned about possible negative effects of our obsession with technology, he lightens his essay by ending on a positive note: "I remain optimistic."

5. **How does the selection encourage further thought?** Rosen's essay focuses on an issue with which many, perhaps most, individuals can identify: smartphone obsession. His main concern is that our need to stay connected at all times could lead to negative effects on "our relationship with the world and the 'real' people who inhabit it" (paragraph 9). His presentation on the issue urges us to think more seriously about our obsession with technology and its possible negative effects on our lives.

Following are some sample questions and writing assignments based on the Rosen essay; all are similar to the sort that appear later in this book.

Questions for Critical Reading

1. According to Rosen, what is the difference between an *addiction* and an *obsession*? What reasons does he give for describing the relationship many individuals have with technology as an *obsession* rather than an *addiction*?

2. What does the acronym *FOMO* stand for, and what are Rosen's concerns about individuals who have this phobia?

Questions About the Writer's Craft

1. What kind of audience do you think Rosen is writing for? What clues does he provide in his essay that make you think he is writing for that audience?

2. Rosen uses numerous examples to convince his readers that many of us have a problematic relationship with technology. Which of his examples stands out to you as the most effective at proving his thesis, and why?

Writing Assignments

1. While stating his overall view that the effects of technology are positive, Rosen focuses his essay on the negative aspects of what he refers to as our *obsession* with technology. Write an essay in which you focus on the positive aspects of a particular technology such as smartphones or a social media platform (Facebook, Twitter, Instagram). Like Rosen, write using first-person point of view and incorporate examples from your own (and others') experiences to support your thesis.

2. Using first-person point of view and numerous personal examples, Rosen crafts an essay in which he shares his concerns about our obsessive relationship with technology. Write an essay in which you share similar or related concerns of your own. For example, you might write about possible negative effects of social networking sites, video games, or texting. Instead of writing in first person as Rosen does, use the third-person point of view. Consider including several outside sources to strengthen the effectiveness of your essay, and be sure to correctly document your sources.

Chapter 2
Getting Started Through Prewriting

∨ Learning Objectives

2.1 Use prewriting to generate ideas before composing a first draft.

2.2 Organize your ideas into a scratch outline that will make the writing process more manageable.

How do you typically react when a college instructor assigns an essay? Are you so excited that you can hardly wait to get started? Perhaps you are—if you are lucky enough to immediately think of what you want to say and how you want to say it. But for many people, putting pen or pencil to paper—or fingers to keyboard—is a little scary.

When you write, you put what's going on in your brain—your innermost thoughts—down for others to see. If they read what you've written and react positively (perhaps with a comment such as "Wow! You are an amazing writer!"), you feel wonderful. That reaction makes you feel validated as a student, as a thinker, and as a writer. But if your early drafts need a lot of improvement, don't despair. Imperfect early drafts don't mean that you're not smart or not a good writer. They *do* mean that, more often than not, writing is hard work, and the words don't simply pour perfectly and effortlessly out of your brain and onto the page or screen. Although your final draft will be engaging, interesting, and polished, chances are that your writing did not start out that way. Writing truly is a process, and you need to think carefully about the steps that will lead to a final draft that you are proud to share with your audience.

In this chapter and following chapters, we describe a sequence of steps (that is, a process) for writing essays. Familiarity with this sequence develops your awareness of strategies and choices, increasing your confidence when you write. You're less likely to look at a blank piece of paper and think, "Help! Now what do I do?" During the process, you do the following:

- Prewrite
- Identify your thesis
- Support the thesis with evidence
- Organize the evidence
- Write the paragraphs of the first draft
- Revise meaning, structure, and paragraph development
- Revise sentences and words
- Edit and proofread

We present the sequence as a series of steps, but we urge you not to view it as a formula that you must follow rigidly. Most people develop personalized approaches to the writing process. Some writers mull over a topic in their heads and then move quickly into a promising first draft; others outline their essays in detail before beginning to write. Between these two extremes are many effective approaches. The sequence here—illustrated in Figure 2.1—can be streamlined or otherwise altered to fit individual writing styles as well as the needs of specific assignments. You'll find that this sequence can help you not only as you compose essays for your English classes but also when you're composing in other *genres* (forms of writing) in your college courses and beyond.

Use Prewriting to Get Started

2.1 Use prewriting to generate ideas before composing a first draft.

Prewriting refers to strategies you can use to generate ideas *before* starting the first draft of a paper. (See Figure 2.1.) Because prewriting techniques encourage imaginative exploration, they also help you discover what interests you most about your subject. Having such a focus early in the writing process keeps you from plunging into your initial draft without first giving some thought to what you want to say. Prewriting thus saves you time in the long run by keeping you on course.

Prewriting can help in other ways, too. When we write, we often sabotage our ability to generate material because we continually critique what we put down on paper. During prewriting, you deliberately ignore your internal critic. Your purpose is simply to get ideas down on paper or on a computer screen *without evaluating* them.

One final advantage of prewriting: The random associations typical of prewriting tap the mind's ability to make unusual connections. You may stumble upon an interesting idea. Prewriting helps you appreciate—right from the start—this element of surprise in the writing process.

Keep a Journal

Of all the prewriting techniques, keeping a **journal** (daily or almost daily) is the one most likely to make writing a part of your life. No matter what format your journal takes—notebook or computer file—be sure to date all entries.

Some journal entries focus on a single theme; others wander from topic to topic. Your starting point may be a dream, a conversation, a video on YouTube, a political

Figure 2.1 Process Diagram: Prewriting

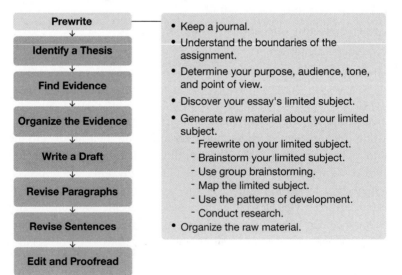

cartoon, an issue raised in class or in your reading—anything that surprises, interests, angers, depresses, confuses, or amuses you. You may also use a journal to experiment with your writing style—say, to vary your sentence structure if you tend to use predictable patterns.

Here is a fairly focused excerpt from a student's journal:

> Mom and Dad will be in town again this weekend for the football game, like they were last weekend and two weekends before that. I'm beginning to wonder if I made a smart choice when I made the decision to attend college here. I knew, of course, that Mom went to college here and that they brought me to lots of the games here while I was growing up. I loved that. But somehow I didn't realize that once I was a student here and they came up for the games, they would expect me to spend all weekend with them. At first it was fine. They took me shopping and out for great food, much better than what I eat on campus every day. And I'll admit I missed them when I first left home. And the fact that I'm an only child probably makes them miss me more than they would if there were other kids still at home with them. I understand all of that. But now I've made friends here and there's so much going on that I'm missing out on when Mom and Dad are around. Now they're talking about buying a three-bedroom condo here where I could live with a roommate and they could stay when they're in town visiting. This is not going the way I want it to go, and I don't know what to do. I don't want to hurt them. They love me. They miss me. They've done so much for me. But I know this situation is only going to get worse if I don't figure something out soon. (October 28)

The journal is a place for you to get in touch with the writer inside you. Although some instructors collect students' journals—done in notebooks or through an online course management system or a blog set up for the class—you needn't be overly concerned with spelling, grammar, sentence structure, or organization, unless your instructor tells you otherwise. Although journal writing is typically more structured than freewriting (discussed later in this chapter), you usually don't have to strive for entries that read like mini-essays. In fact, sometimes you may find it helpful to use a simple list to record your thoughts. The important thing is to use your journal to stimulate reflection and new insights that provide you with material to use in your writing. For this reason, it is a good idea to reread each week's entries to identify recurring themes and concerns. Keep a list of these issues at the back of your journal, under a heading such as "Possible Essay Subjects." For instance, here are a few topics suggested by the preceding journal entry: deciding which college to attend, leaving home, being an only child. Each of these topics could be developed into a full-length essay.

The Pre-Reading Journal Entry

To reinforce the value of journal writing, we've included a journal assignment before each reading selection in this book. This assignment, called *Pre-Reading Journal Entry*, encourages you to explore—in a tentative fashion—your thoughts about an issue that will be raised in the selection. Here, once again, is the

Pre-Reading Journal Entry assignment that precedes Larry Rosen's "Our Obsessive Relationship with Technology":

> Technology is often blamed for having harmful effects. Do you think this criticism is merited? In what ways does technology in general, or a specific technology that especially interests you, exert a negative influence? In what ways does it exert a positive influence? Take a few minutes to respond to these questions in your journal.

The following journal entry shows how one student, Caylah Francis, responded to the journal assignment. An eighteen-year-old college student with two younger brothers who spend hours each week playing video games, Caylah was intrigued by the journal assignment; she decided to focus her journal entry on the negative and positive effects of playing video games. Caylah used a listing strategy to prepare her journal entry. She found that lists were perfect for dealing with the essentially "for or against" nature of the journal assignment:

Video Games' Negative Influence on Kids	**Video Games' Positive Influence on Kids**
Teaches negative behaviors (violence, sex, swearing, drugs, alcohol, etc.)	Teaches important problem solving skills
Cuts down on time spent doing fun things that don't involve sitting in front of a screen	Exposes kids to new images and worlds (*Skylanders, Disney Infinity*)
Cuts down on time spent with parents (talking, reading, playing board games together)	Can inspire discussions (about morals, sexuality, drugs, etc.) between kids and parents
Encourages parents' lack of involvement with kids	Gives parents a needed break from kids
Frightens kids excessively by showing images of real-life violence (terrorist attacks, war, murders, etc.)	Educates kids about the painful realities in the world
Encourages isolation (interacting with a screen rather than interacting with other kids face to face or in the same room)	Creates common ground among kids, basis for conversations about games
De-emphasizes reading and creates the need for constant stimulation	Sharpens eye-hand coordination skills and promotes faster reaction times
Cuts down on time spent playing outside and getting much-needed exercise	Keeps kids occupied in the safety of their homes instead of outside in a potentially dangerous environment

As you've just seen, journal writing can stimulate thinking in a loose, unstructured way; it can also prompt the focused thinking required by a specific writing assignment. When you have a specific piece to write, you should approach prewriting in a purposeful, focused manner. You need to:

- Understand the boundaries of the assignment.
- Determine your purpose, audience, tone, and point of view.
- Discover your essay's limited subject.
- Generate raw material about your limited subject.
- Conduct research.
- Organize the raw material into a scratch outline.

Understand the Boundaries of the Assignment

Before you start writing an essay, you need to know what your instructor expects. First, clarify the *kind* of composition the instructor has in mind. Suppose the instructor asks you to discuss the key ideas in an assigned reading. What does the instructor want you to do? Should you write a brief summary of the selection? Should you compare the author's ideas with your own views of the subject? Should you determine if the author's view is supported by valid evidence? If you're not sure about the details of an assignment, ask your instructor to make the requirements clear.

In particular, clarify whether your instructor expects you to consult outside sources (other pieces of writing) for your essay. If you are required to use sources, then be sure to find out the following:

- The number and kinds of sources you need to include in your essay
- Whether you need to use primary sources (material from interviews, surveys, or studies you conducted), secondary sources (material from research conducted by others), or both
- Whether you need to use books, magazines, journals, and/or other types of sources
- Whether you are expected to use print sources, online sources, or both
- The note-taking procedure your teacher expects you to use (for example, note cards, a research journal, or a research log)
- The required documentation style—for example, the style favored by the Modern Language Association (MLA) or the American Psychological Association (APA)
- Whether you need to include visuals to clarify or illustrate points you make in your essay and, if so, what kinds of visuals you should use (for example, graphs, charts, or photos)

You also need to find out anything else you need to know to effectively complete the assignment, including *how long* the paper should be. Many instructors indicate the approximate length of the compositions they assign. If no length requirements are provided, discuss with the instructor what you plan to cover and indicate how long you think your essay will be. The instructor will either give you the go-ahead or help you refine the direction and scope of your work.

Determine Your Purpose, Audience, Tone, and Point of View

Once you understand the requirements for a writing assignment, you're ready to begin thinking about the essay. What is its *purpose*? For what *audience* will you write it? What *tone* will you use? What *point of view* will be most effective? Later on, you may modify your decisions about these issues. That's fine. But you need to understand the way these considerations influence your work in the early phases of the writing process.

PURPOSE   Start by clarifying the essay's broad **purpose**. What do you want the essay to accomplish? The essays you write in college are usually meant to *inform* or *explain*, to *convince* or *persuade*, to *analyze* or *evaluate*, and sometimes to *entertain*. In practice, writing often combines purposes. You might, for example, write an essay trying to *convince* people to support a new trash recycling program in your community. But before you win readers over, you most likely would have to *explain* something about current waste-disposal technology.

When purposes blend in this way, the predominant one influences the essay's content, organization, pattern of development, emphasis, and language. Assume you're writing about a political campaign. If your primary goal is to *entertain*, to poke gentle fun at two candidates, you might use the comparison-contrast pattern to organize your essay. You might, for example, start with several accounts of one candidate's "foot-in-mouth disease" and then describe the attempts of the other candidate, a multimillionaire, to portray himself as an average Joe. Your language, full of exaggeration, would reflect your objective. But if your primary purpose is to *persuade* readers that the candidates are incompetent and shouldn't be elected, you might adopt a serious, straightforward style. Selecting the argumentation-persuasion pattern to structure the essay, you might use one candidate's gaffes and the other's posturings to build a case that neither is worthy of public office.

AUDIENCE   Writing is a social act and thus implies a reader or an **audience**. To write effectively, you need to identify who your readers are and to take their expectations and needs into account.

If you forget your readers, your essay can run into problems. Consider what happened when one student, an emergency medical technician, submitted a draft of his essay to his instructor for feedback. The assignment was to write about an experience that demonstrated the value of education. Here's the opening paragraph from his first draft:

> When I received my first page as an EMT, I realized pretty quickly that all the weeks of KED and CPR training paid off. At first, when the call came in, I was all nerves, I can tell you. When the heat is on, my mind tends to go as blank as an unplugged computer screen. But I beat it to the van right away. After a couple of false turns, my partner and I finally got the right house and found a woman fibrillating and suffering severe myocardial arrhythmia. Despite our anxiety, our heads were on straight; we knew exactly what to do.

The student's instructor found his essay unclear because she knew nothing about being an EMT (emergency medical technician). When writing the essay, he neglected to consider his audience. Specifically, he forgot that college instructors are no more knowledgeable than anyone else about subjects outside their specialty. His instructor also commented that she was put off by the essay's casual, slangy approach ("I was all nerves, I can tell you"; "I beat it to the van right away"). He used a breezy, colloquial style—almost as though he were chatting about the experience with friends—but the instructor had expected a more formal approach.

The more you know about your readers, the more you can adapt your writing to fit their needs and expectations. The following checklist will help you analyze your audience.

☑ Analyzing Your Audience: A Checklist

- ☐ What are my readers' ages, sex, and educational levels? How do these factors affect what I tell and don't tell them?
- ☐ What are my readers' political, religious, and other beliefs? How do these beliefs influence their attitudes and actions?
- ☐ What interests and needs motivate my audience?
- ☐ How much do my readers already know about my subject? Do they have any misconceptions?
- ☐ What biases do they have about me, my subject, and my opinion?
- ☐ How do my readers expect me to relate to them?
- ☐ What values do I share with my readers that will help me communicate with them?

TONE, SENTENCE STRUCTURE, AND WORD CHOICE Just as your voice may project a range of feelings, your writing can convey one or more **tones**, or emotional states: enthusiasm, anger, resignation, and so on. Tone is integral to meaning. It permeates writing and reflects your attitude toward yourself, your purpose, your subject, and your readers. In writing, how do you project tone? You pay close attention to *sentence structure* and *word choice*. In Chapter 8, we present detailed strategies for fine-tuning sentences and words during the revision stage. Here we simply want to help you see that determining your tone should come early in the writing process because the tone you select influences the sentences and words you use later.

Sentence structure refers to the way sentences are shaped. Although the following two paragraphs deal with exactly the same subject, note how differences in sentence structure create sharply dissimilar tones:

> During the 1960s, many inner-city minorities considered the police an occupying force and an oppressive agent of control. As a result, violence grew against police in poorer neighborhoods, as did the number of residents killed by police.

> An occupying force. An agent of control. An oppressor. That's how many inner-city minorities in the '60s viewed the police. Violence against police soared. Police killings of residents mounted.

Informative in its approach, the first paragraph projects a neutral, almost dispassionate tone. The sentences are fairly long, and clear transitions ("During the 1960s"; "As a result") mark the progression of thought. But the second paragraph, with its dramatic, almost alarmist tone, seems intended to elicit a strong emotional response. Its short sentences, fragments, and abrupt transitions reflect the turbulence of the 1960s.

Word choice also plays a role in establishing the tone of an essay. Words have **denotations**, neutral dictionary meanings, as well as **connotations**, emotional associations that go beyond the literal meaning. The word *beach,* for instance, is defined in the dictionary as "a nearly level stretch of pebbles and sand beside a body of water." However, this definition doesn't capture individual responses to the word. For some, *beach* suggests warmth and relaxation. For others, it calls up images of a once-clean stretch of shoreline ruined by an oil spill.

Because tone and meaning are tightly bound, you must be sensitive to the emotional nuances of words. In a respectful essay about police officers, you wouldn't refer to "cops," "narcs," or "flatfoots" because such terms convey a contempt inconsistent with the intended tone. Now suppose you're writing a satirical piece criticizing a local beauty pageant. Dubbing the participants "livestock on view" leaves no question about your tone and your approach to the topic. But if you simply refer to the participants as "attractive young women," readers might be unsure of your feelings about the pageant. Remember: Readers can't read your mind, only your words.

In most *academic writing*, the author is expected to use a formal tone. The casual language you use in conversation or text messages with a friend is almost never appropriate for the writing you'll do in your college classes. Your instructor might ask you not to use contractions, abbreviations, or slang. The sentence "You don't eat junk like donuts and puff pastries, just the healthy stuff, if you want a great bod" would not be appropriate in an academic essay. You might revise the sentence as follows: "Avoiding sugary treats and eating healthy foods such as whole grains, fruits, and vegetables is an important part of staying in shape." A good rule of thumb is to save informal language for informal situations.

POINT OF VIEW   When you write, you speak as a unique individual to your audience. **Point of view** reveals the person you decide to be as you write. Like tone, point of view is closely tied to your purpose, audience, and subject. Imagine you want to convey to students in your composition class the way your grandfather's death—on your eighth birthday—impressed you with life's fragility. To capture that day's impact on you, you might tell what happened from the point of view of a child: "Today is my birthday. I'm eight. Grandpa died an hour before I was supposed to have my party." Or you might choose instead to recount the event speaking as the adult you are today: "My grandfather died an hour before my eighth birthday party." Your point of view will affect the essay's content and organization.

The most strongly individualized point of view is the **first person** (*I, me, mine, we, us, our*). The first-person point of view is appropriate in narrative and descriptive essays based on personal experience. It also suits other types of essays (for example, causal analyses and process analyses) when the bulk of evidence presented consists of personal observation. In such essays, avoiding the first person often leads to stilted sentences like "There was strong parental opposition to the decision" or "Although organic chemistry had been dreaded, it became a passion." In contrast, the sentences sound much more natural when the first person is used: "*Our* parents strongly opposed the decision" and "Although *I* had dreaded organic chemistry, it became *my* passion."

In essays voicing an opinion, most first-person expressions ("I believe that..." and "In my opinion...") are unnecessary and distracting. The point of view is assumed to be the writer's unless another source is indicated.

In some situations, writers use the **second person** (*you, your, yours*), alone or in combination with the first person. For instance, "If *you're* the kind of person who doodles while thinking, *you* may want to try mapping..." rather than "If a *writer* is the kind of person who doodles while thinking, *he* or *she* may want to try mapping...." The second person simplifies style and involves the reader in a more personal way. You'll also find that the *imperative* form of the verb ("*Send* letters of protest to the television networks") engages readers in much the same way. The implied *you* speaks to the audience directly and lends immediacy to the directions. Despite these advantages, the second-person point of view isn't appropriate in many college courses, where more formal, less conversational writing is usually called for.

The **third-person** point of view is by far the most common in academic writing. The third person gets its name from the stance it conveys—that of an outsider or "third person" observing and reporting on matters of primarily public rather than private importance. In discussions of historical events, scientific phenomena, works of art, and the like, the third-person point of view conveys a feeling of distance and objectivity. Be careful not to adopt such a detached stance that you end up using a stiff, artificial style: "On this campus, approximately two-thirds of the student body is dependent on bicycles as the primary mode of transportation to class." Aim instead for a more natural and personable quality: "Two-thirds of the students on campus ride their bikes to class."

Discover Your Essay's Limited Subject

Once you have a firm grasp of the assignment's boundaries and have determined your purpose, audience, tone, and point of view, you're ready to focus on a **limited subject** of the general assignment. Too broad a subject can result in a rambling essay, so be sure to restrict your general subject before starting to write.

The following examples show the difference between general subjects that are too broad for an essay and limited subjects that are appropriate and workable.

General Subject	Less General	Limited Subject
Education	Computers in education	Computers in elementary school arithmetic classes
Transportation	Low-cost travel	Hitchhiking
Work	Planning for a career	College internships

How do you move from a general subject to a narrow subject? Imagine that you're asked to prepare a straightforward, informative essay for your writing class. The assignment is prompted by Larry Rosen's essay "Our Obsessive Relationship with Technology":

Using first-person point of view and numerous personal examples, Rosen crafts an essay in which he shares his concerns about our obsessive relationship with technology. Write an essay in which you share similar or related concerns of your own. For example, you might write about possible negative effects of social networking sites, video games, or texting. Instead of writing in first person as Rosen does, use the third-person point of view. Consider including several outside sources to strengthen the effectiveness of your essay, and be sure to correctly document your sources.

Keeping your purpose, audience, tone, and point of view in mind, your next step may be to **question** or **brainstorm** the general subject. Although the two techniques encourage you to roam freely over a subject, they also help restrict the discussion by revealing which aspects of the subject interest you most.

 QUESTION THE GENERAL SUBJECT   One way to narrow a subject is to ask a series of who, how, why, where, when, and what questions. The following example shows how Caylah Francis, an eighteen-year-old college student, used this technique to limit the Rosen assignment.

You may recall that, before reading Rosen's essay, Caylah used her journal to explore the topic by listing video games' effects on children. After reading "Our Obsessive Relationship with Technology," Caylah concluded that she agreed with much of what Rosen had to say: She felt that various forms of technology have become an obsession for many people and have brought about many negative effects. Caylah soon realized that she had to narrow the Rosen assignment. She started by asking a number of pointed questions about the general topic. She used the table feature on her computer to create boxes that she filled in. As she proceeded, she was aware that the same questions could have led to different limited subjects—just as other questions would have.

General Assignment: Write about the negative effects of technology.

Question	Limited Subject
<u>Who</u> is to blame for the negative effects of various technologies?	Parents give kids too much freedom to play violent video games.
<u>How</u> have schools contributed to the negative effects of technology?	Schools today rely too much on technology.
<u>Why</u> do kids get so wrapped up in things like social networking sites, video games, and texting?	Parents don't give kids enough time and attention.
<u>Where</u> can kids get the kind of guidance and advice they need about possible negative effects of technology?	Parents need to give kids more guidance and enforce limits.
<u>When</u> are children most vulnerable to the negative effects of technology?	Adolescents are especially vulnerable to the negative effects of technology.
<u>What</u> dangers related to technology should parents discuss with their children?	Dangers of texting and driving, sharing too much information on Facebook, becoming addicted to playing violent video games

BRAINSTORM THE GENERAL SUBJECT   Another way to focus on a limited subject is to list quickly everything about the general topic that pops into your mind. Write down brief words, phrases, and abbreviations that capture your free-floating thoughts. Writing in complete sentences will slow you down. Don't try to organize or censor your ideas. Even the most fleeting, random, or seemingly outrageous thoughts can be productive.

Here's an example of the brainstorming that Caylah Francis did in an effort to gather more material for the Rosen assignment.

General Subject: Technology has many negative effects.

People don't talk to each other

Spend too much time texting

Can't stand being away from their phones

Spend hours updating Facebook instead of going out with friends or exercising

Never take time to read books for fun

People think they can text while driving

Even kids obsessed with technology

Not enough guidance from parents

All Brandon and Josh want to do is play their violent video games

Dangers of playing violent video games

Are they obsessed or addicted to playing them

As you can see, questioning and brainstorming suggest many possible limited subjects. To identify especially promising ones, reread your material. What arouses your interest, anger, or curiosity? What themes seem to dominate and cut to the heart of the matter? Star or highlight ideas with potential. Pay close attention to material generated at the end of your questioning and brainstorming. Often your mind takes a few minutes to warm up, with the best ideas popping out last.

After marking the material, come up with several phrases or sentences that summarize the most promising limited subjects. Here are just a few that emerged from Caylah's questioning and brainstorming the Rosen assignment:

Danger of putting too much personal information on Facebook

Parents need to give their kids guidance and set limits to help them avoid negative effects of technology

Adults need to realize dangers of technology and set limits for themselves and their children

Violent video games especially harmful to kids today

Looking back at the work she did for her pre-reading journal assignment, Caylah decided to write on the last of these limited subjects. This topic, in turn, is the focus of our discussion in the rest of this chapter.

Generate Raw Material About Your Limited Subject

When a limited subject strikes you as having possibilities, your next step is to begin generating material about that topic. If you generate raw material now, during the prewriting stage, you'll find it easier to write the essay later on. Because you'll already have amassed much of the material for your composition, you'll be able to concentrate on other matters—for example, finding the right words to convey your ideas. Taking the time to explore your limited subject during the prewriting stage also means you won't find yourself halfway through the first draft without much to say.

To generate raw material, you may use *freewriting, brainstorming, mapping,* and other techniques.

FREEWRITE ON YOUR LIMITED SUBJECT Although freewriting can help you narrow a general subject, it's more valuable once you have limited your topic. **Freewriting** means jotting down in rough sentences or phrases everything that comes to mind.

To capture this continuous stream of thought, write or type nonstop for ten minutes or more. Don't reread, edit, or pay attention to organization, spelling, or grammar. If your mind goes blank, repeat words until another thought emerges.

Here is part of the freewriting that Caylah generated about her limited subject, "The harmful effects of playing violent video games":

> Kids today have tough problems to face. Lots of dangers. Lots of temptations. They see violence everywhere. The Internet first and foremost. Also crimes of violence against kids. Parents have to keep up with cost of living, everything costs more, kids want and expect more. My brothers sure expect and get more than I did when I was their age. Today, both parents almost always have full-time jobs. Parents have to work more hours than ever before to give their kids everything they need and want. Sometimes parents give in and buy them things that are not good for them. Like some of the games my brothers play. What were my parents thinking? Why would they buy those games for Brandon and Josh? Kids are left alone at home more than they ever were before. Kids grow up too fast, too fast. Kids grow up too fast, too fast. Drugs and alcohol. Witness real-life violence everywhere, like terrorist attacks and school shootings. Kids can't handle knowing too much at an early age. Both parents at work much of the day. Kids spend too much time at home alone. Can do pretty much anything they want when parents aren't around. Another problem is getting kids to do homework, lots of other things to do. Especially like texting friends or checking out the latest Facebook posts. When I was young, we did homework after dinner, no excuses accepted by my parents. My parents are sure a lot easier on my brothers than they were on me. That's not a good thing.

BRAINSTORM YOUR LIMITED SUBJECT Let your mind wander freely, as you did when narrowing your general subject. This time, though, list every idea, fact, and example that occurs to you about your limited subject. Use brief words and phrases, so you don't get bogged down writing full sentences. For now, don't worry whether ideas fit together or whether the points listed make sense.

To gather additional material on her limited subject for the Rosen assignment ("The harmful effects of playing violent video games"), Caylah brainstormed the following list:

Parents at work long hours

Kids left alone

Kids expect more and more things

Prices of things outrageous, even with both parents working

Ads make kids want more of everything

Clothes so important to kids today

Kids have too much freedom

Parents too permissive

Kids become addicted

Start acting like the characters in the games they play

Get in trouble for being aggressive at school and at home

Some kids become addicted to playing violent video games

Can't stop playing even when parents tell them to stop

Lie about playing

Health issues

Sit too much

Many become obese

Not enough fresh air and sunshine

Kids exposed to negative influences

Exposed to drugs

Exposed to profanity

Exposed to sex

USE GROUP BRAINSTORMING   Brainstorming with other people stretches the imagination, revealing possibilities you may not have considered on your own. Group brainstorming doesn't have to be conducted in a formal classroom. You can bounce ideas around with friends and family anywhere.

MAP THE LIMITED SUBJECT   If you're the kind of person who doodles while thinking, you may want to try **mapping**, sometimes called **diagramming** or **clustering**.

Begin by expressing your limited subject in a crisp phrase and placing it in the center of a blank sheet of paper. As ideas come to you, put them along lines or in boxes or circles around the limited subject. Draw arrows and lines to show the relationships among ideas. Don't stop there, however. Focus on each idea; as subpoints and details come to you, connect them to their source idea, again using boxes, lines, circles, or arrows to clarify how everything relates.

Figure 2.2 Mapping the Limited Subject

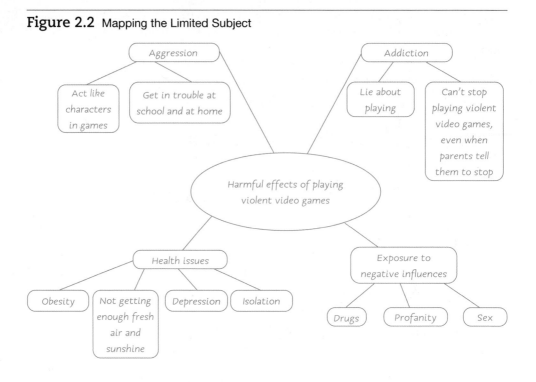

Figure 2.2 is an example of the kind of map that Caylah Francis could have drawn to generate material for her limited subject based on the Rosen assignment.

USE THE PATTERNS OF DEVELOPMENT Throughout this book, we show how writers use various **patterns of development** (narration, process analysis, definition, and so on), singly or in combination, to develop and organize their ideas. Because each pattern has its own distinctive logic, the patterns encourage you to think about a limited subject in surprising new ways.

The various patterns of development are discussed in detail in later chapters. At this point, though, you will find the following chart helpful. It not only summarizes the broad purpose of each pattern but also shows the way each pattern could generate different raw material for the limited subject of Caylah's essay.

Limited Subject: The harmful effects of playing violent video games.

Pattern of Development	Purpose	Raw Material
Description	To detail what a person, place, or object is like	Detail what the games are like—the sexy images, the language used, the thrill of the chase, the danger and excitement of battle
Narration	To relate an event	Recount what happened when neighbors tried to forbid their kids from playing the same violent games their friends were playing
Illustration	To provide specific instances or examples	Offer examples of particular games and the violence in them

Pattern of Development	Purpose	Raw Material
Division-classification	To divide something into parts or to group related things into categories	Identify different kinds of violent games—those about war, those about high-speed chases from law enforcement, those about abduction, etc.
Process analysis	To explain how something happens or how something is done	Explain step by step how adolescents can go from playing their first violent video game to becoming addicted to them
Comparison-contrast	To point out similarities and/or dissimilarities	Contrast popular video games today with the kinds of indoor games kids played 50 years ago—Monopoly, checkers, dominoes, etc.
Cause-effect	To analyze reasons and consequences	Explain why parents are not around to supervise their kids: Everything costs so much and we expect more luxuries today than our parents and grandparents expected—such as large houses and cars for everyone in the family who is old enough to drive
		Explain the consequences of absentee parents: Kids left alone too much with time to do whatever they want; they spend hours on the Internet; they spend far too many hours each week playing violent video games
Definition	To explain the meaning of a term or concept	What is meant by the "tough love" parents must show their kids by setting limits and enforcing them?
Argumentation-persuasion	To win people over to a point of view	Convince parents that they must learn how to say "no" to their kids and not let them do something just because their friends are doing it

Conduct Research

Depending on your topic, you may find it helpful to visit the library or go online to identify books and articles about your limited subject. At this point, you don't need to read closely the material you find. Just skim and perhaps take a few brief notes on ideas and points that could be useful.

Early in the drafting process, Caylah realized that she needed to conduct research to find out more about her subject: the harmful effects of playing violent video games. She had many ideas about possible harmful effects, but she needed to find out what reputable sources say about her subject. She knew her essay would not be effective unless she included documented sources to support her claims.

In researching for her assignment, Caylah looked under the following headings and subheadings:

The most popular violent video games on the market today

Effects of playing violent video games

Isolation and video game play

Obesity and video game play

Addiction and video game play

Aggression and video game play

Family

Parent-child relationships

Children of working parents

School and home

Caylah eventually identified several sources that offered important material on her subject. She read these sources critically and made sure they were reputable. She also made sure the sources were relevant to her topic and provided trustworthy information. Many of the sources she found came from Internet sites, and Caylah looked closely at who hosted the sites, who wrote the articles, the links provided by the sites, and whether the information on the sites was supported with reliable, credible documentation. As she took notes, she was careful to place quotation marks around words and phrases she copied directly from the sources and to record all of the information she would need when compiling a list of the works she consulted and quoted from when researching and writing her essay. In addition, she made copies of her source materials so that she could easily access them if needed.

Organize the Raw Material into a Scratch Outline

2.2 Organize your ideas into a scratch outline that will make the writing process more manageable.

Some students prefer to wait until after they have formulated a thesis to shape their prewriting material. But if you find that imposing a preliminary order on your prewriting provides the focus needed to devise an effective thesis, you'll probably want to prepare a **scratch list** or **outline** that can help you shape the tentative ideas generated during prewriting.

As you reread your exploratory thoughts about the limited subject, keep the following questions in mind: What *purpose* have you decided on? What are the characteristics of your *audience*? What *tone* will be effective in achieving your purpose with your audience? What *point of view* will you adopt? Record your responses to these questions at the top of your prewriting material.

Now go to work on the raw material itself. Cross out anything not appropriate for your purpose, audience, tone, and point of view; add points that didn't originally occur to you. Star or circle compelling items that warrant further development. Then draw arrows between related items, your goal being to group such material under a common heading. Finally, determine what seems to be the best order for the headings. If you are creating your scratch outline on a computer, cut and paste; move items around as you try to figure out the order that might work best for presenting your ideas.

By giving you a sense of the way your free-form material might fit together, a scratch outline makes the writing process more manageable. You're less likely to feel overwhelmed once you start writing because you'll already have some idea about how to shape your material into a meaningful statement. Remember, though, the outline can, and most likely will, be modified along the way.

Below are Caylah Francis's handwritten annotations on her brainstormed list, sometimes called a *scratch list*. Note that Caylah's annotations illustrate the way she began shaping her raw prewriting material. She started at the top by recording her limited subject as well as her decisions about purpose, audience, tone, and point of view. Next, she crossed out the material she didn't want to use in her supporting paragraphs and jotted down new ideas that came to her. For instance, Caylah realized that the first eight items on her list were related to her topic in that they offered reasons why kids play violent video games, but they were not directly related to the harmful effects of playing the games. So she crossed them off but wondered if she might be able to use some of those ideas later in the drafting process when she started writing her introduction. Caylah also decided that the harmful effects of too much exposure to inappropriate elements such as drugs, sex, and profanity were too complex to include in her essay, so she crossed those out. She also added new ideas: "some might also become depressed" and "too much isolation." Note how clear supporting points emerged after she grouped together similar ideas.

Purpose: To inform

Audience: Instructor as well as class members, most of whom are 18–20 years old

Tone: Serious and straightforward

Point of view: Third person (sister of two adolescent boys)

Limited subject: The harmful effects of playing violent video games

① *Kids more aggressive*

~~Parents at work long hours~~
~~Kids left alone~~
~~Kids expect more and more things~~
~~Prices of things outrageous, even with both parents working~~
~~Ads make kids want more of everything~~
~~Clothes so important to kids today~~
~~Kids have too much freedom~~
~~Parents too permissive~~

② *Kids become addicted*

Start acting like the characters in the games they play
Get in trouble for being aggressive at school and at home
Some kids become addicted to playing violent video games
Can't stop playing even when parents tell them to stop
Lie about playing

③ *Health*
issues

> Sit too much
>
> Many become obese —*some might also become depressed*
>
> Not enough fresh air and sunshine —*too much isolation*
>
> Kids exposed to negative influences
>
> Exposed to drugs
>
> Exposed to profanity
>
> Exposed to sex

The following scratch outline shows how Caylah began to shape her prewriting into a more organized format.

Purpose: To inform

Audience: Instructor as well as class members, most of whom are 18–20 years old

Tone: Serious and straightforward

Point of view: Third person (sister of two adolescent boys)

Limited subject: The harmful effects of playing violent video games

1. Kids more aggressive

   —They start acting like the characters in the games they play

   —They get in trouble for being aggressive at school and at home

2. Kids become addicted to games

   —They can't stop playing, even when parents tell them to stop

   —They lie about playing

3. Their health is damaged

   —Many become obese

   —Some kids become depressed

   —Not enough time outside in fresh air and sunshine

   —Too much isolation

Activities: Getting Started Through Prewriting

1. Number the items in each set from 1 (*broadest subject*) to 5 (*most limited subject*):

Set A	Set B
Abortion	Business majors
Controversial social issue	Students' majors
Cutting state abortion funds	College students
Federal funding of abortions	Kinds of students on campus
Social issues	Why students major in business

2. Which of the following topics are too broad for an essay of three to five typewritten pages: reality TV's appeal to college students; day care; trying to "kick" the junk food habit; romantic relationships; international terrorism?

3. Assume you're writing essays on two of the topics given here. For each one, explain how you might adapt your purpose, tone, and point of view to the audiences indicated in parentheses. (You may find it helpful to work with others on this activity.)

    a. Overcoming shyness (ten-year-olds; teachers of ten-year-olds; young singles living in large apartment buildings)

    b. Telephone solicitations (people training for a job in this field; homeowners; readers of a humorous magazine)

    c. Smoking (people who have quit; smokers; elementary school children)

4. Choose one of the following general topics for an essay. Then use the prewriting technique indicated in parentheses to identify several limited topics. Next, with the help of one or more patterns of development, generate raw material on the limited subject you consider most interesting.

    a. Friendship (*journal writing*)

    b. Amusement parks (*mapping*)

    c. Leisure (*freewriting*)

    d. Action movies (*brainstorming*)

    e. Required courses (*group brainstorming*)

    f. Manners (*questioning*)

5. For each set of limited subjects and purposes that follows, determine which pattern(s) of development would be most useful. (Save this material so you can work with it further.)

    a. The failure of recycling efforts on campus

    Purpose: to explain why students and faculty tend to disregard recycling guidelines

    b. The worst personality trait that a teacher, parent, boss, or friend can have

    Purpose: to poke fun at this personality trait

    c. The importance of being knowledgeable about national affairs

    Purpose: to convince students to stay informed about current events

6. Select one of the following limited subjects. Then, given the purpose and audience indicated, draft a paragraph using the first-, second-, or third-person point of view. Next, rewrite the paragraph two more times, each time using a different point of view. What differences do you see in the three versions? Which version do you prefer? Why?

   a. Fantasy movies like *Star Wars* and *The Lord of the Rings* series

     Purpose: to defend the enjoyment of such films

     Audience: those who like "art" films

   b. Senioritis

     Purpose: to explain why high school seniors lose interest in school

     Audience: parents and teachers

   c. Television commercials aimed at teens and young adults

     Purpose: to make fun of the commercials' persuasive appeals

     Audience: advertising executives

7. Select one of the following general subjects. Keeping in mind the indicated purpose, audience, tone, and point of view, use a prewriting technique to limit the subject. Next, by means of another prewriting strategy, generate relevant information about the restricted topic. Finally, shape your raw material into a scratch outline—crossing out, combining, and adding ideas as needed. (Save your scratch outline so you can work with it further after reading the chapter on identifying a thesis.)

   a. Hip-hop music

     Purpose: to explain its attraction

     Audience: classical music fans

     Tone: playful

     Writer's point of view: a hip-hop fan

   b. Becoming a volunteer

     Purpose: to recruit

     Audience: ambitious young professionals

     Tone: straightforward

     Writer's point of view: head of a volunteer organization

   c. Sexist attitudes in music videos

     Purpose: to inform

     Audience: teenagers of both sexes

     Tone: objective but with some emotion

     Writer's point of view: a teenage male

Chapter 3
Identifying a Thesis

⌄ **Learning Objectives**

3.1 Identify the purpose of a thesis.

3.2 Craft an effective thesis, avoiding thesis pitfalls.

3.3 Place your thesis in an essay.

The process of prewriting—discovering a limited subject and generating ideas about it—prepares you for the next stage in writing an essay: identifying the composition's *thesis*, or controlling idea.

What Is a Thesis?

3.1 Identify the purpose of a thesis.

The **thesis**, which presents your position on a subject, should focus on an interesting and significant issue, one that engages your energies and merits your consideration. Your thesis determines what does and does not belong in the essay. The thesis, especially when it occurs early in an essay, also helps focus the reader on the piece's central point and thus helps you achieve your writing purpose.

Crafting a Thesis

3.2 Craft an effective thesis, avoiding thesis pitfalls.

Sometimes the thesis emerges early in the prewriting stage, particularly if a special angle on your limited topic sparks your interest or becomes readily apparent. Often, though, you'll need to do some work to determine your thesis. For some topics, you may need to do some research. For others, the best way to identify a promising thesis is to look through your prewriting and ask yourself these questions:

- What statement does all this prewriting support?
- What aspect of the limited subject is covered in most detail?
- What is the focus of the most provocative material?

For more details, see Figure 3.1.

Creating an Effective Thesis

What makes a thesis effective? The thesis statement, generally expressed in one or two sentences, has two parts. One part presents your essay's *limited subject;* the other presents your *point of view,* or *attitude,* about that subject. In each of the following thesis statements, the limited subject is underlined once and the attitude twice.

General Subject	Limited Subject	Thesis Statement
Education	Computers in elementary school mathematics classes	Computer programs in mathematics can individualize instruction more effectively than the average elementary school teacher can.
Work	College internships	The college internship program has had positive consequences for students.
Our anti-child world	Special problems that parents face raising children today	Being a parent today is much more difficult than it was a generation ago.

Figure 3.1 Process Diagram: Identifying a Thesis

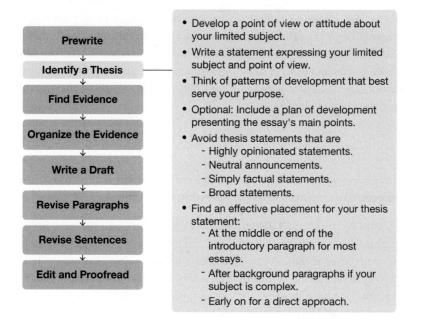

- Prewrite
- Identify a Thesis
- Find Evidence
- Organize the Evidence
- Write a Draft
- Revise Paragraphs
- Revise Sentences
- Edit and Proofread

- Develop a point of view or attitude about your limited subject.
- Write a statement expressing your limited subject and point of view.
- Think of patterns of development that best serve your purpose.
- Optional: Include a plan of development presenting the essay's main points.
- Avoid thesis statements that are
  - Highly opinionated statements.
  - Neutral announcements.
  - Simply factual statements.
  - Broad statements.
- Find an effective placement for your thesis statement:
  - At the middle or end of the introductory paragraph for most essays.
  - After background paragraphs if your subject is complex.
  - Early on for a direct approach.

TONE AND POINT OF VIEW   An effective thesis establishes a tone and point of view suitable for a given purpose and audience. If you're writing an essay arguing that multimedia equipment can never replace a live teacher in the classroom, you need to frame a thesis that matches your and your readers' concerns about the subject: "Education won't be improved by purchasing more electronic teaching tools but rather by allocating more money to hire and develop good teachers."

IMPLIED PATTERN OF DEVELOPMENT   An essay's purpose may suggest a pattern of development. In the same way, an effective thesis may point the way to a pattern of development that would be appropriate for developing the essay. Consider the thesis statements in the preceding list. The first thesis might use *comparison-contrast;* the second *cause-effect;* and the third *argumentation-persuasion.*

INCLUDING A PLAN OF DEVELOPMENT   Sometimes a thesis will include a **plan of development**: a concise *overview of the essay's main points in the exact order* in which those points will be discussed. To incorporate a plan of development into your thesis, use single words or brief phrases that convey—in a nutshell—your essay's key points; then add those summarized points to the end of the thesis, being sure to present them in the order in which they will appear in the essay. Note, for example, the way a plan of development (in italics) is included in the following thesis: "An after-school job develops *responsibility, human-relations skills, and an awareness of career options.*"

   A thesis with a plan of development is effective in keeping readers focused on an essay's main points. Be careful, though, not to overload it with too much information.

If the essay's key points resist your efforts to reduce them to crisp phrases, you can place the plan of development in a separate sentence, directly *after* the thesis. Consider the plan of development (in italics) that comes after the following thesis: "Many parents have unrealistic expectations for their children. These parents want their children to *accept their values, follow their paths, and succeed where they have failed.*" Note that the points in a plan of development are expressed in grammatically parallel terms, in this case as verb phrases ("accept their values," "follow their paths," "succeed where they have failed").

Avoiding Thesis Pitfalls

Because preparing an effective thesis is such a critical step in writing a sharply focused essay, you need to avoid the following four common problems.

1. DON'T WRITE A HIGHLY OPINIONATED STATEMENT Although your thesis should express your attitude toward your subject, don't go overboard and write a dogmatic, overstated thesis: "With characteristic clumsiness, campus officials bumbled their way through the recent budget crisis." A more moderate thesis can make the same point, *without alienating readers:* "Campus officials had trouble managing the recent budget crisis effectively."

2. DON'T MAKE AN ANNOUNCEMENT Some writers use the thesis statement merely to announce the limited subject of their essay and forget to indicate their attitude toward the subject. Such statements are announcements of intent, not thesis statements. Compare the following:

Announcement	Thesis Statement
My essay will discuss whether a student pub should exist on campus.	This college should not allow a student pub on campus.
The legislating of assault weapons will be the subject of my essay.	Banning assault weapons is the first step toward controlling crime in America.

3. DON'T MAKE A FACTUAL STATEMENT   Your thesis, and thus your essay, should focus on an issue capable of being developed. If a fact is used as a thesis, you have no place to go; a fact generally doesn't invite much discussion. Notice the difference between the factual statements and thesis statements in the following table:

Factual Statement	Thesis Statement
Many businesses pollute the environment.	Tax penalties should be levied against businesses that pollute the environment.
Movies nowadays are often violent.	Movie violence provides a healthy outlet for aggression.

4. DON'T MAKE A BROAD STATEMENT Broad statements make it difficult for readers to grasp your essay's point. If you start with a broad thesis, you're saddled with the impossible task of trying to develop a book-length idea in an essay that runs only several pages.

Broad Statement

Nowadays, high school education is often meaningless.

Nobody reads newspapers anymore.

Thesis Statement

High school diplomas have been devalued by grade inflation.

With the growth of online sources, fewer and fewer people depend on print newspapers for news.

Arriving at an Effective Thesis

Previously, we pointed out how Caylah Francis identified her essay's thesis: "Playing violent video games can have many negative effects on kids. It can lead to increased levels of aggression, video game addiction, and serious health issues." But Caylah went through several stages before she came up with the final wording.

- Caylah started with her limited subject ("Violent video games especially harmful to kids today"). She tentatively worded her thesis to read "My essay will show the harmful effects of kids playing violent video games."

- Next, she asked herself, "Is my thesis *highly opinionated*? an *announcement*? a *factual statement*? a *broad statement*?" She realized that she had prepared an *announcement* rather than a thesis.

- Caylah rewrote her statement so that she would not be making an *announcement.* She came up with the following: "Playing violent video games can have many negative effects on kids."

- As she read over her revised statement, Caylah realized that although she had eliminated the *announcement,* the rephrasing highlighted a problem she hadn't thought about previously: her statement was too *broad* and needed to be more specific. She realized that she needed to let her readers know the specific negative effects of playing violent video games that she would be discussing in her essay: (1) increased levels of aggression, (2) video game addiction, and (3) serious health issues.

- Caylah revised her statement one more time to eliminate these problems and arrived at the final wording of her thesis: "Playing violent video games can have many negative effects on kids. It can lead to increased levels of aggression, video game addiction, and serious health issues."

Placing the Thesis in an Essay

3.3 Place your thesis in an essay.

The thesis is often at the middle or end of the introduction, but audience, purpose, and tone should always guide your decision about its placement. For example, if you feel readers would appreciate a direct, forthright approach, you might place the thesis early, even at the very beginning of the introduction.

Sometimes the thesis is reiterated—using fresh words—in the essay's conclusion or elsewhere. If done well, this repetition keeps readers focused on the essay's key point. You may even leave the thesis implied, relying on strong support, tone, and style to convey the essay's central idea.

One final point: Once you start writing your draft, some feelings, thoughts, and examples may emerge that modify, even contradict, your initial thesis. Don't resist these new ideas. Keep them in mind as you revise the thesis and move toward a more valid and richer view of your subject. Remember, though: Your essay *must* have a thesis. Without this central concept, you have no reason for writing.

Activities: Identifying a Thesis

1. For the following limited subject, four possible thesis statements are given. Indicate whether each thesis is an announcement (A), a factual statement (FS), too broad a statement (TB), or an acceptable thesis (OK). Revise the flawed statements. Then, for each effective thesis statement, identify a possible purpose, audience, tone, and point of view.

   Limited subject: Privacy and computerized records

   - Computers raise some significant questions for all of us.
   - Computerized records keep track of consumer spending habits, credit records, travel patterns, and other personal information.
   - Computerized records have turned our private lives into public property.
   - In this essay, the relationship between computerized records and the right to privacy will be discussed.

2. Turn back to activity 5 at the end of Chapter 2. For each set of limited subjects, develop an effective thesis. Select one of the thesis statements. Then, keeping in mind the purpose indicated and the pattern of development you identified earlier, draft a paragraph developing the point expressed in the thesis.

3. Following are three pairs of general and limited subjects. Generate an appropriate thesis for each pair. Select one of the thesis statements and determine which pattern of development would support the thesis most effectively. Use that pattern to draft a paragraph developing the thesis.

General Subject	Limited Subject
Psychology	The power struggles in a classroom
Health	Doctors' attitudes toward patients
Work	Minimum-wage jobs for young people

4. Following are key points for an essay. Based on the information provided, prepare a possible thesis for each essay. Then propose a possible purpose, audience, tone, and point of view.

- We do not know how engineering new forms of life might affect the earth's delicate ecological balance.

- Another danger of genetic research is its potential for unleashing new forms of disease.

- Even beneficial attempts to eliminate genetic defects could contribute to the dangerous idea that only perfect individuals are entitled to live.

5. Keep a journal for several weeks. Then reread a number of entries, identifying two or three recurring themes or subjects. Narrow the subjects and, for each one, generate possible thesis statements. Using an appropriate pattern of development, draft a paragraph for one of the thesis statements.

6. Return to the scratch outline you prepared in response to activity 7 at the end of Chapter 2. Identify a thesis that conveys the central idea behind most of the raw material. Then ask others to evaluate your thesis in light of the material in your scratch outline. Finally, keeping the thesis—as well as your purpose, audience, and tone—in mind, refine the scratch outline by deleting inappropriate items, adding relevant ones, and indicating where more material is needed.

Chapter 4
Supporting the Thesis with Evidence

Learning Objectives

4.1 Identify the key types of evidence.

4.2 Find evidence using the patterns of development.

4.3 Know the characteristics of evidence.

After identifying a preliminary thesis, you should develop the evidence needed to support that central idea. This supporting material grounds your essay, showing readers you have good reason for feeling as you do about your subject. Your evidence also adds interest and color to your writing.

In college essays of 500 to 1,500 words, you usually need at least three major points of evidence to develop your thesis. These major points—each focusing on related but separate aspects of the thesis—eventually become the supporting paragraphs in the body of the essay.

What Is Evidence?

4.1 Identify the key types of evidence.

By **evidence**, we mean a number of different kinds of support. *Reasons* are just one option. To develop your thesis, you might also include *examples, facts, details, statistics, personal observation* or *experience, anecdotes,* and *expert opinions* and *quotations* (gathered from a variety of both print and digital sources that might include websites, books, articles, interviews, documentaries, and the like). Imagine you're writing an essay with the thesis "People normally unconcerned about the environment can be galvanized to constructive action if they feel personally affected by an environmental problem." You could support this thesis with any combination of the following types of evidence:

- *Reasons* why people become involved in the environmental movement: they believe the situation endangers their health; they fear the value of their homes will plummet; they feel deceived by officials' empty assurances.

- *Examples* of successful neighborhood recycling efforts.

- *Facts* about residents' efforts to preserve the quality of well water in a community undergoing widespread industrial development.

- *Details* about steps one can take to get involved in environmental issues.

- *Statistics* showing the growing number of Americans concerned about the environment.

- A *personal experience* telling about the way you became involved in an effort to stop a local business from dumping waste into a neighborhood stream.

- An *anecdote* about a friend who protested a commercial development.

- A *quotation* from a well-known scientist about the impact that well-organized, well-informed citizens can have on environmental legislation.

How Do You Find Evidence?

4.2 Find evidence using the patterns of development.

Where do you find the examples, anecdotes, details, and other types of evidence needed to support your thesis? As you saw when you followed Caylah Francis's strategies for gathering material for an essay, a good deal of information is generated during the prewriting stage. In this phase of the writing process, you tap into your personal experiences, draw on other people's observations, or perhaps interview a person with special knowledge about your subject. The library and the Internet are also rich sources of supporting evidence, and Caylah made extensive use of both of these as she prepared to write her essay on the harmful effects of playing violent video games. In addition, the various patterns of development are a valuable source of evidence.

How the Patterns of Development Help Generate Evidence

We have seen how the patterns of development could help generate material about Caylah's limited subject. The same patterns also help develop support for a thesis. The chart that follows shows how they generate evidence for this thesis: "To those who haven't done it, babysitting looks easy. In practice, though, babysitting can be difficult, frightening, even dangerous."

Pattern of Development	Evidence Generated
Description	Details about a child who, while being babysat, was badly hurt playing on a backyard swing.
Narration	Story about a child who became ill and whose condition was worsened by the babysitter's remedies.
Illustration	Examples of potential babysitting problems: infant rolls off a changing table; toddler sticks objects into an outlet; child is bitten by a neighborhood dog.
Division-classification	A typical babysitting evening divided into stages: playing with the kids; putting them to bed; dealing with nightmares.
	Kids' nighttime fears classified by type: monsters under their beds; bad dreams; being abandoned.
Process analysis	Step-by-step account of what a babysitter should do if a child becomes ill or injured.
Comparison-contrast	Contrast between two babysitters: one well prepared, the other unprepared.
Cause-effect	Why children have temper tantrums; the effect of such tantrums on an unskilled babysitter.
Definition	What is meant by a *skilled* babysitter?
Argumentation-persuasion	A proposal for a babysitting training program to be offered by the local community center.

Characteristics of Evidence

4.3 Know the characteristics of evidence.

No matter how it is generated, all types of supporting evidence share the characteristics described in the following sections. Keep these characteristics in mind as you review your thesis and scratch outline. That way, you can make the changes needed to strengthen the evidence you gathered previously. As you'll see shortly, Caylah

Figure 4.1 Process Diagram: Finding Evidence

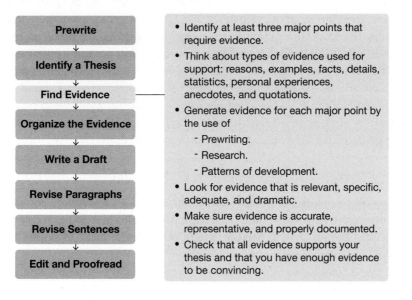

Prewrite
↓
Identify a Thesis
↓
Find Evidence
↓
Organize the Evidence
↓
Write a Draft
↓
Revise Paragraphs
↓
Revise Sentences
↓
Edit and Proofread

- Identify at least three major points that require evidence.
- Think about types of evidence used for support: reasons, examples, facts, details, statistics, personal experiences, anecdotes, and quotations.
- Generate evidence for each major point by the use of
  - Prewriting.
  - Research.
  - Patterns of development.
- Look for evidence that is relevant, specific, adequate, and dramatic.
- Make sure evidence is accurate, representative, and properly documented.
- Check that all evidence supports your thesis and that you have enough evidence to be convincing.

focused on many of these issues as she worked with the evidence she collected during the prewriting phase. (See Figure 4.1.)

The Evidence Is Relevant and Unified

All the evidence in an essay must clearly support the thesis. It makes no difference how riveting the material might be; if it doesn't *relate* directly to the essay's central point, it should be eliminated. Irrelevant material can weaken your position by implying that no relevant support exists. It also distracts readers from your controlling idea, thus disrupting the paper's overall unity.

Early in the writing process, Caylah was aware of the importance of relevant evidence. Even though Caylah hadn't yet identified her thesis, she realized she should delete a number of items on the reshaped version of her brainstormed list.

The Evidence Is Specific

When evidence is vague and general, readers lose interest in what you're saying, become skeptical of your ideas' validity, and feel puzzled about your meaning. In contrast, *specific, concrete evidence* provides sharp *word pictures* that engage your readers, persuades them that your thinking is sound, and clarifies meaning.

Early in the writing process, Caylah was aware of the importance of specific evidence. Look back at the annotations she entered on her prewriting material. Note the way she jotted down new details as they came to her while she organized her raw material. For instance, to the item, "Many become obese," she jotted down "some might also become depressed." And once Caylah arrived at her thesis ("Playing violent video games can have many negative effects on kids. It can lead to increased levels of aggression, video game addiction, and serious health issues"), she knew that she needed to provide even more specifics. With her thesis firmly in mind, she expanded her prewriting material—for instance, the point about playing violent video games potentially leading to health issues. She knew that sitting and playing violent games for hours on end could lead to obesity, but she needed to conduct research to find out more about other possible health-related issues. She suspected that playing violent video games might lead to depression, and as she read various outside sources, she discovered sound evidence that supported her hunch and allowed her to include specific evidence in her supporting paragraphs. And, as you'll soon discover, Caylah added many more specific details when she prepared her final outline and her first and final drafts.

The Evidence Is Adequate

Readers won't automatically accept your thesis; you need to provide *enough specific evidence* to support your viewpoint. On occasion, a single extended example will suffice. Generally, though, you'll need a variety of evidence: facts, examples, reasons, personal observations, expert opinion, and so on.

Now take a final look at Caylah's annotations on her prewriting. Caylah realized she needed several blocks of supporting material to develop her limited subject, and she realized that she could group her prewriting material into three separate blocks of evidence (one on aggression, another on addiction, and the third on health issues). As soon as Caylah formulated her thesis, she reexamined her prewriting to see if it provided sufficient support for her essay's central point. Luckily, Caylah recognized that these three blocks of evidence needed to be developed further. Her final outline reflects these decisions. She added so many specific details when writing her first and final drafts that her evidence was more than sufficient.

The Evidence Is Dramatic

The most effective evidence enlarges the reader's experience by *dramatizing reality.* Say you plan to write an essay with the thesis "People who affirm the value of life refuse to wear fur coats." If, as support, you state only that most animals killed for their fur are caught in leg-hold traps, your readers will have little sense of the suffering involved. But if you write that steel-jaw, leg-hold traps snap shut on an animal's limb, crushing tissue and bone and leaving the animal to die, in severe pain, from exposure or starvation, your readers can better envision the animal's plight.

The Evidence Is Accurate

When you have a strong belief and want readers to see things your way, you may be tempted to overstate or downplay facts, disregard information, misquote, or make up details. Suppose you plan to write an essay making the point that dormitory security is lax. You begin supporting your thesis by narrating the time you were nearly mugged in your dorm hallway. Realizing the essay would be more persuasive if you also mentioned other episodes, you decide to invent some material. Yes, you've

supported your point—but at the expense of truth. Keep in mind that using hypothetical examples is acceptable, as long as readers know they did not actually happen.

The Evidence Is Representative

Using *representative* evidence means that you rely on the *typical*, the *usual*, to show
that your point is valid. Contrary to the old saying, exceptions don't prove the rule.
Perhaps you plan to write an essay contending that the value of seat belts has been
exaggerated. To support your position, you mention a friend who survived a head-on
collision without wearing a seat belt. Such an example isn't representative because the
facts and figures on accidents suggest your friend's survival was a fluke.

Borrowed Evidence Is Documented

If you include evidence from outside sources (books, websites, articles, interviews),
as Caylah did in her essay, you need to *acknowledge* where that information comes
from. If you don't, readers may consider your evidence nothing more than your point
of view, or they may see you as dishonest for your failure to cite your indebtedness
to others for ideas that are not your own. As Caylah composed her essay, she was
careful to use quotation marks around language that came directly from her sources
and to use parenthetical documentation so that her readers would know where she
obtained her information. She also carefully prepared a Works Cited page so that her
readers could easily locate her sources.

    Strong supporting evidence is at the heart of effective writing. Without it, essays
lack energy and fail to project the writer's voice and perspective. Such lifeless writing
is more likely to put readers to sleep than to engage their interest and convince them
that the points being made are valid. Taking the time to accumulate solid supporting
material is, then, a critical step in the writing process.

Activities: Supporting the Thesis with Evidence

1. Imagine you're writing an essay with the following thesis in mind. Which of the
statements in the list support the thesis? Label each statement acceptable (OK),
irrelevant (IR), inaccurate (IA), or too general (TG).

   Thesis: Colleges should put less emphasis on sports.

   a. High-powered athletic programs can encourage grade fixing.

   b. Too much value is attached to college sports.

   c. Competitive athletics can lead to extensive and expensive injuries.

   d. Athletes can spend more time on the field and less time on their studies.

2. For each of the following thesis statements, list at least three supporting points
that convey vivid word pictures.

a. Rude behavior in movie theaters seems to be on the rise.

b. Recent television commercials portray men as incompetent creatures.

c. The local library fails to meet the public's needs.

3. Turn back to the paragraphs you prepared in response to activity 2, activity 3, or activity 5 in Chapter 3. Select one paragraph and strengthen its evidence, using the guidelines presented in this chapter.

4. Choose one of the following thesis statements. Then identify an appropriate purpose, audience, tone, and point of view for an essay with this thesis. Using freewriting, mapping, or the questioning technique, generate at least three supporting points for the thesis. Last, write a paragraph about one of the points, making sure your evidence reflects the characteristics discussed in this chapter. Alternatively, you may go ahead and prepare the first draft of an essay having the selected thesis. Save whatever you prepare so you can work with it further.

a. Winning the lottery may not always be a blessing.

b. All of us can take steps to reduce the country's trash crisis.

c. Drug education programs in public schools are (or are not) effective.

5. Select one of the following thesis statements. Then determine your purpose, audience, tone, and point of view for an essay with this thesis. Next, use the patterns of development to generate at least three supporting points for the thesis. Finally, write a paragraph about one of the points, making sure that your evidence demonstrates the characteristics discussed in this chapter. Alternatively, you may go ahead and prepare a first draft of an essay having the thesis selected. Save whatever you prepare so you can work with it further.

a. Teenagers should (or should not) be able to obtain birth-control devices without their parents' permission.

b. The college's system for awarding student loans needs to be overhauled.

c. Texting has changed for the worse (or the better) the way Americans communicate with one another.

6. Look at the thesis and refined scratch outline you prepared in response to activity 6 in Chapter 3. Where do you see gaps in the support for your thesis? By brainstorming with others, generate material to fill these gaps. If some of the new points generated suggest that you should modify your thesis, make the appropriate changes now. Save this material so you can work with it further.

Chapter 5
Organizing the Evidence

Learning Objectives

5.1 Use the patterns of development in your essay.

5.2 Organize the evidence in one of four ways: chronologically, spatially,

emphatically, or simple-to-complex.

5.3 Create an outline to assist in writing a first draft of your essay.

Once you've generated supporting evidence, you're ready to *organize* that material. Even highly compelling evidence won't illustrate the validity of your thesis or achieve your purpose if readers have to plow through a maze of chaotic evidence. Some writers can move quickly from generating support to writing a clearly structured first draft. (They usually say they have sequenced their ideas in their heads.) Most, however, need to spend some time sorting out their thoughts on paper or on a screen before starting the first draft; otherwise, they tend to lose their way in a tangle of ideas.

When moving to the organizing stage, you should have in front of you your scratch outline, thesis, and any supporting material—for example, notes from research—that you've accumulated.

Use the Patterns of Development

5.1 Use the patterns of development in your essay.

As you know, the patterns of development (definition, narration, process analysis, and others) can help you develop prewriting material and generate evidence for a thesis. In the organizing stage, the patterns provide frameworks for presenting the evidence in an orderly, accessible way. Here's how.

Each pattern of development has its own internal logic that makes it appropriate for some writing purposes but not for others. (You may find it helpful at this point to review the broad purpose of each pattern.) Imagine that you want to write an essay *explaining why* some students drop out of college during the first semester. If your essay consisted only of a lengthy narrative of two friends floundering through the first month of college, you wouldn't achieve your purpose. A condensed version of the narrative might be appropriate at some point in the essay, but—to meet your objective—most of the essay would have to focus on *causes and effects*.

Once you see which pattern (or combination of patterns) is implied by your purpose, you can block out your essay's general structure. For instance, in the preceding example, you might organize the essay around a three-part discussion of the key reasons that students have difficulty adjusting to college: (1) they miss friends and family, (2) they take inappropriate courses, and (3) they experience conflicts with roommates. As you can see, your choice of pattern of development significantly influences your essay's content and organization.

Some essays follow a single pattern, but most blend them, with a predominant pattern providing the piece's organizational framework. In our example essay, you might include a brief *description* of an overwhelmed first-year college student; you might *define* the psychological term *separation anxiety*; you might end the essay by briefly explaining a *process* for making students' adjustment to college easier. Still, the essay's overall organizational pattern would be *cause-effect* because the essay's primary purpose is to explain why students drop out of college.

Although writers often combine the patterns of development, writing an essay organized according to a single pattern can help you understand a particular pattern's unique demands. Keep in mind, though, that most writing begins not with a specific pattern but with a specific *purpose.* The pattern or combination of patterns used to develop and organize an essay evolves out of that purpose.

Select an Organizational Approach

5.2 Organize the evidence in one of four ways: chronologically, spatially, emphatically, or simple-to-complex.

No matter which pattern(s) of development you select, you need to know four general approaches for organizing the supporting evidence in an essay: chronological, spatial, emphatic, and simple-to-complex. (See Figure 5.1.)

Chronological Approach

When an essay is organized **chronologically**, supporting material is arranged in a clear time sequence, usually from what happened first to what happened last. Occasionally, the order can be resequenced to create flashback or flashforward effects.

Essays using narration (for example, an experience with prejudice) or process analysis (for instance, how to deliver an effective speech) are most likely to be organized chronologically. The essay on public speaking might use a time sequence to present its points: how to prepare a few days before the presentation is due, what to do right before the speech, and what to concentrate on when delivering the speech.

Figure 5.1 Process Diagram: Organizing the Evidence

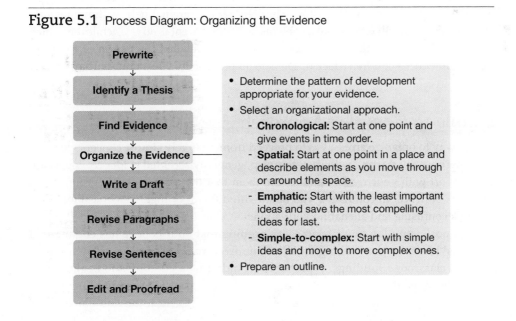

Spatial Approach

When you arrange supporting evidence **spatially**, you discuss details as they occur in space or from certain locations. This strategy is particularly appropriate for description. Imagine that you plan to write an essay describing the happy times you spent as a child playing by a towering old oak tree in the neighborhood park. Using spatial organization, you start by describing the rich animal life (the plump earthworms, swarming anthills, and numerous animal tracks) you observed while hunkered down *at the base* of the tree. Next, you re-create the contented feeling you experienced sitting on a branch *in the middle* of the tree. Finally, you end by describing the glorious view of the world you had *from the top* of the tree.

Although spatial arrangement is flexible (you could, for instance, start with a description from the top of the tree), you should always proceed systematically. And once you select a particular spatial order, you should usually maintain that sequence throughout the essay. Otherwise, readers may get lost along the way.

Emphatic Approach

In **emphatic** order, the most compelling evidence is saved for last. This arrangement is based on the principle that people remember best what they experience last. Sometimes, though, an essay captures the audience's attention by presenting the most important point first. Emphatic order is especially effective in argumentation-persuasion essays, in essays developed through examples, and in pieces involving comparison-contrast, division-classification, or causal analysis.

Consider an essay analyzing the negative effects that workaholic parents can have on their children. The essay might start with a brief discussion of relatively minor effects, such as the family's eating mostly frozen or takeout foods. Paragraphs on more serious effects might follow: children get no parental help with homework, children try to resolve personal problems without parental advice, children watch too much TV. Finally, the essay might close with a detailed discussion of the most significant effect—children's lack of self-esteem because they feel unimportant in their parents' lives.

Simple-to-Complex Approach

A final way to organize an essay is to proceed from relatively **simple** concepts to more **complex** ones. By starting with easy-to-grasp, generally accepted evidence, you establish rapport with your readers and assure them that the essay is firmly grounded in shared experience. In contrast, if you open with difficult or highly technical material, you risk confusing and alienating your audience.

Suppose you plan to write an essay arguing that your college has endangered students' health by not making an all-out effort to remove asbestos from dormitories and classroom buildings. It probably wouldn't be a good idea to begin with a medically sophisticated explanation of precisely how asbestos damages lung tissue. Instead, you might start with an observation that is likely to be familiar to your readers—one that is part of their everyday experience. You could, for example, open with a description of asbestos—as readers might see it—wrapped around air ducts and furnaces or used as electrical insulation and fireproofing material. Having provided a basic, easy-to-visualize description, you could then go on to explain the complicated process by which asbestos can cause chronic lung inflammation.

Depending on your purpose, any one of these four organizational approaches might be appropriate. For example, assume you planned to write an essay developing Caylah's thesis: "Playing violent video games can have many negative effects on young people: It can lead to increased levels of aggression, video game addiction, and serious health issues." To emphasize that the harmful effects are directly related to the types of games played at particular ages, you might select a *chronological* sequence. To show that harmful effects vary depending on whether youngsters are playing at home alone, with friends at their homes, or in other settings, you might choose a *spatial* sequence. To stress the range of harmful effects (from less to more serious), you'd probably use an *emphatic* sequence. To illustrate why video games today require more of a player's time and energy than they used to, you might take a *simple-to-complex* approach in describing the simpler games of decades ago and then today's increasingly sophisticated and complicated games.

Prepare an Outline

5.3 Create an outline to assist in writing a first draft of your essay.

Do you, like many students, react with fear and loathing to the dreaded word *outline?* The outline helps you organize your thoughts, and it guides your writing as you work on the draft. Even though ideas continue to evolve during the drafting process, an outline clarifies how ideas fit together, which points are major, which should come first, and so on. An outline may also reveal places where evidence is weak, prompting you to eliminate the material altogether, retain it in an unemphatic position, or do more prewriting to generate additional support.

To prepare an effective outline, you should reread and evaluate your scratch list/outline and thesis as well as any other evidence you've generated since the prewriting stage. Then decide which pattern of development (description, cause-effect, and so on) is suggested by your evidence. Also determine whether your evidence lends itself to a chronological, a spatial, an emphatic, or a simple-to-complex order. Now you're ready to identify and sequence your main and supporting points.

The amount of detail in an outline will vary according to the essay's length and the instructor's requirements. A scratch outline consisting of words or phrases is often sufficient, but for longer compositions, you'll probably need a more detailed and formal outline. In such cases, the suggestions in the following checklist will help you develop a sound plan. Feel free to modify these guidelines to suit your needs.

☑ Outlining: A Checklist

- ☐ Write your purpose, audience, tone, point of view, and thesis at the top of the outlining page.

- ☐ Below the thesis, enter the pattern of development that is implied by the evidence you've accumulated.

- ☐ Record which of the four organizational approaches would be most effective in sequencing your evidence.

- ☐ Reevaluate your supporting material. Delete anything that doesn't develop the thesis or that isn't appropriate for your purpose, audience, tone, and point of view.

- ☐ Add any new points or material.

- ☐ Group related items together. Give each group a heading that represents a main topic in support of your thesis.

- ☐ Label these main topics with Roman numerals (I, II, III, and so on). Let the order of numerals indicate the best sequence.

- ☐ Identify subtopics and group them under the appropriate main topics. Indent and label them (A, B, C, and so on).

- ☐ Identify supporting points (often reasons and examples) and group them under the appropriate subtopics. Indent and label them (1, 2, 3, and so on).

- ☐ Identify specific details (secondary examples, facts, statistics, expert opinions, quotations) and group them under the appropriate supporting points. Indent and label them (a, b, c, and so on).

- ☐ Examine your outline, looking for places where evidence is weak. Where appropriate, add new evidence.

- ☐ Double-check that all content develops some aspect of the thesis. Also confirm that all items are arranged in the most logical order.

The sample outline that follows does not include the essay's introduction or conclusion. Caylah's purpose in creating this outline was to help her organize the evidence in support of her thesis "Playing violent video games can have many negative effects on kids. It can lead to increased levels of aggression, video game addiction, and serious health issues." The thesis is the one that Caylah devised for the essay she planned to write in response to the Rosen assignment. Caylah's scratch list and outline appeared previously. When you compare Caylah's scratch list with the following outline, you'll find some differences. The scratch list includes material Caylah decided to use in her introduction—material on home life today that she came up with while brainstorming for ideas. That material is not included in the original scratch outline of supporting evidence.

On the whole, the outline of supporting evidence contains more specifics than the scratch outline, but it doesn't include all of the supporting material in the scratch list. For example, when Caylah conducted research on her subject, she discovered new evidence in support of her thesis that she thought would be more effective than the information on the trouble that young people might get into as a result of increased levels of aggression. Consequently, she decided to use this new evidence instead of the information she had included in her scratch list.

The following plan is called a *topic outline* because it uses phrases, or topics, for each entry. For a lengthier or more complex composition, a *sentence outline* would be more appropriate.

Purpose: To persuade

Audience: Instructor as well as class members, most of whom are
   18–20 years old

Tone: Serious and straightforward

Point of view: Third person (older sister of two adolescent boys)

Thesis: Playing video games can have many negative effects on kids.
   It can lead to increased levels of aggression, video game addiction, and
   serious health issues.

Pattern of development: Argumentation-persuasion

Organizational approach: Emphatic order

   I. Increased levels of aggression and violence

      A. Imitation of aggression in violent video games (Include first Willoughby quote)

      B. Effects of playing versus watching violent video games (Include second Willoughby quote)

      C. Effects of playing violent video games versus watching television violence (Include first and second Polman quotes)

  II. Addiction

      A. Relationship between time spent playing and probability of addiction (Include first Porter quote)

      B. Effects of addiction (Include Young quote)

         1. Preoccupation with gaming

         2. Lying about gaming

         3. Loss of interest in other activities

         4. Withdrawal from family and friends

      C. Factors that lead to addiction

         1. Positive reinforcement

         2. Positive sanctions

      D. Extreme effects of addiction (Include paraphrase of Porter)

         1. Mental illness

         2. Physical exhaustion

         3. Death

III. Health dangers

    A. Obesity

    B. Depression

Before starting to compose your first draft, show your outline to several people (your instructor, friends, classmates). Their reactions will indicate whether your proposed organization is appropriate for your thesis, purpose, audience, tone, and point of view. Their comments can also highlight areas needing additional work. After making whatever changes are needed, you're in a good position to go ahead and write the first draft of your essay.

Activities: Organizing the Evidence

1. The following thesis statement is accompanied by a scrambled list of supporting points. Prepare a topic outline for a potential essay, being sure to distinguish between major and secondary points.

   Thesis: Our schools, now in crisis, could be improved in several ways.

Teacher certification requirements	Merit pay for teachers
Improved schedules	More interesting textbooks
Better teachers	Longer school days
Longer school year	More challenging courses

2. For each of the following thesis statements, two purposes are given. Determine whether each purpose suggests an emphatic, chronological, spatial, or simple-to-complex approach. Note the way the approach varies as the purpose changes.

   a. *Thesis:* Traveling in a large city can be an unexpected education.

   Purpose 1: To explain, in a humorous way, the stages in learning to cope with the city's cab system

   Purpose 2: To describe, in a serious manner, the vastly different sections of the city as viewed from a cab

   b. *Thesis:* Supermarkets use sophisticated marketing techniques to prod consumers into buying more than they need.

   Purpose 1: To inform readers that positioning products in certain locations encourages impulse buying

   Purpose 2: To persuade readers not to patronize those chains using especially objectionable sales strategies

3. Return to the paragraph or first draft you prepared in response to activity 4 or activity 5 in Chapter 4. Applying the principles discussed in Chapter 5, strengthen the organization of the evidence you generated. (If you rework a first draft, save the draft so you can refine it further.)

4. The following brief essay outline consists of a thesis and several points of support. Which pattern of development would you probably use to develop the overall organizational framework for each essay? Which pattern(s) would you use to develop each point of support? Why?

   Thesis: Friends often fall into one of several categories: the pal, the confidante, or the pest.

   Points of Support
   - Frequently, a friend is simply a "pal."
   - Sometimes, though, a pal turns, step by step, into a confidante.
   - If a confidante begins to have romantic thoughts, he or she may become a pest, thus disrupting the friendship.

5. For the thesis statement given in activity 4, identify a possible purpose, audience, tone, and point of view. Then, use one or more patterns to generate material to develop the points of support listed. Get together with someone else to review the generated material, deleting, adding, combining, and arranging ideas in logical order. Finally, make an outline for the body of the essay. (Save your outline to work with it further.)

6. Look again at the thesis and scratch outline you refined and elaborated in response to activity 6 in Chapter 4. Reevaluate this material by deleting, adding, combining, and rearranging ideas as needed. Then, in preparation for writing an essay, outline your ideas. Consider whether an emphatic, chronological, spatial, or simple-to-complex approach will be most appropriate. Finally, ask at least one other person to evaluate your organizational plan. (Save your outline to work with it further.)

Chapter 6
Writing the Paragraphs in the First Draft

Learning Objectives

6.1 Move from outline to first draft.

6.2 Develop strategies for moving forward if you get bogged down.

6.3 Use a sequence for writing the first draft.

6.4 Understand the overall structure of an effective essay.

After prewriting, deciding on a thesis, and developing and organizing evidence, you're ready to write a first draft—a rough, tentative version of your essay. While your first draft may flow quite smoothly, don't be discouraged if it doesn't. You may find that your thesis has to be reshaped, that a point no longer fits, or that you need to return to a prewriting activity to generate additional material. Such stops and starts are to be expected. Writing the first draft is a process of discovery, involving the continual clarification and refining of ideas.

How to Move from Outline to First Draft

6.1 Move from outline to first draft.

There's no single right way to prepare a first draft. However you choose to proceed, consider the suggestions in the following checklist when moving from an outline or scratch list to a first draft.

☑ Turning an Outline into First Draft: A Checklist

☐ Make the outline's *main topics* (I, II, III) the *topic sentences* of the essay's supporting paragraphs. (Topic sentences are discussed later in this chapter.)

☐ Make the outline's *subtopics* (A, B, C) the *subpoints* in each paragraph.

☐ Make the outline's *supporting points* (1, 2, 3) the *key examples* and *reasons* in each paragraph.

☐ Make the outline's *specific details* (a, b, c) the *secondary examples*, facts, statistics, expert opinion, and quotations in each paragraph.

Although outlines and lists are valuable for guiding your work, don't be so dependent on them that you shy away from new ideas that surface during your writing of the first draft. It's during this time that promising new thoughts often pop up. As they do, jot them down in the margins of your draft. If you're typing your draft on a computer, you can easily use digital commenting features to keep track of ideas that come to you as you're composing. Then, at the appropriate point, go back and evaluate the ideas that came to you as you were writing your draft: Do they support your thesis? Are they appropriate for your essay's purpose, audience, tone, and point of view? If so, go ahead and include the material in your draft.

It's easy to get bogged down if you try to edit as you write. Remember: A first draft isn't intended to be perfect. There's a good reason it's often referred to as a *rough* draft. For the time being, adopt a relaxed, noncritical attitude. Work as quickly as you can, and don't stop to check spelling, correct grammar, or refine sentence structure. Save these tasks for later.

You may find that using a computer considerably facilitates the drafting process. Word processing programs help you quickly and easily save and revise text as well as cut and paste material. Remember to give each draft a clear, unique filename—for example, "Video games draft 1"—so that you can locate the most recent version easily. If you are using direct quotations from notes that you have in a computer file, carefully cut and paste the quotations from the notes file to your draft, making sure to use quotation marks around each quotation and to indicate the source at the end of the quote.

If You Get Bogged Down

6.2 Develop strategies for moving forward if you get bogged down.

All writers get bogged down now and then. The best thing to do is accept that sooner or later this will happen to you. Just include a reminder to yourself in the margin ("Fix this," "Redo," or "Ugh!") to fine-tune the section later. Or leave a blank space for the right words when they finally come to mind. It may also help to reread—out loud is best—what you've already written. Regaining a sense of the larger context is often enough to get you moving again.

If a section of the essay strikes you as particularly difficult, don't spend time struggling with it. Move on to an easier section, write that, and then return to the challenging part. If you're still getting nowhere, take a break. Listen to music, talk with friends, or take a walk. While you're giving your mind a break, your thoughts may loosen up and untangle the knotty section. If an obligation such as a class or an appointment forces you to stop writing when the draft is going well, take a few seconds to make notes in the margin to remind yourself of your train of thought.

A Suggested Sequence for Writing the First Draft

6.3 Use a sequence for writing the first draft.

Because you read essays from beginning to end, you may assume that writers work the same way, starting with the introduction and going straight through to the conclusion. Often, however, this isn't the case. In fact, because an introduction depends so heavily on everything that follows, it's usually best to write the introduction *after* you write the essay's body. (See Figure 6.1.)

When preparing your first draft, you may find it helpful to follow a five-step sequence.

1. Write the Supporting Paragraphs

Before starting to write the essay's **supporting paragraphs**, enter your thesis at the top of the page. You might even underline key words in the thesis to keep yourself focused on the central ideas you plan to develop. Also, now that you've planned

Figure 6.1 Process Diagram: Writing a Draft

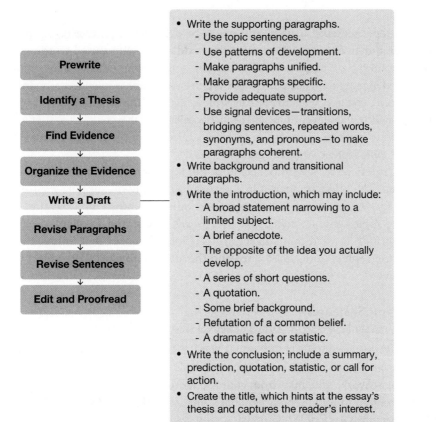

Prewrite

↓

Identify a Thesis

↓

Find Evidence

↓

Organize the Evidence

↓

Write a Draft

↓

Revise Paragraphs

↓

Revise Sentences

↓

Edit and Proofread

- Write the supporting paragraphs.
  - Use topic sentences.
  - Use patterns of development.
  - Make paragraphs unified.
  - Make paragraphs specific.
  - Provide adequate support.
  - Use signal devices—transitions, bridging sentences, repeated words, synonyms, and pronouns—to make paragraphs coherent.
- Write background and transitional paragraphs.
- Write the introduction, which may include:
  - A broad statement narrowing to a limited subject.
  - A brief anecdote.
  - The opposite of the idea you actually develop.
  - A series of short questions.
  - A quotation.
  - Some brief background.
  - Refutation of a common belief.
  - A dramatic fact or statistic.
- Write the conclusion; include a summary, prediction, quotation, statistic, or call for action.
- Create the title, which hints at the essay's thesis and captures the reader's interest.

the essay's overall organization, you may want to add to your thesis a **plan of development**—a brief *overview* of the essay's *major points in the exact order* in which you will discuss those points—if you didn't do so when you developed your thesis statement.

In a long, complex essay, a plan of development helps readers follow the progression of main points in the supporting paragraphs. Whether or not you include a plan of development, always keep in mind that writing the draft often leads to new ideas. You may have to revise your thesis, plan of development, and supporting paragraphs as the draft unfolds.

Drawn from the main sections in your outline or scratch list, each supporting paragraph should develop an aspect of your essay's thesis or plan of development. Although there are no hard-and-fast rules, strong supporting paragraphs are (1) often focused by topic sentences, (2) organized around one or more patterns of development, (3) unified, (4) specific, (5) adequately supported, and (6) coherent. Aim for as many of these qualities as you can in the first draft.

USE TOPIC SENTENCES   Usually, each supporting paragraph in an essay is focused by a **topic sentence**. This sentence usually states a main point in support of the thesis.

The topic sentence usually appears at or near the beginning of the paragraph. However, it may appear at the end, in the middle, or—with varied wording—several times within the paragraph. In other cases, a single topic sentence may state an idea developed in more than one paragraph. When a paragraph is intended primarily to clarify or inform, you may want to place its topic sentence at the beginning; that way, readers are prepared to view everything that follows in light of that main idea. If you intend a paragraph to heighten suspense or to convey a feeling of discovery, you may prefer to delay the topic sentence until the end.

Regardless of its length or location, the topic sentence states the paragraph's main idea. The other sentences in the paragraph provide support for this central point in the form of examples, facts, expert opinion, and so on. Like a thesis statement, the topic sentence *signals the paragraph's subject* and frequently *indicates the writer's attitude* toward that subject. In the topic sentences that follow, the subject of the paragraph is underlined once and the attitude toward that subject is underlined twice:

Topic Sentences
Some students select a particular field of study for the wrong reasons.

The ocean dumping of radioactive waste is a ticking time bomb.

As you work, you may find yourself writing paragraphs without paying too much attention to topic sentences. That's fine, as long as you remember to evaluate the paragraphs later on. When revising, you can provide a topic sentence for a paragraph that needs a sharper focus, recast a topic sentence for a paragraph that ended up taking an unexpected turn, and even eliminate a topic sentence altogether if a paragraph's content is sufficiently unified to imply its point.

USE THE PATTERNS OF DEVELOPMENT   As you know, an entire essay can be organized around one or more patterns of development. These patterns can also provide the organizational framework for an essay's supporting paragraphs. Assume you're writing an article for your town newspaper with the thesis "Year-round residents of an ocean community must take an active role in safeguarding the seashore environment." As the following examples indicate, your supporting paragraphs could develop this thesis through a variety of patterns, with each paragraph's topic sentence suggesting a specific pattern or combination of patterns.

Of course, each supporting paragraph in an essay doesn't have to be organized according to a different pattern of development; several paragraphs may use the same pattern. Nor is it necessary for any one paragraph to be restricted to a single pattern; supporting paragraphs often combine patterns.

Topic Sentence	Possible Pattern of Development
In a nearby ocean community, signs of environmental damage are everywhere.	*Description* of a seaside town: polluted waters, blighted trees, diseased marine life
Typically, residents blame industry or tourists for such damage.	*Narration* of a conversation among seaside residents
Residents' careless behavior is also to blame, however.	*Illustrations* of residents' littering the beach, injuring marine life while motor boating, walking over fragile sand dunes
Even environmentally concerned residents may contribute to the problem.	*Cause-effect* explanation of the way Styrofoam packaging and plastic food wrap, even when properly disposed of in a trash can, can harm scavenging seagulls
Fortunately, not all seaside towns are plagued by such environmental problems.	*Comparison-contrast* of one troubled shore community with another, more ecologically sound one
It's clear that shore residents must become "environmental activists."	*Definition* of an *environmental activist*
Residents can get involved in a variety of pro-environmental activities.	*Division-classification* of activities at the neighborhood, town, and municipal levels
Moreover, getting involved is an easy matter.	*Process analysis* of the steps for getting involved at the various levels
Such activism yields significant rewards.	A final *argumentation-persuasion* pitch showing residents the benefits of responsible action

MAKE THE PARAGRAPHS UNIFIED Just as overall evidence must support an essay's thesis, the facts, opinions, and examples in each supporting paragraph must have *direct bearing* on the paragraph's topic sentence. If the paragraph has no topic sentence, the supporting material must be *consistent* with the paragraph's *implied focus*. A paragraph is **unified** when it meets these requirements.

Consider the following sample paragraph. The paragraph lacks unity because it contains points (underlined) unrelated to its main idea given in the topic (first) sentence. To present a balanced view of cable versus network television, the writer should discuss these points, but in *another paragraph.*

Nonunified Support

Many people consider cable TV an improvement over network television. For one thing, viewers usually prefer the movies on cable. Unlike network films, cable movies are often only months old, they have not been edited by censors, and they are not interrupted by commercials. Growing numbers of people also feel that cable specials are superior to the ones the networks grind out. Cable viewers may enjoy such performers as Usher, Adele, or Chris Rock in concert, whereas the networks continue to broadcast tired, look-alike reality shows and boring awards ceremonies. There is, however, one problem with cable comedians. The foul language many of them use makes it hard to watch these cable specials with children. The networks, in contrast, generally present "clean" shows that parents and children can watch together. Then, too, cable TV offers viewers more flexibility because it schedules shows at various times over the month. People working night shifts or attending evening classes can see movies in the afternoon, and viewers missing the first twenty minutes of a show can always catch them later. It's not surprising that cable viewership is growing while network ratings have taken a plunge.

MAKE THE PARAGRAPHS SPECIFIC If your supporting paragraphs are vague, readers will lose interest, remain unconvinced of your thesis, and even have trouble deciphering your meaning. In contrast, paragraphs filled with **concrete, specific details** engage readers, lend force to ideas, and clarify meaning, as in the following example.

Specific Support

More and more companies have begun to realize that flex-time scheduling offers advantages over a rigid 9-to-5 routine. Along suburban Boston's Route 128, such companies as Compugraphics and Consolidated Paper now permit employees to schedule their arrival any time between 6 a.m. and 11 a.m. The corporations report that the number of rush-hour jams and accidents has fallen dramatically. As a result, employees no longer arrive at work weighed down by tension induced by choking clouds of exhaust fumes and the blaring horns of gridlocked drivers. Studies sponsored by the journal *Business Quarterly* show that this more mellow state of mind benefits corporations. Traffic-stressed employees begin their workday anxious and exasperated, still grinding their teeth at their fellow commuters, their frustration often spilling over into their performance at work. By contrast, stress-free employees work more productively and take fewer days off. They are more tolerant of co-workers and customers, and they are less likely to balloon minor irritations into major confrontations. Perhaps most important, employees arriving at work relatively free of stress can focus their attention on working safely. They rack up significantly fewer on-the-job accidents, such as falls and injuries resulting from careless handling of dangerous equipment. Flex-time improves employee well-being, and as well-being rises, so do company profits.

Five Strategies for Making Paragraphs Specific. How can you make the evidence in your paragraphs specific? The following techniques will help.

1. **Provide examples that answer *who, which, what,* and similar questions**. The preceding paragraph provides examples that answer basic questions. Instead of the general comment "Several companies outside Boston" (*which* companies?), the author provides specific names: Compugraphics and Consolidated Paper. Similarly, "on-the-job accidents" (*which* accidents?) is illustrated with "falls and injuries resulting from careless handling of dangerous equipment."

2. **Replace general nouns and adjectives with precise ones**. In the following sentences, note how much sharper images become when exact nouns and adjectives replace imprecise ones:

General	More Specific	Most Specific
A *man* had trouble lifting the *box* out of the *old car*.	A *young man, out of shape*, struggled to lift the *heavy crate* out of the *beat-up sports car*.	*Joe, only twenty years old but more than fifty pounds overweight*, struggled to lift the *heavy wooden crate* out of the *rusty* and *dented Mustang*.

3. **Replace abstract words with concrete ones**. Notice the way the example on the right, firmly grounded in the physical, clarifies the intangible concepts in the example on the left:

Abstract	Concrete
The fall day had great *beauty*, despite its *dreariness*.	*Red, yellow,* and *orange* leaves *gleamed wetly* through the *gray mist.*

4. **Use words that appeal to the five senses (sight, touch, taste, smell, sound)**. The sentence on the left lacks impact because it fails to convey any sensory impressions. The sentence on the right gains power through the use of sensory details:

Without Sensory Images	With Sensory Images
The computer room is eerie.	In the computer room, keys *click* and printers *grate* while row after row of students stare into screens that *glow without shedding any light.* (sound and sight)

5. **Use vigorous verbs**. Linking verbs (such as *seem* and *appear*) and *to be* verbs (such as *is* and *were*) paint no pictures. Strong verbs, however, create sharp visual images. Compare the following examples:

Weak Verbs	Strong Verbs
The spectators *seemed* pleased and *were* enthusiastic when the runners *went* by.	The spectators *cheered* and *whistled* when the runners *whizzed* by.

PROVIDE ADEQUATE SUPPORT Each supporting paragraph should also have **adequate support** so that your readers can see clearly the validity of the topic sentence. At times, a single extended example is sufficient. Generally, however, an assortment of examples, facts, personal observations, and so forth is more effective.

The following paragraph offers examples, descriptive details, and dialogue—all of which make the writing stronger and more convincing.

Adequate Support

Gas stations are a good example of this impersonal attitude. At almost all stations, attendants have stopped pumping gas. Motorists pull up to a combination convenience store and gas island where an attendant is enclosed in a glass booth with a tray for taking money. The driver must get out of the car, pump the gas, and walk over to the booth to pay. Even at the few stations that still have "pump jockeys," employees seldom ask, "Check your oil?" or wash windshields, although they may grudgingly point out the location of the bucket and squeegee. And customers with a balky engine or a nonfunctioning heater are usually out of luck. Why? Almost all gas stations have eliminated on-duty mechanics. The skillful mechanic who could replace a belt or fix a tire in a few minutes has been replaced by a teenager in a jumpsuit who doesn't know a carburetor from a charge card and couldn't care less.

MAKE THE PARAGRAPHS COHERENT Paragraphs can be unified, specific, and adequately supported, yet—if internally disjointed or inadequately connected to each other—leave readers feeling confused. Readers need to be able to follow with ease the progression of thought within and between paragraphs. One idea must flow smoothly and logically into the next; that is, your writing must be **coherent**.

To avoid incoherent paragraphs, use two key strategies: (1) a clearly *chronological, spatial, emphatic, or simple-to-complex order* and (2) *signal devices* to show how ideas are connected.

Order. As you know, an entire essay can be organized using chronological, spatial, emphatic, or simple-to-complex order. These strategies can also be used to make individual paragraphs coherent.

For example, imagine you plan to write an essay showing the difficulties many immigrants face when they first come to this country. Let's consider how you might structure your three supporting paragraphs, particularly the way each paragraph's organizational approach can help you arrange ideas in a logical, easy-to-follow sequence.

One paragraph, focused by the topic sentence "The everyday life of a typical immigrant family is arduous," might be developed through a **chronological** account of the family's daily routine: purchasing, before dawn, fruits and vegetables for their produce stand; setting up the stand early in the morning; working there for ten hours; attending English class at night. Another paragraph might develop its topic sentence, "Many immigrant families get along without the technology that others take for granted," through **spatial** order, taking readers on a brief tour of an immigrant family's rented home: the kitchen lacks a dishwasher or microwave; the living room has no computer or phone, only a small TV; the basement has just a washtub and clothesline instead of a washer and dryer. Finally, a third paragraph, with the topic sentence "A number of worries typically beset immigrant families," might use an **emphatic** sequence, moving from less significant concerns (having to wear old, unfashionable clothes) to more critical issues (having to deal with isolation and discrimination).

Signal Devices. Once you determine a logical sequence for your points, you need to make sure that readers can follow the progression of those points within and between paragraphs. **Signal devices** provide readers with cues, reminding them where they have been and indicating where they are going.

Try to include some signals—however awkward or temporary—in your first draft. If you find you *can't*, that's probably a warning that your ideas may not be arranged logically—in which case, it's better to find that out now rather than later on. Keep in mind, though, that a light touch should be your goal with such signals. Overuse can make the essay mechanical and plodding.

1. **Transitions.** Words and phrases that ease readers from one idea to another are called **transitions**. The following chart lists a variety of such signals. (You'll notice that some transitions can be used for more than one purpose.)

TRANSITIONS

Time

after, afterward

at the same time

before, earlier, previously

finally, eventually

first, next

immediately

in the meantime

meanwhile

simultaneously

subsequently, later

then, now

Space

above, below

next to, behind

Examples

for instance, for example

namely, specifically

to illustrate

Addition or Sequence

and, also, too

besides

finally, last

first, . . . second, . . . third

furthermore

moreover, in addition

next

one . . . another

Contrast

although, though

but, however

conversely

despite, even though

in contrast

nevertheless, nonetheless

on the contrary, whereas

on the one (other) hand

otherwise

yet, still

Comparison

also, too

likewise

in comparison

in the same way

similarly

Cause or Effect

as a result

because, since

consequently

in turn

so

therefore, then

Summary or Conclusion

in conclusion

in short

therefore

thus

Note how the underlined transitions in the following paragraph provide clear cues to readers, showing how ideas fit together:

> Although the effect of air pollution on the human body is distressing, its effect on global ecology is even more troubling. In the Bavarian, French, and Italian Alps, <u>for example</u>, once-magnificent forests are slowly being destroyed by air pollution. Trees dying from pollution lose their leaves or needles, allowing sunlight to reach the forest floor. <u>During</u> this process, grass prospers in the increased light and pushes out the native plants and moss that help hold rainwater. The soil <u>thus</u> loses absorbency and becomes hard, causing rain and snow to slide over the ground instead of sinking into it. This, <u>in turn</u>, leads to erosion of the soil. <u>After</u> a heavy rain, the eroded land <u>finally</u> falls away in giant rockslides and avalanches, destroying entire villages and causing life-threatening floods.

2. **Bridging sentences.** Although **bridging sentences** may be used within a paragraph, they are more often used to move readers from one paragraph to the next. Look again at the first sentence in the preceding paragraph on pollution. Note that the sentence consists of two parts: The first part reminds readers that the previous discussion focused on pollution's effect on the body; the second part tells readers that the focus will now be pollution's effect on global ecology.

3. **Repeated words, synonyms, and pronouns.** The **repetition** of important words maintains continuity, reassures readers that they are on the right track, and highlights key ideas. **Synonyms**—words similar in meaning—to key words or phrases

also provide coherence while making it possible to avoid unimaginative and tedious repetitions. Finally, **pronouns** (*he, she, it, they, this, that*) enhance coherence by causing readers to think back to the original word (antecedent) the pronoun replaces. When using pronouns, however, be sure there is no ambiguity about antecedents.

The following paragraph uses repeated words (underlined once), synonyms (underlined twice), and pronouns (underlined three times) to integrate ideas:

> Studies have shown that color is also an important part of the way people experience food. In one study, individuals fed a rich red tomato sauce didn't notice the complete absence of flavor until they were nearly finished eating. Similarly, in another experiment, people were offered strangely colored foods: gray pork chops, lavender mashed potatoes, dark blue peas, dessert topped with yellow whipped cream. Not one of the subjects would eat the strange-looking food, even though it smelled and tasted normal.

2. Write Other Paragraphs in the Essay's Body

Paragraphs supporting the thesis are not necessarily the only kind of paragraph in the body of an essay. You may also include paragraphs that give background information or provide transitions.

BACKGROUND PARAGRAPHS   Usually found near the essay's beginning, **background paragraphs** provide information that doesn't directly support the thesis but that helps the reader understand or accept the discussion that follows. Such paragraphs may consist of a definition, a historical overview, or a short description. For example, in a student essay titled "Party with a Purpose," the opening paragraphs provide important background information on Ryan White, a thirteen-year-old boy who was diagnosed with HIV/AIDS and who, consequently, was subjected to discrimination in both his community and his school. This background information serves as a lead-in to the causal chain that makes up the rest of the cause-effect essay. Without the background information on Ryan, readers would not have a clear picture of the essay's main point.

TRANSITIONAL PARAGRAPHS   Another kind of paragraph, generally one to three sentences long, may appear between supporting paragraphs to help readers keep track of your discussion. Like the bridging sentences discussed earlier in the chapter, **transitional paragraphs** usually sum up what has been discussed so far and then indicate the direction the essay will take next.

While too many such paragraphs make writing stiff and mechanical, they can be effective when used sparingly, especially in essays with sharp turns in direction.

3. Write the Introduction

Many writers don't prepare an **introduction** until they have started to revise; others feel more comfortable if their first draft includes in basic form all parts of the final essay. No matter when you prepare it, keep in mind how crucial the introduction is to your essay's success. The introduction serves three distinct functions:

- It arouses readers' interest.
- It introduces your subject.
- It presents your thesis.

Remember, the introduction's style and content should flow into the rest of the essay.

The length of your introduction will vary according to your essay's scope and purpose. Most essays you write will be served best by a one- or two-paragraph beginning. To write an effective introduction, use any of the following methods, singly or in combination. The thesis statement in each sample introduction is underlined. Note, too, that the first thesis includes a plan of development, whereas the last thesis is followed by a plan of development.

Broad Statement Narrowing to a Limited Subject

For generations, morality has been molded primarily by parents, religion, and schools. Children traditionally acquired their ideas about what is right and wrong, which goals are important in life, and how others should be treated from these three sources collectively. But in the past few decades, a single force—television—has undermined the beneficial influence that parents, religion, and school have on children's moral development. Indeed, television often implants in children negative values about sex, work, and family life.

Brief Anecdote

At a local high school, students in a psychology course were recently given a hint of what it is like to be the parents of a newborn. Each "parent" had to carry a raw egg around at all times to symbolize the responsibilities of parenthood. The egg could not be left alone; it limited the "parents'" activities; it placed a full-time emotional burden on "Mom" and "Dad." This class exercise illustrates a common problem facing the majority of new mothers and fathers. Most people receive little preparation for the job of being parents.

Starting with an Idea That Is the Opposite of the One Actually Developed

We hear a great deal about divorce's disastrous impact on children. We are deluged with advice on ways to make divorce as painless as possible for youngsters; we listen to heartbreaking stories about the confused, grieving children of divorced parents. Little attention has been paid, however, to a different kind of effect that divorce may have on children. Children from divorced families may become skilled manipulators, playing off one parent against the other, worsening an already painful situation.

Series of Short Questions

What happens if a child is caught vandalizing school property? What happens if a child goes for a joyride in a stolen car and accidentally hits a pedestrian? Should parents be liable for their children's mistakes? Should parents have to pay what might be hundreds of thousands of dollars in damages? Adults have begun to think seriously about such questions because the laws concerning the limits of parental responsibility are changing rapidly. <u>With unfortunate frequency, courts have begun to hold parents legally and financially responsible for their children's misbehavior.</u>

Quotation

Educator Neil Postman believes that television has blurred the line between childhood and adulthood. According to Postman, "All the secrets that a print culture kept from children...are revealed all at once by media that do not, and cannot, exclude any audience." <u>This media barrage of information, once intended only for adults, has changed childhood for the worse.</u>

Brief Background on the Topic

For a long time, adults believed that "children should be seen, not heard." On special occasions, youngsters were dressed up and told to sit quietly while adults socialized. Even when they were alone with their parents, children were not supposed to bother adults with their concerns. However, beginning with psychologist Arnold Gesell in the 1940s, child-raising experts began to question the wisdom of an approach that blocked communication. In 1965, Haim Ginott's ground-breaking book *Between Parent and Child* stressed the importance of conversing with children. More recently, two of Ginott's disciples, Adele Sager and Elaine Mazlish, wrote a book on this subject: *How to Talk So Children Will Listen and Listen So Children Will Talk*. <u>These days, experts agree, successful parents are those who encourage their children to share their thoughts and concerns.</u>

Refutation of a Common Belief

Adolescents care only about material things; their lives revolve around brand-name sneakers, designer clothes, the latest smartphone. They resist education, don't read, barely know who is president, are plugged into Facebook 24/7, experiment with drugs, and exist on a steady diet of Ring-Dings, nachos, and beer. This is what many adults, including parents, seem to believe about the young. <u>The reality is, however, that young people today show more maturity and common sense than most adults give them credit for.</u>

Dramatic Fact or Statistic

Seventy percent of the respondents in a poll conducted by columnist Ann Landers stated that, if they could live their lives over, they would choose not to have children. This startling statistic makes one wonder what these people believed parenthood would be like. <u>Many parents have unrealistic expectations for their children.</u> Parents want their children to accept their values, follow their paths, and succeed where they failed.

4. Write the Conclusion

A strong **conclusion** is an important part of an effective essay, and many writers find conclusions difficult to write. When it comes time to write one, you may feel you've said all there is to say. To prevent such an impasse, you can try saving a compelling statistic, quotation, or detail for the end of your essay. Just make sure that this interesting item fits in the conclusion and that the essay's body contains sufficient support without it.

Occasionally, an essay doesn't need a separate conclusion. This is often the case with narration or description. For instance, in a narrative showing how a crisis can strengthen a faltering friendship, your point will probably be made with sufficient force without a final "this is what the narrative is all about" paragraph.

Usually, though, a conclusion is necessary. Generally one or two paragraphs long, the conclusion should give the reader a feeling of completeness and finality. One way to achieve this sense of "rounding off" is to return to an image, idea, or anecdote from the introduction.

Because people tend to remember most clearly the points they read last, the conclusion is also a good place to remind readers of your thesis, phrasing this central idea somewhat differently than you did earlier in the essay. You may also use the conclusion to make a final point. This way, you leave your readers with something to mull over. Be careful, though, not to open an entirely new line of thought at the essay's close. If you do, readers may feel puzzled and frustrated, wishing you had provided evidence for your final point. And, of course, always be sure that concluding material fits your thesis and is consistent with your purpose, tone, and point of view.

In your conclusion, it's best to steer away from stock phrases like "In sum," "In conclusion," and "This essay has shown that..." Also avoid lengthy conclusions. As in everyday life, prolonged farewells are tedious.

Following are examples of some techniques you can use to write effective conclusions. These strategies may be used singly or in combination. The first strategy (*summary*) can be especially helpful in long, complex essays because readers may appreciate a review of your points. Tacked onto a short essay, though, a summary conclusion often seems boring and mechanical.

Summary
Contrary to what many adults think, most adolescents are not only aware of the important issues of the times but also deeply concerned about them. They are sensitive to the plight of the homeless, the destruction of the environment, and the pitfalls of rampant materialism. Indeed, today's young people are not less mature and sensible than their parents were. If anything, they are more so.

Prediction
The growing tendency on the part of the judicial system to hold parents responsible for the actions of their delinquent children can have a disturbing impact on all of us. Parents will feel bitter toward their own children and cynical about a system that holds them accountable for the actions of minors. Children, continuing to escape the consequences of their actions, will become even more lawless and destructive. Society cannot afford two such possibilities.

Quotation
The comic W. C. Fields is reputed to have said, "Anyone who hates children and dogs can't be all bad." Most people do not share Fields's cynicism.

Viewing childhood as a time of purity, they are alarmed at the way television, video games, and the Internet expose children to the seamy side of life, stripping youngsters of their innocence and giving them a glib sophistication that is a poor substitute for wisdom.

Statistic

Granted, divorce may, in some cases, be the best thing for families torn apart by parents battling one another. However, in longitudinal studies of children from divorced families, psychologist Judith Wallerstein found that only 10 percent of the youngsters felt relief at their parents' divorce; the remaining 90 percent felt devastated. Such statistics surely call into question parents' claims that they are divorcing for their children's sake.

Recommendation or Call for Action

It is a mistake to leave parenting to instinct. Instead, we should make parenting skills a required course in schools. In addition, a nationwide hotline should be established to help parents deal with crises. Such training and continuing support would help adults deal more effectively with many of the problems they face as parents.

5. Create the Title

Some writers say that they often begin a piece with only a title in mind. But for most, writing the **title** is the finishing touch. Although creating a title is usually one of the last steps in writing an essay, it shouldn't be done haphazardly. It may take time to write an effective title—one that hints at the essay's thesis and snares the reader's interest.

Good titles may make use of the following techniques: *repetition of sounds* ("The Sanctuary of School"), *humor* ("'Tweet, Tweedle-lee-dee' (118 Characters Left)"), and *questions* ("Who's a Pirate?"). More often, though, titles are straightforward phrases derived from the essay's subject or thesis: "The Body Piercing Project" and "Government Intervention Will Not Solve Our Obesity Problem," for example.

As you read the first and final drafts of Caylah Francis's essay, notice that the title changes. In the early stages of drafting her essay, Caylah's title was "Kids and Video Games"—not exactly a riveting title, and Caylah knew it. As she continued to work on improving her essay, she played around with various titles and finally arrived at one that pleased her: "Aggression, Addiction, Isolation, and More: The Dark Side of Video Game Play"—*much* better!

Pulling It All Together

6.4 Understand the overall structure of an effective essay.

Now that you know how to prepare a first draft, you might find it helpful to examine Figure 6.2 to see how the different parts of a draft can fit together. Keep in mind that not every essay you write will take this shape. As your purpose, audience, tone, and

Figure 6.2 Structure of an Essay

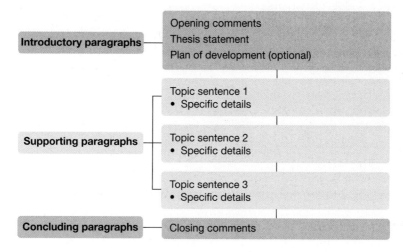

Introductory paragraphs — Opening comments / Thesis statement / Plan of development (optional)

Supporting paragraphs —
Topic sentence 1
• Specific details

Topic sentence 2
• Specific details

Topic sentence 3
• Specific details

Concluding paragraphs — Closing comments

point of view change, so will your essay's structure. The basic format presented here offers a strategy for organizing a variety of writing assignments. Once you feel comfortable with the structure, you have a foundation on which to base your variations.

Sample First Draft

Here is the first draft of Caylah Francis's essay. Caylah wrote the draft in one sitting. Working at a computer, she started by typing her thesis at the top of the first page. Then, following the guidelines in this chapter, she moved the material in her outline to her draft. Caylah worked rapidly; she started with the first body paragraph and wrote straight through to the last supporting paragraph.

By moving quickly, Caylah got down her essay's basic text rather easily. She had already conducted her research and made notes in her outline regarding where she would include supporting material from her outside sources. Once she felt she had captured in rough form what she wanted to say in her three body paragraphs, she reread her draft to get a sense of how she might introduce and conclude the essay. She already knew that she wanted to include information about changing family life and the role of parents in monitoring video game play in her introduction, but she didn't have a plan for her conclusion. Both her introduction and conclusion appear here, along with the body of the essay. The commentary following the draft will give you a clearer sense of how Caylah proceeded. (Note that the marginal annotations reflect Caylah's comments to herself about areas she needs to address when revising her first draft.)

Kids and Video Games
by Caylah Francis

Thesis: Playing violent video games can have many negative effects on kids. It can lead to increased levels of aggression, video game addiction, and serious health issues.

Name specific
games

Reword?

Weak transition

Integrate quotes
better

Integrate quote
better

The incredible advancement of technology has created a world where many American houses not only have one television, one computer, and one video game console, but many have several of these media devices. Parents try everything to please their kids such as buying them a variety of video games from violent first person shooter games to fantasy games. Parents that work many hours a week and have kids try their best to preoccupy their children to aid in the parenting process. With that said, the use of video games has become a popular activity among many kids. In result, there have been many negative and positive effects on young people who play video games. More specifically this has created concerns for kids who play video games an excessive amount of time. Playing violent video games can have many negative effects on kids. It can lead to increased levels of aggression, video game addiction, and serious health issues.

One concern that many people have for violent video games is their children learning to be more aggressive and violent. "From a social learning perspective, adolescents who play violent video games may imitate the aggression that they observe in the games" (Willoughby 1044). According to Willoughby in "A Longitudinal Study of the Association Between Violent Video Game Play and Aggression among Adolecents," "greater violent video game play predicted higher levels of aggression over time," while nonviolent video game play did not predict higher levels of aggressive behavior" (Willoughby 1044). Another study revealed that "playing a violent video game caused boys to become more aggressive than merely watching the same violent video game" (Polman 256). This study goes on to state that "specifically for boys, playing a violent video game could lead to more aggression than watching television violence" (Polman 256). There is no doubt that children can learn to be more aggressive and violent by playing a simple video game.

Violent video games and the creation of aggressive children is only one of many negative effects. Another negative effect is video game addiction. In a 2010 study, 1,945 people were surveyed about video game use. The study found that "almost one-half (48.7%) of the participants spent 1-3 hours per day playing video games, and approximately one-third (32.9%) spent 4-8 hours per day doing so" (Porter 123). As young children play video games, the probability that the child will grow up addicted to video games is very high. "They become preoccupied with gaming, lie about their gaming use, lose interest in other activities just to game, withdrawal from family and friends to game, and use gaming as a means to psychologically escape" (Young 356). Games usually offer positive reinforcement and positive sanctions. For example, games that are first person shooter games often offer their positive reinforcement in terms of new weapons, perks, vehicles, and ranks. As many play these video games online they can communicate to others through a simple microphone. This allows many positive sanctions from other people. Gaming addiction has also had associated with mental illness, physical exhaustion, and death (Porter 2010).

Same trans. as previous paragraph. Revise?

  Video game addiction and aggressive learning are two of many negative effects. Another effect is the danger to the child's health. The United States of America is known for obesity. Video games offer the lack of movement; this can cause an increase in risk for obesity. Not only is the child's physical health at risk, but, the risk of poor psychological health is also at risk. If one were to play video games for many hours, this could lead to depression, and that can be a very serious health issue. It can result in kids not wanting to go to school or interact with others, even their families.

Word choice?

In result, it can affect both the kid and their family.

Weak transition. Redo conclusion.

  Above all, video games have many negative effects on young children. Video games are a very popular activity for young children. Research shows that children can become more aggressive and violent after playing violent video games. Extensive research also shows that many become addicted to video games and can develop health issues as well.

Commentary

As you can see, Caylah's draft is rough. Because she knew she would revise later on, she focused on getting all of her ideas down and incorporating outside source material. She did not take time at this point in the drafting process to polish her prose or create smooth transitions.

Writing a first draft may seem like quite a challenge, but the tips offered in these pages should help you proceed with confidence. Indeed, as you work on the draft, you may be surprised how much you enjoy writing. After all, this is your chance to get down on paper something you want to say.

Activities: Writing the Paragraphs in the First Draft

1. For each paragraph that follows, determine whether the topic sentence is stated or implied. If the topic sentence is explicit, indicate its location in the paragraph (beginning, end, middle, or both beginning and end). If the topic sentence is implied, state it in your own words.

   a. In 1902, a well-known mathematician wrote an article "proving" that no airplane could ever fly. Just a year later, the Wright brothers made their first flight. In the 1950s, a famed British astronomer said in an interview that the idea of space travel was "utter bilge." Similarly, noted scholars in this country and abroad claimed that automobiles would never replace the trolley car and that the electric light was an impractical gimmick. Clearly, being an expert doesn't guarantee a clear vision of the future.

b. Many American companies have learned the hard way that they need to know the language of their foreign customers. When Chevrolet began selling its Nova cars in Latin America, hardly anyone would buy them. The company finally realized that Spanish speakers read the car's name as the Spanish phrase "no va," meaning "doesn't go." When Pepsi-Cola ran its "Pepsi gives you life" ads in China, consumers either laughed or were offended. The company hadn't translated its slogan quite right. In Chinese, the slogan came out "Pepsi brings your ancestors back from the dead."

2. Using the strategies described in this chapter, strengthen the following vague paragraphs. Elaborate each one with striking specifics that clarify meaning and add interest. As you provide specifics, you may need to break each paragraph into several paragraphs.

a. Other students can make studying in the college library difficult. For one thing, they take up so much space that they leave little room for anyone else. By being inconsiderate in other ways, they make it hard to concentrate on the task at hand. Worst of all, they do things that make it almost impossible to find needed books and magazines.

b. Some people have dangerous driving habits. They act as though there's no one else on the road. They also seem unsure of where they're going. Changing their minds from second to second, they leave it up to others to figure out what they're going to do. Finally, too many people drive at speeds that are either too slow or too fast, creating dangerous situations for both drivers and pedestrians.

3. Using the designations indicated in parentheses, identify the flaw(s) in the development of each of the following paragraphs. The paragraphs may lack one or more of the following: unity (U), specific and sufficient support (S), coherence (C). The paragraphs may also needlessly repeat a point (R). Revise the paragraphs, deleting, combining, and rearranging material. Also, add supporting evidence and signal devices where needed.

a. Despite widespread belief to the contrary, brain size within a species has little to do with how intelligent a particular individual is. A human brain can range from 900 cubic centimeters to as much as 2,500 cubic centimeters, but a large brain does not indicate an equally large degree of intelligence. If humans could see the size of other people's brains, they would probably judge each other accordingly, even though brain size has no real significance.

b. For the 50 percent of adult Americans with high cholesterol, heart disease is a constant threat. Americans can reduce their cholesterol significantly by taking a number of easy steps. Because only foods derived from animals contain cholesterol, eating a strict vegetarian diet is the best way to beat the cholesterol problem. Also, losing weight is known to reduce cholesterol levels—even in those who were as little as ten pounds overweight. Physicians warn, though, that quick weight loss almost always leads to an equally rapid regaining of the lost pounds. For those unwilling to try a vegetarian diet, there are other options. Poultry, fish, and low-fat dairy products can substitute for such high-cholesterol foods as red meat, eggs, cream, and butter. Adding oat bran to the diet has been shown to lower cholesterol. The bran absorbs excess cholesterol in the blood and removes it from the body through waste matter.

4. Strengthen the coherence of the following paragraphs by providing a clear organizational structure and by adding appropriate signal devices. To improve the flow of ideas, you may also need to combine and resequence sentences.

I was a camp counselor this past summer. I learned that leading young children is different from leading people your own age. I was president of my high school Ecology Club. I ran it democratically. We wanted to bring a speaker to the school. We decided to do a fund-raiser. I solicited ideas from everybody. We got together to figure out which was best. It became obvious which was the most profitable and workable fund-raiser. Everybody got behind the effort. The discussion showed that the idea of a raffle with prizes donated by local merchants was likely to be the most profitable.

   I learned that little kids operate differently. I had to be more of a boss rather than a democratic leader. I took suggestions from the group on the main activity of the day. Everyone voted for the best suggestion. Some kids got especially upset. There was a problem with kids whose ideas were voted down. I learned to make the suggestions myself. The children could vote on my suggestions. No one was overly attached to any of the suggestions. They felt that the outcome of the voting was fair. Basically, I got to be in charge.

5. For an essay with the thesis shown here, indicate the implied pattern(s) of development for each topic sentence that follows.

Thesis: The college should make community service a requirement for graduation.

Topic Sentences

a. "Mandatory community service" is a fairly new and often misunderstood concept.

b. Here's the story of one student's community involvement.

c. Indeed, a single program offers numerous opportunities for students.

d. Such involvement can have a real impact on students' lives.

e. However, the college could adopt two very different approaches—one developed by a university, the other by a community college.

f. In any case, the college should begin exploring the possibility of making community service a graduation requirement.

6. Select one of the topic sentences listed in activity 5. Use individual or group brainstorming to generate support for it. Review your raw material, and then delete, add, and combine points as needed. Finally, with the thesis in mind, write a rough draft of the paragraph.

7. Imagine you plan to write a serious essay on one of the following thesis statements. The essay will be read by students in your composition class. After determining your point of view, use prewriting techniques of your choice to identify the essay's major and supporting points. Arrange the points in order and determine where background or transitional paragraphs might be helpful.

   a. Society needs stricter laws against noise pollution.

   b. Public buildings in this town should be redesigned to accommodate the disabled.

   c. Long-standing discrimination against women in college athletics must stop.

8. Use any of the techniques described in this chapter to revise the opening and closing paragraphs of two of your own essays. When rewriting, don't forget to keep your purpose, audience, tone, and point of view in mind.

9. Reread Caylah Francis's first draft in this chapter. Overall, does it support Caylah's thesis? Which topic sentences focus paragraphs effectively? Where is evidence specific, unified, and coherent? Where does Caylah run into some problems? Make a list of the draft's strengths and weaknesses. Save your list for later review.

10. Freewrite or write in your journal about a subject that's been on your mind lately. Reread your raw material to see what thesis seems to emerge. What might your purpose, audience, tone, and point of view be if you wrote an essay with this thesis? What primary and secondary points would you cover? Prepare an outline of your ideas. Then draft the essay's body, providing background and transitional paragraphs if appropriate. Finally, write a rough version of the essay's introduction, conclusion, and title. (Save your draft so you can revise it later.)

11. If you prepared a first draft in response to activity 3 in Chapter 5, work with at least one other person to strengthen that early draft by applying the ideas presented in this chapter. (Save this stronger version of your draft so you can refine it further.)

12. Referring to the outline you prepared in response to activity 5 or activity 6 in Chapter 5, draft the body of an essay. After reviewing the draft, prepare background and transitional paragraphs as needed. Then draft a rough introduction, conclusion, and title. Ask several people to react to what you've prepared, and save your draft so you can work with it further.

Chapter 7
Revising Overall Meaning, Structure, and Paragraph Development

Learning Objectives

7.1 Use six strategies to make revision easier.

7.2 Revise for overall meaning and structure.

7.3 Revise paragraph development.

Revision occurs throughout the writing process: At some earlier stage, you most likely dropped an idea, overhauled your thesis, or shifted paragraph order. What, then, is different about the rewriting that occurs in the revision stage? The answer has to do with the literal meaning of the word *revision*—reseeing, or seeing again. Genuine revision involves casting clear eyes on your work, viewing it as though you're a reader rather than the writer. Revision is not, as some believe, simply touch-up work—changing a sentence here, a word there, eliminating spelling errors, typing or printing out a neat final copy. Revision means that you go through your essay looking for trouble, ready to pick a fight with your own writing. And then you must be willing to sit down and make the changes needed for your writing to be as effective as possible.

Because revision is hard work, you may resist it. After putting the final period in your first draft, you may feel done and have trouble accepting that more work remains. Or, as you read the draft, you may see so many weak spots that you view revision as punishment for not getting things right the first time. If you feel shaky about how to proceed, you may be tempted to skip revising altogether. But do not fear—this chapter will help you undertake the revision process with confidence and enthusiasm.

Six Strategies to Make Revision Easier

7.1 Use six strategies to make revision easier.

Keep in mind that the revision strategies that we discuss in the following sections should be adapted to each writing situation. Other considerations include your professor's requirements and expectations, the time available, and the assignment's bearing on your grade. The strategies summarized in Figure 7.1 will help you approach revision more confidently.

Set Your First Draft Aside for a While

When you pick up or open your draft after having set it aside for a time, you'll approach it with a fresh, more objective point of view. How much of an interval to leave depends on the time available to you. In general, though, the more time between finishing the draft and starting to revise, the better. Just don't wait so long that you lose sight of your audience, purpose, and goals for writing the essay.

Work from Printed Text

Working with an essay in printed form helps you see the essay impartially, as if someone else had written it. Each time you make major changes, print out your essay so that you can see it anew.

Read the Draft Aloud

Hearing how your writing sounds helps you pick up problems that might otherwise go undetected: places where sentences are awkward, meaning is ambiguous, and words are imprecise. Even better, have another person read your draft aloud to you. If

Figure 7.1 Process Diagram: Revising Paragraphs

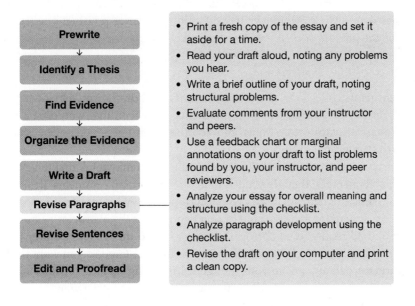

a reader slows to a crawl over a murky paragraph or trips over a convoluted sentence, you know where you have to do some rewriting.

View Revision as a Series of Steps

Like many students, you may find the prospect of revising your draft to be a daunting one. You can overcome a bad case of revision jitters simply by viewing revision as a process. Instead of trying to tackle all of a draft's problems at once, proceed step by step. (The feedback chart and annotation system discussed later in this chapter will help you do just that.) If time allows, read your essay several times. Move from a broad overview (the *macro* level) to an up-close look at mechanics (the *micro* level). With each reading, focus on different issues and ask different questions about the draft.

Here is a recommended series of revision steps:

First step: Revise overall meaning and structure.

Second step: Revise paragraph development.

Third step: Revise sentences and words.

At first, the prospect of reading and rewriting an essay several times may seem to make revision more, not less, overwhelming. Eventually, though, you'll become accustomed to revision as a process, and you'll appreciate the way such an approach improves your writing.

Whenever possible, you should aim for three readings. Resist the impulse to tinker with, say, an unclear sentence until you're sure the essay as a whole makes its point clearly. After all, it can be difficult to rephrase a muddy sentence until you have the essay's overall meaning well in hand.

Remember, though: There are no hard-and-fast rules about the revision steps. For one thing, there are bound to be occasions when you have time for, at best, only one quick pass over a draft. Moreover, as you gain experience revising, you'll probably streamline the process or shift the steps around.

Evaluate and Respond to Instructor Feedback

Often, instructors collect and respond to students' first drafts. You may be tempted to look only briefly at your instructor's comments. However, that would be a mistake. Taking your instructor's comments into account often helps you turn a shaky first draft into a strong final draft.

When an instructor returns a final draft graded, you may think that the grade is all that counts. Remember, though: While grades are important, comments are even more important. They can help you *improve* your writing—if not in this composition, then in the next one. If you don't understand or don't agree with the instructor's observations, don't hesitate to request a conference. Be sure to go to the conference prepared. You might, for example, put a check next to the instructor's comments you want to discuss. Your instructor will appreciate your thoughtful planning; getting together gives both you and the instructor a chance to clarify your respective points of view.

Peer Review: An Additional Revision Strategy

Many instructors include in-class or at-home **peer review** as a part of their composition course. Peer review—the critical reading of another person's writing with the intention of suggesting constructive changes—accomplishes several important goals:

- First, peer review helps you gain a more objective perspective on your work. When you write something, you're often too close to what you've prepared to evaluate it fairly; you may have trouble seeing where the writing is strong and where it needs to be strengthened. Peer review supplies the fresh, neutral perspective you need.

- Second, reviewing your classmates' work broadens your own composing options. You may be inspired to experiment with a technique you admired in a classmate's writing but wouldn't have thought of on your own.

- Finally, peer review trains you to be a better reader and critic of your *own* writing. When you get into the habit of critically reading other students' writing, you become more adept at critiquing your own.

 The revision checklists in this book will help focus your revision—whether you're reworking your own essay or responding to a peer's. What follows is a peer review worksheet that Caylah Francis's instructor prepared to help students respond to first drafts based on the assignment. Wanting students to focus on four areas (thesis statement, support for thesis statement, overall organization, and signal devices), the instructor drew upon relevant sections from the revision checklists. With this customized worksheet in hand, Caylah's classmate Taylor Young was able to give Caylah constructive feedback on her first draft. (*Note:* Because Caylah didn't want to influence Taylor's reaction, the draft she gave her didn't include her marginal notations to herself.)

Peer Review Worksheet

Essay Author's Name: *Caylah Francis*   Reviewer's Name: *Taylor Young*

1. What is the essay's thesis? Is it explicit or implied? Does the thesis focus on a limited subject and express the writer's attitude toward that subject?

   Thesis: "Playing violent video games can have many negative effects on kids. It can lead to increased levels of aggression, video game addiction, and serious health issues."
   The thesis is limited, but it's pretty long; it's made up of two sentences, with the plan of development in the second one. You could omit the second sentence and add something about the research you did. You do a great job of including lots of sources to back up your claims, but you don't mention that in the introduction.

2. What are the main points supporting the thesis? List the points. Is each supporting point developed sufficiently? If not, where is more support needed?

   (1) Playing violent video games can make children become more aggressive and violent.
   (2) Playing violent video games can lead to video game addiction.
   (3) Playing violent video games can affect a child's health.

   The supporting points are good and are explained pretty well, except for a few places.
   In the last sentence in para. 2, you refer to "a simple video game." I'm not sure that's what you really meant. The violent video games I've seen are not simple, and even if some are, I'm not sure that's the point you're trying to make.
   About halfway through para. 3, you use the word "withdrawal" in the quote from Young, pg. 356. You might want to check the source. I don't think that's the right word. It doesn't make sense there.
   In para. 4 on how playing violent video games can endanger a child's health, you don't incorporate any outside sources the way you do in the other body paragraphs. Your essay might be stronger if you did.
   As for the conclusion, I know those aren't easy to write—they sure aren't for me. But in that paragraph you pretty much just restate what you have already said. I can see why you might want to do that in a long essay, but since this is a pretty short essay, I wonder if there's another approach you could take—maybe go back to the ideas in your introduction about parents and their role in helping their kids not get hooked on playing violent video games and then just briefly remind readers of the essay's main points.

3. What overall format (chronological, spatial, emphatic, simple-to-complex) is used to sequence the essay's main points? Does this format work? Why or why not? What organizational format is used in each supporting paragraph? Does the format work? Why or why not?

   The essay's overall emphatic organization seems good. I like the way you use exemplification in your three supporting paragraphs to back up your topic sentences for each paragraph. That works well—except in para. 4. I mentioned this before, but you could use at least one source to back up your claims.

4. What signal devices are used to connect ideas within and between paragraphs? Are there too few signal devices or too many? Where?

You do a nice job overall, with transitions from one sentence to another and from one paragraph to another. But I did notice some areas you might want to work on.

About halfway through para. 1, you use the signal device "with that said," and in the next sentence you use the phrase "in result." You might want to play with your wording in those two places. The two phrases sound kind of strange to me, as if you couldn't quite find the words you were looking for.

Something else you might consider is your signal device at the beginning of your conclusion: "Above all." You might be able to come up with a more effective bridge there.

As you can see, Taylor flagged several areas that Caylah also noted as needing work. But Taylor also commented on entirely new areas (for example, the mistake Caylah made when quoting Young, one of her sources, in paragraph 3 and her need for additional support in paragraph 4), offering Caylah a fresh perspective on how she should polish her draft.

 BECOMING A SKILLED PEER REVIEWER   Effective peer review calls for rigor and care; you should give classmates the conscientious feedback that you hope for in return. Peer review also requires tact and kindness. Feedback should always be constructive and include observations about what works well in a piece of writing. Writers have difficulty mustering the energy to revise if they feel there's nothing worth revising.

To focus your readers' comments, you may adapt the revision checklists that appear throughout this book, or you may develop your own questions. If you prepare the questions yourself, be sure to solicit *specific* observations about what does and doesn't work in your writing. If you simply ask, "How's this?" you may receive a vague comment like "It's not very effective." What you want are concrete observations and suggestions: "I'm confused because what you say in the fifth sentence contradicts what you say in the second." To promote such specific responses, ask your readers targeted questions such as, "I'm having trouble moving from my second to my third point. How can I make the transition smoother?" Such questions require more than "yes" or "no" responses; they encourage readers to dig into your writing where you sense it needs work. (If it's feasible, provide your question in writing to your readers and encourage readers to *write* their responses to your questions.)

If you and your peer reviewer(s) can't meet in person, **e-mail** can provide a crucial means of contact. With a couple of clicks, you can simply send each other files of your work. Decide exactly how to exchange comments about your drafts. You might conclude, for example, that you'll use Microsoft Word's "Track Changes" feature or type your responses, perhaps in bold capitals, into the file itself. Or you might decide to print out the drafts and reply to the comments in writing, later exchanging the annotated drafts in person. No matter what you and your peer(s) decide, you'll probably find e-mail an invaluable tool in the writing process.

EVALUATE AND RESPOND TO PEER REVIEW   Accepting criticism isn't easy (even if you asked for it), and not all peer reviewers will be tactful. Even so, try to listen with an open mind to those giving you feedback. Take notes on their oral observations or have them fill out the checklist described previously. Later, when you're ready to revise your draft, reread your notes. Which reviewer remarks seem valid? Which recommendations are workable? Which are not? In addition, try using a feedback chart or a system of marginal annotations to help you evaluate and remedy any perceived weaknesses in your draft.

Here's how to use a three-column **feedback chart**. In the first column, list the major problems you and your readers see in the draft. Next, rank the problems, designating the most critical as "1." Then in the second column, jot down possible solutions—your own as well as your readers'. Finally, in the third column, briefly describe what action you'll take to correct each problem. The following is the chart that Caylah Francis composed following Taylor Young's review of her first draft.

Whether or not you decide to use a feedback chart, be sure to enter **marginal annotations** on your draft (preferably a clean copy of it) before revising it. In the margins, jot down any major problems, numbered in order of importance, along with possible remedies. Marking your essay this way, much as an instructor might, helps you view your essay as though it were written by someone else. Then, keeping the draft's problems in mind, start revising.

Problems	Suggestions	Decisions
⑤ Two signal devices ("with that said" and "in result") sound awkward.	Find other signal devices that are more effective.	Eliminate "with that said" and "in result." Make revisions as needed to incorporate more effective signal devices in place of those.
① Thesis is too long and doesn't say anything about the research included to support the claims.	Shorten thesis to one sentence and make a reference to research.	Delete the second sentence and revise the first one to read, "While some argue that playing violent video games does not have harmful effects, research proves otherwise."
⑥ Reference to "a simple video game" in paragraph 2 when many violent video games are far from simple, and even if they were, that's not the point.	Revise sentence to eliminate the reference to video games as being "simple."	Delete "simple."
④ The word "withdrawal" in the quote from Young near the end of paragraph 3 makes no sense.	Check the source to see if I made a mistake when recording the quote.	The source material uses the word "withdraw"—not "withdrawal." Correct the mistake.
② Not enough support for the claims in paragraph 4.	Conduct more research and find material to support the claim that playing violent video games can endanger a child's health.	Conduct research and find material to support the claim.
③ Weak conclusion that simply restates what's already been said.	Revise the conclusion by returning to the ideas in the introduction about the important role that parents play in helping their kids not get hooked on playing violent video games.	Revise so that conclusion does not simply summarize the claims made in the three supporting paragraphs. Add information mentioned in the introduction about the important role parents play.

Revising Overall Meaning and Structure

7.2 Revise for overall meaning and structure.

It's not uncommon when revising at this stage to find that the draft doesn't fully convey what you had in mind. Perhaps your intended thesis ends up being overshadowed by another idea. (If that happens, you have two options: you may pursue the new line of thought as your revised thesis, or you may bring the essay back into line with your original thesis by deleting extraneous material.) Another problem might be that readers miss a key point. Perhaps you initially believed the point could be implied, but you now realize it needs to be stated explicitly.

A *brief outline* of a draft can help you evaluate the essay's overall structure. Either you or a reader can prepare the outline. In either case, your thesis, reflecting any changes made during the first draft, should be noted at the top of the outline page. Then you or your readers briefly outline the essay's basic structure. With the draft pared down to its essentials, you can see more easily how parts contribute to the whole and how points do or do not fit together.

☑ Revising Overall Meaning and Structure: A Checklist

- ☐ What is your initial reaction to the draft? What do you like and dislike?

- ☐ What audience does the essay address? How suited to this audience are the essay's purpose, tone, and point of view?

- ☐ What is the essay's thesis? Is it explicit or implied? Does it focus on a limited subject and express the writer's attitude toward that subject? If not, what changes need to be made?

- ☐ What are the points supporting the thesis? List them. If any stray from or contradict the thesis, what changes need to be made?

- ☐ According to which organizing principle(s)—spatial, chronological, emphatic, simple-to-complex—are the main points arranged? Does this organizational scheme reinforce the thesis? Why or why not?

- ☐ Which patterns of development (narration, description, comparison-contrast, and so on) are used in the essay? How do these patterns reinforce the thesis?

- ☐ Where would background information, definition of terms, or additional material clarify meaning?

You are now ready to focus on the second major step in the revising process, revising paragraph development.

Revising Paragraph Development

7.3 Revise paragraph development.

After you use feedback to refine the essay's fundamental meaning and structure, it's time to look closely at the essay's paragraphs. At this point, you and those giving you feedback should read the draft more slowly. How can the essay's paragraphs be made more unified and more specific? Which paragraphs seem to lack sufficient support? Which would profit from more attention to coherence?

At this stage, you may find that a paragraph needs more examples to make its point or that a paragraph should be deleted because it doesn't develop the thesis. Or perhaps you realize that a paragraph should come earlier in the essay because it defines a term readers need to understand from the outset.

Here's a strategy to help assess your paragraphs' effectiveness. In the margin next to each paragraph, make a brief notation that answers these two questions: (1) What is the paragraph's *purpose?* and (2) What is its *content?* Then skim the marginal notes to see if each paragraph does what you intended.

During this stage, you should also examine the *length of your paragraphs.* Paragraphs that are all the same length dull your readers' response, whereas variations encourage them to sit up and take notice.

If your paragraphs tend to run long, try breaking some of them into shorter, crisper chunks. Be sure, however, not to break paragraphs just anywhere. To preserve a paragraph's logic, you may need to reshape and add material, always keeping in mind that the paragraph should have a clear and distinctive focus.

However, don't go overboard and break up all your paragraphs. An abundance of brief paragraphs makes it difficult for readers to see how points are related. Furthermore, overreliance on short paragraphs may mean that you haven't provided sufficient evidence to support your ideas. Finally, a succession of short paragraphs encourages readers to skim when, of course, you want them to consider carefully what you have to say. So use short paragraphs, but save them for places where you want to introduce variation or achieve emphasis.

The following checklist is designed to help you and your readers evaluate a draft's paragraph development.

☑ Revising Paragraph Development: A Checklist

☐ In what way does each supporting paragraph develop the essay's thesis? Which paragraphs fail to develop the thesis? Should they be deleted or revised?

☐ What is each paragraph's central idea? If this idea is expressed in a topic sentence, where is this sentence located? Where does something stray from or contradict the paragraph's main idea? How could the paragraph's focus be sharpened?

☐ Where in each paragraph does support seem irrelevant, vague, insufficient, inaccurate, nonrepresentative, or disorganized? What could be done to remedy these problems? Where would additional sensory details, examples, facts, statistics, expert authority, and personal observations be appropriate?

☐ By which organizational principle (spatial, chronological, emphatic, or simple-to-complex) are each paragraph's ideas arranged? Does this format reinforce the paragraph's main point? Why or why not?

☐ How could paragraph coherence be strengthened? Which signal devices are used to connect ideas within and between paragraphs? Where are there too few signals or too many?

☐ Where do too many paragraphs of the same length dull the reader's interest? Where would a short paragraph or a long paragraph be more effective?

☐ How could the introduction be strengthened? Which striking anecdote, fact, or statistic elsewhere in the essay might be moved to the introduction? How does the introduction establish the essay's purpose, audience, tone, and point of view? Which strategy links the introduction to the essay's body?

☐ How could the conclusion be strengthened? Which striking anecdote, fact, or statistic elsewhere in the essay might be moved to the conclusion? Would echoing something from the introduction help close the essay more effectively? How has the conclusion been made an integral part of the essay?

Sample Student Revision of Overall Meaning, Structure, and Paragraph Development

The introduction to Caylah Francis's first draft is reprinted here with her revisions. In the margin, numbered in order of importance, are the problems with the introduction's meaning, structure, and paragraph development—as noted by Caylah's peer reviewer, Taylor, and other classmates. The above-line changes show Caylah's efforts to eliminate these problems through revision.

② *Revise awk-ward signal devices "with that said" and "in result."*

The incredible advancement of technology has created a world where many

American houses not only have one television, one computer, and one video game

console, but many have several of these media devices. Parents try everything to

please their kids such as buying them a variety of video games from violent first per-

They often buy these games because they

① *Thesis too long. Shorten to one sentence and mention research.*

son shooter games to fantasy games. ~~Parents that~~ work many hours a week and

~~have kids~~ try their best to preoccupy their children to aid in the parenting process.

As a result

~~With that said,~~ the use of video games has become a popular activity among many

Playing these games has had both

kids. ~~In result, there have been many~~ negative and positive effects on young people

~~who play video games.~~ More specifically this has created concerns for kids who play

While some argue that playing video games

video games an excessive amount of time. ~~Playing violent video games can have~~

does not have harmful effects, research proves otherwise.

~~many negative effects on kids. It can lead to increased levels of aggression, video~~

~~game addiction, and serious health issues.~~

Activities: Revising Overall Meaning, Structure, and Paragraph Development

An important note: When revising essay drafts in activities 1–3, don't worry too much about sentence structure and word choice. However, do save your revisions so you can focus on these matters in later chapters.

1. Look at the marginal notes and above-line changes that Caylah Francis added to her first draft introduction above. Now look at the draft's other paragraphs and identify problems in overall meaning, structure, and paragraph development. Working alone or in a group, start by asking questions like these: "Where does the essay stray from the thesis?" and "Where does a paragraph fail to present points in the most logical and compelling order?" For further guidance, refer to the checklists in this chapter. Summarize and rank the perceived problems in marginal annotations or on a feedback chart. Then type your changes or handwrite them between the lines of the draft (work on a newly printed copy or a photocopy). Don't forget to save your revision.

2. Retrieve the draft you prepared in response to activity 12 in Chapter 6. Outline the draft. Does your outline reveal any problems in the draft's overall meaning and structure? If it does, make whatever changes are needed. The checklists in this chapter will help focus your revising efforts. (Save your revised draft so you can work with it further in future chapters.)

3. Following is the first draft of an essay advocating a longer elementary school day. Read it closely. Are tone and point of view consistent throughout? Is the thesis clear? Is the support in each body paragraph relevant, specific, and adequate? Are ideas arranged in the most effective order? Working alone or in a group, use the checklists in this chapter to identify problems with the draft's overall meaning, structure, and paragraph development. Summarize and rank the perceived problems on a feedback chart or in marginal annotations. Then revise the draft by typing a new version or by entering your changes by hand (on a photocopy of the draft, a typed copy, or a freshly printed copy). Don't forget to save your revision.

The Extended School Day

Imagine a seven-year-old whose parents work until five each night. When she arrives home after school, she is on her own. She's a good girl, but still a lot of things could happen. She could get into trouble just by being curious. Or something could happen through no fault of her own. All over the country, there are many "latchkey" children like this little girl. Some way must be found to deal with the problem. One suggestion is to keep elementary schools open longer than they now are. There are many advantages to this idea.

Parents wouldn't have to be in a state of uneasiness about whether their child is safe and happy at home. They wouldn't get uptight about whether their child's needs are being met. They also wouldn't have to feel guilty because they are not able to help a child with homework. The longer day would make it possible for the teacher to provide such help.

Extended school hours would also relieve families of the financial burden of hiring a home sitter. As my family learned, having a sitter can wipe out the budget. And having a sitter doesn't necessarily eliminate all problems. Parents still have the hassle of worrying whether the person will show up and be reliable.

It's a fact of life that many children dislike school, which is a sad commentary on the state of education in this country. Even so, the longer school day would benefit children as well. Obviously, the dangers of their being home alone after school would disappear because by the time the bus dropped them off after the longer school day, at least one parent would be home. The unnameable horrors feared by parents would not have a chance to happen. Instead, the children would be in school, under trained supervision. There, they would have a chance to work on subjects that give them trouble. In contrast, when my younger brother had difficulty with subtraction in second grade, he had to struggle along because there wasn't enough time to give him the help he needed. The longer day would also give children a chance to participate in extracurricular activities. They could join a science club, play on a softball team, sing in a school chorus, take an art class. Because school districts are trying to save money, they often cut back on such extracurricular activities. They don't realize how important such experiences are.

Finally, the longer school day would also benefit teachers. Having more hours in each day would relieve them of a lot of pressure. This longer workday would obviously require schools to increase teachers' pay. The added salary would be an incentive for teachers to stay in the profession.

Implementing an extended school day would be expensive, but I feel that many communities would willingly finance its costs because it provides benefits to parents, children, and even teachers. Young children, home alone, wondering whether to watch another TV show or to wander outside to see what's happening, need this longer school day now.

4. Look closely at your instructor's comments on an ungraded draft of one of your essays. Using a feedback chart, summarize and evaluate your instructor's comments. When that's done, rework the essay. Type your new version, or make your changes by hand. In either case, save the revision so you can work with it further in later chapters.

5. Return to the draft you wrote in response to activity 10 or activity 11 in Chapter 6. To identify any problems, meet with several people and request that one of them read the draft aloud. Then ask your listeners focused questions about the areas you sense need work. Alternatively, you may use the checklists in this chapter to focus the group's feedback. In either case, summarize and rank the comments on a feedback chart or in marginal annotations. Then, using the comments as a guide, revise the draft. Either type a new version or do your revising by hand. (Save your revision so you can work with it further in later chapters.)

Chapter 8
Revising Sentences and Words

 ## Learning Objectives

8.1 Revise your sentences for tone, length, and emphasis.

8.2 Revise your words for appropriate tone and meaning.

Revising Sentences

8.1 Revise your sentences for tone, length, and emphasis.

Having refined your essay's overall meaning, structure, and paragraph development, you can concentrate on sharpening individual sentences. Although polishing sentences inevitably involves decisions about individual words, for now focus on each sentence as a whole; you can evaluate individual words later (see Figure 8.1). In revising your sentences, you will want to:

- Make sentences consistent with your tone.
- Make sentences economical.
- Vary sentence type.
- Vary sentence length.
- Make sentences emphatic.

Make Sentences Consistent with Your Tone

As you have learned, **tone** is integral to meaning. As you revise, be sure each sentence's **content** (its images and ideas) and **style** (how the writer conveys his or her message) reinforce your intended tone: Both *what* you say and *how* you say it should support the essay's overall mood.

Figure 8.1 Process Diagram: Revising Sentences

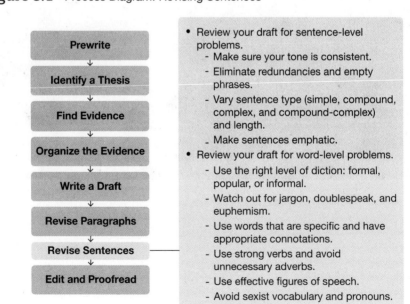

Prewrite
↓
Identify a Thesis
↓
Find Evidence
↓
Organize the Evidence
↓
Write a Draft
↓
Revise Paragraphs
↓
Revise Sentences
↓
Edit and Proofread

- Review your draft for sentence-level problems.
  - Make sure your tone is consistent.
  - Eliminate redundancies and empty phrases.
  - Vary sentence type (simple, compound, complex, and compound-complex) and length.
  - Make sentences emphatic.
- Review your draft for word-level problems.
  - Use the right level of diction: formal, popular, or informal.
  - Watch out for jargon, doublespeak, and euphemism.
  - Use words that are specific and have appropriate connotations.
  - Use strong verbs and avoid unnecessary adverbs.
  - Use effective figures of speech.
  - Avoid sexist vocabulary and pronouns.

Consider the following excerpt from Hillary Clinton's "Remarks to the United Nations Fourth World Conference on Women Plenary Session." She states:

> Tragically, women are most often the ones whose human rights are violated. Even now, in the late 20th century, the rape of women continues to be used as an instrument of armed conflict. Women and children make up a large majority of the world's refugees. And when women are excluded from the political process, they become even more vulnerable to abuse. I believe that now, on the eve of a new millennium, it is time to break the silence. It is time for us to say here in Beijing, and for the world to hear, that it is no longer acceptable to discuss women's rights as separate from human rights.

Clinton's tone is impassioned, her attitude determined and strong. She establishes this tone partly through sentence content (what she says). For example, she finds it unpardonable that close to the end of the twentieth century, the sexual abuse of women is being used "as an instrument of armed conflict." Clinton's style (how she says what she wants to say) also contributes to her overall tone. Her repetition of the phrase "it is time," followed by the phrase "it is no longer acceptable," conveys an attitude of outrage with the ways that women's rights have been violated for far too long. Working together, content and style help express Clinton's impassioned attitude toward her subject.

Make Sentences Economical

Besides reinforcing your tone, your sentences should be **economical** rather than wordy. Use as few, not as many, words as possible. Your sentences won't be wordy if you (1) eliminate redundancy, (2) delete weak phrases, and (3) remove unnecessary *who, which,* and *that* clauses.

ELIMINATE REDUNDANCY   **Redundancy** means unnecessary repetition. Sometimes words are repeated exactly; sometimes they are repeated by way of *synonyms,* other words or phrases that mean the same thing. When writing is redundant, words can be trimmed away without sacrificing meaning or effect. Why, for example, write "In the expert opinion of one expert" and needlessly repeat the word *expert?* Similarly, "They found it difficult to get consensus or agreement about the proposal" contains an unnecessary synonym (*agreement*) for *consensus.*

Repetition weakens prose. Take a look at the sentence pair below. Note how the revised version is clearer and stronger because the redundancy in the original sentence (italicized) has been eliminated:

Original   While under the *influence* of alcohol, many people insist they are not under the *influence* and *swear* they are sober.

Revised   While under the influence of alcohol, many people insist they are sober.

DELETE WEAK PHRASES   In addition to eliminating redundancy, you can make sentences more economical by **deleting the three types of weak phrases** described here.

1. **Empty Phrases.** In speaking, we frequently use empty phrases that give us time to think but don't add to our message ("Okay?" "You know what I mean?") In writing, though, we can eliminate such deadwood. Here are some expressions that are needlessly awkward and wordy, along with one-word alternatives:

Wordy Expressions	Revised
due to the fact that	because
in light of the fact that	since
regardless of the fact that	although
in the event that	if
in many cases	often
in that period	then
at this point in time	now
in the not-too-distant future	soon
for the purpose of	to
has the ability to	can
be aware of the fact that	know
is necessary that	must

Notice the improvement in the following sentence when a wordy, awkward phrase is replaced with a one-word substitute:

Original   *It is necessary that* the government outlaw the production of carcinogenic pesticides.

Revised   The government *must* outlaw the production of carcinogenic pesticides.

Some phrases don't even call for concise substitutes. Because they add nothing at all to a sentence's meaning, they can simply be deleted.

Original   The hybrid azaleas were light blue *in color.*

Revised   The hybrid azaleas were light blue.

Other times, to avoid an empty phrase, you may need to recast a sentence slightly:

Original   The midterm assessment is *for the purpose of letting* students know if they are failing a course.

Revised   The midterm assessment *lets* students know if they are failing a course.

2. **Roundabout Openings with *There, It,* and Question Words Such as *How* and *What*.** The openings of sentences are especially vulnerable to unnecessary phrases. Common culprits include phrases beginning with *There* and *It* (when *It* does not refer to a specific noun) and words such as *How* and *What* (when they don't actually ask a question).

Original	It was their belief that the problem had been solved.
Revised	They believed the problem had been solved.
Original	There are now computer courses offered by many high schools.
Revised	Many high schools now offer computer courses.

Of course, feel free to open with *There* or *It* when some other construction would be less clear or effective. For example, don't write "Many reasons can be cited why students avoid art courses" when you can say "There are many reasons why students avoid art courses."

3. **Excessive Prepositional Phrases.** Strings of prepositional phrases (word groups beginning with *at, on,* and the like) tend to make writing choppy. They weigh sentences down and hide main ideas. Note how much smoother and clearer sentences become when prepositional phrases (italicized in the following example) are eliminated:

Original	Growth *in the greenhouse effect* may result *in increases in the intensity of hurricanes.*
Revised	The growing greenhouse effect may intensify hurricanes.

This example shows that you can sometimes eliminate prepositional phrases by substituting one strong verb (*intensify*) rather than an *of* phrase.

REMOVE UNNECESSARY *WHO, WHICH,* AND *THAT* CLAUSES   Often *who, which,* or *that* clauses can be removed with no loss of meaning. Consider the tightening possible in these sentences:

Original	The townsfolk misunderstood the main point *that the developer made.*
Revised	The townsfolk misunderstood *the developer's main point.*
Original	The employees *who protested* the restrictions went on strike, *which was a real surprise to management.*
Revised	The employees *protesting* the restrictions *surprised management* by going on strike.

Vary Sentence Type

Another way to invigorate writing is to **vary sentence type**.

SIMPLE SENTENCES   A **clause** is a group of words with both a subject and a verb. Clauses can be **independent** (able to stand alone) or **dependent** (unable to stand alone). A **simple sentence** consists of a single independent clause (whose subject and verb are italicized here):

Marie Curie investigated radioactivity and *died* from its effects.

Unlike most mammals, *birds* and *fish see* color.

A simple sentence can have more than one verb (sentence 1) or more than one subject (sentence 2). In addition, any number of modifying phrases (such as *Unlike most mammals*) can extend the sentence's length and add information. What distinguishes a simple sentence is its single *subject-verb combination*.

Simple sentences can convey dramatic urgency:

> Suddenly we heard the screech of brakes. Across the street, a small boy lay sprawled in front of a car. We started to run toward the child. The driver sped away.

Simple sentences are also excellent for singling out a climactic point, but in a series, they lose their impact and become boring. Also, because simple sentences highlight one idea at a time, they don't clarify the relationships among ideas:

> **Original**
> Many first-year college students are apprehensive. They won't admit it to themselves. They hesitate to confide in their friends. They never find out that everyone else is anxious, too. They are nervous about being disliked and feeling lonely. They fear not "knowing the ropes."

> **Revised**
> Many first-year college students are apprehensive, but they won't admit it to themselves. Because they hesitate to confide in their friends, they never find out that everyone else is anxious, too. Being disliked, feeling lonely, not "knowing the ropes"—these are what beginning college students fear.

The simple sentences in the original version fragment the passage into a series of disconnected ideas. The revised version includes a variety of sentence types and patterns, all of which are discussed in the sections that follow. This variety clarifies the relationships among ideas, so that the passage reads more easily.

Compound Sentences

Compound sentences consist of two or more independent clauses. There are four types of compound sentences. The most basic type consists of two simple sentences joined by a *coordinating conjunction* (*and, but, for, nor, or, so,* or *yet*):

> Chimpanzees and gorillas can learn sign language, *and* they have been seen teaching this language to others.

Another type of compound sentence has a semicolon (;), rather than a comma and coordinating conjunction, between the two simple sentences:

> Yesterday, editorials attacked the plan; a week ago, they praised it.

A third type of compound sentence links two simple sentences with a semicolon plus a *conjunctive adverb* such as *however, moreover, nevertheless, therefore,* or *thus*:

> Every year billions of U.S. dollars go to researching AIDS; *however*, recent studies show that a large percentage of the money has been mismanaged.

A final type of compound sentence consists of two simple sentences connected by a *correlative conjunction,* a word pair such as *either...or, neither...nor,* or *not only...but also:*

> *Either* the litigants will win the lawsuit, *or* they will end up in debt from court costs.

Compound sentences help clarify the relationship between ideas. Similarities are signaled by such words as *and* and *moreover,* contrasts by *but* and *however,* cause-effect by *so* and *therefore.* When only a semicolon separates the two parts of a compound sentence, the relationship between those two parts is often a contrast. ("Yesterday, editorials attacked the plan; a week ago, they praised it.")

Complex Sentences

In a **complex sentence**, a dependent (subordinate) clause is joined to an independent clause. Sometimes the dependent clause (italicized in the following example) is introduced by a subordinating conjunction such as *although, because, if, since,* or *when:*

> *Since they have relatively small circulations,* specialty magazines tend to be expensive.

Other dependent clauses are introduced by a relative pronoun such as *that, which,* or *who.*

> The USDA, *which controls food labeling,* sets the standards for organic food.

The order of the dependent and independent clause isn't fixed. The dependent clause may come first, last, or even in the middle of the independent clause:

> Nurses' uniforms, *although they are no longer the norm,* are still required by some hospitals.

Whether to use a comma between a dependent and an independent clause depends on a number of factors, including the location of the dependent clause and whether it's *restrictive* (essential for identifying whatever it modifies) or *nonrestrictive* (not essential for identifying whatever it modifies).

Because a dependent clause is subordinate to an independent one, complex sentences can clarify the relationships among ideas. Consider the two paragraphs that follow. The first merely strings together a series of simple and compound sentences, all of them carrying roughly the same weight. In contrast, the complex sentences in the revised version use subordination to connect ideas and signal their relative importance.

> **Original**
> Are you the "average American"? Then take heed. Here are the results of a time-management survey. You might want to budget your time differently. According to the survey, you spend six years of your life eating. Also, you're likely to spend two years trying to reach people by telephone, so you should think about texting instead of calling. Finally, you may be married and expect long conversations with your spouse to occur spontaneously, but you'll have to make a special effort. Ordinarily, your discussions will average only four minutes a day.

Revised

If you're the "average American," take heed. After you hear the results of a time-management survey, you might want to budget your time differently. According to the survey, you spend six years of your life eating. Also, unless you call less and text more, you're likely to spend two years trying to reach your friends by telephone. Finally, if you're married, you shouldn't expect long conversations with your spouse to occur spontaneously. Unless you make a special effort, your discussions will average only four minutes a day.

The following sentences illustrate how meaning shifts depending on what is placed in the main clause and what is subordinated:

Although most fraternities and sororities no longer allow hazing, pledging is still a big event on many campuses.

Although pledging is still a big event on many campuses, most fraternities and sororities no longer allow hazing.

In the first sentence, the focus is on pledging; in the second, it is on the discontinuation of hazing.

COMPOUND-COMPLEX SENTENCES A **compound-complex sentence** connects one or more dependent clauses to two or more independent clauses. In the following example, the two independent clauses are underscored once and the two dependent clauses twice:

The Procrastinators' Club, which is based in Philadelphia, issues a small magazine, but it appears infrequently, only when members get around to writing it.

Go easy on the number of compound-complex sentences you use. They tend to be long, so a string of them is likely to overwhelm the reader.

Vary Sentence Length

Generally, by varying sentence type, a writer automatically **varies sentence length** as well. However, sentence type doesn't always determine length. In this example, the simple sentence is longer than the complex one:

Simple Sentence
Hot and thirsty, exhausted from the effort of carrying so many groceries, I desired nothing more than an ice-cold glass of lemonade.

Complex Sentence
Because I was hot and thirsty, I craved lemonade.

The difference lies in the number of **modifiers**—words or groups of words used to describe another word or group of words. So, besides considering sentence type, check sentence length when revising.

SHORT SENTENCES Too many short sentences, like too many simple ones, can sound childish and create a choppy effect that muddies the relationship among ideas.

Used wisely, though, a series of short sentences gives writing a staccato rhythm that carries more punch and conveys a faster pace than the same number of words gathered into longer sentences:

> Witches bring their faces close. Goblins glare with fiery eyes. Fiendish devils stealthily approach to claw a beloved stuffed bear. The toy recoils in horror. These are among the terrifying happenings in the world of children's nightmares.

> Witches bring their faces close as goblins glare, their eyes fiery. Approaching stealthily, fiendish devils come to claw a beloved stuffed bear that recoils in horror. These are among the terrifying happenings in the world of children's nightmares.

Brevity also highlights a sentence, especially when surrounding sentences are longer. Consider the dramatic effect of the final sentence in this paragraph:

> Starting in June, millions of Americans pour onto the highways, eager to begin vacation. At the same time, city, state, and federal agencies deploy hundreds, even thousands, of workers to repair roads that have, until now, managed to escape bureaucratic attention. Chaos results.

The sentence "Chaos results" stands out because it's so much shorter than the other sentences. The emphasis is appropriate because, in the writer's view, chaos is the dramatic consequence of prolonged bureaucratic inertia.

LONG SENTENCES   Long sentences often convey a leisurely pace and establish a calm tone:

> As I look across the lake, I see the steady light of a campfire at the water's edge, the flames tinting to copper, an aluminum rowboat tied to the dock, the boat glimmering in the darkness.

Too many long sentences can be hard to follow. And remember: A sentence stands out most when it differs in length from surrounding sentences. Glance back at the first paragraph on children's nightmares above. The final long sentence stands in contrast to the preceding short ones. The resulting emphasis works because the final sentence is also the paragraph's topic sentence.

Make Sentences Emphatic

Within a single sentence, you can use a number of techniques to make parts of the sentence stand out from the rest. To achieve such **emphasis**, you can: (1) place key ideas at the beginning or end, (2) set them in parallel constructions, (3) express them as fragments, or (4) express them in inverted word order.

PLACE KEY POINTS AT THE BEGINNING OR END   A sentence's start and close are its most prominent positions. So, keeping your overall meaning in mind, use those two spots to highlight key ideas.

Let's look first at the **beginning** position. Here are two versions of a sentence. The meanings differ because the openers differ.

The potentially life-saving drug, developed by junior researchers at the medical school, will be available next month.

Developed by junior researchers at the medical school, the potentially life-saving drug will be available next month.

In the first version, the emphasis is on the life-saving potential of a drug. Reordering the sentence shifts attention to those responsible for discovering the drug.

Another emphatic position is the **end** of the sentence. Place whatever you want to emphasize at the end of the sentence:

Kindergarten is wasted on the young—especially the naptime.

Now look at two versions of another sentence, each with a slightly different meaning because of what's at the end:

Increasingly, overt racism is showing up in—of all places—popular song lyrics.

Popular song lyrics are showing—of all things—increasingly overt racism.

In the first version, the emphasis is on lyrics; in the second, it's on racism.

Be sure, though, that whatever you place in the climactic position merits the emphasis. The following sentence is so anticlimactic that it's unintentionally humorous:

The family, waiting anxiously for the results of the medical tests, sat.

Similarly, don't build toward a strong climax only to defuse it with some less important material:

On the narrow parts of the trail, where jagged cliffs drop steeply from the path, keep your eyes straight ahead and don't look down, toward the town of Belmont in the east.

In the preceding sentence, "toward the town of Belmont in the east" should be deleted. The important point surely isn't Belmont's location but how to avoid an accident.

USE PARALLELISM **Parallelism** occurs when ideas of comparable weight are expressed in the same grammatical form, which underscores their equality. Parallel elements may be words, phrases, clauses, or full sentences. Here are some examples:

Parallel Nouns
We bought *pretzels, nachos,* and *candy bars* to feed our pre-exam jitters.

Parallel Adverbs
Smoothly, steadily, quietly, the sails tipped toward the sun.

Parallel Verbs
The guest lecturer *spoke* to the group, *showed* her slides, and then *invited* questions.

Parallel Adjective Phrases
Playful as a kitten but *wise as a street Tom,* the old cat toyed with the string while keeping a watchful eye on his surroundings.

Parallel Prepositional Phrases

Gloomy predictions came *from political analysts, from the candidate's staff,* and, surprisingly, *from the candidate herself.*

Parallel Dependent Clauses

Because our rivals were in top form, because their top player would soon come up to bat, we knew that all was lost.

As you can see, the repetition of grammatical forms creates a pleasing symmetry that emphasizes the sequenced ideas. Parallel structure also conveys meaning economically. Look at the way the following sentences can be tightened using parallelism:

Nonparallel

Studies show that most women today are different from those in the past. They want to have their own careers. They want to be successful. They also want to enjoy financial independence.

Parallel

Studies show that most women today are different from those in the past. They want to have careers, be successful, and enjoy financial independence.

Parallel constructions are often signaled by word pairs (correlative conjunctions) such as *either...or, neither...nor,* and *not only...but also.* To maintain parallelism, the same grammatical form must follow each half of the word pair.

Either professors are too rigorous, *or* they are too lax.

When my roommate argues, she tends to be *not only* totally stubborn *but also* totally wrong.

Parallelism can create elegant and dramatic writing. Too much, though, seems artificial, so use it sparingly. Save it for your most important points.

USE FRAGMENTS   A **fragment** is part of a sentence punctuated as if it were a whole sentence—that is, with a period at the end. A sentence fragment consists of words, phrases, and/or dependent clauses, *without an independent clause.* Here are some examples:

Resting quietly.   Because they admired her.

Except for the trees.   A demanding boss who accepted no excuses.

Ask your composition instructor whether an occasional fragment—used as a stylistic device—will be considered acceptable. Here's an example showing the way fragments (underlined) can be used effectively for emphasis:

One of my aunt's eccentricities is her belief that only personally made gifts show the proper amount of love. Her gifts are often strange. Hand-drawn calendars. Home-brewed cologne that smells like jam. Crocheted washcloths. Frankly, I'd rather receive a gift certificate from a department store.

Notice how the three fragments focus attention on the aunt's charmingly offbeat gifts. Remember, though: When overused, fragments lose their effect, so draw on them sparingly.

USE INVERTED WORD ORDER   In most English sentences, the subject comes before the verb. When you use **inverted word order**, at least part of the verb comes before the subject. The resulting sentence is so atypical that it automatically stands out.

Inverted statements, like those that follow, are used to emphasize an idea:

Normal   My Uncle Bill is a strange man.

Inverted   A strange man is my Uncle Bill.

A note of caution: Inverted statements should be used infrequently and with special care. Bizarre can they easily sound.

Another form of inversion, the question, also acts as emphasis. A question may be a genuine inquiry, one that focuses attention on the issue at hand:

> Since the 1960s, only about half of this country's eligible voters have gone to the polls during national elections. *Why are Americans so apathetic?* Let's look at some of the reasons.

Or a question may be *rhetorical;* that is, one that implies its own answer and encourages the reader to share the writer's view:

> Yesterday, there was yet another accident at the intersection of Fairview and Springdale. Given the disproportionately high number of collisions at that crossing, *can anyone question the need for a traffic light?*

The following checklist is designed to help you and your readers evaluate the sentences in a first draft. (Activities at the end of the chapter will refer you to this checklist when you revise several essays.)

☑ Revising Sentences: A Checklist

☐ Which sentences seem inconsistent with the essay's intended tone? How could the problem be fixed?

☐ Which sentences could be more economical? Where could unnecessary repetition, empty phrases, and weak openings be eliminated? Which prepositional phrases could be deleted? Where are there unnecessary *who, which*, and *that* clauses?

☐ Where should sentence type be more varied? Where would subordination clarify the connections among ideas? Where would simpler sentences make the writing less inflated and easier to understand?

☐ Where does sentence length become monotonous and predictable? Which short sentences should be connected to enhance flow and convey a more leisurely pace? Which long sentences would be more effective if broken into crisp, short ones?

☐ Where would a different sentence pattern add variety? Better highlight key sentence elements? Seem more natural?

☐ Which sentences could be more emphatic? Which strategy would be most effective— expressing the main point at the beginning or end, using parallelism, or rewriting the sentence as a fragment, question, or inverted-word-order statement?

Revising Words

8.2 Revise your words for appropriate tone and meaning.

After refining the sentences in your first draft, you're in a good position to look closely at individual words. (Refer back to Figure 8.1.) During this stage, you should aim for:

- Words consistent with your intended tone
- An appropriate level of diction
- Words that neither overstate nor understate
- Words with appropriate connotations
- Specific rather than general words
- Strong verbs
- No unnecessary adverbs
- Original figures of speech
- Nonsexist language

Make Words Consistent with Your Tone

Like full sentences, individual words and phrases should reinforce your intended tone. Reread the Hillary Rodham Clinton excerpt on women's rights earlier in this chapter. Earlier we discussed how sentence structure contributes to the excerpt's strong and determined tone. Word choice also plays an important role. The word *tragically* leaves the audience with no doubt about the author's attitude toward women's rights. And the impassioned plea "it is time for us to say here in Beijing, and for the world to hear, that it is no longer acceptable" serves as a call to action for ending the distinction between women's rights and human rights. Such word choices reinforce the overall tone Clinton wants to convey.

Use an Appropriate Level of Diction

Diction refers to the words a writer selects. Those words should be appropriate for the writer's purpose, audience, point of view, and tone. For example, if you are writing a straightforward, serious piece about on-the-job incompetence, you would be better off saying that people "don't concentrate on their work" and they "make frequent errors," rather than saying they "screw up" or "goof off."

There are three broad levels of diction: *formal, popular,* and *informal.* Within each level of diction, there are degrees of formality and informality.

FORMAL DICTION   Impersonal and distant in tone, **formal diction** is the type of language found in scholarly journals. Contractions are rare; long, specialized, technical words are common. Unfortunately, many writers mistakenly equate word length with education: The longer the words, they think, the more impressed readers will be. So rather than using the familiar and natural words *improve* and *think,* they thumb through a thesaurus for such fancy-sounding alternatives as *ameliorate* and *conceptualize.*

When writing for a general audience, don't use **jargon**, which is insiders' terms from a particular area of expertise (for example, a term such as *authorial omniscience* from literary theory). Such "shoptalk" should be used only when less specialized words lack the necessary precision. If readers are likely to be unfamiliar with a term, provide a definition.

Some degree of formality is appropriate—when, for example, you write up survey results for a sociology class. In such a case, your instructor may expect you to avoid the pronoun *I*. Other instructors may think it's pretentious for a student to refer to himself or herself in the third person ("The writer observed that...."). These instructors may be equally put off by the artificiality of the passive voice: "It was observed that...." To be safe, find out what your instructors expect. If possible, use *I* when you mean "I."

POPULAR DICTION   **Popular**, or **mainstream**, **diction** is found in most magazines, newspapers, books, and texts (including this one). In such prose, the writer may use the first person and address the reader as "you." Contractions appear frequently, and specialized vocabulary is kept to a minimum.

You should aim for popular diction in most of the writing you do—in and out of college. Also keep in mind that an abrupt downshift to slang (*freaked out* instead of *lost control*) or a sudden turn to highly formal language (*myocardial infarction* instead of *heart attack*) will disconcert readers and may undermine your credibility.

INFORMAL DICTION   **Informal diction**, which conveys a sense of everyday speech, is friendly and casual. First-person and second-person pronouns are common, as are contractions and fragments. Colloquial expressions (*rub the wrong way*) and slang (*you wimp*) are used freely. Informal diction isn't appropriate for academic essays, except where it is used to indicate *someone else's* speech.

Avoid Words That Overstate or Understate

When revising, be on the lookout for **doublespeak**, language that deliberately overstates or understates reality. For example, in their correspondence, Public Works Departments often refer to "ground-mounted confirmatory route markers"—a grandiose way of saying "road signs."

Other organizations go to the other extreme and use **euphemisms**, words that minimize something's genuine gravity or importance. Hospital officials, for instance, sometimes call deaths resulting from staff negligence "unanticipated therapeutic misadventures." When revising, check that you haven't used words that exaggerate or downplay something's significance.

Select Words with Appropriate Connotations

The dictionary meaning of a word is its **denotation**. The word *motorcycle*, for example, is defined as "a two- or three-wheeled vehicle propelled by an internal-combustion engine that resembles a bicycle but is usually larger and heavier and often has two saddles." Yet how many of us think of a motorcycle in these terms? Certainly, there is more to a word than its denotation. A word also comes surrounded by **connotations**— associated sensations, emotions, images, and ideas. For some, the word *motorcycle* calls to mind danger and noise. For motorcyclists themselves, the word most likely summons pleasant memories of high-speed movement through the open air.

Given the wide range of responses that any one word can elicit, you need to be sensitive to each word's shades of meaning so you can judge when to use it rather than some other word. Examine the following word series to get a better feel for the subtle but often critical differences between similar words:

contribution, donation, handout

quiet, reserved, closemouthed

Notice the extent to which words' connotations create different impressions in these two examples:

The young woman emerged from the interview, her face *aglow*. Moving *briskly* to the coat rack, she *tossed* her raincoat over one arm. After a *carefree* "Thank you" to the receptionist, she *glided* from the room.

The young woman emerged from the interview, her face *aflame*. Moving *hurriedly* to the coat rack, she *flung* her raincoat over one arm. After a *perfunctory* "Thank you" to the receptionist, she *bolted* from the room.

In the first paragraph, the words *aglow, carefree,* and *glided* have positive connotations, so the reader surmises that the interview was a success. In contrast, the second paragraph contains words loaded with negative connotations: *aflame, perfunctory,* and *bolted*. Reading this paragraph, the reader assumes something went awry.

A print or online thesaurus can help you select words with the right connotations. Just look up any word with which you aren't satisfied, and you'll find a list of synonyms. To be safe, stay away from unfamiliar words. Choose only those words whose nuances you understand.

Use Specific Rather Than General Words

Besides carrying the right connotations, words should be **specific** rather than general. That is, they must avoid vagueness and ambiguity by referring to *particular* people, animals, events, objects, and phenomena. If they don't, readers may misinterpret what you mean.

Besides clarifying meaning, specific words enliven writing and make it more convincing. Compare these two paragraphs:

Original
Sponsored by a charitable organization, a group of children from a nearby town visited a theme park. The kids had a great time. They went on several rides and ate a variety of foods. Reporters and a TV crew shared in the fun.

Revised

Sponsored by the United Glendale Charities, twenty-five underprivileged Glendale grade-schoolers visited the Universe of Fun theme park. The kids had a great time. They roller-coastered through a meteor shower on the Space Probe, encountered a giant squid on the Submarine Voyage, and screamed their way past coffins and ghosts in the House of Horrors. At the International Cuisine arcade, they sampled foods ranging from Hawaiian poi to German strudel. Reporters from *The Texas Herald* and a camera crew from WGLD, the Glendale cable station, shared in the fun.

You may have noticed that the specific words in the second paragraph provide answers to "which," "how," and similar questions. In contrast, when reading the first paragraph, you probably wondered, "*Which* charitable organization? *Which* theme park? *Which* rides?" Similarly, you may have asked, "*How* large a group? *How* young were the kids?" Specific language also answers "In what way?" The revised paragraph details *in what way* the children "had a great time." They didn't just eat "a variety of foods." Rather, they "sampled foods ranging from Hawaiian poi to German strudel." So, when you revise, check to make sure that your wording doesn't leave unanswered questions like "How?" "Why?" and "In what way?"

Use Strong Verbs

Replacing weak verbs with **strong verbs** is another way to tighten and energize language. Consider the following strategies.

REPLACE *TO BE* AND LINKING VERBS WITH ACTION VERBS   Overreliance on *to be* verbs (*is, were, has been*, and so on) tends to stretch sentences, making them flat and wordy. The same is true of motionless **linking verbs** such as *appear, become, sound, feel, look,* and *seem.* Because these verbs don't communicate any action, more words are required to complete their meaning and explain what is happening. Even *to be* verb forms combined with present participles (*is laughing, were running*) are weaker than bare **action verbs** (*laughs, ran*). Similarly, linking verbs combined with adjectives (*becomes shiny, seemed offensive*) aren't as vigorous as the action verb alone (*shines, offended*). Look how much more effective a paragraph becomes when weak verbs are replaced with dynamic ones:

Original

The waves *were* so high that the boat *was* nearly *tipping* on end. The wind *felt* rough against our faces, and the salt spray *became* so strong that we *felt* our breath *would be* cut off. Suddenly, in the air *was* the sound I had dreaded most— the snap of the rigging. I *felt* panicky.

Revised

The waves *towered* until the boat nearly *tipped* on end. The wind *lashed* our faces, while the salt spray *clogged* our throats and *cut* off our breath. Suddenly, the sound I had dreaded most *splintered* the air—the snap of the rigging. Panic *gripped* me.

The second paragraph is not only less wordy, it's also more vivid.

When you revise, look closely at your verbs. If you find too many *to be* and linking verb forms, ask yourself, "What's happening in the sentence?" Your response will help you substitute stronger verbs that will make your writing more compelling.

CHANGE PASSIVE VERBS TO ACTIVE VERBS *To be* verb forms (*is, has been,* and so on) may also be combined with a past participle (*cooked, stung*); the result is a **passive verb**. A passive verb creates a sentence structure in which the subject is *acted on* and the doer of the action appears in a prepositional phrase—or not at all. In contrast, the subject of an **active verb** *performs* the action. Consider the following active and passive forms:

Passive	**Active**
A suggestion was made by the instructor that the project plan be revised by the students.	The instructor suggested that the students revise the project plan.

Although they're not grammatically incorrect, passive verbs generally weaken writing, making it wordy and stiffly formal. Sometimes, though, it makes sense to use the passive voice. Perhaps you don't know who performed an action. ("When I returned to my car, I noticed the door had been dented.") Or you may want to emphasize an event, not the agent responsible for the event. For example, in an article about academic dishonesty on your campus, you might deliberately use the passive voice: "Every semester, research papers are plagiarized and lab reports falsified."

Unfortunately, corporations, government agencies, and other institutions often use the passive voice to avoid taking responsibility for controversial actions. Notice how easily the passive conceals the agent: "The rabbits were injected with a cancer-causing chemical."

Because the passive voice is associated with "official" writing, you may think it sounds scholarly and impressive. It doesn't. Unless you have good reason for deemphasizing the agent, change passive verbs to active ones.

REPLACE WEAK VERB-NOUN COMBINATIONS Just as *to be*, linking, and passive verbs tend to lengthen sentences needlessly, so do weak verb-noun combinations. Whenever possible, replace such combinations with their strong verb counterparts. Change "made an estimate" to "estimated," "gave approval" to "approved." Notice how revision tightens the following sentence, making it livelier and less pretentious:

Original   They *were* of the *belief* that the report was due next week.

Revised   They *believed* the report was due next week.

Delete Unnecessary Adverbs

Strong verbs can further tighten your writing by ridding it of unnecessary adverbs. "She *strolled* down the path" conveys the same message as "She *walked slowly* and *leisurely* down the path"—but more economically.

Adverbs such as *extremely, really,* and *very* usually weaken writing. Although they are called "intensifiers," they make writing less, not more, intense. Notice that the following sentence reads more emphatically *without* the intensifier:

Original   Although the professor's lectures are controversial, no one denies that they are *really* brilliant.

Revised   Although the professor's lectures are controversial, no one denies that they are brilliant.

"Qualifiers" such as *quite, rather,* and *somewhat* also tend to weaken writing. When you spot one, try to delete it:

Original   When planning a summer trip to the mountains, remember to pack warm clothes; it turns *quite* cool at night.

Revised   When planning a summer trip to the mountains, remember to pack warm clothes; it turns cool at night.

Use Original Figures of Speech

Another strategy for adding vitality to your writing is to create imaginative, nonliteral comparisons, called **figures of speech**. For example, you might describe midsummer humidity this way: "Going from an air-conditioned building to the street is like being hit in the face with peanut butter." Notice that the comparison yokes essentially dissimilar things (humidity and peanut butter). Such unexpected connections surprise readers and help keep their interest.

Figures of speech also tighten writing. Because they create sharp images in the reader's mind, you don't need many words to convey as much information. If someone writes, "My teenage years were like a perpetual root canal," the reader immediately knows how painful and never-ending the author found adolescence.

SIMILES, METAPHORS, PERSONIFICATION   Figures of speech come in several varieties. A **simile** is a direct comparison of two unlike things using the words *like* or *as:* "The moon brightened the yard *like* a floodlight." In a **metaphor**, the comparison is implied rather than directly stated: "The girl's *barbed-wire hair* set off *electric shocks* in her parents." In **personification**, an inanimate object is given human characteristics: "The couple robbed the store without noticing a silent, hidden eyewitness who later would tell all—a video camera."

AVOID CLICHÉS   Some figures of speech are trite and overused. They signal a lack of imagination: *a tough nut to crack, cool as a cucumber, green with envy*. Such expressions, called **clichés**, are so predictable that you can hear the first few words (*Life is a bowl of…*) and fill in the rest (*cherries*). Clichés lull writer and reader alike into passivity because they encourage rote, habitual thinking.

When revising, either eliminate tired figures of speech or give them an unexpected twist. For example, seeking a humorous effect, you might write, "Beneath his rough exterior beat a heart of lead" (instead of "gold"). Rather than "Last but not least," you might write, "Last but also least."

TWO ADDITIONAL CAUTIONS   First, if you include figures of speech, *don't pile one on top of another,* as in the following sentence:

> Whenever the dorm residents prepared for the first party of the season, hairdryers howled like a windstorm, hairspray rained down in torrents, stereos vibrated like an earthquake, and shouts of excitement shook the walls like an avalanche.

Second, guard against *illogical* or *mixed* figures of speech. In the following example, note the ludicrous and contradictory comparisons:

> They rode the roller coaster of high finance, dodging bullets and avoiding ambushes from those trying to lasso their streak of good luck.

To detect outlandish comparisons, visualize each figure of speech. If it calls up some unintentionally humorous or impossible image, revise or eliminate it.

Avoid Sexist Language

Sexist language gives the impression that one gender is more important, powerful, or valuable than the other. **Gender-neutral or nonsexist** terms convey no gender-based prejudice.

SEXIST VOCABULARY   Using nonsexist vocabulary means staying away from terms that demean or exclude one of the sexes. Such slang words as *stud, jock, chick,* and *fox* portray people as one-dimensional. Just as adult males should be called *men,* not *boys,* adult females should be referred to as *women,* not *girls.* In addition, consider replacing *Mrs.* and *Miss* with *Ms.* Like *Mr., Ms.* doesn't indicate marital status.

Be alert as well to the fact that words not inherently sexist can become so in certain contexts. Asking "What does the *man* on the street think of the teachers' strike?" excludes the possibility of asking women for their reactions.

Because the English language tends to exclude women rather than men, we list here a number of common words that exclude women. When you write (or speak), make an effort to use the more inclusive alternatives given.

Sexist	Nonsexist and Inclusive
the average guy	the average person
chairman	chairperson, chair
congressman	congressional representative
fireman	fire fighter
foreman	supervisor
layman	layperson
mailman	mail carrier, letter carrier
mankind, man	people, humans, human beings
policeman	police officer
salesman	salesperson

Also be on the lookout for phrases that suggest a given profession or talent is unusual for someone of a particular sex: *woman judge, woman doctor, male secretary, male nurse.*

SEXIST PRONOUN USE *Indefinite singular nouns*—representing one person in a general group of people consisting of both genders—can lead to **sexist pronoun use**: "On *his* first day of school, a young child often experiences separation anxiety," or "Each professor should be responsible for monitoring *her* own students' progress" are sexist because the language excludes one gender.

Indefinite pronouns such as *anyone, each,* and *everybody* may also pave the way to sexist language. Although such pronouns often refer to a number of individuals, they are considered singular. So, wanting to be grammatically correct, you may write a sentence like the following: "Everybody wants *his* favorite candidate to win." The sentence, however, is sexist because *everybody* is certainly not restricted to men. Writing "Everybody wants *her* candidate to win" is equally sexist because now males aren't included.

Here's one way to avoid these kinds of sexist constructions: Use *both* male and female pronouns, instead of just one or the other. For example, you could write "On *his or her* first day of school, a young child often experiences separation anxiety," or "Everybody wants *his or her* favorite candidate to win." If you use both pronouns, you might try to vary their order; that is, alternate *his or her* with *her or his,* and so on. Another approach is to use the gender-neutral pronouns *they, their,* or *themselves:* "Everybody wants *their* favorite candidate to win." Be warned, though. Some people object to using these plural pronouns with singular indefinite pronouns, even though the practice is common in everyday speech. To be on the safe side, ask your instructors if they object to any of the approaches described here. If not, feel free to choose whichever nonsexist construction seems most graceful and least obtrusive.

If you're still unhappy with the result, two alternative strategies enable you to eliminate the need for *any* gender-marked singular pronouns. First, you can change singular general nouns or indefinite pronouns to their plural equivalents and then use nonsexist plural pronouns:

Original	A *workaholic* feels anxious when *he* isn't involved in a task-related project.
Revised	*Workaholics* feel anxious when *they're* not involved in task-related projects.

Second, you can recast the sentence to omit the singular pronoun:

Original	A *manager* usually spends part of each day settling squabbles among *his* staff.
Revised	A manager usually spends part of each day settling *staff squabbles.*

The following checklist is designed to help you and your readers evaluate the words in a draft. (Activities at the end of the chapter will refer you to this checklist when you revise several essays.)

☑ **Revising Words: A Checklist**

☐ Which words seem inconsistent with the essay's tone? What words would be more appropriate?

☐ Which words seem vague and overly general? Where would more specific and concrete words add vitality and clarify meaning?

☐ Where is language overly formal? Which words are unnecessarily long or specialized? Where is language too informal? Where do unintended shifts in diction level create a jarring effect?

☐ Which words overstate? Which understate? What alternatives would be less misleading?

☐ Which words carry connotations unsuited to the essay's purpose and tone? What synonyms would be more appropriate?

☐ Where could weak verbs be replaced by vigorous ones? Which *to be* and linking verbs should be changed to action verbs? Which passive verbs could be replaced by active ones? Where could a noun-verb combination be replaced by a strong verb?

☐ Which adverbs, especially intensifiers (*very*) and qualifiers (*quite*), could be eliminated?

☐ Where would original similes, metaphors, and personifications add power? Which figures of speech are overused, illogical, or mixed? How could these problems be fixed?

☐ Where does sexist language appear? What terms could be used instead? How could sexist pronouns be eliminated?

Sample Student Revision of Sentences and Words

Reprinted here is the introduction to Caylah Francis's first draft—as it looked after she entered on a word processor the changes she made in overall meaning, structure, and paragraph development. To help identify problems with words and sentences, Caylah asked one of the students in her editing group to read the revised version aloud. Then she asked the group to comment on her paper, using the checklists in this chapter. The marginal notes indicate her ranking of the group's comments in order of importance. The above-line changes show how Caylah revised in response to these suggestions for improving the paragraph's sentences and words.

The incredible advancement of technology has created a world where many American

houses not only have one television, one computer, and one video game console, but

To

many have several of these media devices. ~~Parents try everything to~~ please their kids
and keep them occupied,   *ranging from Dance, Dance Revolution to*
many parents buy   *Outlast and*
~~such as~~ buying them a variety of video games ~~from~~ violent first person shooter games

such as Call of Duty.
~~to fantasy games. They often buy these games because they work many hours a week~~
        Parents are working more hours than ever before to provide for their families.
        They are not always home as much as they would like to be to spend

① *Explain why parents are working long hours and how that affects them even when they are home.*

② *Eliminate the reference to positive effects of playing video games. That's not what the essay is about.*

③ *Include examples of specific games.*

~~and try their best to preoccupy their children to aid in the parenting process.~~ *time with their children, and when these parents are home, there is much that demands their attention* As a result, the use of video games has become a popular activity among many kids.

~~Playing these games has had both negative and positive effects on young people.~~

More specifically this has created concerns for kids who play video games an excessive amount of time. While some argue that playing video games does not have

harmful effects, research proves otherwise.

Once you, like Caylah, have carefully revised sentences and words, your essay needs only to be edited (for errors in grammar, punctuation, and spelling) and proofread.

Activities: Revising Sentences and Words

1. Revise the following sentences, making them economical and clear.

   a. What a person should do before subletting a rental apartment is make sure to have the sublet agreement written up in a formal contract.

   b. In high school, it often happens that young people deny liking poetry because of the fact that they fear running the risk of having people mock or make fun of them because they actually enjoy poetry.

   c. In light of the fact that college students are rare in my home neighborhood, being a college student gives me immediate and instant status.

2. Using only simple or simple and compound sentences, write a paragraph based on one of the following topic sentences. Then rewrite the paragraph, making some of the sentences complex and others compound-complex. Examine your two versions of the paragraph. What differences do you see in meaning and emphasis?

   a. The campus parking lot is dangerous at night.

   b. Silent body language speaks loudly.

   c. Getting on a teacher's good side is an easily mastered skill.

3. The following sentences could be more emphatic. Examine each one to determine its focus. Then revise the sentence, using one of the following strategies: placing the most important item first or last, parallelism, inverted word order, a fragment. Try to use a different strategy in each sentence.

   a. Most of us find rude salespeople difficult to deal with.

   b. The politician promises, "I'll solve all your problems."

   c. It's a wise teacher who encourages discussion of controversial issues in the classroom.

4. The following paragraph is pretentious and murky. Revise to make it crisp and clear.

> Since its founding, the student senate on this campus has maintained essentially one goal: to upgrade the quality of its student-related services. Two years ago, the senate, supported by the opinions of three consultants provided by the National Council of Student Governing Boards, was confident it was operating from a base of quality but felt that, if given additional monetary support from the administration, a significant improvement in student services would be facilitated. This was a valid prediction, for that is exactly what transpired in the past fifteen months once additional monetary resources were, in fact, allocated by the administration to the senate and its activities.

5. Write a sentence for each word in the series that follows, making sure your details reinforce each word's connotations:

a. chubby, voluptuous, portly

b. stroll, trudge, loiter

c. turmoil, anarchy, hubbub

6. Write three versions of a brief letter voicing a complaint to a store, a person, or an organization. One version should be charged with negative connotations; another should "soft pedal" the problem. The final version should present your complaint using neutral, objective words. Which letter do you prefer? Why?

7. Describe each of the following in one or two sentences, using a creative figure of speech to convey each item's distinctive quality:

a. a baby's hand

b. a pile of dead leaves

c. an empty room

8. Enliven the following dull, vague sentences. Use your knowledge of sentence structure to dramatize key elements. Replace weak verbs with vigorous ones and make language more specific.

a. I got sick on the holiday.

b. He stopped the car at the crowded intersection.

c. The class grew restless.

d. The TV broadcaster put on a concerned air as she announced the tragedy.

9. The following paragraph contains too many linking verbs, passives, adverbs, and prepositions. In addition, noun forms are sometimes used where their verb counterparts would be more effective. Revise the paragraph by eliminating unnecessary prepositions and providing more vigorous verbs. Then add specific, concrete words that dramatize what is being described.

The farmers in the area conducted a meeting during which they formulated a discussion of the vandalism problem in the county in which they live. They made the estimate that, on the average, each of them had at least an acre of crops destroyed the past few weekends by gangs of motorcyclists who have been driving maliciously over their land. The increase in such vandalism has been caused by the encroachment of the suburbs on rural areas.

10. Revise the following sentences to eliminate sexist language.

    a. The manager of a convenience store has to guard his cash register carefully.

    b. When I broke my arm in a car accident, a male nurse, aided by a physician's assistant, treated my injury.

    c. All of us should contact our congressman if we're not satisfied with his performance.

    d. The chemistry professors agree that nobody should have to buy her own Bunsen burner.

11. In response to activity 1 in Chapter 7, you revised the overall meaning, structure, and paragraph development of Caylah Francis's first draft. Find that revision so that you can now focus on its sentences and words. Get together with at least one other person and ask yourselves these questions: "Where should sentence type, length, or pattern be more varied?" and "Where would more specific and concrete words add vitality and clarify meaning?" For further guidance, refer to the checklists in this chapter. Summarize and rank any perceived problems in marginal annotations or a feedback chart. Then type your changes into a word processor or enter them between the lines of the draft. (Save your revision so you can use it at later stages of the writing process.)

12. Return to the draft you prepared in response to activity 2, 3, or 4 in Chapter 7. Get together with several people and request that one of them read the draft aloud. Then, using the checklists in this chapter, ask the group members focused questions about any sentences and words that you feel need sharpening. After evaluating the feedback, revise the draft. Either key your changes into a computer or do your revising by hand. (Save your revision so you can use it at later stages of the writing process.)

Chapter 9
Editing and Proofreading

Learning Objectives

9.1 Edit your essay.

9.2 Use the appropriate manuscript format for your essay.

9.3 Proofread your essay.

W anting to finish a writing assignment is a normal human desire. But if you don't edit and proofread—that is, closely check your writing for grammar, spelling, and typographical errors—you run the risk of sabotaging your composition. Readers may assume that a piece of writing isn't worth their time if they're jolted by surface flaws that make it difficult to read. So, to make sure that your good ideas get a fair hearing (and as detailed in Figure 9.1), you should do the following:

- Edit carefully.
- Use the appropriate manuscript format for your essay.
- Proofread your essay.

Edit Carefully

9.1 Edit your essay.

When revising your essay, you probably spotted some errors in grammar, punctuation, or spelling, perhaps flagging them for later correction. Now—after you're satisfied with the essay's organization, development, and style—it's time to return to these errors. It's also time to search for and correct errors that have slipped by you so far.

If you're working with pen and paper or on a printed draft with handwritten annotations, use a different color of ink so your new corrections will stand out. If you use a computer, search for errors both on the screen and on a printout. Use the computer's spell-check function, which will greatly simplify your search for misspellings. Be aware, however, that such programs may not find errors in the spelling of proper nouns, and they won't flag errors that constitute legitimate words (for example, *he* when you meant *the* or *their* when you meant *there*).

Figure 9.1 Process Diagram: Editing and Proofreading

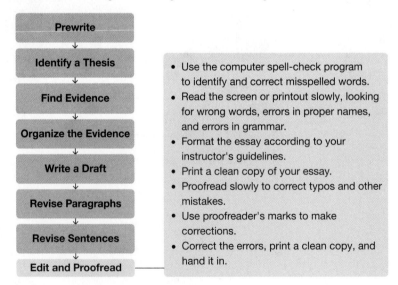

To be a successful editor of your own work, you need two standard tools: a grammar handbook and a good dictionary. Use a handbook to identify and correct any errors in grammar, style, and punctuation; use a dictionary to check your spelling.

Use the Appropriate Manuscript Format

9.2 Use the appropriate manuscript format for your essay.

After correcting all grammar and spelling problems, you're ready to produce the final copy. In doing so, you should follow accepted academic practice, adapted to your instructor's requirements. Most instructors will require that you type your essays. Even if your instructor doesn't impose this requirement, computer-printed essays look neater, are easier to grade, and show that you have made the transition to college-level format.

The following checklist on manuscript format lists the basic rules for college essays. In addition, check for any specific format preferences your instructor may have.

☑ Manuscript Format: A Checklist

- ☐ Use standard-sized (8½ by 11 inches), white printer paper.

- ☐ Use a standard font, such as Times Roman or Courier, 12-point size.

- ☐ Use only black ink for text. Print illustrations in color if possible.

- ☐ Leave one-inch margins at the top, bottom, left, and right.

- ☐ Double-space all text, including extracts, notes, bibliographies, and Works Cited and References lists.

- ☐ Follow the citation style (for example, MLA or APA) required by your instructor.

- ☐ Use the computer's page-numbering feature to add a header, one-half inch from the top of the sheet.

- ☐ If you include a title page, place the title about one-third of the way down the page. Enter the title, and double-space between lines of the title and your name. Give the course and section, instructor's name, and date on separate lines, double-spaced and centered.

- ☐ If you don't include a title page, use a standard heading, as specified by your instructor, at the top of the first page.

- ☐ Center the title of your essay one double-space below the heading. Capitalize only the first letter of all main words. Don't use all capital letters, underlining, quotation marks, or bold type. Double-space a title having more than one line.

- ☐ Double-space between the title and the first paragraph of your essay.

- ☐ Indent the first line of each paragraph one-half inch, the default setting for most word-processing software.

- ☐ Place any illustrations as close as possible to their mention in the text. Position a caption below the illustration.

☐ Print on only one side of each sheet of paper.

☐ Paper-clip or staple the pages, placing the outline wherever your instructor requests.

☐ Don't use a report cover unless your instructor requests one.

☐ If you are sending the essay by e-mail or uploading it to a course management system, follow your instructor's directions for naming the file.

☐ Keep a backup copy of the essay on a disc, external hard drive or thumb drive, or an online cloud-based system.

Proofread Closely

9.3 Proofread your essay.

Proofreading means checking your final copy carefully for "typos" (typographical errors) or other mistakes. One trick is to read your material backward, sentence by sentence or word by word: If you read from the end of each paragraph to the beginning, you can focus on each word individually to make sure no letters have been left out or transposed (switched). This technique prevents you from getting caught up in the flow of ideas and missing small defects, which is easy to do when you've read your own words many times.

What should you do when you find a typo? Working with a print copy of your essay, simply use a pen with dark ink to make an above-line correction. The following standard proofreader's marks will help you indicate some common types of corrections:

Proofreader's Mark	Meaning	Example
∧	insert missing letter or word	televsion
℺	delete	reports the the findings
∾	reverse order	the gang' here all
¶	start new paragraph	to dry. Next, put
#	add space	thegirls
⌒	close up space	boy cott

If you make so many corrections on a page that it begins to look like a draft, make the corrections and reprint the page for fresh review.

Student Essay: From Prewriting Through Proofreading

In the last several chapters, we've taken you through the various stages in the writing process—from prewriting to proofreading. You've seen how Caylah Francis used prewriting and outlining to arrive at her thesis and her first draft. You also saw how Caylah's peer reviewer, Taylor Young, critiqued her first draft. You then observed how Caylah revised, first, her draft's overall meaning and paragraph development and, second, its sentences and words. In the following pages, you'll read Caylah's final draft—the essay she submitted to her instructor after completing all the stages of the writing process.

This is the assignment that prompted Caylah's essay:

> Using first-person point of view and numerous personal examples, Rosen crafts an essay in which he shares his concerns about our obsessive relationship with technology. Write an essay in which you share similar or related concerns of your own. For example, you might write about possible negative effects of social networking sites, video games, or texting. Instead of writing in first person as Rosen does, use the third-person point of view. Consider including several outside sources to strengthen the effectiveness of your essay, and be sure to correctly document your sources.

Caylah's essay is annotated so you can see how it illustrates the general essay format. As you read the essay, try to determine how well it reflects the principles of effective writing. The commentary following the essay will help you look at the essay more closely and give you some sense of the way Caylah went about revising her first draft.

Page number | Francis 1

Heading — Caylah Francis
Professor Hernandez
English 1102
18 April 2016

Title

Aggression, Addiction, Isolation, and More:
The Dark Side of Video Game Play

Introduction

Advancements in technology have resulted in a world in which many   1
American homes have not just one television, one computer, and one video game console, but more than one of each of these media devices. To please their children and help keep them occupied, many parents buy them a variety of video games, ranging from seemingly innocent, fun games such as *Dance Dance Revolution* to survival horror games like *Outlast* and violent first-person shooter games such as *Call of Duty*. Many parents are working more hours than ever before trying to provide for their families. They are not always home as much as they would like to be to spend time with their children, and when these parents are home, there is much that demands their attention. As a result, many children are keeping themselves occupied by spending hours each day playing video games. While some argue

Thesis —— that playing video games does not have harmful effects, research proves otherwise.

First supporting paragraph

One concern many people have is that playing some of these   2
video games makes children become more aggressive and violent.

Topic sentence —— A 2011 article on the relationship between playing violent video games and increased aggression revealed that playing these games can cause players to "imitate the aggression that they observe in the games" (Willoughby 1044). The researchers who conducted this study found that "greater violent video game play predicted higher levels of aggression over time" while "nonviolent video game play did not predict higher levels of aggressive behavior" (1044). Another study that focused on the difference in the effects of playing versus watching violent video games reports that "playing a violent video game caused boys to become more aggressive than merely watching the same violent video game" (Polman 256). This study goes on to state that "specifically for boys, playing a violent video game could lead to more aggression than watching television violence" (256). There is no doubt that children can learn to be more aggressive and violent by playing video games.

Second supporting paragraph

Topic sentence

A tendency toward increased aggression and violence is only one of many negative effects of spending time playing these games; another negative effect is video game addiction. In a 2010 study, 1,945 participants were surveyed about video game use. Findings of the study showed that "almost one-half (48.7%) of the participants spent 1-3 hours per day playing video games, and approximately one-third (32.9%) spent 4-8 hours per day doing so" (Porter 123). As children spend more and more time playing video games, the chance that they will grow up addicted to playing them increases. Another study reports that video gamers can "become preoccupied with gaming, lie about their gaming use, lose interest in other activities just to game, withdraw from family and friends to game, and use gaming as a means to psychologically escape" (Young 356). Violent video games usually offer positive reinforcement and positive sanctions for violent acts. For example, first-person-shooter games often offer positive reinforcement in terms of new weapons, perks, vehicles, and ranks. Many who play these video games online communicate with others through a simple microphone as they play the games. This allows them to receive even more positive sanctions for their violent behavior. Gaming addiction has also been associated with mental illness, physical exhaustion, and death (Porter 120).

Third supporting paragraph

Topic sentence

Increased aggression and video game addiction are two of many negative effects; another effect is the danger to the child's health. The United States has become known as a nation filled with obese individuals. Children who spend hours each day playing video games are most likely not getting enough exercise; this can cause an increase in risk for obesity. Not only is the child's physical health at risk; there is also a risk of poor psychological health. A 2013 study conducted in Great Britain reveals that children who spend time playing video games experience higher levels of emotional distress, anxiety, and depression than other children and that the greater the amount of screen time, the higher the likelihood of these negative effects (United Kingdom).

Conclusion

Playing video games can have many negative effects on children. While playing these games is a very popular activity among children, research shows that playing violent video games can result in increased levels of aggression and that children can become

3

4

5

Francis 3

addicted. Gaming addiction can lead to hours of screen time each day, which, in turn, can lead to obesity and greater chances of psychological issues such as emotional distress, anxiety, and depression. Parents need to think carefully before caving in to their children's pleas for the latest video game. The dangers associated with video gaming cannot be denied and should not be ignored.

Works Cited

Polman, Hanneke, et al. "Experimental Study of the Differential Effects of Playing versus Watching Violent Video Games on Children's Aggressive Behavior." *Aggressive Behavior*, vol. 34, no. 3, 2008, pp. 256–64.

Porter, Guy, et al. "Recognizing Problem Video Game Use." *Australian & New Zealand Journal of Psychiatry*, vol. 44, no. 2, 2010, pp. 120–28.

United Kingdom. "How Healthy Behaviour Supports Children's Wellbeing." *Public Health England*, 28 Aug. 2013, www.gov.uk/ government/uploads/system/uploads/attachment _data/ file/232978/Smart_Restart_280813_web.pdf.

Willoughby, Teena, et al. "A Longitudinal Study of the Association between Violent Video Game Play and Aggression among Adolescents." *Developmental Psychology*, vol. 48, no. 4, 2011, pp. 1044–57.

Young, Kimberly. "Understanding Online Gaming Addiction and Treatment Issues for Adolescents." *American Journal of Family Therapy*, vol. 37, 2009, pp. 355–72.

Commentary

The following sections examine each part of Caylah's essay.

INTRODUCTION AND THESIS The opening paragraph attracts readers' interest by pointing out how recent advancements in technology have drastically changed the number and kinds of media devices that many people now have in their homes. Instead of immediately focusing on the negative effects of one form of media, video games, Caylah acknowledges that there are many different types of games and that parents often purchase them to help keep children occupied while the parents are working long hours to provide for their families. Then she transitions smoothly to her *thesis*, which she revised according to peer review feedback from Taylor Young: "While some argue that playing video games does not have harmful effects, research proves otherwise." Her statement acknowledges that this is a controversial issue, reveals her stance on the issue, and lets her readers know that she will be supporting her assertion with evidence from research.

PLAN OF DEVELOPMENT Instead of following her thesis with a *plan of development* that anticipates the three major points to be covered in the essay's supporting paragraphs, Caylah ends the introduction with her thesis. She had included the three major points (that playing violent video games can lead to increased levels of aggression, video game addiction, and serious health issues) in her first draft that she shared with peer reviewer Taylor Young, but she chose to follow Taylor's recommendation to cut the two awkward sentences and end the introduction with a stronger, clearer statement. Caylah decided that it was unnecessarily repetitive to state the three major points in the introduction and also in the topic sentences of the three supporting paragraphs.

PATTERNS OF DEVELOPMENT   Caylah's primary pattern of development is *argumentation-persuasion*. She develops her thesis by making assertions about the harmful effects of playing violent video games and supporting those assertions with evidence from documented sources. However, she incorporates other *patterns of development* throughout her essay. For example, she employs *comparison-contrast* when she compares the number and types of media devices in many American homes today with those present before recent advancements in technology. She employs *division-classification* when she refers to various types of video games: "seemingly innocent fun games such as *Dance Dance Revolution*, survival horror games like *Outlast*, and violent first-person shooter games such as *Call of Duty*." She also uses *exemplification* through her use of researched *examples* substantiating her claim that playing violent video games can have harmful effects on children.

PURPOSE, AUDIENCE, AND TONE   Given the essay's *purpose* and *audience*, Caylah adopts a serious *tone*, providing no-nonsense evidence to support her thesis. Suppose, however, that she had been asked to write a column for her school newspaper on video games that can help college students stay in shape. Aiming for a different tone, purpose, and audience, Caylah would have taken another approach. Drawing on her personal experience, she might have shared how she and her friends love spending hours playing *Dance Dance Revolution* and about how such video games, as well as games like *Wii Fit*, *Kinect Sports*, and *Zumba Fitness*, can have positive rather than harmful effects. Such a column would have been written in a lighter, less formal tone.

ORGANIZATION   Structuring the essay around three major points (increased levels of aggression, video game addiction, and serious health issues), Caylah uses *emphatic order* to sequence those claims. While each claim is important, Caylah decided to try to keep her readers interested by starting with a major concern for society and parents (aggression), then move on to a more personal concern for parents (addiction), and finally discuss the most tangential concern (health). She decided that it would make sense to start with the issue most readers would be anxious about (because it's the result most likely to affect them) and then to give the substantially less alarming potential consequences (at least for society) as additional support.

The essay also displays Caylah's familiarity with other kinds of organizational strategies. Each supporting paragraph opens with a *topic sentence*. Further, *signal devices* are used throughout the essay to show how ideas are related to one another: *transitions* ("As a result, many children are keeping themselves occupied by spending hours each day playing video games"; *pronouns* ("many parents … they"); and *bridging sentences* ("A tendency toward increased aggression and violence is only one of many negative effects of spending time playing these games; another negative effect is video game addiction").

TWO MINOR PROBLEMS   Caylah's efforts to write a well-organized essay result in a somewhat predictable structure. She might have increased the essay's appeal if she had rewritten one of the paragraphs, perhaps embedding the topic sentence in the middle of the paragraph or saving it for the end. Similarly, Caylah's signal devices are a little heavy-handed. Even so, an essay with a sharp focus and clear signals is preferable to one with a confusing or inaccessible structure. As she gains more experience, Caylah can work on making the structure of her essays more subtle.

CONCLUSION   Caylah brings the essay to a satisfying *close* by reminding readers of the essay's central idea and three main points. The final paragraph also extends the essay's scope by introducing a new but related issue: "Parents need to think carefully before caving in to their children's pleas for the latest video game."

Revising the First Draft

Caylah reworked her essay a number of times. For a clearer sense of her revision process, compare the final version of her conclusion with the original version reprinted here. Caylah wisely waited to rework her conclusion until after she had fine-tuned the rest of the essay. The marginal annotations, ranked in order of importance, indicate the problems that Caylah and her editing group detected in the conclusion.

Original Conclusion

Above all, video games have many negative effects on young children. Video games are a very popular activity for young children. Research shows that children can become more aggressive and violent after playing video games. Extensive research also shows that many become addicted to video games and can develop health issues as well.

(2) *Paragraph seems tacked on*

(1) *Paragraph simply restates what's already been said*

(3) *References to "young children" doesn't work*

(4) *Weak opening transition "Above all"*

As soon as Caylah heard her essay read aloud during a group session, she realized her conclusion didn't work at all. Rather than bringing the essay to a pleasing finish, the final paragraph seemed like a tired afterthought. She realized that her references to "young children" in the conclusion were also inappropriate. Throughout the rest of the essay she had referred to "children" and "kids"—not to "young children." Keeping these points in mind, Caylah decided to scrap her original conclusion. Working at a computer, she prepared a new, much stronger concluding paragraph. In addition to eliminating the inaccurate reference to "young children," she deleted the weak transition "Above all" and combined the second and third sentences into one sentence that clarified the relationship between her ideas. She also added more specific details about the relationship between video game addiction and possible health issues, along with two new final sentences that emphasize the important role that parents play in their children's welfare.

These are just a few of the changes Caylah made when reworking her essay. Realizing that writing is a process, she left herself enough time to revise—and to carefully consider Taylor Young's earlier comments on her rough draft. Early in her composition course, Caylah learned that attention to the various stages in the writing process yields satisfying results, for writer and reader alike.

Activities: Editing and Proofreading

1. Applying for a job, a student wrote the following letter. Edit and proofread it carefully, as if it were your own. If you have trouble spotting many grammar, spelling, and typing errors, that's a sign you need to review the appropriate sections of a grammar handbook.

> Dear Mr. Eno:
>
> I am a sophomore at Harper College who will be returning home to Brooktown this June, hopefully, to fine a job for the the summer. One that would give me further experience in the retail field. I have heard from my freind, Sarah Snyder, that your hiring college studnets as assistant mangers, I would be greatly intrested in such a postion.
>
> I have quite a bit of experience in retail sales. Having worked after school in a "Classy Boutique" shop at Mason Mall, Pennsylvania. I started their as a sales clerk, by my second year I was serving as assistant manger.
>
> I am reliable and responsible, and truely enjoy sales work. Alexandria Gillespie, the owner of the "Classy Boutique," can verify my qualifications, she was my supervisor for two years.
>
> I will be visiting Brooktown from April 25 to 30. I hope to have an oppurtunity to speak to you about possible summer jobs at that time, and will be available for interview at your convience. Thank-you for you're consideration.
>
> Sincerley,
Joan Ackerman
Joan Ackerman

2. Retrieve the revised essay you prepared in response to either activity 11 or activity 12 in Chapter 8. Following the guidelines described on the preceding pages, edit and proofread your revision. After making the needed changes, prepare your final draft of the essay, using the appropriate manuscript format. Before submitting your essay to your instructor, ask someone to check it for grammar, spelling, and typographical errors that may have slipped by you.

Chapter 10
Description

10.1 Understand how you can use the description pattern to develop your essays.

10.2 Consider how description can fit your purpose and audience.

10.3 Develop prewriting strategies for using description in an essay.

10.4 Develop strategies for writing a description essay.

10.5 Use strategies for revising your description essay.

10.6 Analyze how description is used effectively in a student-written selection.

What Is Description?

10.1 Understand how you can use the description pattern to develop your essays.

All of us respond in a strong way to sensory stimulation. The sweet perfume of a candy shop takes us back to childhood; the blank white walls of the campus infirmary remind us of long vigils at a hospital where a grandmother lay dying; the screech of a subway car sets our nerves on edge.

Without any sensory stimulation, we sink into a less-than-human state. Neglected babies, left alone with no human touch, no colors, and no lullabies become withdrawn and unresponsive. And prisoners dread solitary confinement, knowing that the sensory deprivation can be unbearable, bringing them even to the point of madness.

Because sensory impressions are so potent, descriptive writing has a unique power and appeal. **Description** can be defined as the expression, in vivid language, of what the five senses experience. A richly rendered description freezes a subject in time, evoking sights, smells, sounds, textures, and tastes in such a way that readers become one with the writer's world.

How Description Fits Your Purpose and Audience

10.2 Consider how description can fit your purpose and audience.

Description can be a supportive technique that develops part of an essay, or it can be the dominant technique used throughout an essay. Here are some examples of the way description can help you meet the objective of an essay developed chiefly through another pattern of development:

- In a *causal analysis* showing the *consequences* of pet overpopulation, you might describe the desperate appearance of a pack of starving stray dogs.

- In an *argumentation-persuasion essay* urging more rigorous gun control, you might start with a description of a violent family confrontation that ended in murder.

- In a *process analysis* explaining the pleasure of making ice cream at home, you might describe the beauty of an old-fashioned, hand-cranked ice cream maker.

- In a *narrative essay* recounting a day in the life of a street musician, you might describe the musician's energy and the joyous appreciation of passersby.

In each case, the essay's overall purpose would affect the amount of description needed.

Your readers also influence how much description you should include. As you write, ask yourself, "What do my particular readers need to know to understand and experience what I'm describing? What descriptive details will they enjoy most?" Your answers to these and similar questions will help you tailor your description to specific readers.

Although your purpose and audience define *how much* to describe, you have great freedom deciding *what* to describe. Description is especially suited to objects (your car or desk, for example), but you can also describe a person, an animal, a place, a time, and a phenomenon or concept. You might write an effective description about a friend who runs marathons (person), the kitchen of a fast-food restaurant (place), or a period when you were unemployed (time).

Objective and Subjective Description

Description can be divided into two types: objective and subjective. In an **objective description**, you describe the subject in a straightforward and literal way, without revealing your attitude or feelings. Reporters, as well as technical and scientific writers, specialize in objective description; their jobs depend on their ability to detail experiences without emotional bias. For example, a reporter may write an unemotional account of a township meeting that ended in a fistfight.

In contrast, when writing a **subjective description**, you convey a highly personal view of your subject and seek to elicit a strong emotional response from your readers. Such subjective descriptions often take the form of reflective pieces or character studies. For example, in an essay describing the rich plant life in an inner-city garden, you might reflect on people's longing to connect with the soil and express admiration for the gardeners' hard work—an admiration you'd like readers to share.

Tone and Language

The *tone* of a subjective description is determined by your purpose, your attitude toward the subject, and the reader response you wish to evoke. Consider an essay about a dynamic woman who runs a center for disturbed children. If your goal is to make readers admire the woman, your tone will be serious and appreciative. But if you want to criticize the woman's high-pressure tactics and create distaste for her management style, your tone will be disapproving and severe.

The language of a descriptive piece also depends, to a great extent, on whether your purpose is primarily objective or subjective. If the description is objective, the language is straightforward, precise, and factual. Such *denotative* language consists of neutral dictionary meanings. If you want to describe as dispassionately as possible fans' violent behavior at a football game, you might write about the "large crowd" and its "mass movement onto the field." But if you are shocked by the fans' behavior and want to write a subjective piece that inspires outrage in readers, then you might write about the "swelling mob" and its "rowdy stampede onto the field." In the latter case, the language used would be *connotative* and emotionally charged so that readers would share your feelings.

Subjective and objective descriptions often overlap. Sometimes a single sentence contains both objective and subjective elements: "Although his hands were large and misshapen by arthritis, they were gentle to the touch, inspiring confidence and trust." Other times, part of an essay may provide a factual description (the physical appearance of a summer cabin your family rented), whereas another part of the essay may be highly subjective (how you felt in the cabin, sitting in front of a fire on a rainy day).

Prewriting Strategies

10.3 Develop prewriting strategies for using description in an essay.

The following checklist shows how you can apply prewriting strategies to description.

☑ Description: A Prewriting Checklist

Choose a Subject to Describe

☐ Might a photograph, postcard, prized possession, or journal entry suggest a subject worth describing?

☐ Will you describe a person, animal, object, place, time period, or phenomenon? Is the subject readily observable, or will you have to reconstruct it from memory?

Determine Your Purpose, Audience, Tone, and Point of View

☐ Is your purpose to inform or to evoke an emotional response? If you want to do both, which is your predominant purpose?

☐ What audience are you writing for? How much does the audience already know about the subject you plan to describe?

☐ What tone and point of view will best serve your purpose and make readers receptive to your description?

Use Prewriting to Generate Details About the Subject

☐ How could freewriting, journal entries, or brainstorming help you gather sensory specifics about your subject?

☐ What relevant details about your subject come to mind when you apply the questioning technique to each of the five senses—sight, sound, taste, touch, and smell?

Strategies for Writing a Description Essay

10.4 Develop strategies for writing a description essay.

After prewriting, you're ready to draft your essay. The suggestions in Figure 10.1 and those that follow will be helpful whether you use description as a dominant or supportive pattern of development.

1. **Focus a descriptive essay around a dominant impression.** Like other kinds of writing, a descriptive essay must have a thesis, or main point. In a descriptive essay with a subjective slant, the thesis usually centers on the **dominant impression** you want to convey about your subject.

Figure 10.1 Development Diagram: Writing a Description Essay

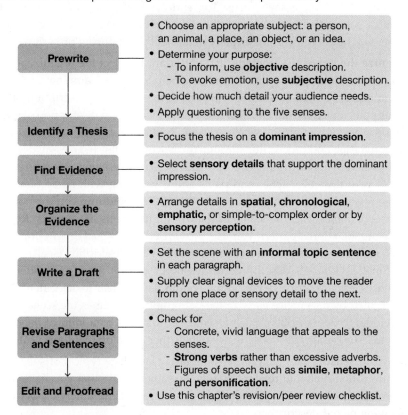

Prewrite
- Choose an appropriate subject: a person, an animal, a place, an object, or an idea.
- Determine your purpose:
  - To inform, use **objective** description.
  - To evoke emotion, use **subjective** description.
- Decide how much detail your audience needs.
- Apply questioning to the five senses.

Identify a Thesis
- Focus the thesis on a **dominant impression**.

Find Evidence
- Select **sensory details** that support the dominant impression.

Organize the Evidence
- Arrange details in **spatial**, **chronological**, **emphatic**, or simple-to-complex order or by **sensory perception**.

Write a Draft
- Set the scene with an **informal topic sentence** in each paragraph.
- Supply clear signal devices to move the reader from one place or sensory detail to the next.

Revise Paragraphs and Sentences
- Check for
  - Concrete, vivid language that appeals to the senses.
  - **Strong verbs** rather than excessive adverbs.
  - Figures of speech such as **simile**, **metaphor**, and **personification**.
- Use this chapter's revision/peer review checklist.

Edit and Proofread

2. **Select the details to include.** Prewriting techniques can help you develop heightened powers of observation and recall. The power of description hinges on your ability to select from all possible details *only those that support the dominant impression.* All others—no matter how vivid or interesting—must be left out. If you were describing how flamboyant your ninth-grade teacher could be, the details in the following paragraph would be appropriate:

> A large-boned woman, Ms. Hazzard wore her bright red hair piled on top of her head, where it perched precariously. By the end of class, wayward strands of hair tumbled down and fell into eyes fringed by spiky false eyelashes. Ms. Hazzard's nails, filed into crisp points, were painted either bloody burgundy or neon pink. Plastic bangle bracelets, also either burgundy or pink, clattered up and down her ample arms as she scrawled on the board the historical dates that had, she claimed, "changed the world."

Such details—the heavy eye makeup, stiletto nails, gaudy bracelets—contribute to the impression of a flamboyant, unusual person. Even if you remembered times that Ms. Hazzard seemed perfectly conventional and understated, most likely you wouldn't describe those times because they would contradict the dominant impression.

You must also be selective in the *number of details* you include. Excessive detailing dilutes the essay's focus. You end up with a seemingly endless list of specifics, rather than with a carefully crafted word picture. Having a dominant impression helps you eliminate many details gathered during prewriting.

3. **Organize the descriptive details.** It's important to select the organizational pattern (or combination of patterns) that best supports your dominant impression. You might, for instance, use a *spatial* pattern to organize a description of a large city as you viewed it from the air, a taxi, or a subway car. A description of your first day on a new job might move *chronologically*, starting with how you felt the first hour on the job and proceeding through the rest of the day. In an essay describing a bout with the flu, you might arrange details *emphatically*, beginning with a description of your low-level aches and pains and concluding with an account of your raging fever. An essay about a neighborhood garbage dump could be organized by *sensory impressions:* the sights of the dump, its smells, its sounds. Regardless of the organizational pattern you use, provide enough *signal devices* (for example, *about, next, worst of all*) so that readers can follow the description easily.

Finally, although descriptive essays don't always have conventional topic sentences, each descriptive paragraph should have a clear focus. Often this focus is indicated by a sentence early in the paragraph that names the scene, object, or individual to be described. Such a sentence functions as a kind of *informal topic sentence*. The paragraph's descriptive details then develop that topic sentence.

4. **Use vivid sensory language.** The connotative language typical of subjective description should etch in readers' minds the same picture that you have in yours. Use language that involves readers' senses. Consider the difference between the following paired descriptions:

Vague	**Vivid**
The food was unappetizing.	The stew congealed into an oval pool of muddy brown fat.
The lemonade was refreshing.	As I gulped the icy lemonade, its sweet tartness tingled my tongue.

Although all good writing blends abstract and concrete language, descriptive writing demands an abundance of specific sensory language.

Although you should aim for rich, sensory images, avoid overloading your sentences with too many adjectives: "A stark, smooth, blinding glass cylinder, the fifty-story skyscraper dominated the crowded city street." Delete unnecessary words, retaining only the most powerful: "A blinding glass cylinder, the skyscraper dominated the street."

Remember, too, that verbs pack more of a wallop than adverbs. The following sentence has to rely on adverbs (italicized) because its verbs are so weak: "She walked *casually* into the room and *deliberately* tried not to pay attention to their stares." Rewritten, so that verbs (italicized), not adverbs, do the bulk of the work, the sentence becomes more powerful: "She *strolled* into the room and *ignored* their stares." *Onomatopoetic* verbs that reflect sound, like *buzz, sizzle,* and *zoom,* can be especially effective because their sounds convey their meaning.

5. **Use figures of speech to enliven your description.** *Figures of speech*—nonliteral, imaginative comparisons between two basically dissimilar things—are another way to enliven descriptive writing. *Similes* use the word *like* or *as* when comparing; *metaphors* state or imply that the two things being compared are alike; and *personification* attributes human characteristics to inanimate things.

   The following examples show the effective use of figurative language in descriptive writing:

   Simile
   Moving as jerkily as a marionette on strings, the man picked himself up off the sidewalk and staggered down the street.

   Metaphor
   Stalking their prey, the hall monitors remained hidden in the corridors, motionless and ready to spring on any student who tried to sneak into class late.

   Personification
   The scoop of vanilla ice cream, plain and unadorned, cried out for hot fudge sauce and a sprinkling of sliced pecans.

6. **Vary your sentence structure.** Don't use the same subject-verb pattern in all sentences. The metaphor example above, for instance, could have been written as follows: "The hall monitors stalked their prey. They hid in the corridors. They remained motionless and ready to spring on any student who tried to sneak into class late." But the sentence is richer and more interesting when the descriptive elements are embedded, so that a clipped and predictable subject-verb pattern is avoided.

Revision Strategies

10.5 Use strategies for revising your description essay.

Once you have a draft of the essay, you're ready to revise. The following checklist will help your peers provide feedback and aid you in revising your essay.

☑ Description: A Revision/Peer Review Checklist

Revise Overall Meaning and Structure

☐ What dominant impression does the essay convey? Is the dominant impression stated or implied? Where? Should it be made more obvious or more subtle?

☐ Is the essay primarily objective or subjective? Should the essay be more personal and emotionally charged or less so?

☐ Which descriptive details don't support the dominant impression? Should they be deleted, or should the dominant impression be adjusted to encompass the details?

Revise Paragraph Development

☐ How are the essay's descriptive paragraphs (or passages) organized—spatially, chrono-logically, emphatically, from least to most complex, or by sensory impressions? Would another organizational pattern be more effective? Which one(s)?

☐ Which paragraphs lack a distinctive focus?

☐ Which descriptive paragraphs are mere lists of sensory impressions?

☐ Which descriptive paragraphs are too abstract or general? Which fail to engage the reader's senses? How could they be made more concrete and specific?

Revise Sentences and Words

☐ What signal devices (such as *above, next, worst of all*) guide readers through the description? Are there enough signals? Too many?

☐ Where should sentence structure be varied to make it less predictable?

☐ Which sentences should include sensory images?

☐ Where should flat verbs and adverbs be replaced with vigorous ones? Where would onomatopoeia enliven a sentence?

☐ Where should there be more or fewer adjectives?

☐ Do any figures of speech seem contrived or trite? Which ones?

Student Essay: From Prewriting Through Revision

10.6 Analyze how description is used effectively in a student-written selection.

The following student essay was written by Leanna Stoufer in response to this assignment:

> The essay "El Hoyo" is a poignant piece about a place that has special meaning for Mario Suárez. Write an essay about a place, a person, or an object that holds rich significance for you, centering the description on a dominant impression.

Leanna decided to write about a sculpture she had recently seen on a trip to the Denver Art Museum: *Akua's Surviving Children* by El Anatsui. Leanna had found herself thinking again and again about the sculpture and its powerful effect on her. As she began to think about the details of the sculpture and what she wanted to include in her essay, she realized that she would be able to write a richer essay if she returned to the museum, took time to carefully study the sculpture, and made notes about what she saw and what made the piece of art so powerful. She decided to use the prewriting technique of *questioning* to gather specific details about this piece of sculpture. When she arrived at the museum and began studying *Akua's Surviving Children*, she focused on two areas: what she saw and what characteristics made it such a powerful piece of art. Leanna took time to carefully look at the details of the structure and to make notes that could help her write a detailed descriptive essay. She also took a screen shot of the exhibition notes that included specific information about the sculpture and the entire El Anatsui exhibit.

When Leanna later reviewed the details listed under each of her two headings, she concluded that her essay's dominant impression should be the powerful story told by the twenty-seven figures in the sculpture. With that dominant impression in mind, she added some details to her prewriting. Below is Leanna's original prewriting; the handwritten insertions indicate her later efforts to develop the material:

Questioning Technique

What do I see when I look at *Akua's Surviving Children*?

- Twenty-seven charred and scarred wooden figures
  "with splits, gouges, and worm-eaten holes"
- Figures of different sizes—between 2 and 5 feet tall
- Sculpture sits on a gray platform
  "that is about 8 inches thick and about 12 x 8 feet"
- Figures look like they're attached to the platform with metal brackets
- Figures all have "heads" that are attached to the "bodies" with spikes—except one that's attached with what look like wire wrappings
- The heads are all charred and look darker than their bodies
- All figures facing the same way—to my left—except the one near the right front who seems to be looking back

What makes this sculpture so powerful?

- Figures all look like they've had a hard life
- Figures all look sad—like they've lost something or someone
- Title makes clear that these figures are "survivors"
  "makes me think of those who survive violence, cancer, AIDS. Also makes me think of all the ones who don't survive."
- Exhibition notes say that the sculpture is "representative of individual Africans who crossed tumultuous oceans" during the days of the Danish slave trade
- Figures tell a poignant story I can't get out of my mind

When Leanna reviewed her annotated prewriting, she decided that she would begin her essay with a spatial pattern that allows the reader to "see" the sculpture as she first saw it as she walked in the doorway of El Anatsui's exhibit at the Denver Art Museum. Then she would use an emphatic method of organization as she (1) described the figures and then (2) recounted information that the artist, El Anatsui, gave about these figures and the story they tell. The arrangement of details was now so clear to Leanna that she felt comfortable moving to a first draft without further shaping her prewriting or preparing an outline. As she wrote, though, she frequently referred to her prewriting to retrieve specific details.

Now read Leanna's essay, "Enduring with Dignity: *Akua's Surviving Children*." Notice that when she wrote the essay, Leanna expanded the details in her prewriting by adding more specifics and focusing on the story told by the twenty-seven figures. Finally, consider how well the essay applies the principles of description discussed in this chapter. (The commentary that follows the essay will help you look at the essay more closely and will give you some sense of how Leanna went about revising her first draft.)

Enduring with Dignity: *Akua's Surviving Children*
by Leanna Stoufer

Introduction; spatial sequence at the beginning

It is often the first piece that catches the visitor's eye when walking   1
through the doorway of El Anatsui's exhibit, "When I Last Wrote to You About Africa," featured at the Denver Art Museum. (See Figure 1.) The structure, created in 1996, is titled *Akua's Surviving Children* and sits on an 8-inch platform, approximately 12 feet wide and 8 feet deep. The platform itself is a flat grey color and appears to have been provided by the Denver Art Museum, rather than being an integral part of the artwork. There are twenty-seven figures standing on the platform. Each one is unique, with heights varying between approximately 2 feet and 5 feet. Each figure has a "body" that is described by the artist as a piece of driftwood; however, these bodies appear to have been shaped by man at one time—perhaps they are the broken remnants of piers, or docks,

Dominant impression (thesis)

or maybe shards left from a shoreline house or a boat. What is clear is that each piece has had a difficult life. Each of the twenty-seven bodies

Personification

has its own mélange of scars, splits, gouges, and worm-eaten holes, and each is attached to the platform with a simple pair of metal brackets. Several have charred areas, and one has a section of threaded rod protruding through the bottom, with a rusty washer and nut still attached.

Figure 1. Anatsui, El. *Akua's Surviving Children*. 1996, Collection of the artist and October Gallery, London. Photo: Andy Keate. Courtesy the artist and Jack Shainman Gallery, New York. © El Anatsui. (El Anatsui)

Topic sentence: First of three paragraphs in an emphatic sequence

Each figure also has a "head" attached at the top; these heads   2
are smaller chunks of worn and battered wood. In fact, some are made up of several small chunks of wood wired together. One appears to have been attached to the body with wire wrappings, but most have a gigantic spike driven through the head, with a small space between head and body where the spike forms a neck of sorts. Nearly every one of the heads is charred, which gives it a much darker appearance than the body beneath. It is not possible to say with assuredness which way these figures are facing, but they appear to all be facing in one direction (to the viewer's left), with the exception

Personification	of one figure near the front of the platform and on the right-hand side, which seems to be looking back—perhaps toward its homeland.
Topic sentence: Second of three paragraphs in an emphatic sequence	El Anatsui's statement regarding his creation shares not only that each of the "bodies" is composed of a piece of driftwood, but also that the piece was created while he was in Denmark. He adds that this piece is "representative of individual Africans who crossed tumultuous oceans" during the days of the Danish slave trade. Regarding his work, El Anatsui states, "Rather than recounting history, my art is telling about what history has provoked" (qtd. in Exhibition Notes).
Topic sentence: Third of three paragraphs in an emphatic sequence	El Anatsui and his crew used a wide variety of materials and processes as they created the multiple pieces included in the exhibit. His most famous works are the moveable blankets or sheets, made up of thousands of pieces of plastic from bottle necks and lids. The tiny pieces are stitched together with copper wire, creating massive blankets, with many colors and textures. These have been shaped and draped on walls and on the exteriors of buildings, and also hung from cables. Each of his pieces is evocative of the transformation of materials, and perhaps of the transformation of peoples as well.
Conclusion	*Akua's Surviving Children* captures the onlooker's attention partly because of the poignancy of seeing such battered pieces of wood used to create works of art, and partly because of the title, which brings to mind images of survivors—those who have survived violence, cancer, AIDS, and other diseases—along with images of those who do not survive. These figures, battered and scarred though they are, stand
Personification	straight, with heads upright, and they seem to wear the mantle of survivorship with great dignity. These are not figures that go quietly into a
Echo of idea in introduction	dusty, ignoble history, but rather they seem to still be speaking to future generations of their toils, their travels, and their strength in bearing the unbearable. The story they tell is deeply moving.

3

4

5

Work Cited

Exhibition Notes for El Anatsui's *When I Last Wrote to You About Africa*. 2012, Denver Art Museum.

Commentary

THE DOMINANT IMPRESSION   Leanna responded to the assignment by writing a moving tribute to a sculpture having special meaning for her—El Anatsui's *Akua's Surviving Children*. Like most descriptive pieces, Leanna's essay is organized around a dominant impression: the poignant story told by twenty-seven charred and scarred wooden figures who are "representative of individual Africans who crossed tumultuous oceans" during the days of the Danish slave trade. The essay's introduction provides a context for the dominant impression with two images of the work of art—one through the writer's words and another through a photo of the sculpture.

COMBINING PATTERNS OF DEVELOPMENT   In addition to vivid *description* throughout her essay, Leanna uses *process analysis* when explaining how El Anatsui creates his sculptures. In the second paragraph she says that some of the "heads" "are made up of several small chunks of wood wired together." She goes on explain: "One appears to have been attached to the body with wire wrappings, but most have a gigantic spike driven through the head, with a small space between head and body where the spike forms a neck of sorts." And in the fourth paragraph she explains that El Anatsui's "most famous works are the moveable blankets or sheets." She tells how the works are made from bottle necks and lids: "The tiny pieces are stitched together with copper wire, creating massive blankets, with many colors and textures."

The essay also contains a strong element of *narration* in that Leanna shares the story the wooden figures tell. In paragraph 1 she states, "What is clear is that each piece has had a difficult life. Each of the twenty-seven bodies has its own mélange of scars, splits, gouges, and worm-eaten holes," and in paragraph 2 she tells us that all of the figures except one are facing in the same direction and that the one who is looking in the opposite direction "seems to be looking back—perhaps toward its homeland." Then in the following paragraph she adds to the story she is weaving into her description when she quotes El Anatsui as saying that *Akua's Surviving Children* is "'representative of individual Africans who crossed tumultuous oceans' during the days of the Danish slave trade" and that "rather than recounting history, [his] art is telling about what history has provoked." Leanna completes her story in the final sentences of the closing paragraph: "These are not figures that go quietly into a dusty, ignoble history, but rather they seem to still be speaking to future generations of their toils, their travels, and their strength in bearing the unbearable. The story they tell is deeply moving."

SENSORY LANGUAGE   Leanna's essay is rich with concrete, sensory-packed sentences and connotative language such as "mélange of scars, splits, gouges, and worm-eaten holes" and "attached … with a simple pair of metal brackets" (paragraph 1) and "Most have a gigantic spike driven through the head, with a small space between head and body where the spike forms a neck of sorts" (paragraph 2).

FIGURATIVE LANGUAGE, VIGOROUS VERBS, AND VARIED SENTENCE STRUCTURE   You might have noted that *figurative language, vigorous verbs,* and *varied sentence patterns* contribute to the essay's descriptive power. Leanna uses personification throughout the essay as she attributes human characteristics to wooden figures; she refers to the "difficult life" of each figure in paragraph 1, the heads of the figures and the lone figure as looking back toward its homeland in paragraph 2, and the figures' "deeply moving story" in paragraph 5. Moreover, throughout the essay she uses lively verbs ("wired," "driven," "stitched," "shaped and draped") to capture the artist's work. She even ascribes "dignity" to the figures: "These figures, battered and scarred though they are, stand straight, with heads upright, and they seem to wear the mantle of survivorship with great dignity" (paragraph 5).

Similarly, Leanna enhances descriptive passages by varying the length of her sentences. Long, fairly elaborate sentences are interspersed with shorter, dramatic statements. In the opening paragraph, for example, a long sentence ("Each figure has a 'body' that is described by the artist as a piece of driftwood; however, they appear to have been shaped by man at one time—perhaps they are the broken remnants of piers, or docks, or maybe shards left from a shoreline house or a boat") is followed by a brief statement: "What is clear is that each piece has had a difficult life." And in the concluding paragraph, the long sentence "These are not figures that go quietly into a dusty, ignoble history, but rather they seem to still be speaking to future generations of their toils, their travels, and their strength in bearing the unbearable" is followed by the simple and poignant closing statement "The story they tell is deeply moving."

ORGANIZATION   Leanna uses an easy-to-follow combination of *spatial* and *emphatic* patterns in her essay. Although the essay begins with a spatial pattern, it relies primarily on emphatic arrangement because the three body paragraphs focus on the different elements of the sculpture that combine to create the story it tells. Leanna begins by using spatial order as she describes what it is like to walk through the doorway of the room that houses the exhibit by El Anatsui and to have one's attention immediately drawn to the piece that is the focus of her essay: *Akua's Surviving Children.* However, from that point on, she uses emphatic order as she tells the story of people who were taken from their homeland and sold into slavery. In the first body paragraph she focuses on describing the heads of the wooden figures and their human characteristics; in the second body paragraph she incorporates quotes from El Anatsui, the creator of the piece, sharing his statement that the "piece is representative of individual Africans who crossed tumultuous oceans"; and in the final supporting paragraph she describes how the artist creates pieces that are "evocative of the transformation of materials, and perhaps of the transformation of peoples as well." Using an emphatic pattern allows her to effectively tell the story of people who were treated horribly yet managed to survive.

Note, however, that while Leanna's final supporting paragraph contains interesting information, it does not directly support the dominant impression on which her essay focuses: the story told by the sculpture, *Akua's Surviving Children.* Instead, the fourth paragraph of her essay describes another part of the El Anatsui exhibit—"the moveable blankets or sheets." If Leanna were to further revise her essay, she might consider removing this material or including it in her introduction before she narrows her focus to the sculpture.

CONCLUSION   The concluding paragraph brings the essay to a powerful close. It begins by connecting with the first sentence of the essay and the reference to "the first piece that catches the visitor's eye" but goes beyond that image to reflect on why the image is so captivating, noting not only "the poignancy of seeing such battered pieces of wood used to create works of art" but also the significance "of the title, which brings to mind images of survivors—those who have survived violence, cancer, AIDS, and other diseases—along with images of those who do not survive." She goes on to describe images that "wear the mantle of survivorship with great dignity" and refuse to "go quietly into a dusty, ignoble history, but rather … seem to still be speaking to future generations of their toils, their travels, and their strength in bearing the unbearable."

REVISING THE FIRST DRAFT   When Leanna met with a small group of her classmates during a peer review session, the students agreed that Leanna's first draft was strong and moving. However, one group member pointed out that as he read her concluding paragraph, he thought that perhaps her essay would be more effective if written from third-person point of view. He went on to explain that he thought the move to third-person might be appropriate because the essay wasn't really about Leanna and her trip to the museum, but rather about the sculpture. Consequently, it was less about her personal experience at the museum than it was a critical commentary. Following is the first-draft version of Leanna's concluding paragraph.

> **Original Version of the Conclusion**
>
> *Akua's Surviving Children* captured my attention partly because of the poignancy of seeing such battered pieces of wood used to create works of art, and partly because of the title. I was immediately struck by the idea of survivors, and thought of the survivors of violence, survivors of cancer and other diseases, and the many who do not survive. The many images that coursed through my mind on reading the title compelled me to spend some time appreciating this piece. These figures, battered and scarred though they are, stand straight, with heads upright, and they seem to wear the mantle of survivorship with great dignity. These are not figures that go quietly into a dusty, ignoble history, but rather they seem to still be speaking to future generations of their toils, their travels, and their strength in bearing the unbearable. Speaking only for myself, I was deeply moved by their story.

When Leanna looked more carefully at the paragraph, she agreed that her use of first-person point of view detracted from the essay's main focus: the piece of art itself. As she revised the concluding paragraph and switched from first person to third person, she combined the ideas in the first three sentences of the first draft and wrote one tighter, more effective sentence: "*Akua's Surviving Children* captures the onlooker's attention partly because of the poignancy of seeing such battered pieces of wood used to create works of art, and partly because of the title, which brings to mind images of survivors—those who have survived violence, cancer, AIDS, and other diseases— along with images of those who do not survive." As she continued her move from first person to third person in that paragraph, she also revised her closing sentence, making it more emphatic and pointed: "The story they tell is deeply moving."

As she continued revising her essay, Leanna switched from first-person to third-person point of view throughout and intensified the sensory images in her opening paragraph. She changed "perhaps they are broken pieces of piers or docks" to "perhaps they are the broken remnants of piers, or docks, or maybe shards left from a shoreline house or a boat." And in the fourth paragraph "The small pieces are joined with wire, making huge, colorful blankets" became "The tiny pieces are stitched together with copper wire, creating massive blankets, with many colors and textures."

These are just some of the changes Leanna made while rewriting her essay. Her skillful revisions provided the polish needed to make an already strong essay even more evocative.

Activities: Description

Prewriting Activities

1. Imagine you're writing two essays: One explains how students get "burned out"; the other contends that being a spendthrift is better (or worse) than being frugal. Jot down ways you might use description in each essay.

2. Go to a place on campus where students congregate. In preparation for an *objective* description of this place, make notes of various sights, sounds, smells, and textures as well as the overall "feel" of the place. Then, in preparation for a *subjective* description, observe and take notes on another sheet of paper. Compare the two sets of material. What differences do you see in word choice and selection of details?

3. Prepare to interview an interesting person by outlining several questions ahead of time. When you visit that person's home or workplace, bring a notebook in which to record his or her responses. During the interview, observe the person's surroundings, voice, body language, dress, and so on. As soon as the interview is over, make notes on these matters. Then review your notes and identify your dominant impression of the person. With that impression in mind, which details would you omit if you were writing an essay? Which would you elaborate? Which organizational pattern (spatial, emphatic, chronological, least-to-most complex, or sensory) would you select to organize your description? Why?

Revising Activities

4. The following sentences contain clichés. Rewrite each sentence, supplying a fresh and imaginative figure of speech. Add whatever descriptive details are needed to provide a context for the figure of speech.

   a. They were as quiet as mice.

   b. My brother used to get green with envy if I had a date and he didn't.

   c. The little girl is proud as a peacock of her Girl Scout uniform.

5. The following descriptive paragraph is from the first draft of an essay showing that personal growth may result when romanticized notions and reality collide. How effective is the paragraph in illustrating the essay's thesis? Which details are powerful? Which could be more concrete? Which should be deleted? Where should sentence structure be more varied? How could the description be made more coherent? Revise the paragraph, correcting any problems you discover and adding whatever sensory details are needed to enliven the description. Feel free to break the paragraph into two or more separate paragraphs.

   As a child, I was intrigued by stories about the farm in Harrison County, Maine, where my father spent his teens. Being raised on a farm seemed more interesting than growing up in the suburbs. So about a year ago, I decided to see for myself what the farm was like. I got there by driving on Route 334, a surprisingly easy-to-drive, four-lane highway that had recently been built with matching state and federal funds. I turned into the dirt road leading to the farm and got out of my car. It had been washed and waxed for the occasion. Then I headed for a dirt-colored barn. Its roof was full of huge, rotted holes. As I rounded the bushes, I saw the house. It too was dirt-colored. Its paint must have worn off decades ago. A couple of dead-looking old cars were sprawled in front of the barn. They were dented and windowless. Also by the barn was an ancient refrigerator, crushed like a discarded accordion. The porch steps to the house were slanted and wobbly. Through the open windows came a stale smell and the sound of television. Looking in the front door screen, I could see two chickens jumping around inside. Everything looked dirty both inside and out. Secretly grateful that no one answered my knock, I bolted down the stairs, got into my clean, shiny car, and drove away.

Professional Selections: Description

MARIO SUÁREZ

Mario Suárez (1923–1998), author of *Chicano Sketches* (2004), a collection of short stories, is considered by many to be the first contemporary Chicano writer. Suárez was one of five children born to Mexican immigrants who moved to Arizona. After serving in the U.S. Navy during World War II, he attended the University of Arizona, and while still an undergraduate, he wrote for the *Arizona Quarterly.* A journalist and college teacher, Suárez wrote primarily about the lives of immigrants and life in El Hoyo, the barrio where he grew up.

To understand how this description essay is organized, see Figure 10.2.

Pre-Reading Journal Entry

Think of a place that is important to you from your childhood or adolescence—perhaps the place (or one of the places) where you grew up. Why was the place important to you? How would you describe it to someone who had never been there?

El Hoyo

From the center of downtown Tucson, the ground slopes gently away to Main Street, drops a few feet, and then rolls to the banks of the Santa Cruz River. Here lies the section of the city known as El Hoyo. Why it is called El Hoyo is not very clear. In no sense is it a hole as its name would imply; it is simply the river's immediate valley. Its inhabitants are chicanos who raise hell on Saturday night and listen to Padre Estanislao on Sunday morning. While the term *chicano* is the short way of saying Mexicano, it is not restricted to the paisanos who came from old Mexico with the territory or the last famine to work for the railroad, labor, sing, and go on relief. Chicano is the easy way of referring to everybody. Pablo Gut'errez married the Chinese grocer's daughter and now runs a meat department; his sons are chicanos. So are the sons of Killer Jones who threw a fight in Harlem and fled to El Hoyo to marry Cristina Mendez. And so are all of them. However, it is doubtful that all these spiritual sons of Mexico live in El Hoyo because they love each other—many fight and bicker constantly. It is doubtful they live in El Hoyo because of its scenic beauty—it is everything but beautiful. Its houses are simple affairs of unplastered adobe, wood, and abandoned car parts. Its narrow streets are mostly clearings which have, in time, acquired names. Except for some tall trees which nobody has ever cared to identify, nurse, or destroy, the main things known to grow in the general area are weeds, garbage piles, dark-eyed chavalos, and dogs. And it is doubtful that the chicanos live in El Hoyo because it is safe—many times the Santa Cruz has risen and inundated the area.

1

In other respects, living in El Hoyo has its advantages. If one is born with a   2
weakness for acquiring bills, El Hoyo is where the collectors are less likely to find
you. If one has acquired the habit of listening to Octavio Perea's Mexican Hour in the
wee hours of the morning with the radio on at full blast, El Hoyo is where you are
less likely to be reported to the authorities. Besides, Perea is very popular and sooner
or later to everyone "Smoke in the Eyes" is dedicated between the pinto beans and
white flour commercials. If one, for any reason whatever, comes on an extended period of hard times, where, if not in El Hoyo, are the neighbors more willing to offer
solace? When Teofila Malacara's house burned to the ground with all her belongings
and two children, a benevolent gentleman carried through the gesture that made
tolerable her burden. He made a list of five hundred names and solicited from each
a dollar. At the end of a month, he turned over to the tearful but grateful señora one
hundred dollars in cold cash and then accompanied her on a short vacation. When
the new manager of a local store decided that no more chicanas were to work behind
the counters, it was the chicanos of El Hoyo who, on taking their individually small
but collectively great buying power elsewhere, drove the manager out and the girls
returned to their jobs. When the Mexican Army was en route to Baja, California, and
the chicanos found out that the enlisted men ate only at infrequent intervals, it was
El Hoyo's chicanos who crusaded across town with pots of beans and trays of tortil-
las to meet the train. When someone gets married, celebrating is not restricted to the
immediate friends of the couple. Everybody is invited. Anything calls for a celebration, and a celebration calls for anything. On Memorial Day there are no less than
half a dozen good fights at the Riverside Dance Hall. On Mexican Independence
Day, more than one flag is sworn allegiance to amid cheers for the queen.

And El Hoyo is something more. It is this something more which brought Fe-   3
lipe Sanchez back from the wars after having killed a score of Vietnamese with his
body resembling a patchwork quilt to marry Julia Armijo. It brought Joe Zepeda,
a gunner,…back to compose boleros. He has a metal plate for a skull. Perhaps
El Hoyo is proof that those people exist, and perhaps exist best, who have as yet
failed to observe the more popular modes of human conduct. Perhaps the humble
appearance of El Hoyo justifies the indifferent shrug of those made aware of its
existence. Perhaps El Hoyo's simplicity motivates an occasional chicano to move
away from its narrow streets, babbling comadres, and shrieking children to deny
the bloodwell from which he springs and to claim the blood of a conquistador
while his hair is straight and his face beardless. Yet El Hoyo is not an outpost of a
few families against the world. It fights for no causes except those which soothe its
immediate angers. It laughs and cries with the same amount of passion in times of
plenty and of want.

Perhaps El Hoyo, its inhabitants, and its essence can best be explained by tell-   4
ing a bit about a dish called capirotada. Its origin is uncertain. But, according to the
time and the circumstance, it is made of old, new, or hard bread. It is softened with
water and then cooked with peanuts, raisins, onions, cheese, and panocha. It is fired
with sherry wine. Then it is served hot, cold, or just "on the weather" as they say in
El Hoyo. The Sermeños like it one way, the Garcias another, and the Ortegas still another. While it might differ greatly from one home to another; nevertheless, it is still

capirotada. And so it is with El Hoyo's chicanos. While being divided from within and from without, like the capirotada, they remain chicanos.

Figure 10.2 Essay Structure Diagram: "El Hoyo" by Mario Suárez

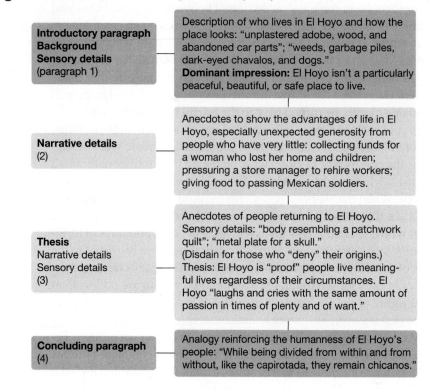

Questions for Critical Reading

1. What is the selection's thesis (or dominant impression)? Locate the sentence(s) in which Suárez states his main idea. If he doesn't state the thesis explicitly, express it in your own words.

2. According to the author, what do the words *el hoyo* and *chicano* mean?

3. Why do people choose to live in El Hoyo?

4. Suárez tries to create an essay that describes for his readers the place where he grew up and why it is important in his life. Do you think his essay succeeds in communicating his ideas? Why or why not?

Questions About the Writer's Craft

1. **Introduction.** Focus on the first paragraph of "El Hoyo." Carefully reread the paragraph and make notes regarding its organization. What does Suárez accomplish in his

opening paragraph? What negative aspects of El Hoyo does he include, and why do you think he includes these in the opening paragraph? What might be his purpose?

2. **Tone.** How would you characterize the author's tone? Is it serious? Humorous? Down to earth? Give some examples to support your answer. Why do you think the author adopts the tone that he uses?

3. **Other patterns.** Although the primary focus of "El Hoyo" is on describing the barrio where Suárez grew up, the essay also *compares* and *contrasts* both positive and negative aspects of life in this Tucson neighborhood. First, list three negative aspects of the community, and then list three of the positive aspects. How does the inclusion of both positive and negative characteristics of El Hoyo strengthen the essay's overall impact?

4. **Conclusion.** In the closing paragraph of the essay, Suárez creates an analogy between El Hoyo and *capirotada*, a Mexican dish made of leftovers. In what ways might *capirotada* represent life in the barrio? Make a list of three similarities you can draw between the neighborhood and the dish.

Writing Assignments Using Description as a Pattern of Development

1. Suárez describes the barrio where he grew up: where it is located, the people who live there, the positive and negative aspects of the neighborhood, and how it is different from other places. He closes his essay with an analogy that captures the essence of El Hoyo. Write an essay in which you describe the neighborhood (or one of the neighborhoods) where you grew up. Do your best to present a multifaceted view of your neighborhood for your reader. Consider including images of the neighborhood or its residents that enhance your essay and strengthen its visual impact. Be sure to integrate your images into your written text by referencing them in your essay.

2. In his essay Suárez mentions specific individuals from the community who stood out for him—among them Pablo Gut'errez, Killer Jones, Felipe Sanchez, Julia Amijo, and Joe Zepeda. Write a descriptive essay about particular people from your neighborhood, your elementary school, a team you were a part of, or another group that played a role in your life. Go beyond describing these individuals and reflect on why they stand out in your mind. Why did they create a lasting impression on you? Consider integrating images that enhance your essay and strengthen its visual impact. Be sure to integrate your images into your written text by referencing them in your essay.

Writing Assignment Combining Patterns of Development

3. Although El Hoyo is the barrio where Suárez grew up—a neighborhood he cherishes—it is clearly not the upscale, upper-class part of town. Write an essay in which you *compare* and *contrast* two neighborhoods—or two cities or countries—you are familiar with. Describe both areas, but also compare the ways they are alike and the

ways they differ. Bring in outside sources as needed to strengthen your essay, and consider using images such as a pie chart showing income or education levels, or perhaps a map of the areas discussed in your essay.

CHEROKEE PAUL MCDONALD

Cherokee Paul McDonald is a fiction writer and journalist, a military veteran, and a former ten-year member of the Fort Lauderdale (Florida) Police Force. His publications include *Blue Truth* (1992), a graphic memoir of his day-to-day life as a police officer, and *Into the Green* (2001), in which he draws on his experiences as an Army lieutenant. He is also a fisherman and the father of three children. "A View from the Bridge" was first published February 12, 1989, in the *Florida Sun Sentinel.*

Pre-Reading Journal Entry

Think of a time when you did something to help someone—perhaps a friend, a family member, a classmate, or a stranger—and later realized that your actions had benefitted you just as much as, or perhaps even more than, they had helped the other person.

A View from the Bridge

I was coming up on the little bridge in the Rio Vista neighborhood of Fort Lauderdale, deepening my stride and my breathing to negotiate the slight incline without altering my pace. And then, as I neared the crest, I saw the kid.   1

He was a lumpy little guy with baggy shorts, a faded T-shirt, and heavy sweat socks falling down over old sneakers.   2

Partially covering his shaggy blond hair was one of those blue baseball caps with gold braid on the bill and a sailfish patch sewn onto the peak. Covering his eyes and part of his face was a pair of those stupid-looking '50s-style wrap-around sunglasses.   3

He was fumbling with a beat-up rod and reel, and he had a little bait bucket by his feet. I puffed on by, glancing down into the empty bucket as I passed.   4

"Hey, mister! Would you help me, please?"   5

The shrill voice penetrated my jogger's concentration, and I was determined to ignore it. But for some reason, I stopped.   6

With my hands on my hips and the sweat dripping from my nose I asked, "What do you want, kid?"   7

"Would you please help me find my shrimp? It's my last one and I've been getting bites and I know I can catch a fish if I can just find that shrimp. He jumped outta my hand as I was getting him from the bucket."   8

Exasperated, I walked slowly back to the kid, and pointed.   9

"There's the damn shrimp by your left foot. You stopped me for *that?*"   10

As I said it, the kid reached down and trapped the shrimp.   11

"Thanks a lot, mister," he said.   12

I watched as the kid dropped the baited hook down into the canal. Then I turned to start back down the bridge.   13

That's when the kid let out a "Hey! Hey!" and the prettiest tarpon I'd ever 14
seen came almost six feet out of the water, twisting and turning as he fell through
the air.

"I got one!" the kid yelled as the fish hit the water with a loud splash and took off 15
down the canal.

I watched the line being burned off the reel at an alarming rate. The kid's left hand 16
held the crank while the extended fingers felt for the drag setting.

"No, kid!" I shouted. "Leave the drag alone…just keep that damn rod tip up!" 17

Then I glanced at the reel and saw there were just a few loops of line left on the 18
spool.

"Why don't you get yourself some decent equipment?" I said, but before the kid 19
could answer I saw the line go slack.

"Ohhh, I lost him," the kid said. I saw the flash of silver as the fish turned. 20

"Crank, kid, crank! You didn't lose him. He's coming back toward you. Bring in 21
the slack!"

The kid cranked like mad, and a beautiful grin spread across his face. 22

"He's heading in for the pilings," I said. "Keep him out of those pilings!" 23

The kid played it perfectly. When the fish made its play for the pilings, he kept 24
just enough pressure on to force the fish out. When the water exploded and the silver
missile hurled into the air, the kid kept the rod tip up and the line tight.

As the fish came to the surface and began a slow circle in the middle of the canal, 25
I said, "Whooee, is that a nice fish or what?"

The kid didn't say anything, so I said, "Okay, move to the edge of the bridge and 26
I'll climb down to the seawall and pull him out."

When I reached the seawall I pulled in the leader, leaving the fish lying on its side 27
in the water.

"How's that?" I said. 28

"Hey, mister, tell me what it looks like." 29

"Look down here and check him out," I said, "He's beautiful." 30

But then I looked up into those stupid-looking sunglasses and it hit me. The kid 31
was blind.

"Could you tell me what he looks like, mister?" he said again. 32

"Well, he's just under three, uh, he's about as long as one of your arms," I said. 33
"I'd guess he goes about 15, 20 pounds. He's mostly silver, but the silver is somehow
made up of *all* the colors, if you know what I mean." I stopped. "Do you know what
I mean by colors?"

The kid nodded. 34

"Okay. He has all these big scales, like armor all over his body. They're silver too, and 35
when he moves they sparkle. He has a strong body and a large powerful tail. He has big
round eyes, bigger than a quarter, and a lower jaw that sticks out past the upper one and
is very tough. His belly is almost white and his back is a gunmetal gray. When he jumped
he came out of the water about six feet, and his scales caught the sun and flashed it all
over the place."

By now the fish had righted itself, and I could see the bright-red gills as the gill 36
plates opened and closed. I explained this to the kid, and then said, more to myself,
"He's a beauty."

"Can you get him off the hook?" the kid asked. "I don't want to kill him." 37

I watched as the tarpon began to slowly swim away, tired but still alive. 38

By the time I got back up to the top of the bridge the kid had his line secured and 39
his bait bucket in one hand.

He grinned and said, "Just in time. My mom drops me off here, and she'll be back 40
to pick me up any minute."

He used the back of one hand to wipe his nose. 41

"Thanks for helping me catch that tarpon," he said, "and for helping me to see it." 42

I looked at him, shook my head, and said, "No, my friend, thank you for letting 43
me see that fish."

I took off, but before I got far the kid yelled again. 44

"Hey, mister!" 45

I stopped. 46

"Someday I'm gonna catch a sailfish and a blue marlin and a giant tuna and all 47
those big sportfish!"

As I looked into those sunglasses I knew he probably would. I wished I could be 48
there when it happened.

Questions for Critical Reading

1. What is the selection's thesis (or dominant impression)? Locate the sentence(s) in which McDonald states his main idea. If he doesn't state the thesis explicitly, express it in your own words.

2. Why is McDonald initially determined to ignore the boy's request for help? Why does he hesitate to stop for the boy?

3. What details are provided to let the reader know that the boy is blind, and at what point does McDonald finally come to this realization?

4. Why do you think McDonald titled this essay "A View from the Bridge," and how does the view change—both literally and figuratively— as the essay progresses?

Questions About the Writer's Craft

1. **The pattern.** Choose a passage that you consider to be especially rich in detail and description, and make a list of the descriptors McDonald uses in the passage to draw a picture of the image in words. Then, using those descriptors, take a few minutes to sketch out the image as you see it in your mind.

2. **Organization.** How does McDonald organize his essay? What transitional words and phrases does he use to keep the reader oriented as his essay progresses?

3. **Other patterns.** Because McDonald's descriptive essay has a strong *narrative* component, the selection includes extensive dialogue. How does the use of dialogue enrich the essay? In what ways might the essay be less effective if the reader could not "hear" what McDonald and the boy said to each other?

4. **Sensory details.** Most of the description in this essay focuses on visual details, but McDonald also describes some other sensations. Find the passages in which McDonald presents other details that help the reader have a clearer understanding of the changing dynamic between the two characters as the essay moves along.

Writing Assignments Using Description as a Pattern of Development

1. In his essay, McDonald uses description to allow his readers to "see" the jogger-narrator (McDonald), the boy, the fish they caught, the view from the bridge, and more. Think of a scene that you came upon suddenly—a vista you encountered hiking, a street musician playing for spare change, a solitary animal at the zoo. Use vivid language to describe the scene and its impact on you.

2. While stories of incidents in our lives provide rich contexts for description, so do a host of other subjects. Write an essay in which you describe a place that is meaningful to you—perhaps the house where you grew up, the home of a friend or relative, the elementary school you attended, or a place where you and your friends spend time together. Be sure to convey a dominant impression: Did or do you feel safe in this place? comfortable? on edge? invisible? Select descriptive terms that appropriately convey your feelings.

Writing Assignment Combining Patterns of Development

3. McDonald's essay describes the process of catching a fish. Write an essay in which you guide the reader through a familiar *process*–for example, baking cookies, planting flowers, or uploading a video to a social media site such as *YouTube*. *Describe* how each stage of the process would look, sound, smell, feel, or taste. You might want to research images online to *illustrate* your essay. If you decide to include images, write a descriptive caption for each image.

RIVERBEND

The author known by the *pseudonym*, or fictitious name, Riverbend is an Iraqi woman in her twenties. In 2003, she began writing a blog, Baghdad Burning, in which she described her personal experiences of the U.S. invasion and occupation of Iraq. The blog entries have been collected in two books—*Baghdad Burning: Girl Blog from Iraq* (2005) and *Baghdad Burning II: More Girl Blog from Iraq* (2006)—published by The Feminist Press. "Bloggers Without Borders..." is Riverbend's last blog entry, posted on October 22, 2007.

Pre-Reading Journal Entry

Can you remember a time you endured a frustrating situation? Maybe you were appealing a ticket in traffic court or waiting to board an airplane. In your journal, jot down what you recall about the scene. What was the setting like? Who else was present? Why was the situation frustrating? How else did you feel in the situation?

Bloggers Without Borders...

Syria is a beautiful country—at least I think it is. I say "I think" because while   1
I perceive it to be beautiful, I sometimes wonder if I mistake safety, security, and normalcy for "beauty." In so many ways, Damascus is like Baghdad before the war—bustling streets, occasional traffic jams, markets seemingly always full of shoppers[.] ... And in so many ways it's different. The buildings are higher, the streets are generally narrower, and there's a mountain, Qasiyoun, that looms in the distance.

The mountain distracts me, as it does many Iraqis—especially those from Bagh-   2
dad. Northern Iraq is full of mountains, but the rest of Iraq is quite flat. At night, Qasiyoun blends into the black sky and the only indication of its presence is a multitude of little, glimmering spots of light—houses and restaurants built right up there on the mountain. Every time I take a picture, I try to work Qasiyoun into it—I try to position the person so that Qasiyoun is in the background.

The first weeks here were something of a cultural shock. It has taken me   3
these last three months to work away certain habits I'd acquired in Iraq after the war. It's funny how you learn to act a certain way and don't even know you're doing strange things—like avoiding people's eyes in the street or crazily murmuring prayers to yourself when stuck in traffic. It took me at least three weeks to teach myself to walk properly again—with head lifted, not constantly looking behind me.

It is estimated that there are at least 1.5 million Iraqis in Syria today. I believe it.   4
Walking down the streets of Damascus, you can hear the Iraqi accent everywhere. There are areas like Geramana and Qudsiya that are packed full of Iraqi refugees. Syrians are few and far between in these areas. Even the public schools in the areas are full of Iraqi children. A cousin of mine is now attending a school in Qudsiya and his class is composed of 26 Iraqi children, and 5 Syrian children. It's beyond belief sometimes. Most of the families have nothing to live on beyond their savings, which are quickly being depleted with rent and the costs of living.

Within a month of our being here, we began hearing talk about Syria requiring   5
visas from Iraqis, like most other countries. Apparently, our esteemed puppets in power met with Syrian and Jordanian authorities and decided they wanted to take away the last two safe havens remaining for Iraqis—Damascus and Amman. The talk began in late August and was only talk until recently—early October. Iraqis entering Syria now need a visa from the Syrian consulate or embassy in the country they are currently in. In the case of Iraqis still in Iraq, it is said that an approval

from the Ministry of Interior is also required (which kind of makes it difficult for people running away from militias OF the Ministry of Interior …). Today, there's talk of a possible fifty-dollar visa at the border.

Iraqis who entered Syria before the visa was implemented were getting a one-month visitation visa at the border. As soon as that month was over, you could take your passport and visit the local immigration bureau. If you were lucky, they would give you an additional month or two. When talk about visas from the Syrian embassy began, they stopped giving an extension on the initial border visa. We, as a family, had a brilliant idea. Before the commotion of visas began, and before we started needing a renewal, we decided to go to one of the border crossings, cross into Iraq, and come back into Syria—everyone was doing it. It would buy us some time—at least 2 months.   6

We chose a hot day in early September and drove the six hours to Kameshli, a border town in northern Syria. My aunt and her son came with us—they also needed an extension on their visa. There is a border crossing in Kameshli called Yaarubiya. It's one of the simpler crossings because the Iraqi and Syrian borders are only a matter of several meters. You walk out of Syrian territory and then walk into Iraqi territory—simple and safe.   7

When we got to the Yaarubiya border patrol, it hit us that thousands of Iraqis had had our brilliant idea simultaneously—the lines to the border patrol office were endless. Hundreds of Iraqis stood in a long line waiting to have their passports stamped with an exit visa. We joined the line of people and waited. And waited. And waited…   8

It took four hours to leave the Syrian border after which came the lines of the Iraqi border post. Those were even longer. We joined one of the lines of weary, impatient Iraqis. "It's looking like a gasoline line[.] …" my younger cousin joked. That was the beginning of another four hours of waiting under the sun, taking baby steps, moving forward ever so slowly. The line kept getting longer. At one point, we could see neither the beginning of the line, where passports were being stamped to enter Iraq, nor the end. Running up and down the line were little boys selling glasses of water, chewing gum, and cigarettes. My aunt caught one of them by the arm as he zipped past us, "How many people are in front of us?" He whistled and took a few steps back to assess the situation, "A hundred! A thousand!" He was almost gleeful as he ran off to make business.   9

I had such mixed feelings standing in that line. I was caught between a feeling of yearning, a certain homesickness that sometimes catches me at the oddest moments, and a heavy feeling of dread. What if they didn't agree to let us out again? It wasn't really possible, but what if it happened? What if this was the last time I'd see the Iraqi border? What if we were no longer allowed to enter Iraq for some reason? What if we were never allowed to leave?   10

We spent the four hours standing, crouching, sitting and leaning in the line. The sun beat down on everyone equally—Sunnis, Shia, and Kurds alike. E. tried to convince the aunt to faint so it would speed the process up for the family, but she just gave us a withering look and stood straighter. People just stood there, chatting,   11 cursing or silent. It was yet another gathering of Iraqis—the perfect opportunity to swap sad stories and ask about distant relations or acquaintances.

We met two families we knew while waiting for our turn. We greeted each 12 other like long lost friends and exchanged phone numbers and addresses in Damascus, promising to visit. I noticed the 23-year-old son, K., from one of the families was missing. I beat down my curiosity and refused to ask where he was. The mother was looking older than I remembered and the father looked constantly lost in thought, or maybe it was grief. I didn't want to know if K. was dead or alive. I'd just have to believe he was alive and thriving somewhere, not worrying about borders or visas. Ignorance really is bliss sometimes...

Back at the Syrian border, we waited in a large group, tired and hungry, 13 having handed over our passports for a stamp. The Syrian immigration man sifting through dozens of passports called out names and looked at faces as he handed over the passports patiently, "Stand back please—stand back." There was a general cry towards the back of the crowded hall where we were standing as someone collapsed—as they lifted him I recognized an old man who was there with his family being chaperoned by his sons, leaning on a walking stick.

By the time we had reentered the Syrian border and were headed back to the 14 cab ready to take us into Kameshli, I had resigned myself to the fact that we were refugees. I read about refugees on the Internet daily...in the newspapers...hear about them on TV. I hear about the estimated 1.5 million plus Iraqi refugees in Syria and shake my head, never really considering myself or my family as one of them. After all, refugees are people who sleep in tents and have no potable water or plumbing, right? Refugees carry their belongings in bags instead of suitcases and they don't have cell phones or Internet access, right? Grasping my passport in my hand like my life depended on it, with two extra months in Syria stamped inside, it hit me how wrong I was. We were all refugees. I was suddenly a number. No matter how wealthy or educated or comfortable, a refugee is a refugee. A refugee is someone who isn't really welcome in any country—including their own... especially their own.

We live in an apartment building where two other Iraqis are renting. The people 15 in the floor above us are a Christian family from northern Iraq who got chased out of their village by Peshmerga and the family on our floor is a Kurdish family who lost their home in Baghdad to militias and were waiting for immigration to Sweden or Switzerland or some such European refugee haven.

The first evening we arrived, exhausted, dragging suitcases behind us, morale a 16 little bit bruised, the Kurdish family sent over their representative—a 9-year-old boy missing two front teeth, holding a lopsided cake, "We're Abu Mohammed's house— across from you—mama says if you need anything, just ask—this is our number. Abu Dalia's family live upstairs, this is their number. We're all Iraqi too... Welcome to the building."

I cried that night because for the first time in a long time, so far away from home, 17 I felt the unity that had been stolen from us in 2003.

Questions for Critical Reading

1. What is the selection's thesis (or dominant impression)? Locate the sentence(s) in which Riverbend states her main idea. If she doesn't state the thesis explicitly, express it in your own words.

2. At the start of the reading, the author compares Damascus, the capital of Syria, with her native Baghdad. How do the cities seem the same? How do they seem different? Why do you think the author is "distracted" by the mountain Qasiyoun?

3. The author uses two numerical examples. What are they? What are the sources for these examples? How do the examples contribute to the dominant impression of the reading?

4. For much of the selection, the author describes the scene as she and her family cross the border into Iraq and then immediately cross back into Syria. Why have they decided to take these actions? What realization does the author have as a result?

Questions About the Writer's Craft

1. **The pattern.** How does the author use description in the selection? What phrases convey the physical discomfort of the border-crossing experience? Why does the author spend so much of the selection describing the experience?

2. **Tone.** At times, the selection expresses an ironic or humorously sardonic tone. Which specific sentences does the author use to achieve this tone? What is the effect of the selection's tone for the reader?

3. **Other patterns.** The author *compares* Damascus to Baghdad at the start of the reading and then *narrates* the story of the border crossing. In addition, the author gives at least four personal *anecdotes* from the border crossing and afterward. What are these anecdotes, and what do they illustrate for the reader?

4. **Title.** What is the significance of the selection's title, "Blogging Without Borders…"? Is the title effective?

Writing Assignments Using Description as a Pattern of Development

1. The author uses the phrase "Ignorance is bliss" to underscore that she would rather continue imagining a young family friend as "alive and thriving somewhere" than risk finding out for sure that he was dead or missing. Like the author, we may suddenly find ourselves reminded of the possibility of death. For example, we may hear about a friend's serious accident or illness. Write an essay in which you describe your thoughts and feelings in response to such a reminder. Did you feel sad, afraid, angry, vulnerable, or lucky? How were you affected by the experience?

2. Riverbend describes the "culture shock" she experiences in Damascus. Have you ever spent time in a place that is very different from your home? For example, if you live in the city, have you ever spent a summer on a farm? Or if you live in a warm region, have you spent a winter holiday in a cold climate? In an essay, describe your experience in that strange place. Use colorful details to tell readers about the environment, food, customs, and other aspects of the place and its inhabitants.

Writing Assignments Combining Patterns of Development

3. The author implies that Syria imposed new visa requirements in an attempt to control the number of Iraqi refugees. With Syria now in civil turmoil, the refugee problem across the Middle East has become acute. Do some research into conditions for Middle Eastern refugees and their host countries—primarily Jordan, Egypt, Turkey, and the United States. In an essay, argue for or against the policies of one host country, using your researched evidence to support your view.

Additional Writing Topics: Description

General Assignments

Using description, develop one of these topics into an essay.

1. A favorite item of clothing

2. A school as a young child might see it

3. A coffee shop, bus shelter, newsstand, or some other small place

4. A parade or victory celebration

5. One drawer in a desk or bureau

6. A TV, film, or music celebrity

7. The inside of something, such as a cave, boat, car, shed, or machine

8. A friend, roommate, or other person you know well

9. An essential or a useless gadget

10. A once-in-a-lifetime event

Assignments Using Multimedia

Use the suggested media to help develop a descriptive essay on one of these topics:

1. Your best friend and the role that person has played in your life (photos)

2. Effective Super Bowl advertisements (links to ads on *YouTube*)

3. The best (or worst) gift you have received (photo or weblink)

4. Your vision of an ideal house (sketches or photos)

5. A place you love to visit and why (photos and/or weblinks)

Assignments with a Specific Purpose, Audience, and Point of View

1. **Academic life.** Your college has decided to replace an old campus structure (for example, a dorm or dining hall) with a new version. Write a letter of protest to the administration, describing the place so vividly and appealingly that its value and need for preservation are unquestionable.

2. **Academic life.** As a staff member of the campus newspaper, you have been asked to write a weekly column of social news and gossip. For your first column, you plan to describe a recent campus event—a dance, party, concert, or other social activity. With a straightforward or tongue-in-cheek tone, describe where the event was held, the appearance of the people who attended, and so on.

3. **Civic activity.** As a subscriber to a community-wide dating service, you've been asked to submit a description of the kind of person you'd like to meet. Describe your ideal date. Focus on specifics about physical appearance, personal habits, character traits, and interests.

4. **Civic activity.** As a resident of a particular town, you're angered by the appearance of a certain spot and by the activities that take place there. Write a letter to the town council, describing in detail the undesirable nature of this place (an adult bookstore, a bar, a bus station, a neglected park or beach). End with some suggestions about ways to improve the situation.

5. **Workplace action.** You've noticed a recurring problem in your workplace and want to bring it to the attention of your boss, who typically is inattentive. Write a letter to your boss describing the problem. Your goal is not to provide solutions, but rather to provide a vivid description—complete with sensory details—so that your boss can no longer ignore the problem.

6. **Workplace action.** As a teacher at an elementary school, you are the chair of the Fall Festival Committee. Your school principal has asked you to send a memo to all teachers and staff, describing for them the various activities your committee has planned for the upcoming festival. Your goal is to provide vivid descriptions of the games and food that will be available at the festival. You will likely want to use either a spatial or emphatic order as you present the various descriptions.

Chapter 11
Narration

What Is Narration?

11.1 Understand how you can use the narration pattern to develop your essays.

Human beings are instinctively storytellers. Our hunger for telling and listening to stories is basic.

In **narration**, the writer tells a single story or several related stories. The story can be a means to an end, a way to support a main idea or thesis. Every public speaker, from politician to classroom teacher, knows that stories capture listeners' attention as nothing else can. We want to know what happened to others, not simply because we're curious but also because their experiences shed light on our own lives. Narration lends force to opinion, triggers the flow of memory, and evokes places, times, and people in ways that are compelling and affecting.

How Narration Fits Your Purpose and Audience

11.2 Consider how narration can fit your purpose and audience.

Because narratives tell a story, you may think they're found only in novels or short stories. But narration can also appear in essays, sometimes as a supplemental pattern of development. For example, if your purpose in a composition is to *persuade* apathetic readers that airport security regulations must be strengthened, you might lead off with a brief account of armed terrorists who easily boarded planes on September 11, 2001. In an essay *defining* good teaching, you might keep readers engaged by including satirical anecdotes about one hapless instructor who is the antithesis (opposite) of an effective teacher. An essay on the *effects* of an overburdened judicial system might provide—in an attempt to involve readers—a dramatic account of the way one clearly guilty murderer pleabargained his way to freedom.

In addition to providing effective support in one section of your essay, narration can also serve as an essay's dominant pattern of development. In fact, most of this chapter shows you how to use a single narrative to convey a central point and share with readers your view of what happened.

Although some narratives relate unusual experiences, most tread familiar ground, telling tales of joy, love, loss, frustration, fear—all common emotions experienced during life. Narratives can take the ordinary and transform it into something significant, even extraordinary. The challenge lies in applying your own vision to a tale, thereby making it unique.

Prewriting Strategies

11.3 Develop prewriting strategies for using narration in an essay.

The following checklist shows how you can apply prewriting strategies to narration.

☑ **Narration: A Prewriting Checklist**

Select Your Narrative Event(s)

☐ What event evokes strong emotion in you and is likely to have a powerful effect on your readers?

☐ Does a scrapbook souvenir, snapshot, old letter, or prized object (an athletic trophy, a political button) point to an event worth writing about?

☐ Will you focus on a personal experience, an incident in someone else's life, or a public event?

☐ Can you recount your story effectively, given the length of a typical college essay? If not, will relating one key incident from the fuller, more complete event enable you to convey the point and feeling of the entire experience?

☐ If you write about an event in someone else's life, will you have time to interview the person?

Focus on the Conflict in the Event

☐ What is the source of tension in the event: one person's internal dilemma, a conflict between two (or more) people, or a struggle between a person and a social institution or natural phenomenon?

☐ Will the conflict create enough tension to "hook" readers and keep them interested?

☐ What point do the conflict and its resolution convey to readers?

☐ What tone is appropriate for recounting the conflict?

Use Prewriting to Generate Specifics About the Conflict

☐ Would questioning, brainstorming, freewriting, mapping, or interviewing help you generate details about the conflict?

Strategies for Using Narration in an Essay

11.4 Develop strategies for writing a narration essay.

After prewriting, you're ready to draft your essay. Figure 11.1 and the suggestions that follow will be helpful whether you use narration as a dominant or supportive pattern of development.

1. **Identify the point of the narrative conflict.** Most narratives center on a conflict (see the prewriting checklist in this chapter). When you relate a story, it's up to you to convey the *significance* or *meaning* of the event's conflict. When recounting your narrative, be sure to begin with a clear sense of your *narrative point*, or *thesis*. Then either state that point directly or select details and a tone that imply the point you want readers to take away from your story.

2. **Develop only those details that advance the narrative point.** Nothing is more boring than a storyteller who gets sidetracked and drags out a story with nonessential

Figure 11.1   Development Diagram: Writing a Narration Essay

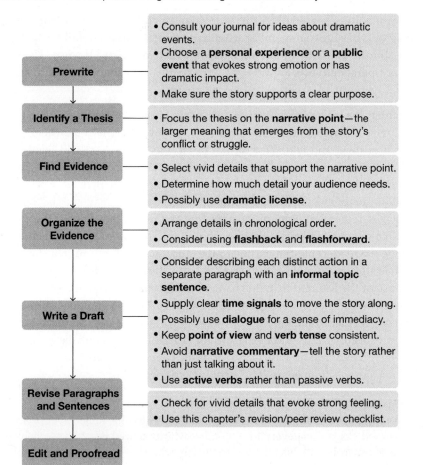

Prewrite
- Consult your journal for ideas about dramatic events.
- Choose a **personal experience** or a **public event** that evokes strong emotion or has dramatic impact.
- Make sure the story supports a clear purpose.

Identify a Thesis
- Focus the thesis on the **narrative point**—the larger meaning that emerges from the story's conflict or struggle.

Find Evidence
- Select vivid details that support the narrative point.
- Determine how much detail your audience needs.
- Possibly use **dramatic license**.

Organize the Evidence
- Arrange details in chronological order.
- Consider using **flashback** and **flashforward**.

Write a Draft
- Consider describing each distinct action in a separate paragraph with an **informal topic sentence**.
- Supply clear **time signals** to move the story along.
- Possibly use **dialogue** for a sense of immediacy.
- Keep **point of view** and **verb tense** consistent.
- Avoid **narrative commentary**—tell the story rather than just talking about it.
- Use **active verbs** rather than passive verbs.

Revise Paragraphs and Sentences
- Check for vivid details that evoke strong feeling.
- Use this chapter's revision/peer review checklist.

Edit and Proofread

details. Maintain an effective narrative pace by focusing on your point and eliminating any details that don't support it. A good narrative depends not only on what is included but also on what has been left out.

How do you determine which specific points to omit, which to treat briefly, and which to emphasize? Having a clear sense of your narrative point and knowing your audience are crucial.

Also keep your audience in mind when selecting narrative details that support your specific points. As you write, keep asking yourself, "Is this detail or character or snippet of conversation essential? Does my audience need this detail to understand the conflict in the situation? Does this detail advance or intensify the narrative action?" Summarize details that have some importance but do not deserve lengthy treatment ("Two hours went by…"). And try to limit *narrative commentary*—statements that tell rather than show what happened—because such remarks interrupt the narrative flow. Focus instead on the specifics that propel action forward in a vigorous way.

Sometimes, especially if the narrative re-creates an event from the past, you won't be able to remember what happened detail for detail. In such a case, you should take advantage of what is called **dramatic license**. Using your current perspective as a guide, feel free to add or reshape details to suit your narrative point.

3. **Organize the narrative sequence.** All of us know the traditional beginning of fairy tales: "Once upon a time…" Every narrative begins somewhere, presents a span of time, and ends at a certain point. Frequently, you will want to use a straightforward time order, following the event *chronologically* from beginning to end: first this happened, next this happened, finally this happened.

But sometimes a strict chronological recounting may not be effective—especially if the high point of the narrative gets lost somewhere in the middle of the time sequence. To avoid that possibility, you may want to disrupt chronology, plunge the reader into the middle of the story, and then return in a **flashback** to the tale's beginning. Narratives can also use **flashforward**—you give readers a glimpse of the future (the main character being jailed) before the story continues in the present (the events leading to the arrest). These techniques shift the story onto several planes and keep it from becoming a step-by-step, predictable account. Reserve flashforwards and flashbacks for crucial incidents only because breaking out of chronological order acts as emphasis. Here are examples of how flashback and flashforward can be used in narrative writing:

Flashback
Standing behind the wooden counter, Greg wielded his knife expertly as he shucked clams—one every ten seconds—with practiced ease. The scene contrasted sharply with his first day on the job, when his hands broke out in blisters and when splitting each shell was like prying open a safe.

Flashforward
Rushing to move my car from the no-parking zone, I waved a quick good-bye to Karen as she climbed the steps to the bus. I didn't know then that by the time I picked her up at the bus station later that day, she would have made a decision that would affect both our lives.

Whether or not you choose to include flashbacks or flashforwards in an essay, remember to limit the time span covered by the narrative. Otherwise, you'll have trouble generating the details needed to give the story depth and meaning. Also, regardless of the time sequence you select, organize the tale so that it drives toward a strong finish. Be careful that your story doesn't trail off into minor, anticlimactic details.

4. **Make the narrative easy to follow.** Describing each distinct action in a separate paragraph helps readers grasp the flow of events. Although narrative essays don't always have conventional topic sentences, each narrative paragraph should have a

clear focus. Often this focus is indicated by a sentence early in the paragraph that directs attention to the action taking place. Such a sentence functions as a kind of *informal topic sentence;* the rest of the paragraph then develops that topic sentence. Also be sure to use time signals when narrating a story. Words like *now, then, next, after,* and *later* ensure that your reader won't get lost as the story progresses.

5. **Make the narrative vigorous and immediate.** A compelling narrative provides an abundance of specific details, making readers feel as if they're experiencing the story being told. Readers must be able to see, hear, touch, smell, and taste the event you're narrating. *Vivid sensory description* is, therefore, an essential part of an effective narrative. Not only do specific sensory details make writing a pleasure to read—we all enjoy learning the particulars about people, places, and things—but they also give the narrative the stamp of reality. The specifics convince the reader that the event being described actually did, or could, occur.

   Compare the following excerpts from a narrative essay. The first version is lifeless and dull; the revised version, packed with sensory images, grabs readers with its sense of foreboding:

   Original Version
   That eventful day started out like every other summer day. My sister, Tricia, and I made several elaborate mud pies that we decorated with care. A little later on, as we were spraying each other with the garden hose, we heard my father walk up the path.

   Revised
   That sad summer day started out uneventfully enough. My sister Tricia and I spent a few hours mixing and decorating mud pies. Our hands caked with dry mud, we sprinkled each lopsided pie with alternating rows of dandelion and clover petals. Later, when the sun got hotter, we tossed our white T-shirts over the red picket fence—forgetting my grandmother's frequent warnings to be more ladylike. Our sweaty backs bared to the sun, we doused each other with icy sprays from the garden hose. Caught up in the primitive pleasure of it all, we barely heard my father as he walked up the garden path, the gravel crunching under his heavy work boots.

   A caution: Sensory language enlivens narration, but it also slows the pace. Be sure that the slower pace suits your purpose.

6. **Use dialogue.** Another way to create an aura of narrative immediacy is to use **dialogue.** Our sense of other people comes, in part, from what they say and the way they sound. Conversational exchanges allow the reader to experience characters directly. Compare the following fragments of a narrative, one with dialogue and one without, noting how much more energetic the second version is.

   Original
   As soon as I found my way back to the campsite, the trail guide commented on my disheveled appearance. I explained that I had heard some gunshots and had run back to camp as soon as I could.

Revised

As soon as I found my way back to the campsite, the trail guide took one look at me and drawled, "What on earth happened to you, Daniel Boone? You look as though you've been dragged through a haystack backwards."

"I'd look a lot worse if I hadn't run back here. When a bullet whizzes by me, I don't stick around to see who's doing the shooting."

Note that, when using dialogue, you generally begin a new paragraph to indicate a shift from one person's speech to another's (as in the second example). You can also use dialogue to convey a person's inner thoughts. Like conversation between people, such interior dialogue is enclosed in quotation marks.

The challenge in writing dialogue, both exterior and interior, is to make each character's speech distinctive and convincing. Reading the dialogue aloud—even asking friends or family members to speak the lines—will help you develop an ear for authentic speech. What sounds most natural is often a compressed and reshaped version of what was actually said. As with other narrative details, include only those portions of dialogue that serve your purpose, fit the mood you want to create, and reveal character.

7. **Vary your sentence structure.** A good way to enliven narratives is to use *varied sentence structure*. Sentences that plod along with the same predictable pattern put readers to sleep. Experiment with your sentences by varying their length and type; mix long and short sentences, simple and complex. Compare the following original and revised version to see how effective varied sentence structure can be in narrative writing:

   Original
   The store manager went to the walk-in refrigerator every day. The heavy metal door clanged shut behind her. I had visions of her freezing to death among the hanging carcasses. The shiny door finally swung open. She waddled out.

   Revised
   Each time the store manager went to the walk-in refrigerator, the heavy metal door clanged shut behind her. Visions of her freezing to death among the hanging carcasses crept into my mind until, finally, the shiny door swung open and out she waddled.

8. **Use vigorous verbs.** Narratives benefit from *vigorous verbs*, which give energy to the story. Use active verb forms ("The boss yelled at him") rather than passive ones ("He was yelled at by the boss"), and try to replace anemic *to be* verbs ("She was a good basketball player") with more dynamic constructions ("She played basketball well").

9. **Keep your point of view and verb tense consistent.** All stories have a *narrator*, the person who tells the story. If you, as narrator, tell a story as you experienced it, the story is written in the *first-person point of view* ("I saw the dog pull loose"). But if you want to tell how someone else experienced the incident, you use the *third-person point of view* ("Anne saw the dog pull loose"). Each point of view has

advantages and limitations. First person allows you to express ordinarily private thoughts and to re-create an event as you experienced it. It is limited, though, in its ability to depict other people's inner thoughts. In contrast, third person makes it easier to provide insight into the thoughts of all the participants. However, its objective, broad perspective may undercut some of the subjective immediacy of the "I was there" point of view. No matter which viewpoint you select, stay with that viewpoint throughout the entire narrative. Remember also that research reports and other academic papers are usually written from the third-person point of view.

Knowing whether to use the **past** or **present tense** ("I *strolled* into the room" as opposed to "I *stroll* into the room") is important. In most narrations, the past tense predominates, enabling the writer to span a considerable period of time. Although more rarely used, the present tense can be powerful for events of short duration—a wrestling match or a medical emergency, for instance. A narrative in the present tense prolongs each moment, intensifying the reader's sense of participation. Be careful, though; unless the event is intense and fast-paced, the present tense can seem contrived. Whichever tense you choose, avoid shifting midstream—starting, let's say, in the past tense ("she skated") and switching to the present tense ("she runs").

Revision Strategies

11.5 Use strategies for revising your narration essay.

Once you have a draft of the essay, you're ready to revise. The following checklist will help your peers provide feedback and aid you in revising your essay.

Student Essay: From Prewriting Through Revision

11.6 Analyze how narration is used effectively in a student-written selection.

The following student essay was written by Laura Rose Dunn in response to this assignment:

> In her essay, "The Fourth of July," Audre Lorde shares a disturbing experience that brought her childhood to an end and changed the way she thought about "her" country. Write a narrative about an experience that had a profound effect on you. Your essay does not necessarily have to be about a disturbing experience, but it should focus on something from your childhood that played a role in shaping you into the person you are today.

After deciding to write about how the letters her dad had written her over the years had played a major role in her life, Laura Rose did some *freewriting* on her computer to help her get started on her assignment. She knew that getting started was the most difficult part of the writing process for her and that *freewriting* might help ease her into the assignment. She typed quickly for ten minutes, not worrying about whether

---

☑ Narration: A Revision/Peer Review Checklist

Revise Overall Meaning and Structure

- ☐ What is the essay's main point? Is it stated explicitly or is it implied? Could the point be conveyed more clearly? How?

- ☐ What is the narrative's conflict? Is it stated explicitly or is it implied? Could the conflict be made more dramatic? How?

- ☐ From which point of view is the narrative told? Is it the most effective point of view for this essay? Why or why not?

Revise Paragraph Development

- ☐ Which paragraphs (or passages) fail to advance the action, reveal character, or contribute to the story's mood? Should these sections be condensed or eliminated?

- ☐ Where should the narrative pace be slowed down or quickened?

- ☐ Where is it difficult to follow the chronology of events? Should the order of paragraphs be changed? How? Where would additional time signals help?

- ☐ How could flashback or flashforward paragraphs be used to highlight key events?

- ☐ What can be done to make the essay's opening paragraph more compelling? Would dramatic dialogue or mood-setting description help?

- ☐ What could be done to make the essay's closing paragraph more effective? Should the essay end earlier? Should it close by echoing an idea or image from the opening?

Revise Sentences and Words

- ☐ Where is sentence structure monotonous? Where would combining sentences, mixing sentence type, and/or alternating sentence length help?

- ☐ Where could dialogue replace commentary to convey character and propel the story forward?

- ☐ Which sentences and words are inconsistent with the essay's tone?

- ☐ Which sentences would benefit from sensory details that heighten the narrative mood?

- ☐ Where do vigorous verbs convey action? Where could active verbs replace passive verbs? Where could dull *to be* verbs be converted to more dynamic forms?

- ☐ Are there inappropriate shifts in point of view or verb tense?

---

her sentences were especially polished, if she'd left out a comma, or if she needed to divide her material into separate paragraphs. Her point was to generate ideas and to figure out where she wanted to go in her essay. Here's what she came up with:

Freewriting

So I know I want to write about my dad and how the letters he writes me every week, no matter where he is, have influenced the person I've become, but I'm not sure where to start. Maybe I could start with that time in kindergarten when I kind of hurt my dad's feelings because I wrote an essay about my mom and how wonderful she was. I clearly remember how I ended that essay with the sentence, "My dad, his name is Bill." He'll never stop giving me a hard time about that. And then maybe it would work to use a chronological approach like Dr. Canter talked about in class yesterday. I could start with explaining that Dad's a Marine and has had to be away so much, but how he always sends me letters. Then I could write about the letters he sent me when I was real little and couldn't read, so he drew lots of pictures for me, even though he is not a good artist. I didn't care. In fact, I'm realizing now as I'm typing that those pictures and the letters he wrote made me want to learn to read. And they made me want to learn to write too so that I could write him back. Oh, and then later, when I learned to read and write, he started correcting my grammar. It was like I had an English teacher for a parent. I can't say that was always tons of fun, but he really did help me develop my reading and writing skills. Maybe that's why I've always done well in my English classes. But Dad has helped me with more than just with reading and writing. He told me so much in those letters that helped me in other ways. I learned all about places in the world I'd never been and also about what war is like. I know he tried not to tell me anything that would make me worry about him, but I couldn't help it. I remember not being able to go to sleep at night because I wondered if he was safe. I missed him so much, and I still do, but the letters helped me stay close to him when I was growing up. And now that I'm away from home in my first year of college, he still writes me every week, and I still look so forward to reading his letters.

Now read Laura Rose's essay, "Letters from Dad," noting how the ten minutes she spent freewriting helped her figure out what she wanted to include in her opening paragraph, the way she wanted to structure her essay, and the content she wanted to include. Notice, also, the ideas she included in her freewriting but decided to leave out of her essay. Finally, consider how well the essay applies the principles of narration discussed in this chapter. (The commentary that follows the essay will help you look at Laura Rose's essay more closely and will give you some sense of how she went about the composing process, from freewriting, to her first draft, and finally to the draft that appears below.)

Letters from Dad
by Laura Rose Dunn

Introduction

Time signal

Narrative tension established

When I was in kindergarten, my teacher asked each of us to write a paper about our parents. The first "open house" of the school year was a few days away, and she wanted to post our early essay attempts on the classroom walls. I began my essay by telling the world about my mom and how beautiful and kind she was. I wrote about how she was my hero and how I was so proud to be her daughter. I went on and on like that for the whole page, not once mentioning good old dad. I soon realized this, and at the very end of my paper, after I had practically serenaded my mom, I added six short words: "My dad, his name is Bill." That was it. That was all I had to say about my dad. Naturally, my dad was crushed when he read my paper at open house, and I am sure he will never forget my insinuation in that

1

kindergarten essay that he did not play an important role in my life. In fact, he still teases me about the way I slighted him in that paper. So in the spirit of making up for past neglect, I want to now make clear that my dad has always been an important figure in my life, even when he was thousands of miles away. He has not only helped me develop my reading and writing skills but has also played a major role in expanding my view of the world.

My dad and I have always been close, despite his frequent absences. You see, my dad has been and always will be a United States Marine, and with that title come certain obligations. He has been overseas more times than I can count and has seen more of the world than I could ever imagine. From the time I was three, my dad has written me letters every week of every deployment. Although at first I could not read them on my own, I never grew weary of trying. Those letters were my only link to him while he was away, and I held on to every single one. Each night that he was gone, I would pull them out of my drawer and read my letters from him as if it were for the first time, and I anxiously awaited the arrival of the next one.

At the time, I loved those letters almost as much as the man behind them. When I was very young and hadn't yet learned how to read, he would illustrate key words below each sentence to help me grasp his meaning. To this day, my favorite letter from Dad features drawings of a fish, a cat, a dog, and Jabba the Hutt. Needless to say, it was a very interesting letter. Although his illustrations were juvenile at best (no offense, Dad), they gave me a way to connect with the words he wrote. With the pictures there to guide me, I felt more encouraged to take a real stab at reading. I even started writing my own letters to him.

My first letters to my dad were very interesting specimens. Some consisted of more glitter-glue than actual vocabulary, but day-by-day, my letters became more readable. By the time I hit age six, I was very good at thinking about what I wanted to say and putting those thoughts on a piece of paper. Upon receiving my letters, my dad would read and enjoy them, and then critique and criticize. Along with my dad's usual letters, I would also receive my letters with corrections on them. Part of me wants to think that he did this to help pass the time, but I know in my heart that what it really comes down to is that my dad runs the "grammar police." Even when he was home, he would drill me on my vocabulary, spelling, and sentence structure. Despite my protests at the time, I will admit that now, I am grateful for the instruction he gave me. By the time I was in fifth grade, I was a writing pro. The only thing I failed to comprehend was sarcasm. So when my dad signed at the end of his letter, "Laura, I love you as if you were my own daughter, but you have got to work on your handwriting," I naturally assumed that I had been adopted. And as you might imagine, sarcasm was the next concept he helped me tackle.

My dad's letters not only gave me the tools I needed to grow as a writer; they also helped me see a new side of the world. Dad wrote to me of the beautiful Alps in Switzerland, the vast deserts of the Middle East, the complex beauty of The Med, and the heart-breaking reality of war. I got a firsthand look at the world just by reading his

Margin annotations:

Narrative point (thesis)

Informal topic sentence

Time signal

Time signal
Informal topic sentence

Time signal

Time signal

Sensory details

Informal topic sentence

Time signal

Time signal

Informal topic sentence

Paragraph numbers: 2, 3, 4, 5

letters, and I know I am lucky to have had that. I was able to make connections between what he shared with me in his letters and what I was reading about in school. When it came time for my geography and history classes, I had an advantage over most of my classmates.

Informal topic sentence

Time signal

Although I enjoyed our relationship as pen pals, it is always so much better to have my dad at home. Life for me is still hard when he is gone. As I have gotten older, I have not "gotten used to it." In fact, knowing that he is on the other side of the world is almost harder now. The only thing that gets me through my dad being away is the promise of a letter, once a week. Those letters *are* my dad, and he has taught me more through his letters than any book could have taught me. My dad has missed more birthdays, soccer games, and award ceremonies than I even care to count. He has missed chunks of my life that are impossible to make up, but in his absence my dad gave me so much more than a cheer from the crowd or a swing on the merry-go-round. He shared his world with me and taught me not only how to read and write, but how vast the world is and how I can use its history to enrich my life.   6

Sensory details

Echoing of narrative point in the introduction

I thank my dad for all that he has taught me that has helped me grow as a reader, a writer, and a person. I thank him for playing a huge role in making me who I am today. I am so proud to be the daughter of a United States Marine.   7

Concluding statement

Oh, and my mom, her name is Mimi.   8

Commentary

POINT OF VIEW, TENSE, AND NARRATIVE TENSION   Laura Rose chose to write "Letters from Dad" from the *first-person point of view*, a logical choice because she appears as a main character in her own story. Using a combination of *past* and *present tense*, Laura Rose recounts a story from her past but also moves to the present as she shares with her readers how her dad has played a major role in shaping her into the reader, writer, and individual she has become. In pointing out that her dad was "crushed" because she did not mention him in her first school paper, Laura Rose introduces some mild *narrative tension* that contributes to the point of her essay.

NARRATIVE POINT   It isn't always necessary to state the *narrative point* of an essay; the point can be implied. But Laura Rose decided to express the controlling idea of her narrative in two places. First, in the introduction, she includes two sentences that work together to make her narrative point: "So in the spirit of making up for past neglect, I want to make clear that my dad has always been an important figure in my life, even when he was thousands of miles away. He has not only helped me develop my reading and writing skills but has also played a major role in expanding my view of the world." She makes her narrative point again in the next-to-last paragraph, where she thanks her dad for his positive influence on her life. All of the essay's narrative details contribute to the point of the piece; Laura Rose does not include any extraneous information that would detract from the central idea she wants to convey.

ORGANIZATION   The narrative is organized *chronologically*, as Laura Rose reflects on the important role her dad has played in her life. Although the story she tells spans fifteen years, from when she was three years old to the present, Laura Rose chooses specific examples from across the years as she shares with her readers the role her dad has played in shaping her into the person she has become. To help the reader follow the course of the narrative, Laura Rose uses *time signals*: "When I was in kindergarten…" (1); "From the time I was three…" (2); "At the time…," "When I was very young …," "To this day…" (3); "By the time I hit age six,…" "By the time I was in fifth grade,…" (4); "As I have gotten older…" (6).

The paragraphs also contain *informal topic sentences* that direct attention to the specific parts of the story being narrated. Indeed, each paragraph focuses on a particular aspect of her story: how a kindergarten assignment led to an essay for a college class, why her dad has been away from home for much of her life, why she loved receiving letters from him, what those early letters to him and his responses to her were like, how her dad's letters enriched her life, how his absence over the years has affected her, and why he means so much to her today.

 COMBINING PATTERNS OF DEVELOPMENT   The chronological structure of Laura Rose's reflection, from her childhood years to the present, uses *cause* and *effect* to explain how the letters from her dad have shaped the person she has become, and the *description* she uses throughout her essay brings her story to life with rich *sensory details* to engage the reader. For example, the two following sentences allow her readers to "see" what his letters to her looked like and understand how they helped her learn to read: "When I was very young and hadn't yet learned how to read, he would illustrate key words below each sentence to help me grasp his meaning. To this day, my favorite letter from Dad features drawings of a fish, a cat, a dog, and Jabba the Hut" (3).

CONCLUSION   The primary purpose of an essay's conclusion is to bring the composition to closure, and Laura Rose does this in a creative way. Although her next-to-last paragraph adheres to a more typical essay structure by restating the main idea she has communicated to her readers—that she appreciates all that her dad has done over the years to help her grow as a reader, a writer, and a person—she doesn't stop there. Laura Rose goes on to include one short, terse, concluding sentence that brings her readers back to her reason for writing this essay: that she slighted her dad in a kindergarten essay she wrote in which she focused on her mom. She evens the score—resolving the narrative tension expressed in paragraph 1—by ending her college essay with a humorously ironic nod to her mom: "Oh, and my mom, her name is Mimi."

REVISING THE FIRST DRAFT   Comparing the final version of the essay's first paragraph with the following preliminary version reveals some of the changes Laura Rose made while revising the essay.

Original Version of the Introductory Paragraph

When I was in Kindergarten, my teacher had our class sit down and write a paper about our parents. I began my paper by telling the world about my mom and how beautiful and kind she was. I wrote about how she was my hero and how I was so proud to be her daughter. I went on and on like that for the whole page, not once mentioning good old dad. I soon realized this and at the very end of my paper, after I had practically serenaded my mom, I added six short words: "My dad, his name is Bill." That was it. That was all I had to say about my dad. Naturally, my dad was crushed when he read my paper at open house, and I am sure that he will never let me live it down as he still teases me about it to this day. So, in the spirit of making up for past neglect, I must now say that my dad has really helped me come into my own and has given me the practice I needed to become a successful reader and writer.

After putting the original draft aside for a while, Laura Rose reread what she had written and realized that she needed to make some major changes in her opening paragraph. She began her revisions by tackling the easy issues: correcting a capitalization or punctuation error (changing *Kindergarten* to *kindergarten*, adding a needed comma in her fifth sentence); omitting unnecessary words (such as "sit down" in the first sentence and "that" in other sentences); and playing with her wording to make sentences more accurately reflect her intentions (such as changing "I must now say..." to "I want to now make clear...").

Next, Laura Rose decided to add a sentence that would allow her readers to understand early in the essay that the papers she and her classmates were writing in kindergarten were going to be posted around the room at her school's upcoming open house. In her first draft, she had waited until more than halfway through the paragraph to mention this event. As she revised, Laura Rose was clearly thinking more about her readers and making changes that would help them more easily follow her story line.

She also realized that her pronoun reference was both repetitive and unclear in the last part of one of her sentences in the original draft: "...and I am sure that he will never let me live *it* down as he still teases me about *it* to this day." In her revision, she gets rid of the unclear pronoun reference by including concrete language and using two sentences instead of one to make her point: "...and I am sure he will never forget my insinuation in that kindergarten essay that he did not play an important role in my life. In fact, he still teases me about the way I slighted him in that paper."

Finally, she realized that her last sentence in the paragraph needed to be revised. When she started drafting her essay, she intended to focus on how her dad had helped her develop as a reader and writer, but as she was drafting her essay, she went on to include additional information on how her dad helped expand her view of the world. As is the case for many writers, Laura Rose's thesis changed as she worked on her essay, and she needed to revise the thesis statement to reflect that change.

The revisions she made in her opening paragraph made for a stronger, more polished piece of narrative writing. Consideration of her audience helped Laura Rose see how she could improve her opening paragraph as well as the rest of her essay.

Activities: Narration

Prewriting Activities

1. Imagine you're writing two essays. One analyzes the effect of insensitive teachers on young children; the other argues the importance of family traditions. With the help of your freewriting, identify different narratives you could use to open each essay.

2. Use brainstorming or any other prewriting technique to generate narrative details about one of the following events. After examining your raw material, identify two or three narrative points (thesis statements) that might focus an essay. Then edit the pre-writing material for each narrative point, noting which items would be appropriate, which would be inappropriate, and which would have to be developed more fully.

   a. An injury you experienced

   b. The loss of an important object

   c. An event that made you wish you had a certain skill

3. For each of the following situations, identify two different conflicts that would make a story worth relating:

   a. Going to the supermarket with a friend

   b. Telling your parents which college you've decided to attend

   c. Participating in a demonstration

4. Prepare six to ten lines of vivid and natural-sounding dialogue to convey the conflict in two of the following situations:

   a. One member of a couple trying to break up with the other

   b. An instructor talking to a student who plagiarized a composition

   c. A young person talking to his or her parents about dropping out of college

Revising Activities

5. Revise each of the following narrative sentence groups twice: once with words that carry negative connotations, and again with words that carry positive connotations. Use varied sentence structure, sensory details, and vigorous verbs to convey mood.

   a. The bell rang. It rang loudly. Students knew the last day of class was over.

   b. Last weekend, our neighbors burned leaves in their yard. We went over to speak with them.

   c. The sun shone in through my bedroom window. It made me sit up in bed. Daylight was finally here, I told myself.

6. The following paragraph is the introduction from the first draft of an essay propos- ing harsher penalties for drunk drivers. Revise this narrative paragraph to make it more effective. How can you make sentence structure less predictable? Which de- tails should you delete? As you revise, provide language that conveys the event's sights, smells, and sounds. Also, clarify the chronological sequence.

> As I drove down the street in my bright blue sports car, I saw a car coming rapidly around the curve. The car didn't slow down as it headed toward the traffic light. The light turned yellow and then red. A young couple, dressed like models, started crossing the street. When the woman saw the car, she called out to her husband. He jumped onto the shoulder. The man wasn't hurt but, sec- onds later, it was clear the woman was. I ran to a nearby emergency phone and called the police. The ambulance arrived, but the woman was already dead. The driver, who looked terrible, failed the sobriety test, and the police found out that he had two previous offenses. It's apparent that better ways have to be found for getting drunk drivers off the road.

Professional Selections: Narration

AUDRE LORDE

Named poet laureate of the state of New York in 1991, Audre Lorde (1934–1992) was a New Yorker born of African-Caribbean parents. Lorde taught at Hunter College for many years and published numerous poems and nonfiction pieces in a variety of magazines and literary journals. Her books include *The Black Unicorn: Poems* (1978), *Sister Outsider: Essays and Speeches* (1984), and *A Burst of Light* (1988). "The Fourth of July" is an excerpt from her autobiography, *Zami: A New Spelling of My Name* (1982).

To understand how this narration essay is organized, see Figure 11.2.

Pre-Reading Journal Entry

When you were a child, what beliefs about the United States did you have? List these beliefs. For each, indicate whether subsequent experience maintained or shattered your childhood understand- ing of these beliefs. Take time to explore these issues in your journal.

The Fourth of July

The first time I went to Washington, D.C., was on the edge of the summer when   1
I was supposed to stop being a child. At least that's what they said to us all at grad- uation from the eighth grade. My sister, Phyllis, graduated at the same time from high school. I don't know what she was supposed to stop being. But as graduation presents for us both, the whole family took a Fourth of July trip to Washington, D.C., the fabled and famous capital of our country.

It was the first time I'd ever been on a railroad train during the day. When I   2
was little, and we used to go to the Connecticut shore, we always went at night on the milk train, because it was cheaper.

Preparations were in the air around our house before school was even over. We packed for a week. There were two very large suitcases that my father carried, and a box filled with food. In fact, my first trip to Washington was a mobile feast; I started eating as soon as we were comfortably ensconced in our seats, and did not stop until somewhere after Philadelphia. I remember it was Philadelphia because I was disappointed not to have passed by the Liberty Bell. 3

My mother had roasted two chickens and cut them up into dainty bite-size pieces. She packed slices of brown bread and butter and green pepper and carrot sticks. There were little violently yellow iced cakes with scalloped edges called "marigolds," that came from Cushman's Bakery. There was a spice bun and rock-cakes from Newton's, the West Indian bakery across Lenox Avenue from St. Mark's School, and iced tea in a wrapped mayonnaise jar. There were sweet pickles for us and dill pickles for my father, and peaches with the fuzz still on them, individually wrapped to keep them from bruising. And, for neatness, there were piles of napkins and a little tin box with a washcloth dampened with rosewater and glycerine for wiping sticky mouths. 4

I wanted to eat in the dining car because I had read all about them, but my mother reminded me for the umpteenth time that dining car food always cost too much money and besides, you never could tell whose hands had been playing all over that food, nor where those same hands had been just before. My mother never mentioned that Black people were not allowed into railroad dining cars headed south in 1947. As usual, whatever my mother did not like and could not change, she ignored. Perhaps it would go away, deprived of her attention. 5

I learned later that Phyllis's high school senior class trip had been to Washington, but the nuns had given her back her deposit in private, explaining to her that the class, all of whom were white, except Phyllis, would be staying in a hotel where Phyllis "would not be happy," meaning, Daddy explained to her, also in private, that they did not rent rooms to Negroes. "We will take you to Washington, ourselves," my father had avowed, "and not just for an overnight in some measly fleabag hotel." 6

American racism was a new and crushing reality that my parents had to deal with every day of their lives once they came to this country. They handled it as a private woe. My mother and father believed that they could best protect their children from the realities of race in america and the fact of american racism by never giving them name, much less discussing their nature. We were told we must never trust white people, but *why* was never explained, nor the nature of their ill will. Like so many other vital pieces of information in my childhood, I was supposed to know without being told. It always seemed like a very strange injunction coming from my mother, who looked so much like one of those people we were never supposed to trust. But something always warned me not to ask my mother why she wasn't white, and why Auntie Lillah and Auntie Etta weren't, even though they were all that same problematic color so different from my father and me, even from my sisters, who were somewhere in-between. 7

In Washington, D.C., we had one large room with two double beds and an extra cot for me. It was a back-street hotel that belonged to a friend of my father's who was in real estate, and I spent the whole next day after Mass squinting up at 8 the Lincoln Memorial where Marian Anderson[1] had sung after the D.A.R.[2] refused to allow her to sing in their auditorium because she was Black. Or because she was "Colored," my father said as he told us the story. Except that what he probably said was "Negro," because for his time, my father was quite progressive.

I was squinting because I was in that silent agony that characterized all of my 9 childhood summers, from the time school let out in June to the end of July, brought about by my dilated and vulnerable eyes exposed to the summer brightness.

I viewed Julys through an agonizing corolla of dazzling whiteness and I al- 10 ways hated the Fourth of July, even before I came to realize the travesty such a celebration was for Black people in this country.

My parents did not approve of sunglasses, nor of their expense. 11

I spent the afternoon squinting up at monuments to freedom and past presi- 12 dencies and democracy, and wondering why the light and heat were both so much stronger in Washington, D.C., than back home in New York City. Even the pavement on the streets was a shade lighter in color than back home.

Late that Washington afternoon my family and I walked back down Pennsylvania 13 Avenue. We were a proper caravan, mother bright and father brown, the three of us girls step-standards in-between. Moved by our historical surroundings and the heat of the early evening, my father decreed yet another treat. He had a great sense of history, a flair for the quietly dramatic and the sense of specialness of an occasion and a trip.

"Shall we stop and have a little something to cool off, Lin?" 14

Two blocks away from our hotel, the family stopped for a dish of vanilla ice 15 cream at a Breyer's ice cream and soda fountain. Indoors, the soda fountain was dim and fancooled, deliciously relieving to my scorched eyes.

Corded and crisp and pinafored, the five of us seated ourselves one by one 16 at the counter. There was I between my mother and father, and my two sisters on the other side of my mother. We settled ourselves along the white mottled marble counter, and when the waitress spoke at first no one understood what she was saying, and so the five of us just sat there.

The waitress moved along the line of us closer to my father and spoke again. 17 "I said I kin give you to take out, but you can't eat here. Sorry." Then she dropped her eyes looking very embarrassed, and suddenly we heard what it was she was saying all at the same time, loud and clear.

Straight-backed and indignant, one by one, my family and I got down from 18 the counter stools and turned around and marched out of the store, quiet and outraged, as if we had never been Black before. No one would answer my emphatic questions with anything other than a guilty silence. "But we hadn't done anything!" This wasn't right or fair! Hadn't I written poems about Bataan and freedom and democracy for all?

My parents wouldn't speak of this injustice, not because they had contributed 19 to it, but because they felt they should have anticipated it and avoided it. This made me even angrier. My fury was not going to be acknowledged by a like fury.

---

[1] An acclaimed African-American opera singer (1902–1993), famed for her renderings of Black spirituals.

[2] Daughters of the American Revolution. A society, founded in 1890, for women who can prove direct lineage to soldiers or others who aided in winning American independence from Great Britain during the Revolutionary War (1775–1783). The DAR has admitted non-white women as members since 1977.

Even my two sisters copied my parents' pretense that nothing unusual and anti-american had occurred. I was left to write my angry letter to the president of the united states all by myself, although my father did promise I could type it out on the office typewriter next week, after I showed it to him in my copybook diary.

The waitress was white, and the counter was white, and the ice cream I never 20 ate in Washington, D.C., that summer I left childhood was white, and the white heat and the white pavement and the white stone monuments of my first Washington summer made me sick to my stomach for the whole rest of that trip and it wasn't much of a graduation present after all.

Figure 11.2 Essay Structure Diagram: "The Fourth of July" by Audre Lorde

Introductory paragraph: Narrative point (paragraph 1)	Going on a trip to Washington, D.C., as a graduation present. **Narrative point:** This experience marked the end of the narrator's childhood.
Narrative details (2–19). Also, descriptive and explanatory material (in parentheses at right)	Preparing for the train trip. (The food packed for the trip.) *Foreshadowing:* Not allowed in the dining car. *Flashforward:* Learning later that her sister had been denied a trip to Washington because of racist hotel policies. (How the author's parents and relatives dealt with the "crushing reality" of racism.) (The hotel room and its location.) Spending the day "squinting up at monuments." Deciding to stop for ice cream at a soda fountain and waiting to be served. Waitress refusing to serve the family. Leaving the soda fountain. (The parents' response and the author's anger.)
Concluding paragraph (20)	The incident at the soda fountain marked an end to the narrator's childhood.

Questions for Critical Reading

1. What is the selection's thesis (or narrative point)? Locate the sentence(s) in which Lorde states her main idea. If she doesn't state the thesis explicitly, express it in your own words.

2. In paragraph 4, Lorde describes the elaborate picnic her mother prepared for the trip to Washington, D.C. Why did Lorde's mother make such elaborate preparations? What do these preparations tell us about Lorde's mother?

3. Why does Lorde have trouble understanding her parents' dictate that she "never trust white people" (paragraph 7)?

4. In general, how do Lorde's parents handle racism? How does the family as a whole deal with the racism they encounter in the ice cream parlor? How does the family's reaction to the ice cream parlor incident make Lorde feel?

Questions About the Writer's Craft

1. **The pattern.** What techniques does Lorde use to help readers follow the unfolding of the story as it occurs in both time and space?

2. **Narrative commentary.** When telling a story, skilled writers limit narrative commentary—statements that tell rather than show what happened—because such commentary tends to interrupt the narrative flow. Lorde, however, provides narrative commentary in several spots. Find these instances. How is the information she provides in these places essential to her narrative?

3. **Breaking the rules.** In paragraphs 7 and 19, Lorde uses all lowercase letters when referring to America/American and to the President of the United States. Why do you suppose she doesn't follow the rules of capitalization? In what ways does her rejection of these rules reinforce what she is trying to convey through the essay's title?

4. **Key words.** What key word does Lorde repeat in paragraph 20? What effect do you think she hopes the repetition will have on readers?

Writing Assignments Using Narration as a Pattern of Development

1. Lorde recounts an incident during which she was treated unfairly. Write a narrative about a time when either you were treated unjustly or you treated someone else in an unfair manner. Like Lorde, use vivid details to make the incident come alive and to convey how it affected you.

2. Write a narrative about an experience that dramatically changed your view of the world. The experience might have been jarring and painful, or it may have been positive and uplifting. In either case, recount the incident with compelling narrative details. To illustrate the shift in your perspective, begin with a brief statement of the way you viewed the world before the experience.

Writing Assignment Combining Patterns of Development

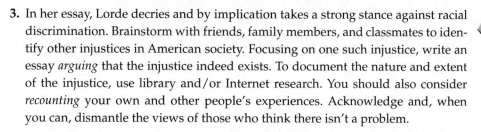

3. In her essay, Lorde decries and by implication takes a strong stance against racial discrimination. Brainstorm with friends, family members, and classmates to identify other injustices in American society. Focusing on one such injustice, write an essay *arguing* that the injustice indeed exists. To document the nature and extent of the injustice, use library and/or Internet research. You should also consider *recounting* your own and other people's experiences. Acknowledge and, when you can, dismantle the views of those who think there isn't a problem.

LYNDA BARRY

Cartoonist, novelist, and playwright, Lynda Barry combines the genres of collage, memoir, novel, graphic novel, and workbook in her compositions. Her creations include the syndicated strip *Ernie Pook's Comeek* and the illustrated novels *Cruddy* (2001), *One Hundred Demons* (2002), *What It Is* (2008), and *Picture This: The Near-Sighted Monkey Book* (2010). Her 2002 novel *The Good Times Are Killing Me* was adapted into an off-Broadway play. The following essay was originally published in the *Baltimore Sun* on January 24, 1992.

Pre-Reading Journal Entry

In her essay, Lynda Barry writes about a time in her childhood when she was "filled with a panic...like the panic that strikes kids when they realize they are lost." Think of a time during your childhood when you were filled with panic. Why were you afraid? How did you feel? What did you do?

The Sanctuary of School

I was 7 years old the first time I snuck out of the house in the dark. It was winter and my parents had been fighting all night. They were short on money and long on relatives who kept "temporarily" moving into our house because they had nowhere else to go. 1

My brother and I were used to giving up our bedroom. We slept on the couch, something we actually liked because it put us that much closer to the light of our lives, our television. 2

At night when everyone was asleep, we lay on our pillows watching it with the sound off. We watched Steve Allen's mouth moving. We watched Johnny Carson's mouth moving. We watched movies filled with gangsters shooting machine guns into packed rooms, dying soldiers hurling a last grenade and beautiful women crying at windows. Then the sign-off finally came and we tried to sleep. 3

The morning I snuck out, I woke up filled with a panic about needing to get to school. The sun wasn't quite up yet but my anxiety was so fierce that I just got dressed, walked quietly across the kitchen and let myself out the back door. 4

It was quiet outside. Stars were still out. Nothing moved and no one was in the street. It was as if someone had turned the sound off on the world. 5

I walked the alley, breaking thin ice over the puddles with my shoes. I didn't know why I was walking to school in the dark. I didn't think about it. All I knew was a feeling of panic, like the panic that strikes kids when they realize they are lost. 6

That feeling eased the moment I turned the corner and saw the dark outline of my school at the top of the hill. My school was made up of about 15 nondescript portable classrooms set down on a fenced concrete lot in a rundown Seattle neighborhood, but it had the most beautiful view of the Cascade Mountains. You could see them from anywhere on the playfield and you could see them from the windows of my classroom—Room 2. 7

I walked over to the monkey bars and hooked my arms around the cold metal. I stood for a long time just looking across Rainier Valley. The sky was beginning to whiten and I could hear a few birds. 8

In a perfect world my absence at home would not have gone unnoticed. I 9 would have had two parents in a panic to locate me, instead of two parents in a panic to locate an answer to the hard question of survival during a deep financial and emotional crisis.

But in an overcrowded and unhappy home, it's incredibly easy for any child to 10 slip away. The high levels of frustration, depression and anger in my house made my brother and me invisible. We were children with the sound turned off. And for us, as for the steadily increasing number of neglected children in this country, the only place where we could count on being noticed was at school.

"Hey there, young lady. Did you forget to go home last night?" It was Mr. 11 Gunderson, our janitor, whom we all loved. He was nice and he was funny and he was old with white hair, thick glasses and an unbelievable number of keys. I could hear them jingling as he walked across the playfield. I felt incredibly happy to see him.

He let me push his wheeled garbage can between the different portables as he 12 unlocked each room. He let me turn on the lights and raise the window shades and I saw my school slowly come to life. I saw Mrs. Holman, our school secretary, walk into the office without her orange lipstick on yet. She waved.

I saw the fifth-grade teacher, Mr. Cunningham, walking under the breezeway 13 eating a hard roll. He waved.

And I saw my teacher, Mrs. Claire LeSane, walking toward us in a red coat and 14 calling my name in a very happy and surprised way, and suddenly my throat got tight and my eyes stung and I ran toward her crying. It was something that surprised us both.

It's only thinking about it now, 28 years later, that I realize I was crying from 15 relief. I was with my teacher, and in a while I was going to sit at my desk, with my crayons and pencils and books and classmates all around me, and for the next six hours I was going to enjoy a thoroughly secure, warm and stable world. It was a world I absolutely relied on. Without it, I don't know where I would have gone that morning.

Mrs. LeSane asked me what was wrong and when I said "Nothing," she seem- 16 ingly left it at that. But she asked me if I would carry her purse for her, an honor above all honors, and she asked if I wanted to come into Room 2 early and paint.

She believed in the natural healing power of painting and drawing for trou- 17 bled children. In the back of her room there was always a drawing table and an easel with plenty of supplies, and sometimes during the day she would come up to you for what seemed like no good reason and quietly ask if you wanted to go to the back table and "make some pictures for Mrs. LeSane." We all had a chance at it—to sit apart from the class for a while to paint, draw and silently work out impossible problems on 11×17 sheets of newsprint.

Drawing came to mean everything to me. At the back table in Room 2, I learned 18 to build myself a life preserver that I could carry into my home.

We all know that a good education system saves lives, but the people of this 19 country are still told that cutting the budget for public schools is necessary, that poor salaries for teachers are all we can manage and that art, music and all creative activities must be the first to go when times are lean.

Before- and after-school programs are cut and we are told that public schools 20
are not made for baby-sitting children. If parents are neglectful temporarily or permanently, for whatever reason, it's certainly sad, but their unlucky children must
fend for themselves. Or slip through the cracks. Or wander in a dark night alone.

We are told in a thousand ways that not only are public schools not important, 21
but that the children who attend them, the children who need them most, are not
important either. We leave them to learn from the blind eye of a television, or to the
mercy of "a thousand points of light"[1] that can be as far away as stars.

I was lucky. I had Mrs. LeSane. I had Mr. Gunderson. I had an abundance of 22
art supplies. And I had a particular brand of neglect in my home that allowed me
to slip away and get to them. But what about the rest of the kids who weren't as
lucky? What happened to them?

By the time the bell rang that morning I had finished my drawing and Mrs. 23
LeSane pinned it up on the special bulletin board she reserved for drawings from
the back table. It was the same picture I always drew—a sun in the corner of a blue
sky over a nice house with flowers all around it.

Mrs. LeSane asked us to please stand, face the flag, place our right hands over our 24
hearts and say the Pledge of Allegiance. Children across the country do it faithfully.
I wonder now when the country will face its children and say a pledge right back.

Questions for Critical Reading

1. What is the selection's thesis? Locate the sentence(s) in which Barry states her main
   idea. If she doesn't state the thesis explicitly, express it in your own words.

2. Various details from Barry's narrative essay let the reader know that her childhood
   home life was far from perfect. Skim back over the essay and make a list of the
   details she includes to describe what she refers to as "a particular brand of neglect
   in [her] home" (paragraph 22).

3. Barry says that the first time she sneaked out of her house when she was seven, she
   did not know why she was leaving and she "did not think about it" (paragraph 6). She
   only knew that she was seized by panic and had to escape. From what was she escap-
   ing, and what was there about her school that made it a "sanctuary" for her? Why do
   you think she "did not want to think about" why she was sneaking away from home?

4. What details both for and against budget cuts in education are included in Barry's
   essay?

Questions About the Writer's Craft

1. **The pattern.** What kind of organizational pattern does Barry use in her narrative essay,
   and in what ways is this pattern an appropriate choice for organizing the selection?

2. **Repeated references.** In her essay Barry uses repeated references to the absence of
   sound. Locate those references and reflect on how she uses them. In what ways do
   you think they add to or take away from the essay's effectiveness?

---

[1] In his inaugural address, President George H. W. Bush used this phrase to encourage nongovernmental community
action (editors' note).

3. **Other patterns.** While the primary focus of Barry's essay is on narrating a story from her childhood and the important role that school played as a safe refuge, her essay is also *persuasive*. She takes a stand and makes a strong *argument*. In what ways does the personal anecdote she tells in the first sixteen paragraphs of the essay make her political argument stronger than it would be had she not included her own story?

4. **Reflections and discoveries.** In the essay, Barry reflects on her childhood experience and comes to realizations about herself that she did not make when she was a small child. Read through the essay, listing the discoveries she makes about herself as she reflects. In what ways do Barry's reflections add to the effectiveness of her essay?

Writing Assignments Using Narration as a Pattern of Development

1. Barry's essay tells about a time when she was seized by panic and felt that she had to escape. Write an essay about a time in your life when you felt that you had to get away from a particular situation—a time when you had to make a change in your life. Go beyond telling your story and reflect on *why* you needed to get away and *why* you took the steps needed to make the change.

2. Barry writes about individuals in her life who were there when she desperately needed them. Write a narrative essay about a time when someone reached out to you and helped you when you especially needed help. Use vivid details and believable dialogue to enrich your essay.

Writing Assignment Combining Patterns of Development

3. In her essay Barry combines *narration* and *argumentation-persuasion*. Write an essay in which you *argue* for an educational or child-rearing issue that matters to you. Include a story that helps the reader understand why the issue is important to you. Take time to conduct any research needed to substantiate your claims, and include those findings in your essay. Consider using images—perhaps charts or graphs—that illustrate your findings for your readers.

JOAN MURRAY

Joan Murray—a poet, writer, editor, and playwright—was born in New York City in 1945. She attended Hunter College and New York University, and she published her first volume of poetry, which she also illustrated, in 1975. Three of her poetry books—*Queen of the Mist, Looking for the Parade,* and *The Same Water*—have won prizes. Her most recent volume of poetry is *Dancing on the Edge*, published in 2002. This essay appeared in the "Lives" section of the weekly *New York Times Magazine* on May 13, 2007.

Pre-Reading Journal Entry

We are used to having our mothers care for us, but sometimes we have to care for our mothers. Reflect on an occasion when you had to do something important for your mother or other caregiver. What was the situation? How did you help? How did you feel about helping someone who normally helped you? Use your journal to respond to these questions.

Someone's Mother

Hitchhiking is generally illegal where I live in upstate New York, but it's not unusual to see someone along Route 20 with an outstretched thumb or a hand-made sign saying "Boston." This hitchhiker, though, was waving both arms in the air and grinning like a president boarding Air Force One. 1

I was doing 60—eager to get home after a dental appointment in Albany—and I was a mile past the hitchhiker before something made me turn back. I couldn't say if the hitchhiker was a man or a woman. All I knew was that the hitchhiker was old. 2

As I drove back up the hill, I eyed the hitchhiker in the distance: dark blue raincoat, jaunty black beret. Thin arms waving, spine a little bent. Wisps of white hair lilting as the trucks whizzed by. I made a U-turn and pulled up on the gravel, face to face with an eager old woman who kept waving till I stopped. I saw no broken-down vehicle. There was no vehicle at all. She wore the same broad grin I noticed when I passed her. 3

I rolled my window down. "Can I call someone for you?" 4

"No, I'm fine—I just need a ride." 5

"Where are you going?" 6

"Nassau." 7

That was three miles away. "Are you going there to shop?" 8

"No. I live there." 9

"What are you doing here?" I asked with a tone I hadn't used since my son was a teenager. 10

"I was out for a walk." 11

I glanced down the road: Jet's Autobody. Copeland Coating. Thoma Tire Company. And the half-mile hill outside Nassau—so steep that there's a second lane for trucks. She must have climbed the shoulder of that hill. And the next one. And the next. Until something made her stop and throw her hands in the air. 12

"Did you get lost?" I asked, trying to conceal my alarm. 13

"It was a nice day," she said with a little cry. "Can't an old lady go for a walk on a nice day and get lost?" 14

It wasn't a question meant to be answered. She came around to the passenger side, opened the door and sat down. On our way to Nassau, she admitted to being 92. Though she ducked my questions about her name, her address and her family. "Just leave me at the drugstore," she said. 15

"I'll take you home," I said. "Then you can call someone." 16

"Please," she said, "just leave me at the drugstore." 17

"I can't leave you there," I replied just as firmly. "I'm going to take you to your house. Or else to the police station." 18

"No, no," she begged. She was agitated now. "If my son finds out, he'll put me in a home." 19

Already I was seeing my own mother, who's 90. A few years ago, she was liv- 20
ing in her house on Long Island, surrounded by her neighbors, her bird feeders,
her azaleas. Then one morning she phoned my brother to say she didn't remember
how to get dressed anymore. A few weeks later, with sorrow and worry, we arranged her move to a nursing home.

I noticed that the hitchhiker had a white dove pinned to her collar. "Do you 21
belong to a church?" I tried. "Yes," she said. She was grinning. "I'd like to take you
there," I said. "No, please," she said again. "My son will find out."

Things were getting clearer. "You've gotten lost before?" 22

"A few times," she shrugged. "But I always find my way home. Just take me 23
to the drugstore."

As we drove, I kept thinking about my mother, watched over and cared for 24
in a bright, clean place. I also thought about her empty bird feeders, her azaleas
blooming for no one, the way she whispers on the phone, "I don't know anyone
here."

When I pulled into the parking strip beside the drugstore, the hitchhiker let her- 25
self out. "I just need to sit on the step for a while," she said before closing the door.
I stepped out after her. "Can't I take you home?" I asked as gently as I could.

She looked into my eyes for a moment. "I don't know where I live," she said in 26
the tiniest voice. "But someone will come along who knows me. They always do."

I watched as she sat herself down on the step. Already she had dismissed me 27
from her service. She was staring ahead with her grin intact, waiting for the next
person who would aid her.

I should call the police, I thought. But then surely her son would be told. I should 28
speak with the pharmacists. Surely they might know her—though they might know
her son as well. Yet who was I to keep this incident from him? And yet how could
I help him put the hitchhiker in a home?

"Promise me you'll tell the druggist if no one comes soon," I said to her with 29
great seriousness.

"I promise," she said with a cheerful little wave. 30

Questions for Critical Reading

1. What is the selection's thesis? Locate the sentence(s) in which Murray states
   her main idea. If she doesn't state the thesis explicitly, express it in your own
   words.

2. What is the external conflict Murray experiences in this essay? What is the internal
   conflict?

3. In paragraph 22, the author says, "Things were getting clearer." What does she
   mean by this?

4. Why does Murray finally go along with the hitchhiker's wishes?

Questions About the Writer's Craft

1. **The pattern.** How does Murray organize the events in this essay? How does she keep the reader oriented as her story progresses?

2. **Other patterns.** In some passages, Murray *describes* the hitchhiker's appearance. What do these descriptions contribute to the narrative?

3. **The author's thoughts.** In paragraphs 12, 20, 24, and 28, Murray tells us her thoughts. What effect do these sections have on the pace of the narrative? How do they affect our understanding of what is happening?

4. **Dialogue.** Murray uses a lot of dialogue in this essay. Explain why the use of dialogue is (or is not) effective. What function does the dialogue have?

Writing Assignments Using Narration as a Pattern of Development

1. Murray's encounter with the hitchhiker happens as she is driving home. Recall a time when you were traveling in a car, bus, or other vehicle and something surprising occurred. Were you frightened, puzzled, amused? Did you learn something about people or about yourself? Tell the story using first-person narration, being sure to include your thoughts as well as your actions and the actions of others.

2. Write a narrative about an incident in your life in which a stranger helped you, and explain how this made you feel. The experience might have made you grateful, resentful, or anxious like the hitchhiker. Use either flashback or flashforward to emphasize an event in your narrative.

Writing Assignment Combining Patterns of Development

3. Did Murray do the right thing when she left the elderly woman sitting in front of the drugstore? Write an essay in which you *argue* that Murray did or did not act properly. You can support your argument using *examples* from the essay showing the hitchhiker's state of mental and physical health. You can also support your argument by presenting the possible positive or negative effects of Murray's action, depending on your point of view.

Additional Writing Topics: Narration

General Assignments

Using narration, develop one of these topics into an essay.

1. An emergency that brought out the best or worst in you

2. The hazards of taking children out to eat

3. An incident that made you believe in fate

4. Your best or worst day at school or work

5. An important learning experience

6. A narrow escape

7. Your first date or first day on the job

8. A memorable childhood experience

9. An unpleasant confrontation

10. An imagined meeting with a historical figure

Assignments Using Multimedia

Use the suggested media to develop a narrative essay on one of these topics:

1. The best (or worst) vacation of your life (photos)

2. A school experience that had a positive impact on you (sketches or photos)

3. A family outing with an unexpected outcome (photos)

4. Something you did that you wish you could undo (diagram, photo)

5. A civic event you participated in (photos and/or weblinks)

Assignments with a Specific Purpose, Audience, and Point of View

1. **Academic life.** Write an article for your old high school newspaper. The article will be read primarily by seniors who are planning to go away to college next year. In the article, narrate a story that points to some truth about the "breaking away" stage of life.

2. **Academic life.** A friend of yours has seen someone cheat on a test, plagiarize an entire essay, or seriously violate some other academic policy. In a letter, convince this friend to inform the instructor or a campus administrator by narrating an incident in which a witness did (or did not) speak up in such a situation. Tell what happened as a result.

3. **Civic activity.** You have had a disturbing encounter with one of the people who seems to have "fallen through the cracks" of society—a street person, an unwanted child, or anyone else who is alone and abandoned. Write a letter to the local newspaper describing this encounter. Your purpose is to arouse people's indignation and compassion and to get help for such unfortunates.

4. **Civic activity.** Your younger brother, sister, relative, or neighborhood friend can't wait to be your age. Write a letter in which you narrate a dramatic story that shows the young person that your age isn't as wonderful as he or she thinks. Be sure to select a story that the person can understand and appreciate.

5. **Workplace action.** As fund-raiser for a particular organization (for example, Red Cross, SPCA, Big Brothers/Big Sisters), you're sending a newsletter to contributors. Support your cause by telling the story of a time when your organization made all the difference—the blood donation that saved a life, the animal that was rescued from abuse, and so on.

6. **Workplace action.** A customer has written a letter to you (or your boss) complaining about a bad experience that he or she had with someone in your workplace. On the basis of that single experience, the customer now regards your company and its employees with great suspicion. It's your job to respond to this complaint. Write a letter to the customer balancing his or her negative picture by narrating a story that shows the "flip side" of your company and its employees.

Chapter 12
Illustration

Learning Objectives

12.1 Understand how you can use the illustration pattern to develop your essays.

12.2 Consider how illustration can fit your purpose and audience.

12.3 Develop prewriting strategies for using illustration in an essay.

12.4 Develop strategies for writing an illustration essay.

12.5 Use strategies for revising your illustration essay.

12.6 Analyze how illustration is used effectively in a student-written selection.

What Is Illustration?

12.1 Understand how you can use the illustration pattern to develop your essays.

If someone asked you, "Have you been to any good restaurants lately?" you probably wouldn't answer "Yes" and then immediately change the subject. Most likely, you would go on to **illustrate** with examples. Perhaps you'd give the names of restaurants you've enjoyed and talk briefly about the specific things you liked. Such examples and details are needed to convince others that your opinion—in this or any matter—is valid.

Examples are equally important when you write an essay. Facts, details, anecdotes, statistics, expert opinion, and personal observations are at the heart of effective writing; they give your work substance and solidity.

How Illustration Fits Your Purpose and Audience

12.2 Consider how illustration can fit your purpose and audience.

The wording of assignments and essay exam questions may signal the need for illustration:

> Some observers claim that college students are less interested in learning than in getting ahead in their careers. Cite evidence to support or refute this claim.

> A number of commentators claim that social media, such as Facebook and Twitter, have caused us to value personal privacy less than we did before. Basing your conclusion on your own experiences and observations, indicate whether you think this point of view is reasonable.

The phrases "Cite evidence" and "Basing your conclusion on your own experiences and observations" signal that you should develop each essay through illustration (example).

 Usually, though, you won't be told so explicitly to provide examples. Instead, as you think about the best way to achieve your essay's purpose, you'll see the need for illustrative details—no matter which patterns of development you use. For instance, to *persuade* skeptical readers that the country needs a national health system, you might mention specific cases to dramatize the inadequacy of our current health-care system: a family bankrupted by medical bills, an uninsured accident victim turned away by a hospital, a chronically ill person rapidly deteriorating because he didn't have enough money to visit a doctor.

Or imagine a lightly satiric piece that pokes fun at cat lovers. Insisting that "cat people" are pretty strange creatures, you might make your point—and make readers chuckle—with a series of examples *contrasting* cat lovers and dog lovers: the qualities admired by each group (loyalty in dogs versus independence in cats) and the different expectations each group has for its pets (dog lovers want Fido to be obedient and lovable, whereas cat lovers are satisfied with Felix's occasional spurts of docility and affection).

Illustration **185**

Whether you use illustration as a primary or supplemental method of development, it serves a number of important purposes.

1. **Illustrations make writing *interesting*.** Assume you're writing an essay showing that television commercials are biased against women. Your essay would be lifeless and boring if all it did was repeat, in a general way, that commercials present stereotyped views of women:

   Original
   An anti-female bias is rampant in television commercials. It is very much alive, yet most viewers seem to take it all in stride. Few people protest the obviously sexist characters and statements on such commercials. Surely, these commercials misrepresent the way most of us live.

   Without interesting particulars, readers may respond, "Who cares?" But if you provide specific examples, you'll attract your readers' attention:

   Revised
   An anti-female bias is rampant in television commercials. Although millions of women hold responsible jobs outside the home, commercials continue to portray women as simple creatures who spend much of their time thinking about wax buildup, cottony-soft bathroom tissue, and static-free clothes. Men, apparently, have better things to do than fret over such mundane household matters. How many commercials can you recall that depict men proclaiming the virtues of squeaky-clean dishes or sparkling bathrooms? Not many.

2. **Illustrations make writing persuasive.** Most writing conveys a point, but many readers are reluctant to accept someone else's point of view unless evidence demonstrates its validity. Without specific examples your readers will question your position's validity.

3. **Illustrations help explain difficult, abstract, or unusual ideas.** As a writer, you have a responsibility to your readers to make difficult concepts concrete and understandable. Examples ground your discussion, making it immediate and concrete, preventing it from flying off into the vague and theoretical.

4. **Illustrations help prevent unintended ambiguity.** All of us have experienced the frustration of having someone misinterpret what we say. In face-to-face communication, we can provide on-the-spot clarification. In writing, however, instantaneous feedback isn't available, so it's crucial that meaning be as unambiguous as possible. Illustrations will help.

Prewriting Strategies

12.3 Develop prewriting strategies for using illustration in an essay.

The following checklist shows how you can apply prewriting strategies to illustration.

☑ **Illustration: A Prewriting Checklist**

Choose a Subject to Illustrate

☐ What general situation or phenomenon (for example, campus apathy, organic farming) can you depict through illustration?

☐ What difficult or misunderstood concept (nuclear winter, passive aggression) would examples help to explain and make concrete?

Determine Your Purpose, Audience, Tone, and Point of View

☐ What is your purpose in writing?

☐ What audience do you have in mind?

☐ What tone and point of view will best serve your purpose and lead readers to adopt the desired attitude toward the subject?

Use Prewriting to Generate Examples

☐ How can brainstorming, freewriting, or mapping help you generate relevant examples from your own or others' experiences?

☐ How could library research help you gather pertinent examples (expert opinion, case studies, statistics)?

Strategies for Using Illustration in an Essay

12.4 Develop strategies for writing an illustration essay.

After prewriting, you're ready to draft your essay. The following suggestions and Figure 12.1 will be helpful whether you use illustration as a dominant or supportive pattern of development.

1. **Select the number and types of examples to include.**

   Examples can take several forms, including specific names (of people, places, products, and so on), anecdotes, personal observations, and expert opinion as well as facts, statistics, and case studies gathered through research. Once you've used prewriting to generate as many examples as possible, you're ready to limit your examples to the strongest. Keeping your thesis, audience, tone, and point of view in mind, ask yourself several key questions: "Which examples support my thesis? Which do not? Which are most convincing? Which are most likely to interest readers and clarify meaning?"

   You may include several brief examples within a single sentence:

   > The French people's fascination with some American literary figures, such as Poe and Hawthorne, is understandable, but their great respect for "artists" like comedian Jerry Lewis is a mystery to many Americans.

Illustration   **187**

Figure 12.1 Development Diagram: Writing an Illustration Essay

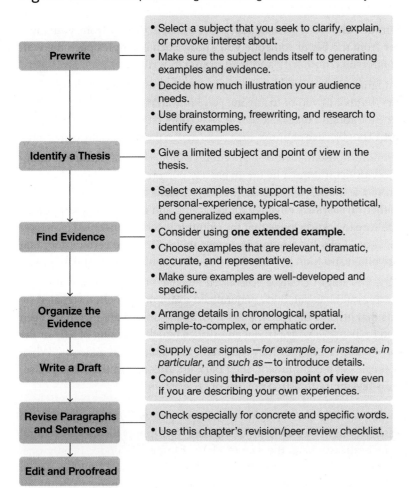

Prewrite	• Select a subject that you seek to clarify, explain, or provoke interest about. • Make sure the subject lends itself to generating examples and evidence. • Decide how much illustration your audience needs. • Use brainstorming, freewriting, and research to identify examples.
Identify a Thesis	• Give a limited subject and point of view in the thesis.
Find Evidence	• Select examples that support the thesis: personal-experience, typical-case, hypothetical, and generalized examples. • Consider using **one extended example**. • Choose examples that are relevant, dramatic, accurate, and representative. • Make sure examples are well-developed and specific.
Organize the Evidence	• Arrange details in chronological, spatial, simple-to-complex, or emphatic order.
Write a Draft	• Supply clear signals—*for example, for instance, in particular*, and *such as*—to introduce details. • Consider using **third-person point of view** even if you are describing your own experiences.
Revise Paragraphs and Sentences	• Check especially for concrete and specific words. • Use this chapter's revision/peer review checklist.
Edit and Proofread	

Or you may develop a paragraph with a number of "for instances":

A uniquely American style of movie acting reached its peak in the 1950s. Certain charismatic actors completely abandoned the stage techniques and tradition that had been the foundation of acting up to that time. Instead of articulating their lines clearly, the actors mumbled; instead of making firm eye contact with their colleagues, they hung their heads, shifted their eyes, and even talked with their eyes closed. Marlon Brando, Montgomery Clift, and James Dean were three actors who exemplified this new trend.

As the preceding paragraph shows, *several examples* are usually needed to achieve your purpose. An essay with the thesis "Video games are dangerously violent" wouldn't be convincing if you gave only one example of a violent video game. Several strong examples would be needed for readers to feel you had illustrated your point sufficiently.

As a general rule, you should strive for variety in the kinds of examples you include:

- You might choose a *personal-experience example* drawn from your own life or from the life of someone you know. Such examples pack the wallop of personal authority and lend drama to writing.

- You might include a *typical-case example,* an actual event or situation that did occur—but not to you or to anyone you know. (Perhaps you learned about the event through a magazine article, an account on a website, or a television report.) The objective nature of such cases makes them especially convincing.

- You might choose to include a speculative or *hypothetical example* ("Imagine how difficult it must be for an elderly person to carry bags of groceries from the market to a bus stop several blocks away"). You'll find that hypothetical cases are effective for clarifying and dramatizing key points, but be sure to acknowledge that the example is indeed invented ("*Suppose* that..." or "Let's for a moment *assume* that..."). Make certain, too, that the invented situation is easily imagined and could conceivably happen.

- Finally, you might create a *generalized example*—one that is a composite of the typical or usual. Such generalized examples are often signaled by words that involve the reader ("*All of us,* at one time or another, have been driven to distraction by a trivial annoyance like the buzzing of a fly or the sting of a paper cut"), or they may refer to humanity in general ("When *most people* get a compliment, they perk up, preen, and think the praise-giver is blessed with astute powers of observation").

Occasionally, *one extended example,* fully developed with many details, can support an essay. It might be possible, for instance, to support the thesis "Federal legislation, which already bans the sale of alcohol to people under twenty-one, should also ban its private consumption by those individuals" with a single compelling, highly detailed example of the effects of one young person's drunken-driving spree.

The examples you choose should also have the following characteristics:

- **Examples must be *relevant*.** That is, they must have direct bearing on the point you want to make. When examples *contradict,* rather than support, your thesis, readers are apt to dismiss what you have to say.

- **Examples should be *dramatic* whenever possible.** Say you're writing an essay to show that society needs to take more steps to protect children from abuse. Simply stating that many parents hit their children isn't likely to make a strong impression in the reader's mind. However, graphic examples (children with stab wounds, welts, and burn marks) are apt to create a sense of urgency and outrage in the reader.

- **Examples must be *accurate*.** Exercise special caution when using statistics. A commercial may claim, "In a taste test, 80 percent of those questioned

Illustration **189**

indicated that they preferred Fizzy Cola." Impressed? Don't be—at least, not until you find out how the test was conducted. Perhaps the participants had to choose between Fizzy Cola and battery acid, or perhaps there were only five participants, all Fizzy Cola vice presidents.

- **Examples should be** *representative.* Picking the oddball, one-in-a-million example to support a point—and passing it off as typical—is dishonest. Consider an essay with this thesis: "Part-time jobs contribute to academic success." Citing only one example of a student who works at a job twenty-five hours a week while earning straight *A*'s isn't playing fair. Why not? You've made a *hasty generalization* based on only one case. To be convincing, you need to show how holding down a job affects *most* students' academic performance.

2. **Develop your examples sufficiently.**

To ensure that you get your ideas across, you must make sure your examples are *specific.* An essay on the types of heroes in American movies wouldn't succeed if you simply strung together a series of undeveloped examples in paragraphs like this one:

Original
Heroes in American movies usually fall into types. One kind of hero is the tight-lipped loner, men like Clint Eastwood and Humphrey Bogart. Another movie hero is the quiet, shy, or fumbling type who has appeared in movies since the beginning. The main characteristic of this hero is lovableness, as seen in actors like Jimmy Stewart. Perhaps the most one-dimensional and predictable hero is the tough guy who battles seemingly impossible odds. This kind of hero is best illustrated by Sylvester Stallone as Rocky and by Vin Diesel as Dominic Toretto and Riddick.

The examples in the preceding paragraph could be developed in paragraphs of their own. You could, for instance, develop the first example this way:

Revised
Heroes can be tight-lipped loners who appear out of nowhere, form no permanent attachments, and then walk, drive, or ride off into the sunset. In most of his Westerns, from the low-budget "spaghetti Westerns" of the 1960s to *Unforgiven* in 1992, *Million Dollar Baby* in 2004, and *Gran Torino* in 2008, Clint Eastwood personifies this kind of hero. He is remote, mysterious, and untalkative. Yet he guns down an evil sheriff, runs other villains out of town, helps a handicapped girl, reluctantly trains a young female boxer, and even more reluctantly helps a young Hmong refugee—acts that cement his heroic status. The loner might also be Sam Spade as played by Humphrey Bogart. Spade solves the crime and sends the guilty off to jail, yet he holds his emotions in check and has no permanent ties beyond his faithful secretary and shabby office. One gets the feeling that he could walk away from these, too, if necessary. Even in *The Right Stuff*, an account of the early U.S. astronauts, the scriptwriters mold Chuck Yeager, the man who broke the sound barrier, into a classic loner.

Yeager, portrayed by the aloof Sam Shepard, has a wife, but he is nevertheless insular. Taking mute pride in his ability to distance himself from politicians, bureaucrats, even colleagues, he soars into space, dignified and detached.

3. **Organize the examples.**

If, as is usually the case, several examples support your point, be sure to present the examples in an *organized* manner. Often you'll find that other *patterns of development* (cause-effect, comparison-contrast, definition, and so on) suggest ways to sequence examples. Let's say you're writing an essay showing that stay-at-home vacations offer numerous opportunities to relax. You might begin the essay with examples that *contrast* stay-at-home and getaway vacations. Then you might move to a *process analysis* that illustrates different techniques for unwinding at home. The essay might end with examples showing the *effect* of such leisurely at-home breaks.

You need to select an organizational approach consistent with your *purpose* and *thesis*. Imagine you're writing an essay about students' adjustment during the first months of college. The supporting examples could be arranged *chronologically*. You might start by illustrating the ambivalence many students feel the first day of college after their parents have dropped them off. You might then offer an anecdote or two about students' frequent calls to Mom and Dad during the opening weeks of the semester. The essay might close with an account of students' reluctance to leave campus at the midyear break.

Similarly, an essay demonstrating that a room often reflects the character of its occupant might be organized *spatially:* from the empty soda cans on the floor to the spitballs on the ceiling. In an essay illustrating the kinds of skills taught in a composition course, you might move from *simple* to *complex* examples: starting with relatively matter-of-fact skills such as spelling and punctuation and ending with more conceptually difficult skills like formulating a thesis and organizing an essay. Last, the *emphatic sequence*—in which you lead from your first example to your final, most significant one—is another effective way to organize an essay with many examples. A composition about Americans' characteristic impatience might progress from minor examples (dependence on fast food, obsession with texting) to more disturbing manifestations of impatience (using drugs as quick solutions to problems, advocating simple answers to complex international problems: "Bomb them!").

4. **Choose a point of view.**

Many essays developed by illustration place the subject in the foreground and the writer in the background. Such an approach calls for the *third-person point of view.* For example, even if you draw examples from your own personal experience, you can present them without using the *first-person "I."* You might convert such personal material into generalized examples, or you might describe the personal experience as if it happened to someone else. Just because an event happened to you personally doesn't mean you have to use the first-person point of view. Remember also that many instructors discourage the use of "I" in an academic assignment.

Illustration **191**

Revision Strategies

12.5 Use strategies for revising your illustration essay.

Once you have a draft of the essay, you're ready to revise. The following checklist will help your peers provide feedback and aid you in revising your essay.

☑ Illustration: A Revision/Peer Review Checklist

Revise Overall Meaning and Structure

☐ What thesis is being advanced? Which examples don't support the thesis? Should these examples be deleted, or should the thesis be reshaped to fit the examples? Why?

☐ Which patterns of development and methods of organization (chronological, spatial, simple-to-complex, emphatic) provide the essay's framework? Would other ordering principles be more effective? If so, which ones?

Revise Paragraph Development

☐ Which paragraphs contain too many or too few examples? Which contain examples that are too brief or too extended? Which include insufficiently or overly detailed examples?

☐ Which paragraphs rely on predictable examples? How could the examples be made more compelling?

☐ Which paragraphs include examples that are atypical or inaccurate?

Revise Sentences and Words

☐ What signal devices (*for example, for instance, in particular, such as*) introduce examples and clarify the line of thought? Where are there too many or too few of these devices?

☐ Where would more varied sentence structure heighten the effect of the essay's illustrations?

☐ Where would more concrete and specific words make the examples more effective?

Student Essay: From Prewriting Through Revision

12.6 Analyze how illustration is used effectively in a student-written selection.

The following student essay was written by Charlene Adams in response to this assignment:

> In "Tweens: Ten Going on Sixteen," Kay Hymowitz provides examples of the ways our culture pushes children to grow up too fast, incorporating information from a variety of sources to support her thesis. Write an essay in which you explore another cultural phenomenon that affects young people. To substantiate your claim, provide examples that support a claim you consider important, using information from at least three outside sources, including personal interviews and published works.

Figure 12.2 Mapping the Limited Subject

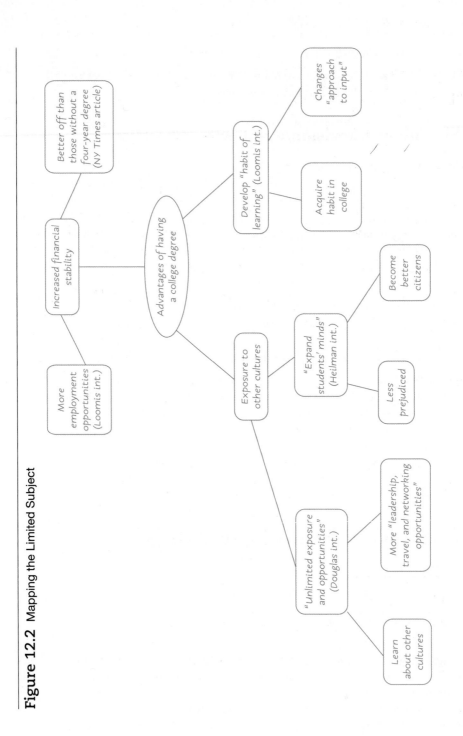

Illustration   **193**

As Charlene considered possible topics for her essay, she remembered a recent discussion in her journalism class. Her professor, David Loomis, had mentioned that many people think the benefits of a college degree are a thing of the past but that a college degree still confers many benefits. Professor Loomis mentioned a recent article that substantiated his claim. Charlene vividly remembered the discussion and the impact it had on her and her classmates. Many of them were doubting whether their time in college would be truly beneficial to them, and Professor Loomis's remarks had been reassuring. Charlene decided that she'd like to research the topic further and see what she could discover.

Charlene began her research by contacting Professor Loomis, explaining to him that she was thinking about writing an essay on the topic and asking if she could interview him. She also made plans to interview Patrice Douglas, a student she had met in Dr. Loomis's class, along with another journalism professor, Patricia Heilman. In addition, she did online research and located the article to which Professor Loomis had referred. As she conducted her research and reviewed her findings, her essay began to take shape. She decided to write an essay on the benefits of a college degree and provide examples of the various ways a four-year college degree can be advantageous.

After preparing her interview questions, conducting her interviews, and further researching her topic, Charlene decided to organize her material by mapping the limited subject, a prewriting technique she had learned about in her composition class. Charlene's map appears in Figure 12.2.

As you read Charlene's essay, consider how well it applies the principles of illustration. The annotations on Charlene's composition and the commentary following it will help you look at the essay more closely.

Professors Open Up About the Benefits of a College Degree
by Charlene Adams

Introduction

1 It's no secret that for the past few years the American economy has been in less-than-perfect condition. With the cost of a college education going up and the possibility of finding a well-paying job seemingly going down, the benefits of a college education seem to be dwindling; however, things are not always what they seem. A college education is more important today than ever before.

Thesis

Interview quote that serves as a topic sentence to introduce the first of three major points

2 "The people who are more likely to be employed are people with college degrees," says David Loomis, Indiana University of Pennsylvania (IUP) journalism professor. "How much more likely? Twice as likely as people who have only a high school education," Loomis adds. To back up this assertion, Loomis points to a January 2013 *New York Times* article, "Benefits of College Degree in Recession Are Outlined," which reports that although almost everyone has taken an economic hit from the recession, college graduates have fared and continue to fare the best.

Paragraph with specific example to support first major point

Topic sentence

The *New York Times* article uses data from the Pew Economic Mobility Project to illustrate employment trends. Richard Pérez-Peña, the author of the *New York Times* article, states that according to the Pew report, "People with four-year college degrees saw a 5 percent drop in wages, compared with a 12 percent decrease for their peers with associate's degrees, and a 10 percent decline for high school graduates." (See Figure 1.)

Paragraph with specific example to support first major point

3

Topic sentence that starts with a transition

First of three paragraphs with specific examples to support second major point

The financial perks of a college education are obvious; however, financial benefits aren't the only advantages college graduates experience. Patrice Douglas, a junior at IUP majoring in management information systems, says that college is a huge help in this troubled economy because of the "unlimited exposure and opportunities." Douglas goes on to state the following: "The benefits of a college education include educating yourself on other cultures and people in the diverse college atmosphere. College students benefit from the numerous leadership, travel, and networking opportunities which aren't so easily accessed without being in a college or university."

4

Second paragraph with specific examples to support second major point

IUP journalism professor Patricia Heilman adds that, contrary to popular belief, "The purpose of a college education is not just to get a job." Heilman goes on to state that "the real purpose of a college education is to expand students' minds—to introduce them to other cultures and other schools of thought. And [the hope is that] when they graduate college, they will have learned how much they don't know. So for the rest of their lives, they are continuing to study and to learn, and that makes them better citizens." Professor Heilman adds that because "college graduates are more knowledgeable about other cultures, they do not approach people from other cultures with a preconceived set of prejudices because, at almost all colleges, [students] have probably had classes with people who were from other parts of the world."

5

Third paragraph with specific examples to support second major point

Professor Heilman believes that the benefits of a college education are so tremendous that to simply limit them to money or a job is "closing the door to all the experiences individuals could have that would affect them for the rest of their lives." She adds that studies show that college graduates are more likely to vote in elections, so they're "more active in the political process" than people who did not attend college.

6

Topic sentence that introduces the third major point

Only one paragraph suports the third major point

In addition to increasing financial stability and exposure to other cultures, a third advantage of having a college education is what Professor Loomis refers to as the "habit of learning." He says that whether students attend a university, a community college, or a technical school, they are likely to acquire this invaluable habit. "Institutions of higher learning systematize this habit of learning in a way that makes it almost impossible to forget," he adds. "It's the way that an individual approaches input, any kind of input, that is one of the great advantages of higher education."

7

The first of two concluding paragraphs that elaborate on the thesis and bring the article to closure

The benefits of a college degree are many. From increasing the likelihood of financial stability, to becoming more familiar with other cultures and developing the habit of learning, a college education is a gift that will undoubtedly keep on giving.

8

Illustration **195**

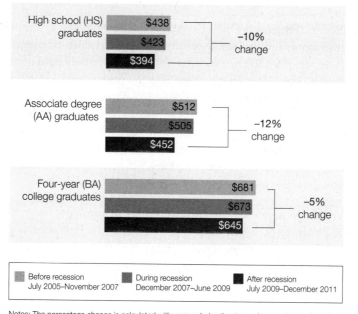

AVERAGE WEEKLY WAGE

High school (HS) graduates
$438
$423
$394
−10% change

Associate degree (AA) graduates
$512
$505
$452
−12% change

Four-year (BA) college graduates
$681
$673
$645
−5% change

Before recession
July 2005–November 2007

During recession
December 2007–June 2009

After recession
July 2009–December 2011

Notes: The percentage change is calculated with unrounded estimates and may not reproduce the percentage change exactly based on the rounded estimates presented here. All statistics are weight-adjusted for probability of selection and household non-response. All differences are significant at the 1 percent level or lower with the exception of the percent change between the high school and associate degree groups.

Source: Current Population Survey (CPS), 2005–2011

FIG. 1

Graphic to offer additional support to first major point

Associate Degree and High School Graduate Wage Declines Were Two Times Higher. From *Current Population Survey (CPS)*, 2005–2011 (qtd. in Pew 16).

Final closing quote that emphasizes the thesis

Professor Loomis sums up the benefits of having a college 9 degree with his comment: "The more education you get, the better off you are."

Works Cited

Douglas, Patrice. Personal interview, 3 Feb. 2013.

Heilman, Patricia. Personal interview, 5 Feb. 2013.

Loomis, David. Personal interview, 30 Jan. 2013.

Pérez-Peña, Richard. "Benefits of College Degree in Recession Are Outlined." *The New York Times*, 10 Jan. 2013, p. A15.

Pew Economic Mobility Project. "How Much Protection Does a College Degree Afford? The Impact of the Recession on Recent College Graduates." *The Pew Charitable Trusts*, 10 Jan. 2013, www.pewtrusts.org/~/media/legacy/uploadedfiles/pcs_assets/2013/pewcollegegradsrecessionreportpdf.pdf.

Commentary

THESIS   In "Professors Open Up About the Benefits of a College Degree," Charlene Adams explores the various ways that having a college degree can positively affect an individual's life. She begins by pointing out a widely held assumption: "With the cost of a college education going up and the possibility of finding a well-paying job seemingly going down, the benefits of a college education seem to be dwindling...." This reference allows her to offer a contrast ("however, things are not always what they seem") to the assumption and then state the main idea she is communicating: "A college education is more important today than ever before." With this statement she makes it clear to her readers that she believes earning a college degree is beneficial, even in depressed economic conditions.

EVIDENCE   Support for the thesis consists of numerous examples gathered from personal interviews, a *New York Times* article, and a Pew report. These examples are organized around the three major points Charlene makes in her essay. She elaborates on these points throughout her essay and summarizes them explicitly as she brings her essay to a close: "From increasing the likelihood of financial stability, to becoming more familiar with other cultures and developing the habit of learning, a college education is a gift that will undoubtedly keep on giving." Charlene uses two paragraphs and a visual to develop her first point, three paragraphs to develop her second point, and one short paragraph to develop her third point.

ORGANIZATIONAL STRATEGIES   Although Charlene includes two paragraphs and an illustration to support her first point followed by three paragraphs to support her second point, she uses only one paragraph to support the third point; this structure implies that she is using reversed *emphatic order*. The first point—that a college education increases the likelihood of financial stability—is a claim that would grab many readers' attention, and perhaps that is the reason Charlene decided to make it her first point. It could also be considered her strongest point because she uses three of her five sources to support the claim. To support her second point—that a college education increases exposure to other cultures—Charlene uses quotes from Patrice Douglas (a student she interviewed) as well as quotes from Professor Patricia Heilman. In contrast, the final point she makes in her essay—that a college education helps individuals develop a "habit of learning"—is supported by quotes from only one source, Professor David Loomis, whom she quoted previously in support of her first point.

When reading the essay, you probably felt that there was an easy flow from one major point to the next. To help her achieve *coherence between paragraphs,* Charlene uses sentences that link back to the preceding points: "*The financial perks of a college education are obvious;* however, financial benefits aren't the only advantages college graduates experience," and "*In addition to increasing financial stability and exposure to other cultures,* a third advantage of having a college education is

Illustration   **197**

what Professor Loomis refers to as the 'habit of learning.'" These links to previous points serve to remind readers of what they have just read and to introduce new information that follows.

PROBLEMS WITH PARAGRAPH DEVELOPMENT   You probably recall that an essay developed primarily through exemplification must include examples that are *relevant, interesting, convincing, representative, accurate,* and *specific.* On the whole, Charlene's examples meet these requirements. Paragraphs 2 and 3, along with the graph, include information that shows how a college education can increase an individual's likelihood of financial stability. Incorporating quotations not only from a college professor but also from highly regarded published sources makes her first point compelling.

The second and third points, however, are underdeveloped. To make these points more convincing, Charlene could incorporate specific examples, perhaps from television documentaries or journal articles focusing on the advantages of a college education. For example, in paragraph 6, Charlene states: "Studies show that college graduates are more likely to vote in elections, so they're 'more active in the political process' [quoting Heilman] than people who did not attend college." This statement would have been much stronger if Charlene had added specific information from the studies to which Heilman refers. The same holds true for the final point in paragraph 7 regarding how a college education helps an individual develop the "habit of learning." Additional support for these examples would give the essay the development it now lacks.

REVISING THE FIRST DRAFT   Although the final version of the essay could be strengthened by incorporating more examples, especially in support of the second and third major points, it's stronger than Charlene's first draft. One major addition Charlene made to the final draft was to include a visual to support her first point. This visual draws the reader's attention and clearly illustrates that wage declines were higher among those with an associate degree or high school education than they were among college graduates.

Another revision Charlene made as she worked on her essay was to strengthen transitions from one major point to another. For example, in her rough draft, she moves directly from paragraph 6, the final paragraph in support of her second point, to paragraph 7, in which she uses quotes from Professor Loomis regarding what he calls the "habit of learning." To see how Charlene revised this section of her essay, compare her essay's sixth and seventh paragraphs with her draft version reprinted here.

Original Version of the Sixth and Seventh Paragraphs
Professor Heilman believes that the benefits of a college education are so tremendous that to simply limit them to money or a job is "closing the door to all the experiences an individual could have that would affect them for the rest of their lives." She adds that studies show that college graduates are more likely to vote in elections, so they're "more active in the political process" than people who did not attend college.

Loomis believes that a perk of college education is what he refers to as the "habit of learning." He says that whether students attend a university, a community college, or a technical school, they are likely to acquire this invaluable habit. "Institutions of higher learning systematize this habit of learning in a way that makes it almost impossible to forget," he adds. "It's the way that an individual approaches input, any kind of input, that is one of the great advantages of higher education."

When Charlene looked more closely at her draft, she realized that she had provided no transition to help ease her readers from her second major point to the third. As she worked on her essay, she revised the opening sentence of the seventh paragraph to read, "In addition to increasing financial stability and exposure to other cultures, a third advantage of having a college education is what Professor Loomis refers to as the 'habit of learning.'" With the addition of this transitional sentence, Charlene reminds her readers of what came before and introduces them to what is yet to come.

Like most pieces of writing, Charlene's essay could be made stronger with additional revisions, but as is almost always the case, writers come to a point when they have to let their writing go, even though they know further revisions could improve the final product. Even so, the experience of writing this essay taught Charlene much that she could use to strengthen her writing in the future.

Activities: Illustration

Prewriting Activities

1. Imagine you're writing two essays. One is a serious essay analyzing why large numbers of public school teachers leave the profession each year; the other is a light essay defining *preppie, thug,* or some other slang term used to describe a kind of person. Jot down ways you might use examples in each essay.

2. Use mapping or another prewriting technique to gather examples illustrating the truth of one of the following familiar sayings. Then, using the same or a different prewriting technique, accumulate examples that counter the saying. Weigh both sets of examples to determine the saying's validity. After developing an appropriate thesis, decide which examples you would elaborate in an essay.

   a. Haste makes waste.

   b. There's no use crying over spilled milk.

   c. A bird in the hand is worth two in the bush.

3. Freewrite or use your journal to generate examples illustrating how widespread a recent fad or trend has become. After reviewing your prewriting to determine a possible thesis, narrow the examples to those you would retain for an essay. How might the patterns of development or a chronological, emphatic, spatial, or simple-to-complex approach help you sequence the examples?

Illustration **199**

Revising Activities

4. The following paragraph is from the first draft of an essay about the decline of small-town shopping districts. The paragraph is meant to show what small towns can do to revitalize business. Revise the paragraph, strengthening it with specific and convincing examples.

> A small town can compete with a large new mall for shoppers. But merchants must work together, modernizing the stores and making the town's main street pleasant, even fun to walk. They should also copy the malls' example by including attention-getting events as often as possible.

5. The paragraph that follows is from the first draft of an essay showing how knowledge of psychology can help us understand behavior that might otherwise seem baffling. The paragraph is intended to illustrate the meaning of the psychological term *superego*. Revise the paragraph, replacing its vague, unconvincing examples with one extended example that conveys the meaning of *superego* clearly and dramatically.

> The superego is the part of us that makes us feel guilty when we do something that we know is wrong. When we act foolishly or wildly, we usually feel qualms about our actions later on. If we imagine ourselves getting revenge, we most likely discover that the thoughts make us feel bad. All of these are examples of the superego at work.

6. Reprinted here is a paragraph from the first draft of a light-spirited essay showing that Americans' pursuit of change for change's sake has drawbacks. The paragraph is meant to illustrate that infatuation with newness costs consumers money but leads to no improvement in product quality. How effective is the paragraph? Which examples are specific and convincing? Which are not? Do any seem nonrepresentative, offensive, or sexist? How could the paragraph's organization be improved? Consider these questions as you rewrite the paragraph. Add specific examples where needed. Depending on the way you revise, you may want to break this one paragraph into several.

> We end up paying for our passion for the new and improved. Trendy clothing styles convince us that last year's outfits are outdated, even though our old clothes are fine. Women are especially vulnerable in this regard. What, though, about items that have to be replaced periodically, like shampoo? Even slight changes lead to new formulations requiring retooling of the production process. That means increased manufacturing costs per item—all of which get passed on to us, the consumers. Then there are those items that tout new, trendsetting features that make earlier versions supposedly obsolete. Some manufacturers, for example, boast that their stereo sound systems transmit an expanded-frequency range. The problem is that humans can't even hear such frequencies, but the high-tech feature dazzles men who are too naive to realize they're being hoodwinked.

Professional Selections: Illustration

KAY S. HYMOWITZ

A senior fellow at the Manhattan Institute and a contributing editor of the urban-policy magazine *City Journal*, Kay S. Hymowitz writes on education and childhood in the United States. A native of Philadelphia, Hymowitz received an undergraduate English degree from Brandeis University and graduate degrees from Tufts University and Columbia University. She has taught English literature and composition at Brooklyn College and at the Parsons School of Design. Her work has appeared in publications including the *New York Times*, the *Washington Post*, and the *New Republic*. The following essay appeared in the Autumn 1998 issue of *City Journal*.

To see how this illustration essay is organized, see Figure 12.3.

Pre-Reading Journal Entry

Think back on your childhood. What were some possessions and activities that you cherished and enjoyed? Freewrite for a few moments in your pre-reading journal about these beloved objects and/or pastimes. What exactly were they? Why did you enjoy them so much? Did your feelings about them change as you matured into adolescence?

Tweens: Ten Going on Sixteen

During the past year my youngest morphed from child to teenager. Down came the posters of adorable puppies and the drawings from art class; up went the airbrushed faces of Leonardo di Caprio and Kate Winslet. CDs of Le Ann Rimes and Paula Cole appeared mysteriously, along with teen fan magazines featuring glowering movie and rock-and-roll hunks....She started reading the newspaper—or at least the movie ads—with all the intensity of a Talmudic scholar, scanning for glimpses of her beloved Leo or, failing that, Matt Damon. As spring approached and younger children skipped past our house on their way to the park, she swigged from a designer water bottle, wearing the obligatory tank top and denim shorts as she whispered on the phone to friends about games of Truth or Dare. The last rites for her childhood came when, embarrassed at reminders of her foolish past, she pulled a sheet over her years-in-the-making American Girl doll collection, now dead to the world. 1

So what's new in this dog-bites-man story? Well, as all this was going on, my daughter was ten years old and in the fourth grade. 2

Those who remember their own teenybopper infatuation with Elvis or the Beatles might be inclined to shrug their shoulders as if to say, "It was ever thus." But this is different. Across class lines and throughout the country, elementary and middle-school principals and teachers, child psychologists and psychiatrists, marketing and demographic researchers all confirm the pronouncement of Henry Trevor, middle-school director of the Berkeley Carroll School in Brooklyn, New York: "There is no such thing as preadolescence anymore. Kids are teenagers at ten." 3

Marketers have a term for this new social animal, kids between eight and 12: they call them "tweens." The name captures the ambiguous reality: though 4

Illustration **201**

chronologically midway between early childhood and adolescence, this group is leaning more and more toward teen styles, teen attitudes, and, sadly, teen behavior at its most troubling.

The tween phenomenon grows out of a complicated mixture of biology, de-   5
mography, and the predictable assortment of Bad Ideas. But putting aside its causes for a moment, the emergence of tweendom carries risks for both young people and society. Eight- to 12-year-olds have an even more wobbly sense of themselves than adolescents; they rely more heavily on others to tell them how to understand the world and how to place themselves in it. Now, for both pragmatic and ideological reasons, they are being increasingly "empowered" to do this on their own, which leaves them highly vulnerable both to a vulgar and sensation-driven marketplace and to the crass authority of their immature peers. In tweens, we can see the future of our society taking shape, and it's not at all clear how it's going to work.

Perhaps the most striking evidence for the tweening of children comes from   6
market researchers. "There's no question there's a deep trend, not a passing fad, toward kids getting older younger," says research psychologist Michael Cohen of Arc Consulting, a public policy, education, and marketing research firm in New York. "This is not just on the coasts. There are no real differences geo-graphically." It seems my daughter's last rites for her American Girl dolls were a perfect symbol not just for her own childhood but for childhood, period. The Toy Manufacturers of America Factbook states that, where once the industry could count on kids between birth and 14 as their target market, today it is only birth to ten. "In the last ten years we've seen a rapid development of upper-age children," says Bruce Friend, vice president of worldwide research and plan-ning for Nickelodeon, a cable channel aimed at kids. "The 12- to 14-year-olds of yesterday are the ten to 12s of today." The rise of the preteen teen is "the biggest trend we've seen."

Scorning any symbols of their immaturity, tweens now cultivate a self-image   7
that emphasizes sophistication. The Nickelodeon-Yankelovich Youth Monitor found that by the time they are 12, children describe themselves as "flirtatious, sexy, trendy, athletic, cool." Nickelodeon's Bruce Friend reports that by 11, children in focus groups say they no longer even think of themselves as children.

They're very concerned with their "look," Friend says, even more so than older   8
teens. Sprouting up everywhere are clothing stores like the chain Limited Too and the catalog company Delia, geared toward tween girls who scorn old-fashioned, little-girl flowers, ruffles, white socks, and Mary Janes[1] in favor of the cool—black mini-dresses and platform shoes....Teachers complain of ten- or 11-year-old girls arriving at school looking like madams, in full cosmetic regalia, with streaked hair, platform shoes, and midriff-revealing shirts. Barbara Kapetanakes, a psychologist at a conservative Jewish day school in New York, describes her students' skirts as being about "the size of a belt." Kapetanakes says she was told to dress respect-fully on Fridays, the eve of the Jewish Sabbath, which she did by donning a long skirt and a modest blouse. Her students, on the other hand, showed their respect

---

[1] Trademark name of patent-leather shoes for girls, usually having a low heel and a strap that fastens at the side (editors' note).

by looking "like they should be hanging around the West Side Highway," where prostitutes ply their trade.

Lottie Sims, a computer teacher in a Miami middle school, says that the   9
hooker look for tweens is fanning strong support for uniforms in her district. But uniforms and tank-top bans won't solve the problem of painted young ladies. "You can count on one hand the girls not wearing makeup," Sims says. "Their parents don't even know. They arrive at school with huge bags of lipstick and hair spray, and head straight to the girls' room."

Though the tweening of youth affects girls more visibly than boys, especially   10
since boys mature more slowly, boys are by no means immune to these obsessions. Once upon a time, about ten years ago, fifth- and sixth-grade boys were about as fashion-conscious as their pet hamsters. But a growing minority have begun trading in their baseball cards for hair mousse and baggy jeans. In some places, $200 jackets, emblazoned with sports logos like the warm-up gear of professional athletes, are *de rigueur*[2]; in others, the preppy look is popular among the majority, while the more daring go for the hipper style of pierced ears, fade haircuts, or ponytails. Often these tween peacocks strut through their middle-school hallways taunting those who have yet to catch on to the cool look....

Those who seek comfort in the idea that the tweening of childhood is merely   11
a matter of fashion—who maybe even find their lip-synching, hip-swaying little boy or girl kind of cute—might want to think twice. There are disturbing signs that tweens are not only eschewing the goody-goody childhood image but its substance as well....

The clearest evidence of tweendom's darker side concerns crime. Although   12
children under 15 still represent a minority of juvenile arrests, their numbers grew disproportionately in the past 20 years. According to a report by the Office of Juvenile Justice and Delinquency Prevention, "offenders under age 15 represent the leading edge of the juvenile crime problem, and their numbers are growing." Moreover, the crimes committed by younger teens and preteens are growing in severity. "Person offenses,[3] which once constituted 16 percent of the total court cases for this age group," continues the report, "now constitute 25 percent." Headline grabbers—like Nathaniel Abraham of Pontiac, Michigan, an 11-year-old who stole a rifle from a neighbor's garage and went on a shooting spree in October 1997, randomly killing a teenager coming out of a store; and 11-year-old Andrew Golden, who, with his 13-year-old partner, killed four children and one teacher at his middle school in Jonesboro, Arkansas—are extreme, exceptional cases, but alas, they are part of a growing trend toward preteen violent crime....

The evidence on tween sex presents a troubling picture, too. Despite a decrease   13
among older teens for the first time since records have been kept, sexual activity among tweens increased during that period. It seems that kids who are having sex are doing so at earlier ages. Between 1988 and 1995, the proportion of girls saying they began sex before 15 rose from 11 percent to 19 percent. (For boys, the number remained stable, at 21 percent.) This means that approximately one in five

---

[2] French term referring to something that fashion or custom requires (editors' note).

[3] Crimes against a person. They include assault, robbery, rape, and homicide (editors' note).

Illustration **203**

middle-school kids is sexually active. Christie Hogan, a middle-school counselor for 20 years in Louisville, Kentucky, says: "We're beginning to see a few pregnant sixth-graders." Many of the principals and counselors I spoke with reported a small but striking minority of sexually active seventh-graders....

Certainly the days of the tentative and giggly preadolescent seem to be pass- 14 ing. Middle-school principals report having to deal with miniskirted 12-year-olds "draping themselves over boys" or patting their behinds in the hallways, while 11-year-old boys taunt girls about their breasts and rumors about their own and even their parents' sexual proclivities. Tweens have even given new connotations to the word "playground": one fifth-grade teacher from southwestern Ohio told me of two youngsters discovered in the bushes during recess.

Drugs and alcohol are also seeping into tween culture. The past six years have 15 seen more than a doubling of the number of eighth-graders who smoke marijuana (10 percent today) and those who no longer see it as dangerous. "The stigma isn't there the way it was ten years ago," says Dan Kindlon, assistant professor of psychiatry at Harvard Medical School and co-author with Michael Thompson of *Raising Cain*. "Then it was the fringe group smoking pot. You were looked at strangely. Now the fringe group is using LSD."

Aside from sex, drugs, and rock and roll, another teen problem—eating dis- 16 orders—is also beginning to affect younger kids. This behavior grows out of premature fashion-consciousness, which has an even more pernicious effect on tweens than on teens, because, by definition, younger kids have a more vulnerable and insecure self-image. Therapists say they are seeing a growing number of anorexics and obsessive dieters even among late-elementary-school girls. "You go on Internet chat rooms and find ten-and 11-year-olds who know every [fashion] model and every statistic about them," says Nancy Kolodny, a Connecticut-based therapist and author of *When Food's a Foe: How You Can Confront and Conquer Your Eating Disorder*. "Kate Moss is their god. They can tell if she's lost a few pounds or gained a few. If a powerful kid is talking about this stuff at school, it has a big effect."

What change in our social ecology has led to the emergence of tweens? Many 17 note that kids are reaching puberty at earlier ages, but while earlier physical maturation may play a small role in defining adolescence down, its importance tends to be overstated. True, the average age at which girls begin to menstruate has fallen from 13 to between 11 and 12½ today, but the very gradualness of this change means that 12-year-olds have been living inside near-adult bodies for many decades without feeling impelled to build up a cosmetics arsenal or head for the bushes at recess. In fact, some experts believe that the very years that have witnessed the rise of the tween have also seen the age of first menstruation stabilize. Further, teachers and principals on the front lines see no clear correlation between physical and social maturation. Plenty of budding girls and bulking boys have not put away childish things, while an abundance of girls with flat chests and boys with squeaky voices ape the body language and fashions of their older siblings....

Of course, the causes are complex, and most people working with tweens 18 know it. In my conversations with educators and child psychologists who work primarily with middle-class kids nationwide, two major and fairly predictable themes emerged: a sexualized and glitzy media-driven marketplace and absentee parents. What has been less commonly recognized is that at this age, the two causes combine to augment the authority of the peer group, which in turn both weakens the influence of parents and reinforces the power of the media. Taken together, parental absence, the market, and the peer group form a vicious circle that works to distort the development of youngsters....

Figure 12.3 Essay Structure Diagram: "Tweens: Ten Going on Sixteen" by Kay S. Hymowitz

Introductory paragraphs: **Personal anecdote** **Thesis** (paragraphs 1–3)	Author's ten-year-old daughter becoming a teenager: examples of changes in her room décor, music tastes, and dress styles. **Thesis:** These days children become teens without going through preadolescence.
Background: **Quotations and statistics** (4–7)	Definition of "tweens" as a new market: quotations from a research psychologist and a TV executive; statistics from a toy trade publication; market research on tweens' self-image as "sexy" and "cool."
Quotations, examples, and statistics (8–16)	Psychologist's and teacher's descriptions of girls' adult-style clothes, hairstyles, makeup. Examples of boys' new concern with fashion. Evidence of trend's "darker side": statistics on growth in juvenile crime and sexual activity; quotations about tweens' sexualized behavior in school; statistics on drug and alcohol use; therapists' comments on increase in eating disorders.
Concluding paragraphs (17–18)	Experts' ideas about children's earlier physical maturation. Author's view of the real causes of the tweens phenomenon.

Questions for Critical Reading

1. What is the selection's thesis? Locate the sentence(s) in which Hymowitz states her main idea. If she doesn't state the thesis explicitly, express it in your own words.

2. According to Hymowitz, what self-image do tweens cultivate? How do they project this image to others?

3. What physically dangerous behavioral trends does Hymowitz link to the tween phenomenon?

4. According to Hymowitz, what are the primary causes of the tween phenomenon?

Illustration **205**

Questions About the Writer's Craft

1. **Support.** Hymowitz uses a range of examples, citing specific names, anecdotes, expert opinion, and studies. Find the places where Hymowitz uses statistics to support her ideas about crime, sexuality, and drug use. What are the sources? Are the statistics reliable? How persuasive are they?

2. **The pattern.** What types of examples does Hymowitz provide in her essay? Cite at least one example of each type. How does each type of example contribute to her thesis?

3. **Tone.** How would you characterize Hymowitz's tone in the selection? Cite vocabulary that conveys this tone.

4. **Other patterns.** In paragraph 8, Hymowitz uses clothing as a means of presenting an important contrast. What does she contrast in this paragraph? How does this contrast contribute to her thesis?

Writing Assignments Using Illustration as a Pattern of Development

1. Hymowitz is troubled and perplexed by her daughter's behavior. Think about an older person, such as a parent or another relative, who finds *your* behavior troubling and perplexing. Write an essay in which you illustrate why your behavior distresses this person. (Or, conversely, think of an elder whose behavior *you* find problematic, and write an essay illustrating why that person evokes this response in you.) Be sure to provide abundant examples throughout.

2. The cultivation of a sophisticated self-image is, according to Hymowitz, a hallmark of tweenhood. Think back to when you were around that age. What was your self-image at that time? Did you think of yourself as worldly or inexperienced? Cool or awkward? Attractive or unappealing? Freewrite about the traits that you would have identified in yourself as either a tween or an adolescent. Write an essay in which you illustrate your self-image at that age, focusing on two to three dominant characteristics you associated with yourself. Conclude your essay by reflecting on whether the way you saw yourself at the time was accurate, and whether your feelings about yourself have changed since then.

Writing Assignment Combining Patterns of Development

3. Hymowitz advances a powerful argument about the alarming contemporary trend of tweenhood. But many would disagree with her entirely pessimistic analysis. Write an essay in which you *argue*, contrary to Hymowitz, that tweens today actually exhibit several *positive* characteristics. To develop your argument, you'll need

to show how each characteristic you're discussing *contrasts* favorably with that characteristic in a previous generation of kids. Be sure, too, to acknowledge opposing arguments as you proceed. Research conducted in the library and/or on the Internet might help you develop your pro-tween argument.

HILLARY RODHAM CLINTON

Hillary Rodham Clinton, a graduate of Wellesley College and Yale Law School, was the First Lady of the United States (1993–2001), a U.S. Senator (2001–2009), and the sixty-seventh U.S. Secretary of State (2009–2013). In 1988 and 1991, she was on *The National Law Journal*'s list of the "One Hundred Most Powerful Lawyers in America." Clinton's publications include five books: *It Takes a Village* (1996), *Dear Socks, Dear Buddy: Kids' Letters to the First Pets* (1998), *An Invitation to the White House* (2000), *Living History* (2003), and *Hard Choices* (2014). She is widely respected as a champion for women's rights and child-care and health-care reform. Clinton presented the speech that follows at the plenary session (general meeting of all participants) of the United Nations Fourth World Conference on Women in Beijing, China, on September 5, 1995.

Pre-Reading Journal Entry

In the following essay, Hillary Rodham Clinton discusses the various roles that women play, the contributions they make, and the inhumane ways in which they are too often treated. Take a few minutes to write in your journal about women who play an important role in your life and examples of when they have been treated unfairly. If you are a woman, you might write about times in your own life when you have been treated unfairly because of your gender.

Remarks to the United Nations Fourth World Conference on Women Plenary Session

1   Thank you very much, Gertrude Mongella,[1] for your dedicated work that has brought us to this point, distinguished delegates, and guests:

2   I would like to thank the Secretary General for inviting me to be part of this important United Nations Fourth World Conference on Women. This is truly a celebration, a celebration of the contributions women make in every aspect of life: in the home, on the job, in the community, as mothers, wives, sisters, daughters, learners, workers, citizens, and leaders.

3   It is also a coming together, much the way women come together every day in every country. We come together in fields and factories, in village markets and supermarkets, in living rooms and board rooms. Whether it is while playing with our children in the park, or washing clothes in a river, or taking a break at the office water cooler, we come together and talk about our aspirations and concerns. And

---

[1] Gertrude Mongella is the former president of the Pan-African Parliament and was Secretary General of the Fourth World Conference on Women (editors' note).

Illustration **207**

time and again, our talk turns to our children and our families. However different we may appear, there is far more that unites us than divides us. We share a common future, and we are here to find common ground so that we may help bring new dignity and respect to women and girls all over the world, and in so doing bring new strength and stability to families as well.

By gathering in Beijing, we are focusing world attention on issues that matter most in our lives—the lives of women and their families: access to education, health care, jobs and credit, the chance to enjoy basic legal and human rights and to participate fully in the political life of our countries.   4

There are some who question the reason for this conference. Let them listen to the voices of women in their homes, neighborhoods, and workplaces. There are some who wonder whether the lives of women and girls matter to economic and political progress around the globe. Let them look at the women gathered here and at Huairou[2]—the homemakers and nurses, the teachers and lawyers, the policymakers and women who run their own businesses. It is conferences like this that compel governments and peoples everywhere to listen, look, and face the world's most pressing problems. Wasn't it after the women's conference in Nairobi ten years ago that the world focused for the first time on the crisis of domestic violence?   5

Earlier today, I participated in a World Health Organization forum. In that forum, we talked about ways that government officials, NGOs[3], and individual citizens are working to address the health problems of women and girls. Tomorrow, I will attend a gathering of the United Nations Development Fund for Women. There, the discussion will focus on local—and highly successful—programs that give hard-working women access to credit so they can improve their own lives and the lives of their families.   6

What we are learning around the world is that if women are healthy and educated, their families will flourish. If women are free from violence, their families will flourish. If women have a chance to work and earn as full and equal partners in society, their families will flourish. And when families flourish, communities and nations do as well. That is why every woman, every man, every child, every family, and every nation on this planet does have a stake in the discussion that takes place here.   7

Over the past 25 years, I have worked persistently on issues relating to women, children, and families. Over the past two and a half years, I've had the opportunity to learn more about the challenges facing women in my own country and around the world.   8

I have met new mothers in Indonesia, who come together regularly in their village to discuss nutrition, family planning, and baby care. I have met working parents in Denmark who talk about the comfort they feel in knowing that their children can be cared for in safe, and nurturing after-school centers. I have met women in South Africa who helped lead the struggle to end apartheid and are   9

---

[2] Huairou is the small town thirty-five miles northeast of Beijing where the United Nations Fourth World Conference on Women was held in 1995 (editors' note).

[3] NGO is an acronym for *nongovernmental organization* (editors' note).

now helping to build a new democracy. I have met with the leading women of my own hemisphere who are working every day to promote literacy and better health care for children in their countries. I have met women in India and Bangladesh who are taking out small loans to buy milk cows, or rickshaws, or thread in order to create a livelihood for themselves and their families. I have met the doctors and nurses in Belarus and Ukraine who are trying to keep children alive in the aftermath of Chernobyl.[4]

The great challenge of this conference is to give voice to women everywhere 10 whose experiences go unnoticed, whose words go unheard. Women comprise more than half the world's population, 70% of the world's poor, and two-thirds of those who are not taught to read and write. We are the primary caretakers for most of the world's children and elderly. Yet much of the work we do is not valued—not by economists, not by historians, not by popular culture, not by government leaders.

At this very moment, as we sit here, women around the world are giving birth, 11 raising children, cooking meals, washing clothes, cleaning houses, planting crops, working on assembly lines, running companies, and running countries. Women also are dying from diseases that should have been prevented or treated. They are watching their children succumb to malnutrition caused by poverty and economic deprivation. They are being denied the right to go to school by their own fathers and brothers. They are being forced into prostitution, and they are being barred from the bank lending offices and banned from the ballot box.

Those of us who have the opportunity to be here have the responsibility to 12 speak for those who could not. As an American, I want to speak for those women in my own country, women who are raising children on the minimum wage, women who can't afford health care or child care, women whose lives are threatened by violence, including violence in their own homes.

I want to speak up for mothers who are fighting for good schools, safe neigh- 13 borhoods, clean air, and clean airwaves; for older women, some of them widows, who find that, after raising their families, their skills and life experiences are not valued in the marketplace; for women who are working all night as nurses, hotel clerks, or fast food chefs so that they can be at home during the day with their children; and for women everywhere who simply don't have time to do everything they are called upon to do each and every day.

Speaking to you today, I speak for them, just as each of us speaks for women 14 around the world who are denied the chance to go to school, or see a doctor, or own property, or have a say about the direction of their lives, simply because they are women. The truth is that most women around the world work both inside and outside the home, usually by necessity.

We need to understand there is no one formula for how women should lead 15 our lives. That is why we must respect the choices that each woman makes for herself and her family. Every woman deserves the chance to realize her own God-given potential. But we must recognize that women will never gain full dignity until their human rights are respected and protected.

---

[4] Chernobyl, a city in Ukraine, was devastated by an explosion at the town's nuclear power plant on April 26, 1986. Belarus, a country across the Ukraine border and eleven miles from Chernobyl, also experienced devastating effects (editors' note).

Illustration **209**

Our goals for this conference, to strengthen families and societies by empower- 16
ing women to take greater control over their own destinies, cannot be fully achieved
unless all governments—here and around the world—accept their responsibility
to protect and promote internationally recognized human rights The international
community has long acknowledged and recently reaffirmed at Vienna[5] that both
women and men are entitled to a range of protections and personal freedoms, from
the right of personal security to the right to determine freely the number and spac-
ing of the children they bear. No one should be forced to remain silent for fear of
religious or political persecution, arrest, abuse, or torture.

Tragically, women are most often the ones whose human rights are violated. 17
Even now, in the late 20th century, the rape of women continues to be used as an
instrument of armed conflict. Women and children make up a large majority of
the world's refugees. And when women are excluded from the political process,
they become even more vulnerable to abuse. I believe that now, on the eve of a
new millennium, it is time to break the silence. It is time for us to say here in Beijing, and for the world to hear, that it is no longer acceptable to discuss women's
rights as separate from human rights.

These abuses have continued because, for too long, the history of women has 18
been a history of silence. Even today, there are those who are trying to silence our
words. But the voices of this conference and of the women at Huairou must be
heard loudly and clearly:

It is a violation of human rights when babies are denied food, or drowned, or 19
suffocated, or their spines broken, simply because they are born girls.

It is a violation of human rights when women and girls are sold into the slav- 20
ery of prostitution for human greed—and the kinds of reasons that are used to
justify this practice should no longer be tolerated.

It is a violation of human rights when women are doused with gasoline, set on 21
fire, and burned to death because their marriage dowries are deemed too small.

It is a violation of human rights when individual women are raped in their own 22
communities and when thousands of women are subjected to rape as a tactic or prize
of war.

It is a violation of human rights when a leading cause of death worldwide 23
among women ages 14 to 44 is the violence they are subjected to in their own
homes by their own relatives.

It is a violation of human rights when young girls are brutalized by the painful 24
and degrading practice of genital mutilation.

It is a violation of human rights when women are denied the right to plan their 25
own families, and that includes being forced to have abortions or being sterilized
against their will.

If there is one message that echoes forth from this conference, let it be that human 26
rights are women's rights and women's rights are human rights once and for all. Let
us not forget that among those rights are the right to speak freely—and the right to
be heard.

---

[5] Vienna, Austria, was the site of the World Conference on Human Rights where the "Vienna Declaration and Program of Action" was adopted on June 25, 1993 (editors' note).

Women must enjoy the rights to participate fully in the social and political 27
lives of their countries, if we want freedom and democracy to thrive and endure. It
is indefensible that many women in nongovernmental organizations who wished
to participate in this conference have not been able to attend—or have been pro-
hibited from fully taking part.

Let me be clear. Freedom means the right of people to assemble, organize, and 28
debate openly. It means respecting the views of those who may disagree with the
views of their governments. It means not taking citizens away from their loved ones
and jailing them, mistreating them, or denying them their freedom or dignity because
of the peaceful expression of their ideas and opinions.

In my country, we recently celebrated the 75th anniversary of Women's Suf- 29
frage. It took 150 years after the signing of our Declaration of Independence for
women to win the right to vote. It took 72 years of organized struggle, before
that happened, on the part of many courageous women and men. It was one of
America's most divisive philosophical wars. But it was a bloodless war. Suffrage
was achieved without a shot being fired.

But we have also been reminded, in V-J Day[6] observances last weekend, of 30
the good that comes when men and women join together to combat the forces of
tyranny and to build a better world. We have seen peace prevail in most places for
a half century. We have avoided another world war. But we have not solved older,
deeply rooted problems that continue to diminish the potential of half the world's
population.

Now it is the time to act on behalf of women everywhere. If we take bold 31
steps to better the lives of women, we will be taking bold steps to better the lives
of children and families too. Families rely on mothers and wives for emotional
support and care. Families rely on women for labor in the home. And increasingly,
everywhere, families rely on women for income needed to raise healthy children
and care for other relatives.

As long as discrimination and inequities remain so commonplace every- 32
where in the world, as long as girls and women are valued less, fed less, fed last,
overworked, underpaid, not schooled, subjected to violence in and outside their
homes—the potential of the human family to create a peaceful, prosperous world
will not be realized.

Let this conference be our—and the world's—call to action. Let us heed that 33
call so we can create a world in which every woman is treated with respect and
dignity, every boy and girl is loved and cared for equally, and every family has the
hope of a strong and stable future. That is the work before you. That is the work
before all of us who have a vision of the world we want to see—for our children
and our grandchildren.

The time is now. We must move beyond rhetoric. We must move beyond rec- 34
ognition of problems to working together, to have the common efforts to build that
common ground we hope to see.

God's blessing on you, your work, and all who will benefit from it. 35
Godspeed and thank you very much. 36

---

[6] V-J Day (Victory over Japan Day) is the day when Japan surrendered and World War II ended (editors' note).

Illustration **211**

Questions for Critical Reading

1. What is the selection's thesis? Locate the sentence(s) in which Clinton states her main idea. If she doesn't state the thesis explicitly, express it in your own words.

2. Near the beginning of her speech, Clinton addresses the viewpoints of those who oppose the conference at which she is speaking. What does she say about the opposition, and why do you think she includes this section in her speech?

3. Later in the speech, Clinton establishes her own credentials. What information does she provide, and why do you think someone so well known around the world would make a point of establishing her credibility on the subject about which she is speaking?

4. What statistics does Clinton include that support the roles women play and the conditions in which they live?

Questions About the Writer's Craft

1. **Examples.** Clinton provides many examples of the ways women around the world are denied their human rights. Which three or four of her examples are most compelling to you and why?

2. **Other patterns.** What important *contrast* does Clinton develop in paragraph 3? How does this contrast reinforce the essay's main idea?

3. **Sentence structure.** Writers generally vary sentence structure in an effort to add interest to their work. But in paragraph 18, Clinton employs a repetitive sentence structure. Where is the repetition in this paragraph? Why do you think Clinton uses this technique?

4. **Tone.** Jot down several phrases or sentences from Clinton's speech that illustrate her tone. How would you describe her tone? Do you think her tone is effective? Why or why not?

Writing Assignments Using Illustration as a Pattern of Development

1. In her speech, Clinton catalogs a number of roles that women play. Write an essay of your own, illustrating the various roles a woman in your life plays. For example, you might write about a family member (such as your mother, grandmother, aunt, or sister), or you might write about a co-worker, friend, teacher, or other woman in your life. Start by making a list of five women you know who juggle many roles. Then narrow that list down to the three women you can

imagine yourself writing an essay about, and do some freewriting to generate details about each one. Then choose one of them and decide whether you will order your examples in simple-to-complex order or emphatically; use whichever order illustrates the various roles more effectively. End with some conclusions about the difference that the woman you are writing about makes in the lives of others.

2. While Clinton's speech focuses on the human rights often denied to women, other groups in our world today are often denied their human rights as well. Focus on one of these groups in your essay—for example, immigrants trying to flee the horrible conditions under which they are living but are denied entry to other countries or individuals who are racially profiled and subjected to inhumane treatment. Write an essay in which you provide examples of the unfair treatment these individuals are forced to endure and what should be done to protect them and make sure their rights are not violated. Consider using outside sources and/or images to strengthen your essay.

Writing Assignment Combining Patterns of Development

3. Clinton explores the roles women play, the contributions they make, and how their human rights are denied. Write an essay about the *effects* on women and their families when they are not treated with the respect and dignity every individual deserves.

TEMPLE GRANDIN

Known as "the face of autism," Temple Grandin earned her Ph.D. in animal sciences and is a professor at Colorado State University. She is responsible for the development of livestock handling facility designs that decrease pain and fear for animals and are widely used across the United States today. The 2010 HBO movie *Temple Grandin*, winner of five Emmys, is based on her life story. Grandin's publications include three books: *Thinking in Pictures: My Life with Autism* (2010), *The Way I See It: A Personal Look at Autism and Aspergers* (2011), and *The Autistic Brain: Helping Different Kinds of Minds Succeed* (2014). The essay that follows was written for and first appeared in the National Public Radio series *This I Believe* on August 16, 2006.

Pre-Reading Journal

Autism is one of many qualities that can set a person off from others. Think of other qualities—physical attributes or handicaps, mental or psychological abilities, personality characteristics—that can affect individuals' lives for better or worse. Use your journal to explore these qualities and their effects in people you know.

Illustration **213**

Seeing in Beautiful, Precise Pictures

Because I have autism, I live by concrete rules instead of abstract beliefs. And   1
because I have autism, I think in pictures and sounds. I don't have the ability to
process abstract thought the way that you do. Here's how my brain works: It's like
the search engine Google for images. If you say the word "love" to me, I'll surf
the Internet inside my brain. Then, a series of images pops into my head. What I'll
see, for example, is a picture of a mother horse with a foal, or I think of "Herbie
the Lovebug," scenes from the movie *Love Story* or the Beatles song, "Love, love,
love...."

When I was a child, my parents taught me the difference between good and   2
bad behavior by showing me specific examples. My mother told me that you don't
hit other kids because you would not like it if they hit you. That makes sense. But
if my mother told me to be "nice" to someone, it was too vague for me to comprehend. But if she said that being nice meant delivering daffodils to a next-door
neighbor, that I could understand.

I built a library of experiences that I could refer to when I was in a new situ-   3
ation. That way, when I confronted something unfamiliar, I could draw on the
information in my homemade library and come up with an appropriate way to
behave in a new and strange situation.

When I was in my 20s, I thought a lot about the meaning of life. At the time,   4
I was getting started in my career, designing more humane facilities for animals
at ranches and slaughterhouses. Many people would think that to even work at a
slaughterhouse would be inhumane, but they forget that every human and animal
eventually dies. In my mind, I had a picture of a way to make that dying as peaceful as possible.

I believe that doing practical things can make the world a better place. And   5
one of the features of being autistic is that I'm good at synthesizing lots of information and creating systems out of it.

When I was creating my first corral back in the 1970s, I went to 50 different   6
feedlots and ranches in Arizona and Texas and helped them work cattle. In my
mind, I catalogued the parts of each facility that worked effectively and assembled
them into an ideal new system. I get great satisfaction when a rancher tells me
that my corral design helps cattle move through it quietly and easily. When cattle
stay calm, it means they are not scared. And that makes me feel I've accomplished
something important.

Some people might think if I could snap my fingers I'd choose to be "normal."   7
But I wouldn't want to give up my ability to see in beautiful, precise pictures.
I believe in them.

Questions for Critical Reading

1. What is the selection's thesis? Locate the sentence(s) in which Grandin states her
   main idea. If she doesn't state her thesis explicitly, express it in your own words.

2. How does Grandin describe the way her brain works? In what specific way does
   she say her brain works differently from other people's?

3. Why does Grandin see her autism as an asset in her work to make ranch and slaughterhouse conditions more humane?

4. Grandin says that if given the opportunity to be "normal," she would choose to remain the way she is. Why does she feel this way?

Questions About the Writer's Craft

1. **Metaphor.** What metaphor does Grandin use to explain how she says her brain works? What examples does she provide to illustrate her metaphor?

2. **Examples.** What example does Grandin use to show how she learned "the difference between good and bad behavior"? Which examples in the essay most clearly helped you understand the affects of autism?

3. **Other patterns.** In what ways does Grandin use elements of narration and description in her essay? Provide specific examples. How does her use of narration and description make her writing more effective?

4. **Title.** How does the title of Grandin's essay, "Seeing in Beautiful, Precise Pictures," capture or fail to capture the essence of the message she is trying to convey to her readers?

Writing Assignments Using Exemplification as a Pattern of Development

1. In her essay, Grandin provides examples of how autism has played a major role in shaping her life. Write an essay in which you provide examples of how something in your life affects or affected who you are today. You might write about a traumatic experience in your life—perhaps a divorce in your family, a car accident, or a serious illness. Or you might write about a positive experience, such as a meaningful relationship, the birth of a child, or an acceptance from the college you wanted to attend. Explain how the experience has played a role in making you the person you have become. Focus on providing examples that illustrate the experience and its influence.

2. Grandin, widely referred to as "the face of autism," believes that her autism is an asset—that being autistic allows her to see life in a way that would not be possible if she were "normal." Write an essay in which you provide examples of how another public figure turned what might be considered a handicap into an asset. For example, you might conduct research on Franklin D. Roosevelt, the thirty-second president of the United States, and how the polio he contracted at the age of thirty-nine played a role in making him the man he was. Or you might write about the actor Michael J. Fox and how his experience with Parkinson's disease has helped others who are dealing with the condition. Conduct research as needed to discover information that can help you write an effective essay.

Illustration   **215**

Writing Assignment Combining Patterns of Development

3. Conduct research to learn more about how Temple Grandin developed a design for more humane livestock-handling facilities. Write an essay that documents her *process* and *explains* how her designs are now being used, with positive *results*, in facilities across the United States.

Additional Writing Topics: Illustration

General Assignments

Using illustration, develop one of these topics into an essay.

1. Today's drivers' dangerous habits

2. Taking care of our neighborhoods

3. The best things in life: definitely not free

4. The importance of part-time jobs for college students

5. How smartphones have changed communication

6. Learning about people from what they wear

7. Americans' obsession with or neglect of physical fitness

8. How to avoid bad eating habits

9. Eliminating obstacles faced by people with handicaps

10. _____ (someone you know) as a _____ (reliable, open-minded, dishonest, pushy, etc.) person

Assignments Using Multimedia

Use the suggested media to help develop an illustration essay on one of these topics:

1. How smartphones have changed our lives (photos and/or charts)

2. The dangers of texting while driving (weblinks and/or charts)

3. How the Internet has affected society (slide show)

4. Characteristics of college students with high GPAs (charts or cartoons)

5. How a hobby such as hiking or singing can expand our horizons (weblinks)

Assignments with a Specific Purpose, Audience, and Point of View

1. **Academic life.** Lately, many people at your college have been experiencing stress. As a member of the Student Life Committee, you've been asked to prepare a pamphlet illustrating strategies for reducing different kinds of stress. Decide which stresses to discuss and explain coping strategies for each, providing helpful examples as you go.

2. **Academic life.** A friend of yours will be going away to college in an unfamiliar environment—in a bustling urban setting or in a quiet rural one. To help your friend prepare for this new environment, write a letter giving examples of what life on an urban or a rural campus is like. You might focus on the benefits and dangers with which your friend is unlikely to be familiar.

3. **Civic activity.** Shopping for a new car, you become annoyed at how many safety features are available only as expensive options. Write a letter of complaint to the auto manufacturer, citing at least three examples of such options. Avoid sounding hostile.

4. **Civic activity.** A pet-food company is having an annual contest to choose a new animal to feature in its advertising. To win the contest, you must convince the company that your pet is personable, playful, and unique. Write an essay giving examples of your pet's special qualities.

5. **Workplace action.** Assume that you're an elementary school principal planning to give a speech in which you'll try to convince parents that television distorts children's perceptions of reality. Write the speech, illustrating your point with vivid examples.

6. **Workplace action.** The online publication you work for has asked you to write an article on what you consider to be the "three best consumer products of the past twenty-five years." Support your opinion with lively, engaging specifics that are consistent with the website's offbeat and slightly ironic tone.

Chapter 13
Division-Classification

Learning Objectives

13.1 Understand how you can use the division-classification pattern to develop your essays.

13.2 Consider how division-classification can fit your purpose and audience.

13.3 Develop prewriting strategies for using division-classification in an essay.

13.4 Develop strategies for writing a division-classification essay.

13.5 Use strategies for revising your division-classification essay.

13.6 Analyze how division-classification is used effectively in a student-written selection.

What Is Division-Classification?

13.1 Understand how you can use the division-classification pattern to develop your essays.

All of us instinctively look for ways to order our environment. Without systems, categories, or sorting mechanisms, we would be overwhelmed by life's complexity. An organization such as a college or university, for example, is made manageable by being divided into various schools (Liberal Arts, Performing Arts, Engineering, and so on). The schools are then separated into departments (English, History, Political Science), and each department's offerings are grouped into distinct categories—English, for instance, might be divided into Literature, Linguistics, and Composition—before being further divided into specific courses.

The kind of ordering system we're discussing is called **division-classification**, and it is a way of thinking that allows us to make sense of a complex world. Division and classification often complement each other. **Division** involves taking a single unit or concept, breaking it down into parts, and then analyzing the connections among the parts and between the parts and the whole. For instance, a hospital could be broken down into its components. We might come up with the following breakdown:

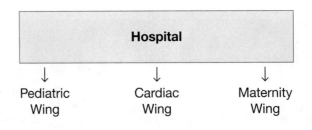

What we have just done is division: We've taken a single entity (a hospital) and divided it into some of its component parts (wings), each with its own facilities and patients.

In contrast, **classification** brings two or more related items together and categorizes them according to type or kind. In a supermarket, clerks classify the items in the store:

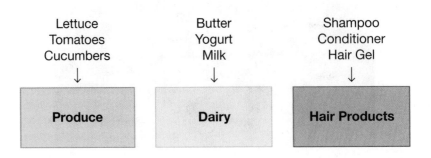

How Division-Classification Fits Your Purpose and Audience

13.2 Consider how division-classification can fit your purpose and audience.

The hospital and supermarket examples show the way division and classification work in everyday life. But division and classification also come into play during the writing process. Because division involves breaking a subject into parts, it can be a helpful strategy during prewriting, especially if you're analyzing a broad, complex subject—for example, the structure of a film, a character's motivation in a novel, the vandalism problem in your community, the controversy surrounding school prayer.

Classification can be useful for imposing order on the hodgepodge of ideas generated during prewriting. You examine that material to see which of your rough ideas are alike and which are dissimilar, so that you can cluster related items in the same category. Classification, then, is a helpful strategy when analyzing topics such as these: techniques for impressing teachers, comedic styles of talk-show hosts, views on abortion, and reasons for the recent rise in volunteerism.

Division-classification can be crucial when responding to college assignments like the following:

> Based on your observations, what kinds of appeals do television advertisers use when selling automobiles? In your view, are any of these appeals morally irresponsible?

> Analyze the components that go into being an effective parent. Indicate those you consider most vital for raising confident, well-adjusted children.

> Describe the hierarchy of the typical high school clique, identifying the various parts of the hierarchy. Use your analysis to support or refute the view that adolescence is a period of rigid conformity.

These assignments suggest division-classification through the use of such words as *kinds, components,* and *parts.* Generally, though, you won't receive such clear signals to use division-classification. Instead, the broad purpose of the essay—and the point you want to make—will lead you to the analytical thinking characteristic of division-classification.

Sometimes division-classification is the dominant technique for structuring an essay; other times it is a supplemental pattern in an essay organized primarily according to another pattern of development. Let's look at some examples:

- Say you want to write an essay *explaining a process,* such as using the Heimlich maneuver on people who are choking. You could *divide* the process into parts or stages, showing, for instance, that the Heimlich maneuver is an easily mastered skill that readers should acquire.

- Or imagine you plan to write a light-spirited essay analyzing the *effect* that increased awareness of sexual stereotypes has had on college students' social lives.

In such a case, you might use *classification*. To show readers that shifting gender roles make young men and women comically self-conscious, you could categorize the places where students scope each other out: in class, at the library, at parties, and in dorms. You could then show how students—not wanting to be macho or coyly feminine—approach each other with laughable tentativeness in these four environments.

- Now imagine that you're writing an *argumentation-persuasion* essay urging the federal government to prohibit the use of growth-inducing antibiotics in livestock feed. The essay could begin by *dividing* the antibiotics cycle into stages: the effects of antibiotics on livestock, the short-term effects on humans who consume the animals, and the possible long-term effects of consuming antibiotic-tainted meat. To increase readers' understanding of the problem, you might also discuss the antibiotics controversy in terms of an even larger issue: the dangerous ways food is treated before being consumed. In this case, you would consider the various procedures (use of additives, preservatives, artificial colors, and so on), *classifying* these treatments into several types—from least harmful (some additives or artificial colors, perhaps) to most harmful (you might slot the antibiotics here). Such an essay would be developed using both division *and* classification: first, the division of the antibiotics cycle and then the classification of the various food treatments. Frequently, this interdependence will be reversed, and classification will precede rather than follow division.

Prewriting Strategies

13.3 Develop prewriting strategies for using division-classification in an essay.

The following checklist shows how you can apply prewriting strategies to division-classification.

☑ Division-Classification: A Prewriting Checklist

Choose a Subject to Analyze

☐ What fairly complex subject (sibling rivalry, religious cults) can be made more understandable through division-classification?

☐ Will you divide a single entity or concept (domestic violence) into parts (toward spouse, parent, or child)? Will you classify a number of similar things (college courses) into categories (easy, of average difficulty, tough)? Or will you use both division and classification?

Determine Your Purpose, Audience, Tone, and Point of View

☐ What is the purpose of your analysis?

☐ Toward what audience will you direct your explanations?

☐ What tone and point of view will make readers receptive to your explanation?

Use Prewriting to Generate Material on Parts or Types

☐ How can brainstorming, mapping, or any other prewriting technique help you divide your subject into parts? What differences or similarities among parts will you emphasize?

☐ How can brainstorming, mapping, or any other prewriting technique help you categorize your subjects? What differences or similarities among categories will you emphasize?

☐ How can the patterns of development help you generate material about your subjects' parts or categories? How can you describe the parts or categories? What can you narrate about them? What examples illustrate them? What process do they help explain? How can they be compared or contrasted? What causes them? What are their effects? How can they be defined? What arguments do they support?

Strategies for Using Division-Classification in an Essay

13.4 Develop strategies for writing a division-classification essay.

After prewriting, you're ready to draft your essay. Figure 13.1 and the following suggestions will be helpful whether you use division-classification as a dominant or supportive pattern of development.

1. **Select a principle of division-classification consistent with your purpose.**

    Most subjects can be divided or classified according to several different principles. In all cases, though, the principle of division-classification you select must meet one stringent requirement: It must help you meet your overall purpose and reinforce your central point.

    Don't, however, take this to mean that essays can never use more than one principle of division-classification as they unfold. They can—as long as the *shift from one principle to another* occurs in *different parts* of the essay.

2. **Apply the principle of division-classification logically.**

    In an essay using division-classification, you need to demonstrate that your analysis is the result of careful thought. First, your division-classification should be as *complete* as possible. Your analysis should include—within reason—all the parts into which you can divide your subject, or all the types into which you can categorize your subjects.

    Your division-classification should also be *consistent:* The parts into which you break your subject or the groups into which you place your subjects should be as mutually exclusive as possible. The parts or categories should not be mixed, nor should they overlap.

3. **Prepare an effective thesis.**

    If your essay uses division-classification as its dominant method of development, it might be helpful to prepare a thesis that does more than signal the essay's subject and suggest your attitude toward that subject. You might also

Figure 13.1 Development Diagram: Writing a Division-Classification Essay

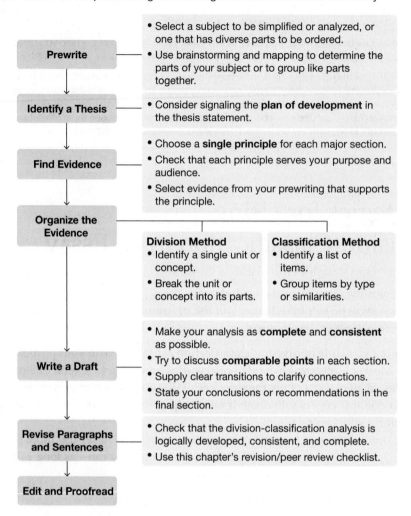

want the thesis to state the principle of division-classification at the heart of the essay. Furthermore, you might want the thesis to reveal which part or category you regard as most important.

Consider the following two thesis statements:

Thesis 1

As the observant beachcomber moves from the tidal area to the upper beach to the sandy dunes, rich variations in marine life become apparent.

Thesis 2

Although most people focus on the dangers associated with the disposal of toxic waste in the land and ocean, the incineration of toxic matter may pose an even more serious threat to human life.

The first thesis statement makes clear that the writer will organize the essay by classifying forms of marine life according to location. Because the essay's purpose is to inform as objectively as possible, the thesis doesn't suggest the writer's opinion about which category is most significant.

The second thesis signals that the essay will evolve by dividing the issue of toxic waste according to methods of disposal. Moreover, because the essay takes a stance on a controversial subject, the thesis is worded to reveal which aspect of the topic the writer considers most important. Such a clear statement of the writer's position is an effective strategy in an essay of this kind.

You may have noted that each thesis statement also signals the essay's plan of development. The first essay, for example, will use specific facts, examples, and details to describe the kinds of marine life found in the tidal area, upper beach, and dunes.

4. **Organize the essay logically.**

    Whether your essay is developed wholly or in part by division-classification, it should have a logical structure. As much as possible, you should try to discuss *comparable points* in each section of the essay. You should also use *signal devices* to connect various parts of the essay: "*Another* characteristic of…"; "A *final* important trait of…"; "*Unlike* the…" Such signals clarify the connections among the essay's ideas.

5. **State any conclusions or recommendations in the essay's final section.**

    The analytic thinking that occurs during division-classification often leads to surprising insights. Such insights may be introduced early on, or they may be reserved for the end, where they are stated as conclusions or recommendations.

Revision Strategies

13.5 Use strategies for revising your division-classification essay.

Once you have a draft of the essay, you're ready to revise. The following checklist will help your peers provide feedback and aid you in revising your essay.

☑ Division-Classification: A Revision/Peer Review Checklist

Revise Overall Meaning and Structure

☐   What is the principle of division-classification at the heart of the essay? How does this principle contribute to the essay's overall purpose and thesis?

☐   Does the thesis state the essay's principle of division-classification? Should it? Does the thesis signal which part or category is most important? Should it? Does the thesis reveal the essay's plan of development? Should it?

☐   Is the essay organized primarily through division, classification, or a blend of both?

☐ If the essay is organized mainly through division, is the subject sufficiently broad and complex to be broken down into parts? What are the parts?

☐ If the essay is organized mainly through classification, what are the categories? How does this categorizing reveal similarities and/or differences that would otherwise not be apparent?

Revise Paragraph Development

☐ Are comparable points discussed in each of the essay's sections? What are these points?

☐ In which paragraphs does the division-classification seem illogical, incomplete, or inconsistent? In which paragraphs are parts or categories not clearly explained?

☐ Are the subject's different parts or categories discussed in separate paragraphs? Should they be?

Revise Sentences and Words

☐ What signal devices help integrate the essay? Are there enough signals? Too many?

☐ Where should sentences and words be made more specific in order to clarify the parts and categories being discussed?

Student Essay: From Prewriting Through Revision

13.6 Analyze how division-classification is used effectively in a student-written selection.

The following student essay was written by Catherine Gispert in response to this assignment:

> In "Mother Tongue," Amy Tan describes the various types of English that she uses, a subject with which she has much personal experience. Write an essay about a subject about which you are knowledgeable, but instead of writing about yourself, write about a group of individuals you know well, and divide the group into types. For example, you might write about various types of parents, teachers, friends, or students. Be sure to include specific details that bring the various groups to life for your intended audience.

Catherine, who was double majoring in music and English, spent a couple of days thinking about possible topics she might write about. She thought she could write a more interesting essay if she wrote about a group known well by her but not by others in her composition class. As she mulled over possible topics while waiting to use one of the campus practice rooms that all music majors use regularly, an idea came to her: She could write about the various types of students who use the "dreaded practice rooms." Her narrowed topic would allow her to include information and details with which not everyone in her composition class would be familiar.

Catherine quickly reached into her backpack for her laptop and began brainstorming her limited subject. As she thought about how she could divide practice room users into various types, she came up with the following:

Types of Practice Room Users

- Those who are serious—the ones who actually use the practice rooms to practice their music. Sometimes I think that's the smallest group of all.

- Those who are the opposite of serious. They actually take naps in the practice rooms while people like me do what I'm doing now and sit outside, waiting for them to wake up and get out.

- Those who aggravate me the most—the ones who drop their backpacks in practice rooms and then go outside and talk with their friends, while students like me have to wait for them to finally stop socializing and get back in the room and practice.

- The students who are freaking out because the competition in the program is tough and so they freeze when they finally get into a practice room. They sit and look at the piano and do nothing, while I wait outside on the bench.

Catherine decided that she wanted to write a light-spirited essay about the various types of students who use practice rooms, and the ten minutes she spent brainstorming proved to be quite productive. Catherine prepared her first draft without shaping her prewriting further or making an outline. As she wrote, though, she frequently referred to her brainstorming to retrieve specifics about each type of practice room user.

Now read Catherine's essay, "The Benchers, the Nappers, the Jellyfish, and the Musicians," noting the similarities and differences between her prewriting and final essay. As you read the essay, consider how well it applies the principles of division-classification discussed in this chapter. (The commentary that follows the essay will help you look at the essay more closely and give you some sense of how Catherine went about revising her first draft.)

The Benchers, the Nappers, the Jellyfish, and the Musicians
by Catherine Gispert

First of two introductory paragraphs

As if getting into college and deciding where to go wasn't hard   1
enough, now you have to pick a major. It's a little overwhelming. Should you pick the easy route and check "Undecided," or just write down the first thing that comes to mind? Or maybe you're one of the lucky ones and you know what you want to do. If not, how about the arts? Painting, dancing, and acting might be a little daunting, but almost everyone can sing a bit or play "Hot Cross Buns" on the recorder. So maybe music is your thing.

Transition to focus on an issue music majors have to deal with

Be careful, though. As a music major, you'll find there is one   2
thing that everyone underestimates: the amount of time you'll spend locked up in a small room with only a piano, your sheet music, and a couple of chairs for company. Yes, these are the dreaded practice rooms. Never heard of them? If you choose to become a music major, not only will you quickly learn what they are; most of your life

*Second of two intro-
ductory paragraphs*

Thesis

*First heading—
informs the reader
of the first type of
practice room user*

Topic sentence

*Second heading—
informs the reader
of the second type of
practice room user*

*Third heading—
informs the reader
of the third type of
practice room user*

Topic sentence

*The first of three
paragraphs on the
third type of practice
room user*

will revolve around trying to find a practice room with a tuned piano, a nicely situated mirror so that you can check your posture and technique, or quite simply, one that's empty—because more often than not, at least during peak practicing times (think lunch time to early afternoon, when sane people are eating and enjoying the sunshine), you won't be able to find an empty practice room. Is this because everyone in the School of Music has the same idea as you: to hone his or her music craft? No, unfortunately, that is not the case. You see, there are four types of people in those occupied rooms, and only one of them is actually practicing.

The Benchers

Benchers are the first type of practice room occupiers. These are the social butterflies of the major. They're all friends with each other and enthusiastically gossip about conductors and teachers. Instead of practicing, they're gathered around the benches outside the hallway, blocking traffic. This is perfect, right? If they're out socializing, that means there must be a lot of rooms open. Alas, wrong again. The Benchers have all left their book bags and instruments in practice rooms (probably one of the rooms you wanted, too), saving the room for later. Whether "later" is in a couple of minutes or hours is uncertain. Of course, you could take matters into your own hands and knock on closed doors, but you might disturb the second practice room occupant on this list—the Nappers. 3

The Nappers

Let's not kid ourselves; everyone is a Napper at one time or another. Even you will fall victim to the occasional nap in a practice room. It's really only a matter of time before your fingers grow tired from plucking notes, or your eyelids start to droop after a long day of Sight Singing 101, Music Theory 202, and Music History 303. You'll close your eyes only for a minute, you tell yourself. Just a quick rest before you start on the next exercise in your music. That is, of course, until you are jolted awake by the rapping on the door from a fellow music major, wondering why she can't hear music coming from within. (Ugh, another Bencher? she's wondering.) "Taken!" you blurt out, while standing up to set the motion-sensing lights back on. You make a promise not to let them turn off again, but it's a losing battle. 4

The Jellyfish

If you've managed to avoid being a Bencher or a Napper, you could very likely end up a Jellyfish—immobilized by fear. Welcome to college, where every exam and final can make or break you—or so the Jellyfish believes. Dramatic? Yeah, but not exactly false, either. As a music major, you will face your very own set of final exams, called "juries." Your fate in the music program depends on your passing them. So, naturally, you will spend all year preparing for them: learning your major and minor scales to perfection, reciting your Italian and German lyrics until you hate both languages, and memorizing music you don't even like. But there will come a time when even all this won't be enough. Cue the existential crisis. 5

| The second of three paragraphs on the third type of practice room user | "What am I doing with my life?" you'll ask yourself, staring blankly at your music, panicking alone in a practice room. "How am I supposed to do this? I'm going to fail, get kicked out of the music school, and end up destitute on the streets." | 6 |

| The third of three paragraphs on the third type of practice room user | Yes, no, perhaps. Most likely, you just have pre-performance jitters, and even if that's not the case, maybe it's some comfort to know that you'll probably end up destitute on the streets whether you pass your juries or not. The stereotype isn't "starving musicians" for nothing! | 7 |

The Musicians

| Fourth heading—informs the reader of the fourth type of practice room user. The first of two paragraphs on the fourth type of practice room user | At last, there are the real music majors—the Musicians. They will actually be using practice rooms for their intended purpose: practicing. You might every so often hear a curse word or two and the slamming of piano keys, but not to worry; that means the music "genius" is flowing. The Musicians might leave their rooms, but it's generally only to get sheet music from their lockers or use the facilities. | 8 |

| The second of two paragraphs on the fourth type of practice room user | These are the people you should aspire to be. They essentially live in the practice rooms and will never have to worry about failing a jury. Benchers? Not a chance. They only socialize when filling their water bottles, and the conversation is usually about what they're practicing. And napping isn't an option; that would take away practice time, after all. What about panicking over their musical future? No time for that. They're too busy creating that future. | 9 |

| Conclusion | So if you decide to become a music major, at least you'll know from the start how difficult it is to acquire a practice room. Snagging one won't be easy, but practicing in one of them sure beats getting yelled at by the other students in your dorm or receiving noise complaints from the neighbors next door. Make sure the piano's tuned and still has all its keys, check the mirror for cracks and scratches, and find a good piano bench or chair. And finally, make sure the room just feels right. After all, you'll be spending the next few hours trapped inside, playing the same piece over and over. But that's okay. It's all in pursuit of the musical dream—right? | 10 |

Commentary

INTRODUCTION AND THESIS As Catherine Gispert thought about a possible topic for her classification essay, she decided that she would probably write a stronger essay if she wrote about a subject she knew well. As a music major, she spent a lot of time in practice rooms, and she had already been doing some thinking about the different types of students who used the rooms, so she decided that might be a good topic for her essay.

As Catherine thought about an audience for her essay, she decided to write for college students who had not yet decided on a major or who were thinking about switching majors. She wanted to engage her readers, and she knew that most of them would never have heard of "practice rooms." She also knew that if her readers were bored with her introduction, they would probably read no further. So as she worked on her essay, Catherine tried to write an introduction that would interest all students—no matter what major they were considering. She also tried to use an informal, playful tone, something that can be difficult to achieve. Catherine thought that an informal tone would engage her readers and make them want to keep reading. That tone is evident in her thesis: "You see, there are four types of people in those occupied rooms, and only one of them is actually practicing." Catherine does a nice job of crafting a thesis that draws her readers into her essay and makes them want to read on.

PURPOSE   Catherine's purpose in writing this essay was to share with her readers one of the challenges they would face if they became music majors—a challenge she faces almost every day: finding a place to practice. She realizes that her readers know nothing about the topic and that, unless she writes an engaging, well-organized, entertaining essay, they will not read it.

CATEGORIES AND TOPIC SENTENCES   To make her essay easier to follow, Catherine decided to use a technique she had never used before in an essay: headings. She knew that as a reader, headings helped her navigate difficult texts, and although the subject matter of her essay would not be considered "difficult," it was one that some readers might lose interest in, so she thought the headings might help keep them engaged.

As Catherine composed her essay, she realized that the topic sentences she was accustomed to using at the beginning of paragraphs to signal to her readers that she was transitioning to a new point could be repetitive in some cases; often, the headings themselves would signal the moves. So she focused on developing interesting headings that capture the essence of the various types of practice room users ("The Benchers," "The Nappers," "The Jellyfish," and "The Musicians") as well as supporting paragraphs that describe the various types of practice room users and bring them to life for her readers.

OVERALL ORGANIZATION AND PARAGRAPH STRUCTURE   Catherine made a smart decision when she decided to use headings to organize her essay. Although this technique is not appropriate for all essays, it works well in Catherine's informal, playful piece of writing and allows her to shift easily from one type of practice room user to the next.

She also does a good job of balancing the information she provides on the four types of practice room users. Each of the four sections is roughly the same length and provides readers with just enough (but not too much) information to help them picture the types of individuals Catherine is describing. She uses one paragraph (3) to describe the Benchers, one paragraph (4) to describe the Nappers, three (5–7) to describe the Jellyfish, and two (8–9) to describe the Musicians.

Catherine keeps her paragraphs relatively short and lively with imagined conversations ("'Taken!' you blurt out, while standing up to set the motion-sensing lights back on"—paragraph 4; "'What am I doing with my life?' you'll ask yourself, staring blankly at your music"—paragraph 6), and she provides specific details that allow her readers to know how music majors spend their days ("It's really only a matter of time before your fingers grow tired from plucking notes, or your eyelids start to droop after a long day of Sight Singing 101, Music Theory 202, and Music History 303"—paragraph 4; "…you'll spend all year…learning your major and minor scales to perfection, reciting your Italian and German lyrics until you hate both languages, and memorizing music you don't even like"—paragraph 5).

Although the overall development is balanced and strong, the introduction seems to be long in relation to the rest of the essay. In her eagerness to draw the reader in, Catherine might have focused too much on elaborating her introduction. For example, one parenthetical aside—"(think lunch time to early afternoon, when sane people are eating and enjoying the sunshine)"—introduces humor but lengthens the introduction with an awkwardly constructed sentence.

TONE Although it is often difficult to achieve a humorous tone, Catherine knew before she began writing the first draft of her essay that a serious tone would have been off-putting for readers who knew nothing about the lives of music majors and had no particular interest in learning more about them. She decided early in the writing process to use a light, friendly, playful tone that would be more likely to engage readers than would a serious tone. We hear this conversational tone throughout her essay: "So maybe music is your thing" (1); "This is perfect, right?" (3); "Welcome to college, where every exam and final can make or break you—or so the Jellyfish believes. Dramatic? Yeah, but not exactly false, either" (5); "Snagging [a practice room] won't be easy, but practicing in one of them sure beats getting yelled at by the other students in your dorm or receiving noise complaints from the neighbors next door" (10).

COMBINING PATTERNS OF DEVELOPMENT Catherine uses a few examples that employ cause-effect reasoning: "If they're out socializing, that means there must be a ton of rooms open. Alas, wrong again" (3) and "'How am I supposed to do this? I'm going to fail, get kicked out of the music school, and end up destitute on the streets'" (6). Introducing these patterns of development adds variety to her essay.

REVISING THE FIRST DRAFT Before she started drafting her essay, Catherine thought carefully about what she wanted to say and how she wanted to say it. She decided on her intended audience (college students who had not yet decided on a major or were considering switching from one major to another), an essay structure (classification—with headings for the four categories), and an appropriate tone (conversational, informal, and playful). With her audience, structure, and intended tone in mind, Catherine began writing.

As is often the case for writers at all levels, the most difficult part of writing an essay is getting started, and this was true for Catherine as she began typing this one. She struggled to find a way into her topic that captures the tone she wanted to use and engages her readers. Here is the original version of Catherine's opening paragraph:

> Congrats! You're in college. All right—enough celebrating. Now you must
> decide what you want to do with the rest of your life. Thankfully, there are a

few options: "Undecided," a freshman favorite, "Biology," something you'll probably change halfway through the year: or "The Arts," the best and worst decision you can make—music, especially.

When Catherine shared her first draft with her peer review group, she let them know that it was not complete—she had not yet written a conclusion—and that she was not at all happy with the opening paragraph and would appreciate any advice about how she might revise it. Both members of her group, Shaina and Ed, told her that they liked the informal tone but that she had not come across as especially friendly near the beginning when she stated, "All right—enough celebrating. Now you must decide what you want to do with the rest of your life." Shaina told Catherine that she sounded almost bossy in the opening paragraph, even though she knew that's not the way Catherine intended to come across. Ed agreed and pointed out that her tone softened by the time she got to the second paragraph and that she sounded much friendlier and playful from that point on.

A couple of days had passed since Catherine had written the first draft that she was sharing with Shaina and Ed, and that time away from her writing provided her with the distance she needed to more objectively review what she had written. She realized that Shaina and Ed were right and that the tone she used in the opening paragraph was not what she had intended.

Later that day she returned to her draft, deleted the opening paragraph, and completely revised it, using a friendlier, kinder tone. Then she wrote a conclusion that maintained the tone she had used throughout her essay, summarized the virtues of practice rooms despite their handicaps, and brought the essay back to the issue addressed in the introduction—readers' concern with choosing a major.

Activities: Division-Classification

Prewriting Activities

1. Imagine you're writing two essays. One is a humorous essay showing how to impress college instructors; the other is a serious essay explaining why volunteerism is on the rise. What aspects of the topics might you divide and/or classify?

2. Use group brainstorming to identify at least three possible principles of division for one of the following topics. For each principle, determine what your thesis might be if you were writing an essay.

   a. Prejudice

   b. Hip-hop music

   c. A good horror movie

3. Through group brainstorming, identify three different principles of classification that might provide the structure for an essay about the possible effects of a

controversial decision to expand your college's enrollment. Focusing on one of the principles, decide what your thesis might be. How would you sequence the categories?

Revising Activities

4. Following is a scratch outline for an essay developed through division-classification. On what principle of division-classification is the essay based? What problem do you see in the way the principle is applied? How could the problem be remedied?

    Thesis: The same experience often teaches opposite things to different people.

    - What working as a fast-food cook teaches: Some learn responsibility; others learn to take a "quick-and-dirty" approach.

    - What a negative experience teaches optimists: Some learn from their mistakes; others continue to maintain a positive outlook.

    - What a difficult course teaches: Some learn to study hard; others learn to avoid demanding courses.

    - What the breakup of a close relationship teaches: Some learn how to negotiate differences; others learn to avoid intimacy.

5. Following is a paragraph from the first draft of an essay urging that daycare centers adopt play programs tailored to children's developmental needs. What principle of division-classification focuses the paragraph? Is the principle applied consistently and logically? Are parts or categories developed sufficiently? Revise the paragraph, eliminating any problems you discover and adding specific details where needed.

    Within a few years, preschool children move from self-absorbed to interactive play. Babies and toddlers engage in solitary play. Although they sometimes prefer being near other children, they focus primarily on their own actions. This is very different from the highly interactive play of the elementary school years. Sometime in children's second year, solitary play is replaced by parallel play, during which children engage in similar activities near one another. However, they interact only occasionally. By age three, most children show at least some cooperative play, a form that involves interaction and cooperative role-taking. Such role-taking can be found in the "pretend" games that children play to explore adult relationships (games of "Mommy and Daddy") and anatomy (games of "Doctor"). Additional signs of youngsters' growing awareness of peers can be seen at about age four. At this age, many children begin showing a special devotion to one other child and may want to play only with that child. During this time, children also begin to take special delight in physical activities such as running and jumping, often going off by themselves to expend their abundant physical energy.

Professional Selections: Division-Classification

AMY TAN

The American writer Amy Tan was born in 1952, a few years after her parents had emigrated from China. Tan grew up in California and Switzerland, and she earned a master's degree in linguistics from San José State University. Her first novel, *The Joy Luck Club* (1987), won a National Book Award. Her other novels include *The Kitchen God's Wife* (1991), *The Bonesetter's Daughter* (2000), *Saving Fish from Drowning* (2005), *The Hundred Secret Senses* (2010), and *The Valley of Amazement* (2013). The following essay, first published in *The Threepenny Review*, is from her memoir *The Opposite of Fate: A Book of Musings* (2003).

Pre-Reading Journal Entry

Most people have different ways of speaking in different situations. Think of how you talk to your parents and other relatives; to children; to friends; to colleagues at work; to professors, doctors, and other professionals; and to your spouse or partner. Write down in your journal some examples of how you speak in various situations.

Figure 13.2 shows how this division-classification essay is organized.

Mother Tongue

I am not a scholar of English or literature. I cannot give you much more than personal opinions of the English language and its variations in this country or others. 1

I am a writer. And by that definition, I am someone who has always loved language. I am fascinated by language in daily life. I spend a great deal of my time thinking about the power of language—the way it can evoke an emotion, a visual image, a complex idea, or a simple truth. Language is the tool of my trade. And I use them all—all the Englishes I grew up with. 2

Recently, I was made keenly aware of the different Englishes I do use. I was giving a talk to a large group of people, the same talk I had already given to half a dozen other groups. The nature of the talk was about my writing, my life, and my book, *The Joy Luck Club*. The talk was going along well enough, until I remembered one major difference that made the whole talk sound wrong. My mother was in the room. And it was perhaps the first time she had heard me give a lengthy speech, using the kind of English I have never used with her. I was saying things like, "The intersection of memory upon imagination" and "There is an aspect of my fiction that relates to thus-and-thus"—a speech filled with carefully wrought grammatical phrases, burdened, it suddenly seemed to me, with nominalized forms, past perfect tenses, conditional phrases, all the forms of standard English that I had learned in school and through books, the forms of English I did not use at home with my mother. 3

Just last week, I was walking down the street with my mother, and I again found myself conscious of the English I was using, and the English I do use with her. We were talking about the price of new and used furniture and I heard myself saying this: "Not waste money that way." My husband was with us as well, and he 4 didn't notice any switch in my English. And then I realized why. It's because over the twenty years we've been together I've often used the same kind of English with him, and sometimes he even uses it with me. It has become our language of intimacy, a different sort of English that relates to family talk, the language I grew up with.

So you'll have some idea of what this family talk I heard sounds like, I'll quote what my mother said during a recent conversation which I videotaped and then transcribed. During this conversation, my mother was talking about a political gangster in Shanghai who had the same last name as her family's, Du, and how the gangster in his early years wanted to be adopted by her family, which was rich by comparison. Later, the gangster became more powerful, far richer than my mother's family, and one day showed up at my mother's wedding to pay his respects. Here's what she said in part:

> "Du Yusong having business like fruit stand. Like off the street kind. He is Du like Du Zong—but not Tsung-ming Island people. The local people call putong, the river east side, he belong to that side local people. The man want to ask Du Zong father take him in like become own family. Du Zong father wasn't look down on him, but didn't take seriously, until the man big like become a mafia. Now important person, very hard to inviting him. Chinese way, came only to show respect, don't stay for dinner. Respect for making big celebration, he shows up. Mean gives lots of respect. Chinese custom. Chinese social life that way. If too important won't have to stay too long. He come to my wedding. I didn't see, I heard it. I gone to boy's side, they have YMCA dinner. Chinese age I was nineteen."

You should know that my mother's expressive command of English belies how much she actually understands. She reads the Forbes report, listens to *Wall Street Week*, converses daily with her stockbroker, reads all of Shirley MacLaine's books with ease—all kinds of things I can't begin to understand. Yet some of my friends tell me they understand 50 percent of what my mother says. Some say they understand 80 to 90 percent. Some say they understand none of it, as if she were speaking pure Chinese. But to me, my mother's English is perfectly clear, perfectly natural. It's my mother tongue. Her language, as I hear it, vivid, direct, full of observation and imagery. That was the language that helped shape the way I saw things, expressed things, made sense of the world.

Lately, I've been giving more thought to the kind of English my mother speaks. Like others, I have described it to people as "broken" or "fractured" English. But I wince when I say that. It has always bothered me that I can think of no way to describe it other than "broken," as if it were damaged and needed to be fixed, as if it lacked a certain wholeness and soundness. I've heard other terms used, "limited English," for example. But they seem just as bad, as if everything is limited, including people's perceptions of the limited English speaker.

I know this for a fact, because when I was growing up, my mother's "limited" English limited *my* perception of her. I was ashamed of her English. I believed that her English reflected the quality of what she had to say. That is, because she expressed them imperfectly her thoughts were imperfect. And I had plenty of empirical evidence to support me: the fact that people in department stores, at banks, and at restaurants did not take her seriously, did not give her good service, pretended not to understand her, or even acted as if they did not hear her.

My mother has long realized the limitations of her English as well. When I was 10 fifteen, she used to have me call people on the phone to pretend I was she. In this guise, I was forced to ask for information or even to complain and yell at people who had been rude to her. One time it was a call to her stockbroker in New York. She had cashed out her small portfolio and it just so happened we were going to go to New York the next week, our very first trip outside California. I had to get on the phone and say in an adolescent voice that was not very convincing, "This is Mrs. Tan."

And my mother was standing in back whispering loudly, "Why he don't send 11 me check, already two weeks late. So mad he lie to me, losing me money."

And then I said in perfect English, "Yes, I'm getting rather concerned. You had 12 agreed to send the check two weeks ago, but it hasn't arrived."

Then she began to talk more loudly. "What he want, I come to New York tell 13 him front of his boss, you cheating me?" And I was trying to calm her down, make her be quiet, while telling the stockbroker, "I can't tolerate any more excuses. If I don't receive the check immediately, I am going to have to speak to your manager when I'm in New York next week." And sure enough, the following week there we were in front of this astonished stockbroker, and I was sitting there red-faced and quiet, and my mother, the real Mrs. Tan, was shouting at his boss in her impeccable broken English.

We used a similar routine just five days ago, for a situation that was far less 14 humorous. My mother had gone to the hospital for an appointment, to find out about a benign brain tumor a CAT scan had revealed a month ago. She said she had spoken very good English, her best English, no mistakes. Still, she said, the hospital did not apologize when they said they had lost the CAT scan and she had come for nothing. She said they did not seem to have any sympathy when she told them she was anxious to know the exact diagnosis, since her husband and son had both died of brain tumors. She said they would not give her any more information until the next time and she would have to make another appointment for that. So she said she would not leave until the doctor called her daughter. She wouldn't budge. And when the doctor finally called her daughter, me, who spoke in perfect English—lo and behold—we had assurances the CAT scan would be found, promises that a conference call on Monday would be held, and apologies for any suffering my mother had gone through for a most regrettable mistake.

I think my mother's English almost had an effect on limiting my possibili- 15 ties in life as well. Sociologists and linguists probably will tell you that a person's developing language skills are more influenced by peers. But I do think that the language spoken in the family, especially in immigrant families which are more insular, plays a large role in shaping the language of the child. And I believe that it affected my results on achievement tests, IQ tests, and the SAT. While my English skills were never judged as poor, compared to math, English could not be considered my strong suit. In grade school I did moderately well, getting perhaps B's, sometimes B-pluses, in English and scoring perhaps in the sixtieth or seventieth percentile on achievement tests. But those scores were not good enough to override the opinion that my true abilities lay in math and science, because in those areas I achieved A's and scored in the ninetieth percentile or higher.

This was understandable. Math is precise; there is only one correct answer. 16 Whereas, for me at least, the answers on English tests were always a judgment call, a matter of opinion and personal experience. Those tests were constructed around items like fill-in-the-blank sentence completion, such as, "Even though Tom was _____, Mary thought he was _____." And the correct answer always seemed to be the most bland combinations of thoughts, for example, "Even though Tom was shy, Mary thought he was charming," with the grammatical structure "even though" limiting the correct answer to some sort of semantic opposites, so you wouldn't get answers like, "Even though Tom was foolish, Mary thought he was ridiculous." Well, according to my mother, there were very few limitations as to what Tom could have been and what Mary might have thought of him. So I never did well on tests like that.

The same was true with word analogies, pairs of words in which you were 17 supposed to find some sort of logical, semantic relationship—for example, "*Sunset* is to *nightfall* as _____ is to _____." And here you would be presented with a list of four possible pairs, one of which showed the same kind of relationship: *red* is to *stoplight, bus* is to *arrival, chills* is to *fever, yawn* is to *boring.* Well, I could never think that way. I knew what the tests were asking, but I could not block out of my mind the images already created by the first pair, "*sunset* is to *nightfall*"—and I would see a burst of colors against a darkening sky, the moon rising, the lowering of a curtain of stars. And all the other pairs of words—red, bus, stoplight, boring—just threw up a mess of confusing images, making it impossible for me to sort out something as logical as saying: "A sunset precedes nightfall" is the same as "a chill precedes a fever." The only way I would have gotten that answer right would have been to imagine an associative situation, for example, my being disobedient and staying out past sunset, catching a chill at night, which turns into feverish pneumonia as punishment, which indeed did happen to me.

I have been thinking about all this lately, about my mother's English, about 18 achievement tests. Because lately I've been asked, as a writer, why there are not more Asian Americans represented in American literature. Why are there few Asian Americans enrolled in creative writing programs? Why do so many Chinese students go into engineering? Well, these are broad sociological questions I can't begin to answer. But I have noticed in surveys—in fact, just last week—that Asian students, as a whole, always do significantly better on math achievement tests than in English. And this makes me think that there are other Asian-American students whose English spoken in the home might also be described as "broken" or "limited." And perhaps they also have teachers who are steering them away from writing and into math and science, which is what happened to me.

Fortunately, I happen to be rebellious in nature and enjoy the challenge of dis- 19 proving assumptions made about me. I became an English major my first year in college, after being enrolled as pre-med. I started writing nonfiction as a freelancer the week after I was told by my former boss that writing was my worst skill and I should hone my talents toward account management.

But it wasn't until 1985 that I finally began to write fiction. And at first I wrote 20 using what I thought would be wittily crafted sentences, sentences that would finally prove I had mastery over the English language. Here's an example from the first draft of a story that later made its way into *The Joy Luck Club,* but without this line: "That was my mental quandary in the nascent state." A terrible line, which I can barely pronounce.

Fortunately, for reasons I won't get into today, I later decided I should envi-   21
sion a reader for the stories I would write. And the reader I decided upon was
my mother, because these were stories about mothers. So with this reader in
mind—and in fact she did read my early drafts—I began to write stories using
all the Englishes I grew up with: the English I spoke to my mother, which for
lack of a better term might be described as "simple"; the English she used with
me, which for lack of a better term might be described as "broken"; my translation of her Chinese, which could certainly be described as "watered down"; and

Figure 13.2

Essay Structure Diagram: "Mother Tongue" by Amy Tan

Introductory paragraphs **Background** **Thesis** (paragraphs 1–2)	Identification as a writer, not a scholar **Thesis:** "Language is the tool of my trade. And I use them all—all the Englishes I grew up with."
Background: examples (3–7)	Examples of Tan's use of the language (speaking to a group about her writing, writing a novel, talking with family members) Examples of Tan's mother's "broken" English (conversing about a political gangster, talking with a stockbroker, trying to obtain information about her CAT scan)
Causes and effects: examples (8–20)	Reflections the author makes about • the *effects* of describing forms of English as "broken" or "limited"; • ways that using "sub-standard" English *affects* students' academic test results; and • how students' use of "limited" English can *cause* teachers to steer them away from writing and towards math and science
Additional details of classification with examples (21)	Types of English Tan grew up using: • Simple—English Tan spoke to her mother • Broken—English Tan's mother used with her • Watered down—Tan's translation of her mother's Chinese • Tan's mother's internal language—what Tan imagined to be her mother's translation of her mother's Chinese if her mother could speak in perfect English What language ability tests cannot reveal: • Intent • Passion • Imagery • Rhythms of speech • Nature of thoughts
Concluding paragraph (22)	Author's closing comment on how she knew she had succeeded as a writer

what I imagined to be her translation of her Chinese if she could speak in perfect English, her internal language, and for that I sought to preserve the essence, but neither an English nor a Chinese structure. I wanted to capture what language ability tests can never reveal: her intent, her passion, her imagery, the rhythms of her speech and the nature of her thoughts.

Apart from what any critic had to say about my writing, I knew I had suc- 22 ceeded where it counted when my mother finished reading my book and gave me her verdict: "So easy to read."

Questions for Critical Reading

1. What is the selection's thesis? Locate the sentence(s) in which Tan states her main idea. If she doesn't state her thesis explicitly, express it in your own words.

2. Describe the particular event that prompted the author to think about her use of language. What does she mean by "different Englishes"? What are these "different Englishes"?

3. What questions has Tan been asked "as a writer"? What survey information does she use in formulating her response? Is the survey information valid? How does Tan use it to support personal information she gives in the essay?

4. How have Tan's feelings about her mother's command of English changed over the years?

Questions About the Writer's Craft

1. **Principle of classification**. What principle of classification does the author use to identify the "different Englishes" she describes? How is that principle reflected in the different types of English Tan mentions?

2. **Examples**. In paragraph 6, the author gives an extended example of her mother's speech. Why does she do this? What is the effect of having this quotation in the essay? How easy do you think it is to follow Tan's mother's speech?

3. **Anecdotes and other patterns**. The author uses personal anecdotes about her relationship with her mother to illustrate some important points. Identify at least two anecdotes. What points do they support? How effective are they? Why?

4. **A terrible line**. In paragraph 20, the author quotes a line that she wrote but ultimately did not include in the final version of her novel. Why does she call it a "terrible line," and why do you think she included it? How does the English in that line compare with the English in the excerpt of her mother's speech?

Writing Assignments Using Classification-Division as a Pattern of Development

1. Like Amy Tan, you probably do different kinds of writing. You might write e-mails at work, academic papers in class, text messages to friends, and journal or diary entries. You might also compose song lyrics, poems, or other kinds of creative

writing. Write an essay in which you classify the types of writing you do. Choose an appropriate principle of classification, and then show how the types of writing are similar and dissimilar. Use examples, including excerpts from your writing, to illustrate the points you make.

2. Tan classifies types of English, but there are other types of expression that can be classified. For example, you can classify manners, modes of dress, facial expressions, and kinds of greetings. Choose one of these topics or another such subject, and write an essay in which you classify types in this group. Decide whether you wish to inform or entertain, and develop a principle of classification that suits your purpose. Remember to include relevant examples.

Writing Assignment Combining Patterns of Development

3. The author mentions surveys showing how Asian Americans perform on standardized tests, such as the SAT. Proponents of standardized tests believe the tests hold all students to the same objective standard. Opponents believe some tests are unintentionally biased against one or more groups of students. Do some research on one standardized test. Develop a position about the test, and *argue* your position in an essay. Include the results of *relevant studies* and the opinions of *experts* as evidence for your views.

BIANCA BOSKER

Princeton University graduate Bianca Bosker is Executive Tech Editor for *The Huffington Post*, an online news website and blog that covers U.S. politics, world news, entertainment, and style. Bosker's publications have appeared in the *Wall Street Journal, Condé Nast Traveler*, and the *Far Eastern Economic Review*. She is the co-author of *Bowled Over: A Roll Down Memory Lane*, a tribute to the tradition and culture of bowling. The following article was published on *The Huffington Post* website on May 21, 2013.

Pre-Reading Journal Entry

In what ways do you make use of social media sites such as Facebook, Twitter, Instagram, and Myspace? How have the ways you use these sites changed over the past several years? If you don't use any of these sites, why not? Why do you think they are a major part of the lives of millions? Explore these ideas in your journal.

How Teens Are Really Using Facebook: It's a "Social Burden," Pew Study Finds

The Facebook generation is fed up with Facebook. 1

That's according to a report released Tuesday by the Pew Research Center, 2
which surveyed 802 teens between the ages of 12 and 17 [in September 2012] to produce a 107-page report on their online habits.

Pew's findings suggest teens' enthusiasm for Facebook is waning, lending cre- 3
dence to concerns, raised by the company's investors and others, that the social
network may be losing a crucial demographic that has long fueled its success
("Facebook's CEO").

Facebook has become a "social burden" for teens, write the authors of the Pew 4
report. "While Facebook is still deeply integrated in teens' everyday lives, it is
sometimes seen as a utility and an obligation rather than an exciting new platform
that teens can claim as their own" (Madden et al.).

Teens aren't abandoning Facebook—deactivating their accounts would mean 5
missing out on the crucial social intrigues that transpire online—and 94 percent of
teenage social media users still have profiles on the site, Pew's report notes. But
they're simultaneously migrating to Twitter and Instagram, which teens say offer
a parent-free place where they can better express themselves. Eleven percent of
teens surveyed had Instagram accounts, while the number of teen Twitter users
climbed from 16 percent in 2011 to 24 percent in 2012. Five percent of teens have
accounts on Tumblr, which was just purchased by Yahoo for $1.1 billion, while 7
percent have accounts on Myspace (Kleinman).

Where teens have social media profiles or accounts
% of teen social media users who use the following sites...

	2011	2012
Facebook	93%	94%
Twitter	12	26
Instagram	n/a	11
Myspace	24	7
YouTube	6	7
Tumblr	2	5
Google Plus	n/a	3
Yahoo (unspecified)	7	2
myYearbook	2	*
Pinterest	n/a	1
Gmail	n/a	1
Meet Me	n/a	1
Other	8	6
Don't know /Don't have own profile	2	1

SOURCE: Madden et al.

Facebook, teens say, has been overrun by parents, fuels unnecessary social "dra- 6
ma" and gives a mouthpiece to annoying oversharers who drone on about inane
events in their lives.

"Honestly, Facebook at this point, I'm on it constantly but I hate it so much," 7
one 15-year-old girl told Pew during a focus group (Madden et al.).

"I got mine [Facebook account] around sixth grade. And I was really obsessed 8
with it for a while," another 14-year-old said. "Then towards eighth grade, I kind
of just—once you get into Twitter, if you make a Twitter and an Instagram, then
you'll just kind of forget about Facebook, is what I did" (Madden et al.).

On the whole, teens' usage of social media seems to have plateaued, and the fraction of those who check social sites "several times a day" has stayed steady at around 40 percent since 2011 (Madden et al.). 9

Female (age 19): "Yeah, that's why we go on Twitter and Instagram [instead of Facebook]. My mom doesn't have that."

Female (age 15): "If you are on Facebook, you see a lot of drama."

Female (age 14): "OK, here's something I want to say. I think Facebook can be fun, but also it's drama central. On Facebook, people imply things and say things, even just by a like, that they wouldn't say in real life."

Male (age 18): "It's because [Facebook] it's where people post unnecessary pictures and they say unnecessary things, like saying he has a girlfriend, and a girl will go on and tag him in the picture like, me and him in the sun having fun. Why would you do that?" (Madden et al.)

Asked about teens' Facebook habits during a recent earnings call with investors, Facebook's chief financial officer answered that the company "remain[s] really pleased with the high level of engagement on Facebook by people of all ages around the world" and called younger users "among the most active and engaged users that we have on Facebook" ("Facebook's CEO"). 10

Here's what that "high level of engagement" really looks like, according to Pew: 11

They're deleting, lying and blocking: Some three-quarters of Facebook users have purged friends on Facebook, 58 percent have edited or deleted content they've shared, and 26 percent have tried to protect their privacy by sharing false information. Among all teens online (not just Facebook users), 39 percent have lied about their age. The report also notes, "Girls are more likely than boys to delete friends from their network (82 percent vs. 66 percent) and block people (67 percent vs. 48 percent)."

Superusers on Facebook are superusers on other social sites: Teens with large friend networks on Facebook are more likely than their peers to have profiles on other social media sites: 46 percent of teens with over 600 Facebook friends have a Twitter profile, and 12 percent of such users have an Instagram account. By comparison, just 21 percent and 11 percent of teens who have 150 to 300 friends have Twitter and Instagram accounts, respectively.

Teens have hundreds of friends, but they haven't met them all: The typical Facebook-using teen has 300 friends, though girls are more likely to have more friends (the median is 350) than boys (300). Seventy percent of teens are friends with their parents, 30 percent are friends with teachers or coaches, and 33 percent are friends with people they've never met in person.

It turns out parents actually do see what their kids are posting: Just 5 percent of teens tweak their privacy to limit what their parents see.

They're watching out for their privacy: Sixty percent of teens on Facebook say they've checked their privacy settings in the past month—a third of them within the past seven days. The majority (60 percent) of teens have their profiles set to private, while 14 percent have profiles that are completely public.

But yes, they are sharing personal details: Teens with more Facebook friends are more likely to share a greater variety of personal details about themselves online. Among all teens on Facebook, 21 percent share their cell phone number, 63 percent share their relationship status and 54 percent share their email address.

Seventeen percent of teens on Facebook will automatically share their location in their posts, and 18 percent say they've shared something they later regret posting.

They're enjoying themselves, but they've been contacted by creeps: Among all teens surveyed by Pew, 17 percent have been contacted by strangers in a way that made them "scared or uncomfortable." However, 57 percent of social media–using teens said they've had an experience online that "made them feel good about themselves," and 37 percent say social media has made them feel more connected to someone else.

Works Cited

"Facebook's CEO Discusses Q1 2013 Results—Earnings Call Transcript." *Seeking Alpha,* 1 May 2013, seekingalpha.com/article/1392101-facebooks-ceo-discusses-q1-2013-results-earnings-call-transcript.
Kleinman, Alexis. "Yahoo Tumblr Deal Is Officially Announced." *Huffington Post,* 20 May 2013, www.huffingtonpost.com/2013/05/20/yahoo-tumblr-deal_n_3305953.html.
Madden, Mary, et al. "Teens, Social Media, and Privacy." *Pew Internet & American Life Project,* 21 May 2013, www.pewinternet.org/2013/05/21/teens-social-media-and-privacy.

Questions for Critical Reading

1. What is the selection's thesis? Locate the sentence(s) in which Bosker states her main idea. If she doesn't state the thesis explicitly, express it in your own words.

2. According to the Pew report by Madden et al. that Bosker references in her article, in what ways has Facebook become a "social burden" for many users?

3. The chart from the Pew report that is included in this reading shows the percentage of teens using various social media sites. According to the chart, which two sites have shown the largest increases in use, and which two have shown the greatest decreases?

4. The phrase "high level of engagement" appears in paragraphs 10 and 11 of the article. How does Facebook's chief financial officer's use of the term differ from the way, according to Bosker, the Pew report interprets "what that 'high level of engagement' really looks like"?

Questions About the Writer's Craft

1. **The pattern**. In what ways does Bosker's article classify teens' use of social media sites? Does the classification scheme seem reasonable to you? Why or why not?

2. **Other patterns**. In addition to classifying the ways teens use social media sites, Bosker provides examples that *illustrate* the points she is making. List three of the examples she uses that you think work especially well to support her thesis.

3. **Sources**. Bosker references three sources in her article. Which one does she rely most heavily on and why? In what ways does the use of the other two sources enrich her article?

4. **Graphics**. Why do you think Bosker decided to include a chart from the Pew report in her article? In what ways does the chart add to the effectiveness of her article?

Writing Assignments Using Division-Classification as a Pattern of Development

1. The authors of the Pew report gathered information on the online habits of teens between the ages of 12 and 17. Conduct your own research by designing a questionnaire on the online habits of another group—perhaps the students in your composition class or the members of another group or community to which you belong. Write an essay in which you present the information you gathered, classifying the ways the members of your research group use online media sites. Consider designing a chart similar to the one in the Bosker article, and include it in your composition to illustrate the various sites where the members of your research group have social media profiles or accounts.

2. Write an essay in which you classify the types of music most popular today among a particular demographic. You might rely on secondary sources for the information you include in your essay—as Bosker did in hers—or you might conduct your own primary research using questionnaires or surveys that you design. Consider using visuals such as charts or graphs to clearly present your findings to your readers.

Writing Assignment Combining Patterns of Development

3. Write an essay in which you *compare* and *contrast* various social media sites. For example, you might compare Facebook, Twitter, and Instagram and explore what the sites have in common as well as how they differ from one another. You might also include quotes from individuals you interview to *illustrate* what these social media users consider to be advantages and disadvantages of the various sites.

WILLIAM ZINSSER

In addition to having taught at both the Columbia University Graduate School of Journalism and the New School in New York City, William Zinsser has written news journalism, drama criticism, magazine columns, a memoir, and several books on U.S. culture. Born in 1922 in New York, Zinsser worked for *The New York Herald Tribune* and *Life*. In 1970, Zinsser designed a course in nonfiction writing for Yale University. Using what he learned at Yale about the way college students approach the writing process, Zinsser wrote the popular guide *On Writing Well* (1976), now in its seventh edition. He has written seven other titles and has also edited an additional seven books on writing, including *Inventing the Truth: The Art & Craft of Memoir* (1995). The following essay first appeared in the magazine *Country Journal* in 1979.

Pre-Reading Journal Entry

Many students feel pressured by college graduation requirements. Do you? What courses are you required to take that you wouldn't ordinarily choose? What courses would you like to take but don't have time for? Should colleges require students to take courses that aren't part of their majors? Why or why not? Use your journal to respond to these questions.

College Pressures

Dear Carlos: I desperately need a dean's excuse for my chem midterm which will begin in about 1 hour. All I can say is that I totally blew it this week. I've fallen incredibly, inconceivably behind.

Carlos: Help! I'm anxious to hear from you. I'll be in my room and won't leave it until I hear from you. Tomorrow is the last day for . . .

Carlos: I left town because I started bugging out again. I stayed up all night to finish a take-home make-up exam & am typing it to hand in on the 10th. It was due on the 5th. P.S. I'm going to the dentist. Pain is pretty bad.

Carlos: Probably by Friday I'll be able to get back to my studies. Right now I'm going to take a long walk. This whole thing has taken a lot out of me.

Carlos: I'm really up the proverbial creek. The problem is I really *bombed* the history final. Since I need that course for my major I . . .

Carlos: Here follows a tale of woe. I went home this weekend, had to help my Mom, & caught a fever so didn't have much time to study. My professor . . .

Carlos: Aargh! Trouble. Nothing original but everything's piling up at once. To be brief, my job interview . . .

Hey Carlos, good news! I've got mononucleosis.

Who are these wretched supplicants, scribbling notes so laden with anxiety, seeking such miracles of postponement and balm? They are men and women who belong to Branford College, one of the twelve residential colleges at Yale University, and the messages are just a few of the hundreds that they left for their dean, Carlos Hortas—often slipped under his door at 4 A.M.—last year.

1

But students like the ones who wrote those notes can also be found on campuses from coast to coast—especially in New England and at many other private colleges across the country that have high academic standards and highly motivated students. Nobody could doubt that the notes are real. In their urgency and their gallows humor they are authentic voices of a generation that is panicky to succeed. 2

My own connection with the message writers is that I am master of Branford College. I live in its Gothic quadrangle and know the students well. (We have 485 of them.) I am privy to their hopes and fears—and also to their stereo music and their piercing cries in the dead of the night ("Does anybody *ca-a-are?*"). If they went to Carlos to ask how to get through tomorrow, they come to me to ask how to get through the rest of their lives. 3

Mainly I try to remind them that the road ahead is a long one and that it will have more unexpected turns than they think. There will be plenty of time to change jobs, change careers, change whole attitudes and approaches. They don't want to hear such liberating news. They want a map—right now—that they can follow unswervingly to career security, financial security, Social Security and, presumably, a prepaid grave. 4

What I wish for all students is some release from the clammy grip of the future. I wish them a chance to savor each segment of their education as an experience in itself and not as a grim preparation for the next step. I wish them the right to experiment, to trip and fall, to learn that defeat is as instructive as victory and is not the end of the world. 5

My wish, of course, is naïve. One of the few rights that America does not proclaim is the right to fail. Achievement is the national god, venerated in our media—the million-dollar athlete, the wealthy executive—and glorified in our praise of possessions. In the presence of such a potent state religion, the young are growing up old. 6

I see four kinds of pressure working on college students today: economic pressure, parental pressure, peer pressure, and self-induced pressure. It is easy to look around for villains—to blame the colleges for charging too much money, the professors for assigning too much work, the parents for pushing their children too far, the students for driving themselves too hard. But there are no villains; only victims. 7

"In the late 1960s," one dean told me, "the typical question that I got from students was 'Why is there so much suffering in the world?' or 'How can I make a contribution?' Today it's 'Do you think it would look better for getting into law school if I did a double major in history and political science, or just majored in one of them?'" Many other deans confirmed this pattern. One said: "They're trying to find an edge—the intangible something that will look better on paper if two students are about equal." 8

Note the emphasis on looking better. The transcript has become a sacred document, the passport to security. How one appears on paper is more important than how one appears in person. *A* is for Admirable and *B* is for Borderline, even though, in Yale's official system of grading, *A* means "excellent" and *B* means "very good." Today, looking very good is no longer good enough, especially for students who hope to go on to law school or medical school. They know that entrance into the better schools will be an entrance into the better law firms and better medical practices where they will make a lot of money. They also know that the odds are harsh. Yale Law School, for instance, matriculates 170 students from an applicant pool of 3,700; Harvard enrolls 550 from a pool of 7,000. 9

It's all very well for those of us who write letters of recommendation for our 10
students to stress the qualities of humanity that will make them good lawyers or
doctors. And it's nice to think that admission officers are really reading our letters
and looking for the extra dimension of commitment or concern. Still, it would
be hard for a student not to visualize these officers shuffling so many transcripts
studded with *A*s that they regard a *B* as positively shameful.

The pressure is almost as heavy on students who just want to graduate and get 11
a job. Long gone are the days of the "gentleman's *C*, " when students journeyed
through college with a certain relaxation, sampling a wide variety of courses—
music, art, philosophy, classics, anthropology, poetry, religion—that would send
them out as liberally educated men and women. If I were an employer I would
rather employ graduates who have this range and curiosity than those who nar-
rowly pursued safe subjects and high grades. I know countless students whose
inquiring minds exhilarate me. I like to hear the play of their ideas. I don't know if
they are getting *A*s or *C*s, and I don't care. I also like them as people. The country
needs them, and they will find satisfying jobs. I tell them to relax. They can't.

Nor can I blame them. They live in a brutal economy. Tuition, room, and board 12
at most private colleges now comes to at least $7,000 [in 1979], not counting books
and fees. This might seem to suggest that the colleges are getting rich. But they
are equally battered by inflation. Tuition covers only 60 percent of what it costs to
educate a student, and ordinarily the remainder comes from what colleges receive
in endowments, grants, and gifts. Now the remainder keeps being swallowed by
the cruel costs—higher every year—of just opening the doors. Heating oil is up.
Insurance is up. Postage is up. Health-premium costs are up. Everything is up.
Deficits are up. We are witnessing in America the creation of a brotherhood of
paupers—colleges, parents, and students, joined by the common bond of debt.

Today it is not unusual for a student, even if he works part time at college and full 13
time during the summer, to accrue $5,000 in loans after four years—loans that he must
start to repay within one year after graduation. Exhorted at commencement to go forth
into the world, he is already behind as he goes forth. How could he not feel under
pressure throughout college to prepare for this day of reckoning? I have used "he,"
incidentally, only for brevity. Women at Yale are under no less pressure to justify their
expensive education to themselves, their parents, and society. In fact, they are probably under more pressure. For although they leave college superbly equipped to bring
fresh leadership to traditionally male jobs, society hasn't yet caught up with this fact.

Along with economic pressure goes parental pressure. Inevitably, the two are 14
deeply intertwined.

I see many students taking pre-medical courses with joyless tenacity. They go 15
off to their labs as if they were going to the dentist. It saddens me because I know
them in other corners of their life as cheerful people.

"Do you want to go to medical school?" I ask them. 16

"I guess so," they say, without conviction, or "Not really." 17

"Then why are you going?" 18

"Well, my parents want me to be a doctor. They're paying all this money and . . ." 19

Poor students, poor parents. They are caught in one of the oldest webs of love 20
and duty and guilt. The parents mean well; they are trying to steer their sons and

daughters toward a secure future. But the sons and daughters want to major in history or classics or philosophy—subjects with no "practical" value. Where's the payoff on the humanities? It's not easy to persuade such loving parents that the humanities do indeed pay off. The intellectual faculties developed by studying subjects like history and classics—an ability to synthesize and relate, to weigh cause and effect, to see events in perspective—are just the faculties that make creative leaders in business or almost any general field. Still, many fathers would rather put their money on courses that point toward a specific profession—courses that are pre-law, pre-medical, pre-business, or, as I sometimes heard it put, "pre-rich."

But the pressure on students is severe. They are truly torn. One part of them 21 feels obligated to fulfill their parents' expectations; after all, their parents are older and presumably wiser. Another part tells them that the expectations that are right for their parents are not right for them.

I know a student who wants to be an artist. She is very obviously an artist and 22 will be a good one—she has already had several modest local exhibits. Meanwhile she is growing as a well-rounded person and taking humanistic subjects that will enrich the inner resources out of which her art will grow. But her father is strongly opposed. He thinks that an artist is a "dumb" thing to be. The student vacillates and tries to please everybody. She keeps up with her art somewhat furtively and takes some of the "dumb" courses her father wants her to take—at least they are dumb courses for her. She is a free spirit on a campus of tense students—no small achievement in itself—and she deserves to follow her muse.

Peer pressure and self-induced pressure are also intertwined, and they begin 23 almost at the beginning of freshman year.

"I had a freshman student I'll call Linda," one dean told me, "who came in and 24 said she was under terrible pressure because her roommate, Barbara, was much brighter and studied all the time. I couldn't tell her that Barbara had come in two hours earlier to say the same thing about Linda."

The story is almost funny—except that it's not. It's symptomatic of all the pres- 25 sures put together. When every student thinks every other student is working harder and doing better, the only solution is to study harder still. I see students going off to the library every night after dinner and coming back when it closes at midnight. I wish they would sometimes forget about their peers and go to a movie. I hear the clacking of typewriters in the hours before dawn. I see the tension in their eyes when exams are approaching and papers are due: *"Will I get everything done?"*

Probably they won't. They will get sick. They will get "blocked." They will 26 sleep. They will oversleep. They will bug out. *Hey, Carlos, help!*

Part of the problem is that they do more than they are expected to do. A professor 27 will assign five-page papers. Several students will start writing ten-page papers to impress him. Then more students will write ten-page papers, and a few will raise the ante to fifteen. Pity the poor student who is still just doing the assignment.

"Once you have twenty or thirty percent of the student population deliberately 28 overexerting," one dean points out, "it's bad for everybody. When a teacher gets more and more effort from his class, the student who is doing normal work can be perceived as not doing well. The tactic works, psychologically."

Why can't the professor just cut back and not accept longer papers? He can, 29 and he probably will. But by then the term will be half over and the damage done. Grade fever is highly contagious and not easily reversed. Besides, the professor's main concern is with his course. He knows his students only in relation to the course and doesn't know that they are also overexerting in their other courses. Nor is it really his business. He didn't sign up for dealing with the student as a whole person and with all the emotional baggage the student brought along from home. That's what deans, masters, chaplains, and psychiatrists are for.

To some extent this is nothing new: a certain number of professors have always 30 been self-contained islands of scholarship and shyness, more comfortable with books than with people. But the new pauperism has widened the gap still further, for professors who actually like to spend time with students don't have as much time to spend. They are also overexerting. If they are young, they are busy trying to publish in order not to perish, hanging by their fingernails onto a shrinking profession. If they are old and tenured, they are buried under the duties of administering departments—as departmental chairmen or members of committees—that have been thinned out by the budgetary axe.

Ultimately it will be the students' own business to break the circles in which 31 they are trapped. They are too young to be prisoners of their parents' dreams and their classmates' fears. They must be jolted into believing in themselves as unique men and women who have the power to shape their own future.

"Violence is being done to the undergraduate experience," says Carlos Hortas. 32 "College should be open-ended: at the end it should open many, many roads. Instead, students are choosing their goal in advance, and their choices narrow as they go along. It's almost as if they think that the country has been codified in the type of jobs that exist—that they've got to fit into certain slots. Therefore, fit into the best-paying slot.

"They ought to take chances. Not taking chances will lead to a life of colorless 33 mediocrity. They'll be comfortable. But something in the spirit will be missing."

I have painted too drab a portrait of today's students, making them seem a solemn 34 lot. That is only half of their story; if they were so dreary I wouldn't so thoroughly enjoy their company. The other half is that they are easy to like. They are quick to laugh and to offer friendship. They are not introverts. They are unusually kind and are more considerate of one another than any student generation I have known.

Nor are they so obsessed with their studies that they avoid sports and extracur- 35 ricular activities. On the contrary, they juggle their crowded hours to play on a variety of teams, perform with musical and dramatic groups, and write for campus publications. But this in turn is one more cause of anxiety. There are too many choices. Academically, they have 1,300 courses to select from; outside class they have to decide how much spare time they can spare and how to spend it.

This means that they engage in fewer extracurricular pursuits than their prede- 36 cessors did. If they want to row on the crew and play in the symphony they will eliminate one; in the '60s they would have done both. They also tend to choose activities that are self-limiting. Drama, for instance, is flourishing in all twelve of Yale's residential colleges as it never has before. Students hurl themselves into these productions—as actors, directors, carpenters, and technicians—with a dedication to create the best possible play, knowing that the day will come when the run will end and they can get back to their studies.

They also can't afford to be the willing slave of organizations like the *Yale Daily* 37 *News* . . . . At the one-hundredth anniversary banquet of that paper—whose past chairmen include such once and future kings as Potter Stewart, Kingman Brewster, and William F. Buckley, Jr.—much was made of the fact that the editorial staff used to be small and totally committed and that "newsies" routinely worked fifty hours a week. In effect they belonged to a club; Newsies is how they defined themselves at Yale. Today's student will write one or two articles a week, when he can, and he defines himself as a student. I've never heard the word Newsie except at the banquet.

If I have described the modern undergraduate primarily as a driven creature 38 who is largely ignoring the blithe spirit inside who keeps trying to come out and play, it's because that's where the crunch is, not only at Yale but throughout American education. It's why I think we should all be worried about the values that are nurturing a generation so fearful of risk and so goal-obsessed at such an early age.

I tell students that there is no one "right" way to get ahead—that each of them is 39 a different person, starting from a different point and bound for a different destination. I tell them that change is a tonic and that all the slots are not codified nor the frontiers closed. One of my ways of telling them is to invite men and women who have achieved success outside the academic world to come and talk informally with my students during the year. They are heads of companies or ad agencies, editors of magazines, politicians, public officials, television magnates, labor leaders, business executives, Broadway producers, artists, writers, economists, photographers, scientists, historians—a mixed bag of achievers.

I ask them to say a few words about how they got started. The students assume 40 that they started in their present profession and knew all along that it was what they wanted to do. Luckily for me, most of them got into their field by a circuitous route, to their surprise, after many detours. The students are startled. They can hardly conceive of a career that was not pre-planned. They can hardly imagine allowing the hand of God or chance to nudge them down some unforeseen trail.

Questions for Critical Reading

1. What is the selection's thesis? Locate the sentence(s) in which Zinsser states his main idea. If he doesn't state the thesis explicitly, express it in your own words.

2. According to Zinsser, why are the pressures on college students so harmful?

3. Zinsser says that some of the pressures are "intertwined." What does he mean? Give examples from the essay.

4. What actions or attitudes on the part of students can help free them from the pressures that Zinsser describes?

Questions About the Writer's Craft

1. **The pattern**. When analyzing a subject, writers usually try to identify divisions and classifications that are—within reason—mutually exclusive. But Zinsser acknowledges that the four pressures he discusses can be seen as two distinct pairs, with each pair consisting of two "deeply intertwined" pressures. How does this overlapping of categories help Zinsser make his point?

2. **Other patterns**. In addition to using classification in this essay, what other pattern of development does Zinsser use? How does this additional pattern help him make his point?

3. Why do you suppose Zinsser uses the notes to Carlos as his essay's introduction? What profile of college students does the reader get from these notes?

4. In paragraph 4, the author writes that students want a map "they can follow unswervingly to career security, financial security, Social Security and, presumably, a prepaid grave." What tone is Zinsser using here? Where else does he use this tone?

Writing Assignments Using Division-Classification as a Pattern of Development

1. Zinsser writes as if all students are the same—panicky, overwrought, and materialistic. Take a position counter to his, and write an essay explaining that campuses contain many students different from those Zinsser writes about. To support your point, categorize students into types, giving examples of what each type is like. Be sure that the categories you identify refute Zinsser's analysis of the typical student. The tone of your essay may be serious or playful.

2. Is economic security the only kind of satisfaction that college students should pursue? Write an essay classifying the various kinds of satisfactions that students could aim for. At the end of the essay, include brief recommendations about ways that students could best spend their time preparing for these different kinds of satisfactions.

Writing Assignment Combining Patterns of Development

3. Using Zinsser's analysis of the pressures on college students, write an essay explaining how these pressures can be reduced or eliminated. Give practical suggestions showing how students can avoid or get around the pressures. Also, indicate what society, parents, and college staff can do to help ease students' anxieties. You might benefit from gathering examples of and information on this topic in the library and/or on the Internet before writing.

Additional Writing Topics: Division-Classification

General Assignments

Using division-classification, develop one of these topics into an essay.

Division	Classification
1. A shopping mall	1. Commercials
2. A video system	2. Holidays
3. A particular kind of team	3. Roommates
4. A school library	4. Summer movies
5. A college campus	5. Internet surfers

Assignments Using Multimedia

Use the suggested media to help develop a division-classification essay on one of these topics:

1. Types of friends and the roles they play in our lives (slide show or cartoons)

2. Novels made into movies in the past two years (weblinks to movie trailers)

3. Various parenting styles by period or region (charts)

4. This year's most popular TV shows (links to websites and/or *YouTube* videos)

5. Personality types identified by psychologists (charts and/or graphs)

Assignments with a Specific Purpose, Audience, and Point of View

1. **Academic life**. You're a dorm counselor. During orientation week, you'll be talking to students on your floor about the different kinds of problems they may have with roommates. Write your talk, describing each kind of problem and explaining how to cope.

2. **Academic life**. As your college newspaper's TV critic, you plan to write a review of the fall shows, most of which—in your opinion—lack originality. To show how stereotypical the programs are, select one type (for example, situation comedies or crime dramas). Then use a specific division-classification principle to illustrate that the same stale formulas are trotted out from show to show.

3. **Civic activity.** Asked to write an editorial for the local newspaper, you decide to do a half-serious piece on taking "mental health" days off from work. Structure your essay around three kinds of occasions when "playing hooky" is essential for maintaining sanity.

4. **Civic activity**. Your favorite magazine runs an editorial asking readers to send in what they think are the main challenges facing their particular gender group. Write a letter to the editor in which you identify at least three categories of problems that your sex faces. Be sure to provide lively, specific examples to illustrate each category. In your letter, you may adopt a serious or lighthearted tone, depending on your over-all subject matter.

5. **Workplace action**. As a driving instructor, you decide to prepare a lecture on the types of drivers that your students are likely to encounter on the road. In your lecture, categorize drivers according to a specific principle and show the behaviors of each type.

6. **Workplace action**. A seasoned camp counselor, you've been asked to prepare, for new counselors, an informational sheet on children's emotional needs. Categorizing those needs into types, explain what counselors can do to nurture youngsters emotionally.

Chapter 14
Process Analysis

14.1 Understand how you can use the process analysis pattern to develop your essays.

14.2 Consider how process analysis can fit your purpose and audience.

14.3 Develop prewriting strategies for using process analysis in an essay.

14.4 Develop strategies for writing a process analysis essay.

14.5 Use strategies for revising your process analysis essay.

14.6 Analyze how process analysis is used effectively in a student-written selection.

What Is Process Analysis?

14.1 Understand how you can use the process analysis pattern to develop your essays.

We spend a good deal of our lives learning—everything from speaking our first word to registering for our first college courses. Indeed, the milestones in our lives are often linked to the processes we have mastered: how to cross the street alone, how to drive a car, how to make a speech without being paralyzed by fear.

Process analysis, a technique that explains the steps or sequence involved in doing something, satisfies our need to learn as well as our curiosity about how the world works. Process analysis can be more than merely interesting or entertaining, though; it can be of critical importance. Consider a waiter hurriedly skimming the "Choking Aid" instructions posted on a restaurant wall or an air-traffic controller following emergency procedures in an effort to prevent a midair collision. In these examples, the consequences could be fatal if the process analyses are slipshod, inaccurate, or confusing.

Undoubtedly, all of us have experienced less dramatic effects of poorly written process analyses. Perhaps you've tried to assemble a bicycle or a piece of IKEA furniture and spent hours sorting through a stack of parts, only to end up with one or two extra pieces never mentioned or shown in the instructions. No wonder many people stay clear of anything that admits "assembly required."

How Process Analysis Fits Your Purpose and Audience

14.2 Consider how process analysis can fit your purpose and audience.

You use process analysis in two types of writing situations: (1) when you want to give step-by-step instructions to readers showing them how to do something or (2) when you want readers to understand how something happens even though they won't actually follow the steps outlined. The first kind of process analysis is **directional**; the second is **informational**.

When you follow guidelines for completing a job application, you're reading directional process analysis. A serious essay explaining how to select a college is also an example of a directional process analysis. Using a variety of tones, informational process analyses can range over many subjects. They can describe mechanical, scientific, historical, sociological, artistic, or psychological processes: for example, how the core of a nuclear power plant melts down or how television became so important in political campaigns.

Problem Solving

Process analysis, both directional and informational, is often appropriate in *problem-solving situations.* In such cases, you say, "Here's the problem and here's what should be done to solve the problem." Indeed, college assignments frequently take the form of problem-solving process analyses. Consider these examples:

> Because many colleges and universities have changed the eligibility require-ments for financial aid, fewer students receive loans or scholarships. How can students cope with the increasing costs of obtaining a higher education?

> Community officials have been accused of mismanaging recent unrest over the public housing ordinance. Describe the steps the officials took, indicating why you think their strategy was unwise. Then explain how you think the situation should have been handled.

Note that the second assignment asks students to explain what's wrong with the current approach before they present their own step-by-step solution. Problem-solving process analyses are often organized in this way. You may also have noticed that nei-ther assignment explicitly requires an essay response using process analysis. However, the wording of the assignments—"How *can students* cope," "Describe the steps"—indicates that process analysis is an appropriate strategy for developing the responses.

Assignments don't always signal the use of process analysis so clearly. But dur-ing the prewriting stage, as you generate material to support your thesis, you'll often realize that you can best achieve your purpose by developing the essay—or part of it—using process analysis.

Process Analysis Combined with Other Strategies

Sometimes process analysis will be the primary strategy for organizing an essay; other times it will be used to help make a point in an essay organized around another pat-tern of development. Let's take a look at process analysis as a supporting strategy in several types of essays.

- Assume that you're writing a *causal analysis* examining the impact of television commercials on people's buying behavior. To help readers see that commercials create a need where none existed before, you might describe the various stages in an advertising campaign to pitch a new, completely frivolous product.

- In an essay *defining* a good boss, you could convey the point that effective manag-ers must be skilled at settling disputes by explaining the steps your boss took to resolve a heated disagreement between two employees.

- If you write an *argumentation-persuasion* essay urging the funding of programs to ease the plight of the homeless, you would have to dramatize for readers the trag-edy of these people's lives. To achieve your purpose, you could devote part of the essay to an explanation of how the typical street person goes about finding a place to sleep and getting food to eat.

Prewriting Strategies

14.3 Develop prewriting strategies for using process analysis in an essay.

The following checklist shows how you can apply prewriting strategies to process analysis.

☑ **Process Analysis: A Prewriting Checklist**

Choose a Process to Analyze

☐ What processes do you know well and feel you can explain clearly?

☐ What processes have you wondered about?

☐ What process needs changing if a current problem is to be solved?

Determine Your Purpose, Audience, Tone, and Point of View

☐ What is the central purpose of your process analysis? Do you want to inform readers so that they will acquire a new skill? Do you want readers to gain a better understanding of a complex process? Do you want to persuade readers to accept your point of view about a process, perhaps even urge them to adopt a particular course of action?

☐ What audience are you writing for? What will they need to know to understand the process? What will they not need to know?

☐ What point of view will you adopt when addressing the audience?

☐ What tone do you want to project? Do you want to come across as serious, humorous, sarcastic, ironic, objective, impassioned?

Use Prewriting to Generate the Stages of the Process

☐ How could brainstorming or mapping help you identify primary and secondary steps in the process?

☐ How could brainstorming or mapping help you identify the ingredients or materials that the reader will need?

Strategies for Using Process Analysis in an Essay

14.4 Develop strategies for writing a process analysis essay.

After prewriting, you're ready to draft your essay. Figure 14.1 and the suggestions that follow will be helpful whether you use process analysis as a dominant or supportive pattern of development.

1. **Formulate a thesis that clarifies your attitude toward the process.**

    Like the thesis in any other composition, the thesis in a process analysis should do more than announce your subject. It should also state or imply your attitude toward the process.

2. **Keep your audience in mind when deciding what to cover.**

Only after you gauge how much your readers already know (or don't know) about the process can you determine how much explanation to provide.

The audience's level of knowledge determines whether you should define technical terms. To determine how much explanation is needed, put yourself in your readers' shoes. Don't assume readers will know something just because you do. Ask these questions about your audience: "Will my readers need some background about the process before I describe it in depth?" and "If my essay is directional, should I specify near the beginning the ingredients, materials, and equipment needed to perform the process?" (For more help in analyzing your audience, see this chapter's prewriting checklist.)

3. **Focusing on your purpose, thesis, and audience, explain the process—one step at a time.**

After using prewriting techniques to identify primary and secondary steps and needed supplies and/or equipment, you're ready to organize your raw material into an easy-to-follow sequence. For example:

- At times your purpose will be to explain a process with a *fairly fixed chronological sequence:* how to make a pizza or how to pot a plant. In such cases, you should include all necessary steps in the correct chronological order. However, if a strict chronological ordering of steps means that a particularly important part of the sequence gets buried in the middle, you should probably juggle the sequence so that the crucial step receives the attention it deserves.

- Other times your goal will be to describe a process having *no commonly accepted sequence.* For example, in an essay explaining how to discipline a child or how to pull yourself out of a blue mood, you will have to come up with your own definition of the key steps and then arrange those steps in some logical order.

- You may also use process analysis to *reject* or *reformulate* a traditional sequence. In this case, you would propose a more logical series of steps: "Our system for electing congressional representatives is inefficient and undemocratic; it should be reformed in the following ways."

Whether the essay describes a generally agreed-on process or one that is not commonly accepted, you must provide all the details needed to explain the process. Your readers should be able to understand, even visualize, the process. There should be no fuzzy patches or confusing cuts from one step to another. Don't, however, go into obsessive detail about minor stages or steps. If you dwell for several hundred words on how to butter the pan, your readers will not stay with you long enough to learn how to make the omelet. Consider using a graphic or visual aid to help your readers. Figure 14.1, and all the other diagrams like it in this book, are graphic aids that summarize a process.

It's not unusual, especially in less defined sequences, for some steps in a process to occur simultaneously and to overlap. In such cases, you should present the steps in the most logical order, being sure to tell your readers that several steps are not perfectly distinct and may merge.

Figure 14.1 Development Diagram: Writing a Process Analysis Essay

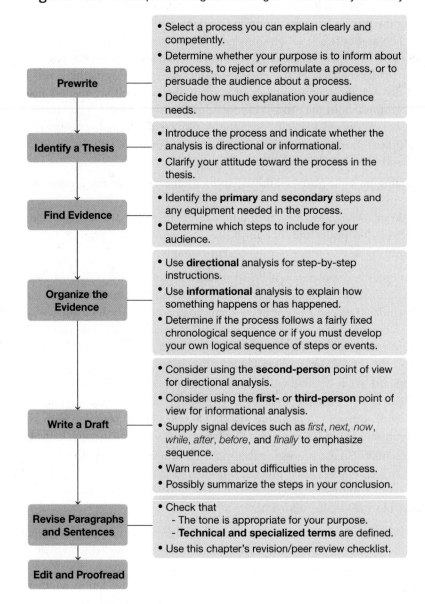

- **Prewrite**
  - Select a process you can explain clearly and competently.
  - Determine whether your purpose is to inform about a process, to reject or reformulate a process, or to persuade the audience about a process.
  - Decide how much explanation your audience needs.

- **Identify a Thesis**
  - Introduce the process and indicate whether the analysis is directional or informational.
  - Clarify your attitude toward the process in the thesis.

- **Find Evidence**
  - Identify the **primary** and **secondary** steps and any equipment needed in the process.
  - Determine which steps to include for your audience.

- **Organize the Evidence**
  - Use **directional** analysis for step-by-step instructions.
  - Use **informational** analysis to explain how something happens or has happened.
  - Determine if the process follows a fairly fixed chronological sequence or if you must develop your own logical sequence of steps or events.

- **Write a Draft**
  - Consider using the **second-person** point of view for directional analysis.
  - Consider using the **first-** or **third-person** point of view for informational analysis.
  - Supply signal devices such as *first, next, now, while, after, before,* and *finally* to emphasize sequence.
  - Warn readers about difficulties in the process.
  - Possibly summarize the steps in your conclusion.

- **Revise Paragraphs and Sentences**
  - Check that
    - The tone is appropriate for your purpose.
    - **Technical and specialized terms** are defined.
  - Use this chapter's revision/peer review checklist.

- **Edit and Proofread**

4. **Sort out the directional and informational aspects of the process analysis.**

   As you may have discovered when prewriting, directional and informational process analyses are not always distinct. In fact, they may be complementary: You may need to provide background information about a process before outlining its steps. For example, in an essay describing a step-by-step approach for losing weight, you might first need to explain how the body burns calories. Although both approaches may be appropriate in an essay, one generally predominates.

The kind of process analysis chosen has implications for the way you will relate to your reader. When the process analysis is *directional,* you should address the reader in the *second person:* "You should first rinse the residue from the radiator by…" or "Wrap the injured person in a blanket and then…" (In the second example, the pronoun *you* is implied.)

If the process analysis has an *informational* purpose, you won't address the reader directly but will choose from a number of other options. For example, you might use the *first person:* "Filled with good intentions, I sit on my bed, get in a comfortable position, open my textbook, and promptly fall asleep." You can also use the *third-person singular or plural* in informational process essays: "The spelling bee finalist walks up to the podium, heart pounding, more than a bit nervous, but also challenged by the prospect of winning the competition." Whether you use the first, second, or third person, avoid shifting point of view midstream.

You might have noticed that in the third-person examples, the present tense ("walks up") is used. The past tense is appropriate for events already completed, whereas the present tense is used for habitual or ongoing actions. The present tense is also effective when you want to lend a sense of dramatic immediacy to a process, even if the steps were performed in the past. As with point of view, be on guard against changing tenses in the middle of your explanation.

5. **Provide readers with the help they need to follow the sequence.**

As you move through the steps of a process analysis, don't forget to *warn readers about difficulties* they might encounter. For example, in an essay on the artistry involved in butterflying a shrimp, you might write something like this:

> Next, make a shallow cut with your sharpened knife along the convex curve of the shrimp's intestinal tract. The tract, usually a faint black line along the outside curve of the shrimp, is faintly visible beneath the translucent flesh. But some shrimp have a thick orange, blue, or gray line instead of a thin black one. In all cases, be careful not to slice too deeply, or you will end up with two shrimp halves instead of one butterflied shrimp.

You have told readers what to look for, citing the exceptions, and have warned them against making too deep a cut. Anticipating spots where communication might break down is a key part of writing an effective process analysis.

Transitional words and phrases are critical in helping readers understand the order of the steps being described. Time signals like *first, next, now, while, after, before,* and *finally* provide readers with a clear sense of the sequence. Entire sentences can also be used to link parts of the process, reminding your audience of what has already been discussed and indicating what will now be explained.

6. **Select and maintain an appropriate tone.**

When writing a process analysis essay, be sure your tone is consistent with your purpose, your attitude toward your subject, and the effect you want to have on readers. Take into account readers' attitudes toward your subject. Does your audience have a financial or emotional investment in the process being described? Does your own interest in the process coincide or conflict with that of your audience? Awareness of your readers' stance can be crucial. You'd do well to be tactful in your criticisms. Offend your reader, and your cause is lost. Once you settle on the essay's tone, maintain it throughout.

7. **Open and close the process analysis effectively.**

An essay developed primarily through process analysis should have a strong beginning. The introduction should state the process to be described and imply whether the essay has an informational or directional intent.

If you suspect readers are indifferent to your subject, use the introduction to motivate them, telling them how important the subject is. For example:

> Do you enjoy the salad bars found in many restaurants? If you do, you probably have noticed that the vegetables are always crisp and fresh—no matter how many hours they have been exposed to the air. What are the restaurants doing to make the vegetables look so inviting? There's a simple answer. Many restaurants dip and spray the vegetables with potent chemicals to make them look appetizing.

If you think your audience may be intimidated by your subject (perhaps because it's complex or relatively obscure), the introduction is the perfect spot to reassure them that the process being described is not beyond their grasp. For example:

> Studies show that many people prefer to accept a defective product rather than deal with the uncomfortable process of making a complaint. But by mastering a few easy-to-learn basics, anyone can register a complaint that gets results.

Most process analysis essays don't end as soon as the last step in the sequence is explained. Instead, they usually include some brief final comments that round out the piece and bring it to a satisfying close. This final section of the essay may summarize the main steps in the process—not by repeating the steps verbatim but by rephrasing and condensing them in several concise sentences. The conclusion can also be an effective spot to underscore the significance of the process, recalling what may have been said in the introduction about the subject's importance. Or the essay can end by echoing the note of reassurance that may have been included at the start.

Revision Strategies

14.5 Use strategies for revising your process analysis essay.

Once you have a draft of the essay, you're ready to revise. The following checklist will help your peers provide feedback and aid you in revising your essay.

☑ Process Analysis: A Revision/Peer Review Checklist

Revise Overall Meaning and Structure

☐ What purpose does the process analysis serve—to inform, to persuade, or to do both?

☐ Is the process analysis primarily *directional* or *informational*? How can you tell?

☐ Where does the process seem confusing? Where have steps been left out? Which steps need simplifying?

☐ What is the essay's tone? Is the tone appropriate for the essay's purpose and readers? Where are there distracting shifts in tone?

Revise Paragraph Development

☐ Does the introduction specify the process to be described? Does it provide an overview? Should it?

☐ Which paragraphs are difficult to follow? Have any steps or materials been omitted or explained in too much or too little detail? Which paragraphs should warn readers about potential trouble spots or overlapping steps?

☐ Where are additional time signals (*after, before, next*) needed to clarify the sequence within and between paragraphs? Where does overreliance on time signals make the sequence awkward and mechanical?

☐ Which paragraph describes the most crucial step in the sequence? How has the step been highlighted?

☐ How could the conclusion be more effective?

Revise Sentences and Words

☐ What technical or specialized terms appear in the essay? Have they been sufficiently explained? Where could simpler, less technical language be used?

☐ Are there any places where the essay's point of view awkwardly shifts? How could this problem be corrected?

☐ Does the essay use correct verb tenses—the past tense for completed events, the present tense for habitual or ongoing actions?

☐ Where does the essay use the passive voice ("The hole is dug")? Would the active voice ("You dig the hole") be more effective?

Student Essay: From Prewriting Through Revision

14.6 Analyze how process analysis is used effectively in a student-written selection.

The following student essay was written by Jared Mosley in response to this assignment:

> Alex Horton, a military veteran, provides other military veterans with a plan for college in "On Getting By." Serving a fifteen-month tour in Iraq, returning to the United States, and becoming a college student provided Horton with the experience he needed to help others who could benefit from what he had learned. Write an essay in which you present a *process analysis* of how to do something with which you have experience and consider yourself knowledgeable.

Jared, an English major, a lover of poetry, and a writer of poems, decided to write an essay that could help other students understand how they, too, could become poets. Before writing his essay, Jared prepared a topic outline that helped him organize and develop his thoughts.

Outline

Thesis: Becoming a poet doesn't require learning new skills. All you need are your thoughts and ideas.

I. Stage One: Developing the habits of a poet

   A. Be a reader

      1. How reading helps you become a poet

      2. What you should read

   B. Be a thinker

II. Stage Two: Defeating writer's block

   A. Understand where writer's block comes from

   B. Get started writing, even if it's awful

III. Stage Three: Writing poems

   A. Don't worry about rhyme

   B. Use lots of details

   C. Don't worry too much about rhythm

   D. Don't worry about making your poems so serious

   E. Do think about line breaks

After studying Jared's outline, read his essay, "Don't Write Poetry—Be a Poet," noting how closely he followed the plan he came up with as he worked on his outline. He took his time developing his outline and thought about how to sequence his ideas so that they would be easy for his readers to follow. Consequently, the essay's structure closely follows the outline. As he worked on various drafts of his essay, Jared added supporting details and carefully considered the tone he would use to keep his readers' attention. Finally, as you read the essay, consider how well it applies the principles of process analysis discussed in this chapter. (The commentary that follows the essay will help you look at Jared's essay more closely and will give you some sense of how he went about revising.)

Don't Write Poetry—Be a Poet
by Jared Mosley

Introduction

    The mention of poetry in a college class tends to strike fear into the heart of anyone who's not an English major. But poetry isn't as scary as it often seems. Poems don't have to be fancy or complicated, and they are a wonderful way to express yourself. Many forms

Start of two-sentence thesis

of artistic expression require learning new skills. Poetry doesn't; all you need to get started are the words and ideas you already know.

Topic sentence introducing the first stage (developing habits)

    To write poetry successfully, you must first learn how to be a poet. In other words, you must develop the habits of a poet. There are two habits that successful poets constantly keep in mind. The great news is that you can start practicing them today.

1

2

Topic sentence introducing the first habit	• The first essential habit for poets is reading. A poet's main tools are words and ideas. More importantly, the poet specializes in arranging these words and ideas in a meaningful way. Reading helps in two ways: it teaches you how to use the tools (words and ideas) you already have, and it introduces you to new ones. If you want to write poems but you don't know where to start, just read everything you can find. The material you read doesn't need to be academic or literary. You can read news sources, popular magazines, your favorite fiction series, or even comics. Whatever you're passionate about, read it more often. Once you've got that down, try reading something you don't know much about; that will help broaden your understanding of the world. And read other poets too; that will deepen your ideas about how to make your poems effective and meaningful.

3

Two-sentence introduction to the second habit (thinking), functioning as a topic sentence	• Understanding the world is very important for poets. That's why the other habit any aspiring poet must have is thinking. This doesn't mean that you must know all the answers to everything. Instead, it means that you must learn as much as you can (through experience, books, movies, whatever) and spend time figuring out what this new information means to you—because that's what poetry is: your personal reflection of the world around you.

4

Supporting paragraph topic sentence	• Thinking is easier for some people than for others. It comes naturally to certain personality types, and for others, spending time inside their own minds can be a real struggle. Our modern world of distractions (like the Internet) makes it hard to find time to think. Many individuals actively avoid deep thought because it makes them feel uncomfortable or uneasy. But if you want to be a poet, it is essential to figure out how you feel about yourself and everything else in the universe. So start thinking! Think about what makes you mad, what makes you sad, what you love, hate, or want to change. Think about
Sentence providing transition to second stage (fighting writer's block)	what's funny, fascinating, brilliant, or stupid. And when you're ready, you can start writing—unless you come up against what is commonly referred to as "writer's block," which just means that you feel unable to keep on writing.

5

Topic sentence	• To defeat writer's block, there are some things you need to know. The poet's worst enemy is herself. Even the most veteran writers are stricken with writer's block. The only difference is that they're able to overcome it. The first thing to realize is that writer's block usually comes from insecurity. Writer's block cleverly disguises itself in many forms, but the reason the plague strikes in the first place almost always comes down to your not believing you can write something. Writer's block can be especially hard for poets to overcome, because they're often trying to transfer their innermost thoughts onto the page, which is hard enough without writer's block.
Second stage in process	

6

Supporting paragraph topic sentence	• The good news is that you always have one sure way to defeat writer's block: writing. No matter how much you feel that you can't write or your work won't be good, write anyway. Write whatever you think of. Nobody has to see it; nobody cares if it is terrible. Let your words be your canvas or your punching bag, and write whatever you want. Don't follow rules if you don't want to. You will be amazed at how freeing this activity can be, and your writer's block will suddenly disappear.

7

Topic sentence ————→ Now you know how to develop the habits of a poet and how   8
to fight writer's block, but how do you actually write poems? The

Third stage in
process (writing
poems)
answer to that question varies greatly depending on whom you ask,
and there is no one right way to do it. Poetry is subjective and doesn't
have many strict rules. That said, here are five important tips to help
you get started.

Five supporting
tips

1. Poems don't need to rhyme. Really. Poems that are good and
   that rhyme are a pleasure to read and can be fun to write. But way
   too many good ideas are ruined because the poet tried to force a
   rhyming pattern. Don't limit yourself.

2. Use sensory details. Keep your poems out of abstract la-la-land
   by grounding them in the real world with the five senses.

3. When learning about poetry, you'll hear a lot about rhythm. It's
   true that rhythm is very important, but you don't have to worry
   too much about technical details. Focus on whether your poem
   sounds good when it's read aloud; that's all that matters.

4. Not all poems have to be deep or depressing. They can cover the
   entire range of human emotions. Humorous poems are a lot of fun
   to write—and to read!

5. Line breaks are more important than you think. When a poem is
   read aloud, a new line signals a brief pause, so write accordingly.
   Try to begin and end lines with important words.

Conclusion
Don't be discouraged as you begin your journey as a poet. It is   9
important for you always to remember that your poetry belongs to
you. Don't get caught up in trivial things like spelling errors or punctuation; these are the easiest things for you to go back and fix later on.
They matter, but only technically. Much more important are the ideas
that only you, with your individual mind, can express. Too many people think poetry is a mystical art designed to torture them with confusion. It's not. Instead, it's a beautiful and limitless form of expression.

Closing statements ——→ Get your ideas out there. Let your voice be heard.

Commentary

PURPOSE, THESIS   Jared's essay is an example of *directional process analysis*; his
purpose, as his title makes clear, is to help other students understand how they can
become poets. The first sentence of the essay establishes Jared's awareness of many
students' attitudes toward poetry; he knows that "the mention of poetry in a college
class tends to strike fear into the heart of anyone who's not an English major" (paragraph 1). He continues to write in a friendly, helpful voice throughout the introductory paragraph as he assures students that "poetry isn't as scary as it often seems" and
that it doesn't "have to be fancy or complicated." These reassuring statements lead
to his thesis: "Many forms of artistic expression require learning new skills. Poetry
doesn't; all you need to get started are the words and ideas you already know."

TONE   Throughout the essay, Jared continues to use the friendly tone he establishes in the introduction. He knows quite well that his topic—how to become a poet—could be an instant turnoff for many students. Consequently, he makes a point of using an informal, helpful tone not only in the opening paragraph but throughout the essay.

When discussing reading, "the first essential habit for poets," he puts readers at ease by advising them to "just read everything [they] can find." He goes on to identify reading material that will be comfortable and familiar: "The material you read doesn't need to be academic or literary. You can read news sources, popular magazines, your favorite fiction series, or even comics" (3). When discussing thinking, the second important habit for poets, he makes his ideas clear without using technical language: "This doesn't mean that you must know all the answers to everything. Instead, it means that you must learn as much as you can (through experience, books, movies, whatever) and spend time figuring out how what this new information means to you…" (4). Jared maintains this tone in his choice of everyday words, such as the adjectives and verbs in these sentences: "Think about what makes you mad, what makes you sad, what you love, hate, or want to change. Think about what's funny, fascinating, brilliant, or stupid. And when you're ready, you can start writing…" (5). He also uses contractions (*can't, won't, doesn't*) and second person (*you*) to reinforce the informal tone.

A little later in his essay when he warns of the plague referred to as "writer's block," he gives his readers reassuring advice: "No matter how much you feel that you can't write or it won't be good, write anyway. Write whatever you think of. Nobody has to see it; nobody cares if it is terrible. Let your words be your canvas or your punching bag and write whatever you want" (7). Then in the next paragraph he provides a list of five tips to help his audience as they get started writing their own poems. The friendly, reassuring tone Jared uses throughout his essay helps dissolve the fear many students feel when they consider the idea of writing poetry.

ORGANIZATION AND TOPIC SENTENCES   To meet the requirements of the assignment, Jared needed to provide a *step-by-step* explanation of a process. As he drafted his essay, Jared realized that the process of becoming a poet has no commonly accepted sequence and that he would need to come up with his own logical series of stages. He decided to structure the stages as (1) developing the habits of a poet, (2) learning how to defeat writer's block, and (3) getting started writing poetry. He explains the first stage, which includes two important habits, in paragraphs 2–5; the second stage in paragraphs 6–7; and the third stage in paragraph 8, which includes a list of five important tips. Each stage begins with a topic sentence indicating the logical progression from one stage to the next.

TRANSITIONS   As Jared drafted his process analysis essay, he was careful to keep in mind that he needed to provide an easy-to-follow structure. Consequently, he included transitions to help his readers easily navigate within and among the stages he describes. Notice the transitional word *first* that Jared uses to introduce his discussions of the first stage ("To write poetry successfully, you must *first* learn how to be a poet") and then the habit of reading ("The *first* essential habit for poets is reading").

Then in the following paragraph he uses another transitional word, *other*: "...the *other* essential habit any aspiring poet must have is thinking." As Jared moves from the first stage in his process to the second, he makes sure his readers understand where his ideas are going. He writes, "And when you're ready, you can start writing—unless you come up against what is commonly referred to as 'writer's block.' To defeat writer's block, there are some things you need to know" (5). He creates a smooth transition from the second stage to the third when he writes, at the start of paragraph 8, "Now you know how to develop the habits of a poet and how to defeat writer's block, but how do you actually write poems?" Jared's use of transitions plays an important role in helping him clearly communicate his ideas to his audience.

 COMBINING PATTERNS OF DEVELOPMENT   Jared uses some *examples*, as in paragraph 3: "You can read news sources, popular magazines, your favorite fiction series, or even comics." However, he makes the decision not to include the names of poets or lines from poems because he is concerned with keeping the essay accessible to readers who do not have much experience with poetry. He does, however, use *definition* in important ways. In paragraph 4, he defines *thinking:* "[Thinking] doesn't mean that you must know all the answers to everything. Instead, it means that you must learn as much as you can...and spend time figuring out how what this new information means to you." In addition, he defines *poetry* for readers: "that's what poetry is: your personal reflection of the world around you" (4). Finally, Jared uses definition for another key term: "what is commonly referred to as 'writer's block,' which just means that you feel unable to keep on writing" (5). In explaining how writers can overcome writer's block, Jared uses *cause-effect* to suggest solutions: "The good news is that you always have one sure way to defeat writer's block: writing" (7).

REVISING THE FIRST DRAFT   Jared chose to write about a topic that was important to him—one in which he had a deep interest. Reaching his audience and convincing them that poetry is accessible and that they, too, could become poets, was an idea he wanted to clearly communicate to his readers. Before he sat down with his laptop and began putting words on the screen, he thought carefully about his essay and developed his topic outline to help him figure out how he might structure his composition.

When working on the first draft, Jared decided to use headings in much the same way that Alex Horton uses them in his essay "On Getting By." Jared liked the way the headings guided him as he read Horton's essay, and although he had never used this type of structure in an essay before, he thought headings might work well in his piece of writing. In his first draft he included his title, "Don't Write Poetry—Be a Poet," followed by his introduction. Then he included the following headings: "Essential Habits for Poets," "Defeating Writer's Block," "How to Write a Poem," and "Don't Be Discouraged" to segue from one part of the essay to the next.

When he shared his first draft with the two other students in his peer review group, one of the students, Olivia, asked him why he had included the headings. Jared explained that he thought they would help readers make the transition from one main idea to the next and then to the conclusion. Olivia told him that she didn't think he needed the headings—that they were unnecessary because of the transitional sentences he had provided to guide readers. Hunter, Jared's other classmate in their group, said he thought that Olivia had a good point. At first, Jared was hesitant to cut the headings. He liked the idea of using them to guide readers, and he tried cutting the transitional sentences and leaving the headings. However, as he read back over his essay without the transitional sentences, he felt that he was asking his readers to jump from one idea to the next without any guidance. He came to agree with Olivia and Hunter—that the headings were unnecessary and that his essay would be stronger without them.

Jared made other changes as he revised, constantly keeping his audience in mind. He realized that he had overused the pronoun *it*, a habit he knew he needed to break, and that although his pronoun reference was clear to him, it might not be to his readers. To help eliminate this problem, he revised several of his sentences. For example, he revised—

> The first thing to realize is that writer's block usually comes from insecurity. *It* cleverly disguises itself in many forms, but *it* always comes down to your not believing you can write something. *It* can be especially hard for poets to overcome…

so that it read—

> The first thing to realize is that writer's block usually comes from insecurity. *Writer's block* cleverly disguises itself in many forms, but the *reason the plague strikes in the first place almost* always comes down to your not believing you can write something. *Writer's block* can be especially hard for poets to overcome…

These revisions improved Jared's essay and allowed him to more effectively communicate his ideas to his audience.

Activities: Process Analysis

Prewriting Activities

1. Imagine you're writing two essays. One defines the term *comparison shopping;* the other contrasts two different teaching styles. Jot down ways you might use process analysis in each essay.

2. Look at the essay topics that follow. Assuming that your readers will be students in your composition class, which topics would lend themselves to directional process analysis, informational process analysis, or a blend of both? Explain your responses.

   a. Going on a job interview

   b. Using a computer in the library

   c. Cleaning up oil spills

   d. Negotiating personal conflicts

   e. Curing a cold

   f. Growing vegetables organically

3. Select one of the essay topics that follow and determine what your purpose, tone, and point of view would be for each audience indicated in parentheses. Then use prewriting to identify the points you'd cover for each audience. Finally, organize the raw material, noting the differences in emphasis and sequence for each group of readers.

   a. How to buy a car (*young people who have just gotten a driver's license; established professionals*)

   b. How children acquire their values (*first-time parents; elementary school teachers*)

   c. How to manage money (*grade-school children; college students*)

   d. How disagreements can strengthen relationships (*preteen children; young adults*)

4. For one of the following process topics, identify an appropriate audience, purpose, tone, and point of view. Then use prewriting to generate raw material showing that there's a problem with the way the process is performed. After organizing that material, use prewriting once again—this time to identify how the process *should* be performed. Sequence this new material in a logical order.

   a. How students select a college or a major

   b. How local television news covers national events

   c. How your campus or your community is handling a difficult situation

Revising Activities

5. The following paragraph is from an essay making the point that over-the-phone sales can be a challenging career. The paragraph, written as a process analysis, describes the steps involved in making a sales call. Revise the paragraph, deleting any material that undermines the paragraph's unity, organizing the steps in a logical sequence, and supplying transitions where needed. Also be sure to correct any inappropriate shifts in person. Finally, do some brainstorming—individually or in a group—to generate details to bolster underdeveloped steps in the sequence.

   Establishing rapport with potential customers is the most challenging part of phone sales. The longer you can keep customers on the phone, the more you can get a sense of their needs. And the more you know about customers, the more successful the salesperson is bound to be. Your opening comments are critical. After setting the right tone, you gently introduce your product. There are a number of ways you can move gracefully from your opening remarks to the actual selling phase of the call. Remember: Don't try to sell the customer at the beginning. Instead, try in a friendly way to keep the prospective customer on the phone. Maintaining such a connection is easier than you think because many people have an almost desperate need to talk. Their lives are isolated and lonely—a sad fact of contemporary life. Once you shift to the distinctly selling phase of the call, you should present the advantages of the product, especially the advantages of price and convenience. Mentioning installment payments is often effective. If the customer says that he or she isn't interested, the salesperson should try to determine—in a genial way—why the person is reluctant to buy. Don't, however, push aggressively for reasons or try to steamroll the person into thinking his or her reservations are invalid. Once the person agrees to buy, try to encourage credit card payment, rather than check or money order. The salesperson can explain that credit card payment means the customer will receive the product sooner. End the call as you began—in an easy, personable way.

6. Reprinted here is a paragraph from the first draft of a humorous essay advising shy college students how to get through a typical day. Written as a process analysis, the paragraph outlines techniques for surviving class. Revise the paragraph, deleting digressions that disrupt the paragraph's unity, eliminating unnecessary repetition, and sequencing the steps in the proper order. Also correct inappropriate shifts in person and add transitions where needed. Feel free to add details.

Simply attending class can be stressful for shy people. Several strategies, though, can lessen the trauma. Shy students should time their arrival to coincide with that of most other class members—about two minutes before the class is scheduled to begin. If you arrive too early, you may be seen sitting alone or, even worse, may actually be forced to talk with another early arrival. If you arrive late, all eyes will be upon you. Before heading to class, the shy student should dress in the least conspicuous manner possible—say, in the blue jeans, sweatshirt, and sneakers that 99.9 percent of your classmates wear. That way you won't stand out from everyone else. Take a seat near the back of the room. Don't, however, sit at the very back since professors often take sadistic pleasure in calling on students back there, assuming they chose those seats because they didn't want to be called on. A friend of mine who is far from shy uses just the opposite ploy. In an attempt to get in good with her professors, she sits in the front row and, incredibly enough, volunteers to participate. However, since shy people don't want to call attention to themselves, they should stifle any urge to sneeze or cough. You run the risk of having people look at you or offer you a tissue or cough drop. And of course, never, ever volunteer to answer. Such a display of intelligence is sure to focus all eyes on you. In other words, make yourself as inconspicuous as possible. How, you might wonder, can you be inconspicuous if you're blessed (or cursed) with great looks? Well,…have you ever considered earning your degree through the mail?

Professional Selections: Process Analysis

AMY SUTHERLAND

Amy Sutherland was born in 1959 and grew up in suburban Cincinnati, Ohio. Her book, *Kicked, Bitten, and Scratched: Life and Lessons at the Premier School for Exotic Animal Trainers* (2003), inspired the essay that follows, which appeared in the *New York Times*. In turn, the essay led to another book, *What Shamu Taught Me About Life, Love, and Marriage* (2008) as well as a movie.

For ideas on how this process analysis essay is organized, see Figure 14.2.

Pre-Reading Journal Entry

All of us have habits—patterns of behavior that we repeat, sometimes even without being aware that we are performing them. Reflect on your own habits, good and bad, past and present. In your journal, list some of your habits and describe the situations in which they arise and the patterns of behavior that characterize them.

What Shamu Taught Me About a Happy Marriage

As I wash dishes at the kitchen sink, my husband paces behind me, irritated. "Have you seen my keys?" he snarls, then huffs out a loud sigh and stomps from the room with our dog, Dixie, at his heels, anxious over her favorite human's upset. 1

In the past I would have been right behind Dixie. I would have turned off the faucet and joined the hunt while trying to soothe my husband with bromides like, "Don't worry, they'll turn up." But that only made him angrier, and a simple case of missing keys soon would become a full-blown angst-ridden drama starring the two of us and our poor nervous dog. 2

Now, I focus on the wet dish in my hands. I don't turn around. I don't say a word. I'm using a technique I learned from a dolphin trainer. 3

I love my husband. He's well read, adventurous and does a hysterical rendition of a northern Vermont accent that still cracks me up after 12 years of marriage. 4

But he also tends to be forgetful, and is often tardy and mercurial. He hovers around me in the kitchen asking if I read this or that piece in *The New Yorker* when I'm trying to concentrate on the simmering pans. He leaves wadded tissues in his wake. He suffers from serious bouts of spousal deafness but never fails to hear me when I mutter to myself on the other side of the house. "What did you say?" he'll shout. 5

These minor annoyances are not the stuff of separation and divorce, but in sum they began to dull my love for Scott. I wanted—needed—to nudge him a little closer to perfect, to make him into a mate who might annoy me a little less, who wouldn't keep me waiting at restaurants, a mate who would be easier to love. 6

So, like many wives before me, I ignored a library of advice books and set about improving him. By nagging, of course, which only made his behavior worse: he'd drive faster instead of slower; shave less frequently, not more; and leave his reeking bike garb on the bedroom floor longer than ever. 7

We went to a counselor to smooth the edges off our marriage. She didn't un- 8
derstand what we were doing there and complimented us repeatedly on how well
we communicated. I gave up. I guessed she was right—our union was better than
most—and resigned myself to stretches of slow-boil resentment and occasional
sarcasm.

Then something magical happened. For a book I was writing about a school 9
for exotic animal trainers, I started commuting from Maine to California, where I
spent my days watching students do the seemingly impossible: teaching hyenas
to pirouette on command, cougars to offer their paws for a nail clipping, and ba-
boons to skateboard.

I listened, rapt, as professional trainers explained how they taught dolphins 10
to flip and elephants to paint. Eventually it hit me that the same techniques might
work on that stubborn but lovable species, the American husband.

The central lesson I learned from exotic animal trainers is that I should reward 11
behavior I like and ignore behavior I don't. After all, you don't get a sea lion to
balance a ball on the end of its nose by nagging. The same goes for the American
husband.

Back in Maine, I began thanking Scott if he threw one dirty shirt into the ham- 12
per. If he threw in two, I'd kiss him. Meanwhile, I would step over any soiled
clothes on the floor without one sharp word, though I did sometimes kick them
under the bed. But as he basked in my appreciation, the piles became smaller.

I was using what trainers call "approximations," rewarding the small steps to- 13
ward learning a whole new behavior. You can't expect a baboon to learn to flip on
command in one session, just as you can't expect an American husband to begin
regularly picking up his dirty socks by praising him once for picking up a single
sock. With the baboon you first reward a hop, then a bigger hop, then an even bigger hop. With Scott the husband, I began to praise every small act every time: if he
drove just a mile an hour slower, tossed one pair of shorts into the hamper, or was
on time for anything.

I also began to analyze my husband the way a trainer considers an exotic ani- 14
mal. Enlightened trainers learn all they can about a species, from anatomy to social
structure, to understand how it thinks, what it likes and dislikes, what comes easily to it and what doesn't. For example, an elephant is a herd animal, so it responds
to hierarchy. It cannot jump, but can stand on its head. It is a vegetarian.

The exotic animal known as Scott is a loner, but an alpha male. So hierarchy 15
matters, but being in a group doesn't so much. He has the balance of a gymnast,
but moves slowly, especially when getting dressed. Skiing comes naturally, but
being on time does not. He's an omnivore, and what a trainer would call food-
driven.

Once I started thinking this way, I couldn't stop. At the school in California, 16
I'd be scribbling notes on how to walk an emu or have a wolf accept you as a pack
member, but I'd be thinking, "I can't wait to try this on Scott."

On a field trip with the students, I listened to a professional trainer describe 17
how he had taught African crested cranes to stop landing on his head and shoulders. He did this by training the leggy birds to land on mats on the ground. This,
he explained, is what is called an "incompatible behavior," a simple but brilliant
concept.

Rather than teach the cranes to stop landing on him, the trainer taught the 18 birds something else, a behavior that would make the undesirable behavior impossible. The birds couldn't alight on the mats and his head simultaneously.

At home, I came up with incompatible behaviors for Scott to keep him from 19 crowding me while I cooked. To lure him away from the stove, I piled up parsley for him to chop or cheese for him to grate at the other end of the kitchen island. Or I'd set out a bowl of chips and salsa across the room. Soon I'd done it: no more Scott hovering around me while I cooked.

I followed the students to SeaWorld San Diego, where a dolphin trainer intro- 20 duced me to least reinforcing syndrome (L.R.S.). When a dolphin does something wrong, the trainer doesn't respond in any way. He stands still for a few beats, careful not to look at the dolphin, and then returns to work. The idea is that any response, positive or negative, fuels a behavior. If a behavior provokes no response, it typically dies away.

In the margins of my notes I wrote, "Try on Scott!" 21

It was only a matter of time before he was again tearing around the house 22 searching for his keys, at which point I said nothing and kept at what I was doing. It took a lot of discipline to maintain my calm, but results were immediate and stunning. His temper fell far shy of its usual pitch and then waned like a fast-moving storm. I felt as if I should throw him a mackerel.

Now he's at it again; I hear him banging a closet door shut, rustling through 23 papers on a chest in the front hall and thumping upstairs. At the sink, I hold steady. Then, sure enough, all goes quiet. A moment later, he walks into the kitchen, keys in hand, and says calmly, "Found them."

Without turning, I call out, "Great, see you later." 24

Off he goes with our much-calmed pup. 25

After two years of exotic animal training, my marriage is far smoother, my 26 husband much easier to love. I used to take his faults personally; his dirty clothes on the floor were an affront, a symbol of how he didn't care enough about me. But thinking of my husband as an exotic species gave me the distance I needed to consider our differences more objectively.

I adopted the trainers' motto: "It's never the animal's fault." When my train- 27 ing attempts failed, I didn't blame Scott. Rather, I brainstormed new strategies, thought up more incompatible behaviors and used smaller approximations. I dissected my own behavior, considered how my actions might inadvertently fuel his. I also accepted that some behaviors were too entrenched, too instinctive to train away. You can't stop a badger from digging, and you can't stop my husband from losing his wallet and keys.

Professionals talk of animals that understand training so well they eventually 28 use it back on the trainer. My animal did the same. When the training techniques worked so beautifully, I couldn't resist telling my husband what I was up to. He wasn't offended, just amused. As I explained the techniques and terminology, he soaked it up. Far more than I realized.

Last fall, firmly in middle age, I learned that I needed braces. They were not 29 only humiliating, but also excruciating. For weeks my gums, teeth, jaw and sinuses throbbed. I complained frequently and loudly. Scott assured me that I would become used to all the metal in my mouth. I did not.

One morning, as I launched into yet another tirade about how uncomfortable 30
I was, Scott just looked at me blankly. He didn't say a word or acknowledge my
rant in any way, not even with a nod.

I quickly ran out of steam and started to walk away. Then I realized what was 31
happening, and I turned and asked, "Are you giving me an L.R.S.?" Silence. "You
are, aren't you?"

He finally smiled, but his L.R.S. has already done the trick. He'd begun to 32
train me, the American wife.

Questions for Critical Reading

1. What is the selection's thesis? Locate the sentence(s) in which Sutherland states her main idea. If she doesn't state her thesis explicitly, express it in your own words.

2. Sutherland tries a couple of solutions to her problems with her husband before she starts using the behavioral techniques that are the main focus of the essay. What were these initial solutions, and why did they fail to improve her relationship with her husband?

3. What techniques for changing behavior did Sutherland learn from the animal trainers? How did she apply each of these techniques to her husband Scott's behavior?

4. Why did changing her husband's behavior improve Sutherland's marriage?

Figure 14.2 Essay Structure Diagram: "What Shamu Taught Me About a Happy Marriage" by Amy Sutherland

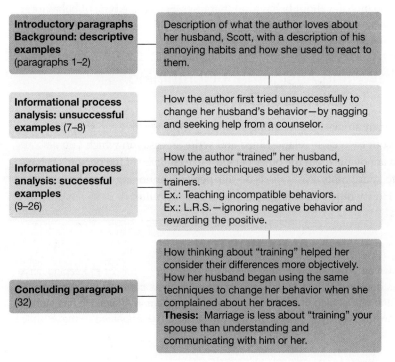

Questions About the Writer's Craft

1. **The pattern.** What type of process analysis does Sutherland use in this essay? How does the first-person point of view support the pattern of development?

2. **Tone.** What is the tone of Sutherland's essay? What contributes to the tone?

3. **Other patterns.** What pattern of development, besides process analysis, helps organize this essay? What does the other pattern contribute to the essay?

4. **Conclusion.** Is Sutherland's conclusion effective? How does her conclusion change your response to the essay?

Writing Assignments Using Process Analysis as a Pattern of Development

1. In this essay, Sutherland describes how animal trainers teach cranes, dolphins, and other animals to behave in certain ways. Imagine turning this scenario around, and thinking of animals teaching their human masters how to behave. Write an essay from an animal's point of view in which you explain how the animal trains its human "master" to meet its needs.

2. The animal-training techniques Sutherland describes in this essay are similar to behavioral therapies used by psychologists and other mental health professionals to treat people for phobias, anxiety, and other disorders, and to change specific behaviors, like smoking and other undesirable habits. Do some research in the library and on the Internet about behavioral therapies. Select one type of behavioral therapy and write an essay explaining how it works. Give examples of its use in your essay.

Writing Assignment Combining Patterns of Development

3. Sutherland's essay shows how irritating even the people we love can sometimes be. Select one of your own close relationships and write an essay in which you *describe* what you find annoying about the other person. Give *examples* of the person's behavior to illustrate your points. What *effects* do this person's annoying traits have on the relationship? How would you change this person if you could?

ALEX HORTON

Alex Horton is known as "Army of Dude," the title of the blog that he has been keeping since 2006, when he was deployed to Iraq for a fifteen-month tour. He is currently the senior writer for *VAntage Point*, the official blog of the U.S. Department of Veterans Affairs. He has studied writing at Georgetown University in Washington, D.C. His work has appeared in the *Atlantic*,

New York Times, *St. Petersburg Times*, and *Washingtonian* magazine. Horton was a finalist for Weblog Awards for Best Military Blog in 2007 and 2008. The selection that follows was posted on *Army of Dude* on January 13, 2010.

Pre-Reading Journal Entry

What do you know about blogs? Have you ever created one or posted to one? If so, what kind(s) of blog(s) did you post to? What is the purpose of a blog? Explore these questions in your journal and use the Internet to find out more about blogs if you are unfamiliar with them.

On Getting By

In my previous post, I outlined some basic principles (Horton) needed to suc-　1
cessfully navigate the murky waters of education under the GI Bill. The challenges in dealing with the VA for education benefits are considerable, yet veterans new to college face an unfamiliar, unpredictable and strange environment on campus. If taken all at once, these hurdles can quickly overwhelm a student veteran and distract from the overall goal: to finish a degree on time with benefits to spare. Next week I will be in class for my fifth semester of higher education, and in my time I have tinkered with a system of how to bring up my veteran status, discussing Iraq and Afghanistan in the classroom and dealing with the myriad reactions fellow students have had. The system cannot be expected to work for everyone, but as veterans file into classrooms for the first time this spring, these tips could help in the development of a coping system better tailored for you. These should simply help to get you started.

Modesty Is the Best Policy

There are only two kinds of veterans in school: those who prattle on about　2
their time in the military and overseas, and those who do not. The former will find any opportunity to bring up their time in Afghanistan or Iraq, even if it is not relevant to class discussion. They forget one of the tenets of military experience—the role of the consummate professional. Joining the military and serving in a time of war are sacred acts and carry a certain degree of respect and modesty. We owe it to our injured buddies and fallen friends not to brag about our exploits overseas. We have done our fair share of things that set us apart from others in the classroom, and that is exactly why it is best to retain an understated presence among others.

This is a difficult situation as it applies to reintegration, as the chasm be-　3
tween veterans and civilians has never been wider. From World War II to Vietnam, it would have been a difficult task to know someone that neither served overseas nor had a family member or friend who did. Now there are whole classrooms filled with those people. As Matthew McConaughey spoke prophetically in *Dazed and Confused*, "I get older, they stay the same age." An 18 year old in college this year would have been nine years old during the invasion of Afghanistan and eleven years old during the invasion of Iraq. They have grown up with war to the point of it becoming a mind numbingly prosaic concept. It would be a frustrating battle to try and close the rift with those who don't see a rift at all.

The best thing to do is use your judgment when bringing up your veteran status in the classroom. I've done it just a few times and felt uncomfortable enough to think twice about the next time. Now I tend to mention it in private conversation, not when I have the floor in public, and even then it is a casual touch on the subject. When you are ready to talk...

... Prepare for a Question Salvo

No matter how much you try to keep it stashed away from students and coworkers, your military experience will come out sooner or later. There are things you simply cannot hide forever, like going to prison or reading *Twilight*. Once you begin to move past casual conversation, it's only a matter of time before that period of your life is visited. It usually begins with a discussion of age. When I tell people I'm 24, the followup questions are almost always, "What have you done since high school?" or, "Why did you wait so long to go to school?" People tend to catch on if you mention extended vacations in the Middle East or recite monologues, so at that point it is best to come clean. However, be prepared for the questions they are more than willing to hurl your way. They might not know anyone who has deployed, but our hyperviolent culture has removed any restraint left in the world and enables them to ask any question that comes to mind. Here is what you can expect, in order of the most frequently asked:

1. What's it like?
2. Was it really hot?
3. Did you kill anyone?
4. Seriously, how hot was it?
5. Do you regret it?
6. Did you see any camel spiders?
7. Were you in Iran?

It's hard to get upset at some of those questions, as I find it difficult to think of what I'd ask if the roles were switched. #3 can be blamed on ignorance and apathy, but #5 is the most troubling I've heard. It suggests that there is something shameful about service, duty and sacrifice. Both questions trivialize an important part of our lives. The best answer to #3 I've heard comes from the The Kitchen Dispatch comment section: "I will forgive you for asking that question if you forgive me for not answering it." Something that personal should never be asked, only told (Fong).

The flip side to some of those cavalier probes are questions that handle the topic with kid gloves. Once a coworker found out I was in the Army, she asked, "Did you go to...one of those places they send people?" It was uncomfortable for her just to utter those dirty "I" and "A" words, like we were speaking about some subversive topic. The kind of questions you will get will be all over the map, spanning from a place of genuine interest to the depths of sheer morbidity. Be prepared to answer anything, or politely let them know the subject isn't appropriate for casual banter.

Let the Right Ones In

Popular culture is replete with images of the maladjusted veteran, from Rambo   7
to Travis Bickle to Red Forman. These characters are ingrained in our national conscious and typically become placeholders in the event someone doesn't personally
know a veteran. When these sources are taken at face value, war veterans are invariably crazy, depressive, easily startled, quick to anger and alcoholics. We come from
broken homes, trying to escape jail time and were too dumb or poor to go to college
after high school. The best way to combat these silly notions is to let people get to
know you, the person, before you, the veteran. Those stereotypes aren't going anywhere soon, so the best idea is to take the concept of guarding your veteran status in
the classroom and carry it over to blossoming relationships. That way your service
and overseas experience complement your personality and don't define it. Revealing too much at one time can damage a friendship before it takes off. Just like in the
classroom, take it slow. If they are worth keeping around, they'll understand why.
We have met our lifelong friends already; we can afford to be picky.

Try to Keep a Straight Face

There's a huge disparity between what you have been asked to do in the ser-   8
vice and what you will be asked to do in school. At the very basic level you were
asked to maintain a clean weapon and uniform. Many of you were tasked with
watching the back of your fellow soldiers while in imminent danger or operate
complex machinery and vehicles. At school, you'll be held responsible for showing up and turning in work before deadlines. That's it. Like I mentioned in the earlier post, college seems like an insurmountable gauntlet of crushed dreams when
you're in the military. Once you transition to civilian life and take a few classes,
you'll be astounded at the lack of discipline and drive in some of your classmates.
It's a big joke, but try to maintain composure. I'm not saying it's easy the whole
way through, but I guarantee you've done something harder than a five page essay. As they say, the rest is downhill.

Find Another Brother

If you were in active duty, the friends you met along the way are now scattered   9
across the country. Perhaps I've always been an introvert, but I don't make friends
as easy as some people. I've met just two people in fourteen classes that I consider
friends, and one of them is an Afghanistan veteran. It's easy to understand why we
get along. Do your best to find other veterans in your class and say hello. Talking
to them will come easier than the 18 year old hipster next to you about his passion
for ironic hats. Find out if there is a veteran's organization on campus, but be wary
of their motives. While some will join to find support and befriend fellow veterans,
others will use it for recognition....

Enjoy the Ride

Besides getting a degree or learning new skills, people go to college to meet   10
new people and to experience a different life. If you've served since Sept. 12, 2001,

you've already had a bit of each. But don't let that stop you from enjoying every-thing school has to offer. It's the last time very little will be expected of you, unless you get another government job. Then you're golden.

If you are recently out of the military and on your way to college, these tenets, coupled with the GI Bill pointers, should help you get started in academia (*The Post-9/11*). Like most things, your experience may vary, and I would hope you don't safeguard your veteran status like it's a dark secret or the true location of Jimmy Hoffa's body. It's something to be proud of, but not flaunted. It's something to share with your friends who genuinely want to know about the world you lived in, but not with the people who have twisted notions of what you have done over-seas. The last thing you want people to know you as is the guy who went to Iraq. You want them to say "Hey, that's Alex, he's good people," and not "I wonder how many ear necklaces he has. I'm betting two." Hopefully these tips will help even just a tiny bit in that regard.

11

Works Cited

Fong, Kanani. "Seven Things Never to Say to a Veteran." The Kitchen Dispatch: A View from the Breakfast Table During War, 3 Jan. 2010, www.pbs.org/pov/regardingwar/author/kanani-fong.

Horton, Alex. "Here to There: Tips and Tricks for the Student Veteran." Army of Dude, 29 Dec. 2009, armyofdude.blogspot.com/2009/12/here-to-there-tips-and-tricks-for.html.

The Post-9/11 GI Bill, U.S. Dept. of Veterans Affairs. Facebook, www.facebook.com/gibillEducation.

Questions for Critical Reading

1. What is the selection's thesis? Locate the sentence(s) in which Horton states his main idea. If he doesn't state the thesis explicitly, express it in your own words.

2. What reason does Horton give veterans for why they should generally avoid talk-ing about their military experiences when they are at school?

3. Of the questions Horton lists as those other students are likely to ask when they discover one of their classmates is a veteran, which one does Horton find most troubling and why?

4. What does Horton have to say about what those in the military think college will be like, compared with what he thinks they are likely to discover when they go to college?

Questions About the Writer's Craft

1. **The pattern.** How does Horton organize his process analysis? What tool does he use, and how does his strategy make his blog more effective?

2. **The pattern.** Is Horton's process analysis primarily *directional* or *informational*? Explain. To what extent does Horton try to persuade readers that the process he describes should be followed?

3. **Other patterns.** Although Horton organizes his selection as a process analysis, he also weaves in his own experience—his own *narrative* about what he learned when he returned to civilian life and started taking college classes. How does this combination of patterns make Horton's writing stronger than it would be without the inclusion of his own story?

4. **Audience.** Horton's intended audience is those currently or formerly in the military—not students and their teachers. What parts of his essay might some students and instructors find offensive and why?

Writing Assignments Using Process Analysis as a Pattern of Development

1. In his essay Horton, a military veteran, provides other military veterans with a plan for how to "get by" in college. Write an essay in which you present a process analysis of ways a member of a group to which you belong or have belonged can adjust to a particular situation—perhaps an essay written to high school seniors on how to adjust to college life or an essay for new employees on how to adjust to working at your place of employment.

2. Horton is an expert on the subject he addresses. Write an essay in which you present a process analysis that provides both directions and information for an audience unfamiliar with or less experienced than you on a particular subject. For example, if you are an avid gamer, you might write an essay on how to successfully navigate a challenging game such as *Call of Duty*, *Forza*, or *Portal*. Or if you have learned how to survive as a student on a bare-bones budget, you might write an essay in which you offer tips to other college students in a similar economic situation.

Writing Assignment Combining Patterns of Development

3. In his *process analysis* Horton also tells a story—a *narrative*—about the common societal experience of adjusting to college life. Write an essay in which you examine another common process, for example, applying for a driver's license, or a larger societal process, such as electing a president. Give the process involved, but also include sufficient *description*—for example, of an exam room at the license bureau or the crowds at a political rally—to support your thesis. You might find it helpful to conduct some original research on the subject.

CAROLINE REGO

Caroline Rego was born in 1950 in Edmond, Oklahoma. A graduate of the University of Oklahoma, she began her journalistic career as a police reporter for a daily newspaper in Montana. Later, while filling in for a vacationing colleague in the features section of another newspaper, she found her true calling: writing consumer-affairs articles that teach readers how to protect themselves against shoddy service, dangerous products, and inefficiency. A sought-after public speaker, Rego talks frequently to students and community groups on strategies for becoming an informed consumer. The following selection is part of a work in progress on consumer empowerment.

Pre-Reading Journal Entry

When you're disappointed with someone or something, how do you typically react—passively, assertively, or in some other way? In your journal, list a few disappointments you've experienced. How did you respond on each occasion? In retrospect, are you happy with your responses? Why or why not?

The Fine Art of Complaining

You waited forty-five minutes for your dinner, and when it came it was cold—and not 1 *what you ordered in the first place. You washed your supposedly machine-washable, pre-shrunk T-shirt (the one the catalogue claimed was "indestructible"), and now it's the size of a napkin. Your new car broke down a month after you bought it, and the dealer says the warranty doesn't apply.*

Life's annoyances descend on all of us—some pattering down like gentle rain- 2 drops, others striking with the bruising force of hailstones. We dodge the ones we can, but inevitably, plenty of them make contact. And when they do, we react fairly predictably. Many of us—most of us, probably—grumble to ourselves and take it. We scowl at our unappetizing food but choke it down. We stash the shrunken T-shirt in a drawer, vowing never again to order from a catalogue. We glare fiercely at our checkbooks as we pay for repairs that should have been free.

A few of us go to the other extreme. Taking our cue from the crazed newscaster 3 in the 1976 movie *Network,* we go through life mad as hell and unwilling to take it anymore. In offices, we shout at hapless receptionists when we're kept waiting for appointments. In restaurants, we make scenes that have fellow patrons craning their necks to get a look at us. In stores, we argue with salespeople for not waiting on us. We may notice after a while that our friends seem reluctant to venture into public with us, but hey—we're just standing up for our rights. Being a patsy doesn't get you anywhere in life.

It's true—milquetoasts live unsatisfying lives. However, people who go 4 through the day in an eye-popping, vein-throbbing state of apoplectic rage don't win any prizes either. What persons at both ends of the scale need—what could empower the silent sufferer and civilize the Neanderthal—is a course in the gentle art of *effective* complaining.

Effective complaining is not apologetic and half-hearted. It's not making one 5 awkward attempt at protest—"Uh, excuse me, I don't think I ordered the squid and onions"—and then slinking away in defeat. But neither is it roaring away indiscriminately, attempting to get satisfaction through the sheer volume of our complaint.

Effective complainers are people who act businesslike and important. Acting   6
important doesn't mean puffing up your chest and saying, "Do you know who I
am?"—an approach that would tempt anyone to take you down a peg or two. It
doesn't mean shouting and threatening—techniques that will only antagonize the
person whose help you need. It *does* mean making it clear that you know your request
is reasonable and that you are confident it will be taken care of. People are generally treated the way they expect to be treated. If you act like someone making a fair
request, chances are that request will be granted. Don't beg, don't explain. Just state
your name, the problem, and what you expect to have done. Remain polite. But be
firm. "My car has been in your garage for three days, and a mechanic hasn't even
looked at it yet," you might say. "I want to know when it is going to be worked on."
Period. Now it is up to them to give you a satisfactory response. Don't say, "Sorry to
bother you about this, but …" or "I, uh, was sort of expecting… ." You're only asking
people to remedy a problem, after all; that is not grounds for apology.

If your problem requires an immediate response, try to make your complaint   7
in person; a real, live, in-the-flesh individual has to be dealt with in some way.
Complaining over the telephone, by contrast, is much less effective. When you
speak to a disembodied voice, when the person at the other end of the line doesn't
have to face you, you're more likely to get a runaround.

Most importantly, complain to the right person. One of the greatest frustra-   8
tions in complaining is talking to a clerk or receptionist who cannot solve your
problem and whose only purpose seems to be to drive you crazy. Getting mad
doesn't help; the person you're mad at probably had nothing to do with your actual problem. And you'll have to repeat everything you've said to the clerk once
you're passed along to the appropriate person. So make sure from the start that
you're talking to someone who can help—a manager or supervisor.

If your problem doesn't require an immediate response, complaining by let-   9
ter is probably the most effective way to get what you want. A letter of complaint
should be brief, businesslike, and to the point. If you have a new vacuum cleaner
that doesn't work, don't spend a paragraph describing how your Uncle Joe tried to
fix the problem and couldn't. As when complaining in person, be sure you address
someone in a position of real authority. Here's an example of an effective letter of
complaint.

Ms. Anne Lublin   10
Manager
Mitchell Appliances
80 Front Street
Newton, MA 02159

Dear Ms. Lublin: 11

First section: Explain the problem. Include facts to back up your story.   12

On August 6, I purchased a new Perma-Kool freezer from your store (a copy of   13
my sales receipt is enclosed). In the two weeks I have owned the freezer, I have
had to call your repair department three times in an attempt to get it running

properly. The freezer ran normally when it was installed, but since then it has repeatedly turned off, causing the food inside to spoil. My calls to your repair department have not been responded to promptly. After I called the first time, on August 10, I waited two days for the repair person to show up. It took three days to get a repair person here after my second call, on August 15. The freezer stopped yet again on August 20. I called to discuss this recent problem, but no one has responded to my call.

Second section: Tell how you trust the company and are confident that your reader will fix the problem. This is to "soften up" the reader a bit. 14

I am surprised to receive such unprofessional service and poor quality from Mitchell Appliances since I have been one of your satisfied customers for fifteen years. In the past, I have purchased a television, air conditioner, and washing machine from your company. I know that you value good relations with your customers, and I'm sure you want to see me pleased with my most recent purchase. 15

Third section: Explain exactly what you want to be done—repair, replacement, refund, etc. 16

Although your repair department initially thought that the freezer needed only some minor adjustments, the fact that no one has been able to permanently fix the problem convinces me that the freezer has some serious defect. I am understandably unwilling to spend any more time having repairs made. Therefore, I expect you to exchange the freezer for an identical model by the end of this week (August 30). Please call me to arrange for the removal of the defective freezer and the delivery of the new one. 17

Sincerely, 18

Janice Becker

P.S. (Readers always notice a P.S.) State again when you expect the problem to be taken care of, and what you will do if it isn't. 19

P.S. I am confident that we can resolve this problem by August 30. If the defective freezer is not replaced by then, however, I will report this incident to the Better Business Bureau. 20

Notice that the P.S. says what you'll do if your problem isn't solved. In other words, you make a threat—a polite threat. Your threat must be reasonable and believable. A threat to burn down the store if your purchase price isn't refunded is neither reasonable nor believable—or if it *were* believed, you could end up in jail. A threat to report the store to a consumer-protection agency, such as the Better Business Bureau, however, is credible. 21

Don't be too quick to make one of the most common—and commonly empty—threats: "I'll sue!" A full-blown lawsuit is more trouble, and more expensive, than most problems are worth. On the other hand, most areas have a small-claims court 22 where suits involving modest amounts of money are heard. These courts don't use complex legal language or procedures, and you don't need a lawyer to use them. A store or company will often settle with you—if your claim is fair—rather than go to small-claims court.

Whether you complain over the phone, in person, or by letter, be persistent. 23 One complaint may not get results. In that case, keep on complaining, and make sure you keep complaining to the same person. Chances are he or she will get worn out and take care of the situation, if only to be rid of you.

Someday, perhaps, the world will be free of the petty annoyances that plague us 24 all from time to time. Until then, however, toasters will break down, stores will refuse to honor rainchecks, and bills will include items that were never purchased. You can depend upon it—there will be grounds for complaint. You might as well learn to be good at it.

Questions for Critical Reading

1. What is the selection's thesis? Locate the sentence(s) in which Rego states her main idea. If she doesn't state the thesis explicitly, express it in your own words.

2. In Rego's opinion, what types of actions and statements are *not* helpful when making a complaint?

3. What should be included in a letter of complaint? What should be omitted?

4. What does Rego suggest doing if a complaint is ignored?

Questions About the Writer's Craft

1. **The pattern.** Is Rego's process analysis primarily directional or primarily informational? Explain. To what extent does Rego try to persuade readers to follow her process?

2. **Other patterns.** Where does Rego include *narrative* elements in her essay? What do these brief narratives add to the piece?

3. **Other patterns.** Numerous oppositions occur throughout the essay. How do these *contrasts* enliven the essay and help Rego persuade readers to adopt her suggestions?

4. **Point of view.** Reread the essay, noting where Rego shifts point of view. Where does she use the second-person (*you*), the first-person-plural (*we*), and the third-person-plural (*they*) points of view? How does her use of multiple points of view add to the essay's effectiveness?

Writing Assignments Using Process Analysis as a Pattern of Development

1. Write an essay explaining to college students how to register (with someone in a position of authority) an effective complaint about a campus problem. You could show, for example, how to complain to a professor about a course's grading policy, to the bookstore manager about the markup on textbooks, or to security about the

poorly maintained college parking lots. Feel free to adapt some of Rego's recommendations, but be sure to invent several strategies of your own. In either case, provide—as Rego does—lively examples to illustrate the step-by-step procedure for registering an effective complaint with a specific authority figure on campus.

2. Rego argues that "people who go through the day in an eye-popping, vein-throbbing state of apoplectic rage don't win any prizes." But sometimes, getting mad can be appropriate—even productive. Write an essay explaining the best process for expressing anger effectively. Explain how to vent emotion safely, communicate the complaint in a nonthreatening way, encourage more honest interaction, and prompt change for the better. Illustrate the process by drawing upon your own experiences and observations.

Writing Assignment Combining Patterns of Development

3. Think about a service or product that failed to live up to your expectations. Perhaps you were disgruntled about your mechanic's car repair, a store's return policy, or a hotel's accommodations. Using Rego's suggestions, write a letter of complaint in which you *describe* the problem, convey confidence in the reader's ability to resolve the problem, and state your request for specific action. Remember that a firm but cordial tone will *persuade* your reader that you have legitimate grounds for seeking the resolution you propose.

Additional Writing Topics: Process Analysis

General Assignments

Using process analysis, develop one of these topics into an essay.

Directional: How to Do Something

1. How to drive defensively
2. How to improve the place where you work or study
3. How to relax
4. How to show appreciation to others
5. How to get through school despite personal problems

Informational: How Something Happens

1. How a student becomes burned out
2. How a dead thing decays (or some other natural process)
3. How humans choose a mate
4. How a bad habit develops
5. How people fall into debt

Assignments Using Multimedia

Use the suggested media to help develop a process analysis essay on one of these topics:

1. Making it through freshman year without gaining the "freshman 15" (photos)
2. Juggling school, friends, relationships, and a job (pie chart)
3. Deciding on the right career path to your dream job (weblinks)
4. The evolution of the national parks system (weblinks)
5. Becoming a successful entrepreneur (diagrams and/or links to videos)

Assignments with a Specific Purpose, Audience, and Point of View

1. **Academic life.** You are an experienced campus tour guide for prospective students, and your school's admissions office has asked you to write a pamphlet explaining to new tour guides how to conduct a tour of your school's campus. When explaining the process, keep in mind that tour guides need to portray the school in its best light.

2. **Academic life.** You write an "advice to the lovelorn" column for the campus newspaper. A correspondent writes saying that he or she wants to break up with a steady girlfriend/boyfriend but doesn't know how to do it without hurting the person. Give the writer guidance on how to end a meaningful relationship with a minimal amount of pain.

3. **Civic activity.** To help a sixteen-year-old friend learn how to drive, explain a specific driving maneuver one step at a time. You might, for example, describe how to make a three-point turn, parallel-park, or handle a skid. Remember, your friend lacks self-confidence and experience.

4. **Civic activity.** Your best friend plans to move into his or her own apartment but doesn't know the first thing about how to choose one. Explain the process of selecting an apartment—where to look, what to investigate, what questions to ask before signing a lease.

5. **Workplace action.** As a staff writer for a consumer magazine, you've been asked to write an article on how to shop for a certain product. Give specific steps explaining how to save money, buy a quality product, and the like.

6. **Workplace action.** An author of books for elementary school children, you want to show children how to do something—take care of a pet, get along with siblings, keep a room clean. Explain the process in terms a child would understand but not find condescending.

Chapter 15
Comparison-Contrast

Learning Objectives

15.1 Understand how you can use the comparison-contrast pattern to develop your essays.

15.2 Consider how comparison-contrast can fit your purpose and audience.

15.3 Develop prewriting strategies for using comparison-contrast in an essay.

15.4 Develop strategies for writing a comparison-contrast essay.

15.5 Use strategies for revising your comparison-contrast essay.

15.6 Analyze how comparison-contrast is used effectively in a student-written selection.

What Is Comparison-Contrast?

15.1 Understand how you can use the comparison-contrast pattern to develop your essays.

We frequently try to make sense of the world by finding similarities and differences in our experiences. Seeing how things are alike (**comparing**) and seeing how they are different (**contrasting**) help us impose meaning on experiences that otherwise might remain fragmented and disconnected.

Comparing and contrasting also help us make choices. We compare and contrast everything—from two brands of soap we might buy to two colleges we might attend. When we have to make important decisions, we tend to think rigorously about how things are alike or different: Should I accept the higher-paying job or the lower-paying one that offers more benefits? A deliberate approach to comparison-contrast may also provide us with insight into complex contemporary issues: Is television's coverage of political candidates more objective or less objective than it used to be?

How Comparison-Contrast Fits Your Purpose and Audience

15.2 Consider how comparison-contrast can fit your purpose and audience.

When is it appropriate to use the comparison-contrast pattern of development? Comparison-contrast works well if you want to demonstrate any of the following. Note that a sample essay question follows each example:

- **One thing is better than another.** *Example essay question:* Compare and contrast the way male and female relationships are depicted in *Cosmopolitan, Ms., Playboy,* and *Esquire.* Which publication has the most limited view of men and women? Which has the broadest perspective?

- **Things that seem different are actually alike.** *Example essay question:* Football, basketball, and baseball differ in the ways they appeal to fans. Describe the unique drawing power of each sport, but also reach some conclusions about the appeals the three sports have in common.

- **Things that seem alike are actually different.** *Example essay question:* Studies show that college students and their parents feel that post-secondary education should equip young people to succeed in the marketplace. Yet the same studies report that the two groups have a very different understanding of what it means to succeed. What differences do you think the studies identify?

Other assignments lend themselves to comparison-contrast in less obvious ways. For instance, although words like *compare, contrast, differ,* and *have in common* don't appear in the following assignments, essay responses to the assignments could be organized around the comparison-contrast format:

> The emergence of the two-career family is one of the major phenomena of our culture. Discuss the advantages and disadvantages of having both parents work, showing how you feel about such two-career households.

> There has been considerable criticism recently of the news coverage by the city's two leading newspapers, the *Herald* and the *Beacon*. Indicate whether you think the criticism is valid by discussing the similarities and differences in the two papers' news coverage.

Note that the second assignment shows that a comparison-contrast essay may cover similarities *and* differences, not just one or the other.

As you have seen, comparison-contrast can be the key strategy for achieving an essay's purpose. But comparison-contrast can also be a supplemental method used to help make a point in an essay organized chiefly around another pattern of development. For example:

- A serious, informative essay intended for laypeople might *define* clinical depression by contrasting that state of mind with ordinary run-of-the-mill blues.

- Writing humorously about the exhausting *effects* of trying to get in shape, you might dramatize your plight for readers by contrasting the leisurely way you used to spend your day with your current rigidly compulsive exercise regimen.

- In an urgent *argumentation-persuasion* essay on the need for stricter controls over drug abuse in the workplace, you might provide readers with background by comparing several companies' approaches to the problem.

Prewriting Strategies

15.3 Develop prewriting strategies for using comparison-contrast in an essay.

The following checklist shows how you can apply prewriting strategies to comparison-contrast.

☑ Comparison-Contrast: A Prewriting Checklist

Choose Subjects to Compare and Contrast

☐ What have you recently needed to compare and contrast (subjects to major in, events to attend, ways to resolve a disagreement) in order to make a choice? What would a comparison-contrast analysis disclose about the alternatives, your priorities, and the criteria by which you judge?

☐ Can you show a need for change by contrasting one way of doing something with a better way?

☐   Do any people you know show some striking similarities and differences? What would a comparison-contrast analysis reveal about their characters and the personal qualities you prize?

☐   How does your view on an issue differ from that of other people? What would a comparison-contrast analysis of these views indicate about your values?

Determine Your Purpose, Audience, Tone, and Point of View

☐   Is your purpose primarily to inform readers of similarities and differences? To evaluate your subjects' relative merits? To persuade readers to choose between alternative courses of action?

☐   What audience are you writing for? To what tone and point of view will they be most receptive?

Use Prewriting to Generate Points of Comparison-Contrast

☐   How could brainstorming, freewriting, mapping, or journal entries help you gather information about your subjects' most significant similarities and differences?

Strategies for Using Comparison-Contrast in an Essay

15.4 Develop strategies for writing a comparison-contrast essay.

After prewriting, you're ready to draft your essay. The following suggestions and Figure 15.1 will be helpful whether you use comparison-contrast as a dominant or supportive pattern of development.

1. **Be sure your subjects are at least somewhat alike.**

    Unless you plan to develop an *analogy* (see point #2 below), the subjects you choose to compare or contrast should share some obvious characteristics or qualities. It makes sense to compare different parts of the country, but a reasonable essay wouldn't result from comparing a television game show with a soap opera. Your subjects must belong to the same general group so that your comparison-contrast stays within logical bounds.

2. **Stay focused on your purpose.**

    When writing, remember that comparison-contrast isn't an end in itself. That is, your objective isn't to turn an essay into a mechanical list of "how *A* differs from *B*" or "how *A* is like *B*." As with the other patterns of development, comparison-contrast is a strategy for making a point or meeting a larger purpose.

    Consider the assignment about the two newspapers:

    There has been considerable criticism recently of the news coverage by the city's two leading newspapers, the *Herald* and the *Beacon*. Indicate whether you think the criticism is valid by discussing the similarities and differences in the two papers' news coverage.

Figure 15.1 Development Diagram: Writing a Comparison-Contrast Essay

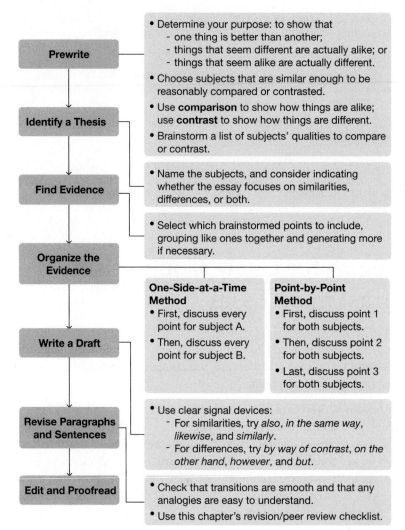

Your purpose in this assignment might take several forms:

- Your goal may be simply to *inform*, to present information as objectively as possible: "This is what the *Herald*'s news coverage is like. This is what the *Beacon*'s news coverage is like."

- More frequently, though, you'll use comparison-contrast to *evaluate* your subjects' pros and cons, with your goal being to reach a conclusion or make a judgment: "Both the *Herald* and the *Beacon* spend too much time reporting local news," or "The *Herald*'s analysis of the recent hostage crisis was more insightful than the *Beacon*'s."

- You can also use comparison-contrast to *persuade* readers to take action: "People interested in thorough coverage of international events should read the *Herald* rather than the *Beacon.*" Persuasive essays may also propose a change, contrasting what now exists with a more ideal situation: "For the *Beacon* to compete with the *Herald,* it must assign more reporters to international stories."

Another purpose you might have in writing a comparison-contrast essay is to *clear up misconceptions* by revealing previously hidden similarities or differences. For example, perhaps your town's two newspapers are thought to be sharply different. However, a comparison-contrast analysis might reveal that—although one paper specializes in sensationalized stories while the other adopts a more muted approach—both resort to biased, emotionally charged analyses of local politics. Or the essay might illustrate that the tabloid's treatment of the local arts scene is surprisingly more comprehensive than its competitor's.

Comparing and contrasting also make it possible to *draw an analogy* between two seemingly unrelated subjects. An **analogy** is an imaginative comparison that delves beneath the subjects' surface differences to expose their significant and often unsuspected similarities or differences. An analogy can make a complex subject easier to understand—as, for example, when the national deficit is compared to a household budget gone awry. Analogies are often dramatic and instructive, challenging you and your audience to consider subjects in a new light. But analogies don't speak for themselves. You must make clear how the analogy demonstrates your purpose.

3. **Formulate a strong thesis.**

An essay that is developed primarily through comparison-contrast should be focused by a solid thesis. Besides revealing your attitude, the thesis will often do the following:

- Name the subjects being compared and contrasted
- Indicate whether the essay focuses on the subjects' similarities, differences, or both
- State the essay's main point of comparison or contrast

Not all comparison-contrast essays need thesis statements as structured as those that follow. Even so, these examples can serve as models of clarity. Note that the first thesis statement signals similarities, the second differences, and the last both similarities and differences:

Middle-aged parents are often in a good position to empathize with adolescent children because the emotional upheavals experienced by the two age groups are much the same.

The priorities of most retired people are more conducive to health and happiness than the priorities of most young professionals.

College students in their thirties and forties face many of the same pressures as younger students, but they are better equipped to withstand these pressures.

4. **Select the points to be discussed.**

   Once you have identified the essay's subject, purpose, and thesis, you need to decide which of the many points generated during prewriting you will discuss: You have to identify which aspects of the subjects to compare or contrast. For instance, you could compare and contrast college professors on the basis of their testing methods, ability to motivate students, confidence in front of a classroom, personalities, level of enthusiasm, and so forth.

   When selecting points to cover, be sure to consider your audience. Ask yourself: "Will my readers be familiar with this item? Will I need it to get my message across? Will my audience find this item interesting or convincing?" What your readers know, what they don't know, and what you can project about their reactions should influence your choices. And, of course, you need to select points that support your thesis.

5. **Organize the points to be discussed.**

   After deciding which points to include, you should use a systematic, logical plan for presenting those ideas. If the points aren't organized, your essay will be little more than a confusing jumble of ideas. There are two common ways to organize an essay developed wholly or in part by comparison-contrast. Although both strategies may be used in an essay, one method usually predominates.

   In the **one-side-at-a-time method** of organization, you discuss everything relevant about one subject before moving to another subject. For example, responding to the earlier assignment that asked you to analyze the news coverage in two local papers, you might first talk about the *Herald*'s coverage of international, national, and local news; then you would discuss the *Beacon*'s coverage of the same categories. Note that the areas discussed should be the same for both newspapers. It wouldn't be logical to review the *Herald*'s coverage of international, national, and local news and then to detail the *Beacon*'s magazine supplements, modern living section, and comics page. Moreover, the areas compared and contrasted should be presented in the same order.

   This is how you would organize the essay using the one-side-at-a-time method:

Everything about subject *A*	*Herald*'s news coverage:
	• International
	• National
	• Local
Everything about subject *B*	*Beacon*'s news coverage:
	• International
	• National
	• Local

   In the **point-by-point method** of organization, you alternate from one aspect of the first subject to the same aspect of your other subject(s). For example, to use this method when comparing or contrasting the *Herald* and the *Beacon*, you would first discuss the *Herald*'s international coverage, then the *Beacon*'s international coverage; next, the *Herald*'s national coverage, then the *Beacon*'s; and finally, the *Herald*'s local coverage, then the *Beacon*'s.

An essay using the point-by-point method would be organized like this:

First aspect of subjects *A* and *B*	*Herald:* International coverage
	Beacon: International coverage
Second aspect of subjects *A* and *B*	*Herald:* National coverage
	Beacon: National coverage
Third aspect of subjects *A* and *B*	*Herald:* Local coverage
	Beacon: Local coverage

Deciding which of these two methods of organization to use is largely a personal choice, though there are several factors to consider. The one-side-at-a-time method tends to convey a more unified feeling because it highlights broad similarities and differences. It is therefore an effective approach for subjects that are fairly uncomplicated. This strategy also works well when your essay will be brief; the reader won't find it difficult to remember what has been said about subject *A* when reading about subject *B*.

Because the point-by-point method permits more extensive coverage of similarities and differences, it is often a wise choice when subjects are complex. This pattern is also useful for lengthy essays because readers would probably find it difficult to remember, let's say, ten pages of information about subject *A* while reading the next ten pages about subject *B*. However, the point-by-point approach may cause readers to lose sight of the broader picture, so remember to keep them focused on your central point.

6. **Supply the reader with clear transitions.**

Readers should be able to follow your line of thought easily. Your comparison-contrast essay needs *transitions*—especially those signaling similarities or differences—to show readers where they have been and where they are going. By indicating clearly when subjects are being compared or contrasted, the transitions help weave the discussion into a coherent whole.

The transitions (in boldface) in the following examples could be used to *signal similarities* in an essay discussing the news coverage in the *Herald* and the *Beacon*:

- The *Beacon* **also** allots only a small portion of the front page to global news.
- **In the same way,** the *Herald* tries to include at least three local stories on the first page.
- **Likewise,** the *Beacon* emphasizes the importance of up-to-date reporting of town meetings.

The transitions (in boldface) in these examples could be used to *signal differences:*

- **By way of contrast,** the *Herald*'s editorial page deals with national matters on the average of three times a week.

- **On the other hand,** the *Beacon* does not share the *Herald*'s enthusiasm for interviews with national figures.
- **But** the *Herald*'s coverage of the Washington scene is much more comprehensive than its competitor's.

Revision Strategies

15.5 Use strategies for revising your comparison-contrast essay.

Once you have a draft of the essay, you're ready to revise. The following checklist will help your peers provide feedback and aid you in revising your essay.

☑ Comparison-Contrast: A Revision/Peer Review Checklist

Revise Overall Meaning and Structure

☐ Are the subjects sufficiently alike for the comparison-contrast to be logical and meaningful?

☐ What purpose does the essay serve—to inform, to evaluate, to persuade readers to accept a viewpoint, to eliminate misconceptions, or to draw a surprising analogy?

☐ What is the essay's thesis? How could the thesis be stated more effectively?

☐ Is the overall essay organized primarily by the one-side-at-a-time method or by the point-by-point method? What is the advantage of that strategy for this essay?

☐ Are the same features discussed for each subject? Are they discussed in the same order?

☐ Which points of comparison and/or contrast need further development? Which points should be deleted? Where do significant points seem to be missing? How has the most important similarity or difference been emphasized?

Revise Paragraph Development

☐ If the essay uses the one-side-at-a-time method, which paragraph marks the switch from one subject to another?

☐ If the essay uses the point-by-point method, do paragraphs consistently alternate between subjects? If this alternation becomes too elaborate or predictable, what could be done to eliminate the problem?

☐ If the essay uses both the one-side-at-a-time and the point-by-point methods, which paragraph marks the switch from one method to the other? If the switch is confusing, how could it be made less so?

☐ Where would signal devices (*also, likewise, in contrast*) make it easier to see similarities and differences between the subjects being discussed?

Revise Sentences and Words

☐ Where do too many signal devices make sentences awkward and mechanical?

☐ Which sentences and words fail to convey the intended tone?

Student Essay: From Prewriting Through Revision

15.6 Analyze how comparison-contrast is used effectively in a student-written selection.

The following student essay was written by Blake Norman in response to this assignment:

> In "A Mickey Mouse Approach to Globalization," Jeffrey N. Wasserstrom, a college professor and specialist in Chinese history, contrasts the various ways images are perceived differently around the world. He writes about a subject he knows well from his own research and publications. Write an essay about a subject you are familiar with from your own experience, but also incorporate several outside sources into your essay. For example, you might choose to write about a hobby you enjoy, comparing various types of equipment or supplies needed to effectively participate in that pastime, or you might write about a purchase you are considering making and compare your various options, using information from outside sources for added support.

Blake decided to do some brainstorming to help him come up with possible topics to write about, using the topics his teacher had provided as examples in the assignment: a hobby or a purchase.

Brainstorming

Hobbies I Enjoy	Purchases I Might Make
–hunting	–motorcycle
–fishing	–car
–baseball	–hunting gear
–football	–fishing gear
–mountain bike racing	–mountain bike

As Blake looked over his brainstorming, he asked himself which of his possible topics he knew the most about. He had purchased several mountain bikes over the years and had done some mountain bike racing, so he decided to write about the factors that should be considered when buying a mountain bike. Blake then went on to develop a topic outline that helped him organize his ideas.

Outline

Thesis: Important factors to consider when buying a mountain bike are suspension, wheel size, weight, stiffness, and price.

  I. Suspension

    A. Full-suspension

    B. Hard tail

  II. Wheel size

    A. Larger wheels

    B. Smaller wheels

III. Weight
   A. Aluminum alloy
   B. Steel
   C. Titanium
   D. Carbon fiber

IV. Stiffness
   A. Aluminum alloy
   B. Steel
   C. Titanium
   D. Carbon fiber

V. Price
   A. Low-priced bikes
   B. High-priced bikes
   C. Medium-priced bikes

Now read Blake's essay, "Buying a Cross-Country Mountain Bike," noting the similarities and differences between his outline and final essay. You'll see that the essay is more developed than the outline. In the essay, Blake added numerous specific details—like those about the importance of considering brakes, saddle, seat post, and stem length as well as questions the buyer needs to consider before purchasing a mountain bike. He also developed a graphic that pulled together the important points he was making. As you read the essay, consider how well it applies the principles of comparison-contrast discussed in this chapter. (The commentary that follows the essay will help you look at Blake's essay more closely and will give you some sense of how he went about revising his first draft.)

Buying a Cross-Country Mountain Bike
by Blake Norman

Introduction

Cross-country mountain bike racing has become increasingly   1
popular over the past couple of decades. It offers an enjoyable way for people to exercise their heart as well as other muscles. An added benefit is the chance to join a biking club and meet new people. One result of this popularity is that there are more bikes than ever before on the market. There are also many factors that consumers need to consider if they are thinking about purchasing one of them. Consumers should get information about minor features, such as brakes, saddle, seatpost, and stem length. However, to find the right cross-

Thesis

country bike, beginning bikers need to consider how the bike's major features—suspension and wheel size as well as weight, stiffness, and price—suit their biking habits.

Topic sentence

A bike's suspension determines how smoothly it rides. The Vital   2
MTB website features 926 bikes and explains that cross-country

mountain bikes "come in two varieties—full-suspension or hardtail." Full-suspension bikes offer a smoother ride than do hardtail bikes, which have only front suspension. However, many riders claim that hardtail bikes travel faster without the added suspension.

Wheel size is the next factor to consider in buying a cross-country bike. Cross-country mountain bikes come in 26-inch and 29-inch wheel sizes, and the tires are "relatively skinny … and are made to roll fast" (Vital MTB). Bikes with larger wheels are more stable than smaller-wheeled bikes, so they tend to climb better and descend better. Also, larger wheels, which are becoming more popular, are less likely than smaller wheels to fall into potholes on a trail.   3

In addition to deciding on the type of suspension and wheel size, consumers also need to consider the weight, stiffness, and price of the bike. These features vary by type of material used in the frame—aluminum alloy, steel, titanium, or carbon fiber. Table 1 compares the different frame materials by weight, stiffness, and price.   4

Table 1 Cross-Country Bike Features by Frame Material

Feature	Aluminum alloy	Steel	Titanium	Carbon fiber
Weight	Light	Heaviest; most durable	Light; strong	Lightest; least durable
Stiffness	Moderately stiff	Stiffest	Moderately stiff	Depends on bike design
Price	Moderately expensive	Least expensive	Very expensive	Most expensive
Best use	Popular with a range of riders	Good for entry-level bikers	Used in high-end and custom bikes	Used by serious bikers and racers

The weight of a cross-country mountain racing bike is especially important to consider because a heavy bike will slow bikers down when they are racing. The majority of cross-country bikes are made of aluminum alloy. It is more expensive than steel, but it's lighter. Some manufacturers have higher-end, lighter aluminum frames that are more expensive. Titanium frames are light and strong but are very expensive and are used primarily on high-end bikes. Carbon fiber is light and strong, but manufacturing it is very labor-intensive. Because of this, carbon-fiber frames are primarily used by enthusiasts and racers. Also carbon-fiber frames are lighter than all other types of frames.   5

Stiffness is definitely an aspect that individuals need to take into account when deciding on a bike for cross-country mountain racing because a bike that is stiff will have a better pedaling efficiency. Stiffness controls how much a bike will resist twisting, especially in rough terrain. Aluminum alloy frames can be very stiff and also light. In comparison, steel frames are stiff but may be too heavy   6

Evaluative statement that brings the paragraph to closure

for experienced riders. Titanium frames can be both stiff and strong, but they are not as strong as steel and are expensive to repair. Carbon-fiber frames can be the stiffest of all bike frames ("Bike 101"). As bikers become more experienced, their appreciation for a bike frame's stiffness increases.

Topic sentence

Cross-country mountain bikes come in a wide range of prices. Vital MTB's "Cross-Country Mountain Bike Buyer's Guide" states, "In general, the more expensive a bike is, the more durable it will be (at least until you start getting into the high-end where lightweight construction may reduce durability)." It's important to keep in mind, of course, that one of the main purposes of the site that makes this claim is to sell bikes and make money; but even so, the claim makes good sense. On the other hand, there is a lot of truth to the old saying "You get what you pay for." The site recommends that those who plan to ride on a regular basis spend a minimum of $900 on a bike. Prices of bikes they feature range from $330 for the 2013 GT Palomar GTW model (steel frame, 26-inch tires) to $11,000 for the 2013 Cannondal Scalpel 29er Carbon Ultimate model (carbon frame, 29-inch tires), and there are 924 bikes with prices between these two extremes.

7

Fifth factor to consider—prices compared

Topic sentence

Deciding on the right mountain bike will take some time and effort, but the more thinking and research consumers do before making a purchase, the smarter their choice is likely to be. Although it appears that the weight and stiffness of bikes made from carbon fiber make them better choices than those constructed of aluminum alloy, steel, or titanium, the choice should depend on both the biker's budget and on how the person plans to use the bike. Readers can consult the "Best use" row in Table 1, but consumers must ask themselves these questions: How much can I afford to spend? How often do I plan to ride? Do I plan to ride in competitive racing events or primarily with friends for fun and relaxation? What kinds of trails do I plan to ride on—smooth or rocky? flat or steep? Once beginning bikers think through these issues and do some research, they will be ready to purchase the cross-country mountain bike that is the best fit.

8

Conclusion

Concluding statement that brings the essay to closure

Works Cited

"Bike 101 Frame Materials." *The CARE Exchange*, May 2006, www.caree.org/bike101framematerials.htm.

"Cross-Country Mountain Bike Buyer's Guide." *Vital MTB*, 2014, www.vitalmtb.com.

Commentary

PURPOSE AND THESIS   In his essay, Blake compares factors that first-time buyers should consider in buying a cross-country mountain bike—suspension, wheel size, weight, stiffness, and price—and provides information that is valuable for someone thinking about purchasing one. The *comparison-contrast* pattern allows him to analyze the drawbacks and merits of the various factors, thus providing the essay with an *evaluative purpose*. Using the title to let readers know that his essay will be useful to anyone interested in purchasing a cross-country mountain bike, Blake places the *thesis* at the end of his introductory paragraph: "However, to find the right cross-country bike, beginning bikers need to consider how the bike's major features—suspension and wheel size, as well as weight, stiffness, and price—suit their biking habits." The thesis specifies the five factors to be discussed and indicates why Blake chose to focus on those five areas: they are the "major" features to be considered.

OVERALL ORGANIZATION   Blake begins his essay by introducing the advantages of cross-country biking and its growing popularity. He distinguishes between "minor features" and "major features" in bikes and then goes on to state in his thesis statement the five major features that he will discuss. He then discusses the features one by one, comparing options for each feature, starting with two features—suspension and wheel size—that can be dealt with in self-contained paragraphs. Then he focuses on the remaining three features—weight, stiffness, and price, in that order—saving the discussion of price for the end because he thinks that feature will be the most significant one for beginning bikers. Throughout, Blake also uses signal devices ("However"; "in comparison"; "on the other hand") to make comparisons clear to his readers. Blake then moves on to his concluding paragraph and brings his essay to closure.

PARAGRAPH DEVELOPMENT AND SEQUENCE OF POINTS   Blake generally uses a *point-by-point comparison method*. Blake's first two supporting paragraphs (paragraphs 2 and 3) are relatively short; each compares the options for a specific point—either suspension or wheel size. Then Blake includes a transitional paragraph in which he explains that he will discuss each remaining point in terms of four newly introduced subjects: "type of material used in the frame—aluminum alloy, steel, titanium, or carbon fiber." Because he must repeat the four subjects for each point, the three supporting paragraphs for weight, stiffness, and price are longer than the previous paragraphs and are of roughly equal length. Blake briefly considered using a *one-side-at-a-time comparison method*—devoting a paragraph to each type of frame material. However, he realized that he would have had difficulty fitting the discussion of suspension and wheel size into that comparison structure.

In discussing the weight of bikes, Blake first explains why weight is an important factor and then goes on to compare the four types of materials from which cross-country mountain bikes are commonly built. He concludes this section of his essay with an evaluative statement: "…carbon-fiber frames are primarily used by enthusiasts and racers."

Using a similar structure in the next section of the essay in which he discusses the stiffness of bikes, Blake begins by explaining why stiffness is an important factor and then goes on to compare the four most common types of frame materials. As he did in the previous section, Blake concludes this section of his essay with an evaluative statement: "As bikers become more experienced, their appreciation for a bike frame's stiffness increases" (6). He incorporates a quote from a biking website, with a parenthetical reference: "(Bike 101)."

The structure of the final supporting paragraph on price is somewhat different. Blake seems to assume that his readers will want to spend their money wisely and that there is no need to begin this paragraph with an explanation of why it is important to consider the price of the bike. Following the topic sentence for paragraph 7, "Cross-country mountain bikes come in a wide range of prices," Blake supplies information from the Vital MTB Cross-Country Mountain Bikes website, which recommends that those who plan to ride on a regular basis spend a minimum of $900 on a bike. Next, Blake indirectly explains why it is important to consider the price of the bike you purchase: "On the other hand, you get what you pay for." He concludes the paragraph with brief descriptions of Vital MTB's least expensive ($330) and most expensive ($11,000) bikes. The concluding paragraph reemphasizes Blake's main point—that consumers new to cross-country biking need to do research before buying—and supplies readers with a list of questions they can use to determine their biking needs.

TABLE   Blake decided that his readers would benefit from a graphic that pulled together the important points he was making. He tried creating a table that included all five features. However, because he was not comparing suspension and wheel size by frame material, he soon realized that he could not include them in the table. Blake also thought that the table would be a good place to give his evaluations, so he added a row labeled "Best use." He made sure that the reference to the table preceded the table itself in the essay.

COMBINING PATTERNS OF DEVELOPMENT   To illustrate his points, Blake makes extensive use of *exemplification*, and his discussion also has elements typical of *causal analysis*: "Bikes with larger wheels are more stable than smaller-wheeled bikes, so they tend to climb better and descend" (3). In addition, he includes examples of various wheel sizes, frame materials, and prices of bikes, along with examples of the kinds of questions that should be considered before purchasing a cross-country mountain bike. He also traces the effect of various types of materials on the weight, stiffness, and price of bikes.

A PROBLEM WITH STRUCTURE   Blake begins the paragraph on price with a rather weak topic sentence ("Cross-country mountain bikes come in a wide range of prices") that says nothing about why it is important to carefully consider the price of bikes. Later in the paragraph, he implies that the buyer should not have high expectations of a less expensive model, but his essay could have been stronger if he had begun with a clear explanation of why price is such an important element to consider. Also, although Blake included outside sources, his choice of sources might have been more reliable. One is a commercial website, which he admits has a bias. The other website is not commercial, but it was last updated in 2006. Blake did his own Internet research, but he might have benefitted from a librarian's help in finding sources.

CONCLUSION   Blake's final paragraph does a nice job of bringing his essay to closure. Instead of simply restating his thesis and reminding readers of what he stated in his essay, Blake provides a series of questions that, if carefully considered, can help readers make informed choices when buying a cross-country mountain bike: "How much can I afford to spend? How often do I plan to ride? Do I plan to ride in competitive racing events or primarily with friends for fun and relaxation? What kinds of trails do I plan to ride on—smooth or rocky? flat or steep?" These questions should prove useful to anyone interested in purchasing a cross-country mountain bike, and the final sentence ("Once beginning bikers think through these issues and do some research, they will be ready to purchase the cross-country mountain bike that is the best fit") should give them confidence that they can make a smart choice.

REVISING THE FIRST DRAFT   Parts of Blake's first draft were radically different from the final draft he later submitted for a grade. Upon deciding on a topic for his essay, Blake, an avid cross-country mountain bike racer, thought that because he had purchased several mountain bikes over the years and had done some thinking about how he wanted to organize his essay, he could easily and quickly complete a first draft. Consequently, he did something most writers do at one time or another: He put off the writing until the night before the draft was due. After completing the first draft and quickly reading through it, he felt that he had done a pretty good job.

The next morning Blake arrived at his classroom a few minutes early and spent the extra minutes reading over his draft again. As he reread it, he realized that the draft was not as strong as he had thought it was. For example, he realized that his introduction did not do a good job of engaging readers or of explaining the various kinds of issues that need to be considered when deciding what kind of cross-country mountain bike to purchase.

In class that morning, Blake shared his draft with Olivia and Gabby, the two classmates in his peer review group. He told them that he had put off the writing until the last minute and that, as a result, he had not had time to go back and give his essay the attention he knew it needed. You'll get a good sense of the kinds of revisions he made if you compare the original introduction printed here with the final version in the full essay.

> ### Original Version of the Introduction
> Cross-country mountain bike racing is one of the most popular forms of mountain bike racing. As a result there are many different types of bikes to choose from. A base-level rider may prefer to ride a fully carbon dual suspension bike whereas a pro-level racer may prefer to use an aluminum hard tail. The most important factors to consider in a bike are weight, stiffness, and price.

Blake already knew that his introduction was weak and that he needed to do a much better job of engaging the reader and explaining the various kinds of issues that need to be considered when deciding on what kind of cross-country mountain bike to purchase, but Olivia and Gabby provided him with additional insights. As the three of them read through the draft together, Olivia and Gabby, who knew very little about cross-country mountain bikes, asked Blake questions about what they would need to know if they were going to purchase a bike. Their questions and the explanations Blake gave them helped him understand how to make his draft stronger. As he talked with Olivia and Gabby, he explained to them that deciding on the right bike is complicated because there are so many factors to consider: full suspension or hard-tail; the type of brakes, saddle, seatpost, and stem length; and weight, stiffness, and price—which he considered most important of all.

Blake left his classroom that morning with a much clearer idea of the revisions he needed to make to clearly communicate his ideas to his readers. The combination of letting his writing sit for a while and talking about his draft with Olivia and Gabby was exactly what Blake needed to improve his essay. His instructor's comments on his draft confirmed his ideas, and he revised his essay considerably before submitting his final draft.

Activities: Comparison-Contrast

Prewriting Activities

1. Imagine you're writing two essays. One explores the effects of holding a job while in college; the other explains how to budget money wisely. Jot down ways you might use comparison-contrast in each essay.

2. Suppose you plan to write a series of articles for your college newspaper. What purpose might you have for comparing and/or contrasting each of the following subject pairs?

   a. Live concert and a recording of the concert

   b. Paper or plastic bags at the supermarket

   c. Two courses—one taught by an inexperienced newcomer, the other by an old pro

   d. Cutting class and not showing up at work

3. Use the patterns of development or another prewriting technique to compare or contrast a current situation with the way you would like it to be. After reviewing your prewriting material, decide what your purpose, audience, tone, and point of view might be if you were to write an essay. Finally, write out your thesis and main supporting points.

4. Using your journal or freewriting, jot down the advantages and disadvantages of two ways of doing something. Reread your prewriting and determine what your thesis, purpose, audience, tone, and point of view might be if you were to write an essay. Make a scratch list of the main ideas you would cover. Which would work more effectively, a point-by-point organization or a one-side-at-a-time organization?

Revising Activities

5. Of the statements that follow, which would *not* make effective thesis statements for a comparison-contrast essay? Identify the problem(s) in the faulty statements and revise them accordingly.

a. Although their classroom duties often overlap, teacher aides are not as equipped as teachers to handle disciplinary problems.

b. This college provides more assistance to its students than most schools.

c. There are many differences between American and foreign cars.

6. The following paragraph is from the draft of an essay detailing the qualities of a skillful manager. How effective is this comparison-contrast paragraph? What revisions would help focus the paragraph on the point made in the topic sentence? Where should details be added or deleted? Rewrite the paragraph, providing necessary transitions and details.

> A manager encourages creativity and treats employees courteously, while a boss discourages staff resourcefulness and views it as a threat. At the hardware store where I work, I got my boss's approval to develop a system for organizing excess stock in the storeroom. I shelved items in roughly the same order as they were displayed in the store. The system was helpful to all the salespeople, not just to me, since everyone was stymied by the boss's helter-skelter system. What he did was store overstocked items according to each wholesaler, even though most of us weren't there long enough to know which items came from which wholesaler. His supposed system created chaos. When he saw what I had done, he was furious and insisted that we continue to follow the old slapdash system. I had assumed he would welcome my ideas the way my manager did last summer when I worked in a drugstore. But he didn't and I had to scrap my work and go back to his eccentric system. He certainly could learn something about employee relations from the drugstore manager.

Professional Selections: Comparison–Contrast

JEFFREY N. WASSERSTROM

Jeffrey N. Wasserstrom, a member of the faculty at the University of California, Irvine, and a specialist in Chinese history, is especially interested in patterns of student protest and the effects of globalization on urban life and popular culture. His publications include *Global Shanghai, 1850–1990* (2009) and *China in the 21st Century: What Everyone Needs to Know* (2013). "A Mickey Mouse Approach to Globalization" first appeared in *Yale Global Online* and later in *Global Policy Forum*, an independent policy watchdog group that works to encourage accountability in international organizations such as the United Nations.

For ideas on how this comparison-contrast essay is organized, see Figure 15.2.

Pre-Reading Journal

How do customs and practices from other cultures around the world influence your life on a daily basis? How are the words you use, the foods you eat, the music you listen to, and the sports you enjoy influenced by other worldwide cultures? Explore these ideas in your journal.

A Mickey Mouse Approach to Globalization

From Buenos Aires to Berlin, people around the world are looking more and 1
more American. They're wearing Levis, watching CNN, buying coffee at inter-
changeable Starbucks outlets, and generally experiencing life in "very American" ways. Looking only at the surface of this phenomenon, one might erroneously conclude that US cultural products are creating a homogenized global
community of consumers. But the cultural aspects of the globalization story
are far more complex than might be assumed from looking at just consumer
behavior. Even when the same shirt, song, soda, or store is found on all five
continents, it tends to mean different things depending on who is doing the
wearing, singing, drinking, or shopping. The "strange" fate of global products
in China illustrates these points.

Consider, first of all, the Chinese meaning of Big Macs. In *The Lexus and the* 2
Olive Tree, Thomas Friedman says he has eaten McDonald's burgers in more countries than he can count and is well qualified to state that they "really do all taste the
same." What he actually means, though, is they all taste the same to him. Nearly
identical Big Macs may be sold in Boston and Beijing, but as anthropologist Yan
Yunxiang has convincingly argued, the experiences of eating them and even the
meaning of going to McDonald's in these two locales was very different in the
1990s. In Beijing, but not in Boston, a Big Mac was classified as a snack, not a
meal, and university students thought of McDonald's as a good place to go for
a romantic night out. To bite into a Big Mac thinking that you are about to do
something pleasantly familiar or shamefully plebeian—two common American
experiences—is one thing. To bite into one imagining you are on the brink of discovering what modernity tastes like—a common Chinese experience—is another
thing altogether.

Or take the curious arrival of Mickey Mouse in China, which I witnessed 3
firsthand. While living in Shanghai in the mid-1980s, two things I remember
seeing are sweatshirts for sale on the streets emblazoned with the face of Disney's most famous creation, and a wall poster showing a stake being driven
through Mickey's heart. Were these signs that a big American corporation was
extracting profits from a new market and that local people were angered by
cultural imperialism? Hardly. Yes, Disney was trying to make money, offering
Chinese state television free cartoons to show in the hope that viewers would
rush out and buy authorized products. But the plan went astray: the sweatshirts
I saw were all knock-offs. The only people making money from them were Chinese entrepreneurs. And the wall poster was, of all things, part of a Communist
Party health campaign. A call had just gone out for all citizens to work hard to
rid their cities of rats, which are called "laoshu," the same term used for mice.
It wasn't long before enterprising local residents put up posters showing various forms of violence being directed at "Mi Laoshu," as Mickey is known in
Chinese, not because they hated America but simply because he was the most
famous rodent in China.

Flash forward to the year 2000, when Starbucks first opened in both the 4
American town I live in (Bloomington, Indiana) and the Chinese city I study
(Shanghai), and we see further evidence of the divergent local meanings of

globally familiar icons. In Bloomington, Starbucks triggered mixed reactions. Some locals welcomed its arrival. Others staged non-violent protests or smashed its windows, complaining that the chain's record on environmental and labor issues was abysmal and that Starbucks would drive local coffee shops out of business. In Shanghai, by contrast, there were no demonstrations. The chain's arrival was seen as contributing to, rather than putting a check upon, the proliferation of new independently run coffeehouses.

The local meanings of Shanghai Starbucks do not stop there. For example, 5 when outlets open in Europe, they are typically seen, for understandable reasons, as symbols of creeping—or steam-rolling—Americanization. In Shanghai, though, guidebooks sometimes classify Starbucks as a "European-style" (as opposed to "Japanese-style") foreign coffee house. To further complicate things, the management company that operates the dozens of Shanghai Starbucks outlets is based not in Seattle but in Taiwan.

These examples of American products taking on distinctly new cultural meanings when moved from the US to China are useful in undermining superficial assertions equating globalization with "Americanization." But it is important not to stop there. The same thing has happened—and continues to happen—with the global meanings of Asian icons in America. Here, again, a Chinese illustration seems apt; that of a Middle Kingdom figure, Chairman Mao, whose face nearly rivals Mickey Mouse's in terms of global recognition.

One indication of the fame and varied meanings of Mao's visage is that in 7 2002 news stories appeared that told of the simultaneous appearance of the Chairman's image in three totally different national contexts. Representations of Mao showed up in the huts of Nepalese guerrillas; on posters carried by protesting laid-off workers in Northeast China; and in a London art exhibit. In Nepal, Mao was invoked because he endorsed peasant revolt. In Northeast China, his link to the days when Chinese workers had iron rice bowls for life was what mattered. And in London, it was his status as a favorite subject of a pop art pioneer that counted: the exhibit was a Warhol retrospective.

There is, in sum, more to keep in mind about globalization than Friedman's 8 divide between the worlds of mass-produced Lexus cars and individuated olive trees. One reason is simply that a Lexus can mean myriad things, depending on where it is. Whether one first encounters it in the showroom or working the assembly line matters. And it makes a difference whether the people who watch it are seeing it whiz by as they walk the streets of Toledo or seeing it crawl as they sit on a Tokyo-bound Bullet Train. It is not just in physics, after all, but also in cultural analysis, that the complex workings of relativity need to be kept in mind.

Questions for Critical Reading

1. What is the selection's thesis? Locate the sentence(s) in which Wasserstrom states his main idea. If he doesn't state his thesis explicitly, express it in your own words.

2. What two images of Mickey Mouse in China in the mid-1980s does Wasserstrom describe, and how does he explain the popularity of the images?

Figure 15.2 Essay Structure Diagram: "A Mickey Mouse Approach to Globalization" by Jeffrey N. Wasserstrom

Introductory paragraph Thesis (paragraph 1)	The cultural aspects of the globalization story are complex. **Thesis:** Americanization does not equal globalization.
Comparison-contrast: Point 1: Varied meanings of eating Big Macs and going to McDonald's **Examples (2)**	**China:** Big Mac considered a snack and McDonald's a romantic date spot and place for a modern experience. **America:** Eating a Big Mac considered "something pleasantly familiar or shamefully plebeian."
Comparison-contrast: Point 2: Varied meanings of Mickey Mouse images **Personal observations and examples (3)**	**Chinese:** "Mi Laoshu"—a dirty rat. **America:** Mickey Mouse—a cute, loveable mouse.
Comparison-contrast: Point 3: Varied reactions to openings of Starbucks **Personal observations and examples (4–5)**	**America:** Mixed reactions including protests and smashed windows. **China:** Positive reactions including being referred to as "European-style" coffee houses and good for Chinese economy.
Comparison-contrast: Point 4: Varied meanings of Mao Zedong's images **Examples (6–7)**	**Nepal:** Mao as leader of peasants' revolt. **Northeast China:** Mao as provider of food. **London:** Mao as Warhol's pop art subject.
Concluding paragraph (8)	Author reiterates main idea that the cultural aspects of globalization are more complex than they might seem at first glance and that Americanization does not equal globalization.

3. In his essay Wasserstrom refers to both Thomas Friedman and Yan Yunxiang. What does the essay reveal regarding who these individuals are and how their ideas differ?

4. What three images of Mao Zedong does Wasserstrom describe in his essay, and how does he explain the "fame and varied meanings of Mao's image" (paragraph 7)?

Questions About the Writer's Craft

1. **The pattern.** Does Wasserstrom use the *one-side-at-a-time* or the *point-by-point* method to *compare* and *contrast* ideas and images in his essay? Give examples from the text to back up your assertions. Is his chosen method effective? Why or why not?

2. **Point of view.** Wasserstrom uses first-, second-, and third-person point of view in his essay. Give examples of his use of each one and explain why you think he uses all three.

3. **Other patterns.** In what ways does Wasserstrom use *exemplification* throughout his essay? Give specific examples. How do these examples help convince readers of his *argument* that globalization does not equal Americanization?

4. **References to experts.** Wasserstrom refers to Thomas Friedman in his second paragraph and again in his conclusion. Why do you think he uses this strategy? What purpose does it serve?

Writing Assignments Using Comparison-Contrast as a Pattern of Development

1. Wasserstrom notes that university students in China considered a visit to McDonald's "a romantic night out." Think of how different groups within your own community experience various American cultural institutions, such as Thanksgiving Day, Super Bowl Sunday, and high school graduation. The groups can be ethnic, religious, neighborhood, or school groups; families; or groups of friends. Choose one item and compare and contrast how it is treated differently in two or more groups.

2. Wasserstrom references Thomas Friedman and Yan Yunxiang in the second paragraph of his essay and tells us a little about their ideas. Conduct library and Internet research to find out more about these individuals and then write an essay in which you compare and contrast them and the views they espouse. Alternatively, research the ideas of two other experts on globalization and compare and contrast their views.

Writing Assignment Combining Patterns of Development

3. Using his example of the Andy Warhol retrospective, Wasserstrom claims that other cultures can influence our own American culture. Think of non-American cultural institutions that you are familiar with and that you feel have had an impact on American culture. Some examples might be pizza, salsa music, and manga comic books—or even yoga and soccer. Choose three *examples* and *define* or *describe* them. Then explain how they have influenced American culture. Consider using *narrative* in the form of anecdotes about people you know to illustrate your ideas.

PATRICIA COHEN

The journalist Patricia Cohen, currently the theater editor at the *New York Times*, previously created and edited the Arts & Ideas section for the same publication. Cohen also wrote for the *Washington Post, Rolling Stone* magazine, and *New York Newsday* and is the author of *In Our Prime: The Invention of Middle Age* (2012). The following essay (originally titled "*Cupid*: Spawn of Austen?") appeared in the Culturebox section of *Slate* online magazine on September 16, 2003.

Pre-Reading Journal Entry

The genre of reality-television shows has flourished in recent years, with the numbers and types of shows multiplying at a head-spinning pace. Consider various types of reality-TV shows: matchmaking and dating, athletic-challenge, housemate, secret-camera, personal makeover, home improvement, cooking contest, and so on. What are your feelings about each type of "real-life" show? Collectively, what is your opinion about the reality-TV genre as a whole? Spend some time recording your thoughts on these questions in your pre-reading journal.

Reality TV: Surprising Throwback to the Past?

Will Lisa Shannon find love and fortune? On tonight's finale of *Cupid*, CBS's latest reality dating show, fans will find out which suitor has been chosen to propose to the series's lovely 25-year-old heroine from among the remaining would-be romantics. If Shannon accepts the proposal, the couple will be married right then and there. And if they stay married for a year, they will receive a $1 million check. 1

To many critics, *Cupid* and other matchmaking shows that mix money and real-life marital machinations represent a cynical and tasteless new genre that is yet another sign of America's moral decline. But there's something familiar about the fortune hunters, the status seekers, the thwarted loves, the meddling friends, the public displays, the comic manners, and the sharp competitiveness—all find their counterparts in Jane Austen and Edith Wharton.[1] Only now, three-minute get-to-know-you tryouts in a TV studio substitute for three-minute waltzes at a ball. Traditional family values, it turns out, are back on television after all. 2

Lisa Shannon may lack the wit, depth, and cleverness of an Austen heroine, but like many of Austen's women, she has put herself in the hands of others (in this case her friends and the TV audience), trusting that they will choose the right match. Even the idea that Shannon, at 25, feels the need to go to such lengths to find a husband suggests a troubling 19th-century ethos: A woman who is not married by her late 20s is doomed to be an Old Maid. 3

Undoubtedly, the hundreds of suitors who joined the pursuit are as attracted to the $1 million dowry as to Shannon. But money played a large (and openly 4

---

[1] Jane Austen (1775–1817) and Edith Wharton (1862–1937) are renowned for their novels exploring the intricate social workings—particularly as they relate to courtship and marriage—of the upper classes. Austen wrote of England's country elite in the late 1700s and early 1800s, whereas Wharton most famously examined New York's high society in the late 1800s and early 1900s (editors' note).

discussed) role in the Victorian and Edwardian[2] contract as well. In *Pride and Prejudice*,[3] for example, we learn that "Mr. Darcy soon drew the attention of the room by his fine, tall person, handsome features, noble mien—and the report which was in general circulation within five minutes after his entrance of his having ten thousand a year." And in *Emma*,[4] Mr. Knightly scolds the novel's eponymous heroine for imagining a match between Mr. Elton and her friend Harriet, without understanding he is more interested in money than in love: "I have heard him speak with great animation of a large family of young ladies that his sisters are intimate with, who have all twenty thousand pounds apiece."

On *Cupid*, Lisa's friends Laura and Kimberly are there to protect her from such gold diggers. They helped Lisa screen the men who answered a coast-to-coast open call (which produced more candidates than did the California primary). After the three whittled down the list of hopefuls to 10, the final selection was turned over to TV viewers, who called in every week to vote for their favorite. 5

Like the secondary characters in Austen and Wharton, Shannon's companions are clearly there to provide piquant social commentary, deliciously wicked judgments, and intrigue, sabotaging some suitors and championing others. "Freak," "boring," "awful," shrieks Laura, Lisa's confidante, as she ridicules suitors' looks, accents, clothing, schooling, and pronunciation. 6

Of course, nothing but superficial snap judgments can be made in the few minutes that each man is initially given to impress the three women. But the snap judgments aren't necessarily unanimous, and Laura and Kimberly's debating of the various virtues and flaws (is he "an arrogant jerk" or a dependable lawyer?) are a prosaic version of Mr. Knightly's and Emma's spirited sparring over the lovesick Robert Martin: 7

"A respectable, intelligent gentleman-farmer," says Mr. Knightly. 8

"His appearance is so much against him, and his manner so bad," Emma responds. 9

Likewise, the hopeful bachelors on *Cupid* understand what goes into a suitable match. Corey, a rocket scientist with the Air Force, acknowledged up front, "I know you have your friends here because I have to fit in." One contestant, Rob, went so far as to boast, "I come from good stock, too. I have good hair and teeth," as if he were a racehorse, waiting for her to check his gums. 10

Even Richard Kaye, an English professor and the author of *The Flirt's Tragedy: Desire Without End in Victorian and Edwardian Fiction*, confesses to being a "guilty watcher" of the new matchmaking shows, finding the parallels spookily similar. But inevitably, these series—*The Bachelorette, Meet My Folks, Married by America,* and *For Love or Money* (where a woman can keep the man or the million but not both)—have all been scorned for debasing the sanctity of marriage and for their shallow, indecorous exhibitionism. 11

But the shows also betray dissatisfaction with the individualistic, go-it-alone ethic of modern courtship. The Victorians and Edwardians organized balls, 12

---

[2] The Victorian period refers to the time of Queen Victoria's reign in England (1837–1901), and the Edwardian period refers to the reign of England's King Edward VII (1901–1910) (editors' note).

[3] Novel written by Jane Austen and published in 1813 (editors' note).

[4] Novel written by Austen and published in 1815 (editors' note).

dinners, afternoon teas, country walks, and the like to help their younger members find mates. Today, without such formal social arrangements, singles are pretty much left to their own devices to suss out partners. And while the elaborate courtship rituals and codes may now seem curiously antique, they did serve to cushion the brutally competitive marriage market. "I've been looking for Mr. Right and I've just not been able to find him," Lisa confesses. "Based on my track record, I obviously need help." She has discovered what Lily Bart in Wharton's *The House of Mirth*[5] learned after losing a sought-after bachelor. Upon hearing of the wealthy match that Grace Van Osburgh expertly concocted for her daughter, Bart concludes: "The cleverest girl may miscalculate where her own interests are concerned, may yield too much at one moment and withdraw too far at the next."

In the end, the American public will choose Lisa's potential spouse in what could   13
be seen simply as a more democratic version of those literary heroes and heroines who gave themselves wholly over to society and allowed their extended family to pick an appropriate mate. And why not? The idea that a good husband is hard to find has become a cultural watchword. Meanwhile, the high divorce rate is evidence that love, American style, hasn't necessarily produced happier unions. Nor should anyone forget that Lisa, too, stands to gain the million only through an advantageous marriage. And if it doesn't work out after a year, she at least has one of the modern conveniences not available to Austen's or Wharton's protagonists: a no-fault divorce.[6]

Questions for Critical Reading

1. What is the selection's thesis? Locate the sentence(s) in which Cohen states her main idea. If she doesn't state the thesis explicitly, express it in your own words.

2. What does Cohen assert is the common perception of reality-TV dating shows among critics? Does she agree or disagree with this evaluation?

3. What are three similarities between the dating shows and the plots of classic novels?

4. Though her essay is principally a comparison of reality dating shows and classic novels, Cohen also acknowledges some important contrasts between them. What are these differences?

Questions About the Writer's Craft

1. **The pattern.** Which comparison-contrast method of organization (point-by-point or one-side-at-a-time) does Cohen use to develop her essay? Why might she have chosen this pattern?

---

[5] Novel published in 1905 (editors' note).

[6] Lisa Shannon and Hank Stapleton, the man selected for her, continued to date in the year following *Cupid's* conclusion, though they rejected the option of marrying during the final episode—along with the possibility of winning one million dollars on their first anniversary (editors' note).

2. **Audience.** What kind of audience do you think Cohen is writing for—one that already agrees with her, disagrees, or is indifferent? How can you tell?

3. **Direct quotes.** Throughout her essay, Cohen uses direct quotes from various sources. What kinds of sources does she quote? Why do you think she chose to quote rather than to paraphrase or summarize them?

4. **Other patterns.** In paragraphs 12 and 13, Cohen presents a *causal analysis* of modern-day dating. How does this examination of *causes* and *effects* help reinforce her thesis?

Writing Assignments Using Comparison-Contrast as a Pattern of Development

1. Cohen draws a surprisingly apt comparison between today's reality dating shows and classic novels of the 1800s and early 1900s. Think of another area, device, or activity in modern life that you think compares to one from a previous time. Write an essay in which you compare the two things you've selected, presenting two or three ways in which they are similar. Along the way, you should acknowledge obvious differences as a way of accounting for a skeptical audience.

2. One need not look as far back as the classic novels Cohen cites to observe that courtship rituals have changed—even a single generation is enough for such differences to surface. Spend some time interviewing a parent, grandparent, or other member of an older generation. Then write an essay comparing and/ or contrasting the dating practices of that generation with those of your own. Either along the way or in your conclusion, offer some analysis of why things have changed so much and indicate whether you think this change is for the better.

Writing Assignment Combining Patterns of Development

3. With the "marriage market" as "brutally competitive" as Cohen asserts, many average people are turning to how-to books for advice on dating and romance. Write your own instructional guide, but one with a twist: a how *not*-to dating guide for today's singles. Adopt whatever tone you'd like, though a humorous one might be especially appropriate. No matter what areas you address, clearly present the *steps* that would ensure romantic failure. Along the way, provide vivid *examples* of what to avoid, indicating the possible *effects* of not following your advice.

ALEX WRIGHT

As director of User Experience and Product Research at the *New York Times*, Alex Wright worked on creating the *Times*'s iPod app as well as on other interactive projects. He is the author of *Glut: Mastering Information Through the Ages* (2007) and of articles appearing in numerous publications, including *Salon.com,* the *Christian Science Monitor,* and *Utne Reader.* The following article appeared in the "Week in Review" section of the *New York Times* on December 2, 2007.

Pre-Reading Journal Entry

Most of us would say that making and keeping friends is an essential part of life. Think about your friends and others with whom you have relationships. How did you meet them? When and how did you realize that these specific relationships were important to you? How do you keep those relationships meaningful? Use your journal to answer these questions.

Friending, Ancient or Otherwise

The growing popularity of social networking sites like Facebook, MySpace and Second Life has thrust many of us into a new world where we make "friends" with people we barely know, scrawl messages on each other's walls and project our identities using totem-like visual symbols. 1

We're making up the rules as we go. But is this world as new as it seems? 2

Academic researchers are starting to examine that question by taking an unusual tack: exploring the parallels between online social networks and tribal societies. In the collective patter of profile-surfing, messaging and "friending," they see the resurgence of ancient patterns of oral communication. 3

"Orality is the base of all human experience," says Lance Strate, a communications professor at Fordham University and devoted MySpace user. He says he is convinced that the popularity of social networks stems from their appeal to deep-seated, prehistoric patterns of human communication. "We evolved with speech," he says. "We didn't evolve with writing." 4

The growth of social networks—and the Internet as a whole—stems largely from an outpouring of expression that often feels more like "talking" than writing: blog posts, comments, homemade videos and, lately, an outpouring of epigrammatic one-liners broadcast using services like Twitter and Facebook status updates (usually proving Gertrude Stein's[1] maxim that "literature is not remarks"). 5

"If you examine the Web through the lens of orality, you can't help but see it everywhere," says Irwin Chen, a design instructor at Parsons who is developing a new course to explore the emergence of oral culture online. "Orality is participatory, interactive, communal and focused on the present. The Web is all of these things." 6

---

[1] Gertrude Stein (1874–1946), an American author who lived primarily in Paris, was known for her interest in Modernist art and writing (editors' note).

An early student of electronic orality was the Rev. Walter J. Ong, a professor   7
at St. Louis University and student of Marshall McLuhan[2] who coined the term
"secondary orality" in 1982 to describe the tendency of electronic media to echo
the cadences of earlier oral cultures. The work of Father Ong, who died in 2003,
seems especially prescient in light of the social-networking phenomenon. "Oral
communication," as he put it, "unites people in groups."

In other words, oral culture means more than just talking. There are subtler—   8
and perhaps more important—social dynamics at work.

Michael Wesch, who teaches cultural anthropology at Kansas State University,   9
spent two years living with a tribe in Papua New Guinea, studying how people
forge social relationships in a purely oral culture. Now he applies the same ethno-
graphic research methods to the rites and rituals of Facebook users.

"In tribal cultures, your identity is completely wrapped up in the question   10
of how people know you," he says. "When you look at Facebook, you can see
the same pattern at work: people projecting their identities by demonstrating their relationships to each other. You define yourself in terms of who your
friends are."

In tribal societies, people routinely give each other jewelry, weapons and ritual   11
objects to cement their social ties. On Facebook, people accomplish the same thing
by trading symbolic sock monkeys, disco balls and hula girls.

"It's reminiscent of how people exchange gifts in tribal cultures," says   12
Dr. Strate, whose MySpace page lists his 1,335 "friends" along with his academic
credentials and his predilection for "Battlestar Galactica."

As intriguing as these parallels may be, they only stretch so far. There are big   13
differences between real oral cultures and the virtual kind. In tribal societies, forg-
ing social bonds is a matter of survival; on the Internet, far less so. There is presumably no tribal antecedent for popular Facebook rituals like "poking," virtual
sheep-tossing or drunk-dialing your friends.

Then there's the question of who really counts as a "friend." In tribal socie-   14
ties, people develop bonds through direct, ongoing face-to-face contact. The Web
eliminates that need for physical proximity, enabling people to declare friendships
on the basis of otherwise flimsy connections.

"With social networks, there's a fascination with intimacy because it simulates   15
face-to-face communication," Dr. Wesch says. "But there's also this fundamental distance. That distance makes it safe for people to connect through weak ties
where they can have the appearance of a connection because it's safe."

And while tribal cultures typically engage in highly formalized rituals, social   16
networks seem to encourage a level of casualness and familiarity that would be
unthinkable in traditional oral cultures. "Secondary orality has a leveling effect,"
Dr. Strate says. "In a primary oral culture, you would probably refer to me as
'Dr. Strate,' but on MySpace, everyone calls me 'Lance.' "

As more of us shepherd our social relationships online, will this leveling   17
effect begin to shape the way we relate to each other in the offline world as well?

---

[2] The Canadian philosopher Herbert Marshall McLuhan (1911–1980), a pioneer in the field of communication
theory, coined the phrase "The medium is the message" (editors' note).

Dr. Wesch, for one, says he worries that the rise of secondary orality may have a paradoxical consequence: "It may be gobbling up what's left of our real oral culture."

The more time we spend "talking" online, the less time we spend, well, talking. And as we stretch the definition of a friend to encompass people we may never actually meet, will the strength of our real-world friendships grow diluted as we immerse ourselves in a lattice of hyperlinked "friends"?   18

Still, the sheer popularity of social networking seems to suggest that for many, these environments strike a deep, perhaps even primal chord. "They fulfill our need to be recognized as human beings, and as members of a community," Dr. Strate says. "We all want to be told: You exist."   19

Questions for Critical Reading

1. What is the selection's thesis? Locate the sentence(s) in which Wright states his main idea. If he doesn't state his thesis explicitly, express it in your own words.

2. What fundamental need, in Wright's view, do social networks seem designed to satisfy? How successful are they in meeting this need?

3. To what other type of human community are academics comparing online social networks, according to Wright? Why? According to researchers, what is the importance of oral communication in any human group?

4. Why should we be concerned about the "growing popularity" of social networking sites, according to Wright's article?

Questions About the Writer's Craft

1. **The pattern.** Does Wright use the one-side-at-a-time or the point-by-point method to compare and contrast the two communities he is discussing? What specific points does he discuss in his analysis? How does he say the groups are similar? How does he say they are different?

2. **Outside sources.** Throughout his article, Wright relies on outside sources for evidence. What is the primary type of outside evidence that he uses? Give at least two examples. How effective is this evidence in supporting his thesis?

3. **Other patterns.** Wright uses the term *friend* seven times in the article. How does he *define* this term? How important is the use of definition in the essay? Why? Wright also uses *cause-effect* (paragraphs 17 and 18). What key term signals this pattern of development? What cause(s) and effect(s) does he discuss?

4. **Conclusion.** What strategy does Wright use to conclude his article? How does the conclusion relate to his thesis?

Writing Assignments Using Comparison-Contrast as a Pattern of Development

1. Wright sees social networking sites as ways to communicate. Think of some other ways in which people communicate and the different kinds of communications for which these methods might be suited. For example, how would you suggest vacation plans to a friend? Make an appointment to see an instructor? End a romantic relationship? Choose three communication methods and write an essay comparing and contrasting how effective they are for conveying information, ideas, and feelings to other people. Your essay can be serious or light in tone.

2. Online social networks, such as Facebook, have made it possible for us to have "friendships" with people we never, or hardly ever, see. In the same way, the Internet has made it easy for us to engage in other kinds of long-distance activities—buying items from stores we never enter, taking classes with instructors we never meet, even consulting with attorneys we never see in person. Write an essay in which you compare and contrast the advantages and disadvantages of engaging in a specific online activity with those of pursuing the same activity in a more traditional way.

Writing Assignment Combining Patterns of Development

3. Wright's essay focuses on the purely social functions of networks such as Facebook and Twitter. Social network sites collect a lot of personal information about their subscribers, however, and some companies have sought ways to use that information for commercial purposes—to sell products and services. Some social network subscribers welcome the opportunity to learn about specific products matched to their tastes. Others argue that a network's commercial use of subscribers' personal data amounts to an unacceptable invasion of privacy. Do some online research on this subject. Then write an essay in which you *argue* one side of the issue, giving *examples* from personal experience or evidence from experts to support your arguments.

Additional Writing Topics: Comparison-Contrast

General Assignments

Using comparison-contrast, develop one of these topics into an essay.

1. Living at home versus living in an apartment or dorm
2. Two-career family versus one-career family
3. Children's pastimes today and yesterday
4. Neighborhood stores versus shopping malls

5. A sports team then and now

6. Watching a movie on television versus viewing it in a theater

7. Two approaches to parenting

8. Two approaches to studying

9. Marriage versus living together

10. Talking on the phone versus texting

Assignments Using Multimedia

Use the suggested media to help develop a comparison-contrast essay on one of these topics:

1. Divorce rates of those who marry in their twenties and those who marry in their thirties (charts)

2. Owning and maintaining a small versus a large vehicle (photos or weblinks)

3. Making choices about diet and/or exercise (graphs and/or cartoons)

4. Advantages and disadvantages of a career in health care (slide show)

5. Working in a fast-food restaurant versus a fine dining restaurant (charts)

Assignments with a Specific Purpose, Audience, and Point of View

1. **Academic life.** You would like to change your campus living arrangements. Perhaps you want to move from a dormitory to an off-campus apartment or from home to a dorm. Before you do, though, you'll have to convince your parents (who are paying most of your college costs) that the move will be beneficial. Write out what you would say to your parents. Contrast your current situation with your proposed one, explaining why the new arrangement would be better.

2. **Academic life.** Write a guide on "Passing Exams" for first-year college students, contrasting the right and wrong ways to prepare for and take exams. Although your purpose is basically serious, write the section on how *not* to approach exams with some humor.

3. **Civic activity.** As president of your local neighborhood association, you're concerned about the way your local government is dealing with a particular situation (for example, an increase in robberies, muggings, or graffiti). Write a letter to your mayor contrasting the way your local government handles the situation with another city or town's approach. In your conclusion, point out the advantages of adopting the other neighborhood's strategy.

4. **Civic activity.** Your old high school has invited you back to make a speech before an audience of seniors. The topic will be "how to choose the college that is right for you." Write your speech in the form of a comparison-contrast analysis. Focus on the choices

available (two-year versus four-year schools, large versus small, local versus faraway, and so on), showing the advantages and/or disadvantages of each.

5. **Workplace action.** As a store manager, you decide to write a memo to all sales personnel explaining how to keep customers happy. Compare and/or contrast the needs and shopping habits of several different consumer groups (by age, spending ability, or sex), and show how to make each group comfortable in your store.

6. **Workplace action.** You work as a volunteer for a mental-health hot line. Many people call simply because they feel "stressed out." Do some research on the subject of stress management, and prepare a brochure for these people, recommending a "Type B" approach to stressful situations. Focus the brochure on the contrast between "Type A" and "Type B" personalities: the former is nervous, hard driving, and competitive; the latter is relaxed and noncompetitive. Give specific examples of how each type tends to act in stressful situations.

Chapter 16
Cause-Effect

Learning Objectives

16.1 Understand how you can use the cause-effect pattern to develop your essays.

16.2 Consider how cause-effect can fit your purpose and audience.

16.3 Develop prewriting strategies for using cause-effect in an essay.

16.4 Develop strategies for writing a cause-effect essay.

16.5 Use strategies for revising your cause-effect essay.

16.6 Analyze how cause-effect is used effectively in a student-written selection.

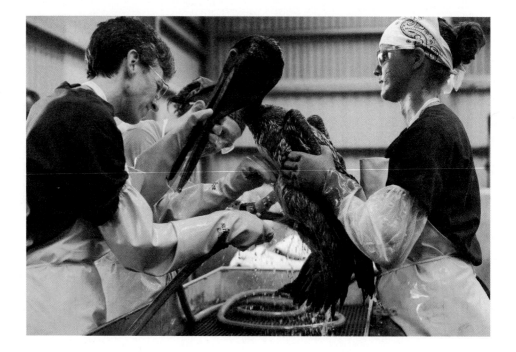

What Is Cause-Effect?

16.1 Understand how you can use the cause-effect pattern to develop your essays.

Science, technology, history, and much of our literature as well as our fascination with the past and the future all spring from our determination to know "Why" and "What if." All of us think in terms of cause and effect, sometimes consciously, sometimes unconsciously. "Why did they give me such an odd look?" we wonder. This exploration of reasons and results is also at the heart of most professions. "What might these symptoms indicate?" physicians ask. "Will these methods yield the desired result?" educators ask.

Cause-effect writing, often called **causal analysis**, is rooted in this elemental need to make connections. Because the drive to understand reasons and results is so fundamental, causal analysis is a common kind of writing. An article analyzing the unexpected outcome of an election and an editorial analyzing the impact of a proposed tax cut are both examples of cause-effect writing.

Done well, cause-effect pieces uncover the subtle and often surprising connections between events or phenomena. By rooting out causes and predicting effects, causal analysis enables us to make sense of our experiences, revealing a world that is somewhat less arbitrary and chaotic.

How Cause-Effect Fits Your Purpose and Audience

16.2 Consider how cause-effect can fit your purpose and audience.

Many college assignments and exam questions involve writing essays that analyze causes, effects, or both. Sometimes, as in the following examples, you'll be asked to write an essay developed primarily through the cause-effect pattern:

> Although divorces have leveled off in the past few years, the number of marriages ending in divorce is still greater than it was a generation ago. What do you think are the causes of this phenomenon?

> Americans never seem to tire of gossip about the rich and famous. What effect has this fascination with celebrities had on American culture?

Other assignments and exam questions may not explicitly ask you to address causes and effects, but they may use words that suggest causal analysis would be appropriate. Consider these examples, paying special attention to the italicized words:

> **Cause**
> In contrast to the socially involved youth of the 1960s, many young people today tend to remove themselves from political issues. What do you think are the *sources* of the political apathy found among 18- to 25-year-olds?

Effect

A number of experts forecast that drug abuse will be the most significant factor affecting American productivity in the coming decade. Evaluate the validity of this observation by discussing the *impact* of drugs on the workplace.

Cause and Effect

According to school officials, a predictable percentage of entering students drop out of college at some point during their first year. What *motivates* students to drop out? What *happens* to them once they leave?

In addition to serving as the primary strategy for achieving an essay's purpose, causal analysis can also be a supplemental method used to help make a point in an essay developed chiefly through another pattern of development. For example, assume that you want to write an essay *defining* the term *the homeless.* To help readers see that unfavorable circumstances can result in nearly anyone becoming homeless, you might discuss some of the unavoidable, everyday factors causing people to live on streets and in subway stations. Similarly, in a *persuasive* proposal urging your college administration to institute an honors program, you would probably spend some time analyzing the positive effects of such a program on students and faculty.

Prewriting Strategies

16.3 Develop prewriting strategies for using cause-effect in an essay.

The following checklist shows how you can apply prewriting strategies to cause-effect.

☑ Cause-Effect: A Prewriting Checklist

Choose a Topic

☐ Do your journal entries reflect an ongoing interest in the causes of and/or effects of something?

☐ Will you analyze a personal phenomenon, a change at your college, a nationwide trend, or a historical event?

☐ Does your subject intrigue, anger, puzzle you? Is it likely to interest your readers as well?

Make Sure the Topic Is Manageable

☐ Can you tackle your subject—especially if it's a social trend or historical event—in the number of pages allotted?

☐ Can you gather enough information for your analysis? Does the topic require library research? Do you have time for such research?

☐ Will you examine causes, effects, or both? Will your topic still be manageable if you discuss both causes and effects?

Identify Your Purpose, Audience, Tone, and Point of View

☐ Is the purpose of your causal analysis to inform? To persuade? To speculate about possibilities? Do you want to combine purposes?

☐ Given your purpose and audience, what tone and point of view should you adopt?

Use Individual and Group Brainstorming, Mapping, and/or Freewriting to Explore Causes and Effects

☐ **Causes**: What happened? What are the possible reasons? Which are most likely? Who was involved? Why?

☐ **Effects**: What happened? Who was involved? What were the observable results? What are some possible future consequences? Which consequences are negative? Which are positive?

Strategies for Using Cause-Effect in an Essay

16.4 Develop strategies for writing a cause-effect essay.

After prewriting, you're ready to draft your essay. The following suggestions and Figure 16.1 will be helpful whether you use causal analysis as a dominant or supportive pattern of development.

1. **Stay focused on the purpose of your analysis.**

     When writing a causal analysis, don't lose sight of your overall purpose. For example, consider an essay on the causes of widespread child abuse. If you're concerned primarily with explaining the problem of child abuse to your readers, you might take a purely *informative* approach:

     The tragic consequences of child abuse provide strong support for more aggressive handling of such cases by social workers and judges.

     Although parental stress is the immediate cause of child abuse, the more compelling reason for such behavior lies in the way parents were themselves mistreated as children.

     Or you might want to *persuade* your audience about some point or idea concerning child abuse:

     The tragic consequences of child abuse provide strong support for more aggressive handling of such cases by social workers and judges.

     You could also choose a *speculative* approach, in which your main purpose is to suggest possibilities:

     Psychologists disagree about the potential effect on youngsters of all the media attention given to child abuse. Will children exposed to this media coverage grow up assertive, self-confident, and able to protect themselves? Or will they become fearful and distrustful?

     These examples illustrate that an essay's causal analysis may have more than one purpose. For instance, although the last example points to an essay with a

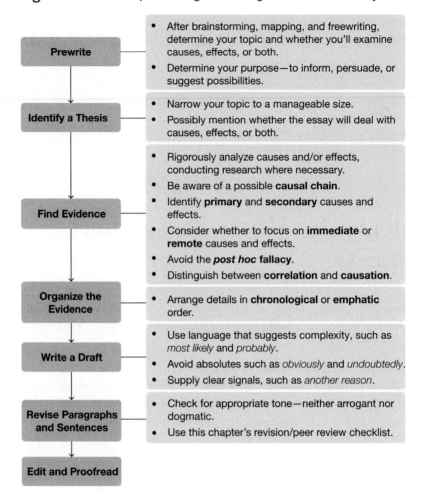

Figure 16.1 Development Diagram: Writing a Cause-Effect Essay

Prewrite
- After brainstorming, mapping, and freewriting, determine your topic and whether you'll examine causes, effects, or both.
- Determine your purpose—to inform, persuade, or suggest possibilities.

Identify a Thesis
- Narrow your topic to a manageable size.
- Possibly mention whether the essay will deal with causes, effects, or both.

Find Evidence
- Rigorously analyze causes and/or effects, conducting research where necessary.
- Be aware of a possible **causal chain**.
- Identify **primary** and **secondary** causes and effects.
- Consider whether to focus on **immediate** or **remote** causes and effects.
- Avoid the **post hoc fallacy**.
- Distinguish between **correlation** and **causation**.

Organize the Evidence
- Arrange details in **chronological** or **emphatic** order.

Write a Draft
- Use language that suggests complexity, such as *most likely* and *probably*.
- Avoid absolutes such as *obviously* and *undoubtedly*.
- Supply clear signals, such as *another reason*.

Revise Paragraphs and Sentences
- Check for appropriate tone—neither arrogant nor dogmatic.
- Use this chapter's revision/peer review checklist.

Edit and Proofread

primarily speculative purpose, the essay would probably start by informing readers of experts' conflicting views. The essay would also have a persuasive slant if it ended by urging readers to complain to the media about their sensationalized treatment of the child-abuse issue.

2. **Adapt content and tone to your purpose and readers.**

Your purpose and audience determine what supporting material and what tone will be most effective in a cause-effect essay. Assume you want to direct your essay on child abuse to general readers who know little about the subject.

To *inform* readers, you might use facts, statistics, and expert opinion to provide an objective discussion of the causes of child abuse. Your analysis might show the following: (1) adults who were themselves mistreated as children tend to abuse their own offspring, (2) marital stress contributes to the mistreatment of children, and (3) certain personality disorders increase the likelihood of child abuse. Sensitive to what your readers would and wouldn't understand, you would stay away from a technical or formal tone.

Now imagine that your purpose is to *convince* future social workers that the failure of social service agencies to act authoritatively in child-abuse cases often has tragic consequences. Hoping to encourage more responsible behavior in the prospective social workers, you would adopt a more emotional tone, perhaps citing wrenching case histories that dramatize what happens when child abuse isn't taken seriously.

3. **Think rigorously about causes and effects.**

   Cause-effect relationships are usually complex. To write a meaningful analysis, you should do some careful thinking about your subject. (The two sets of questions at the end of this chapter's prewriting checklist will help you think creatively about causes and effects.)

   If you look beyond the obvious, you'll discover that a cause may have many effects. Likewise, an effect may have multiple causes.

   Your analysis may uncover a **causal chain** in which one cause (or effect) brings about another, that, in turn, brings about another, and so on. Don't grapple with so complex a chain, however, that you become hopelessly entangled. If your subject involves multiple causes and effects, limit what you'll discuss. Identify which causes and effects are *primary* and which are *secondary.* How extensively you cover secondary factors depends on your purpose and audience.

   Similarly, decide whether to focus on *immediate,* more obvious causes and effects, or on less obvious, more *remote* ones. Or perhaps you need to focus on both. It may be more difficult to explore more remote causes and effects, but doing so can also lead to original and revealing essays. Thoughtful analyses often take less obvious considerations into account.

4. **Be careful to avoid the *post hoc* fallacy.**

   Named after the Latin phrase *post hoc, ergo propter hoc,* meaning "after this, therefore because of this," the *post hoc* fallacy occurs when you assume that simply because one event *followed* another, the first event *caused* the second. For example, if the Republicans win a majority of seats in Congress and, several months later, the economy collapses, can you conclude that the Republicans caused the collapse? A quick assumption of "Yes" fails the test of logic because the timing of events could be coincidental and not indicative of any cause-effect relationship. The collapse may have been triggered by uncontrolled inflation that began well before the congressional elections.

5. **Do not mistake *correlation* for *causation.***

   Two events *correlate* when they occur at about the same time. However, such co-occurrence doesn't guarantee a cause-effect relationship. For instance, while the number of ice cream cones eaten and the instances of heat prostration both increase during the summer months, this correlation doesn't mean that eating ice cream causes heat prostration! A third factor—in this case, summer heat—is the actual cause. When writing causal analyses, then, be cautious when using words that imply a causal link (such as *therefore* and *because*). Words that express time of occurrence (*following* and *previously*) are safer and more objective.

6. **Avoid loose generalizations.**

   A rigorous causal analysis involves more than loose generalizations about causes and effects. Creating plausible connections may require library research, interviewing, or both. Often you'll need to provide facts, statistics, details, personal observations, or other corroborative material if readers are going to accept the reasoning behind your analysis.

7. **Write a thesis that focuses the essay on causes, effects, or both.**

   The thesis in an essay developed through causal analysis often indicates whether the essay will deal mostly with causes, effects, or both. Here are three thesis statements for causal analyses dealing with the public school system. Notice that each thesis signals that essay's particular emphasis:

   Causes
   Our school system has been weakened by an overemphasis on trendy electives.

   Effects
   An ineffectual school system has led to crippling teachers' strikes and widespread disrespect for the teaching profession.

   Causes and Effects
   Bureaucratic inefficiency has created a school system unresponsive to children's emotional, physical, and intellectual needs.

   Note that the thesis statement—in addition to signaling whether the essay will discuss causes, effects, or both—may also point to the essay's plan of development. Consider the last thesis statement; it makes clear that the essay will discuss children's emotional needs first, their physical needs second, and their intellectual needs last.

8. **Choose an organizational pattern.**

   There are two basic ways to organize the points in a cause-effect essay: you may use a chronological or an emphatic sequence.

   If you select *chronological order,* you discuss causes and effects in the order in which they occur or will occur. Chronology might also be used to organize a discussion about effects. Imagine you want to write an essay about the need to guard against disrupting delicate balances in the country's wildlife. You might start the essay by discussing what happened when the starling, a non-native bird, was introduced into the American environment. Because the starling had few natural predators, the starling population soared out of control; the starlings took over food sources and habitats of native species; the bluebird, a native species, declined and is now threatened with extinction.

   Although a chronological pattern can be an effective way to organize material, a strict time sequence can present a problem if your primary cause or effect ends up buried in the middle of the sequence. In such a case, you might use *emphatic order,* saving the most important point for last.

Emphatic order is an especially effective way to sequence cause-effect points when readers hold, in your opinion, mistaken or narrow views about a subject. To encourage readers to look more closely at the issues, you present what you consider the erroneous or obvious views first, show why they are unsound or limited, and then present what you believe are the actual causes and effects. Such a sequence nudges the audience into giving further thought to the causes and effects you have discovered. Here is an informal outline for a causal analysis using this approach:

Subject: The effects of campus crime

1. Immediate problems
   a. Students feel insecure and fearful.
   b. Many nighttime campus activities have been curtailed.
2. More significant long-term problems
   a. Unfavorable publicity about campus crime will affect future student enrollment.
   b. Unfavorable publicity about campus crime will make it difficult to recruit top-notch faculty.

When using emphatic order, you might want to word the thesis in such a way that it signals which point your essay will stress. Consider the following thesis statements:

Although many immigrants arrive in this country without marketable skills, their most pressing problem is learning how to make their way in a society whose language they don't know.

The space program has led to dramatic advances in computer technology and medical science. Even more importantly, the program has helped change many people's attitudes toward the planet we live on.

These thesis statements reflect an awareness of the complex nature of cause-effect relationships. Although they do not dismiss secondary issues, the statements establish which points the writer considers most noteworthy. The second thesis, for instance, indicates that the essay will touch on the technological and medical advances made possible by the space program but will emphasize the way the program has changed people's attitudes toward Earth.

9. **Provide signals for your readers.**
   Whether you use a chronological or emphatic pattern to organize your essay, you need to provide clear *signals* to identify when you're discussing causes and when you're discussing effects. Expressions such as *another reason* and *a final outcome* help readers follow your line of thought.

10. Use language that hints at the complexity of cause-effect relationships.

Because it's difficult—if not impossible—to identify causes and effects with certainty, you should avoid such absolutes as *it must be obvious* and *there is no doubt*. Instead, try phrases such as *most likely* or *it is probable*. Such language isn't indecisive; rather, it's reasonable and reflects your understanding of the often tangled nature of causes and effects. Don't, however, go to the other extreme and be reluctant to take a stand on the issues. If you have thought carefully about causes and effects, you have a right to state your analysis with conviction.

Revision Strategies

16.5 Use strategies for revising your cause-effect essay.

Once you have a draft of the essay, you're ready to revise. The following checklist will help your peers provide feedback and aid you in revising your essay.

☑ Cause-Effect: A Revision/Peer Review Checklist

Revise Overall Meaning and Structure

☐ Is the essay's purpose informative, persuasive, speculative, or a combination of these?

☐ What is the essay's thesis? Is it stated specifically or implied? Where? Could it be made any clearer? How?

☐ Does the essay focus on causes, effects, or both? How do you know?

☐ Where has correlation been mistaken for causation? Where is the essay weakened by *post hoc* thinking?

☐ Where does the essay distinguish between primary and secondary causes and effects? How do the most critical causes and effects receive special attention?

☐ Where does the essay dwell on the obvious?

Revise Paragraph Development

☐ Are the essay's paragraphs sequenced chronologically or emphatically? Could they be sequenced more effectively? How?

☐ Where would signal devices (such as *afterward, before, then*, and *next*) make it easier to follow the progression of thought within and between paragraphs?

☐ Which paragraphs would be strengthened by vivid examples (such as statistics, facts, anecdotes, or personal observations) that support the causal analysis?

Revise Sentences and Words

☐ Where do expressions like *as a result, because*, and *therefore* mislead the reader by implying a cause-effect relationship? Would words such as *following* and *previously* eliminate the problem?

☐ Do any words or phrases convey an arrogant or dogmatic tone (*there is no question, undoubtedly, always, never*)? What other expressions (*most likely, probably*) would improve credibility?

Student Essay: From Prewriting Through Revision

16.6 Analyze how cause-effect is used effectively in a student-written selection.

The following student essay was written by Erica Zwieg in response to this assignment:

> In "Nature and the Suburbs," Jane S. Shaw discusses the factors that have led to the proliferation of wild animals in the United States and the effects of this phenomenon, incorporating a causal chain to explain how one effect led to another. Write an essay in which you use cause-effect as the primary pattern of development and incorporate a causal chain to show your readers how one effect (or cause) brought about another, which in turn brought about another, and so on.

Erica's professor, Dr. Hodges, introduced the new essay assignment during one class and asked her students to begin thinking about the assignment and what they might like to write about. At the beginning of the following class, Dr. Hodges reminded her students of the importance of choosing a topic they found engaging and considering their audience—not only the members of the class but also others who might read the final drafts of the essays when the final essays were posted to the students' electronic portfolio sites. Dr. Hodges then asked her students to take out a sheet of paper or their laptops and spend a few minutes making a list of subjects that had been on their minds lately, perhaps current events or issues they were dealing with. She explained that after the students spent a few minutes generating a list of five or six possible topics, they would discuss their lists with the members of their peer review groups.

Erica came up with the following list of possible topics:

Causes and effects of:

1. Procrastination
2. Divorce
3. Stress
4. A serious illness such as HIV/AIDS
5. Poor time management

As she talked with Sam and Ruben, the two other members of her peer review group, Erica realized that there was a personal element to each of the topics she had listed. She was a chronic procrastinator; her best friend's parents were in the middle of a divorce; she was under a lot of stress; she had recently learned about a teenage boy who had HIV/AIDS and had to deal with discrimination; and she knew she needed to work on her time-management skills. She mentioned to Sam and Ruben that four of the five topics—procrastination, the divorce of her best friend's parents, stress, and poor time management—were issues she was dealing with personally and that she had listed "a serious illness such as HIV/AIDS" as a possible topic because she had recently become familiar with Ryan White's story and couldn't get it off her mind. As she talked with her peer review group about the various topics on her list, it became clear to her that of the five topics, Ryan's story was the one in which she was most interested, but she wasn't sure the topic was suitable for an essay using cause-effect as the primary pattern of development.

Dr. Hodges asked her students to finish up their small-group conversations and return to their sheet of paper or laptop. She explained that at this point she hoped all the students had a fairly good idea of the topic they wanted to write about and that she wanted them to further explore the one or two topics that seemed most promising in a ten-minute freewrite. She reminded them not to worry about writing polished prose—that the purpose of freewriting is to generate and explore ideas and they should not worry about sentence structure and paragraph development while freewriting.

Following is Erica's freewrite:

> So I'm pretty sure I want to write about Ryan White and all he had to go through after he was diagnosed with HIV/AIDS. But where to start? And how to make this a cause-effect essay? So what all did he have to go through? What were the results when he found out he had the disease? When I first joined the Children's Miracle Network Dance Marathon committee, Patty, our committee chair, told us about Ryan. Oh, I can be so stupid sometimes. Of course, one of the main things that eventually happened as a result of Ryan having HIV/AIDS was the CMN Dance Marathon. There never would have been a CMN Dance Marathon without Ryan. That's what I can write about—not just Ryan's story but what happened as a result of Ryan having the disease and all he had to go through. I could tell his story, about the horrible way people treated him, about how Michael Jackson and Elton John heard about him on the news and started really spreading the word about what he was going through, about the TV talk shows Ryan went on, about how he was about to start college at—I think it was Indiana University—when he died. I need to check my facts, and that's fine. Dr. Hodges always loves it when we include outside sources in our essays, and this information would be easy for me to find. And this is an essay that others might actually enjoy reading. They might even start participating in their schools' CMN Dance Marathons. I'm actually getting excited about writing an essay. This is pretty cool.

Now read Erica's essay, "Party with a Purpose," noting how the ideas she generated in her prewriting helped her as she drafted her essay. As you read the essay, also consider how well it applies the principles of causal analysis discussed in this chapter. (The commentary that follows the essay will help you look at Erica's essay more closely and will give you some sense of how she went about revising her first draft.)

Party with a Purpose

by Erica Zwieg

Introduction and background information

In 1984, Ryan White, a 13-year-old boy living in Kokomo, Indiana, was diagnosed with HIV/AIDS after receiving a contaminated blood transfusion. His doctors diagnosed him with six months to live. At the time, there was much misinformation surrounding the HIV/AIDS virus. Many people were afraid that they could contract the virus simply by being around others with the disease. This misconception caused Ryan to experience intolerance and prejudice within his community and school after he received his diagnosis.

First link in causal chain ("banned")

He was banned from attending his local middle school—a decision supported and rallied for by parents within the misinformed community who feared that Ryan might infect their children. Though Ryan's doctors confirmed that he was not contagious, he continued to face vicious protests that included gunfire into his home to instill fear within his family. Ryan was fighting for his life within the hospital and on the streets of his own neighborhood ("Retro Indy").

Topic sentence

News about the discrimination Ryan was experiencing quickly spread throughout the United States and beyond. Ryan's physically draining battle with his disease, coupled with prejudice faced within his hometown, sparked the media's attention and made him an overnight sensation.

Second link in causal chain ("media's attention")

Celebrities like Michael Jackson and Elton John became advocates in Ryan's defense, seeking to educate the nation on HIV/AIDS awareness.

Topic sentence

Ryan's face and story were soon all over the news, and his responses to interview questions showed the nation what a courageous and giving person he was. When asked how he was coping with all that he was going through, Ryan responded, "I figure...that since this was the way the hand was dealt...then I've got to live with it this way and I'm going to try to help anybody I can" (CMN Hospitals). In another interview, Ryan was asked to describe his experience with prejudice and to comment on why he thought he was being treated unfairly.

Paragraph adding support to second link in causal chain

He stated, "In my case, it was fear [that caused people to treat me unfairly], and I suppose because I had something in my body that nobody else had, or very few people had. It was because [I was] different" (CMN Hospitals). For five years Ryan did his best to help others understand more about the HIV/AIDS virus and to speak out against intolerance, living much longer that his doctors had thought possible.

Topic sentences (two sentences)

Though friends and family rallied behind his courageous struggle, Ryan lost his battle against HIV/AIDS on April 8, 1990, one year before he planned to enter Indiana University as a freshman. After losing Ryan to the disease, his friends and family were determined to honor his memory and expand the nationwide movement of change he had created.

Paragraph on third link in causal chain

A year after his death, Ryan's friends who were students at the school he had planned to attend founded the Indiana University Dance Marathon (IUDM). The event began as a way for the student body and the community to celebrate Ryan's life, raise awareness about his disease, and generate funds to help children like Ryan who

1

2

3

4

were facing life-threatening diagnoses. At that first marathon in 1991, students and the community stood together for thirty-six hours, dancing and raising money for children's health care. The event served as a way to celebrate the wonderful person Ryan had been and also gave the student body and the community the opportunity to party with a purpose. Since that first marathon, IUDM has raised over $16 million for the Ryan White Center for Infectious Disease at the Riley Hospital for Children in Indianapolis, Indiana (CMN Hospitals).

Topic sentence —————• Little did Ryan's friends at Indiana University realize that they 5 had created the foundation for a Dance Marathon movement that would spread throughout the nation and into the hearts of students in over two hundred and fifty universities and high schools. Today these students stand united under one motto: "For the Kids." Students in participating schools spend countless hours planning events similar to the first one at Indiana University. The funds raised are allotted to the local Children's Miracle Network Hospitals within their surrounding areas, in addition to pediatric programs of their choice. These funds are used to help fund items and programs such as advanced medical equipment, pediatric ICUs (intensive care units), cancer and infectious disease research, and diversionary programs for patients and families undergoing long hospital stays ("Dance Marathon"). In their description of these marathons and the student volunteers who organize them, the Children's Miracle Network states:

Paragraph on fourth link in causal chain

> These students spend a year learning invaluable leadership and life skills while raising funds and interacting with children's hospital patients and families. The year culminates with a 12–40 hour long event where the students stay on their feet through dancing, games and entertainment in celebration of the total amount raised that year. ("Dance Marathon")

The Children's Miracle Network goes on to report that the Dance Marathon's movement has raised over $62 million for children across the nation ("Dance Marathon").

Conclusion and two-sentence thesis —————• Ryan White's struggle with HIV/AIDS sparked a desire within his 6 friends to stand in his honor and fight for children facing life-threatening illnesses. His memory serves as the foundation for Dance Marathons across the nation that raise money to provide support, awareness, and medical treatment regardless of race, religion, gender, or what type of disease these children are fighting.

Start of two-sentence thesis

Works Cited

CMN Hospitals. "The Story of Dance Marathon." *YouTube*, 13 Aug. 2013, www.youtube.com/watch?v=klHuxf4i6Ms.

"Dance Marathon." *Children's Miracle Network*, 2014, dancemarathon.childrensmiraclenetworkhospitals.org.

"Retro Indy: Ryan White (1971–1990)." *IndyStar*, 8 Apr. 2010, www.indystar.com/story/news/history/retroindy/2014/04/08/ryan-white/7458579.

Commentary

TITLE After completing a first draft of her essay, Erica brought it to class to share with Sam and Ruben, the two other students in her peer review group. She gave each of them a copy of her essay. Then before reading it aloud to them as her teacher had instructed, Erica mentioned that she had still not thought of a title for her composition. She told Sam and Ruben that she often struggled to come up with titles that she thought would interest her readers and make them want to read what she had written. Both of her classmates told her that they knew exactly what she was talking about—they had the same problem. As Erica was reading her essay aloud, a phrase in the fourth paragraph caught her attention: "party with a purpose." After reading those words aloud, she paused, looked at Sam and Ruben, and said, "I think I just found my title." They both thought she had a great idea. Had she not read the essay aloud and heard the spoken phrase, she might have settled, as she often had in the past, for a less effective title.

PURPOSE AND THESIS Erica's purpose was to write an informational causal analysis that informed her readers of Ryan White's experiences with intolerance and prejudice and how he and others reacted to those injustices. She also hoped that her essay would help her readers more clearly understand the importance of helping those in need. Instead of stating her thesis near the beginning of her essay, as she often did, Erica decided to begin by telling Ryan's story and then describe how his experiences affected others. She saved her thesis for the concluding paragraph, in which she ends her essay by making certain her readers understand the main ideas she is trying to communicate: "Ryan White's struggle with HIV/AIDS sparked a desire within his friends to stand in his honor and fight for children facing life-threatening illnesses. His memory serves as the foundation for Dance Marathons across the nation that raise money to provide support, awareness, and medical treatment regardless of race, religion, gender, or what type of disease these children are fighting."

COMBINING PATTERNS OF DEVELOPMENT Erica draws on various patterns of development to develop her causal analysis. She uses *narration* as she tells Ryan's story in chronological order, beginning with his diagnosis and moving forward. For example, she narrates the story of how he was treated by parents in his hometown who were afraid he would spread HIV/AIDS to their children if he attended school with them and of how gunshots were fired into his home in an effort to "instill fear within his family." Erica also uses *exemplification* when she includes examples of celebrities such as Michael Jackson and Elton John who stood up for Ryan and tried "to educate the nation on HIV/AIDS awareness" and when she provides examples of the ways in which funds raised in Dance Marathons benefit children with life-threatening conditions. In addition, she uses *description* in paragraph 5, where she provides additional information about the marathons across the country, the work of the student volunteers who organize them, and the funds they have raised for children with life-threatening conditions.

CAUSAL CHAINS   Erica's essay reveals a causal chain in which one cause (or effect) brings about another, which in turn brings about another, and so on. In the first several sentences of paragraph 1, she clearly states the first cause (Ryan's diagnosis and misconceptions surrounding HIV/AIDS), and she goes on in that same paragraph to reveal the first effect: "This caused Ryan to experience intolerance within his community and school after receiving his diagnosis." Paragraphs 2 and 3 focus on the next link in the causal chain: the media's coverage of Ryan's story and how that led to support from individuals, including Michael Jackson and Elton John, and opportunities for Ryan to tell his story across the country. The attention from the media made students at Indiana University aware of what had happened to Ryan and more likely to participate in the dance marathon held "to celebrate Ryan's life, raise awareness about his disease, and generate funds to help children like Ryan who were facing life-threatening diagnoses" (paragraph 4). This first dance marathon (the third link) led directly to the final link in the causal chain as described in paragraph 5: "a Dance Marathon movement that would spread throughout the nation and into the hearts of students in over two hundred and fifty universities and high schools."

A PROBLEM WITH THE ESSAY'S CLOSE   When reading the essay, you might have noticed that Erica's conclusion is a bit weak. Although providing a clear statement of her thesis at the end of her essay is a good idea, it's not enough. We learn nothing from reading the final paragraph that we did not already know. Ending an otherwise vigorous essay with such a slight conclusion undercuts the effectiveness of the entire composition. Erica focused so much on developing the body of her essay that she ran out of the time needed to write a more forceful conclusion. Careful budgeting of her time would have allowed her to prepare a stronger concluding paragraph.

REVISING THE FIRST DRAFT   As you read the final draft of Erica's essay, you might have noted that its chronological order makes it easy to follow. However, that order did not come as easily as you might assume. You might also have imagined that she easily located effective quotes to use in her essay. That assumption, too, would be incorrect. When Erica shared her early draft with Sam and Ruben, these were issues that needed to be resolved, and the students pointed them out to Erica. Comparing Erica's original version of her second paragraph with paragraphs 2 and 3 in the final version of the essay will show you how she went about revising.

> **Original Version of the Second Paragraph**
> During a talk-show interview, Ryan was asked to describe his experience with prejudice and describe where he believes discrimination stems from. He stated, "In my case, it was fear, and I suppose because I had something in my body that nobody else had, or very few people had. It was because [I was] different. I mean, I'm surprised we really have dogs now days because they're different. It's amazing how you can accept a dog into your house. But you can't accept someone because of their race, their color, their religion, or what they have in them," said Ryan (CMN Hospitals). He continued to speak out against intolerance for an astonishing five years, surpassing his six-month diagnosis. Celebrities like Michael Jackson and Elton John became advocates in Ryan's defense, seeking to

educate the nation on HIV/AIDS awareness. Ryan's physically draining battle with his disease, coupled with prejudice faced within his hometown, sparked the media's attention and made him an overnight sensation.

After sharing her essay with Sam and Ruben, Erica realized that she could make this part of her composition much stronger. She saw that she had jumped from her opening paragraph in which she discussed Ryan's diagnosis, misconceptions surrounding HIV/AIDS, and the ways in which his community treated him to the next paragraph in which Ryan is suddenly making an appearance on a talk show. That was a huge leap to make—one that was likely to confuse her readers. Sam and Ruben also asked her about the quote in which Ryan comments on how he is "surprised we really have dogs now days because they're different" and goes on to compare the acceptance of dogs with the non-acceptance of people who are different "because of their race, their color, their religion, or what they have in them." Although this is certainly an interesting comment in its own way, one made by a young teenage boy who suddenly finds himself not only with a short time left to live but also appearing on national television, Sam and Ruben suggested that it might not be the most effective comment for her essay.

As she revised, Erica decided that she needed to begin her second paragraph with a transition statement that would help guide her readers smoothly from her introductory paragraph to the next section of her essay on the effects of media coverage. She accomplished this by beginning her revised second paragraph with the sentence "News about the discrimination Ryan was experiencing quickly spread throughout the United States and beyond." She also realized that before relating quotes Ryan made in interviews, it would make good sense to describe how celebrities became Ryan's advocates and helped spread his story and to then move on to interview quotes.

Once Erica made those changes, she decided that she needed a separate paragraph for the interview quotes she wanted to include; she wanted those quotes to allow her readers to get to know Ryan better through comments he had made that "showed the nation what a courageous and giving person he was." She did some more research and located an interview quote that does precisely that: " 'I figure...that since this was the way the hand was dealt...then I've got to live with it this way and I'm going to try to help anybody I can' (CMN Hospitals)." She decided to keep the quote in which he commented on his experience with discrimination and its causes but to follow Sam and Ruben's advice to delete the part in which Ryan compared the acceptance of dogs with the non-acceptance of various groups of individuals—though she wasn't entirely sure that was a smart decision. As is often the case, deciding which elements of peer review to accept and which to reject can be difficult. As Erica handed her final draft to her teacher, she wondered if her essay would have been stronger if she had included those quotes.

Erica worked hard at revising other sections of her essay as well. With the exception of the weak spots already discussed, she made the changes needed to craft a well-written essay that shows the positive effects of helping others.

Activities: Cause-Effect

Prewriting Activities

1. Imagine you're writing two essays: One proposes the need for high school courses in personal finance (how to budget money, balance a checkbook, and the like); the other explains how to show appreciation. Jot down ways you might use cause-effect in each essay.

2. Use mapping, collaborative brainstorming, or another prewriting technique to generate possible causes or effects for one of the following topics. Then organize your raw material into a brief outline, with related causes and effects grouped in the same section.

   a. Pressure on students to do well

   b. Being physically fit

   c. Spiraling costs of a college education

3. For the topic you selected in Prewriting Activity 2, note the two potential audiences indicated below in parentheses. For each audience, devise a thesis and decide whether your essay's purpose would be informative, persuasive, speculative, or some combination of these. Then, with your thesis statements and purposes in mind, review the outline you prepared for the Prewriting Activity 2. How would you change it to fit each audience? What points should be added? What points would be primary causes and effects for one audience but secondary for the other? Which organizational pattern—chronological, spatial, or emphatic—would be most effective for each audience?

   a. Pressure on students to do well (*college students, parents of elementary school children*)

   b. Being physically fit (*those who show a reasonable degree of concern, those who are obsessed with being fit*)

   c. Spiraling costs of a college education (*college officials, high school students planning to attend college*)

Revising Activities

4. Explain how the following statements demonstrate *post hoc* thinking and confuse correlation and cause-effect.

   a. Our city now has many immigrants from Latin American countries. The crime rate in our city has increased. Latin American immigrants are the cause of the crime wave.

   b. The divorce rate has skyrocketed. More women are working outside the home than ever before. Working outside the home destroys marriages.

c. A high percentage of people in Dixville have developed cancer. The landfill, used by XYZ Industries, has been located in Dixville for twenty years. The XYZ landfill has caused cancer in Dixville residents.

5. The following paragraph is from the first draft of an essay arguing that technological advances can diminish the quality of life. How solid is the paragraph's causal analysis? Which causes or effects should be eliminated? Where is the analysis simplistic? Where does the writer make absolute claims even though cause-effect relationships are no more than a possibility? Keeping these questions in mind, revise the paragraph.

> How did the banking industry respond to inflation? It simply introduced a new technology—the automated teller machine (ATM). By making money more available to the average person, the ATM gives people the cash to buy inflated goods—whether or not they can afford them. Not surprisingly, automated teller machines have had a number of negative consequences for the average individual. Since people know they can get cash at any time, they use their lunch hours for something other than going to the bank. How do they spend this newfound time? They go shopping, and machine-vended money means more impulse buying, even more than with a credit card. Also, because people don't need their checkbooks to withdraw money, they can't keep track of their accounts and therefore develop a casual attitude toward financial matters. It's no wonder children don't appreciate the value of money. Another problem is that people who would never dream of robbing a bank try to trick the machine into dispensing money "for free." There's no doubt that this kind of fraud contributes to the immoral climate in the country.

Professional Selections: Cause-Effect

JANE S. SHAW

Jane S. Shaw, born in 1944, received a B.A. in English from Wellesley College and was an associate economics editor at *Business Week*. Currently president of the Pope Center for Higher Education Policy, Shaw was formerly a senior fellow at the Property and Environment Research Center, a nonprofit organization that advocates improving the environment by means of property rights and market forces rather than by government regulation. Shaw's articles have appeared in publications such as the *Wall Street Journal*, the *Washington Times*, *USA Today*, *Liberty*, *Public Choice*, and the *Cato Journal*. She is coeditor with Ronald D. Utt of *A Guide to Smart Growth: Shattering Myths and Providing Solutions* (2000). The following selection, adapted from *A Guide to Smart Growth*, was published separately by The Heritage Foundation in 2004. The footnotes are all the author's.

Pre-Reading Journal Entry

Encounters with wildlife and other animals can inspire a range of responses. Think of several encounters you have had with animals—for example, spying a deer in your backyard, purchasing a canary as a pet, or catching a fish. How did you feel about these encounters? In your journal make some notes about your experiences.

Figure 16.2 shows how this cause-effect essay is organized.

Nature in the Suburbs

A decade ago, who would have thought that New Jersey would host a black bear hunt—the first in 33 years? Or that Virginia, whose population of bald eagles was once down to 32 breeding pairs, would have 329 known active bald eagle nests? Who would have expected *Metropolitan Home* magazine to be advising its readers about ornamental grasses to keep away white-tailed deer, now found in the millions around the country? 1

Such incidents illustrate a transformed America. This nation, often condemned for being crowded, paved over, and studded with nature-strangling shopping malls, is proving to be a haven for wild animals. 2

It is difficult to ignore this upsurge of wildlife, because stories about bears raiding trashcans and mountain lions sighted in subdivisions frequently turn up in the press or on television. Featured in these stories are animals as large as moose, as well as once-threatened birds such as eagles and falcons and smaller animals like wolverines and coyotes. 3

One interpretation of these events is that people are moving closer to wilderness and invading the territory of wild animals. But this is only a small part of the story. As this essay will show, wild animals increasingly find suburban life in the United States to be attractive. 4

The stories, while fascinating, are not all upbeat. Americans are grappling with new problems—the growing hazard of automobile collisions with deer, debates over the role of hunting, the disappearance of fragile wild plants gobbled up by hungry ruminants, and even occasional human deaths caused by these animals. 5

At the same time, the proliferation of wildlife should assure Americans that the claim that urban sprawl is wiping out wildlife is simply poppycock. Human settlement in the early 21st century may be sprawling and suburban—about half the people in this country live in suburbs—but it is more compatible with wildlife than most people think. There may be reasons to decry urban sprawl or the suburbanization of America, but the loss of wildlife is not one of them. 6

Why So Many Wild Animals?

Two phenomena are fueling this increase in wild animals. One is natural reforestation, especially in the eastern United States. This is largely a result of the steady decline in farming, including cotton farming, a decline that allows forests to retake territory they lost centuries ago. The other is suburbanization, the expansion of low-density development outside cities, which provides a variety of landscapes and vegetation that attract animals. Both trends undermine the claim that wild open spaces are being strangled and that habitat for wild animals is shrinking. 7

The trend toward regrowth of forest has been well-documented. The percent of forested land in New Hampshire increased from 50 percent in the 1880s to 86 percent 100 years later. Forested land in Connecticut, Massachusetts, and Rhode Island increased from 35 percent to 59 percent over that same period. "The same 8 story has been repeated in other places in the East, the South, and the Lake States," writes forestry expert Roger Sedjo.[1]

Environmentalist Bill McKibben exulted in this "unintentional and mostly unnoticed renewal of the rural and mountainous East" in a 1995 article in the *Atlantic Monthly*. Calling the change "the great environmental story of the United States, and in some ways of the whole world," he added, "Here, where 'suburb' and 'megalopolis' were added to the world's vocabulary, an explosion of green is under way."[2] Along with the reforestation come the animals; McKibben cites a moose "ten miles from Boston," as well as an eastern United States full of black bears, deer, alligators, and perhaps even mountain lions.

This re-greening of the eastern United States explains why some large wild animals are thriving, but much of the wildlife Americans are seeing today is a direct result of the suburbs. Clearly, suburban habitat is not sterile.

Habitat for Wildlife

When people move onto what once was rural land, they modify the landscape. Yes, they build more streets, more parking lots, and more buildings. Wetlands may be drained, hayfields may disappear, trees may be cut down, and pets may proliferate. At the same time, however, the new residents will create habitat for wildlife. They will create ponds, establish gardens, plant trees, and set up bird nesting-boxes. Ornamental nurseries and truck farms may replace cropland, and parks may replace hedgerows.

This new ecology is different, but it is often friendly to animals, especially those that University of Florida biologist Larry Harris calls "meso-mammals," or mammals of medium size.[3] They do not need broad territory for roaming to find food, as moose and grizzly bears do. They can find places in the suburbs to feed, nest, and thrive, especially where gardens flourish.

One example of the positive impact of growth is the rebound of the endangered Key deer, a small white-tailed deer found only in Florida and named for the Florida Keys. According to *Audubon* magazine, the Key deer is experiencing a "remarkable recovery."[4] The news report continues: "Paradoxically, part of the reason for the deer's comeback may lie in the increasing development of the area." Paraphrasing the remarks of a university researcher, the reporter says that human development "tends to open up overgrown forested areas and provide vegetation at deer level—the same factors fueling deer population booms in suburbs all over the country."

Indeed, white-tailed deer of normal size are the most prominent species proliferating in the suburbs. In *The New York Times*, reporter Andrew C. Revkin has commented that "suburbanization created a browser's paradise: a vast patchwork of well-watered, fertilizer-fattened plantings to feed on and vest-pocket forests to hide in, with hunters banished to more distant woods."[5]

[1] Roger A. Sedjo, "Forest Resources," in Kenneth D. Frederick and Roger A. Sedjo, eds., *America's Renewable Resources: Historical Trends and Current Challenges* (Washington, D.C.: Resources for the Future, 1991), p. 109.

[2] Bill McKibben, "An Explosion of Green," *Atlantic Monthly*, April 1995, p. 64.

[3] Larry D. Harris, in e-mail communication with the author, January 16, 2000.

[4] Nancy Klingener, "Doe, Re, Key Deer," *Audubon*, January-February 2000, p. 17.

[5] Andrew C. Revkin, "Out of Control: Deer Send Ecosystem into Chaos," *The New York Times*, November 12, 2002.

The increase in the number of deer in the United States is so great that many 15
people, especially wildlife professionals, are trying to figure out what to do about
them. In 1997, the Wildlife Society, a professional association of wildlife biologists, devoted a special 600-page issue of its *Bulletin* to "deer overabundance." The
lead article noted, "We hear more each year about the high costs of crop and tree-
seedling damage, deer-vehicle collisions, and nuisance deer in suburban locales."[6]
Insurance companies are worried about the increase in damage from automobile
collisions with deer and similar-sized animals. And there are fears that the increase
in deer in populated areas means that the deer tick could be causing the increased
number of reported cases of Lyme disease.

Yes, the proliferation of deer poses problems, as do geese, whose flocks can foul 16
ponds and lawns and are notorious nuisances on golf courses, and beaver, which
can cut down groves of trees. Yet the proliferation of deer is also a wildlife success
story. At least that is the view of Robert J. Warren, editor of the *Bulletin*, who calls
the resurgence of deer "one of the premier examples of successful wildlife management."[7] Today's deer population in the United States may be as high as 25 million,
says Richard Nelson, writing in *Sports Afield*.[8]

People have mixed feelings about deer. In the *Wildlife Society Bulletin*, Dale R. 17
McCullough and his colleagues reported on a survey of households in El Cerrito
and Kensington, two communities near Berkeley, California. Twenty-eight percent
of those who responded reported severe damage to vegetation by the deer, and
25 percent reported moderate damage. Forty-two percent liked having the deer
around, while 35 percent disliked them and 24 percent were indifferent. The authors summarized the findings by saying: "As expected, some residents loved deer,
whereas others considered them 'hoofed rats.'"[9]

James Dunn, a geologist who has studied wildlife in New York State, believes 18
that suburban habitat fosters deer more than forests do. Dunn cites statistics on
the harvest of buck deer reported by the New York State government. Since 1970
the deer population has multiplied 7.1 times in suburban areas (an increase of 610
percent), but only 3.4 times (an increase of 240 percent) in the state overall.[10]

Dunn explains that the forests have been allowed to regrow without logging 19
or burning, so they lack the "edge" that allows sunlight in and encourages vegetation suitable for deer. In his view, that explains why counties with big cities (and
therefore with suburbs) have seen a greater increase in deer populations than have
the isolated, forested rural counties. Supporting this point, Andrew Revkin quotes
a wildlife biologist at the National Zoo in Washington, D.C. "Deer are an edge species," he says, "and the world is one big edge now."[11]

---

[6] Donald M. Waller and William S. Alverson, "The White-Tailed Deer: A Keystone Herbivore," *Wildlife Society Bulletin*, Vol. 25, No. 2 (Summer 1997), p. 217.

[7] Robert J. Warren, "The Challenge of Deer Overabundance in the 21st Century," *Wildlife Society Bulletin*, Vol. 25, No.
2 (Summer 1997), p. 213.

[8] Richard Nelson, "Deer Nation," *Sports Afield*, September 1998, p. 40.

[9] Dale R. McCullough, Kathleen W. Jennings, Natalie B. Gates, Bruce G. Elliott, and Joseph E. DiDonato, "Overabundant
Deer Populations in California," *Wildlife Society Bulletin*, Vol. 25, No. 2 (1997), p. 481.

[10] James R. Dunn, "Wildlife in the Suburbs," Political Economy Research Center, PERC Reports, September 1999, pp. 3–5.
See also James R. Dunn and John E. Kinney, *Conservative Environmentalism: Reassessing the Means, Redefining the Ends* (West-
port, Conn.: Quorum Books, 1996).

[11] Revkin, "Out of Control."

Deer are not the only wild animals that turn up on lawns and doorsteps, how- 20
ever. James Dunn lists species in the Albany, New York, suburbs in addition to deer:
birds such as robins, woodpeckers, chickadees, grouse, finches, hawks, crows, and
nuthatches, as well as squirrels, chipmunks, opossums, raccoons, foxes, and rabbits.[12] Deer attract coyotes too. According to a 1999 article in *Audubon*, biologists
estimate that the coyote population (observed in all states except Hawaii) is about
double what it was in 1850.[13]

Joel Garreau, author of *Edge City*, includes black bears, red-tailed hawks, peregrine 21
falcons, and beaver on his list of animals that find suburban niches. Garreau still considers these distant "edge city" towns a "far less diverse ecology than what was there
before." However, he writes, "if you measure it by the standard of city, it is a far more
diverse ecology than anything humans have built in centuries, if not millennia."[14]

For one reason or another, some environmental activists tend to dismiss the 22
resurgence of deer and other wildlife. In an article criticizing suburban sprawl,
Carl Pope, executive director of the Sierra Club, says that the suburbs are "very
good for the most adaptable and common creatures—raccoons, deer, sparrows,
starlings, and sea gulls" but "devastating for wildlife that is more dependent upon
privacy, seclusion, and protection from such predators as dogs and cats."[15]

Yet the suburbs attract animals larger than meso-mammals, and the suburban 23
habitat may be richer than what they replace. In many regions, suburban growth
comes at the expense of agricultural land that was cultivated for decades, even
centuries. Cropland doesn't necessarily provide abundant habitat. Environmental essayist Donald Worster, for example, has little favorable to say about land
cultivated for crops or used for livestock grazing. In Worster's view, there was a
time when agriculture was diversified, with small patches of different crops and a
variety of animals affecting the landscape. Not now. "[T]he trend over the past two
hundred years or so," he writes, "has been toward the establishment of monocultures on every continent."[16] In contrast, suburbs are not monocultures.

Even large animals can be found at the edges of metropolitan areas. Early in 24
2004, a mountain lion attacked a woman riding a bicycle in the Whiting Ranch
Wilderness Park in the foothills above populous Orange County, and the same
animal may have killed a man who was found dead nearby. According to the *Los
Angeles Times*, if the man's death is confirmed as caused by the mountain lion, it
would be the first death by a mountain lion in Orange County. The *Times* added,
however, that "[m]ountain lions are no strangers in Orange County's canyons and
wilderness parks."[17] Indeed, in 1994, mountain lions killed two women in state
parks near San Diego and Sacramento. Deer may be attracting the cats, suggests
Paul Beier, a professor at the University of California at Berkeley.[18]...

---

[12] Dunn, "Wildlife in the Suburbs," p. 3.

[13] Mike Finkel, "The Ultimate Survivor," *Audubon*, May-June 1999, p. 58.

[14] Joel Garreau, *Edge City: Life on the New Frontier* (New York: Random House, 1991), p. 57.

[15] Carl Pope, "Americans Are Saying No to Sprawl," Political Economy Research Center, PERC Reports, February
1999, p. 6.

[16] Donald Worster, *The Wealth of Nature: Environmental History and the Ecological Imagination.* (New York: Oxford
University Press, 1993), p. 59.

[17] Kimi Yoshino, David Haldane, and Daniel Yi, "Lion Attacks O.C. Biker; Man Found Dead Nearby," *Los Angeles
Times*, January 9, 2004.

[18] McCullough et al., "Overabundant Deer Populations in California," p. 479.

Figure 16.2 Essay Structure Diagram: "Nature in the Suburbs" by Jane S. Shaw

Introductory paragraphs **Examples** **Counterargument** **Thesis** (paragraphs 1–6)	Examples of proliferation of wild animals in the United States and the problems they cause. Counterargument of causes for increase in the number of wild animals: "People are moving closer to wilderness and invading the territory of wild animals." **Thesis:** "There may be reasons to decry urban sprawl or the suburbanization of America, but the loss of wildlife is not one of them."
Two prime causes (with examples in parentheses) (7–10)	**Cause 1:** Natural reforestation (Examples: increases in forested land in New Hampshire, Connecticut, Massachusetts, Rhode Island, and other places in the East, the South, and the Lake States.) **Cause 2:** Suburbanization (Examples: suburbanization from the Florida Keys to New York to California.)
Causal chain for suburbanization cause (with examples in parentheses) (11–24)	**First causal link:** Some changes make land less habitable for wild animals (constructing streets, parking lots, buildings; clearing land; bringing in pets). However, other changes make land more habitable for and attractive to wild animals (creating ponds and parks, planting gardens and trees). **Second causal link:** Increase in wild animals causes problems (deer damage crops and tree seedlings and cause vehicle collisions, possibly increase Lyme disease; geese contaminate ponds and lawns; beaver cut down trees). **Third causal link:** Even large mammals (coyotes and mountain lions) are attracted to the rich, diverse environment of the suburbs and may endanger people's lives.
Concluding paragraphs (25–26)	Closing restates the thesis and looks to the future of environment restoration: "As wildlife proliferates, Americans will learn to live more harmoniously with birds and meso-mammals."

Sharing Our Turf

The fact that wildlife finds a home in suburban settings does not mean that all 25
wildlife will do so. The greening of the suburbs is no substitute for big stretches of
land—both public and private—that allow large mammals such as grizzly bears,
elk, antelope, and caribou to roam. The point of this essay is that the suburbs offer
an environment that is appealing to many wild animal species.

If the United States continues to prosper, the 21st century is likely to be an 26
environmental century. Affluent people will seek to maintain or, in some cases,
restore an environment that is attractive to wildlife, and more parks will likely
be nestled within suburban developments, along with gardens, arboreta, and en-
vironmentally compatible golf courses. As wildlife proliferates, Americans will
learn to live harmoniously with more birds and meso-mammals. New organizations and entrepreneurs will help integrate nature into the human landscape.
There is no reason to be pessimistic about the ability of wildlife to survive and
thrive in the suburbs.

Questions for Critical Reading

1. What is the selection's thesis? Locate the sentence(s) in which Shaw states her main
   idea. If she doesn't state her thesis explicitly, express it in your own words.

2. What evidence does Shaw give to support her assertion, at the beginning of the
   article and then later on, about an "upsurge in wildlife"?

3. Shaw gives two causes for the increase in wildlife—reforestation and suburbanization. How have these two trends brought about an increase in wildlife? Why
   does she believe that suburbanization may promote more wildlife than either thick
   forest growth or cropland?

4. An increase in wildlife, Shaw says, has its negative side. Give at least two examples
   she uses to prove this point. Why do you think Shaw includes these?

Questions About the Writer's Craft

1. **The pattern.** To what extent does the author focus on causes, on effects, or on both
   causes and effects? Identify at least one causal chain.

2. **Purpose.** Is Shaw's purpose to inform, entertain, or persuade? How effective is
   the author's use of research in achieving this purpose? Identify at least three kinds
   of sources the author uses, and give an example of each. How credible are the
   sources?

3. **Other patterns.** At different points, Shaw states objections to her main ideas and
   then refutes those objections. Find at least two instances of this *argument* technique.

4. **Opening with questions.** The selection opens with a series of questions. What do
   you think is the author's purpose in posing these questions? How effective do you
   think the questions are?

Writing Assignments Using Cause-Effect as a Pattern of Development

1. Just as cropland can become suburbs, other environments can also change. Think of a place you know that has been changed by human activity. Maybe a polluted stream has been cleaned up and filled with fish, or an abandoned lot has become a vibrant neighborhood park. In an essay, show either what *caused* the change or what *effects* the change has had. Use your personal experiences as examples to support your ideas.

2. Like environmental changes made by people, human inventions can also have unintended consequences. Write an essay showing how an innovation may have had unintended *effects*. For example, the automobile makes travel easy, but it may also lead to a sedentary lifestyle. If possible, include a relevant causal chain. Be sure to add specific details to support your ideas.

Writing Assignment Combining Patterns of Development

3. Wild animals can be dangerous. Yet many people acquire animals such as tigers, cobras, and chimpanzees as pets. In an essay, *define* what "pet" means to you. Then *compare* the pros and cons of wild animals and domestic animals as pets. Include examples to *illustrate* your ideas.

LEILA AHMED

Leila Ahmed is a member of the faculty at Harvard Divinity School, where she became the first women's studies professor. Her research and publications focus primarily on issues relating to Islam and Islamic feminism. She is the author of *Women and Gender in Islam: The Historical Roots of a Modern Debate* (1993), *A Border Passage: From Cairo to America—A Woman's Journey* (2000), and *A Quiet Revolution: The Veil's Resurgence, from the Middle East to America* (2011) as well as many articles, including "Reinventing the Veil," which was first published in *Financial Times* on May 20, 2011.

Pre-Reading Journal

In the essay that follows, Ahmed explores how her ideas about wearing a *hijab*—a veil that covers the head and chest—have changed over the years. Think of something about which your ideas have changed as you've grown older and thought more about the subject. Take a few minutes to write in your journal and explore your ideas about how and why that change might have occurred.

Reinventing the Veil

I grew up in Cairo, Egypt. Through the decades of my childhood and youth—the 1940s, 1950s and 1960s—the veil was a rarity not only at home but in many Arab and Muslim-majority cities. In fact, when Albert Hourani, the Oxford historian,   1 surveyed the Arab world in the mid-1950s, he predicted that the veil would soon be a thing of the past.

Hourani's prophecy, made in an article called *The Vanishing Veil: A Challenge to the Old Order*, would prove spectacularly wrong, but his piece is nevertheless a gem because it so perfectly captures the ethos of that era. Already the veil was becoming less and less common in my own country, and, as Hourani explains, it was fast disappearing in other "advanced Arab countries," such as Syria, Iraq and Jordan as well. An unveiling movement had begun to sweep across the Arab world, gaining momentum with the spread of education.

In those days, we shared all of Hourani's views and assumptions, including the connections he made between unveiling, "advancement" and education (and between veiling and "backwardness"). We believed the veil was merely a cultural habit, of no relevance to Islam or to religious piety. Even deeply devout women did not wear a hijab. Being unveiled simply seemed the modern "advanced" way of being Muslim.

Consequently the veil's steady "return" from the mid-1980s, and its growing adoption, disturbed us. It was very troubling for people like me who had been working for years as feminists on women and Islam. Why would educated women, particularly those living in free western societies where they could dress as they wished, be willing (apparently) to take on this symbol of patriarchy and women's oppression?

The appearance of the hijab in my own neighborhood of Cambridge, Massachusetts, in the late 1990s was the trigger that launched my own studies into the phenomenon. I well remember the very evening that generated that spark. While I was walking past the common with a friend, a well-known feminist who was visiting from the Arab world, we saw a large crowd with all the women in hijab. At the time, this was still an unusual sight and, frankly, it left us both with distinct misgivings.

While troubling on feminist grounds, the veil's return also disturbed me in other ways. Having settled in the US, I had watched from afar through the 1980s and 1990s as cities back home that I had known as places where scarcely anyone wore hijab were steadily transformed into streets where the vast majority of women now wore it.

This visually dramatic revolution in women's dress changed, to my eyes, the very look and atmosphere of those cities. It had come about as a result of the spread of Islamism in the 1970s, a very political form of Islam that was worlds away from the deeply inward, apolitical form that had been common in Egypt in my day. Fueled by the Muslim Brotherhood, the spread of Islamism always brought its signature emblem: the hijab.

Those same decades were marked in Egypt by rising levels of violence and intellectual repression. In 1992, Farag Foda, a well-known journalist and critic of Islamism, was gunned down. Nasr Hamid Abu Zayd, a professor at Cairo University, was brought to trial on grounds of apostasy and had to flee the country. Soon after, Naguib Mahfouz, the Egyptian novelist and Nobel Laureate, was stabbed by an Islamist who considered his books blasphemous. Such events seemed a shocking measure of the country's descent into intolerance.

The sight of the hijab on the streets of America brought all this to mind. Was its growing presence a sign that Islamic militancy was on the rise here too? Where were these young women (it was young women in particular who wore it) getting their ideas? And why were they accepting whatever it was they were being told, in this country where it was entirely normal to challenge patriarchal ideas? Could the Muslim Brotherhood have somehow succeeded in gaining a foothold here?   9

My instinctive readings of the Cambridge scene proved correct in some ways. The Brotherhood, as well as other Islamist groups, had indeed established a base in America. While most immigrants were not Islamists, those who were quickly set about founding mosques and other organizations. Many immigrants who grew up as I did, without veils, sent their children to Islamic Sunday schools where they imbibed the Islamist outlook—including the hijab.   10

The veiled are always the most visible, but today Islamist-influenced people make up no more than 30 to 40 percent of American Muslims. This is also roughly the percentage of women who veil as opposed to those who do not. This means of course that the majority of Muslim American women do not wear the veil, whether because they are secular or because they see it as an emblem of Islamism rather than Islam.   11

My research may have confirmed some initial fears, but it also challenged my assumptions. As I studied the process by which women had been persuaded to veil in Egypt in the first place, I came to see how essential women themselves had been in its promotion and the cause of Islamism. Among the most important was Zainab al-Ghazali, the "unsung mother" of the Muslim Brotherhood and a forceful activist who had helped keep the organization going after the death of its founder.   12

For these women, adopting hijab could be advantageous. Joining Islamist groups and changing dress sometimes empowered them in relation to their parents; it also expanded job and marriage possibilities. Also, since the veil advertised women's commitment to conservative sexual mores, wearing it paradoxically increased their ability to move freely in public space—allowing them to take jobs in offices shared with men.   13

My assumptions about the veil's patriarchal meanings began to unravel in the first interviews I conducted. One woman explained that she wore it as a way of raising consciousness about the sexist messages of our society. (This reminded me of the bra-burning days in America when some women refused to shave their legs in a similar protest.) Another wore the hijab for the same reason that one of her Jewish friends wore a yarmulke: this was religiously required dress that made visible the presence of a minority who were entitled, like all citizens, to justice and equality. For many others, wearing hijab was a way of affirming pride and rejecting negative stereotypes (like the Afros that flourished in the 1960s among African-Americans).   14

Both Islamist and American ideals—including American ideals of gender justice—seamlessly interweave in the lives of many of this younger generation. This has been a truly remarkable decade as regards Muslim women's activism. Perhaps the post-9/11 atmosphere in the west, which led to intense criticism of Islam and its views of women, spurred Muslim Americans into corrective action. Women are reinterpreting key religious texts, including the Koran, and they have now taken on positions of leadership in Muslim American institutions: Ingrid Mattson,   15 for example, was twice elected president of the Islamic Society of North America. Such female leadership is unprecedented in the home countries: even al-Ghazali, vital as she was to the Brotherhood, never formally presided over an organization which included men.

Many of these women—although not all—wear hijab. Clearly here in the west, 16 where women are free to wear what they want, the veil can have multiple meanings. These are typically a far cry from the old notions which I grew up with, and profoundly different from the veil's ancient patriarchal meanings, which are still in full force in some countries. Here in the west—embedded in the context of democracy, pluralism and a commitment to gender justice—women's hijabs can have meanings that they could not possibly have in countries which do not even subscribe to the idea of equality.

But things are changing here as well. Interestingly, the issue of hijab and 17 whether it is religiously required or not is now coming under scrutiny among women who grew up wearing it. Some are re-reading old texts and concluding that the veil is irrelevant to Islamic piety. They cast it off even as they remain committed Muslims.

It is too soon to tell whether this development, emerging most particularly 18 among intellectual women who once wore hijab, will gather force and become a new unveiling movement for the 21st century: one that repeats, on other continents and in completely new ways, the unveiling movement of the early 20th century. Still, in a time when a number of countries have tried banning the hijab and when typically such rules have backfired, it is worth noting that here in America, where there are no such bans, a new movement may be quietly getting under way, a movement led this time by committed Muslim women who once wore hijab and who, often after much thought and study, have taken the decision to set it aside.

Occasionally now, although less so than in the past, I find myself nostalgic 19 for the Islam of my childhood and youth, an Islam without veils and far removed from politics. An Islam which people seemed to follow not in the prescribed, regimented ways of today but rather according to their own inner sense, and their own particular temperaments, inclinations and the shifting vicissitudes of their lives.

I think my occasional yearning for that now bygone world has abated (not 20 that it is entirely gone) for a number of reasons. As I followed, a little like a detective, the extraordinary twists and turns of history that brought about this entirely unpredicted and unlikely "return" of the veil, I found the story itself so absorbing that I seemed to forget my nostalgia. I also lost the vague sense of annoyance, almost of affront, that I'd had over the years at how history had, seemingly so casually, set aside the entirely reasonable hopes and possibilities of that brighter and now vanished era.

In the process I came to see clearly what I had long known abstractly: that 21 living religions are by definition dynamic. Witness the fact that today we have women priests and rabbis—something unheard of just decades ago. As I followed the shifting history of the veil—a history which had reversed directions twice in one century—I realized that I had lived through one of the great sea changes now overtaking Islam. My own assumptions and the very ground they stood on had been fundamentally challenged. It now seems absurd that we once labeled people who veiled "backward" and those who did not "advanced," and that we thought that it was perfectly fine and reasonable to do so. Seeing one's own life from a new perspective can be unsettling, of course—but it is also quite bracing, and even rather exciting.

Questions for Critical Reading

1. What is the selection's thesis? Locate the sentence(s) in which Ahmed states her main idea. If she doesn't state her thesis explicitly, express it in your own words.

2. According to her essay, what event "generated [the] spark" that caused Ahmed to explore the reason that educated women were wearing what she thought of as a "symbol of patriarchy and women's oppression"?

3. According to Ahmed, how is Islamism different from Islam, and what examples does she provide of violent acts attributed to the spread of Islamism in Egypt toward the end of the twentieth century?

4. Who are Zainab al-Ghazali and Ingrid Mattson, and what roles have they played?

Questions About the Writer's Craft

1. **Purpose.** Does Ahmed's causal analysis have an essentially informative, speculative, or persuasive purpose? What makes you think so?

2. **Other patterns.** Ahmed *compares* and *contrasts* attitudes toward wearing hijabs. How do these comparisons and contrasts reinforce her thesis?

3. **Other patterns.** Ahmed incorporates several *narratives* into her essay. Identify the narratives she includes and comment on the purpose they serve.

4. **Tone.** How would you describe the tone Ahmed uses in her essay? Do you think the tone she uses is effective? Why or why not?

Writing Assignments Using Cause-Effect as a Pattern of Development

1. In her essay, Ahmed explores the ways in which ideas about "the veil" have changed in recent years and what caused those changes—a topic that clearly engages her for both personal and philosophical reasons. Write an essay in which you explore the causes and/or the effects of changes in attitude toward an issue that interests you. For example, you might explore the causes and/or effects of changes in attitude toward smoking, profanity, or obesity. Consider using outside sources and/or images to strengthen your essay.

2. Ahmed states, "The appearance of the hijab in my own neighborhood of Cambridge, Massachusetts, in the late 1990s was the trigger that launched my own studies into the phenomenon." What she saw that evening caused her to want

to more clearly understand why an increasing number of women were wearing the veil. Think of an event that caused you to change your thinking about something. Maybe you read a news article about hungry children in your community and decided to volunteer at a food bank. Or maybe you witnessed a lifeguard rescuing a swimmer and decided to improve your own swimming skills. Write an essay in which you explain the event and why you changed your behavior as a result of it.

Writing Assignments Combining Patterns of Development

3. Ahmed references Albert Hourani, "the Oxford historian [who] surveyed the Arab world in the mid-1950s and predicted that the veil would soon become a thing of the past"—a prediction which proved to be incorrect. What other predictions can you think of (or identify after doing some research) that seemed likely to come true—at least at the time they were made—but later proved inaccurate? For example, as the year 2000 approached, many computer experts predicted widespread chaos, anticipating that computer clocks would automatically reset to 1900 rather than advance to the next millennium. Yet, as January 1, 2000, came and went, it became clear that these predictions were inaccurate and alarmist. Write an essay in which you not only *describe* the incorrect prediction and what prompted it but also *compare* and *contrast* the predicted outcome with what actually transpired.

JOSIE APPLETON

Josie Appleton is the director and spokesperson for the Manifesto Club, a British civil liberties campaign group that speaks out against excessive state regulation. As a journalist, Appleton frequently writes for *Spiked* (or *sp!ked*), an online publication based in London. The following article appeared in *Spiked* on July 9, 2003.

Pre-Reading Journal Entry

There's no denying the growing popularity of tattoos and piercings. What responses—both positive and negative—might people with tattoos or piercings expect or hope to experience at school, at work, or in other societal situations? Explore these ideas in your journal.

The Body Piercing Project

The opening of a tattoo and piercing section in the up-market London store   1
Selfridges shows that body modification has lost its last trace of taboo.

"Metal Morphosis," nestled in the thick of the ladies clothing section, is a world   2
away from the backstreets of Soho—where the company has its other branch. Teenagers, middle-aged women, men in suits and young guys in jeans flock to peer at the rows of tastefully displayed rings and leaf through the tattoo brochures.

Tattooist Greg said that he had seen a "broad variety" of people: "everything   3
from the girl who turned 18 to the two Philippino cousins who just turned 40." The
piercer, Barry, said that a number of "Sloanies" come for piercings (the most expensive navel bar retails at £3000 [$4,550], and there is a broad selection that would
set you back several hundred pounds). A handful of women have even asked to be
tattooed with the label of their favorite bottle of wine (Rumbelow).

This is not just affecting London high-streets. According to current estimates,   4
between 10 and 25 percent of American adolescents have some kind of piercing
or tattoo (Carroll and Anderson 627). And their mothers are taking it up, too—in
the late 1990s, the fastest growing demographic group seeking tattoo services in
America was middle-class suburban women (Levins).

But while tattoos have been taken up by university students and ladies who   5
lunch, more traditional wearers of tattoos—sailors, soldiers, bikers, gangs—find
themselves increasingly censured.

In June 2003, the police rejected an applicant because his tattoos were deemed   6
to have an "implication of racism, sexism or religious prejudice" ("Police"). The US
Navy has banned "tattoos/body art/brands that are excessive, obscene, sexually
explicit or advocate or symbolize sex, gender, racial, religious, ethnic or national
origin discrimination" and "symbols denoting any gang affiliation, supremacist or
extremist groups, or drug use" (Jontz). New-style tattoos are a very different ball-
game to their frowned-upon forebears. While the tattoos of football supporters,
sailors and gang-members tend to be symbols of camaraderie or group affiliation,
the Selfridges brigade are seeking something much more individual.

For some, tattoos and piercing are a matter of personal taste or fashion. "It's   7
purely aesthetic decoration," said 37-year-old Sarah, waiting to get her navel
pierced at Metal Morphosis. The erosion of moral censure on tattooing, and the
increasing hygiene of tattoo parlors, has meant that body modification has become
a fashion option for a much wider group of people.

For others, tattooing seems to go more than skin-deep. Tattoo artist Greg thinks   8
that many of those getting tattoos today are looking for "self-empowerment"—tattoos, he says, are about establishing an "identity for the self." As a permanent
mark on your body that you choose for yourself, a tattoo is "something no one will
ever be able to take away from you," that allows you to say *this is mine.*"

Seventeen-year-old Laura said that she got her piercings done because she   9
"wanted to make a statement." When she turned 18, she planned to have "XXX"
tattooed on the base of her spine, symbolizing her pledge not to drink, smoke or
take drugs. "It's not to prove anything to anyone else," she said: "it's a pact with
myself completely."

Sue said that she had her navel pierced on her fortieth birthday to mark a turn-   10
ing point in her life. Another young man planned to have his girlfriend's name,
and the dates when they met, tattooed on his arm "to show her that I love her"—
and to remind himself of this moment. "The tattoo will be there forever. Whether
or not I feel that in the future, I will remember that I felt it at the time, that I felt
strong enough to have the tattoo."

The tattoos of bikers, sailors and gang-members would be a kind of social   11
symbol, that would establish them as having a particular occupation or belong-
ing to a particular cultural subgroup. By contrast, Laura's "XXX" symbol is a sign

to herself of how she has chosen to live her life; Sue pierced her navel to mark her transition to middle-age. These are not symbols that could be interpreted by anyone else. Even the man who wanted to get tattooed with his girlfriend's name had a modern, personal twist to his tale: the tattoo was less a pact to stay with her forever, than to remind himself of his feelings at this point.

Much new-style body modification is just another way to look good. But the trend also presents a more profound, and worrying, shift: the growing crisis in personal identity. 12

In his book, *Modernity and Self-Identity* (1991), sociologist Anthony Giddens argues that it is the erosion of important sources of identity that helps to explain the growing focus on the body. Body modification began to really take off and move into the mainstream in the late 1980s and early 1990s. At around this time, personal and community relationships that previously helped to provide people with an enduring sense of self could no longer be depended upon. The main ideological frameworks that provided a system to understand the world and the individual's place in it, such as class, religion, or the work ethic, began to erode. 13

These changes have left individuals at sea, trying to establish their own sense of who they are. In their piercing or tattooing, people are trying to construct a "narrative of self" on the last thing that remains solid and tangible: their physical bodies. While much about social experience is uncertain and insecure, the body at least retains a permanence and reliability. Making marks upon their bodies is an attempt by people to build a lasting story of who they are. 14

Many—including, to an extent, Giddens—celebrate modification as a liberating and creative act. "If you want to and it makes you feel good, you should do it," Greg tells me. Websites such as the *Body Modification Ezine* (*BMEzine*) are full of readers' stories about how their piercing has completely changed their life. One piercer said that getting a piercing "helped me know who I am." Another said that they felt "more complete...a better, more rounded and fuller person" (qtd. in Featherstone 68). Others even talk about unlocking their soul, or finally discovering that "I AM." 15

But what these stories actually show is less the virtues of body piercing, than the desperation of individuals' attempts to find a foothold for themselves. There is a notable contrast between the superlatives about discovering identity and Being, and the ultimately banal act of sticking a piece of metal through your flesh. 16

Piercings and tattoos are used to plot out significant life moments, helping to lend a sense of continuity to experience. A first date, the birth of a child, moving house: each event can be marked out on the body, like the notches of time on a stick. One woman said that her piercings helped to give her memory, to "stop me forgetting who I am." They work as a "diary" that "no one can take off you" (qtd. in Featherstone 69). 17

This springs from the fact that there is a great deal of confusion about the stages of life today. Old turning points that marked adulthood—job, marriage, house, kids—have both stopped being compulsory and lost much of their significance. It is more difficult to see life in terms of a narrative, as a plot with key moments of transition and an overall aim. Piercings and tattoos are used to highlight formative experiences and link them together. 18

Some also claim that body modification helps them to feel "comfortable in my own skin," or proud of parts of their body of which they were previously ashamed. The whole process of piercing—which involves caring for the wound, and paying special attention to bodily processes—is given great significance. By modifying a body part, some argue that you are taking possession of it, making it truly yours. "The nipple piercings have really changed my relationship to my breasts," one woman said (qtd. in Siebers 175). 19

This is trying to resolve a sense of self-estrangement—the feeling of detachment from experiences, the feeling that your life doesn't really belong to you. One young woman says how she uses piercing: "[It's been] done at times when I felt like I needed to ground myself. Sometimes I feel like I'm not in my body—then it's time" (Holtham). 20

But piercing is trying to deal with the problem at the most primitive and brutal level—in the manner of "I hurt therefore I am." The experience of pain becomes one of the few authentic experiences. It also tries to resolve the crisis in individual identity in relation to my breasts or my navel, rather than in relation to other people or anything more meaningful in the world. 21

Many claims are made as to the transformative and creative potential of body modification. One girl, who had just had her tongue pierced, writes: "I've always been kind of quiet in school and very predictable....I wanted to think of myself as original and creative, so I decided I wanted something pierced....Now people don't think of me as shy and predictable. They respect me and the person I've become and call me crazily spontaneous" ("My"). 22

Others say they use modification to help master traumatic events. Transforming the body is seen as helping to re-establish a sense of self-control in the face of disrupting or degrading experiences. One woman carved out a Sagittarius symbol on her thigh to commemorate a lover who died. "It was my way of coming to terms with the grief I felt," she said. "It enabled me to always have him with me and to let him go" (Polhemus and Randall 79). 23

Here the body is being modified as a way of trying to effect change in people's lives. It is the way to express creativity, find a challenge, or put themselves through the hoops. "I was ecstatic. I did it!" writes one contributor to *BMEZine*. Instead of a life project, this is a "body project." In the absence of obvious social outlets for creativity, the individual turns back on himself and to the transformation of his own flesh. 24

Body piercing expresses the crisis of social identity—but it actually also makes it worse, too. Focusing on claiming control over my body amounts to making a declaration of independence from everybody else. 25

People with hidden piercings comment on how pleased they were they had something private. One says: "I get so happy just walking along and knowing that I have a secret that no one else could ever guess!" Another said that they now had "something that people could not judge me for, and something that I could hide." Another said that her piercing made her realize that "what other people say or think doesn't matter. The only thing that mattered at that moment was that I was happy with this piercing; I felt beautiful and comfortable in my own skin....They remind me that I'm beautiful to who it matters...*me*" ("My"). 26

Body modification encourages a turn away from trying to build personal identity through relationships with others, and instead tries to resolve problems in 27 relation to one's own body. When things are getting rough, or when somebody wants to change their lives, the answer could be a new piercing or a new tattoo. There is even an underlying element of self-hatred here, as individuals try to deal with their problems by doing violence to themselves. As 17-year-old Laura told me: "You push yourself to do more and more.... You want it to hurt."

This means that the biggest questions—of existence, self-identity, life progres- 28 sion, creativity—are being tackled with the flimsiest of solutions. A mark on the skin or a piercing through the tongue cannot genuinely resolve grief, increase creativity, or give a solid grounding to self-identity. For this reason, body modification can become an endless, unfulfilling quest, as one piercing only fuels a desire for another. All the contributions to *BMEZine* start by saying how much their life has been changed—but then promptly go on to plan their next series of piercings. "Piercing can be addictive!" they warn cheerily.

Body modification should be put back in the fashion box. As a way of im- 29 proving personal appearance, piercing and tattooing are no better or worse than clothes, makeup or hair gel. It is when body modification is loaded with existential significance that the problems start.

Works Cited

Carroll, Lynne, and Roxanne Anderson. "Body Piercing, Tattooing, Self-Esteem, and Body Investment in Adolescent Girls." *Adolescence*, vol. 37, no. 147, 2002, pp. 627–37.

Featherstone, Mike, editor. *Body Modification*, Sage, 2000.

Giddens, Anthony. *Modernity and Self-Identity: Self and Society in the Late Modern Age*, Polity, 1991.

Holtham, Susan. "Body Piercing in the West: A Sociological Inquiry." *Ambient Inc: Body Art Resources*, www.ambient.ca/bodmod/essay.html.

Jontz, Sandra. "Navy Draws a Line on Some Forms of Body Piercing, Ornamentation, Tattoos." *Stars and Stripes*, 29 Jan. 2003, www.stripes.com/news/navy-draws-a-line-on-some-forms-of-body-piercing-ornamentation-tattoos-1.1390.

Levins, Hoag. "The Changing Cultural Status of the Tattoo Arts in America." *TattooArtist*, 1997, tattooartist.com/history.html.

"My Beautiful Piercing." *Body Modification Ezine*, 30 June 2003, www.bme.com/media/story/854435/?cat=pierce/02-tongue.

Polhemus, Ted, and Housk Randall. *The Customized Body*, 2nd ed., Serpent's Tail, 2000.

"Police Reject Tattooed Applicant." *BBC News*, 16 June 2003, news.bbc.co.uk/2/hi/uk_news/england/oxfordshire/2995556.stm.

Rumbelow, Helen. "Ladies Who Lunch Get a Tattoo for Starters." *The Times*, 18 June 2003, www.thetimes.co.uk/tto/news/uk/article1909578.ece.

Siebers, Tobin, editor. *The Body Aesthetic: From Fine Art to Body Modification*. U of Michigan P, 2000.

Questions for Critical Reading

1. What is the selection's thesis? Locate the sentence(s) in which Appleton states her main idea. If she doesn't state the thesis explicitly, express it in your own words.

2. According to Appleton, what are the two main factors that have made body modifications a fashion option for a growing number of individuals?

3. To what cause does the sociologist Anthony Giddens attribute what Appleton calls "the growing focus on the body"? Do you agree with Giddens's assertion? Explain your response.

4. Think of individuals you know—perhaps yourself, your friends, your family members—who have tattoos or piercings and those individuals' reasons for making these body modifications. In what ways does Appleton's thesis ring true or false when you consider her ideas in relation to those reasons?

Questions About the Writer's Craft

1. **The pattern.** Appleton reveals both causes and effects of body modifications. Do paragraphs 28 and 29 discuss causes, effects, or both? Why do you suppose Appleton organizes the paragraphs this way?

2. **Thesis.** Although most essays state their thesis near the beginning, Appleton saves hers for later in the selection. Why do you think she chose to organize her essay in this manner? Do you think her essay would have been more effective if she had stated her thesis in the first or second paragraph? Why or why not?

3. **Other patterns.** Appleton *compares* and *contrasts* the types of tattoos typical of various demographic groups. She distinguishes "tattoos of football supporters, sailors, and gang-members," whose tattoos "tend to be symbols of camaraderie or group affiliation," from those of "the Selfridges brigade," who "are seeking something much more individual" (paragraph 6). Does this distinction make sense to you? Does it apply when you think of individuals you know with tattoos? Why or why not?

4. **Sources.** Appleton includes a number of sources in her essay. List the various types of sources she includes. Of these, which do you consider most effective in helping her convince readers of her thesis? Why?

Writing Assignments Using Cause-Effect as a Pattern of Development

1. Appleton's essay attempts to explain the increasing popularity and acceptance of body modifications such as tattooing and piercings. Write a cause-effect essay in which you focus on another growing trend or current fad such as the increase in popularity and acceptance of revealing clothing, the growing use of Twitter, or the explosion in popularity of 3D movies. Consider including one or more images and several outside sources to add to the effectiveness of your essay.

2. Write a cause-effect essay in which you focus on an individual who chose to modify his or her body—perhaps with tattoos or piercing or perhaps through a surgical procedure. Explore the reasons the person decided to make these changes and the effect of the body modifications. Include information as to whether the modifications brought about the desired results.

Writing Assignment Combining
Patterns of Development

3. Write an essay in which you *compare* and *contrast* the most popular types of tattoos— or alternatively, the types of clothing—favored by various demographic groups in the United States today. You might include some of the groups Appleton mentions in her essay: teenagers, middle-aged women, men in suits, football supporters, sailors, and gang members. Conduct research to gather information for your essay and also consider including a chart to *illustrate* your findings.

Additional Writing Topics: Cause-Effect

General Assignments

Using cause-effect, develop one of these topics into an essay.

1. An eating disorder such as anorexia or bulimia
2. Having the parents you have
3. Lack of communication in a relationship
4. Overexercising or not exercising
5. Traveling or living in a foreign country
6. Skill or ineptitude in sports
7. A major life decision
8. Changing attitudes toward the environment
9. Voter apathy
10. An act of violence or cruelty

Assignments Using Multimedia

Use the suggested media to help develop a cause-effect essay on one of these topics:

1. Sleep deprivation and its effects (slide show)
2. Giving children responsibilities and holding them accountable (weblinks)
3. Stress and its impact on the human body (charts and/or graphs)
4. The consequences of texting while driving (graphs)
5. The effects of stereotyping by gender, race, or disability (weblinks)

Assignments with a Specific Purpose, Audience, and Point of View

1. **Academic life.** A debate about the prominence of athletics at colleges and universities is going to be broadcast on the local cable TV station. For this debate, prepare a speech pointing out either the harmful or the beneficial effects of big-time college athletic programs.

2. **Academic life.** Why do students flunk out of college? Write an article for the campus newspaper outlining the main causes of failure. Your goal is to steer students away from dangerous habits and situations that lead to poor grades or dropping out.

3. **Civic activity.** Write a letter to the editor of your favorite newspaper analyzing the causes of the country's current "trash crisis." Be sure to mention the nationwide love affair with disposable items and the general disregard of the idea of thrift. Conclude by offering brief suggestions for how people in your community can begin to remedy this problem.

4. **Civic activity.** Write a letter to the mayor of your town or city suggesting a "Turn Off the TV" public relations effort, convincing residents to stop watching television for a month. Cite the positive effects that a month of no TV would have on parents, children, and the community in general.

5. **Workplace action.** As the manager of a store or office, you've noticed that a number of employees have negative workplace habits and/or attitudes. Write a memo for your employees in which you identify these negative behaviors and show how they affect the workplace environment. Be sure to adopt a tone that will sound neither patronizing nor overly harsh.

6. **Workplace action.** Why do you think teenage suicide is on the rise? You're a respected psychologist. After performing some research, write a fact sheet for parents of teenagers and for high school guidance counselors describing the factors that could make a young person desperate enough to attempt suicide. At the end, suggest what parents and counselors can do to help confused, unhappy young people.

Chapter 17
Definition

Learning Objectives

17.1 Understand how you can use the definition pattern to develop your essays.

17.2 Consider how definition can fit your purpose and audience.

17.3 Develop prewriting strategies for using definition in an essay.

17.4 Develop strategies for writing a definition essay.

17.5 Use strategies for revising your definition essay.

17.6 Analyze how definition is used effectively in a student-written selection.

What Is Definition?

17.1 Understand how you can use the definition pattern to develop your essays.

For language to communicate, words must have accepted definitions. Dictionaries, which are the source texts for definitions, are compilations of word meanings that enable speakers of a language to understand one another. But as you might suspect, things are not as simple as they first appear.

Words can be slippery. Each of us has unique experiences, attitudes, and values that influence the way we use words and the way we interpret the words of others.

In addition to the idiosyncratic interpretations we may attach to words, some words shift in meaning over time. For example, the word *pedagogue* originally meant "a teacher or leader of children." However, with the passage of time, *pedagogue* has come to mean "a dogmatic, pedantic teacher." And, of course, we invent new words (*emoji, selfie, defriend*) as the need arises.

Writing a **definition**, then, is no simple task. Primarily, the writer tries to answer basic questions: "What does this word mean?" and "What is the special or true nature of this word?" The word to be defined may refer to an object, a concept, a type of person, a place, or a phenomenon. There are various strategies for expanding definitions far beyond the single-word synonyms or brief phrases that dictionaries provide.

How Definition Fits Your Purpose and Audience

17.2 Consider how definition can fit your purpose and audience.

Many times, short-answer exam questions call for definitions. Consider the following examples:

- Define the term *mob psychology.*
- What is the difference between a metaphor and a simile?
- Explain what a religious cult is.

In such cases, a good response might involve a definition of several sentences or several paragraphs.

Other times, definition may be used in an essay organized mainly around another pattern of development. In this situation, all that's needed is a brief formal definition or a short definition given in your own words. For instance, a *process analysis* showing readers how computers have revolutionized the typical business office might start with a textbook definition of the term *information technology.* In an *argumentation-persuasion* essay urging students to support recent efforts to abolish fraternities and sororities, you could refer to the definitions of *blackballing* and *hazing* found in the university handbook. Or your personal definition of *hero* could be the starting point for a *causal analysis* that explains why there are few real heroes in today's world.

The most complex use of definition, and the one on which we focus in this chapter, involves exploring a subject through an **extended definition**. Extended definition allows you to apply a personal interpretation to a word, to propose a new perspective of a commonly accepted meaning, to analyze words representing complex or controversial issues. *Pornography, gun control, secular humanism,* and *right to privacy* would be good subjects for extended definition; each is multifaceted, often misunderstood, and fraught with emotion. *Junk food, anger, leadership,* and *anxiety* could also make interesting subjects, especially if the extended definition helps readers develop a new understanding of the word. You might, for example, define *anxiety* not as a negative state but as a positive force that propels us to take action.

An extended definition may run several paragraphs or a few pages. Keep in mind, however, that some definitions require a chapter or even an entire book to develop. Theologians, philosophers, and psychologists have devoted entire texts to concepts like *evil* and *love.*

Prewriting Strategies

17.3 Develop prewriting strategies for using definition in an essay.

The following checklist shows how you can apply prewriting strategies to definition.

☑ Definition: A Prewriting Checklist

Choose Something to Define

☐ Is there something you're especially qualified to define? What about that thing do you hope to convey?

☐ Do any of your journal entries reflect an attempt to pinpoint something's essence: courage, pornography, a well-rounded education?

☐ Will you define a concept, an object, a type of person, a place, a phenomenon, a complex or controversial issue?

☐ Can your topic be meaningfully defined within the space and time allotted?

Identify Your Purpose, Audience, Tone, and Point of View

☐ Do you want simply to inform and explain—that is, to make the meaning clear? Or do you want to persuade readers to accept your understanding of a term? Do you want to do both?

☐ Will you offer a personal interpretation? Propose a revised meaning? Explain an obscure or technical term? Discuss shifts in meaning over time? Distinguish one term from another closely-related term? Show conflicts in definition?

☐ Are your readers likely to be open to your interpretation of a term? What information will they need to understand your definition and to feel that it is correct and insightful?

☐ What tone and point of view will make your readers receptive to your definition?

Use Prewriting to Develop the Definition

☐ How might mapping, brainstorming, freewriting, and speaking with others generate material that develops your definition?

☐ Which of the following prewriting questions would generate the most details and, therefore, suggest patterns for developing your definition?

Question	Pattern
How does *X* look, taste, smell, feel, and sound?	Description
What does *X* do? When? Where?	Narration
What are some typical instances of *X*?	Illustration
What are *X*'s component parts? What different forms can *X* take?	Division-classification
How does *X* work?	Process analysis
What is *X* like or unlike?	Comparison-contrast
What leads to *X*? What are *X*'s consequences?	Cause-effect

Strategies for Using Definition in an Essay

17.4 Develop strategies for writing a definition essay.

After prewriting, you're ready to draft your essay. Figure 17.1 and the following suggestions will be helpful whether you use definition as a dominant or supportive pattern of development.

1. **Stay focused on the essay's purpose, audience, and tone.**

   Because your purpose for writing an extended definition shapes the entire essay, you need to keep that objective in mind when developing your definition. Suppose you decide to write an essay defining *jazz*. The essay could be purely *informative* and discuss the origins of jazz, its characteristic tonal patterns, and some of the great jazz musicians of the past. Or the essay could move beyond pure information and take on a *persuasive* edge. It might, for example, argue that jazz is the only contemporary form of music worthy of serious consideration.

   Just as your purpose in writing will vary, so will your tone. A strictly informative definition will generally assume a detached, objective tone. In contrast, a definition essay with a persuasive slant might have an urgent tone, or it might take a satiric approach.

   As you write, keep thinking about your audience as well. Not only do your readers determine the terms that need to be defined (and in how much detail), but they also keep you focused on the essay's purpose and tone.

2. **Formulate an effective definition.**

   A definition essay sometimes begins with a brief **formal definition**—the definition found in a dictionary or a textbook or the writer's own formal definition—and then expands that initial definition with supporting details. Formal definitions

Figure 17.1 Development Diagram: Writing a Definition Essay

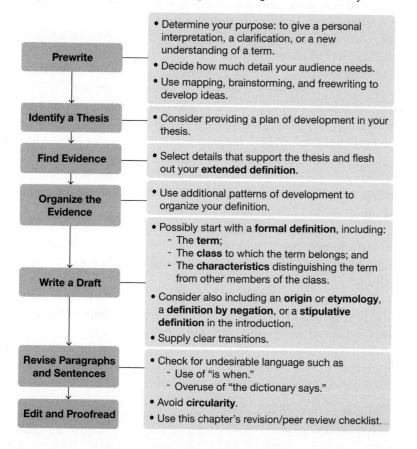

Prewrite
- Determine your purpose: to give a personal interpretation, a clarification, or a new understanding of a term.
- Decide how much detail your audience needs.
- Use mapping, brainstorming, and freewriting to develop ideas.

Identify a Thesis
- Consider providing a plan of development in your thesis.

Find Evidence
- Select details that support the thesis and flesh out your **extended definition**.

Organize the Evidence
- Use additional patterns of development to organize your definition.

Write a Draft
- Possibly start with a **formal definition**, including:
  - The **term**;
  - The **class** to which the term belongs; and
  - The **characteristics** distinguishing the term from other members of the class.
- Consider also including an **origin** or **etymology**, a **definition by negation**, or a **stipulative definition** in the introduction.
- Supply clear transitions.

Revise Paragraphs and Sentences
- Check for undesirable language such as
  - Use of "is when."
  - Overuse of "the dictionary says."
- Avoid **circularity**.
- Use this chapter's revision/peer review checklist.

Edit and Proofread

are traditionally worded as three-part statements, including (1) the **term**, (2) the **class** to which the term belongs, and (3) the **characteristics** that distinguish the term from other members of its class. Consider these examples of formal definition:

Term	Class	Characteristics
The peregrine falcon,	an endangered bird,	is the world's fastest flyer.
Back to basics	is a trend in education	that emphasizes skill mastery through rote learning.

A definition that meets these three guidelines—term, class, and characteristics—will clarify what your subject *is* and what it *is not*. These guidelines also establish the boundaries or scope of your definition. For example, defining *back to basics* as "a trend that emphasizes…rote learning" signals a certain boundary; it lets readers know that other educational trends (such as those that emphasize children's social or emotional development) won't be part of the essay's definition.

Because they are formulaic, formal definitions tend to be dull. For this reason, it's best to reserve them for clarifying potentially confusing words—perhaps words with multiple meanings. For example, the term *the West* can refer to the western section of the United States, historically to the United States and its non-Communist allies (as in the "Western world"), or to the entire Western Hemisphere. Before discussing the West, then, you need to provide a formal definition that clarifies your use of the term.

Highly specialized or technical terms may also require clarification. Few readers are likely to feel confident about their understanding of the term *cognitive dissonance* unless you supply them with a formal definition: "a conflict of thoughts arising when two or more ideas do not go together."

If you decide to include a formal definition in your essay, avoid tired openings such as "the dictionary says" or "according to *Webster's*." Such weak starts lack imagination. Also keep in mind that a strict dictionary definition may actually confuse readers. *Remember:* The purpose of a definition is to clarify meaning, not obscure it.

Stay clear of ungrammatical "is when" definitions: "Blind ambition is when you want to get ahead, no matter how much other people are hurt." Instead, write, "Blind ambition is wanting to get ahead, no matter how much other people are hurt."

A final pitfall to avoid in writing formal definitions is **circularity**, saying the same thing twice and therefore defining nothing: "A campus tribunal is a tribunal composed of various members of the university community." Circular definitions such as this often repeat the term being defined (*tribunal*) or use words having the same meaning (*campus; university community*). In this case, we learn nothing about what a campus tribunal is; the writer says only that "*X* is *X.*"

3. **Develop the extended definition.**

You can use the patterns of development when formulating an extended definition. Description, narration, process analysis, comparison-contrast, or any of the other patterns discussed in this book may be drawn upon—alone or in combination. Imagine you're planning to write an extended definition of *robotics*. You might develop the term by providing *examples* of the way robots are currently being used in scientific research; by *comparing* and *contrasting* human and robot capabilities; or by *classifying* robots, starting with the most basic and moving to the most advanced or futuristic models. (To deepen your understanding of which patterns to use when developing a particular extended definition, take a moment to review the last item in this chapter's prewriting checklist.)

4. **Organize the material that develops the definition.**

If you use a single pattern to develop the extended definition, apply the principles of organization suited to that pattern, as described in the appropriate chapter of this book. Assume that you're defining *fad* by means of *process analysis*. You might organize your paragraphs according to the steps in the process: a fad's slow start as something avant-garde or eccentric; its wildfire acceptance by the general public; the fad's demise as it becomes familiar or tiresome. If you want to define *character* by means of a single *narration*, you would probably organize paragraphs chronologically. In a definition essay using several methods of development, you should devote separate paragraphs to each pattern. A definition of *relaxation,* for instance, might start with a paragraph that *narrates* a particularly relaxing day; then it might move to a paragraph that presents several *examples* of people who find it difficult to unwind; finally, it might end with a paragraph that explains a *process* for relaxing the mind and body.

5. **Write an effective introduction.**

It can be helpful to provide—near the beginning of a definition essay—a brief formal definition of the term you're going to develop in the rest of the essay. Beyond this basic element, the introduction might include a number of other features. You may explain the *origin* of the term being defined: "*Acid rock* is a term first coined in the 1960s to describe music that was written or listened to under the influence of the drug LSD." Similarly, you could explain the *etymology,* or linguistic origin, of the key word that focuses the essay: "The term *vigilantism* is derived from a Latin word meaning 'to watch and be awake.'"

You may also use the introduction to clarify what your subject is *not*. Such **definition by negation** can be an effective strategy at an essay's beginning, especially if readers don't share your view of the subject. In such a case, you might write something like this: "The gorilla, far from being the vicious killer of jungle movies and popular imagination, is a sedentary, gentle creature living in a closely knit family group." This statement provides the focus for your essay and signals some of the misconceptions or fallacies soon to be discussed.

In addition, you may include in the introduction a **stipulative definition**, one that puts restrictions on a term: "Strictly defined, a mall refers to a one- or two-story enclosed building containing a variety of retail shops and at least two large anchor stores. Highway-strip shopping centers or downtown centers cannot be considered true malls." When a term has multiple meanings or when its meaning has become fuzzy through misuse, a stipulative definition sets the record straight right at the start so that readers know exactly what is, and is not, being defined.

Finally, the introduction may end with a *plan of development* that indicates how the essay will unfold. A student who returned to school after raising a family decided to write a composition defining the midlife crisis that led to her enrollment in college. After providing a brief formal definition of *midlife crisis,* the student rounded off her introduction with this sentence: "Such a midlife crisis often starts with vague misgivings, turns into depression, and ends with a significant change in lifestyle."

Revision Strategies

17.5 Use strategies for revising your definition essay.

Once you have a draft of the essay, you're ready to revise. The following checklist will help your peers provide feedback and aid you in revising your essay.

☑ Definition: A Revision/Peer Review Checklist

Revise Overall Meaning and Structure

☐ Is the essay's purpose informative, persuasive, or both?

☐ Is the term being defined clearly distinguished from similar terms?

☐ Where does a circular definition cloud meaning? Where are technical, nonstandard, or ambiguous terms a source of confusion?

☐ Where would a word's historical or linguistic origin clarify meaning? Where would a formal definition, stipulative definition, or definition by negation help?

☐ Which patterns of development are used to develop the definition? How do these help the essay achieve its purpose?

☐ If the essay uses only one pattern, is the essay's method of organization suited to that pattern (step-by-step for process analysis, chronological for narration, and so on)?

☐ Where could a dry formal definition be deleted without sacrificing overall clarity?

Revise Paragraph Development

☐ If the essay uses several patterns of development, where would separate paragraphs for different patterns be appropriate?

☐ Which paragraphs are flat or unconvincing? How could they be made more compelling?

Revise Sentences and Words

☐ Which sentences and words are inconsistent with the essay's tone?

☐ Where should overused phrases, such as "the dictionary says" and "according to *Webster's*," be replaced by more original wording?

☐ Have "is when" definitions been avoided?

Student Essay: From Prewriting Through Revision

17.6 Analyze how definition is used effectively in a student-written selection.

The following student essay was written by Olivia Fletcher in response to this assignment:

> In "The Inner Corset," Laura Fraser writes about the changing definition of beauty, the factors that brought about the change, and the effects of this new ideal on the way we live our lives. Choose another term, one that is multifaceted, and define it in such a way that you reveal something significant about contemporary life.

After Olivia's professor, Dr. Ashman, introduced the new assignment, she asked her students to take a few minutes to brainstorm a list of at least five possible topics they might write about and, after they had a list, to go back and jot down notes that could help them decide which topics have the most potential for their essays.

As Olivia tried to come up with ideas for her essay, her thoughts began to wander off the topic. She found herself thinking, instead, about what she wanted to do when class was over. She hadn't checked her Twitter account for a couple of hours and wondered what new tweets she might find. Then she realized that she had unintentionally come upon what might be the perfect topic for her essay: the changing definition of the word *tweet*, and she quickly noted that at the top of her list. She knew she needed to come up with four more topics, so she thought about other terms relating to new technologies, and then she jotted down ideas that came to her about each one.

Olivia's Brainstorming

tweet—I really like this idea for my essay. I spend so much of my time tweeting, and I think I'd enjoy working on an essay on this topic.

text—This one's not bad, either. A text used to be a book, and now it's so much more. Not so sure I'd find this topic as engaging as the first one.

friend—Before I had a Facebook account, if someone asked me how many friends I had, I'd probably say I had four or five. Now, when someone asks me that question, I assume they want to know how many Facebook friends I have. There's a difference between a friend in life and a Facebook friend.

Twitter—This one's really just another version of the first word on my list. I guess I could write about the changing meaning of either one, but for some reason, I like *tweet* the best. Maybe I just like the sound of *tweet* more than I like the sound of *twitter*. Not sure...

Instagram—Now that I'm thinking more about this word, I realize it won't work. I don't think *Instagram* has a variety of meanings—just the one. And besides, *tweet* is the word I want to write about.

As Olivia looked over her prewriting, she knew she wanted to write about the first topic that had come to mind: the changing definition of the word *tweet*. While Dr. Ashman encouraged her students to consider developing an outline before jumping into their first drafts, Olivia decided that she would rather figure out how to best structure her essay as she wrote the first draft.

Now read Olivia's essay, "'Tweet, Tweedle-lee-dee' (118 Characters Left)," and consider how well it applies the principles of definition discussed in this chapter. As you read the commentary that follows, you'll see that while Olivia's final draft turned out to be an essay she could be proud of, her decision to move directly from brainstorming to the first draft might not have been the smartest choice. Taking time to think more carefully about how she might structure her essay and to develop an outline before writing the first draft would have likely made her writing process move along more smoothly.

"Tweet, Tweedle-lee-dee" (118 Characters Left)
by Olivia Fletcher

Introduction

Original definition

Thesis

Topic sentence

Start of a series of
causes and effects

New definition

Topic sentence

Start of a series
of contrasts

Start of a series of
negative examples

Once upon a time, the word *tweet* simply referred to the sharp, trilling sound a bird makes, and some folks can still remember Bobby Day's 1958 song "Rockin' Robin," with its chorus "Tweet, tweedle-lee-dee" ("Rockin' Robin"). Since those days, *tweet* has morphed into a word whose meaning your great grandfather could have never imagined when he was listening to Day's hit on *Billboard*'s Hot 100.

Jack Dorsey's creation of a new social networking site called *Twitter* in March 2006 soon led to a new definition for the word *tweet*. Dorsey wanted to share his text messages and updates with all of his friends, but in those days, some of his friends didn't have phones with texting abilities but did spend significant amounts of time on their home computers. So Dorsey invented *Twitter*, the social networking site that uses what came to be known as *tweets*, messages composed of 140 or fewer characters to share updates, thus eliminating the need to contact each person individually (Bellis). Before the word *tweet* came into existence, individuals posting to *Twitter* were referred to as "twitter-ers" and their posts were called "twits"—both rather awkward-sounding terms. Then in January 2007, in an e-mail Blaine Cook, a founding engineer at *Twitter*, sent to Craig Hockenberry, a software designer and creator of the *Twitter* app, Cook asks, "How about changing 'twit' to 'tweet'. . .?" Commenting on the exchange with Cook in his blog post, "The Origin of the Word Tweet," Hockenberry writes, "It's rare to have unanimous agreement when naming things in software, but in this case *everyone* loved the word 'tweet.'" Hockenberry also states in his 2013 blog post that the word had recently been added to the *Oxford English Dictionary*. He goes on to quote John Simpson, chief editor of the *OED*: "This breaks at least one *OED* rule, namely that a new word needs to be current for ten years before consideration for inclusion." The new word caught on so quickly and was used so widely that the *OED* made an exception for it.

Today, a tweet is a thought brought to the social table of all thoughts imaginable. The tweet has to be 140 or fewer characters, which forces users to be concise, something they don't need to consider when posting on *Facebook*, a site that allows users to include an unlimited number of characters. *Twitter* was designed for social-networking users who are on the go and do not have time to read four paragraphs about what is going on in their friends' lives.

In the days since Dorsey sent the first "twit" in 2006, tweets have become more and more infamous. Celebrities such as Miley Cyrus, Justin Bieber, Perez Hilton, and John Mayer, along with many others, have shared and continue to share their thoughts in 140 or fewer characters in the form of tweets. Some celebrities, along with thousands of not-so-famous individuals, have used tweets to share personal thoughts better left unsaid. People can do as much damage in 140 or fewer characters as they can in four paragraphs.

1

2

3

4

Topic sentence ────────→ A few years ago the blogger Perez Hilton and the singer John   5
Mayer got into a "*Twitter* war." They carefully, or not so carefully, crafted their personal thoughts of each other in 140 or fewer characters
Continuation of   and shared them publicly on the World Wide Web via *Twitter*. Their
series of negative   tweets were not only insulting but also devious, in that they posted
examples   the tweets without using each other's actual usernames; that meant
the person being insulted could not see the "subtweet" in his or her
Twitter timeline. This, of course, created even more drama and more
subtweets back and forth between the two individuals. This *Twitter*
war between Hilton and Mayer provides a perfect example of how
ridiculous amounts of drama have been introduced into society with a
simple tweet. In his *Elite Daily* article, "Top 10 Celebrity Twitter Feuds,"
Anthony Selden, a New York-based writer, had the following to say
about the Hilton-Mayer feud, which, by the way, he ranked number
one among the top ten feuds:

> "People don't want to see you hurt, they want to see
> you experience something equalizing," tweeted Mayer,
> presumably as an act of revenge for all of Hilton's web-
> based attacks on Mayer over the years. Hilton, ever
> the martyr, whined that Mayer's tweets weren't funny
> and that "karma would be me losing my site and going
> bankrupt."

Topic sentence ────────→ While used all too often to insult others, tweets can be used   6
positively, especially in educational settings. Huge screens at the
front of every meeting room, dining room, and classroom were set up
Start of a series of   at a scholarship competition at the University of West Florida on the
positive examples   third weekend of January 2014. The rising seniors who attended the
event could tweet anything with the "hashtag" (another word that has
been incorporated into the tweeting world) #UWFadmissions, and it
would appear on the screen. One hilarious incident took place at the
competition when one student tweeted, "Having fun at this scholaship competition #UWFadmissions," and another quickly tweeted
back, "This guy can't even spell *scholarship*. That's a bad sign. #UW-
Fadmissions." The crowd erupted with laughter at the witty remark
and from that moment on, every few seconds a tweet discussing the
events of the "scholaship" competition would appear on the white
screens at the front of the rooms (Williams).

Topic sentence ────────→ Another example of tweets being used positively in academic   7
settings is described in "English Class Includes Tweeting," a January
2014 Associated Press article that explains how teachers and stu-
Continuation of a   dents at Holy Trinity Episcopal Academy, a college-prep school in
series of positive   Melbourne, Florida, have incorporated *Twitter* into the classroom
examples   with positive outcomes. "The children are learning how to use social media appropriately. They're learning how what they post on
Twitter and other social media sites can be viewed by literally the
whole world," says Susan Bearden, the school's director of information technology and a nationally recognized leader on the value
of incorporating social media into classroom activities. "That's
such an important concept for kids to understand," Bearden
goes on to say. "When [students] realize there's a broader audience...they really up their game."

Continuation of a
series of positive
examples

    "Twitter has helped give quieter students a voice," adds Valerie   8
Williams, a teacher who works with Bearden at Holy Trinity. Many
students who are hesitant to participate in classroom discussions are
happy to tweet their ideas to others in the classroom and beyond.
Giselle Spicer, a fourteen-year-old student in Williams's class who
is usually reluctant to enter traditional classroom discussions, comments, "It feels like I can be part of the conversation without having
to talk" ("English Class").

Conclusion

    The word *tweet* has taken on an entirely new meaning since its   9
first known use in 1851 ("Tweet"). While a small bird's chirping sound
is still considered a tweet, the word is now used to describe a powerful tool that can help friends stay connected, make friendships, break
up friendships, and serve as an educational tool. While tweets are
sometimes used negatively, they are increasingly being used as positive tools. The word has come a long way since Bobby Day recorded
his "Rockin' Robin" classic, "Tweet, tweedle-lee-dee."

MLA
documentation

Works Cited

Bellis, Mary. "What Is Twitter? Who Invented It?" *About.com*, 19
    Jan. 2014, inventors.about.com/od/tstartinventions/a/Twitter.
    htm.

"English Class Includes Tweeting." *Epoch Times*. 26 Jan. 2014,
    www.theepochtimes.com/n3/471775-english-class-includes-
    tweeting.

Hockenberry, Craig. "The Origin of the Word *Tweet*." *Furbo*, 28 Jun.
    2013, furbo.org/2013/06/28/the-origin-of-tweet.

"Rockin' Robin." *YouTube*, 20 Mar. 2008, www.youtube.com/
    watch?v=DgUn8j5EYew.

Selden, Anthony. "Top 10 Celebrity Twitter Feuds." *Elite Daily*, 2 Apr.
    2012, elitedaily.com/category/life.

"Tweet." *Merriam-Webster Online Dictionary*, 2014, www.merriam-
    webster.com/dictionary/tweet.

Williams, Tiffany. Personal interview, 25 Jan. 2014.

Commentary

TITLE, INTRODUCTION, AND THESIS   Not long after receiving her essay assignment, Olivia decided that she wanted to write about how definitions of the word *tweet*
had changed over the years. She and her friends regularly posted tweets, and she was
curious about the origin of the word. As she thought about the word and its original
meaning, Michael Jackson's recording of "Rockin' Robin," with its chorus of "Tweet,
tweedle-lee-dee," came to mind. Then she discovered through an Internet search that
the song was first recorded by Bobby Day in 1958. As Olivia listened to the song on
YouTube and watched Day's performance, she understood why the song had been a
hit. The lyrics were catchy, and the song had a great beat.

As she began drafting her essay, Olivia already knew that she wanted to use words from the song as the title of her essay. As she was typing "Tweet, Tweedle-lee-dee" at the top of the page, she realized that by adding "(118 Characters Left)" to the title, she could provide readers with an additional hint regarding her essay's subject. Then as she began composing the introduction, Olivia decided to refer to the title of the song in her introductory paragraph as well. She thought that the title did a nice job of illustrating the original definition of *tweet* and would allow her to compare that early definition with the new one that she would define and explore in her essay. The reference to the title of the 1958 hit song led to the point she wanted to communicate in her thesis: "Since those days, *tweet* has morphed into a word whose meaning your great grandfather could have never imagined when he was listening to Day's hit on *Billboard*'s Hot 100." Although Olivia's introductory paragraph is brief, it does a nice job of engaging the reader and introducing the topic to be discussed.

ORGANIZATION Olivia organizes the body of her essay into three parts. First, she devotes paragraphs 2 and 3 to providing information about the new definition of the word *tweet*, circumstances that led to its creation, and a comparison of *Twitter* and *Facebook*. Next, in paragraphs 4 and 5, she discusses negative ways that tweets are used and gives an extended block quote to illustrate a negative example. Then in paragraphs 6–8, she focuses on positive ways tweets are being used in educational settings.

A definite organizational strategy determines the sequence of the three major sections of Olivia's essay, and the essay moves smoothly from one section to another. Olivia begins the first section with the topic sentence "Jack Dorsey's creation of a new social networking site called *Twitter* in March 2006 soon led to a new definition for the word *tweet*." She transitions to the second section of her essay with the topic sentence "In the days since Dorsey sent the first 'twit' in 2006, tweets have become more and more infamous," providing a clear message for her readers of what's to come. Then she moves from the second section to the third with the topic sentence "While used all too often to insult others, tweets can be used positively, especially in educational settings." Olivia does a nice job of providing smooth, clear topic sentences that also function as transitional statements for her readers as they navigate her essay.

COMBINING PATTERNS OF DEVELOPMENT In addition to *defining* the original meaning of *tweet*, along with the new, additional meaning, Olivia draws on several other patterns of development in her essay. She uses *causal analysis* in paragraph 2 to explain the circumstances that led to the need for a new word and its evolution from *twit* to *tweet*. She uses *comparison-contrast* in paragraph 3 as she compares Twitter with Facebook, contrasting the ways in which the two social networking sites are used. Olivia goes on to use *exemplification* as a pattern of development in paragraphs 4 to 8, as she provides examples of negative and positive ways in which tweets are used. This combination of various patterns of development allows her to explore not only the two definitions of the word *tweet* but also how the word came into being and how tweets can be both harmful and beneficial.

A WEAK EXAMPLE As you read Olivia's essay, you might have noticed that one example of the supposedly positive effects of tweeting in paragraph 6 is not the strongest or most effective example she might have chosen to include. She provides the example of a university scholarship competition where students' tweets appeared on a screen for everyone to see. The purpose of allowing the students to tweet during the competition is never made clear. Although some might assume that the purpose of allowing students to tweet at the scholarship competition was to help build a sense of camaraderie among the students, that idea is never stated. Moreover, Olivia describes how one student's misspelling of the word *scholarship* in his tweet was ridiculed in subsequent tweets. Though Olivia refers to one tweet as a "witty remark" that prompted other tweets "discussing the events of the 'scholaship' competition" (paragraph 6), many would consider the tweet making fun of a typo to be more thoughtless and inconsiderate than "witty." The essay would be stronger if this example were replaced with one that clearly demonstrates a positive effect of tweeting in educational settings.

CONCLUSION Olivia's *conclusion* rounds off the essay nicely and brings it to a satisfying close. In addition to restating her thesis, Olivia adds a new detail: The first known use of the word *tweet* was in 1851. This new detail lets her readers know that for more than 150 years, the only definition of *tweet* was the chirping sound of a small bird. She brings her essay full circle with her closing reference to words from "Rockin' Robin" that she used in her title: "Tweet, tweedle-lee-dee."

REVISING THE FIRST DRAFT As Olivia reread her first draft, she realized that she had some work to do. When writing that early draft, she did not have a clear organizational pattern in view. Her goal was to write down everything that came to mind that she might want to include in her essay and worry about matters of structure later. The introduction in that early draft included not only information about the original meaning of the word *tweet*, but also information about the founding of *Twitter* and the new, additional meaning of the word. Then in the second paragraph of the first draft, she had focused on the two definitions of the word. The first draft of that second paragraph is reprinted here:

> **Original Version of the Second Paragraph**
> The *Merriam-Webster* online dictionary offers two definitions of the word *tweet*: "Tweet: noun, 1. A chirping note. 2. A post made on the Twitter online message service" ("Tweet"). The online dictionary also notes that the first known use of the word *tweet* was used in 1851, so the first definition has actually been used for a much longer period of time than the modern definition. The word *tweet* used to have only one definition, however, and it was a very simple one. The only definition that it had before 2006 was a sharp chirping sound made by a small bird. One could hear it outside her window on a bright summer morning, on a walk down a trail in the woods, and some would say it was one of the most beautiful musical instruments of nature. It still is all of those things, but now "tweets" can be found other places. In fact, the most popular place they can be found today is in nature's archenemy—the Internet.

After allowing her first draft to sit for a couple of days, Olivia realized that her second paragraph was confusing and disordered. At the beginning of the paragraph she had focused on dictionary definitions that weren't really needed. In the first sentence of her essay, she had provided the original definition of the word, and so to include a dictionary definition from *Merriam-Webster* in the following paragraph was redundant. She also realized that in the last part of the first paragraph of her rough draft, she had provided the new, additional meaning of the word. As she looked closely at the rest of her second paragraph, she saw other places where she had repeated herself and made rambling comments. In fact, the only detail she thought worth saving in the entire paragraph was the one about the first known use of the word *tweet* in 1851. Olivia knew that her essay would be more effective if she cut the entire paragraph and saved the one interesting detail to include somewhere else.

After making that decision and taking time to think about the overall structure of her essay, Olivia decided to move information regarding the new definition of the word *tweet* and the events that led to its creation from the first paragraph to the second and third paragraphs. After revising the structure of her essay so that one section led logically to the next, Olivia continued to critically read her essay and to eliminate anything that was redundant or did not support the major points she was trying to communicate. For example, in her first draft, toward the end of the third paragraph in which she compares Twitter with Facebook, she had included the following sentences: "Going back to the original meaning of the word, a bird's *tweet* is short, sharp, and full of beautiful sound depending on who is listening. A *tweet* off of Twitter is short, to the point, and can be considered very creative, colorful, and powerful, depending on who the reader is." As she reread what she had written, Olivia realized that although the similarities between the original and new meanings of *tweet* were interesting, they had no place in the paragraph, so she cut them.

As Olivia revised her essay, she realized that her practice of writing down everything that came to mind that she might want to include in her essay was more like freewriting than drafting. Although the approach generated a lot of ideas, she still had the task of organizing her thoughts and identifying her main points. Then she had to be willing to look at her writing objectively and cut ideas that did not support her main points. She decided that thinking of her initial work as prewriting would make it easier for her to organize her ideas and cut unnecessary material.

Activities: Definition

Prewriting Activities

1. Imagine you're writing two essays. One explains an effective strategy for registering a complaint; the other contrasts the styles of two stand-up comics. Jot down ways you might use definition in each essay.

2. Use the prewriting questions for the patterns of development in this chapter to generate material for an extended definition of one of the following terms. Then answer

these questions about your prewriting material: What thesis does the prewriting suggest? Which pattern(s) yielded the most supporting material? In what order would you present this support when writing an essay?

a. popularity

b. cruelty

c. friendship

d. self-esteem

e. loneliness

3. Select a term whose meaning varies from person to person or one for which you have a personal definition. Some possibilities include:

success	femininity	a liberal
patriotism	affirmative action	a good marriage
individuality	pornography	intelligence

Brainstorm with others to identify variations in the term's meaning. Then examine your prewriting material. What thesis comes to mind? If you were writing an essay, would your purpose be informative, persuasive, or both? Finally, prepare a scratch list of the points you might cover.

Revising Activities

4. Explain why each of the following is an effective or ineffective definition. Rewrite those you consider ineffective.

a. *Passive aggression* is when people show their aggression passively.

b. A *terrorist* tries to terrorize people.

c. Being *assertive* means knowing how to express your wishes and goals in a positive, noncombative way.

d. *Loyalty* is when someone stays by another person during difficult times.

5. The following introductory paragraph is from the first draft of an essay contrasting walking and running as techniques for reducing tension. Although intended to be a definition paragraph, it doesn't tell us anything we don't already know. It also relies on the tired formula of referring to a dictionary. Rewrite the paragraph to make it more imaginative. You might use a series of anecdotes or one extended example to define *tension* and introduce the essay's thesis more gracefully.

> A dictionary will define *tension* as a kind of stress or strain, either mental or physical. Everyone feels tense at one time or another. It may occur when there's a deadline to meet. Or it could be caused by the stress of trying to fulfill academic, athletic, or social goals. Sometimes it comes from criticism by family, bosses, or teachers. Such tension puts wear and tear on our bodies and on our emotional well-being. Although some people run to relieve tension, research has found that walking is a more effective tension reducer.

Professional Selections: Definition

JHUMPA LAHIRI

Indian-American author Jhumpa Lahiri earned an M.A. in English, an M.F.A. in creative writing, an M.A. in comparative literature, and a Ph.D. in Renaissance studies. Her publications include her debut short-story collection, *Interpreter of Maladies* (1999); *The Namesake* (2003), made into a movie with the same title; *Unaccustomed Earth* (2008), a #1 *New York Times* best seller; and *Lowlands* (2013), nominated for the Man Booker Prize and the National Book Award for Fiction.

For ideas on how this definition essay is organized, see Figure 17.2.

Pre-Reading Journal Entry

In the following reading, Jhumpa Lahiri shares some of the challenges she faced growing up in the United States as the daughter of parents from India. For years she felt that she did not fit in at home with her parents who spoke Bengali or at school with her classmates who thought she had a strange name. Think of a time, perhaps from your childhood or perhaps more recently, when you felt you did not belong. Why did you feel that way? How did you cope with the situation? Explore these ideas in your journal.

My Two Lives

1   I have lived in the United States for almost 37 years and anticipate growing old in this country. Therefore, with the exception of my first two years in London, "Indian-American" has been a constant way to describe me. Less constant is my relationship to the term. When I was growing up in Rhode Island in the 1970s I felt neither Indian nor American. Like many immigrant offspring I felt intense pressure to be two things, loyal to the old world and fluent in the new, approved of on either side of the hyphen. Looking back, I see that this was generally the case. But my perception as a young girl was that I fell short at both ends, shuttling between two dimensions that had nothing to do with one another.

2   At home I followed the customs of my parents, speaking Bengali and eating rice and dal with my fingers. These ordinary facts seemed part of a secret, utterly alien way of life, and I took pains to hide them from my American friends. For my parents, home was not our house in Rhode Island but Calcutta, where they were raised. I was aware that the things they lived for—the Nazrul songs they listened to on the reel-to-reel, the family they missed, the clothes my mother wore that were not available in any store in any mall—were at once as precious and as worthless as an outmoded currency.

3   I also entered a world my parents had little knowledge or control of: school, books, music, television, things that seeped in and became a fundamental aspect of who I am. I spoke English without an accent, comprehending the language in a way my parents still do not. And yet there was evidence that I was not entirely American. In addition to my distinguishing name and looks, I did not attend Sunday school, did not know how to ice-skate, and disappeared to India for months at a time. Many of my friends proudly called themselves Irish-American or Italian-American. But they were several generations removed from the frequently humiliating process of immigration, so that the ethnic roots they claimed had

descended underground whereas mine were still tangled and green. According to my parents I was not American, nor would I ever be no matter how hard I tried. I felt doomed by their pronouncement, misunderstood and gradually defiant. In spite of the first lessons of arithmetic, one plus one did not equal two but zero, my conflicting selves always canceling each other out.

When I first started writing I was not conscious that my subject was the Indian-American experience. What drew me to my craft was the desire to force the two worlds I occupied to mingle on the page as I was not brave enough, or mature enough, to allow in life. My first book was published in 1999, and around then, on the cusp of a new century, the term "Indian-American" has become part of this country's vocabulary. I've heard it so often that these days, if asked about my background, I use the term myself, pleasantly surprised that I do not have to explain further. What a difference from my early life, when there was no such way to describe me, when the most I could do was to clumsily and ineffectually explain.   4

As I approach middle age, one plus one equals two, both in my work and in my daily existence. The traditions on either side of the hyphen dwell in me like siblings, still occasionally sparring, one outshining the other depending on the day. But like siblings they are intimately familiar with one another, forgiving and intertwined. When my husband and I were married five years ago in Calcutta we invited friends who had never been to India, and they came full of enthusiasm for a place I avoided talking about in my childhood, fearful of what people might say. Around non-Indian friends, I no longer feel compelled to hide the fact that I speak another language. I speak Bengali to my children, even though I lack the proficiency to teach them to read or write the language. As a child I sought perfection and so denied myself the claim to any identity. As an adult I accept that a bicultural upbringing is a rich but imperfect thing.   5

While I am American by virtue of the fact that I was raised in this country, I am Indian thanks to the efforts of two individuals. I feel Indian not because of the time I've spent in India or because of my genetic composition but rather because of my parents' steadfast presence in my life. They live three hours from my home; I speak to them daily and see them about once a month. Everything will change once they die. They will take certain things with them—conversations in another tongue, and perceptions about the difficulties of being foreign. Without them, the back-and-forth life my family leads, both literally and figuratively, will at last approach stillness. An anchor will drop, and a line of connection will be severed.   6

I have always believed that I lack the authority my parents bring to being Indian. But as long as they live they protect me from feeling like an impostor. Their passing will mark not only the loss of the people who created me but the loss of a singular way of life, a singular struggle. The immigrant's journey, no matter how ultimately rewarding, is founded on departure and deprivation, but it secures for the subsequent generation a sense of arrival and advantage. I can see a day coming when my American side, lacking the counterpoint India has until now maintained, begins to gain ascendancy and weight. It is in fiction that I will continue to interpret the term "Indian-American," calculating that shifting equation, whatever answers it may yield.   7

Figure 17.2 Essay Structure: "My Two Lives" by Jhumpa Lahiri

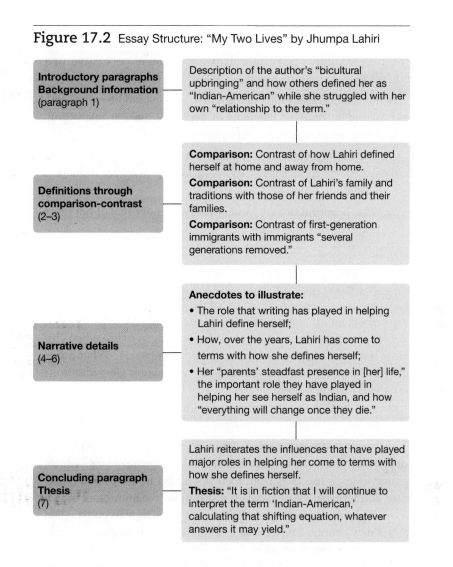

Introductory paragraphs Background information
(paragraph 1)

Description of the author's "bicultural upbringing" and how others defined her as "Indian-American" while she struggled with her own "relationship to the term."

Definitions through comparison-contrast
(2–3)

Comparison: Contrast of how Lahiri defined herself at home and away from home.

Comparison: Contrast of Lahiri's family and traditions with those of her friends and their families.

Comparison: Contrast of first-generation immigrants with immigrants "several generations removed."

Narrative details
(4–6)

Anecdotes to illustrate:
- The role that writing has played in helping Lahiri define herself;
- How, over the years, Lahiri has come to terms with how she defines herself;
- Her "parents' steadfast presence in [her] life," the important role they have played in helping her see herself as Indian, and how "everything will change once they die."

Concluding paragraph Thesis
(7)

Lahiri reiterates the influences that have played major roles in helping her come to terms with how she defines herself.

Thesis: "It is in fiction that I will continue to interpret the term 'Indian-American,' calculating that shifting equation, whatever answers it may yield."

Questions for Critical Reading

1. What is the selection's thesis? Locate the sentence(s) in which Lahiri states her main idea. If she doesn't state her thesis explicitly, express it in your own words.

2. As a child, Lahiri "felt neither Indian nor American." Why?

3. Lahiri is a highly respected writer who has won numerous awards. What "drew [her] to [her] craft"?

4. Lahiri states that she suspects her "American side" will "gain ascendancy and weight" as the years pass. Why does she think that will happen?

Questions About the Writer's Craft

1. **Purpose.** Is the purpose of Lahiri's essay informative, speculative, persuasive, or a combination of these? Explain your response.

2. **The pattern.** Lahiri's definition essay allows readers to understand how she came to terms with her own identity. What elements of her essay make it interesting, engaging, and relatable to readers who are not Indian-American?

3. **Other patterns.** Lahiri uses the comparison-contrast strategy at many points in her article. What purposes do the comparisons and contrasts serve in her definition essay?

4. **Imagery.** Lahiri includes beautiful imagery in her essay. Identify two of her most effective images and explain why you think they work well.

Writing Assignments Using Definition as a Pattern of Development

1. In her essay, Lahiri shares with readers her definition of self. Write an essay in which you define the way you see yourself. How did you see yourself when you were a child? How has your image of self changed over the years? What influences in your life contributed to the changes in your self-image? Consider your audience and how you can keep them interested and engaged in your writing. Also consider including photos in your essay to enrich your audience's reading experience.

2. In her essay, Lahiri describes "the immigrant's journey" as one that is "founded on departure and deprivation." Conduct research on a particular group of individuals who have emigrated in large numbers from their homeland to the United States or another country, and write an essay in which you define "the immigrant's journey" for that group of people. Why did they leave? How were they received when they arrived in their new country? What kind of support were they given as they worked to make a new home for themselves?

Writing Assignment Combining Patterns of Development

3. Lahiri's essay focuses on how her definition of self changed over the years. Write an essay in which you *narrate* the story of someone who emigrated from one country to another or of someone who grew up in a bicultural or multicultural setting. As you tell that person's story, be sure to include vivid *description* and *examples* of what life was like for that individual.

LAURA FRASER

Laura Fraser, born in 1961, is a San Francisco-based journalist and novelist whose work has appeared in a wide variety of publications, including *Food and Wine,* the *New York Times, Salon, Health,* the *Oprah Magazine,* and *Mother Jones.* She is the author of the *New York Times* bestseller *An Italian Affair* (2001) and, more recently, of *All Over the Map* (2010), a travel memoir and sequel to her bestseller. Much of her writing focuses on women's health issues, travel, and cultural aspects of food. The essay that follows, adapted from Fraser's first book, *Losing It: America's Obsession with Weight and the Industry That Feeds on It* (1997), appeared in the 2009 book *The Fat Studies Reader,* edited by Esther Rothblum and Sondra Solovay.

Pre-Reading Journal Entry

Our ideas of what we think beautiful people should look like are influenced to a large extent by the culture in which we live. How similar or dissimilar is your concept of beauty from what you see in movies, fashion, and advertisements? What factors have contributed to your sense of what the word *beauty* means? Explore these ideas in your journal.

The Inner Corset

Once upon a time, a man with a thick gold watch swaying from a big, round paunch was the very picture of American prosperity and vigor. Accordingly, a hundred years ago, a beautiful woman had plump cheeks and arms, and she wore a corset and even a bustle to emphasize her full, substantial hips. Women were *sexy* if they were heavy. In those days, Americans knew that a layer of fat was a sign that you could afford to eat well and that you stood a better chance of fighting off infectious diseases than most people. If you were a woman, having that extra adipose blanket also meant that you were probably fertile and warm to cuddle up next to on chilly nights.

Between the 1880s and 1920s, that pleasant image of fat thoroughly changed in the United States. Some began early on to hint that fat was a health risk. In 1894, Woods Hutchinson, a medical professor who wrote for women's magazines, defended fat against this new point of view. "Adipose," he wrote, "while often pictured as a veritable Frankenstein, born of and breeding disease, sure to ride its possessor to death sooner or later, is really a most harmless, healthful, innocent tissue" ("Fat and Its Follies"). Hutchinson reassured his *Cosmopolitan* readers that fat was not only benign, but also attractive, and that if a poll of beautiful women were taken in any city, there would be at least three times as many plump ones as slender ones. He advised them that no amount of starving or exercise—which were just becoming popular as means of weight control—would change more than 10 percent of a person's body size anyway. "The fat man tends to remain fat, the thin woman to stay thin—and both in perfect health—in spite of everything they can do," he said in that article.

But by 1926, Hutchinson, who was by then a past president of the American Academy of Medicine, had to defend fat against fashion, too, and he was showing signs of strain. "In this present onslaught upon one of the most peaceable, useful and law-abiding of all our tissues," he told readers of the *Saturday Evening Post,* "fashion has apparently the backing of grave physicians, of food reformers and

physical trainers, and even of great insurance companies, all chanting in unison the new commandment of fashion: 'Thou shalt be thin!'" ("Fat and Fashion").

Hutchinson mourned this trend, and was dismayed that young girls were 4 ridding themselves of their roundness and plumpness of figure. He tried to understand the new view that people took toward fat: "It is an outward and visible sign of an inward and spiritual disgrace, of laziness, of self-indulgence," he explained in that article, but he remained unconvinced. Instead, he longed for a more cheerful period in the not-so-distant past when a little fat never hurt anyone, and he darkly warned that some physicians were deliberately underfeeding girls and young women solely for the purpose of giving them a more svelte figure. "The longed-for slender and boyish figure is becoming a menace," Hutchinson wrote, "not only to the present, but also the future generations" ("Fat and Fashion").

The thin ideal that developed in the United States from the 1880s to 1920s can be traced through the evolution of three ideal types: the plump Victorian woman (*top left*), the athletic but curvaceous Gibson Girl (*top right*), and the boyishly straight-bodied flapper (*bottom*).

And so it would. But why did the fashion for plumpness change so dramati- 5
cally during those years? What happened that caused Americans to alter their
tastes, not only to admire thinner figures for a time, but for the next century, cul-
minating in fin de siècle extremes of thinness, where women's magazines in the
1990s would print ads featuring gaunt models side-by-side with photo essays on
anorexia?

Many things were happening at once, and with dizzying speed. Foremost was 6
a changing economy: In the late 1800s, for the first time, ample amounts of food
were available to more and more people who had to do less and less work to eat.
The agricultural economy, based on family farms and home workshops, shifted to
an industrial one. A huge influx of immigrants—many of them genetically shorter
and rounder than the earlier American settlers—fueled the industrial machine.
People moved to cities to do factory work and service jobs, stopped growing
their own food, and relied more on store-bought goods. Large companies began
to process food products, distribute them via railroads, and use refrigeration to
keep perishables fresh. Food became more accessible and convenient to all but the
poorest families. People who once had too little to eat now had plenty, and those
who had a tendency to put on weight began to do so. When it became possible
for people of modest means to become plump, being fat no longer was a sign of
prestige. Well-to-do Americans of northern European extraction wanted to be able
to distinguish themselves, physically and racially, from stockier immigrants. As
anthropologist Margaret Mackenzie notes, the status symbols flipped: it became
chic to be thin and all too ordinary to be overweight (qtd. in Mehren).

In this new environment, older cultural undercurrents suspicious of fat began 7
to surface. Europeans had long considered slenderness a sign of class distinction
and finer sensibilities, and Americans began to follow suit. In Europe, during the
late 18th and early 19th centuries, many artists and writers—the poets John Keats
and Percy Bysshe Shelley, and authors Emily Brontë, Edgar Allan Poe, and Anton
Chekhov—had tuberculosis, which made them sickly thin. Members of the upper
classes believed that having tuberculosis, and being slender itself, were signs that
one possessed a delicate, intellectual, and superior nature. "For snobs and par-
venus and social climbers, TB was the one index of being genteel, delicate, [and]
sensitive," writes essayist Susan Sontag in *Illness as Metaphor* (28). "It was glamorous to look sickly." So interested was the poet Lord Byron in looking as fashion-
ably ill as the other Romantic poets that he embarked on a series of obsessive
diets, consuming only biscuits and water, or vinegar and potatoes, and succeeded
in becoming quite thin. Byron—who, at five feet six inches tall, with a clubfoot
that prevented him from walking much, weighed over two hundred pounds in
his youth—disdained fat in others. "A woman," he wrote, "should never be seen
eating or drinking, unless it be *lobster salad* and *champagne*, the only truly feminine and becoming viands" (qtd. in Schwartz 38). Aristocratic European women,
thrilled with the romantic figure that Byron cut, took his diet advice and despaired
of appearing fat. Aristocratic Americans, trying to imitate Europeans, adopted
their enthusiasm for champagne and slenderness.

Americans believed that it was not only a sign of class to be thin, but also a 8
sign of morality. There was a long tradition in American culture that suggested
that indulging the body and its appetites was immoral, and that denying the flesh

was a sure way to become closer to God. Puritans such as the minister Cotton Mather frequently fasted to prove their worthiness and to cleanse themselves of their sins. Benjamin Franklin, in his *Poor Richard's Almanack*, chided his readers to eat lightly to please not only God, but also a new divinity, Reason: "Wouldst thou enjoy a long life, a healthy Body, and a Vigorous Mind, and be acquainted also with the wonderful works of God? Labour in the first place to bring thy Appetite into Subjection to Reason" (1738). Franklin's attitude toward food not only reveals a puritanical distrust of appetite as overly sensual, but also presaged diets that would attempt to bring eating in line with rational, scientific calculations. "The Difficulty lies, in finding out an exact Measure;" he wrote, "but eat for Necessity, not Pleasure, for Lust knows not where Necessity ends" (1738).

At the end of the 19th century, as Hutchinson observed, science was also help-   9
ing to shape the new slender ideal. Physicians came to believe that they were able to arrive at an exact measure of human beings; they could count calories, weigh people on scales, calculate "ideal" weights, and advise those who deviated from that ideal that they could change themselves. Physicians were both following and encouraging the trend for thinness. In the 1870s, after all, when plumpness was in vogue, physicians had encouraged people to *gain* weight. Two of the most distinguished doctors of the age, George Beard and S. Weir Mitchell, believed that excessive thinness caused American women to succumb to a wide variety of nervous disorders, and that a large number of fat cells was absolutely necessary to achieve a balanced personality (Banner 113). But when the plump figure fell from favor, physicians found new theories to support the new fashion. They hastily developed treatments—such as thyroid, arsenic, and strychnine—to prescribe to their increasing numbers of weight loss patients, many of whom were not exactly corpulent, but who were more than willing to part with their pennies along with their pounds.

As the 20th century got underway, other cultural changes made slenderness   10
seem desirable. When many women ventured out of their homes and away from their strict roles as mothers, they left behind the plump and reproductive physique, which began to seem old-fashioned next to a thinner, freer, more modern body. The new consumer culture encouraged the trend toward thinness with fashion illustrations and ads featuring slim models; advertisers learned early to offer women an unattainable dream of thinness and beauty to sell more products. In short, a cultural obsession with weight became firmly established in the United States when several disparate factors that favored a desire for thinness—economic status symbols, morality, medicine, modernity, changing women's roles, and consumerism—all collided at once.

Thinness is, at its heart, a peculiarly American preoccupation. Europeans ad-   11
mire slenderness, but without our Puritanism they have more relaxed and moderate attitudes about food, eating, and body size (the British are most like us in both being heavy and fixating on weight loss schemes). In countries where people do not have quite enough to eat, and where women remain in traditional roles, plumpness is still widely admired. Other westernized countries have developed a slender ideal, but for the most part they have imported it from the United States. No other culture suffers from the same wild anxieties about weight, dieting, and exercise as we do because they do not share our history.

The thin ideal that developed in the United States from the 1880s to 1920s was   12
not just a momentary shift in fashion; it was a monumental turning point in the
way that women's bodies were appraised by men and experienced by women. The
change can be traced through the evolution of three ideal types: the plump Victorian
woman, the athletic but curvaceous Gibson Girl, and the boyishly straight-bodied
flapper. By 1930, American women knew how very important it was for them to
be thin. From then on, despite moments when voluptuousness was admired again
(e.g., Marilyn Monroe), American women could never be too thin.

Works Cited

Banner, Lois. *American Beauty*. U of Chicago P, 1983.

Franklin, Benjamin. *The Complete Poor Richard Almanacks*, vol. 1, Imprint Society, 1970,
    pp. 1733–47.

Hutchinson, Woods. "Fat and Fashion." *Saturday Evening Post*, 21 Aug. 1926, p. 60.

——. "Fat and Its Follies." *Cosmopolitan*, June 1894, p. 395.

Mehren, Elizabeth. "Fear of Being Fat Is an Obsession, Anthropologist Says." *Ottawa Citizen*,
    2 Mar. 1984, p. 49.

Schwartz, Hillel. *Never Satisfied: A Cultural History of Diets, Fantasies, and Fat*. Free Press,
    1986.

Sontag, Susan. *Illness as Metaphor*. Farrar, Straus & Giroux, 1978.

Questions for Critical Reading

1. What is the selection's thesis? Locate the sentence(s) in which Fraser states her
   main idea. If she doesn't state the thesis explicitly, express it in your own words.

2. What information does Fraser include in her essay to explain the influence of
   tuberculosis on Americans' fixation on being thin?

3. How does Fraser explain the change in America's definition of what it means to
   be beautiful? What six factors does she consider responsible for America's switch
   from a preference for plumpness to a desire to look almost anorexic?

4. According to Fraser, how is America's attitude toward thinness different from the
   attitude in most of Europe? In what parts of the world is plumpness still admired?

Questions About the Writer's Craft

1. **Focus.** Why do you think Fraser chose to begin her essay by focusing on what
   many would consider to be overweight individuals? What might have been her
   purpose?

2. **Organization.** Look closely at the manner in which Fraser structures her essay.
   How would you describe the order in which she presents the factors she believes
   are responsible for America's current definition of beauty? Why might she have
   organized her essay this way?

3. **Multiple patterns.** Although Fraser's essay focuses on the change in America's
   definition of what it means to be beautiful, she also incorporates other organizational patterns. What other patterns does she make use of and how?

4. Tone. How would you describe Fraser's tone in this essay? Why do you think she chose to address readers in this way? Do the photos add to our understanding of Fraser's thesis, or are they unnecessary?

Writing Assignments Using Definition as a Pattern of Development

1. Fraser's essay explores the changing definition of what it means to be beautiful. Think of another term that is used to describe or label individuals—a term whose definition has changed over the past century. Write an essay in which you explore how the changing definition has affected the way individuals think about themselves and others as well as how they live their lives. For example, you might consider the changing definition of terms such as *educated, successful, middle-class, rich,* or *well-traveled.*

2. In her essay, Fraser mentions that ideas about what it means to be healthy have changed since the early 1900s. Write an essay in which you focus on the differences between what it meant to be healthy a century ago and what the term *healthy* means today. Consider using a variety of sources, ranging from personal interviews to published sources on the subject, along with charts or graphs that reference and support ideas and statistics in your essay.

Writing Assignment Combining Patterns of Development

3. Fraser's essay focuses on how and why the definition of beauty has changed. Write an essay in which you focus on the *effects* of the new definition. As you plan your essay about the effects of the pressure to be thin, consider *narrating* the stories of particular individuals and the lengths to which they have gone in an effort to lose weight.

KEITH JOHNSON

Keith Johnson, a staff reporter for the *Wall Street Journal* for more than a decade, has been based in both Europe and Washington, DC. Although he covers topics ranging from terrorism and homeland security to telecommunications, foreign affairs, and energy and the environment, his specialization is the geopolitics of energy. The following article was published in the *Wall Street Journal* on August 20, 2010.

Pre-Reading Journal Entry

Pirates have been romanticized in movies such as *Pirates of the Caribbean* and *The Sea Hawk* and in novels such as *Treasure Island*. Why do you think pirates are such glamorous figures? What other kinds of villains have been treated similarly? Do some freewriting in your journal on this subject.

Who's a Pirate? In Court, a Duel Over Definitions

Not since Lt. Robert Maynard of the Royal Navy sailed back triumphantly to nearby Hampton Roads in 1718 with the severed head of Blackbeard[1] swinging from his bowsprit has this Navy town been so embroiled in the fight against piracy.

Prosecuting pirates, rather than hanging them from the yardarm, is the modern world's approach to the scourge of Somali piracy that has turned huge swathes of the Indian Ocean into a no-go zone for commercial vessels.

But there's a problem: Some 2,000 years after Cicero[2] defined pirates as the "common enemy of all," nobody seems able to say, legally, exactly what a pirate is.

U.S. law long ago made piracy a crime but didn't define it. International law contains differing, even contradictory, definitions. The confusion threatens to hamstring U.S. efforts to crack down on modern-day Blackbeards.

The central issue in Norfolk: If you try to waylay and rob a ship at sea—but you don't succeed—are you still a pirate?

It may seem strange there should be doubt about an offense as old as this one. Piracy was the world's first crime with universal jurisdiction, meaning that any country had the right to apprehend pirates on the high seas.

The Romans took piracy so seriously they overrode a cautious Senate and gave near-dictatorial powers to an up-and-coming general named Pompey,[3] who soon swept away piracy in the Mediterranean.

In more recent centuries, European countries such as Britain cracked down on pirates—except when busy enlisting certain ones, dubbed "privateers," to help them fight their wars by raiding enemy ships.

Pirates even spurred the creation of the U.S. Navy, after Thomas Jefferson erupted over the cost of paying tribute to the Barbary Corsairs[4] for safe passage of U.S. merchant ships. At the time, the U.S. was paying about one-tenth of the federal budget to the pirates. Supplied with warships, President Jefferson waged war on the Barbary pirates (whence the line "to the shores of Tripoli" in the Marines' Hymn). By 1815, the North African pirate kingdoms had been subdued.

When Congress dealt with piracy in a statute four years later, the crime was so easy to recognize that legislators didn't bother to describe it, just the punishment. The 1819 statute that made piracy a capital offense (since changed to mandatory life in prison) simply deferred to "the law of nations." That legal punt has kept American jurists scrambling ever since.

The stage was set for the Norfolk trial on April 10 of this year [2010] when the USS Ashland, cruising in the Gulf of Aden about 330 miles off Djibouti, was fired upon at 5 a.m. by Somali men in a small skiff. The Navy vessel, an amphibious dock landing ship, returned fire with 25-mm cannon, wrecking the 18-foot skiff and sending its six occupants overboard.

---

[1] Blackbeard is the pseudonym of an infamous British pirate who operated off the Eastern Coast of the United States (editors' note).

[2] Cicero (106–43 B.C.E) was a philosopher and statesman in ancient Rome (editors' note).

[3] Pompey (106–48 B.C.E) was a statesman and great military leader in ancient Rome (editors' note).

[4] The Barbary Corsairs were Muslim pirates or privateers who operated out of North Africa (editors' note).

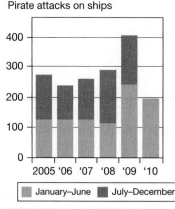

Avast!

Pirate attacks on ships

SOURCE: ICC International Maritime Bureau

The Ashland sent a search boat to recover the Somalis and photograph the smoking hulk of the skiff, which contained at least one weapon and what looked like a grappling hook or anchor. Though that boat was blasted to pieces, even when pirate skiffs survive, the ships they target are often loath to bring the skiffs aboard. One captured by a Navy force in 2006, according to the judge advocate's testimony in a subsequent trial in Kenya, was crawling with "roaches the size of leopards." 12

In Norfolk, the prosecution has begun its effort to convince the U.S. District Court for the Eastern District of Virginia that the quickly foiled Somalis are guilty not just of lesser charges they face but of the main charge of piracy. 13

"Violent attacks on the high seas without lawful authority have always been piracy under the law of nations, in 1819 and today," said the lead prosecutor, Benjamin Hatch, at a pretrial hearing last month [July 2010]. 14

"So if one ship fires a bow-and-arrow," asked Judge Raymond Jackson, rubbing his brow, "or a slingshot, or a rock, those are all acts of violence, and thus piracy?" The prosecutor nodded. 15

The public defender, Geremy Kamens, weighed in. "That a slingshot fired upon another ship would expose the defendant to a mandatory life sentence shows the absurd result of this reading," he said. The defense added that under this broad definition, Greenpeace[5] activists could be considered pirates for their anti-whaling antics on the seas. 16

The defense lawyers trawled through history books, coming to rest upon an obscure 1820 Supreme Court ruling. 17

"We have, therefore, no hesitation in declaring that piracy, by the law of nations, is robbery upon the sea," Justice Joseph Story wrote for the majority in the case of United States v. Smith. 18

That gave the defense lawyers their main argument: Piracy is robbery on the high seas; it isn't merely attempted robbery at sea, which is covered by a separate statute that the Somalis are charged with as well. 19

---

[5] Greenpeace, an activist environmental organization, is known for putting its ships between "whales and harpoons," as its website notes, on the high seas to deter whaling (editors' note).

Since the attack on the Ashland clearly failed, it wasn't piracy, the defense 20
argues, and therefore, the most serious charge should be dropped.

But the prosecutors, too, have probed early sources—17th-century Dutch 21
jurists, 18th-century British writers, 19th-century maritime cases, an 1800 speech
by then-congressman John Marshall, and a slew of international treaties.

The prosecution has leaned heavily on a 1934 ruling by Britain's Privy Coun- 22
cil,[6] which pondered the case of a similarly failed attack at sea, near Hong Kong.
In that case, the jury found the defendants guilty, but said its verdict was subject to
the question of whether it's really piracy if no actual robbery occurs. The court in
Hong Kong said it isn't, and acquitted the attackers.

The Privy Council members, however, after hacking through thickets of legal 23
technicalities, ultimately reached a different conclusion. "Actual robbery is not an
essential element in the crime of piracy," they said; "A frustrated attempt to commit
piratical robbery is equally piracy."

They added, with more than a hint of exasperation: "Their Lordships are 24
almost tempted to say that a little common sense is a valuable quality in the interpretation of international law."

Beyond the legal wrangling and obscure historical references, the implications 25
of the case in Norfolk are serious. Piracy's golden age may have passed two centuries ago, but it remains a scourge in places like the Strait of Malacca in Indonesia

Troubled Waters

Attacks on ships in the first half of 2010, by region

- Boarding or hijacking
- Failed attack

AFRICA: 114
EAST: Gulf of Aden, Red Sea, Somalia, Tanzania

WEST: Cameroon, Congo, Republic of Congo, Guinea, Ivory Coast, Liberia, Nigeria

SOUTHEAST ASIA: 30
Indonesia, Malacca Straits, Malaysia, Philippines, Singapore Straits, Thailand

FAR EAST: 23
China, Vietnam

AMERICAS: 15
Colombia, Ecuador, Guyana, Haiti, Peru, Venezuela

INDIAN SUBCONTINENT: 12
Bangladesh, India

ARABIAN SEA: 2

Source: ICC International Maritime Bureau

---

[6] The Privy Council, formerly very powerful, is a group of advisors to the British sovereign (editors' note).

and Malaysia, off the coast of Nigeria, and above all off the east coast of Africa, where the disintegration of Somalia has led to a major resurgence.

The first half of 2010 saw about 200 raids and unsuccessful attacks on ships at sea worldwide, the bulk of them off Somalia. In early August, two cargo ships were hijacked. In all, an estimated 18 ships and their crews are currently [as of August 2010] being held for ransom. 26

To fight the problem, the U.S. and the United Nations are counting on prosecuting pirates. Some U.N. officials dream of establishing an international piracy tribunal, similar to the one for war crimes in The Hague. 27

In the meantime, the U.S. and other countries have helped Kenya, the closest stable country to the source, to put scores of pirates on trial. But Kenyan law is cumbersome, requiring witnesses to testify on three separate occasions, a tough order logistically for merchant sailors. The European Union is now trying to jump–start Kenya's pirate prosecutions—the first sentence will come later this month—but progress is slow. 28

As a result, attackers captured by European warships in the Indian Ocean often are let go for lack of any real legal recourse. A Spanish warship caught seven Somali pirates red-handed in early August, men who had been trying to waylay a Norwegian chemical tanker. The Spanish frigate immediately released them because it would have been difficult to prosecute them, the EU naval force off Somalia said. 29

That leaves courtrooms like the one in Norfolk as among the best hopes for bringing pirates to justice and deterring future ones. But even seemingly clear-cut cases don't necessarily pass muster in court. 30

After a celebrated incident in April 2009, when U.S. Navy Seals snipers killed three Somali men holding an American captain hostage on a small boat after a raid, rescuing him, the lone Somali survivor of that attack on the Maersk Alabama pleaded guilty to lesser charges in New York, not to piracy. 31

Indeed, the last U.S. piracy conviction was in 1861, of a Confederate blockade runner. 32

Now the court in Norfolk must contend with the defense motion to dismiss the piracy charge, which would leave only such lesser charges as attempted plunder. 33

The prosecution argues that U.S. courts should defer to international law, especially a 1982 U.N. Law of the Sea treaty the U.S. never ratified. Aping the 1958 Geneva Convention,[7] it offers an expansive definition of piracy as any illegal acts of violence, detention or depredation committed for private ends on the high seas. 34

Defense lawyers balk at that suggestion. "We do not interpret U.S. law based on U.N. resolutions, but rather what Congress meant at the time," says the public defender, Mr. Kamens. 35

Judge Jackson is expected to rule soon.[8] 36

---

[7] The Geneva Convention of April 29, 1958, sets forth internationally agreed-upon rules for conduct on the high seas—for example, fishing rights (editors' note).

[8] The Norfolk court ultimately ruled against trying the men on the charge of piracy.

Questions for Critical Reading

1. What is the selection's thesis? Locate the sentence(s) in which Johnson states his main idea. If he doesn't state his thesis explicitly, express it in your own words.

2. What, according to the author, is the essential issue with defining *piracy*? What does the author have to say about the history of piracy before this century?

3. What were the prosecution's arguments in favor of trying the defendants for piracy? What arguments did the defense put forth?

4. Two graphs accompany the article. What information do the graphs supply? How do they support Johnson's point that it is important to resolve the definition of piracy at this time?

Questions About the Writer's Craft

1. **The definition.** What are the term, class, and characteristics involved in the definition of *piracy*? In what way does the selection focus on definition by negation?

2. **Tone and purpose.** Does the author intend to inform, entertain, or persuade the reader? What is the selection's tone? Is it suitable to his purpose? How are the two graphs relevant, or not relevant, to the author's purpose?

3. **Introduction.** What historical anecdote does Johnson use to open his article? What is the effect of this opening? Describe the two current-day piracy anecdotes, besides that of the Norfolk trial, that the author relates.

4. **Language.** The author refers to a number of legal rulings and often gives technical terms for parts of ships. What language techniques does he use to keep the selection interesting and accessible to the average reader? Give some examples.

Writing Assignments Using Definition as a Pattern of Development

1. The Geneva Convention sets forth rules for treating noncombatants during wartime. One major controversy today concerns how to treat captured terrorists. Do some research, and write an essay in which you define *terrorism*. In your definition include your view of whether a non-U.S. citizen on trial for terrorism should be treated as a civilian or an enemy combatant. Consider including graphs or charts that support your main points.

2. *Piracy* has come to mean acts such as downloading music from the Internet without permission, knocking off designer handbags, or bootlegging copies of movies. Write an essay in which you establish a definition of *piracy* that focuses on these kinds of acts. Decide whether these acts should be considered theft.

Writing Assignment Combining Patterns of Development

3. Should crimes against humanity have universal jurisdiction, as piracy does? For example, in 1998 the Chilean dictator Augusto Pinochet was indicted by a magistrate in Spain for human rights violations committed in Chile. He was arrested in London but then ultimately released and allowed to return to Chile. Do some research on how human rights crimes are prosecuted internationally. Write an essay in which you *describe* and *compare* the possibilities for prosecution of human rights violations.

Additional Writing Topics: Definition

General Assignments

Using definition, develop one of these topics into an essay.

1. Fads	6. Inner peace	11. Exploitation
2. Helplessness	7. Obsession	12. A no-win situation
3. An epiphany	8. Generosity	13. A conflict of interest
4. A workaholic	9. Depression	14. An ethical quandary
5. A Pollyanna	10. Greed	15. A win-win situation

Assignments Using Multimedia

Use the suggested media to help develop a definition essay on one of these topics:

1. Masculinity and how it is presented in ads (photos or weblinks to ads)
2. Discrimination in the United States today (charts or graphs)
3. Various definitions of *success* and which one most resonates with you (photos)
4. What it means to be middle class (graphs or charts)
5. New technologies over the past 500 years (photos and weblinks)

Assignments with a Specific Purpose, Audience, and Point of View

1. **Academic life.** You've been asked to write part of a pamphlet for students who come to the college health clinic. For this pamphlet, define one of the following conditions and its symptoms: *depression, stress, burnout, test anxiety, addiction* (to alcohol, drugs, video games, online gambling, or TV), *workaholism.* Part of the pamphlet should describe ways to cope with the condition described.

2. **Academic life.** One of your responsibilities as a peer counselor in the student counseling center involves helping students communicate more effectively. To assist students, write a definition of some term that you think represents an essential component of a strong interpersonal relationship. You might, for example, define *respect, sharing, equality,* or *trust.* Part of the definition should employ definition by negation, a discussion of what the term is *not.*

3. **Civic activity.** Some magazines run columns consisting of readers' opinions on subjects of general interest. Write a piece for this column defining *today's college students.* Use the piece to dispel some negative stereotypes (for example, that college students are apathetic, ill-informed, self-centered, and materialistic).

4. **Civic activity.** In your apartment building, several residents have complained about their neighbors' inconsiderate and rude behavior. You're president of the residents' association, and it's your responsibility to address this problem at your next meeting. Prepare a talk in which you define *courtesy,* the quality you consider most essential to neighborly relations. Use specific examples of what courtesy is and isn't to illustrate your definition.

5. **Workplace action.** You're an attorney arguing a case of sexual harassment—a charge your client has leveled against an employer. To win the case, you must present to the jury a clear definition of exactly what *sexual harassment* is and isn't. Write such a definition for your opening remarks in court.

6. **Workplace action.** A new position has opened in your company. Write a job description to be sent to employment agencies that will screen candidates. Your description should define the job's purpose, state the duties involved, and outline essential qualifications.

Chapter 18

Argumentation-Persuasion

Learning Objectives

18.1 Understand how you can use the argumentation-persuasion pattern to develop your essays.

18.2 Consider how argumentation-persuasion and an understanding of logos, pathos, and ethos can fit your purpose and audience.

18.3 Develop prewriting strategies for using argumentation-persuasion in an essay.

18.4 Develop strategies for writing an argumentation-persuasion essay.

18.5 Use strategies for revising your argumentation-persuasion essay.

18.6 Analyze how argumentation-persuasion is used effectively in a student-written selection.

What Is Argumentation-Persuasion?

18.1 Understand how you can use the argumentation-persuasion pattern to develop your essays.

"You can't possibly believe what you're saying."

"Look, I know what I'm talking about, and that's that."

This heated exchange probably sounds familiar. When we hear the word *argument*, most of us think of a verbal battle propelled by stubbornness and irrational thought, with one person pitted against the other.

Argumentation in writing is a different matter. Using clear thinking and logic, the writer of an argumentation essay tries to convince readers of the soundness of a particular opinion on a controversial issue. If, while trying to convince, the writer uses emotional language and dramatic appeals to readers' concerns, beliefs, and values, then the essay falls into the category called **persuasion**. Besides encouraging acceptance of an opinion, persuasion often urges readers (or another group) to commit themselves to a course of action.

Because people respond rationally *and* emotionally to situations, argumentation and persuasion are usually *combined*. When argumentation and persuasion blend in this way, emotion *supports* rather than *replaces* logic and sound reasoning. Although some writers resort to emotional appeals to the exclusion of rational thought, when you prepare argumentation-persuasion essays, you should advance your position through a balanced appeal to reason and emotion.

How Argumentation-Persuasion Fits Your Purpose and Audience

18.2 Consider how argumentation-persuasion and an understanding of logos, pathos, and ethos can fit your purpose and audience.

You probably realize that argumentation, persuasion, or a combination of the two is everywhere: an editorial urging the overhaul of an ill-managed literacy program, a commercial for a new shampoo, a scientific report advocating increased funding for AIDS research. Your own writing involves argumentation-persuasion as well. When you prepare a *causal analysis, descriptive piece, narrative,* or *definition essay,* you advance a specific point of view. For example:

Television has a negative influence on teens' view of sex.

Cape Cod in winter is imbued with a special kind of magic.

A disillusioning experience can teach people much about themselves.

Character can be defined as the willingness to take unpopular positions on difficult issues.

Indeed, an essay organized around any of the patterns of development described in this book may have a persuasive intent. You might, for example, encourage readers to try out a *process* you've explained, or to see one of the two movies you've *compared*.

However, argumentation-persuasion involves more than presenting a point of view and providing evidence. Unlike other forms of writing, it assumes controversy and addresses opposing viewpoints. Consider the following assignments, which require the writer to take a position on a controversial issue:

> Citing the fact that the highest percentage of automobile accidents involve young men, insurance companies consistently charge their highest rates to young males. Is this practice fair? Why or why not?

> Some colleges and universities have instituted a "no pass, no play" policy for athletes. Explain why this policy is or is not appropriate.

It's impossible to predict with absolute certainty what will make readers accept the view you advance or take the action you propose. But the ancient Greeks, who formulated our basic concepts of logic, isolated three factors crucial to the effectiveness of argumentation-persuasion: *logos*, *pathos*, and *ethos*.

Logos, or Soundness of the Argument

Your main concern in an argumentation-persuasion essay should be with the *logos*, or **soundness**, of your argument: the facts, statistics, examples, and authoritative statements you gather to support your viewpoint. This supporting evidence must be unified, specific, sufficient, accurate, and representative. Imagine, for instance, that you want to convince people that a popular charity misappropriates money it receives from the public. Your readers, inclined to believe in the good works of the charity, will probably dismiss your argument unless you can prove your claim with valid, well-documented evidence that enhances the logos of your position.

Pathos, or the Emotional Power of Language

Sensitivity to the *pathos*, or the **emotional power of language**, is another key consideration for writers of argumentation-persuasion essays. Pathos appeals to readers' needs, values, and attitudes, encouraging them to commit themselves to a viewpoint or course of action. The pathos of a piece derives partly from the writer's language. *Connotative* language—words with strong emotional overtones—can move readers to accept a point of view and may even spur them to act.

Advertising and propaganda generally rely on *pathos* to the exclusion of logic, using emotion to influence and manipulate. Consider the following pitches for a man's cologne and a woman's perfume. The language—and the attitudes to which it appeals—is different in each case:

> Brawn: Experience the power. Bold. Yet subtle. Clean. Masculine. The scent for the man who's in charge.

Black Lace is for you—the woman who dresses for success but who dares to be provocative, slightly naughty. Black Lace. Perfect with pearls by day and with diamonds by night.

The appeal to men plays on the impact that the words *Brawn, bold, power*, and *in charge* may have for some men. Similarly, the charged words *Black Lace, provocative, naughty*, and *diamonds* are intended to appeal to business women who—in the advertiser's mind, at least—may be looking for ways to reconcile sensuality and professionalism.

Like an advertising copywriter, you must select language that reinforces your message. In an essay supporting an expanded immigration policy, you might use evocative phrases such as "land of liberty," "a nation of immigrants," and "America's open-door policy." However, if you were arguing for strict immigration quotas, you might use language such as "save jobs for unemployed Americans," "flood of unskilled labor," and "illegal aliens." Remember, though: Such language should *support, not supplant*, clear thinking.

Ethos, or Credibility and Reliability

Finally, whenever you write an argumentation-persuasion essay, you should establish your *ethos*, or **credibility** and **reliability**. You cannot expect readers to accept or act on your viewpoint unless you convince them that you know what you're talking about and that you're worth listening to. You will come across as knowledgeable and trustworthy if you present a logical, reasoned argument that takes opposing views into account. Make sure, too, that your appeals to emotion aren't excessive. Overwrought emotionalism undercuts credibility.

Analyzing Your Audience

An effective argumentation-persuasion essay involves an interplay of logos, pathos, and ethos. The exact balance among these factors is determined by your audience and purpose (that is, whether you want the audience simply to agree with your view or whether you also want them to take action). More than any other kind of writing, argumentation-persuasion requires that you *analyze your readers* and tailor your approach to them. You need to determine how much they know about the issue, how they feel about you and your position, what their values and attitudes are, what motivates them.

In general, most readers will fall into one of three broad categories: supportive, wavering, or hostile. Each type of audience requires a different blend of logos, pathos, and ethos.

1. **A supportive audience.** If your audience agrees with your position and trusts your credibility, you don't need a highly reasoned argument dense with facts, examples, and statistics. Although you may want to solidify support by providing additional information (logos), you can rely primarily on pathos—a strong emotional appeal—to reinforce readers' commitment to your shared viewpoint.

2. **A wavering audience.** At times, readers may be interested in what you have to say but may not be committed fully to your viewpoint. Or perhaps they're not as informed about the subject as they want to be. In either case, because your readers need to be encouraged to give their complete support, you don't want to risk alienating them with a heavy-handed emotional appeal. Concentrate instead on ethos and logos, bolstering your image as a reliable source and providing the evidence needed to advance your position.

3. **A hostile audience.** An apathetic, skeptical, or hostile audience is obviously most difficult to convince. With such an audience you should avoid emotional appeals because they might seem irrational, sentimental, or even comical. Instead, weigh the essay heavily in favor of logical reasoning and hard-to-dispute facts (logos). Readers may not be won over to your side, but your sound, logical argument may encourage them to be more tolerant of your viewpoint. Indeed, such increased receptivity may be all you can reasonably expect from a hostile audience. (*Note:* The checklists in this chapter provide additional guidelines for analyzing your audience.)

Prewriting Strategies

18.3 Develop prewriting strategies for using argumentation-persuasion in an essay.

The following checklist shows how you can apply prewriting strategies to argumentation-persuasion.

☑ Argumentation-Persuasion: A Prewriting Checklist

Choose a Controversial Issue

☐ What issue do you feel strongly about? With what issues are your journal entries concerned? What issues discussed in recent newspaper, television, magazine, or website reports have piqued your interest?

☐ What is your view on the issue?

Determine Your Purpose, Audience, Tone, and Point of View

☐ Is your purpose limited to convincing readers to adopt your viewpoint, or do you also hope to spur them to action?

☐ Who is your audience? How much do your readers already know about the issue? Are they best characterized as supportive, wavering, or hostile? What values and needs may motivate readers to be responsive to your position?

☐ What tone is most likely to increase readers' commitment to your point of view? Should you convey strong emotion or cool objectivity?

☐ What point of view is most likely to enhance your credibility?

Use Prewriting to Generate Supporting Evidence

☐ How might brainstorming, journal entries, freewriting, or mapping help you identify personal experiences, observations, and examples to support your viewpoint?

☐ How might the various patterns of development help you generate supporting material? What aspects of the issue can you describe? Narrate? Illustrate? Compare and contrast? Analyze in terms of process or cause-effect? Define or categorize in some especially revealing way?

☐ How might interviews or other sources help you uncover relevant examples, facts, statistics, expert opinion?

Strategies for Using Argumentation-Persuasion in an Essay

18.4 Develop strategies for writing an argumentation-persuasion essay.

After prewriting, you're ready to draft your essay. Figure 18.1 and the suggestions that follow will help you prepare a convincing and logical argument.

1. **At the beginning of the composition, identify the controversy surrounding the issue and state your position.**

    Your introduction should clarify the controversy about the issue. In addition, it should provide as much background information as your readers are likely to need.

    The thesis of an argumentation-persuasion essay is often called the **assertion** or **proposition**. Occasionally, the proposition appears at the essay's end, but it is usually stated at the beginning. If you state the thesis right away, your audience knows where you stand and is better able to evaluate the evidence presented.

    Remember: Argumentation-persuasion assumes conflicting viewpoints. Be sure that your proposition focuses on a controversial issue and indicates your view. Avoid a proposition that is merely factual; what is demonstrably true allows little room for debate. To see the difference between a factual statement and an effective thesis, examine the two statements that follow.

    Fact
    In the past few years, the nation's small farmers have suffered financial hardships.

    Thesis
    Inefficient management, rather than competition from agricultural conglomerates, is responsible for the financial plight of the nation's small farmers.

    The first statement is certainly true. It would be difficult to find anyone who believes that these are easy times for small farmers. Because the statement invites little opposition, it can't serve as the focus of an argumentation-persuasion essay.

Figure 18.1 Development Diagram: Writing an Argumentation-Persuasion Essay

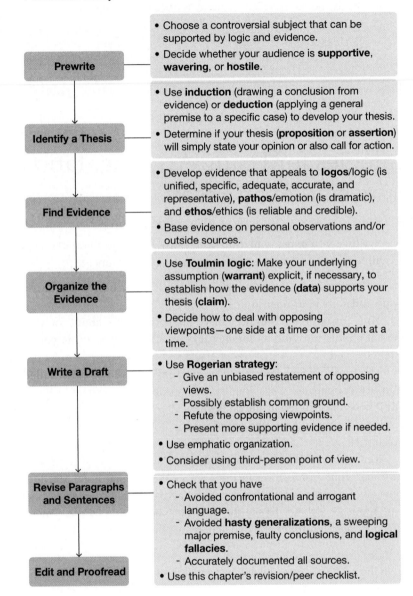

Prewrite	• Choose a controversial subject that can be supported by logic and evidence. • Decide whether your audience is **supportive**, **wavering**, or **hostile**.
Identify a Thesis	• Use **induction** (drawing a conclusion from evidence) or **deduction** (applying a general premise to a specific case) to develop your thesis. • Determine if your thesis (**proposition** or **assertion**) will simply state your opinion or also call for action.
Find Evidence	• Develop evidence that appeals to **logos**/logic (is unified, specific, adequate, accurate, and representative), **pathos**/emotion (is dramatic), and **ethos**/ethics (is reliable and credible). • Base evidence on personal observations and/or outside sources.
Organize the Evidence	• Use **Toulmin logic**: Make your underlying assumption (**warrant**) explicit, if necessary, to establish how the evidence (**data**) supports your thesis (**claim**). • Decide how to deal with opposing viewpoints—one side at a time or one point at a time.

Write a Draft	• Use **Rogerian strategy**:
	  – Give an unbiased restatement of opposing views.
	  – Possibly establish common ground.
	  – Refute the opposing viewpoints.
	  – Present more supporting evidence if needed.
	• Use emphatic organization.
	• Consider using third-person point of view.

Revise Paragraphs and Sentences	• Check that you have
	  – Avoided confrontational and arrogant language.
	  – Avoided **hasty generalizations**, a sweeping major premise, faulty conclusions, and **logical fallacies**.
	  – Accurately documented all sources.
	• Use this chapter's revision/peer checklist.

Edit and Proofread	

The second statement, though, takes a controversial stance on a complex issue. Such a proposition is a valid starting point for a composition intended to argue and persuade. However, don't assume that this advice means that you should take a highly opinionated position in your thesis. A dogmatic, overstated proposition ("Campus security is staffed by overpaid, badge-flashing incompetents") is bound to alienate some readers.

Remember also to keep the proposition narrow and specific, so that you can focus your thoughts in a purposeful way. Consider the following statements:

Broad Thesis
The welfare system has been abused over the years.

Narrowed Thesis
Welfare payments should be denied to unmarried mothers under the age of eighteen.

If you tried to write an essay based on the first statement, you would face an unmanageable task—showing all the ways that welfare has been abused. Your readers would also be confused about what to expect in the essay: Will it discuss unscrupulous bureaucrats, fraudulent bookkeeping, dishonest recipients? In contrast, the revised thesis is *limited and specific*. It signals that the essay will propose severe restrictions. Such a proposal will surely have opponents and is thus appropriate for argumentation-persuasion.

The thesis in an argumentation-persuasion essay can simply state your opinion about an issue, or it can go a step further and call for some action:

Opinion
The lack of affordable daycare centers discriminates against low-income families.

Call for Action
The federal government should support the creation of more daycare centers in low-income neighborhoods.

In either case, your stand on the issue must be clear to your readers.

2. **Offer readers strong support for your thesis.**
   Finding evidence that relates to your readers' needs, values, and experience is a crucial part of writing an argumentation-persuasion essay. Readers will be responsive to evidence that is *unified, adequate, specific, accurate, dramatic,* and *representative*. The evidence might consist of personal experiences or observations. Or it could be gathered from outside sources—statistics, facts, examples, or expert opinion taken from books, articles, reports, interviews, and documentaries. An essay arguing that elderly Americans are better off than they used to be might incorporate the following kinds of evidence:

- **Personal observation or experience:** A description of the writer's grandparents, who are living comfortably on Social Security and pensions.
- **Statistics from a report:** A statement that the per-capita after-tax income of older Americans is $335 greater than the national average.
- **Fact from a newspaper article:** The point that the majority of elderly Americans do not live in nursing homes or on the streets; rather, they have their own houses or apartments.

- **Examples from interviews:** Accounts of several elderly couples living comfortably in well-managed retirement villages in Florida.
- **Expert opinion cited in a documentary:** A statement by Dr. Marie Sanchez, a specialist in geriatrics: "An over-65 American today is likely to be healthier, and have a longer life expectancy, than a 50-year-old living only a decade ago."

3. **Choose the best point of view.**

You may wonder whether to use the *first-person (I)* or *third-person (he, she, they)* point of view when presenting evidence based on personal observation, experience, or interviews. While the first-person point of view often delivers a jolt of persuasive power, many writers prefer to present personal evidence in an objective way, using the third person to keep the focus on the issue rather than on themselves. When you write an argumentation-persuasion essay, your purpose, audience, and tone will help you decide which point of view will be most effective. If you're not sure which point of view to use, check with your instructor. Some encourage a first-person approach; others expect a more objective stance.

4. **Carefully evaluate sources and opposing arguments.**

As you seek outside evidence, you may—perhaps to your dismay—come across information that undercuts your argument. Resist the temptation to ignore such material. Instead, use the evidence to arrive at a more balanced, perhaps somewhat qualified viewpoint. Conversely, don't blindly accept or disregard flaws in the arguments made by sources agreeing with you. Retain a healthy skepticism, analyzing the material as rigorously as if it were advanced by the opposing side.

Also, keep in mind that outside sources aren't infallible. They may have biases that cause them to skew evidence. So be sure to evaluate your sources. Remember, too, that there are more than two sides to a complex issue. To get as broad a perspective as possible, you should track down sources that make a deliberate effort to examine all sides of the issue.

Whatever sources you use, be sure to *document* (give credit to) that material. Otherwise, readers may dismiss your evidence as nothing more than your opinion, or they may conclude that you have *plagiarized*—tried to pass off someone else's ideas as your own. (Documentation isn't necessary when material is commonly known or is a matter of historical or scientific record.)

5. **Seek to create goodwill.**

Because your goal is to convince others of your position's soundness, you need to be careful about alienating readers—especially those who don't agree with you. Be careful, then, about using close-minded, morally superior language ("*Anyone* can see that..."). Exaggerated, overly emotional language can also antagonize readers, as can confrontational language: "*My opponents* find the existing laws more effective than the proposed legislation" sounds adversarial, whereas "*Opponents* of the proposed legislation...," "*Those opposed* to the proposed legislation...," and "*Supporters* of the existing laws...," seem more evenhanded and respectful. The last three statements also focus—as they should—on the issue, not on the people involved in the debate.

Goodwill can also be established by finding a *common ground*—some points on which all sides can agree, despite their differences.

6. **Organize the supporting evidence.**

The support for an argumentation-persuasion essay can be organized in a variety of ways. Any of the patterns of development described in this book (description, narration, definition, cause-effect, and so on) may be used—singly or in combination—to develop the essay's proposition. Imagine you're writing an essay arguing that car racing should be banned from television. Your essay might contain a *description* of a horrifying accident that was televised in graphic detail; you might devote part of the essay to a *causal analysis* showing that the broadcast of such races encourages teens to drive carelessly; you could include a *process analysis* to explain how young drivers soup up their cars in a dangerous attempt to imitate the racers seen on television. If your essay includes several patterns, you may need a separate paragraph for each.

When presenting evidence, arrange it so you create the strongest possible effect. In general, you should end with your most compelling point, leaving readers with dramatic evidence that underscores your proposition's validity.

7. **Use Rogerian strategy to acknowledge differing viewpoints.**

If your essay has a clear thesis and strong, logical support, you've taken important steps toward winning readers over. However, because argumentation-persuasion focuses on controversial issues, you should also take opposing views into account. As you think about and perhaps research your subject, seek out conflicting viewpoints. A good argument seeks out contrary viewpoints, acknowledges them, and perhaps even admits that they have some merit. Such a strategy strengthens your argument in several ways. It helps you anticipate objections, alerts you to flaws in your own position, and makes you more aware of the other sides' weaknesses. Further, by acknowledging the dissenting views, you come across as reasonable and thorough—qualities that may disarm readers and leave them more receptive to your argument. You may not convince them to surrender their views, but you can enlarge their perspectives and encourage them to think about your position.

Psychologist Carl Rogers took the idea of acknowledging contrary viewpoints a step further. He believed that argumentation's goal should be to *reduce conflict* rather than to produce a "winner" and a "loser." But he recognized that people identify so strongly with their opinions that they experience any challenge to those opinions as highly threatening. Such a challenge feels like an attack on their identity. And what's the characteristic response to such a perceived attack? People become defensive; they dig in their heels and become more adamant than ever about their position. Indeed, when confronted with solid information that calls their opinion into question, they devalue that evidence rather than allow themselves to be persuaded.

For these reasons, Rogerian strategy rejects any adversarial approach and adopts, instead, a respectful, conciliatory posture that demonstrates a real understanding of opposing views and emphasizes shared interests and values. The ideal is to negotiate differences and arrive at a *synthesis*: a new position that both parties find at least as acceptable as their original positions. What follows are three basic Rogerian strategies to keep in mind as you write.

- First, you may acknowledge the opposing viewpoint in a two-part proposition consisting of a subordinate clause followed by a main clause. The *first part of the proposition* (the subordinate clause) *acknowledges opposing opinions*. The *second part* (the main clause) *states your opinion* and implies that your view stands on more solid ground. (When using this kind of proposition, you may, but don't have to, discuss opposing opinions.) The following thesis illustrates this strategy (the opposing viewpoint is underlined once; the writer's position is underlined twice):

  > <u>Although some instructors think that standardized finals restrict academic freedom,</u> <u><u>such exams are preferable to those prepared by individual professors.</u></u>

- Second, *in the introduction*, you may provide—separate from the proposition—a *one-* or *two-sentence summary of the opposing viewpoint*. Suppose you're writing an essay advocating a ten-day waiting period before an individual can purchase a handgun. Before presenting your proposition at the end of the introductory paragraph, you might include sentences like these: "Opponents of the waiting period argue that the ten-day delay is worthless without a nationwide computer network that can perform background checks. Those opposed also point out that only a percentage of states with a waiting period have seen a reduction in gun-related crime."

- Third, you can write *one or two body paragraphs* near the beginning of the essay to *present in greater detail arguments raised by opposing viewpoints*. After that, you grant (when appropriate) the validity of some of those points ("It may be true that...," "Granted,..."). Then you go on to present evidence for your position ("Even so...," "Nevertheless..."). Because you prepared readers to listen to your opinion, they will tend to be more open to your argument.

☑ Using Rogerian Strategy: A Checklist

- ☐ Begin by making a conscientious effort to *understand* the viewpoints of those with whom you disagree. As you listen to or read about their opinions, try to put yourself in their shoes; focus on *what they believe* and *why they believe it*, rather than on how you will challenge their beliefs.

- ☐ Open your essay with an unbiased, even-handed *restatement of opposing points of view*. Such an objective summary shows that you're fair and open-minded—and not so blinded by the righteousness of your own position that you can't consider any other. Typically, people respond to a respectful approach by lowering their defenses. Because they appreciate your ability to understand what they have to say, they become more open to your point of view.

☐ When appropriate, *acknowledge the validity* of some of the arguments raised by those with differing views. What should you do if they make a well-founded point? You'll enhance your credibility if you concede that point while continuing to maintain that, overall, your position is stronger.

☐ Point out areas of *common ground* by focusing on interests, values, and beliefs that you and those with opposing views share. When you say to them, "Look at the beliefs we share. Look at our common concerns," you communicate that you're not as unlike them as they first believed.

☐ Finally, *present evidence* for your position. Because those not agreeing with you have been "softened up" by your noncombative stance and disarmed by the realization that you and they share some values and beliefs, they're more ready to consider your point of view.

8. **Refute differing viewpoints.**

There will be times when acknowledging opposing viewpoints and presenting your own case won't be enough. Particularly when an issue is complex and when readers strongly disagree with your position, you may have to *refute* all or part of the *dissenting view*. Refutation means pointing out the problems with opposing viewpoints, thereby highlighting your own position's superiority. You may focus on the opposing sides' inaccurate or inadequate evidence; or you may point to their faulty logic. (Some common types of illogical thinking are discussed later in this chapter.)

There are various ways to develop an essay's refutation section. The best method to use depends on the essay's length and the complexity of the issue. Two possible sequences are outlined here:

First Strategy	**Second Strategy**
• State your proposition.	• State your proposition.
• Cite opposing viewpoints and the evidence for those views.	• Cite opposing viewpoints and the evidence for those views.
• Refute opposing viewpoints by presenting counterarguments.	• Refute opposing viewpoints by presenting counterarguments.
	• Present additional evidence for your proposition.

In the first strategy, you simply refute all or part of the opposing positions' arguments. The second strategy takes the first one a step further by presenting *additional evidence* to support your proposition. The additional evidence *must be different* from the points made in the refutation. The additional evidence may appear at the essay's end (as in the preceding outline), or it may be given near the beginning (after the proposition). It may also be divided between the beginning and end.

No matter which strategy you select, you may refute opposing views *one side at a time* or *one point at a time*. When using the one-side-at-a-time approach, you cite all the points raised by the opposing side and then present your counterargument to each point. When using the one-point-at-a-time strategy, you mention the first point made by the opposing side, refute that point, then move on to the second point and refute that, and so on. No matter which strategy you use, be sure to provide clear signals so that readers can distinguish your arguments from the other side's: "Despite the claims of those opposed to the plan, many think that..." and "Those not in agreement think that ...."

9. **Use induction or deduction to think logically about your argument.**

The line of reasoning used to develop an argument is the surest indicator of how rigorously you have thought through your position. There are two basic ways to think about a subject: inductively and deductively. Though the following discussion treats induction and deduction as separate processes, the two often overlap and complement each other.

INDUCTIVE REASONING **Inductive reasoning** involves examination of specific cases, facts, or examples. Based on these specifics, you then draw a conclusion or make a generalization. This is the kind of thinking scientists use when they examine evidence (the results of experiments, for example) and then draw a *conclusion*: "Smoking increases the risk of cancer."

With inductive reasoning, the conclusion reached can serve as the proposition for an argumentation-persuasion essay. If the essay advances a course of action, the proposition often mentions the action, signaling an essay with a distinctly persuasive purpose.

Suppose that you're writing an essay about a crime wave in the small town where you live. You might use inductive thinking to structure the essay's argument:

Several people were mugged last month while shopping in the center of town. (*Evidence*)

Several homes and apartments were burglarized in the past few weeks. (*Evidence*)

Several cars were stolen from people's driveways over the weekend. (*Evidence*)

The police force hasn't adequately protected town residents. (*Conclusion, or proposition, for an argumentation essay with probable elements of persuasion*)

The police force should take steps to upgrade its protection of town residents. (*Conclusion, or proposition, for an argumentation essay with a clearly persuasive intent*)

This inductive sequence highlights a possible structure for the essay. After providing a clear statement of your proposition, you might detail recent muggings, burglaries, and car thefts. Then you could move to the opposing viewpoint: a description of the steps that the police say they have taken to protect town residents. At that point, you would refute the police's claim, citing additional evidence that shows the measures taken have not been sufficient or effective. Finally, if you wanted your essay to have a decidedly persuasive purpose, you could end by recommending specific action that the police force should take to better protect the community.

As in all essays, your evidence should be *unified, specific, accurate, dramatic, sufficient,* and *representative.* The last two characteristics are critical when you think inductively; they guarantee that your conclusion would be equally valid even if other evidence were presented. Insufficient or atypical evidence often leads to **hasty generalizations** that mar the essay's logic. For example, you might think the following: "Some elderly people are wealthy and do not need Social Security checks" (evidence) and "Some Social Security recipients illegally collect several checks" (evidence). If you then conclude, "Social Security is a waste of taxpayers' money," your conclusion is invalid and hasty because it's based on only a few atypical examples. Millions of Social Security recipients aren't wealthy and don't abuse the system. If you fail to consider the full range of evidence, thoughtful readers will likely be skeptical of any action you propose ("The Social Security system should be disbanded"). It's possible, of course, that doing away with Social Security is a good idea, but the evidence leading to such a conclusion must be sufficient and representative.

When reasoning inductively, be careful that the evidence you collect is *recent* and *accurate*. No valid conclusion can result from dated or inaccurate evidence. To ensure that your evidence is sound, you also need to critically evaluate the reliability of your sources. When a person who is legally drunk claims to have seen a flying saucer, the evidence is shaky, to say the least. But if two respected scientists, both with 20–20 vision, saw the saucer, their evidence is worth considering.

Finally, it's important to realize that there's always an element of uncertainty in inductive reasoning. The conclusion can never be more than an *inference*, involving what logicians call an **inductive leap**. There could be other explanations for the evidence cited and thus other positions to take and actions to advocate. For example, given a small town's crime wave, you might conclude not that the police force has been remiss but that residents are careless about protecting themselves and their property. In turn, you might call for a different kind of action—perhaps that the police conduct public workshops in self-defense and home security. In an inductive argument, your task is to weigh the evidence, consider alternative explanations, and then choose the conclusion and course of action that seem most valid.

DEDUCTIVE REASONING Unlike inductive reasoning, which starts with a specific case and moves toward a generalization or conclusion, **deductive reasoning** begins with a generalization that is then applied to a specific case. This movement from general to specific involves a three-step form of reasoning called a **syllogism**. The first part of a syllogism is called the **major premise**, a general statement about an entire group. The second part is the **minor premise**, a statement about an individual within that group. The syllogism ends with a **conclusion** about that individual.

Just as you use inductive thinking in everyday life, you use deductive thinking— often without being aware of it—to make sense of your experiences. When trying to decide which car to buy, you might think as follows:

Major Premise	In an accident, large cars are safer than small cars.
Minor Premise	The Turbo Titan is a large car.
Conclusion	In an accident, the Turbo Titan will be safer than a small car.

Based on your conclusion, you might decide to take a specific action, buying the Turbo Titan rather than the smaller car you had first considered.

To create a valid syllogism and thus arrive at a sound conclusion, you need to avoid two major pitfalls of deductive reasoning. First, be sure not to start with a *sweeping* or *hasty generalization* as your *major premise*. Second, don't accept a *faulty conclusion* as the truth. Let's look at each problem.

Sweeping major premise. Perhaps you're concerned about a trash-to-steam incinerator scheduled to open near your home. Your thinking about the situation might follow these lines:

Major Premise	Trash-to-steam incinerators have had serious problems and posed significant threats to the well-being of people living near the plants.
Minor Premise	The proposed incinerator in my neighborhood will be a trash-to-steam plant.
Conclusion	The proposed trash-to-steam incinerator in my neighborhood will create serious problems and pose significant threats to the well-being of people living near the plant.

Having arrived at this conclusion, you might decide to join organized protests against the opening of the incinerator. But your thinking is somewhat illogical. Your *major premise* is a *sweeping* one because it indiscriminately groups all trash-to-steam plants into a single category. It's unlikely that you're familiar with all the trash-to-steam incinerators in this country and abroad; it's probably not true that *all* such plants have had serious difficulties that endangered the public. For your argument to reach a valid conclusion, the major premise must be based on *repeated observations* or *verifiable facts*. You would have a better argument, and thus reach a more valid conclusion, if you restricted or qualified the major premise, applying it to some, not all, of the group:

Major Premise	A *number* of trash-to-steam incinerators have had serious problems and posed significant threats to the well-being of people living near the plants.
Minor Premise	The proposed incinerator in my neighborhood will be a trash-to-steam plant.
Conclusion	*It's possible* that the proposed trash-to-steam incinerator in my neighborhood will run into serious problems and pose significant threats to the well-being of people living near the plant.

This new conclusion, the result of more careful reasoning, would probably encourage you to learn more about trash-to-steam incinerators in general and about the proposed plant in particular. If, after further research, you still feel uncomfortable about the plant, you would probably decide to join the protest. On the other hand, your research might convince you that the plant has incorporated into its design a number of safeguards that have been successful at other plants. This added information could reassure you that your original fears were unfounded. In either case, the revised deductive process would lead to a more informed conclusion and course of action.

Faulty conclusion. Your syllogism—and thus your reasoning—would also be invalid if your *conclusion reverses the "if...then" relationship implied in the major premise*. Assume you plan to write a letter to the college newspaper urging the resignation of the student government president. Perhaps you pursue a line of reasoning that goes like this:

Major Premise	Students who plagiarize compositions must appear before the Faculty Committee on Academic Policies and Procedures.
Minor Premise	Yesterday Jennifer Kramer, president of the student government, appeared before the Faculty Committee on Academic Policies and Procedures.
Conclusion	Jennifer must have plagiarized a composition.
Action	Jennifer should resign her position as student government president.

This chain of reasoning is illogical and unfair. Here's why. *If* students plagiarize their term compositions and are caught, *then* they must appear before the committee. However, the converse isn't necessarily true—that *if* students appear before the committee, *then* they must have plagiarized. In other words, not *all* students appearing before the Faculty Committee have been called up on plagiarism charges. For instance, Jennifer could have been speaking on behalf of another student; she could have been protesting some action taken by the committee; she could have been seeking the committee's help on an article she plans to write about academic honesty. The conclusion doesn't allow for these other possible explanations.

Now that you're aware of the problems associated with deductive reasoning, let's look at the way you can use a syllogism to structure an argumentation-persuasion essay. Suppose you decide to write an essay advocating support for a projected space mission. You know that controversy surrounds the space program, especially because seven astronauts died in a 1986 launch. Confident that the tragedy has led to more rigorous controls, you want to argue that the benefits of an upcoming mission outweigh its risks. You could use a deductive pattern to develop your argument. In fact, outlining your thinking as a syllogism might help you formulate a proposition, organize your evidence, deal with the opposing viewpoint, and—if appropriate—propose a course of action:

Major Premise	Space programs in the past have led to important developments in technology, especially in medical science.
Minor Premise	The *Cosmos* Mission is the newest space program.
Proposition *(essay might be persuasive)*	The *Cosmos* Mission will most likely lead to important developments in technology, especially in medical science.
Proposition *(essay is clearly persuasive)*	Congress should continue its funding of the *Cosmos* Mission.

Having outlined the deductive pattern of your thinking, you might begin by stating your proposition and then discuss some new procedures developed to protect the astronauts and the rocket system's structural integrity. With that background established, you could detail the opposing claim that little of value has been produced by the space program so far. You could then move to your refutation, citing significant medical advances derived from former space missions. Finally, the essay might conclude on a persuasive note, with a plea to Congress to continue funding the latest space mission.

10. **Use Toulmin logic to establish a strong connection between your evidence and thesis.**

Whether you use an essentially inductive or deductive approach, your argument depends on strong evidence. In *The Uses of Argument*, Stephen Toulmin describes a useful approach for strengthening the connection between evidence and thesis. Toulmin divides a typical argument into three parts:

- **Claim**—the thesis, proposition, or conclusion
- **Data**—the evidence (facts, statistics, examples, observations, expert opinion) used to convince readers of the claim's validity
- **Warrant**—the underlying assumption that justifies moving from evidence to claim.

Here's a sample argument using Toulmin's terminology:

The train engineer was under the influence of drugs when the train crashed.	Transportation employees entrusted with the public's safety should be tested for drug use.
(Data)	**(Claim)**

Transportation employees entrusted with the public's safety should not be allowed on the job if they use drugs.

(Warrant)

As Toulmin explains, readers are more likely to consider your argument valid if they know what your warrant is. Sometimes your warrant will be so obvious that you won't need to state it explicitly; an *implicit warrant* will be sufficient. Assume you want to argue that using live animals to test product toxicity should be outlawed. To support your claim, you cite the following evidence: first, current animal tests are painful and usually result in the animal's death; second, human cell cultures frequently offer more reliable information on how harmful a product may be to human tissue; and third, computer simulations often can more accurately rate a substance's toxicity. Your warrant, although not explicit, is nonetheless clear: "It is wrong to continue product testing on animals when more humane and valid test methods are available."

Other times, it is better to make your *warrant explicit*. Suppose you plan to argue that students should be involved in deciding which faculty members are granted tenure. To develop your claim, you present some evidence. You begin by noting that, currently, only faculty members and administrators review candidates for tenure. Next, you call attention to the controversy surrounding two professors, widely known by students to be poor teachers, who were nonetheless granted tenure. Finally, you cite a decision, made several years ago, to discontinue using student evaluations as part of the tenure process; you emphasize that since that time complaints about teachers' incompetence have risen dramatically. Some readers, though, still might wonder how you got from your evidence to your claim. In this case, your argument could be made stronger by stating your warrant explicitly: "Because students are as knowledgeable as the faculty and administrators about which professors are competent, they should be involved in the tenure process."

The more widely accepted your warrant, Toulmin explains, the more likely it is that readers will accept your argument. If there's no consensus about the warrant, you'll probably need to *back it up*. For the preceding example, you might mention several reports that found that students evaluate faculty fairly (for example, most students don't use the ratings to get back at professors against whom they have a personal grudge); further, students' ratings strongly match those given by administrators and other faculty.

Toulmin describes another way to increase receptivity to an argument: *qualify the claim*—that is, explain the circumstances under which it might be invalid or restricted. For instance, you might grant that most students know little about their instructors' research activities, scholarly publications, or participation in professional committees. You could, then, qualify your claim this way: "Because students don't have a comprehensive view of their instructors' professional activities, they should be involved in the tenure process but play a less prominent role than faculty and administrators."

As you can see, Toulmin's approach provides strategies for strengthening an argument. So, when prewriting or revising, take a few minutes to ask the questions listed here. Your responses to these questions will help you structure a convincing and logical argument.

☑ Questions for Using Toulmin Logic: A Checklist

☐ What data (*evidence*) should I provide to support my claim (*thesis*)?

☐ Is my warrant clear? Should I state it explicitly? What backup can I provide to justify my warrant?

☐ Would qualifying my claim make my argument more convincing?

---

11. Recognize logical fallacies.

When writing an argumentation-persuasion essay, you need to recognize **logical fallacies** both in your own argument and in points raised by the opposing side. Work to eliminate such gaps in logic from your own writing and, when they appear in the opposing argument, try to expose them in your refutation. Logicians have identified many logical fallacies—including the sweeping or hasty generalization and the faulty conclusion discussed earlier in this chapter. Other logical fallacies include the following:

- The **post hoc fallacy** (short for a Latin phrase meaning "after this, therefore because of this") occurs when you conclude that a cause-effect relationship exists simply because one event preceded another. Let's say you note the growing number of immigrants settling in a nearby city, observe the city's economic decline, and conclude that the immigrants' arrival caused the decline. This chain of thinking is faulty because it assumes a cause-effect relationship based purely on co-occurrence. Perhaps the immigrants' arrival was a factor in the economic slump, but there could also be other reasons: the lack of financial incentives to attract business to the city, restrictions on the size of the city's manufacturing facilities, citywide labor disputes that make companies leery of settling in the area. Your argument should also consider these possibilities.

- The **non sequitur fallacy** (Latin for "it does not follow") is an even more blatant muddying of cause-effect relationships. In this case, a conclusion is drawn that has no logical connection to the evidence cited: "Millions of Americans own cars, so there is no need to fund public transportation." The faulty conclusion disregards the millions of Americans who don't own cars; it also ignores pollution and road congestion, both of which could be reduced if people had access to safe, reliable public transportation.

- An **ad hominem argument** (from the Latin meaning "to the man") occurs when someone attacks a person rather than a point of view. Suppose your college plans to sponsor a physicians' symposium on the abortion controversy. You decide to write a letter to the school newspaper opposing the symposium. Taking swipes at two of the invited doctors who disapprove of abortion, you mention that one was recently involved in a messy divorce and that the other is alleged to have a drinking problem. By hurling unrelated, personal accusations, you avoid discussing the issue. Mudslinging is a poor substitute for reasoned argument. As politician Adlai Stevenson once said, "He who slings mud generally loses ground."

- **Appeals to questionable or faulty authority** also weaken an argument. Many of us have developed a healthy suspicion of phrases like *sources close to, an unidentified spokesperson states, experts claim,* and *studies show.* If these people and reports are so reliable, they should be clearly identified.

- **Begging the question** involves failure to establish proof for a debatable point. The writer expects readers to accept as given a premise that's actually controversial. For instance, you would have trouble convincing readers that prayer should be banned from public schools if you based your argument on the premise that school prayer violates the U.S. Constitution. If the Constitution does, either explicitly or implicitly, prohibit prayer in public education, your essay must demonstrate that fact. You can't build a strong argument if you pretend there's no controversy surrounding your premise.

- A **false analogy** disregards significant dissimilarities and wrongly implies that because two things share *some* characteristics, they are therefore *alike in all respects.* You might, for example, compare nicotine and marijuana. Both, you could mention, involve health risks and have addictive properties. However, if you go on to conclude, "Driving while smoking a cigarette isn't illegal, so driving while smoking marijuana shouldn't be illegal either," you're employing a false analogy.

You've overlooked a major difference between tobacco and marijuana: Marijuana impairs perception and coordination—important aspects of driving—whereas there's no evidence that tobacco does the same.

- The **either/or fallacy** occurs when you assume that a particular viewpoint or course of action can have only one of two diametrically opposed outcomes— either totally this or totally that. Say you argue as follows: "Unless colleges continue to offer scholarships based solely on financial need, no one who is underprivileged will be able to attend college." Such a statement ignores the fact that bright, underprivileged students could receive scholarships based on their potential or their demonstrated academic excellence.

- Finally, a **red herring** argument is an intentional digression from the issue—a ploy to deflect attention from the matter being discussed. Imagine you're arguing that condoms shouldn't be dispensed to high school students. You would introduce a red herring if you began to rail against parents who fail to provide their children with any information about sex. Most people would agree that parents *should* provide such information. However, the issue being discussed is not parents' irresponsibility but the pros and cons of schools distributing condoms to students.

Revision Strategies

18.5 Use strategies for revising your argumentation-persuasion essay.

Once you have a draft of the essay, you're ready to revise. The following checklist will help your peers provide feedback and aid you in revising your essay.

☑ Argumentation-Persuasion: A Revision/Peer Review Checklist

Revise Overall Meaning and Structure

- ☐ What issue is being discussed? What is controversial about it?

- ☐ What is the essay's thesis? How does it differ from a generalization or mere statement of fact?

- ☐ What is the essay's purpose—to win readers over to a point of view, to spur readers to some type of action?

- ☐ For what audience is the essay written? What strategies are used to make readers receptive to the essay's thesis?

- ☐ What tone does the essay project? Is the tone likely to win readers over?

- ☐ If the essay's argument is essentially deductive, is the major premise sufficiently restricted? What evidence is the premise based on? Are the minor premise and conclusion valid? If not, how could these problems be corrected?

☐ Where is the essay weakened by hasty generalizations, a failure to weigh evidence honestly, or a failure to draw the most valid conclusion?

☐ Where does the essay commit any of the following logical fallacies: Concluding that a cause-effect relationship exists simply because one event preceded another? Attacking a person rather than an issue? Drawing a conclusion that isn't logically related to the evidence? Failing to establish proof for a debatable point? Relying on questionable or vaguely specified authority? Drawing a false analogy? Resorting to either/or thinking? Using a red herring argument?

Revise Paragraph Development

☐ How apparent is the link between the evidence (data) and the thesis (claim)? How could an explicit warrant clarify the connection?

☐ How would supporting the warrant or qualifying the claim strengthen the argument?

☐ Which paragraphs lack sufficient evidence (facts, examples, statistics, and expert opinion)?

☐ Which paragraphs lack unity? How could they be made more focused? In which paragraphs(s) does evidence seem bland, overly general, unrepresentative, or inaccurate?

☐ Which paragraphs take opposing views into account? Are these views refuted? How? Which counterarguments are ineffective?

☐ Where do outside sources require documentation?

Revise Sentences and Words

☐ What words and phrases help readers distinguish the essay's arguments from those advanced by the opposing side?

☐ Which words carry strong emotional overtones? Is this connotative language excessive? Where does emotional language replace rather than reinforce clear thinking?

☐ Where might dogmatic language ("Anyone can see that…" and "Obviously,…") alienate readers?

Student Essay: From Prewriting Through Revision

18.6 Analyze how argumentation-persuasion is used effectively in a student-written selection.

The following student essay was written by Lydia Gumm in response to this assignment:

> In "What Causes Weight Gain," television personality and cookbook author Mark Bittman, widely known for his stance on the importance of avoiding hyperprocessed foods, addresses a health issue that he considers important. Think of an issue about which you have strong feelings and write an argumentation-persuasion essay in which you take a stand on the issue. Decide on a specific purpose and audience for your essay and tailor your approach for that purpose and audience. Incorporate a variety of credible outside sources (both print and online) to add support to your argument.

After presenting the assignment to his composition class, which focused on writing about sports, Professor Bowles asked his students to spend a couple of days thinking about a topic they would like to write about for their argumentation-persuasion essay. Later in the week, he asked them to explore their chosen topic in an informal journal entry. He explained that the purpose of the journal assignment was to help them make certain they had decided on a topic they found interesting and wanted to explore further.

Here's what Lydia wrote in her journal:

> For my argumentation-persuasion essay, I want to write about Augusta National Golf Club's discrimination against women. My audience will be the members of our class and anyone who might read my essay on our course website.
>
> This topic is definitely interesting to me, and I want to know more about it. For years, I've heard comments here and there about Augusta's unfair treatment of women, but I want to learn more of the details. I think I will actually enjoy conducting research on this topic and that I'll do my best to write a great essay. This is a subject I am passionate about, and I want my readers to understand how unfair Augusta's practices have been and how Augusta still has a long way to go if it wants to have a good reputation.
>
> This topic is especially important to me because I've been playing golf since I was very young, and I'm a member of our school's golf team. I don't understand how Augusta got away with blatant discrimination for so many years. It's not just women they discriminated against. They were an "all white" club until around 20 years ago. I want to find out more about their racism, too, but the focus of my essay will be on Augusta's discrimination against women. I'll have to figure out how to bring in the racial discrimination while keeping my primary focus on discrimination against women.

After Lydia conducted research and found credible, reliable sources that would work well in her essay, she developed an outline that included notes regarding where she planned to incorporate her sources.

Lydia's Outline

Thesis: While Augusta National Golf Club has taken steps in the right direction, its members still have a long way to go if they want to improve the club's tarnished reputation.

I. Evidence of racial discrimination at Augusta

   A. Augusta an all-white club from 1933–1990 (McCarthy and Brady)

   B. Augusta not integrated until they received threats from the PGA (Juckett)

II. Evidence of discrimination against women at Augusta National

   A. "Male only" signs on doors that were not restrooms

   B. No female members until August 2012

   C. Female members still a rare thing

   D. Incident with female reporter (Plaschke)

III. Explanation of how Augusta got away with discriminatory practices

    A. Members (all male) owned the club (Crouse)

    B. Members could make the rules (Crouse)

IV. Explanation of why Augusta changed discriminatory policies against women

    A. Threats from IBM and CBS (Crouse)

    B. Negative publicity from ESPN and The Golf Channel (Crouse)

V. Evidence of change in discriminatory policy against women

    A. Billy Payne's announcement of the "joyous occasion" (Meece)

    B. Two women—Rice and Moore—invited to join (Meece)

VI. Reactions to change in policy

    A. Burk's comments (Crouse)

    B. Burk's role in change of practices (Hudson)

Now read Lydia's essay, "It's About Time, Augusta," noting the similarities and differences between her prewriting, outline, and final essay. One difference you'll notice is that while Lydia planned to include information about racial discrimination near the beginning of her essay, she changed her mind about her organization as she worked on drafts of her essay. You'll also notice that while her outline refers to six outside sources, her final draft includes seven sources. As you read the essay, consider how well it applies the principles of argumentation-persuasion discussed in this chapter. (The commentary that follows the composition will help you look at Lydia's essay more closely and will give you some sense of how she went about revising her drafts as well as the requirements of the MLA documentation style.)

Center title and double-space all text.

It's About Time, Augusta!
by Lydia Gumm

Introduction

    Sports fans across the nation, even those who are not avid golf- 1 ers, are familiar with Augusta National Golf Club. Augusta National is the home of what many consider to be the most prestigious golf tournament in the United States—The Masters. Augusta National is one of the most perfectly designed, best maintained, and absolutely gorgeous golf courses in the world. Its visitors find not a single divot that needs to be replaced or one blade of grass leaning in the wrong direction. It's a sight that amazes almost every individual who sets foot on its grounds. Augusta might be the most beautiful golf course in all of America, but the stubbornness of the board and the history of the club have proven to people all over the world that discrimination is alive and well in our country. While Augusta National Golf Club has

Thesis

taken steps in the right direction, its members still have a long way to go if they want to improve the club's tarnished reputation.

Topic sentence

Common knowledge. No need to document

Parenthetical citation for a specific page of a source

Common knowledge. No need to document

2   While many like to think that gender inequality is a thing of the past, Augusta National Golf Club is living proof that it is still very much alive. In many respects, equality for females has progressed significantly since 1920, when American women fought for their right to vote. Indeed, sports has been an agent for change for women in many ways: "Women's desire to play golf not only forced men to accommodate them, but also forced restrictive and antiquated clothing into the closet" (Knott 176). Today, more women than ever before not only play golf, but are active in a wide variety of sports, have fulfilling careers, and hold positions of leadership throughout our country. For most Americans, the idea that women are "the weaker sex" and undeserving of all the rights that men enjoy is largely a thing of the past. However, things have not changed so dramatically at Augusta. To this day, female memberships at the club are few and far between, and the fact that they did not allow one female member inside the gates of their immaculate grounds until August 2012 is inexcusable. The presence of women at Augusta has been such an anomaly that during the 2010 Masters, a female reporter was stopped by a guard when she and her male colleague were walking into a room to interview a player. It took a moment for the guard to rethink the situation and realize that for this particular occasion, it was actually okay for the female to be in the room (Plaschke).

Parenthetical citation for source having one author. No page given because electronic text is unpaged.

Topic sentence

Attribution giving author's full name and title of newspaper

3   Many people wonder how on earth such a renowned club could get away with such blatant discrimination of females. It makes no sense that in 2012, there were still rooms at Augusta other than restrooms with signs on the door that read "Males Only." Were people still that prejudiced? Augusta was. At Augusta National, the members make the rules. In her *New York Times* article that was published the day the club finally admitted its first female members, columnist Karen Crouse says, "Augusta National conducts business on its own terms, long responding to questions about its policies by saying that it is a private club and membership issues are a private matter." In other words, the all-male members owned the club, and they could do whatever they wanted. And what they wanted was to deny membership to women.

Full-sentence quotation is preceded by a comma and begins with a capital letter

Parenthetical citation for a source with two authors

Full-sentence introduction to a quotation ends with a colon

4   Gender inequality is not the first publicized discrimination issue that Augusta National has faced. Racism at Augusta is an issue that the entire nation became aware of in 1990. Augusta National Golf Club was established in 1933 as an "all-white" club, and it took members fifty-eight years to finally admit their first African American male member, twenty-six years after the Civil Rights Act was passed (McCarthy and Brady). This is another example of the members of the club doing exactly what they wanted to do. In their *USA Today* article, Michael McCarthy and Erik Brady do a good job of describing the members of the club: "Members at Augusta National are not accustomed to being told what to do. These are the guys who tell others what to do: Augusta's 300 or so members are a who's who of corporate power and old money." Had Augusta National not been pressured by the Professional Golf Association, the members might have never integrated the club. In 1990, the PGA Championship was hosted at Shoal Creek Country Club in Alabama, which at the time was an

all-white golf club. The PGA announced that it would no longer host tournaments, not even the prestigious Masters, at all-white clubs. It is no coincidence that three weeks after this announcement was made, Augusta welcomed its first African American member (Juckett).

Topic sentence → It took threats from the PGA for Augusta to finally integrate in 1990, and similarly, it took threats from IBM, one of the main sponsors of the Masters, as well as threats from CBS, the main network that broadcasts the tournament, for Augusta National to finally allow women to become members (Crouse). For years, IBM had very close ties with the club. In fact, until 2012, the four previously hired CEOs of IBM had been invited to be members at Augusta. However, in 2012, IBM hired a new CEO, Virginia Rometty, and Augusta did not send her an invitation. This did not go over well at IBM, and the company threatened to no longer sponsor the event. Media outlets including ESPN and The Golf Channel learned of the story and publicized it widely. News of Augusta's discriminatory practices quickly spread across the nation, and organizations, sponsors, and partners of The Masters began questioning whether they would maintain connections with Augusta. CBS threatened to no longer cover the event. The issue was quickly becoming a nationwide topic that was bringing much criticism and negative publicity to Augusta (Crouse). 5

Topic sentence →
Parenthetical citation for source having one author. No page given because electronic text is unpaged → As in 1990, when Augusta changed its "all-white" male member policy, the club finally gave in to the pressure of supporters, the media, and society and did away with its "no female" policy. On August 20, 2012, Billy Payne, Augusta National chairman, made an announcement that pleased many golfers, sports fans, and women across America: Augusta National Golf Club would no longer exclude females from its premises and female memberships would be allowed. While Payne called the big news a "joyous occasion," many doubted his sincerity (Meece). Still, the announcement was a milestone for women. 6

Quotation blended into a sentence

Attribution leading to a long (block) quotation. Attribution is followed by a colon because the lead-in is a full sentence. If the lead-in isn't a full sentence, a comma is used after the attribution. → On that same day, two females were added to the exclusive list of members of the Augusta National Golf Club: former Secretary of State Condoleezza Rice and private investment firm partner of Rainwater, Inc., Darla Moore. The two women made history. Some wonder why these two females in particular were chosen to become the first female members. When asked that question, Billy Payne responded with the following statement: 7

> We are fortunate to consider many qualified candidates for membership at Augusta National. Consideration with regard to any candidate is deliberate, held in strict confidence and always takes place over an extended period of time. The process for Condoleezza and Darla was no different. These accomplished women share our passion for the game of golf and both are well known and respected by our membership. It will be a proud moment when we present Condoleezza and Darla their Green Jackets....(qtd. in Meece)

Block quotation indented 1/2 inch from left margin

For an indented quotation, the parenthetical citation is placed after the period

Period and ellipses indicating omission from the end of a sentence in a quotation

While many regarded Payne's remarks as highly hypocritical, the fact that two females were admitted into Augusta was a milestone for women. Martha Burk, former chair of the National Council of Women's 8

Topic sentence

Parenthetical citation for a quotation cited in a secondary source

Organizations, had the following to say when she learned of the change in policy and that Rice and Moore had become members: "It's about ten years too late for the boys to come into the 20th century, never mind the 21st century. But it's a milestone for women in business" (qtd. in Crouse). Burk had led a "highly publicized protest of the club," including putting pressure on corporate sponsors, to "force a change" in Augusta's policy (Hudson 119). Unfortunately, two years later, Rice and Moore remain the only two females on the list of around three hundred members at Augusta (Crouse).

Parenthetical citation of a specific page of a source

Conclusion

Not integrating the club until 1990 was indecent, and to deny women memberships until 2012 indicates a lack of integrity. It is time for Augusta National Golf Club to prove to the country that it has moved beyond its discriminating policies. One way the club could begin to improve its tarnished image is by inviting additional female members to join the club, and another is by hosting an LPGA tournament. Come on, Augusta. It's time for you to prove to America that you have moved beyond your discriminating policies of the past.

9

Start on a new page, double-spaced, no extra space after heading or between entries. Each entry begins flush left. Indent successive lines half an inch.

Book review in a print journal

Article in an online magazine

Article in an online newspaper

Works Cited

Crouse, Karen. "Host to Masters Drops a Barrier with Its First 2 Female Members." *The New York Times*, 20 Aug. 2012, pp. A1+.

Hudson, David L. *Women in Golf: The Players, the History, and the Future of the Sport*. Praeger, 2008.

Juckett, Ron. "3 Reasons Why Augusta National Waited So Long to Admit Women." *Bleacher Report*, 20 Aug. 2012, bleacherreport.com/articles/1304349-3-reasons-why-augusta-national-waited-so-long-to-admit-women.

Knott, Rick. Review of *Golf and the American Country Club*, by Richard J. Moss. *Journal of Sport History*, vol. 37, no. 1, 2010, pp. 176–77.

McCarthy, Michael, and Erik Brady. "Privacy Becomes Public at Augusta." *USA Today*, 27 Sep. 2002, usatoday30.usatoday.com/sports/golf/masters/2002-09-27-augusta_x.htm.

Meece, Mickey. "History Is Made at Augusta with the Admission of Condoleezza Rice and Darla Moore." Forbes.com, 20 Aug. 2012, www.forbes.com/sites/mickeymeece/2012/08/20history-is-made-at-augusta-national-golf-club/#2e524d2c4c27.

Plaschke, Bill. "Augusta Does the Right Thing . . . But What Took So Long?" *Los Angeles Times*, 21 Aug. 2012, articles.latimes.com/2012/aug/21/sports/la-sp-plaschke-augusta-20120821.

Article with a single author in a print newspaper

Print book by a single author

Article in an online newsletter

Article with two authors in an online newspaper

Commentary

BLEND OF ARGUMENTATION AND PERSUASION In her essay, Lydia tackles a controversial issue. She takes the position that Augusta National Golf Club should be ashamed of the discriminatory policies that it held on to for far too long and that the club is still a long way from convincing Americans that it has moved beyond its unfair membership practices. Lydia's essay is a good example of the way *argumentation* and *persuasion* often mix: Although the essay presents Lydia's position in a logical, well-reasoned manner (argumentation), it also appeals to readers' personal values and suggests a course of action (persuasion).

AUDIENCE ANALYSIS   When planning the essay, Lydia carefully considered how her audience—the students in her composition class—would respond to her argument. Lydia was enrolled in a themed composition class, "Writing about Sports," and many of her classmates had been actively engaged in playing sports for most of their lives. Even so, she thought that some of her classmates would initially disagree with her argument that Augusta National had not done enough to convince Americans that it had changed its discriminatory ways. She knew that some of her classmates would need to be persuaded that although Augusta National had taken steps in the right direction, it still had a long way to go. She also knew that some of her classmates might think that because Augusta National is privately owned by its members, the club has the right to make whatever policies it wants to make, even if they are discriminatory.

INTRODUCTION AND THESIS   Lydia introduces her subject by describing Augusta National Golf Club as "the home of what many consider to be the most prestigious golf tournament in the United States—The Masters." She goes on to explain that "Augusta National is one of the most perfectly designed, best maintained, and absolutely gorgeous golf courses in the world," and then she contrasts the beauty of the grounds with the ugliness of the discriminatory policies the club embraced for years. These comments lead to her thesis at the end of the introduction: "While Augusta National Golf Club has taken steps in the right direction, its members still have a long way to go if they want to improve the club's tarnished reputation" (paragraph 1).

TOULMIN LOGIC AND INDUCTIVE REASONING   Using *Toulmin logic* to establish a strong connection between her evidence and thesis, Lydia devotes the body of her essay to providing *data* for her *claim* that Augusta National has not done enough to convince the public that it welcomes a diverse membership. Her evidence is in the form of public knowledge about the policies of Augusta National and specific quotations concerning when and how the policy changed so that two women—but no more than two—were eventually admitted as members. Although Lydia does not explicitly state her warrant, it is nonetheless clear: "It is wrong to discriminate against individuals on the basis of their gender or race, even if doing so in a private club is not illegal."

Lydia arrives at her position *inductively*, through a series of *inferences* or *inductive leaps*. She provides specific cases, facts, and examples that lead readers to draw a conclusion. She provides examples of gender inequality and racism at Augusta National, as well as specific cases and facts from a variety of outside sources. She also provides facts indicating that the club finally changed its discriminatory policies only because of threats from its major sponsors, and that years after it invited its first two female members, those two women remained the only female members at Augusta National.

USE OF OUTSIDE SOURCES   Throughout her body paragraphs, Lydia brings in a variety of outside sources to convince readers of her claim's validity. She uses seven outside sources—a book review published in a journal (Knott, paragraph 2); an online *Los Angeles Times* article (Plaschke, paragraph 2); a print *New York Times* article (Crouse, paragraphs 3, 5, and 8); an online *USA Today* article (McCarthy and Brady, paragraph 4); a sports newsletter website (Juckett, paragraph 4); an online *Forbes* article (Meece, paragraphs 6 and 7); and a book, *Women in Golf: The Players, the History, and the Future of the Sport* (Hudson, paragraph 8)—to provide her readers with strong support that is unified, adequate, specific, accurate, and representative. The *data* she provides makes her readers aware of the discriminatory policies that Augusta National enforced for years and points to her *warrant*—the underlying assumption that justifies moving from evidence to claim.

ACKNOWLEDGING AND REFUTING OPPOSING VIEWPOINTS   Although never pretending to respect the opposing views, Lydia does acknowledge them. In paragraph 3, she points out the first opposing view—that the club's members are free to make their own rules. She cites Crouse, who says, "Augusta National conducts business on its own terms, long responding to questions about its policies by saying that it is a private club and that membership issues are a private matter." Lydia also mentions the second opposing viewpoint—that the "joyous occasion" of admitting two women to Augusta is a policy change borne out of a desire to do the right thing.

Against the first view, Lydia implies that the legality of an action does not make it right. "In other words, the all-male members owned the club, and they could do whatever they wanted. And what they wanted was to deny membership to women," she says disdainfully, letting her tone carry her implied criticism. For the second opposing viewpoint, Lydia provides a pointed *refutation*. She cites Martha Burk, former chair of the National Council of Women's Organizations, on the club's sincerity: "It's about ten years too late for the boys to come into the 20th century, never mind the 21st century," and she cites evidence suggesting that it was outside pressure, rather than moral conviction, that forced August National to admit women. She also makes the point that two years after Augusta's change in policy, Rice and Moore remained the club's only female members.

With these refutations, Lydia firmly establishes her *claim* that Augusta National did not suddenly have a change of heart and make the decision to abandon its racist, prejudiced attitudes. Instead, the club finally let go of its discriminatory policies because of threats from the PGA and leading sponsors of the Masters, such as IBM and CBS.

COMBINING PATTERNS OF DEVELOPMENT   To develop her argument, Lydia draws on several patterns of development. She uses *description* as she conveys to readers the beauty of the golf course, and she employs *exemplification* as she provides examples of Augusta National's discriminatory practices. Lydia includes *process analysis* when she explains the sequence of events that led to the club's finally changing its membership rules and allowing non-white and then female members. She draws on *cause-effect* as she explains how threats from leading sponsors led to the club's change in its membership policies.

CONCLUSION   Although Lydia relied on *logos* throughout much of her essay as she provided facts, statistics, and examples to convince readers of her claim, in the closing paragraph she relies heavily on *pathos*, the emotional power of language. She appeals to her readers' values in the opening sentence of the conclusion, where she says, "Not integrating the club until 1990 was indecent, and to deny women memberships until 2012 indicates a lack of integrity." That done, she restates her thesis: "It is time for Augusta National Golf Club to prove to the country that it has moved beyond its discriminating policies," and then she goes on to suggest specific steps the club should take to improve its "tarnished reputation." She ends her essay with a call to action: "Come on, Augusta. It's time for you to prove to America that you have moved beyond your discriminating policies of the past."

REVISING THE FIRST DRAFT   Given the complex nature of the assignment, Lydia found that she had to revise her essay several times. One way to illustrate some of the changes she made is to compare her final conclusion with the original draft printed here:

> **Original Version of the Conclusion**
> Augusta is such a prominent golf course that it is a shame the women on the LPGA tour have never been able to experience it. Although women are now allowed as members, there still has not been an LPGA tournament hosted at Augusta. Augusta would make so much money from hosting an LPGA event, especially if it were to host a major. At The Masters, the average ticket price is $250, and during the tournament there are 50,000 patrons. Just in ticket sales, Augusta makes $12,500,000. That doesn't even include merchandise sales, television earnings, or sponsorships. Obviously, an LPGA major tournament wouldn't bring in that much money, but it would bring in enough money to definitely make a large profit. It would also be good for Augusta to host an LPGA event just to show society that it actually has a heart. There might be only two female members at the moment, but things are definitely moving in the right direction. August 20, 2012, was a day that changed history, and the day that Augusta National Golf Club finally woke up from its dreams of the twentieth century. It's about time, Augusta!

When Lydia met with her classmate, Lamarcus, for a peer review session, she found that he had a number of helpful suggestions for revising various sections of the essay. But Lydia's partner focused most of his comments on the essay's conclusion because he felt it needed special attention. Following Lamarcus's suggestion, Lydia completely revised her conclusion. She realized that the original focus on the idea that Augusta should host an LPGA event because it would "make so much money" was problematic for several reasons. Hosting an LPGA tournament so that the club could add more money to its coffers is hardly an admirable reason to admit female members and certainly was not the principled rationale that Lydia felt would add force to her argument. In addition, when Lamarcus asked Lydia where she found the information about the average ticket price at The Masters and the number of patrons attending, she told him that she had family members who had attended and they told her they paid $250 for their tickets and that they heard there were about 50,000 attendees. She realized that she could not formally document that information, and consequently, she knew she should not include it. In addition, she realized that the ideas she had presented did not support her claim that Augusta still had a long way to go if it wanted to "improve its tarnished image." Instead of supporting her thesis, the statement in the original conclusion that "there might be only two female members at the moment, but things are definitely moving in the right direction" contradicted the main argument she was trying to make.

As Lydia revised her conclusion, she focused on bringing her essay to closure by appealing to her readers' sense of values and by suggesting a specific course of action that the club could take to prove that it rejects discrimination and values diversity.

These are just a few of the many changes Lydia made while reworking her essay. Because she budgeted her time carefully, she was able to revise thoroughly and create an essay that is reasoned and convincing.

MLA FORMAT   Lydia followed the style given in the *MLA Handbook* (eighth edition) to format her paper.

Activities: Argumentation-Persuasion

Prewriting Activities

1. Imagine you're writing two essays. One defines hypocrisy; the other contrasts license and freedom. Identify an audience for each essay. Then jot down how each essay might argue the merits of certain ways of behaving.

2. Following are several thesis statements for argumentation-persuasion essays. For each thesis, determine whether the three audiences indicated in parentheses are likely to be supportive, wavering, or hostile. Then select one thesis and use group brainstorming to identify, for each audience, general concerns on which you might successfully base your persuasive appeal (for example, the concern for approval, for financial well-being, for self-respect, for the welfare of others).

   a. The minimum wage should be raised every two years (*low-income employees, employers, congressional representatives*).

   b. Students should not graduate from college until they have passed a comprehensive exam in their majors (*college students, their parents, college officials*).

   c. The town should pass a law prohibiting residents near the reservoir from using pesticides on their lawns (*environmentalists, homeowners, members of the town council*).

3. Using the thesis you selected in activity 2, focus—for each group indicated in parentheses—on one or two of the general concerns you identified. Then brainstorm with others to determine the specific points you'd make to persuade each group. How would Rogerian argument and other techniques help you disarm the most hostile audience?

4. Clip an effective advertisement from a magazine or newspaper. Through brainstorming, determine to what extent the ad depends on logos, ethos, and pathos. Consider

the logical fallacies discussed in this chapter. After reviewing your brainstorming, devise a thesis that expresses your feelings about the ad's persuasive strategies. Are they responsible and ethical? Why or why not?

5. In a campus, local, or major newspaper, find an editorial with which you disagree. Using the patterns of development, freewriting, or another prewriting technique, generate points that refute the editorial. You may, for example, identify any logical fallacies in the editorial. Then, following one of the refutation strategies discussed in this chapter, organize your rebuttal, keeping in mind the power of Rogerian argument.

Revising Activities

6. Examine the following sets, each containing *data* (evidence) and a *claim* (thesis). For each set, identify the implied *warrant*. Which sets would benefit from an explicit warrant? Why? How might the warrant be expressed? In which sets would it be helpful to support the warrant or qualify the claim? Why? How might the warrant be supported or the claim qualified?

   a. **Data:** More Americans are buying Japanese cars. The reason, they report, is that Japanese cars tend to have superior fuel efficiency and longevity. Japanese cars are currently manufactured under stricter quality control than American models.

      Claim: Implementing stricter quality controls is one way for the American auto industry to compete with Japanese imports.

   b. **Data:** Although laws guarantee learning-impaired children an education suitable to their needs, no laws safeguard the special needs of intellectually gifted children. There are, proportionately, far more programs that assist the slow learner than there are those that challenge the fast learner.

      Claim: Our educational system is unfair to gifted children.

   c. **Data:** In 2008, Barack Obama was the first Black man to be elected president of the United States.

      Claim: Obama's election shows that racial prejudice no longer plays a major role in U.S. society.

7. Examine the following faulty chains of reasoning. Which use essentially inductive logic? Which use essentially deductive logic? In each set, determine, in general terms, why the conclusion is invalid.

   a. Whenever I work in the college's computer lab, something goes wrong. The program crashes, the cursor freezes, the margins unset themselves.

      Conclusion: The college needs to allocate additional funds to repair and upgrade the computers in the lab.

   b. Many cars in the student parking lot are dented and look as though they have been in accidents.

      Conclusion: Students are careless drivers.

c. Many researchers believe that children in families where both parents work develop confidence and independence. In a nearby community, the number of two-career families increased 15 percent over a two-year period.

Conclusion: Children in the nearby community will develop confidence and independence.

8. Each of the following sets of statements contains at least one of the logical fallacies described in this chapter. Identify the fallacy or fallacies in each set and explain why the statements are invalid.

a. Grades are irrelevant to learning. Students are in college to get an education, not good grades. The university should eliminate grading altogether.

b. The best policy is to put juvenile offenders in jail so that they can get a taste of reality. Otherwise, they will repeat their crimes again and again.

c. Two members of the state legislature have introduced gun-control legislation. Both have led sheltered, pampered lives that prevent them from seeing how ordinary people need guns to protect themselves.

9. Following is the introduction from the first draft of an essay advocating the elimination of mandatory dress codes in public schools. Revise the paragraph, being sure to consider these questions: How effectively does the writer deal with the opposing viewpoint? Does the paragraph encourage those who might disagree with the writer to read on? Why or why not? Do you see any logical fallacies in the writer's thinking? Where? Does the writer introduce anything that veers away from the point being discussed? Where? Before revising, you may find it helpful to do some brainstorming—individually or in a group—to find ways to strengthen the paragraph.

  After reworking the paragraph, take a few minutes to consider how the rest of the essay might unfold. What persuasive strategies could be used? How could Rogerian argument win over readers? What points could be made? What action could be urged in the effort to build a convincing argument?

  In three nearby towns recently, high school administrators joined forces to take an outrageously strong stand against students' constitutional rights. Acting like Fascists, they issued an edict in the form of a preposterous dress code that prohibits students from wearing expensive jewelry, name-brand jeans, leather jackets—anything that the administrators, in their supposed wisdom, consider ostentatious. Perhaps the next thing they'll want to do is forbid students to play hip-hop music at school dances. What prompted the administrators' dictatorial prohibition against certain kinds of clothing? Somehow or other, they got it into their heads that having no restrictions on the way students dress creates an unhealthy environment, where students vie with each other for the flashiest attire. Students and parents alike should protest this and any other dress code. If such codes go into effect, we might as well throw out the Constitution.

Professional Selections: Argumentation-Persuasion

ANNA QUINDLEN

Writer Anna Quindlen was born in Philadelphia, Pennsylvania, and now lives in New York City. At the *New York Times* she became a regular op-ed columnist, winning the Pulitzer Prize for Commentary in 1992. In 1995, Quindlen left newspaper work and devoted herself primarily to writing fiction. She has written novels, nonfiction, self-help books, and children's books. Quindlen also writes regularly for *Newsweek,* where this article appeared on June 11, 2007.

Figure 18.2 summarizes the structure of this selection.

Pre-Reading Journal Entry

Getting a driver's license is an important rite of passage for young people in the United States. It's often preceded by a highly stressful process of learning to drive. Recall your own driving lessons and licensing tests. Who taught you to drive? What were the lessons like? What emotions did you experience while learning to drive and taking your driving test? If you do not know how to drive, why not? How do you feel about not having a driver's license? Use your journal to answer these questions.

Driving to the Funeral

The four years of high school grind inexorably to a close, the milestones passed. The sports contests, the SATs, the exams, the elections, the dances, the proms. And too often, the funerals. It's become a sad rite of passage in many American communities, the services held for teenagers killed in auto accidents before they've even scored a tassel to hang from the rearview mirror. The hearse moves in procession followed by the late-model compact cars of young people, boys trying to control trembling lower lips and girls sobbing into one another's shoulders. The yearbook has a picture or two with a black border. A mom and dad rise from their seats on the athletic field or in the gym to accept a diploma posthumously.

It's simple and inarguable: car crashes are the No. 1 cause of death among 15- to 20-year-olds in this country. What's so peculiar about that fact is that so few adults focus on it until they are planning an untimely funeral. Put it this way: if someone told you that there was one single behavior that would be most likely to lead to the premature death of your kid, wouldn't you try to do something about that? Yet parents seem to treat the right of a 16-year-old to drive as an inalienable one, something to be neither questioned nor abridged.

This makes no sense unless the argument is convenience, and often it is. In a nation that developed mass-transit amnesia and traded the exurb for the small town, a licensed son or daughter relieves parents of a relentless roundelay of driving. Soccer field, Mickey Ds, mall, movies. Of course, if that's the rationale, why not let 13-year-olds drive? Any reasonable person would respond that a 13-year-old is too young. But statistics suggest that that's true of 16-year-olds as well. The National Highway Traffic Safety Administration has found that neophyte drivers of 17 have about a third as many accidents as their counterparts only a year younger.

1

2

3

In 1984 a solution was devised for the problem of teenage auto accidents that   4
lulled many parents into a false sense of security. The drinking age was raised
from 18 to 21. It's become gospel that this has saved thousands of lives, although
no one actually knows if that's the case; fatalities fell, but the use of seat belts and
airbags may have as much to do with that as penalties for alcohol use. And there
has been a pronounced negative effect on college campuses, where administrators describe a forbidden-fruit climate that encourages binge drinking. The pitch-
ers of sangria and kegs of beer that offered legal refreshment for 18-year-olds at
sanctioned campus events 30 years ago have given way to a new tradition called
"pre-gaming," in which dry college activities are preceded by manic alcohol consumption at frats, dorms and bars.

Given the incidence of auto-accident deaths among teenagers despite the   5
higher drinking age, you have to ask whether the powerful lobby Mothers
Against Drunk Driving simply targeted the wrong D. In a survey of young drivers, only half said they had seen a peer drive after drinking. Nearly all, however,
said they had witnessed speeding, which is the leading factor in fatal crashes by
teenagers today. In Europe, governments are relaxed about the drinking age but
tough on driving regulations and licensing provisions; in most countries, the
driving age is 18.

In America some states have taken a tough-love position and bumped up the   6
requirements for young drivers: longer permit periods, restrictions or bans on
night driving. Since the greatest danger to a teenage driver is another teenager in
the car—the chance of having an accident doubles with two teenage passengers
and skyrockets with three or more—some new rules forbid novice drivers from
transporting their peers.

In theory this sounds like a good idea; in fact it's toothless. New Jersey has   7
some of the most demanding regulations for new drivers in the nation, including a provision that until they are 18 they cannot have more than one nonfamily
member in the car. Yet in early January three students leaving school in Freehold
Township died in a horrific accident in which the car's 17-year-old driver was
violating that regulation by carrying two friends. No wonder he took the chance:
between July 2004 and November 2006, only 12 provisional drivers were ticketed
for carrying too many passengers. Good law, bad enforcement.

States might make it easier on themselves, on police officers and on teenagers,   8
too, if instead of chipping away at the right to drive they merely raised the legal
driving age wholesale. There are dozens of statistics to back up such a change: in
Massachusetts alone, one third of 16-year-old drivers have been involved in serious
accidents. Lots and lots of parents will tell you that raising the driving age is unten-
able, that the kids need their freedom and their mobility. Perhaps the only ones who
wouldn't make a fuss are those parents who have accepted diplomas at graduation
because their children were no longer alive to do so themselves, whose children
traded freedom and mobility for their lives. They might think it was worth the wait.

Questions for Critical Reading

1. What is the selection's thesis? Locate the sentence(s) in which Quindlen states her
   main idea. If she doesn't state her thesis explicitly, express it in your own words.

Figure 18.2 Essay Structure Diagram: "Driving to the Funeral" by Anna Quindlen

Introductory paragraph (paragraph 1)

A "sad rite of passage" for American communities is funeral services held for high school students killed in auto accidents.

Background: Statistic and statement foreshadowing the thesis (2)

Statistic: "Car crashes are the No. 1 cause of death among 15- to 20-year-olds."

Statement: Communities aren't doing enough to change this situation.

Opposing and supporting arguments illustrated by examples, anecdotes, and statistics (3–7)

Opposing argument: A higher driving age is inconvenient for parents and teens, and most 16-year-olds are mature enough to drive safely.

Supporting argument with statistic: New 17-year-old drivers have one-third the accidents that new 16-year-old drivers do, according to the National Highway Traffic Safety Administration.

Opposing argument: Raising the drinking age from 18 to 21 has saved lives from accidents.

Supporting argument with examples and statistics: (1) No proof exists that raising the drinking age *alone* is responsible for fewer deaths. Use of seat belts and airbags may play a role. (2) Outlawing drinking doesn't stop students from "pre-gaming" on alcohol. (3) Outlawing alcohol doesn't stop teens from speeding, the leading factor in fatal crashes. (4) In Europe, teens can drink at 16 but cannot drive until 18.

Opposing argument: States have started restricting teen driving: longer permit periods; restrictions on night driving; a ban on teen drivers having more than one nonfamily member in the car.

Supporting argument with anecdote: New requirements are not rigorously reinforced. Despite New Jersey's strict laws, between July 2004 and November 2006, only 12 provisional drivers were ticketed for illegally driving with other teens in their car.

Thesis Concluding paragraph (8)

Thesis: Instead of "chipping away" at the right to drive, just raise the legal driving age.

Conclusion: The increased safety is worth the inconvenience for parents and teens, as parents of teens who have died in crashes will attest.

2. According to Quindlen, what solutions to the problem of teenage auto accidents have not worked over the last 25 years?

3. What approach to young adults' drinking and driving do European nations take?

4. According to Quindlen, what would be a more effective solution to the problem of teen auto accidents?

Questions About the Writer's Craft

1. **The pattern.** What type of audience—supportive, wavering, or hostile—does Quindlen seem to be addressing? How can you tell?

2. **Support.** Quindlen bases much of her argument on the statistics she presents. Where do those statistics appear? How effective are they? Use the criteria for sound evidence (in Learning Objective 18.2) to evaluate Quindlen's use of statistics.

3. **Other patterns.** What other patterns does Quindlen use in this essay? Where? What purpose do these passages serve?

4. **The pattern.** What appeals to pathos does Quindlen use? How effective are they?

Writing Assignments Using Argumentation-Persuasion as a Pattern of Development

1. In paragraph 4 of her essay, Quindlen claims that raising the drinking age from 18 to 21 has had an unintended negative effect on college campuses, where binge drinking has become commonplace. Many college administrators agree with her. In fact, a hundred college and university presidents launched the Amethyst Initiative in 2008, calling for "an informed and dispassionate public debate over the effects of the 21-year-old drinking age." Although the college presidents did not actually call for lowering the drinking age, they argued that the current drinking age simply drives drinking underground, where it is more tempting for students and harder to control. Do you agree with the college presidents that the current drinking age of 21 should be reexamined and possibly lowered? Or do you disagree? Do some research on the Amethyst Initiative and the drinking age issue, and then write an essay in which you argue that the current drinking age should be lowered or should remain the same. Be sure to support your position with sound evidence.

2. Quindlen supports raising the legal driving age in order to decrease teen auto accidents, indicating that the main arguments for a low legal driving age are that it "relieves parents of an endless roundelay of driving" (paragraph 3) and that "the kids need their freedom and their mobility" (paragraph 8). Are there any other reasons that might support a lower legal driving age? Write an essay opposing Quindlen's argument for a higher driving age and supporting a legal driving age of 16, with or without restrictions, depending on your view. Be sure to support your argument with reasons and examples.

Writing Assignment Combining
Patterns of Development

3. Provisional driver's licenses vary from state to state, but all are designed to decrease teen auto accidents by restricting driving privileges among the youngest drivers and gradually allowing them more freedom as they get older and remain accident-free. Develop your own rules for a fair and effective provisional driver's license, and write a *process analysis* essay explaining your system. Indicate what drivers are allowed to do at various ages until they are granted full driving privileges as well as the penalties you would impose for infractions and accidents, and give *examples* to illustrate the provisions. In support of your plan, explain the beneficial *effects* that your provisional license would have on teen driving.

MARY SHERRY

Following her graduation from Dominican University in 1962 with a degree in English, Mary Sherry wrote freelance articles and advertising copy while raising her family. Founder and owner of a small research and publishing firm in Minnesota, she has taught creative and remedial writing to adults for many years. The following selection first appeared as a 1991 "My Turn" column in *Newsweek*.

Pre-Reading Journal Entry

Imagine you had a son or daughter who didn't take school seriously. How would you go about motivating the child to value academic success? Would your strategies differ depending on the age and gender of the child? If so, how and why? What other factors might influence your approach? Use your journal to respond to these questions.

In Praise of the "F" Word

Tens of thousands of 18-year-olds will graduate this year and be handed meaningless diplomas. These diplomas won't look any different from those awarded their luckier classmates. Their validity will be questioned only when their employers discover that these graduates are semiliterate. 1

Eventually a fortunate few will find their way into educational repair shops— adult-literacy programs, such as the one where I teach basic grammar and writing. There, high-school graduates and high-school dropouts pursuing graduate-equivalency certificates will learn the skills they should have learned in school. They will also discover they have been cheated by our educational system. 2

As I teach, I learn a lot about our schools. Early in each session I ask my students to write about an unpleasant experience they had in school. No writers' block here! "I wish someone would have made me stop doing drugs and made me study." "I liked to party and no one seemed to care." "I was a good kid and didn't cause any trouble, so they just passed me along even though I didn't read well and couldn't write." And so on. 3

I am your basic do-gooder, and prior to teaching this class I blamed the poor   4
academic skills our kids have today on drugs, divorce and other impediments to
concentration necessary for doing well in school. But, as I rediscover each time
I walk into the classroom, before a teacher can expect students to concentrate, he
has to get their attention, no matter what distractions may be at hand. There are
many ways to do this, and they have much to do with teaching style. However, if
style alone won't do it, there is another way to show who holds the winning hand
in the classroom. That is to reveal the trump card[1] of failure.

I will never forget a teacher who played that card to get the attention of one of   5
my children. Our youngest, a world-class charmer, did little to develop his intellectual talents but always got by. Until Mrs. Stifter.

Our son was a high-school senior when he had her for English. "He sits in   6
the back of the room talking to his friends," she told me. "Why don't you move
him to the front row?" I urged, believing the embarrassment would get him to
settle down. Mrs. Stifter looked at me steely-eyed over her glasses. "I don't move
seniors," she said. "I flunk them." I was flustered. Our son's academic life flashed
before my eyes. No teacher had ever threatened him with that before. I regained
my composure and managed to say that I thought she was right. By the time
I got home I was feeling pretty good about this. It was a radical approach for these
times, but, well, why not? "She's going to flunk you," I told my son. I did not discuss it any further. Suddenly English became a priority in his life. He finished out
the semester with an A.

I know one example doesn't make a case, but at night I see a parade of stu-   7
dents who are angry and resentful for having been passed along until they could
no longer even pretend to keep up. Of average intelligence or better, they eventually quit school, concluding they were too dumb to finish. "I should have been
held back" is a comment I hear frequently. Even sadder are those students who
are high-school graduates who say to me after a few weeks of class, "I don't know
how I even got a high-school diploma."

Passing students who have not mastered the work cheats them and the em-   8
ployers who expect graduates to have basic skills. We excuse this dishonest behavior by saying kids can't learn if they come from terrible environments. No one
seems to stop to think that—no matter what environments they come from—most
kids don't put school first on their list unless they perceive something is at stake.
They'd rather be sailing.

Many students I see at night could give expert testimony on unemployment,   9
chemical dependency, abusive relationships. In spite of these difficulties, they
have decided to make education a priority. They are motivated by the desire for
a better job or the need to hang on to the one they've got. They have a healthy
fear of failure.

People of all ages can rise above their problems, but they need to have a reason   10
to do so. Young people generally don't have the maturity to value education in
the same way my adult students value it. But fear of failure, whether economic or
academic, can motivate both.

---

[1] In cards, an advantage held in reserve until it's needed (editors' note).

Flunking as a regular policy has just as much merit today as it did two genera-   11
tions ago. We must review the threat of flunking and see it as it really is—a positive
teaching tool. It is an expression of confidence by both teachers and parents that
the students have the ability to learn the material presented to them. However,
making it work again would take a dedicated, caring conspiracy between teachers
and parents. It would mean facing the tough reality that passing kids who haven't
learned the material—while it might save them grief for the short term—dooms
them to long-term illiteracy. It would mean that teachers would have to follow
through on their threats, and parents would have to stand behind them, knowing
their children's best interests are indeed at stake. This means no more doing Scott's
assignments for him because he might fail. No more passing Jodi because she's
such a nice kid.

This is a policy that worked in the past and can work today. A wise teacher,   12
with the support of his parents, gave our son the opportunity to succeed—or fail.
It's time we return this choice to all students.

Questions for Critical Reading

1. What is the selection's thesis? Locate the sentence(s) in which Sherry states her
   main idea. If she doesn't state the thesis explicitly, express it in your own words.

2. Sherry opens her essay with these words: "Tens of thousands of 18-year-olds will
   graduate this year and be handed meaningless diplomas." Why does Sherry consider these diplomas meaningless?

3. According to Sherry, what justification do many teachers give for "passing students who have not mastered the work" (paragraph 8)? Why does Sherry think
   that it is wrong to pass such students?

4. What does Sherry think teachers should do to motivate students to focus on school
   despite the many "distractions…at hand" (4)?

Questions About the Writer's Craft

1. **The pattern.** To write an effective argumentation-persuasion essay, writers need to
   establish their credibility. How does Sherry convince readers that she is qualified
   to write about her subject? What does this attempt to establish credibility say about
   Sherry's perception of her audience's point of view?

2. **Title.** Sherry's title is deliberately misleading. What does her title lead you to
   believe the essay will be about? Why do you think Sherry chose this title?

3. **Quotations.** Why do you suppose Sherry quotes her students rather than summarizing what they had to say? What effect do you think Sherry hopes the quotations
   will have on readers?

4. **Other patterns.** What example does Sherry provide to show that the threat of failure can work? How does this example reinforce her case?

Writing Assignments Using Argumentation-Persuasion as a Pattern of Development

1. Like Sherry, write an essay arguing your position on a controversial school-related issue. Once you select a topic, brainstorm with others to gather insight into varying points of view. When you write, restrict your argument to one level of education, and refute as many opposing arguments as you can.

2. Sherry acknowledges that she used to blame students' poor academic skills on "drugs, divorce and other impediments." To what extent should teachers take these and similar "impediments" into account when grading students? Are there certain situations that call for leniency, or should out-of-school forces affecting students not be considered? To gain perspective on this issue, interview several friends, classmates, and instructors. Then write an essay in which you argue your position. Provide specific examples to support your argument, being sure to acknowledge and—when possible—to refute opposing viewpoints.

Writing Assignment Combining Patterns of Development

3. Where else, besides in the classroom, do you see people acting irresponsibly, expending little effort, and taking the easy way out? Select one area and write an essay illustrating the effects of this behavior on everyone concerned.

Debating the Issues: Gender-Based Education

GERRY GARIBALDI

Writer and teacher Gerry Garibaldi grew up in San Francisco, and attended San Francisco State University. Following college, he worked for Paramount Pictures, first as a reader and eventually as a vice president of production. He was also a freelance writer for film studios and a journalist. Then Garibaldi changed careers, to teach high school English. This article was published in *City Journal*, an urban policy quarterly, in summer 2006.

Pre-Reading Journal Entry

Think back to your own high school days. Recall how boys and girls were treated in school and how they behaved. Did you notice any differences in the way boys and girls were treated by teachers? In the way they behaved in class? In your journal, record some of the differences between the sexes that you noted. To what extent was your own behavior as a high school student influenced by your gender?

How the Schools Shortchange Boys

In the newly feminized classroom, boys tune out. 1

Since I started teaching several years ago, after 25 years in the movie business, 2
I've come to learn firsthand that everything I'd heard about the feminization of
our schools is real—and far more pernicious to boys than I had imagined. Christina Hoff Sommers was absolutely accurate in describing, in her 2000 bestseller, *The
War Against Boys*, how feminist complaints that girls were "losing their voice" in a
male-oriented classroom have prompted the educational establishment to turn the
schools upside down to make them more girl-friendly, to the detriment of males.

As a result, boys have become increasingly disengaged. Only 65 percent 3
earned high school diplomas in the class of 2003, compared with 72 percent of
girls, education researcher Jay Greene recently documented. Girls now so outnumber boys on most university campuses across the country that some schools, like
Kenyon College, have even begun to practice affirmative action for boys in admissions. And as in high school, girls are getting better grades and graduating at a
higher rate.

As Sommers understood, it is boys' aggressive and rationalist nature—rede- 4
fined by educators as a behavioral disorder—that's getting so many of them in
trouble in the feminized schools. Their problem: they don't want to be girls.

Take my tenth-grade student Brandon. I noted that he was on the no-pass list 5
again, after three consecutive days in detention for being disruptive. "Who gave it
to you this time?" I asked, passing him on my way out.

"Waverly," he muttered into the long folding table. 6

"What for?" 7

"Just asking a question," he replied. 8

"No," I corrected him. "You said"—and here I mimicked his voice—"'Why do 9
we have to do this crap anyway?' Right?"

Brandon recalls one of those sweet, ruby-cheeked boys you often see depicted 10
on English porcelain.

He's smart, precocious, and—according to his special-education profile—has 11
been "behaviorally challenged" since fifth grade. The special-ed classification is
the bane of the modern boy. To teachers, it's a yellow flag that snaps out at you the
moment you open a student's folder. More than any other factor, it has determined
Brandon's and legions of other boys' troubled tenures as students.

Brandon's current problem began because Ms. Waverly, his social studies 12
teacher, failed to answer one critical question: What was the point of the lesson
she was teaching? One of the first observations I made as a teacher was that boys
invariably ask this question, while girls seldom do. When a teacher assigns a paper
or a project, girls will obediently flip their notebooks open and jot down the due
date. Teachers love them. God loves them. Girls are calm and pleasant. They succeed through cooperation.

Boys will pin you to the wall like a moth. They want a rational explanation 13
for everything. If unconvinced by your reasons—or if you don't bother to offer
any—they slouch contemptuously in their chairs, beat their pencils, or watch the
squirrels outside the window. Two days before the paper is due, girls are handing
in the finished product in neat vinyl folders with colorful clip-art title pages. It

isn't until the boys notice this that the alarm sounds. "Hey, you never told us 'bout a paper! What paper?! I want to see my fucking counselor!"

A female teacher, especially if she has no male children of her own, I've noticed, 14 will tend to view boys' penchant for challenging classroom assignments as disruptive, disrespectful—rude. In my experience, notes home and parent-teacher conferences almost always concern a boy's behavior in class, usually centering on this kind of conflict. In today's feminized classroom, with its "cooperative learning" and "inclusiveness," a student's demand for assurance of a worthwhile outcome for his effort isn't met with a reasonable explanation but is considered inimical to the educational process. Yet it's this very trait, innate to boys and men, that helps explain male success in the hard sciences, math, and business.

The difference between the male and female predilection for hard proof shows 15 up among the teachers, too. In my second year of teaching, I attended a required seminar on "differentiated instruction," a teaching model that is the current rage in the fickle world of pop education theory. The method addresses the need to teach all students in a classroom where academic abilities vary greatly—where there is "heterogeneous grouping," to use the ed-school jargon—meaning kids with IQs of 55 sit side by side with the gifted. The theory goes that the "least restrictive environment" is best for helping the intellectually challenged. The teacher's job is to figure out how to dice up his daily lessons to address every perceived shortcoming and disability in the classroom.

After the lecture, we broke into groups of five, with instructions to work coop- 16 eratively to come up with a model lesson plan for just such a classroom situation. My group had two men and three women. The women immediately set to work; my seasoned male cohort and I reclined sullenly in our chairs.

"Are the women going to do all the work?" one of the women inquired bright- 17 ly after about ten minutes.

"This is baloney," my friend declared, yawning, as he chucked the seminar 18 handout into a row of empty plastic juice bottles. "We wouldn't have this problem if we grouped kids by ability, like we used to."

The women, all dedicated teachers, understood this, too. But that wasn't the 19 point. Treating people as equals was a social goal well worth pursuing. And we contentious boys were just too dumb to get it.

Female approval has a powerful effect on the male psyche. Kindness, con- 20 sideration, and elevated moral purpose have nothing to do with an irreducible proof, of course. Yet we male teachers squirm when women point out our moral failings—and our boy students do, too. This is the virtue that has helped women redefine the mission of education.

The notion of male ethical inferiority first arises in grammar school, where 21 women make up the overwhelming majority of teachers. It's here that the alphabet soup of supposed male dysfunctions begins. And make no mistake: while girls occasionally exhibit symptoms of male-related disorders in this world, females diagnosed with learning disabilities simply don't exist.

For a generation now, many well-meaning parents, worn down by their boy's 22 failure to flourish in school, his poor self-esteem and unhappiness, his discipline problems, decide to accept administration recommendations to have him tested for disabilities. The pitch sounds reasonable: admission into special ed qualifies him for tutoring, modified lessons, extra time on tests (including the SAT), and other supposed benefits. It's all a hustle, Mom and Dad privately advise their boy. Don't worry about it. We know there's nothing wrong with you.

To get into special ed, however, administrators must find something wrong. In my four years of teaching, I've never seen them fail. In the first IEP (Individualized Educational Program) meeting, the boy and his parents learn the results of disability testing. When the boy hears from three smiling adults that he does indeed have a learning disability, his young face quivers like Jell-O. For him, it was never a hustle. From then on, however, his expectations of himself—and those of his teachers—plummet. 23

Special ed is the great spangled elephant in the education parade. Each year, it grows larger and more lumbering, drawing more and more boys into the procession. Since the publication of Sommers's book, it has grown tenfold. Special ed now is the single largest budget item, outside of basic operations, in most school districts across the country. 24

Special-ed boosters like to point to the success that boys enjoy after they begin the program. Their grades rise, and the phone calls home cease. Anxious parents feel reassured that progress is happening. In truth, I have rarely seen any real improvement in a student's performance after he's become a special-ed kid. On my first day of teaching, I received manila folders for all five of my special-ed students—boys all—with a score of modifications that I had to make in each day's lesson plan. 25

I noticed early on that my special-ed boys often sat at their desks with their heads down or casually staring off into space, as if tracking motes in their eyes, while I proceeded with my lesson. A special-ed caseworker would arrive, take their assignments, and disappear with the boys into the resource room. The students would return the next day with completed assignments. 26

"Did you do this yourself?" I'd ask, dubious. 27

They assured me that they did. I became suspicious, however, when I noticed that they couldn't perform the same work on their own, away from the resource room. A special-ed caseworker's job is to keep her charges from failing. A failure invites scrutiny and reams of paperwork. The caseworkers do their jobs. 28

Brandon has been on the special-ed track since he was nine. He knows his legal rights as well as his caseworkers do. And he plays them ruthlessly. In every debate I have with him about his low performance, Brandon delicately threads his response with the very sinews that bind him. After a particularly easy midterm, I made him stay after class to explain his failure. 29

"An 'F'?!" I said, holding the test under his nose. 30

"You were supposed to modify that test," he countered coolly. "I only had to answer nine of the 27 questions. The nine I did are all right." 31

His argument is like a piece of fine crystal that he rolls admiringly in his hand. He demands that I appreciate the elegance of his position. I do, particularly because my own is so weak. 32

Yet while the process of education may be deeply absorbing to Brandon, he long ago came to dismiss the content entirely. For several decades, white Anglo-Saxon males—Brandon's ancestors—have faced withering assault from feminism- and multiculturalism-inspired education specialists. Armed with a spiteful 33 moral rectitude, their goal is to sever his historical reach, to defame, cover over, dilute…and then reconstruct.

In today's politically correct textbooks, Nikki Giovanni and Toni Morrison 34 stand shoulder-to-shoulder with Mark Twain, William Faulkner, and Charles Dickens, even though both women are second-raters at best. But even in their superficial aspects, the textbooks advertise publishers' intent to pander to the prevailing PC[1] attitudes. The books feature page after page of healthy, exuberant young girls in winning portraits. Boys (white boys in particular) will more often than not be shunted to the background in photos or be absent entirely or appear sitting in wheelchairs.

The underlying message isn't lost on Brandon. His keen young mind reads 35 between the lines and perceives the folly of all that he's told to accept. Because he lacks an adult perspective, however, what he cannot grasp is the ruthlessness of the war that the education reformers have waged. Often when he provokes, it's simple boyish tit for tat.

A week ago, I dispatched Brandon to the library with directions to choose a 36 book for his novel assignment. He returned minutes later with his choice and a twinkling smile.

"I got a grreat book, Mr. Garibaldi!" he said, holding up an old, bleary, cloth- 37 bound item. "Can I read the first page aloud, pahlease?"

My mind buzzed like a fly, trying to discover some hint of mischief. 38

"Who's the author?" 39

"Ah, Joseph Conrad," he replied, consulting the frontispiece. "Can I? Huh, 40 huh, huh?"

"I guess so." 41

Brandon eagerly stood up before the now-alert class of mostly black and 42 Puerto Rican faces, adjusted his shoulders as if straightening a prep-school blazer, then intoned solemnly: *"The Nigger of the 'Narcissus'"*—twinkle, twinkle, twinkle. "Chapter one…."

Merry mayhem ensued. Brandon had one of his best days of the year. 43

Boys today feel isolated and outgunned, but many, like Brandon, don't lack 44 pluck and courage. They often seem to have more of it than their parents, who writhe uncomfortably before a system steeled in the armor of "social conscience." The game, parents whisper to themselves, is to play along, to maneuver, to outdistance your rival. Brandon's struggle is an honest one: to preserve truth and his own integrity.

Boys who get a compartment on the special-ed train take the ride to its end 45 without looking out the window. They wait for the moment when they can step out and scorn the rattletrap that took them nowhere. At the end of the line, some, like Brandon, may have forged the resiliency of survival. But that's not what school is for.

Questions for Critical Reading

1. What is the selection's thesis? Locate the sentence(s) in which Garibaldi states his main idea. If he doesn't state his thesis explicitly, express it in your own words.

---

[1] Short for "politically correct," usually used negatively (editors' note).

2. According to Garibaldi, how do boys and girls—and men and women—react to being given an assignment?

3. Why are so many boys tested for disabilities, according to Garibaldi?

4. How does Garibaldi's student Brandon take advantage of his special education designation?

Questions About the Writer's Craft

1. **The pattern.** Garibaldi uses expert testimony, statistics, examples from his personal experience, and anecdotes as evidence for his thesis. List the specific evidence he uses. Which kinds of evidence does Garibaldi use most often? How does his use of evidence make the essay more or less persuasive?

2. **Other patterns.** Garibaldi uses cause-effect, comparison-contrast, and process analysis in this essay. Identify passages in which these patterns are used.

3. **Strong wording.** The first sentence in the essay is a strongly worded declaration: "In the newly feminized classroom, boys tune out." Where else does Garibaldi use such strongly worded statements? What is the effect of this style?

4. **Language.** Where does Garibaldi use vulgar or offensive language? What effect, if any, does this language have on his argument?

Writing Assignments Using Argumentation-Persuasion as a Pattern of Development

1. Read Michael Kimmel's "A War Against Boys?" (later in this chapter), an essay that takes exception to Garibaldi's view of boys' education. Decide which writer presents his case more convincingly. Then write an essay arguing that the *other writer* has trouble making a strong case for his position. Consider the merits and flaws (including any logical fallacies) in the argument plus such issues as the writer's credibility, strategies for dealing with the opposing view, and use of emotional appeals. Throughout, support your opinion with specific examples drawn from the selection. Keep in mind that you are analyzing the effectiveness of the writer's argument. It's not appropriate, then, simply to explain why you agree or disagree with the writer's position or merely to summarize what the writer says.

2. Although Garibaldi argues forcefully that boys are shortchanged by the "feminization" of education and the special education system, he does not propose any changes to improve the way that boys are educated. How might public elementary, middle, and high school education be changed so that boys flourish? What activities or subjects would help boys in school? Using Garibaldi's essay as a take-off point, write an essay in which you argue for changes in education that would benefit boys.

Writing Assignment Combining
Patterns of Development

3. As Garibaldi puts it, "Special ed is the great spangled elephant in the education parade." He is correct in asserting that the number of children in special education and the amount of money spent to educate them have increased dramatically in recent years. Brainstorm with others to identify factors that might be contributing to this growth; then do some research on the history of special education and current trends. Focusing on several related factors, write an essay showing how these factors contribute to the problem. Possible factors include the following: increases in the number of diagnoses of learning disabilities and autism, lack of standards for determining who needs special education, assigning all low-achieving students to special education whether or not they have a disability, racism, and financial incentives for school districts to increase special education enrollment. At the end of the essay, offer some recommendations about steps that can be taken to ensure that only children who need it are assigned to special education.

MICHAEL KIMMEL

Michael Kimmel is a professor of sociology at State University of New York at Stony Brook and one of the world's leading researchers in gender studies. He is the author or editor of more than twenty volumes on men and masculinity, including *Manhood in America: A Cultural History* (1996) and *Guyland: The Perilous World Where Boys Become Men* (2008). His articles have appeared in dozens of magazines, newspapers, and scholarly journals, and he lectures extensively. The following piece is excerpted from an article published in the Fall 2006 issue of *Dissent Magazine*.

Pre-Reading Journal Entry

The phrase "boys will be boys" is often cited to explain certain types of male behavior. What kinds of actions typically fall in this category? List a few of them in your journal. Which behaviors are positive? Why? Which are negative? Why?

A War Against Boys?

Doug Anglin isn't likely to flash across the radar screen at an Ivy League admissions office. A seventeen-year-old senior at Milton High School, a suburb outside Boston, Anglin has a B-minus average and plays soccer and baseball. But he's done something that millions of other teenagers haven't: he's sued his school district for sex discrimination.

Anglin's lawsuit, brought with the aid of his father, a Boston lawyer, claims that schools routinely discriminate against males. "From the elementary level, they establish a philosophy that if you sit down, follow orders, and listen to what they say, you'll do well and get good grades," he told a journalist. "Men naturally rebel against this." He may have a point: overworked teachers might well look more kindly on classroom docility and decorum. But his proposed remedies—such as raising boy's grades retroactively—are laughable.

And though it's tempting to parse the statements of a mediocre high school   3
senior—what's so "natural" about rebelling against blindly following orders,
a military tactician might ask—Anglin's apparent admissions angle is but the
latest skirmish of a much bigger battle in the culture wars. The current salvos
concern boys. The "trouble with boys" has become a staple on talk-radio, the
cover story in *Newsweek*, and the subject of dozens of columns in newspapers
and magazines. And when the First Lady offers a helping hand to boys, you
know something political is in the works. "Rescuing" boys actually translates
into bashing feminism.

There is no doubt that boys are not faring well in school. From elementary   4
schools to high schools they have lower grades, lower class rank, and fewer honors
than girls. They're 50 percent more likely to repeat a grade in elementary school,
one-third more likely to drop out of high school, and about six times more likely to
be diagnosed with attention deficit and hyperactivity disorder (ADHD).

College statistics are similar—if the boys get there at all. Women now consti-   5
tute the majority of students on college campuses, having passed men in 1982,
so that in eight years women will earn 58 percent of bachelor's degrees in U.S.
colleges. One expert, Tom Mortensen, warns that if current trends continue, "the
graduation line in 2068 will be all females." Mortensen may be a competent higher
education policy analyst, but he's a lousy statistician. His dire prediction is analo-
gous to predicting forty years ago that, if the enrollment of black students at Ol'
Miss was one in 1964, and, say, two hundred in 1968 and one thousand in 1976,
then "if present trends continue" there would be no white students on campus
by 1982. Doomsayers lament that women now outnumber men in the social and
behavioral sciences by about three to one, and that they've invaded such traditionally male bastions as engineering (where they now make up 20 percent) and biology and business (virtually par).

These three issues—declining numbers, declining achievement, and increas-   6
ingly problematic behavior—form the empirical basis of the current debate. But
its political origins are significantly older and ominously more familiar. Peeking
underneath the empirical façade helps explain much of the current lineup.

Why now?   7

If boys are doing worse, whose fault is it? To many of the current critics, it's   8
women's fault, either as feminists, as mothers, or as both. Feminists, we read,
have been so successful that the earlier "chilly classroom climate" has now become overheated to the detriment of boys. Feminist-inspired programs have
enabled a whole generation of girls to enter the sciences, medicine, law, and the
professions; to continue their education; to imagine careers outside the home.
But in so doing, these same feminists have pathologized boyhood. Elementary schools are, we read, "anti-boy"—emphasizing reading and restricting the
movements of young boys. They "feminize" boys, forcing active, healthy, and
naturally exuberant boys to conform to a regime of obedience, "pathologizing
what is simply normal for boys," as one psychologist puts it. Schools are an
"inhospitable" environment for boys, writes Christina Hoff Sommers, where
their natural propensities for rough-and-tumble play, competition, aggression,
and rambunctious violence are cast as social problems in the making. Michael
Gurian argues in *The Wonder of Boys*, that, with testosterone surging through

their little limbs, we demand that they sit still, raise their hands, and take naps. We're giving them the message, he says, that "boyhood is defective." By the time they get to college, they've been steeped in anti-male propaganda. "Why would any self-respecting boy want to attend one of America's increasingly feminized universities?" asks George Gilder in *National Review*. The American university is now a "fluffy pink playpen of feminist studies and agitprop 'herstory,' taught amid a green goo of eco-motherism..." [author's ellipsis].

Such claims sound tinnily familiar. At the turn of the last century, cultural   9
critics were concerned that the rise of white-collar businesses meant increasing indolence for men, whose sons were being feminized by mothers and female teachers. Then, as now, the solutions were to find arenas in which boys could simply be boys, and where men could be men as well. So fraternal lodges offered men a homo-social sanctuary, and dude ranches and sports provided a place where these sedentary men could experience what Theodore Roosevelt called the strenuous life. Boys could troop off with the Boy Scouts, designed as a fin-de-siècle "boys' liberation movement." Modern society was turning hardy, robust boys, as Boy Scouts' founder Ernest Thompson Seton put it, into "a lot of flat chested cigarette smokers with shaky nerves and doubtful vitality." Today, women teachers are once again to blame for boys' feminization. "It's the teacher's job to create a classroom environment that accommodates both male and female energy, not just mainly female energy," explains Gurian.

What's wrong with this picture? Well, for one thing, it creates a false opposi-   10
tion between girls and boys, assuming that educational reforms undertaken to enable girls to perform better hinder boys' educational development. But these reforms—new classroom arrangements, teacher training, increased attentiveness to individual learning styles—actually enable larger numbers of boys to get a better education. Though the current boy advocates claim that schools used to be more "boy friendly" before all these "feminist" reforms, they obviously didn't go to school in those halcyon days, the 1950s, say, when the classroom was far more regimented, corporal punishment common, and teachers far more authoritarian; they even gave grades for "deportment." Rambunctious boys were simply not tolerated; they dropped out.

Gender stereotyping hurts both boys and girls. If there is a zero-sum game,   11
it's not because of some putative feminization of the classroom. The net effect of the No Child Left Behind Act has been zero-sum competition, as school districts scramble to stretch inadequate funding, leaving them little choice but to cut noncurricular programs so as to ensure that curricular mandates are followed. This disadvantages "rambunctious" boys, because many of these programs are afterschool athletics, gym, and recess. And cutting "unnecessary" school counselors and other remedial programs also disadvantages boys, who compose the majority of children in behavioral and remedial educational programs. The problem of inadequate school funding lies not at feminists' door, but in the halls of Congress. This is further compounded by changes in the insurance industry, which often pressure therapists to put children on medication for ADHD rather than pay for expensive therapy.

Another problem is that the frequently cited numbers are misleading. More   12
people—that is, males and females—are going to college than ever before. In 1960,

54 percent of boys and 38 percent of girls went directly to college; today the numbers are 64 percent of boys and 70 percent of girls. It is true that the rate of increase among girls is higher than the rate of increase among boys, but the numbers are increasing for both.

The gender imbalance does not obtain at the nation's most elite colleges and universities, where percentages for men and women are, and have remained, similar. Of the top colleges and universities in the nation, only Stanford sports a fifty-fifty gender balance. Harvard[1] and Amherst enroll 56 percent men, Princeton and Chicago 54 percent men, Duke and Berkeley 52 percent, and Yale 51 percent. In science and engineering, the gender imbalance still tilts decidedly toward men: Cal Tech is 65 percent male and 35 percent female; MIT is 62 percent male, 38 percent female. 13

And the imbalance is not uniform across class and race. It remains the case that far more working-class women—of all races—go to college than do working-class men. Part of this is a seemingly rational individual decision: a college-educated woman still earns about the same as a high-school educated man, $35,000 to $31,000. By race, the disparities are more starkly drawn. Among middle-class, white, high school graduates going to college this year, half are male and half are female. But only 37 percent of black college students and 45 percent of Hispanic students are male. The numerical imbalance turns out to be more a problem of race and class than gender. It is what Cynthia Fuchs Epstein calls a "deceptive distinction"—a difference that appears to be about gender, but is actually about something else. 14

Why don't the critics acknowledge these race and class differences? To many who now propose to "rescue" boys, such differences are incidental because, in their eyes, all boys are the same aggressive, competitive, rambunctious little devils. They operate from a facile, and inaccurate, essentialist dichotomy between males and females. Boys must be allowed to be boys—so that they grow up to be men. 15

This facile biologism leads the critics to propose some distasteful remedies to allow these testosterone-juiced boys to express themselves. Gurian, for example, celebrates all masculine rites of passage, "like military boot camp, fraternity hazings, graduation day, and bar mitzvah" as "essential parts of every boy's life." He also suggests reviving corporal punishment, both at home and at school—but only when administered privately with cool indifference and never in the heat of adult anger. He calls it "spanking responsibly," though I suspect school boards and child welfare agencies might have another term for it. 16

But what boys need turns out to be pretty much what girls need. In their best-selling *Raising Cain*, Michael Thompson and Dan Kindlon describe boys' needs: to be loved, get sex, and not be hurt. Parents are counseled to allow boys their emotions; accept a high level of activity; speak their language; and treat them with respect. They are to teach the many ways a boy can be a man, use discipline to guide and build, and model manhood as emotionally attached. Aside from the obvious tautologies, what they advocate is exactly what feminists have been advocating for girls for some time.... 17

---

[1] Harvard University now enrolls more women than men (author's note).

How does a focus on the ideology of masculinity explain what is happening 18 to boys in school? Consider the parallel for girls. Carol Gilligan's work on adolescent girls describes how these assertive, confident, and proud young girls "lose their voices" when they hit adolescence. At that same moment, Pollack[2] notes, boys become more confident, even beyond their abilities. You might even say that boys find their voices, but it is the inauthentic voice of bravado, posturing, foolish risk-taking, and gratuitous violence. He calls it "the boy code." The boy code teaches them that they are supposed to be in power, and so they begin to act as if they are. They "ruffle in a manly pose," as William Butler Yeats[3] once put it, "for all their timid heart."

In adolescence, both boys and girls get their first real dose of gender inequal- 19 ity: girls suppress ambition, boys inflate it. Recent research on the gender gap in school achievement bears this out. Girls are more likely to undervalue their abilities, especially in the more traditionally "masculine" educational arenas such as math and science. Only the most able and most secure girls take courses in those fields. Thus, their numbers tend to be few, and their mean test scores high. Boys, however, possessed of this false voice of bravado (and facing strong family pressure) are likely to overvalue their abilities, to remain in programs though they are less capable of succeeding.

This difference, and not some putative discrimination against boys, is the rea- 20 son that girls' mean test scores in math and science are now, on average, approaching that of boys. Too many boys remain in difficult math and science courses longer than they should; they pull the boys' mean scores down. By contrast, the smaller number of girls, whose abilities and self-esteem are sufficient to enable them to "trespass" into a male domain, skew female data upward.

A parallel process is at work in the humanities and social sciences. Girls' mean 21 test scores in English and foreign languages, for example, outpace those of boys. But this is not the result of "reverse discrimination"; it is because the boys bump up against the norms of masculinity. Boys regard English as a "feminine" subject. Pioneering research by Wayne Martino in Australia and Britain found that boys avoid English because of what it might say about their (inauthentic) masculine pose. "Reading is lame, sitting down and looking at words is pathetic," commented one boy. "Most guys who like English are faggots." The traditional liberal arts curriculum, as it was before feminism, is seen as feminizing. As Catharine Stimpson[4] recently put it, "Real men don't speak French."

Boys tend to hate English and foreign languages for the same reasons that 22 girls love them. In English, they observe, there are no hard-and-fast rules, one expresses one's opinion about the topic and everyone's opinion is equally valued. "The answer can be a variety of things, you're never really wrong," observed one boy. "It's not like maths and science where there is one set answer to everything." Another boy noted:

---

[2] William Pollack, author of *Real Boys* (editors' note).

[3] Yeats (1865–1939) was a major Irish poet and playwright (editors' note).

[4] Stimpson, a professor of English at New York University, has written about women in culture and society (editors' note).

I find English hard. It's because there are no set rules for reading texts…[author's ellip- 23
sis]. English isn't like math where you have rules on how to do things and where there
are right and wrong answers. In English you have to write down how you feel and that's
what I don't like.

Compare this to the comments of girls in the same study: 24

I feel motivated to study English because…[author's ellipsis] you have freedom in 25
English—unlike subjects such as math and science—and your view isn't necessarily
wrong. There is no definite right or wrong answer, and you have the freedom to say
what you feel is right without it being rejected as a wrong answer.

It is not the school experience that "feminizes" boys, but rather the ideology of 26
traditional masculinity that keeps boys from wanting to succeed. "The work you
do here is girls' work," one boy commented to a researcher. "It's not real work."

"Real work" involves a confrontation—not with feminist women, whose sen- 27
sible educational reforms have opened countless doors to women while closing
off none to men—but with an anachronistic definition of masculinity that stresses
many of its vices (anti-intellectualism, entitlement, arrogance, and aggression) but
few of its virtues. When the self-appointed rescuers demand that we accept boys'
"hardwiring," could they possibly have such a monochromatic and relentlessly
negative view of male biology? Maybe they do. But simply shrugging our collective shoulders in resignation and saying "boys will be boys" sets the bar much too
low. Boys can do better than that. They can be men.

Perhaps the real "male bashers" are those who promise to rescue boys from the 28
clutches of feminists. Are males not also "hardwired" toward compassion, nurturing,
and love? If not, would we allow males to be parents? It is never a biological question
of whether we are "hardwired" for some behavior; it is, rather, a political question of
which "hardwiring" we choose to respect and which we choose to challenge….

Questions for Critical Reading

1. What is the selection's thesis? Locate the sentence(s) in which Kimmel states his
   main idea. If he doesn't state his thesis explicitly, express it in your own words.

2. Kimmel cites statistics showing that more girls than boys go to college. Where does
   he discuss these statistics? How does he interpret the statistics to support his idea
   that the imbalance in college attendance does not have to do with gender?

3. According to Kimmel, how do girls and boys change when they reach adolescence?

4. What does Kimmel mean by the phrase "the boy code" (paragraph 18)?

Questions About the Writer's Craft

1. **Expert opinions.** Kimmel cites a number of experts on both sides of the question
   he is arguing. Which experts oppose his main points? Which ones support them?
   What is the effect of citing so many experts?

2. **Purposes.** What is the purpose of paragraphs 4–6? Paragraphs 7–9? Where does
   Kimmel start presenting his own view of the causes of boys' difficulty in school?

3. **Other patterns.** What is the main pattern, other than argumentation-persuasion, that is used in this essay? Give specific examples.

4. **Ethos.** Reread the biographical sketch of Kimmel that precedes the essay. How does Kimmel's background contribute to the ethos of this argument? Does it influence your response to his claims?

Writing Assignments Using Argumentation-Persuasion as a Pattern of Development

1. Kimmel focuses primarily on how gender inequality affects boys, but gender inequality affects girls as well (see Kimmel, paragraphs 19 and following). Write an essay in which you argue that gender roles and norms limit (or do not limit) what women can accomplish in school and in their careers.

2. Kimmel criticizes those who claim that biology, or inborn traits, are primarily responsible for shaping gender differences. He believes that biological differences may exist but that the environment, including political and cultural forces, has a strong influence. Write an essay arguing your own position about the role that biology and environment play in determining sex-role attitudes and behaviors. Remember to acknowledge opposing views and to defend your own position with examples based on your experiences and observations.

Writing Assignment Combining Patterns of Development

3. Feminism is mentioned throughout Garibaldi's and Kimmel's essays, but neither of them defines the term. Do some research about the history of feminism. Brainstorm with others—both men and women—about the topic and write an essay in which you *define* feminism. Be sure to give *examples* of what you mean by feminism, either from your own experience or from history.

Debating the Issues: Government Regulation to Help Control Obesity and Related Diseases

MARK BITTMAN

Lead food columnist for the *New York Times*, Mark Bittman is also a popular television personality and an award-winning best-selling cookbook author. His publications include *How to Cook Everything* (1998), *How to Cook Everything Vegetarian* (2007), *Food Matters: A Guide to Conscious Eating* (2008), and *VB6: Eat Vegan Before 6:00 to Lose Weight and Restore Your Health...for Good* (2013). The essay that follows was first published in the online *New York Times* on June 10, 2014.

Pre-Reading Journal

Our nation's obesity problem has been the recent subject of countless talk shows, news broadcasts, and magazine articles. How has the "buzz" surrounding this issue affected you? Are you more conscious of how much you weigh and of what you eat than you were a few years ago? Do you see connections in your own life among your health, your weight, and the food you consume? Explore these ideas in your journal.

What Causes Weight Gain

If I ask you what constitutes "bad" eating, the kind that leads to obesity and a variety of connected diseases, you're likely to answer, "Salt, fat and sugar." This trilogy of evil has been drilled into us for decades, yet that's not an adequate answer.   1

We don't know everything about the dietary links to chronic disease, but the best-qualified people argue that real food is more likely to promote health and less likely to cause disease than hyperprocessed food. And we can further refine that message: Minimally processed plants should dominate our diets. (This isn't just me saying this; the Institute of Medicine and the Department of Agriculture agree.)   2

And yet we're in the middle of a public health emergency that isn't being taken seriously enough. We should make it a national priority to create two new programs, a research program to determine precisely what causes diet-related chronic illnesses (on top of the list is "Just how bad is sugar?"), and a program that will get this single, simple message across: Eat Real Food.   3

Real food solves the salt/fat/sugar problem. Yes, excess salt may cause or exacerbate high blood pressure, and lowering sodium intake in people with high blood pressure helps. But salt is only one of several risk factors in developing high blood pressure, and those who eat a diverse diet and few processed foods—which supply more than 80 percent of the sodium in typical American diets—need not worry about salt intake (Nestle).   4

"Fat" is a loaded word and a complicated topic, and the jury is still out. Most naturally occurring fats are probably essential, but too much of some fats—and, again, it may be the industrially produced fats used in hyperprocessed foods—seems harmful. Eat real food and your fat intake will probably be fine.   5

"Sugar" has come to represent (or it should) the entire group of processed, nutritionally worthless caloric sweeteners, including table sugar, high fructose corn syrup and so-called healthy alternatives like agave syrup, brown rice syrup, reduced fruit juice and a dozen others.   6

All appear to be damaging because they're *added* sugars, as opposed to naturally occurring ones, like those in actual fruit, which are not problematic. And although added fructose may be more harmful than the others, it could also be that those highly refined carbohydrates that our bodies rapidly break down to sugar—white bread, for example—are equally unhealthy. Again: These are hyperprocessed foods.   7

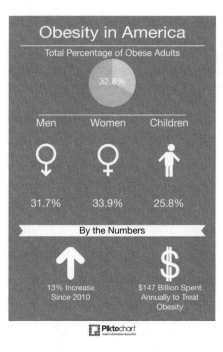

Source: Khan, Amir. "America Tops List of 10 Most Obese Countries." *US News & World Report: Health and Wellness*, 28 May 2014. Based on figures from the CDC.

In sum: Sugar is not the enemy, or not the only enemy. The enemy is hyper- 8 processed food, including sugar.

In the United States—the world's most obese country—the most recent number 9 for the annual cost of obesity is close to $200 billion (Khan).

(Obesity-related costs are incalculable but could easily exceed $1 trillion 10 annually. Wanna balance the budget? Eat real food.) The amount the National Institutes of Health expends for obesity-related research is less than $1 billion annually, and there is no single large, convincing study (and no small study will do) that proposes to solve the underlying causes of obesity ("Estimates of Funding"). If the solution were as simple as "salt, fat, sugar" or the increasingly absurd-sounding "calories in, calories out," surely we'd have made some progress by now.

We know that eating real food is a general solution, but a large part of our 11 dietary problems might stem from something as simple as the skyrocketing and almost unavoidable consumption of caloric sweeteners and/or hyperprocessed carbs, which are in 80 percent of our food products ("Why Katie Couric").

Or it could be those factors in tandem with others, like the degradation of our 12 internal networks of bacteria, which in turn could be caused by the overuse of antibiotics or other environmental issues. Or it could be even more complex.

The point is we need to know for certain, because until we have an actual 13 smoking gun, it's difficult to persuade lawmakers to enact needed policies. (Smoking gun studies are difficult in the diet world, but throwing up our hands in the face of complexity serves the interests of processed-food pushers.) Look no further than the example of tobacco.

Meanwhile, if we had to pick one target in the interim, caloric sweeteners 14 are unquestionably it; they're well correlated with weight gain (and their reduction equally well correlated with weight loss), Type 2 diabetes and many other problems (Johnson et al.). How to limit the intake of sugar? A soda tax is a start, proper labeling would be helpful, and—quite possibly most important, because it's going to take us a generation or two to get out of this mess—restrictions on marketing sweet "food" to children.

There's no reason to delay action on those kinds of moves. But let's get the sci- 15 ence straight so that firm, convincing, sound, evenhanded recommendations can be made based on the best possible evidence. And meanwhile, let's also get the simple message straight: It's "Eat Real Food."

Works Cited

"Estimates of Funding for Various Research, Condition, and Disease Categories (RCDC)." *National Institutes of Health: Research Portfolio Online Reporting Tools*. U.S. Department of Health and Human Services, 7 Mar. 2014.

Johnson, Rachel K., et al. "Dietary Sugars Intake and Cardiovascular Health: A Scientific Statement from the American Heart Association." *Circulation: Journal of the American Heart Association*, vol. 120, 2009, pp. 1011–1020, doi:10.1161/CIRCULATIONAHA. 109.192627.

Khan, Amir. "America Tops List of 10 Most Obese Countries." *US News & World Report: Health and Wellness,* 28 May 2014, health.usnews.com/health-news/health-wellness/articles/2014/05/28/america-tops-list-of-10-most-obese-countries.

Nestle, Marion. "Interview with *Scientific American* on the Complexities of Salt Science." *Food Politics*, 15 July 2011, www.foodpolitics.com/page/11/?s=dietary+guidelines.

"Why Katie Couric Wants You to Get 'Fed Up,' Take a Sugar Challenge." *ABC News: Medical Unit*, 8 May 2014, abcnews.go.com/blogs/health/2014/05/08/why-katie-couric-wants-you-to-get-fed-up-take-a-sugar-challenge.

Questions for Critical Reading

1. What is the selection's thesis? Locate the sentence(s) in which Bittman states his main idea. If he doesn't state his thesis explicitly, express it in your own words.

2. Bittman states that the creation of two new programs should be a national priority. What are those two programs, and why does he believe they are so important?

3. Bittman believes that hyperprocessed food is the leading cause of obesity in the United States. How does he define the term *hyperprocessed food*? What examples of hyperprocessed foods does he provide?

4. What specific legislative action does Bittman recommend to "limit the intake of sugar"? Why does he target sugar?

Questions About the Writer's Craft

1. **Authority.** For argumentation-persuasion essays to be effective, writers need to make sure that their audiences believe they know what they are talking about and

that they are worth listening to. Has Bittman succeeded in establishing his authority on the subject about which he writes? Why or why not?

2. **Title.** Bittman's title, "What Causes Weight Gain," includes no question mark. Do you think the mark of punctuation was intentionally left out, or do you think its omission was a careless error? Explain your reasoning.

3. **Other patterns.** Bittman uses *causal analysis* throughout his essay. For example, early on, he indicates that "real food" results in better health and less disease than hyperprocessed food. Provide several other examples that illustrate his use of *causal analysis*.

4. **Tone.** How would you describe the tone Bittman uses in his writing? Why do you think he decided to use this tone? Do you think it's effective? Why or why not?

Writing Assignments Using Argumentation-Persuasion as a Pattern of Development

1. In his essay, Bittman argues, "Minimally processed plants should dominate our diets." Write an essay in which you either agree or disagree with his position and provide evidence from outside sources to support your claim. In addition to library and Internet sources, consider incorporating information from personal interviews. Also consider using images such as charts or diagrams to add to the effectiveness of your essay.

2. Bittman clearly feels strongly regarding the health issue about which he is writing. Think of a health issue about which you have strong feelings and write an argumentation-persuasion essay in which you make effective use of *logos, pathos*, and *ethos*. For example, you might write about the building of public exercise facilities such as ball courts, the requirements for childhood vaccinations, or laws governing the use of tobacco, alcohol, or marijuana. Decide on a specific purpose and audience for your essay, and tailor your approach for that purpose and audience. You might talk to classmates and friends outside class to make sure your topic is sufficiently narrow. Then develop a thesis that contains a *claim* for which you can provide evidence. Consider using images such as charts or diagrams as well as other outside sources to add to the effectiveness of your essay.

Writing Assignment Combining Patterns of Development

3. In his argumentation-persuasion essay, Bittman states, "'Fat' is a loaded word and a complicated topic, and the jury is still out." Write an essay in which you explore the *definition* of the word *fat*, the power of the word, and how the word is used in our culture today. What *effect* does the word have on people? Include *examples* from your own experience or the experiences of people you know.

SHERZOD ABDUKADIROV AND MICHAEL MARLOW

Sherzod Abdukadirov and Michael Marlow are researchers at the Mercatus Center at George Mason University, a nonprofit research center and think tank. Marlow, also a professor of economics at California Polytechnic State University, earned his Ph.D. in economics from Virginia Polytechnic Institute in 1978 and is widely published in scholarly journals. Abdukadirov holds a Ph.D. from George Mason. The essay that follows was originally published in *U.S. News and World Report* on June 5, 2012.

(Note that the following essay uses APA documentation rather than MLA documentation.)

Pre-Reading Journal

Obesity has become a serious problem in the United States. Think of people you know who are dangerously obese. How does their size affect their lives? Why do you think they are unable to control their weight? What kinds of programs, if any, do you think might actually help them lose weight and keep it off? Explore these ideas in your journal.

Government Intervention Will Not Solve Our Obesity Problem

It is clear the United States is facing a rising obesity problem. But the challenge remains: We have yet to determine a successful way to tackle it. According to the National Center for Health Statistics, the prevalence of obesity among adults more than doubled from 13.4 percent in 1960 to 34.3 percent in 2008 (Ogden & Carroll, 2010). A new report...by the *American Journal of Preventive Medicine* predicts that by 2030, 42 percent of Americans will be obese and 11 percent will be severely obese, or 100 pounds overweight (Finkelstein et al., 2012, p. 563).

Despite the myriad of studies showing American obesity is increasing, research does not clearly support that government can solve this complex problem. And yet, government solutions that provide information the public already knows—weight gain occurs when we eat too much and exercise too little—have been the focus to eliminate this epidemic.

Not only is this method not solving the problem, we may actually be increasing the social stigma associated with weight gain. Rather than pursuing a one-size-fits-all solution, we need to push back against government intervention, and allow people to find the solution that best meets their needs.

One popular government solution requires restaurant chains to post calorie counts on their menus to prevent citizens from underestimating their caloric intakes. A recent study examined the impact of New York City's 2008 law requiring restaurant chains to post calorie counts. While 28 percent of patrons said the information influenced their choices, researchers could not detect a change in calories purchased after the law (Elbel, Kersh, Brescoll, & Dixon, 2009, p. 1110). A different study in Seattle found similar evidence that their mandatory menu labeling did little to change fast food purchasing behavior (Finkelstein, Strombotne, Chan, & Krieger, 2011, p. 122).

Trends in overweight, obesity, and extreme obesity among adults aged 20–74 years: United States, 1960–2008

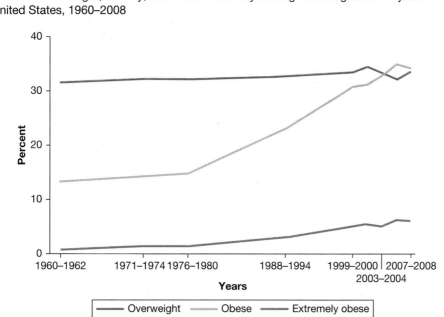

NOTES: Age adjusted by the direct method to the 2000 U.S. Census population using age groups 20–39, 40–59, and 60–74. Pregnant females were excluded. Overweight is a body mass index (BMI) of 25 kg/m^2 or greater but less than 30 kg/m^2; obesity is a BMI greater than or equal to 30 kg/m^2; and extreme obesity is a BMI greater than or equal to 40 kg/m^2.

SOURCES: CDC/NCHS, National Health Examination Survey I 1960–1962; National Health and Nutrition Examination Survey (NHANES) I 1971–1974; NHANES II 1976–1980; NHANES III 1988–1994; NHANES 1999–2000, 2001–2002, 2003–2004, 2005–2006, 2007–2008, and 2009–2010. In Cynthia L. Ogden and Margaret D. Carroll, "Prevalence of Overweight, Obesity, and Extreme Obesity Among Adults: United States, Trends 1960–1962 Through 2007–2008," *Health E-Stats*, National Center for Health Statistics, Dept. of Health and Human Resources, June 2010.

Another government favorite, taxing sugary drinks, does more to shore up gov-   5
ernment coffers than to reduce obesity. A few studies examined the impact of increasing sugary drinks taxes by 20 percent or more. They find that higher taxes do reduce obesity, but the effect is rather limited (Lin, Smith, Lee, & Hall, 2011, p. 329; Fletcher, Frisvold, & Tefft, 2010, p. 23). Interestingly, soda taxes mostly cause people without weight problems to cut back their consumption, even though they are not the intended targets of the policy. Meanwhile, frequent soda drinkers buy lower-priced soda, engage in bulk discounted purchases, and brew more sweetened ice tea.

Beyond being ineffective, there are serious harms from these state interven-   6
tionist policies. Government policies are subject to intense lobbying by well-heeled interest groups, which can lead to results that are counterproductive to the problems they are trying to solve. In one case, Congress effectively declared pizza a vegetable under the intense pressure from agricultural business lobby. This allowed Congress to block attempts by the U.S. Department of Agriculture

to replace pizza, which is classified as a vegetable because it contains tomato paste, with more vegetables.

Government policies may also lead to unintended consequences. Since the 1970s, Department of Agriculture dietary guidelines have urged Americans to eat low fat diets to reduce their risk of coronary heart disease and obesity. Americans heeded the government's advice to switch to foods with less fat content. But because they were eating healthier foods, they ate more. Thus, while the share of calories coming from fat decreased between 1970 and 2000, the actual amount of fat calories in their diet increased, because of an increase in overall calories (Marantz, Bird, & Alderman, 2008, p. 234). 7

The solutions that seem to work the best—the ones that allow individuals to tailor a plan that meets their unique needs—are given short shrift by advocates of government intervention. The growing market for diet books, health foods, weight loss centers, exercise equipment, and athletic clubs is clear evidence that people are concerned about their weight. Unlike government policies, weight loss products and ideas are tested by consumers and failures are replaced by products that really help people control their weight. Consumers will not continue to buy products that don't work. 8

Unfortunately, citizens have little choice but to pay higher taxes and obey bans when laws are passed. One can expect further tax hikes and bans as policymakers conclude that their well-intentioned policies failed simply because they were not harsh enough, but pushing more stringent, failed policies will not improve public health. Instead of wasting resources on inadequate solutions, consumers should return to the market for the innovative solutions, like healthy foods, gyms, and nutrition centers. 9

References

Elbel, B., Kersh, R., Brescoll, V., & Dixon, L.B. (2009). Calorie labeling and food choices: A first look at the effects on low-income people in New York City. *Health Affairs, 28,* 1110–21.

Finkelstein, E., Strombotne, K., Chan, N., & Krieger, J. (2011, February). Mandatory menu labeling in one fast-food chain in King County, Washington. *American Journal of Preventive Medicine,* 122–27.

Finkelstein, E., Khavjou, O., Thompson, H., Trogdon, J., Pan, L., Sherry, B., & Dietz, W. (2012, June). Obesity and severe obesity forecasts through 2030. *American Journal of Preventive Medicine,* 563–570.

Fletcher, J., Frisvold, D, & Tefft, N. (2010, January). Can soft drink taxes reduce population weight? *Contemporary Economic Policy,* 23–35.

Lin, B. H., Smith, T. A., Lee, J. Y., & Hall, K. D. (2011, December). Measuring weight outcomes for obesity intervention strategies: The case of a sugar-sweetened beverage tax. *Economics and Human Biology,* 329–41.

Marantz, P., Bird, E., & Alderman, M. (2008, March). A call for higher standards of evidence for dietary guidelines. *American Journal of Preventive Medicine,* 234–40.

Ogden, C., & Carroll, M. (2012, June 5). Prevalence of overweight, obesity, and extreme obesity among adults: United States, trends 1960–1962 through 2007–2008. *Health E-Stat.* Retrieved from http://www.cdc.gov/nchs/data/hestat/obesity_child_07_08/obesity_child_07_08.htm

Questions for Critical Reading

1. What is the selection's thesis? Locate the sentence(s) in which Abdukadirov and Marlow state their main idea. If they don't state the thesis explicitly, express it in your own words.

2. According to evidence cited by Abdukadirov and Marlow, what has been the effect of posting calorie counts on restaurant menus and taxing sugary drinks in an effort to change purchasing behavior and help control obesity?

3. According to the reading, what harmful and unintended consequences have resulted from government interventionist policies?

4. What solution does the reading offer, instead of government regulation, to help combat our nation's obesity problem?

Questions About the Writer's Craft

1. **Reasoning.** Do Abdukadirov and Marlow use *inductive* or *deductive* reasoning to develop their argument and persuade their readers? Provide evidence from the reading to support your answer.

2. **Comparing arguments.** What does the argument put forth by Abdukadirov and Marlow have in common with the argument put forth by Bittman in the previous reading? In what ways do the arguments differ? In your opinion, which argument is more convincing and why?

3. **Rogerian argument.** To what extent do Abdukadirov and Marlow employ the Rogerian strategy outlined earlier in this chapter? In your opinion, is the strategy effective? Does it help them establish a strong argument that is likely to convince their readers? Do you think their essay would have been more effective if they had adhered more strictly to the Rogerian strategy? Why or why not?

4. **Visual aid.** The essay by Abdukadirov and Marlow is accompanied by a visual component—a graph that illustrates trends in overweight, obese, and extremely obese adults in the United States. What does the graph add to the essay? In what ways does it make the argument more convincing?

Writing Assignments Using Argumentation-Persuasion as a Pattern of Development

1. In their essay, Abdukadirov and Marlow attempt to persuade their readers that government intervention is not the answer to our nation's obesity problem, and they employ a modified Rogerian strategy. Write an essay about an issue that is important to you, and use the Rogerian strategy to acknowledge differing viewpoints, point out areas of common ground, and finally, present evidence for your position. You might address an issue such as requiring all students at your school to live on campus during their first year, or banning freshmen and sophomores from having cars on campus. Or you might address a more widespread issue such

as providing birth control without parental consent to people aged eleven to seventeen or requiring all public school students to wear uniforms.

2. Abdukadirov and Marlow take a stand against government intervention to help control obesity. Many others, including Bittman, maintain an opposing view. Write an essay in which you argue that in light of the seriousness of the obesity problem in the United States, government intervention is both appropriate and necessary. Research specific evidence to support your position and include at least one image to strengthen your argument.

Writing Assignment Combining Patterns of Development

3. In their argumentation-persuasion essay, Abdukadirov and Marlow state in the opening paragraph that although "it is clear the United States is facing a rising obesity problem...we have yet to determine a successful way to tackle it." Write an essay in which you *define* obesity and then *illustrate* possible solutions to this problem. You might interview one or more individuals who were once obese but managed to get their weight under control to find out how they accomplished the feat. You might also conduct research to find out more about programs such as Weight Watchers, Jenny Craig, and Nutrisystem that claim to help individuals lose weight and keep it off. You could also explore how operations such as gastric bypass and gastric banding help some individuals control their weight.

Additional Writing Topics: Argumentation-Persuasion

General Assignments

Using argumentation-persuasion, develop one of these topics into an essay.

1. Hiring or college admissions quotas
2. Giving birth control to teenagers
3. Prayer in the schools
4. Same-sex marriage
5. Reinstating the military draft
6. Penalties for plagiarism
7. Increasing the retirement age
8. Spouses sharing housework equally
9. Smoking in public places
10. Big-time sports in college

Assignments Using Multimedia

Use the suggested media to help develop an argumentation-persuasion essay on one of these topics:

1. AIDS-prevention education and a decline in AIDS cases (graphs)

2. The influences of ethnic cultures on U.S. culture (photos)

3. Societally beneficial uses of public lands (graphs and photos)

4. Bicycle-riding campaigns and the quality of life in cities (photos)

5. The financial expectations of college and high school graduates (graphs).

Assignments with a Specific Purpose, Audience, and Point of View

1. **Academic.** Your college's financial aid department has decided not to renew your scholarship, citing a drop in your grades and an unenthusiastic recommendation from an instructor. Write a letter to the director of financial aid arguing for the renewal of your scholarship.

2. **Academic.** You strongly believe that a particular policy or regulation on campus is unreasonable or unjust. Write a letter to the dean of students (or other appropriate administrator) arguing that the policy needs to be, if not completely revoked, amended in some way. Support your contention with specific examples showing how the regulation has gone wrong. End by providing constructive suggestions for how the policy problem can be solved.

3. **Civic activity.** You and your family don't agree on some aspect of your romantic life (you want to live with your boyfriend/girlfriend and your family doesn't approve; you want to get married and your family wants you to wait). Write a letter explaining why your preference is reasonable. Try hard to win your family over to your side.

4. **Civic activity.** Assume you're a member of a racial, ethnic, religious, or social minority. You might, for example, be a Native American, an elderly person, or a female executive. On a recent television show or in a TV commercial, you saw something that depicts your group in an offensive way. Write a letter (to the network or the advertiser) expressing your feelings and explaining why you feel the material should be taken off the air.

5. **Workplace action.** As a staff writer for an online pop-culture magazine, you've been asked to nominate the "Most Memorable TV Moment of the Last 50 Years" to be featured as the magazine's lead article. Write a letter to your supervising editor in support of your nominee.

6. **Workplace action.** As a high school teacher, you support some additional restriction on students. The restriction might be "no cell phones in school," "no T-shirts," "no food in class," or "no smoking on school grounds." Write an article for the school newspaper justifying this new rule to the student body.

Chapter 19
Locating, Critically Evaluating, Analyzing, and Synthesizing Research Sources

⌄ Learning Objectives

19.1 Plan your research and develop a thesis.

19.2 Conduct primary research—interviews and surveys.

19.3 Conduct secondary research.

19.4 Prepare an annotated bibliography.

19.5 Critically evaluate your sources.

19.6 Analyze and synthesize source material.

19.7 Use quotation, summary, and paraphrase without plagiarizing.

Writing a research essay enlarges your perspective and enables you to move beyond opinions to facts that are firmly supported by evidence. When you write a research paper, you learn how to critically evaluate conflicting opinions and detect other people's biases; you also acquire analytic skills that will benefit you during your college career as well as throughout life.

The process of writing a research essay essentially expands what you already know about writing essays; many steps are the same. The two major differences are the greater length of the research essay—usually five or more pages—and the kind of support you offer for your thesis. Rather than relying on personal experiences, you use published information and expert opinion to support your thesis.

It's helpful to view the process as consisting of two major phases: (1) the research stage, when you find out all you can about your subject and identify a tentative, or working, thesis, and (2) the writing stage, when you present what you've discovered. This chapter focuses on the first stage, as summarized in Figure 19.1. The next chapter examines the second stage. Although we discuss the research process as a series of steps, we encourage you to modify the sequence to suit your subject, your personal approach to writing, and the requirements of a particular assignment.

Plan the Research

19.1 Plan your research and develop a thesis.

Planning your research and developing a thesis involves a sequence of seven steps. First you understand the essay's boundaries. Then you choose a general subject and prewrite to limit the general subject. You then conduct research for primary and secondary sources. Finally, you identify a tentative (working) thesis and make a schedule for getting the essay done on time.

Understand the Essay's Boundaries

Your first step is to clarify the project's requirements. How long should the essay be? How extensively should you deal with opposing viewpoints? Are popular magazines, books, and websites acceptable as sources, or should you use only scholarly sources? Has the instructor limited your subject choices?

Also, be sure you understand the essay's overall purpose and audience. Unless you've been assigned a purely informative report (for example, "Explain several psychologists' theories of hostility"), your research essay shouldn't merely patch together ideas from a variety of sources. You should develop your own position, using outside sources to arrive at a balanced but definitive conclusion. Determine also whether your essay will have an audience other than your instructor. If so, be sure to address the needs of that audience.

One more point: Many instructors expect students to use the third-person point of view in research papers. If you plan to include any personal experiences, observations, or interviews alongside your outside research, ask your instructor if the use of the first-person point of view is appropriate.

Figure 19.1 The Research Essay: Locating, Critically Evaluating, Analyzing, and Synthesizing Research Sources

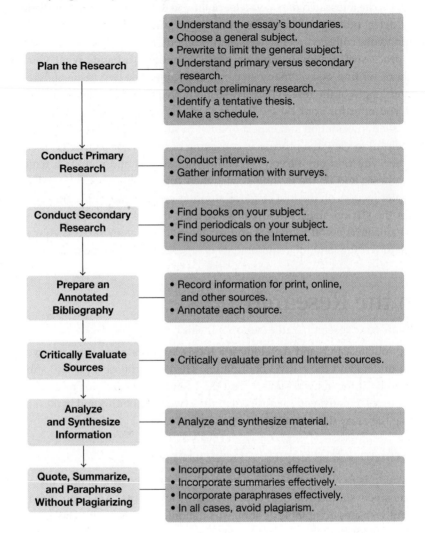

Plan the Research	• Understand the essay's boundaries.
	• Choose a general subject.
	• Prewrite to limit the general subject.
	• Understand primary versus secondary research.
	• Conduct preliminary research.
	• Identify a tentative thesis.
	• Make a schedule.

Conduct Primary Research	• Conduct interviews.
	• Gather information with surveys.

Conduct Secondary Research	• Find books on your subject.
	• Find periodicals on your subject.
	• Find sources on the Internet.

Prepare an Annotated Bibliography	• Record information for print, online, and other sources.
	• Annotate each source.

Critically Evaluate Sources	• Critically evaluate print and Internet sources.

Analyze and Synthesize Information	• Analyze and synthesize material.

Quote, Summarize, and Paraphrase Without Plagiarizing	• Incorporate quotations effectively.
	• Incorporate summaries effectively.
	• Incorporate paraphrases effectively.
	• In all cases, avoid plagiarism.

Choose a General Subject

Your next step is to choose a general subject. If you have an area of interest—say, early childhood education—the subject might be suitable for a research essay. If you don't immediately know what you'd like to research, consider current events, journal entries, the courses you're taking, the reading you've done on your own, or some of the selections in this book.

You might also do some background reading on several possible general subjects or try using one or more prewriting techniques to identify areas that interest or puzzle you. Brainstorming, questioning, freewriting, and mapping should help you generate ideas worth exploring. When you have a list of possible topics, use the following checklist to help you determine which would be best for a research essay.

Once you have a general topic in mind, you may want to clear it with your instructor. Or you might wait until the next stage to do so—after you've narrowed the topic further.

☑ **Selecting an Appropriate Subject to Research: A Checklist**

☐ Will you enjoy learning about the subject? Can you obtain enough information on the subject? Recent developments can be investigated through mass-circulation sources, both print and online, including newspapers, magazines, and blogs. Books and specialized or scholarly journal articles on recent events may not be available for some time.

☐ Has the topic been researched so often that there's nothing new or interesting left to say about it?

☐ Is the topic surrounded by unreliable testimony, which would make it unsuitable for a research paper?

☐ Is the topic too trivial for an academic project?

☐ Does the subject lend itself to or call for research? For example, the dangers of smoking, now almost universally acknowledged, wouldn't be an appropriate topic for a research paper.

☐ Has the topic been written about by only one major source? If so, your research will be one-sided.

☐ Can you be objective about your topic?

Prewrite to Limit the General Subject

Once you have a general subject, you need to limit or narrow it. "Pollution" is too broad a topic, but "the effect of acid rain on urban structures" poses a realistic challenge. Similarly, "cable television" is too general, but "trends in cable comedy" is manageable. Remember, you aren't writing a book but an essay of probably five to fifteen pages.

Sometimes you'll know the particular aspect of a subject you want to explore. Usually, though, you'll have to do some work to restrict your subject. In such cases, try using the prewriting techniques of questioning, mapping, freewriting, and brainstorming. Discussing the topic with other people and doing some background reading can also help focus your thinking.

Understand Primary versus Secondary Research

Most college research essays involve library or **secondary research**—information gathered from published print sources or from the Internet—including statistics, facts, case studies, expert opinion, critical interpretations, and experimental results. Occasionally, though, your instructor may require **primary research**—that is, research in which you gather and present data and reasonable conclusions. For example, you may conduct an experiment, visit an organization, observe a situation, conduct an interview, or gather information with a survey. If you decide to conduct primary research, you need to prepare carefully and establish a strict schedule for yourself. (We discuss primary and secondary research in detail in Learning Objectives 19.2 and 19.3.)

Conduct Preliminary Research

Frequently, you won't be able to narrow your topic until you learn more about it by reading secondary sources. Just as prewriting precedes a first draft, *preliminary research* precedes the in-depth research you conduct further along in the process.

At this point, you don't have to track down highly specialized material. Instead, you simply browse the Internet and skim books and general magazine or newspaper articles on your topic to get an overview and to identify possible slants on your subject. If your broad subject is inspired by a class, you can check out the topic in your textbook. And, of course, you can consult library sources including the computerized catalog, various online databases, the reference section, and periodical indexes such as the *Readers' Guide to Periodical Literature*. All of these sources break broad subjects into subtopics, which will help you focus your research.

After you locate several promising books or articles on your general subject, glance through the material rapidly to get a sense of issues and themes. Do the sources suggest a particular angle of inquiry? If you don't find much material on your subject, think about selecting another subject about which more has been written. While conducting preliminary research, keep a record of the books and articles you skim in an annotated bibliography (discussed in Learning Objective 19.4). Recording basic information as you go along will help you relocate material later on, when you need to look at your sources more closely.

Once you arrive at your limited topic—or several possibilities—ask your instructor for feedback, listening carefully to any reservations he or she may have about your idea. Even after you've identified a limited subject, don't be surprised if it continues to shift and narrow as you go along. Such reshaping is part of the research process.

Identify a Tentative (Working) Thesis

After limiting your topic, start to form a *working thesis*—an idea that is in some way original. Having a tentative thesis guides your research and helps you determine which sources will be appropriate. The thesis should take a stand by expressing your point of view, or attitude, about the subject. In the following thesis statements, the limited subjects are underlined once, the attitudes twice:

> The Congressional decision to reduce funding of school lunch programs has had unfortunate consequences for disadvantaged children.
>
> A moment of silence in public schools does not violate the constitutional separation of church and state.

It's important to view your working thesis as tentative; you probably won't have a final thesis until your research is almost complete. Indeed, if your thesis doesn't shift as you investigate your topic, you may not be tapping a wide enough range of sources, or you may be resisting challenges to your original point of view.

Make a Schedule

Before you begin the research stage, make a schedule. First, list what you need to do. Then, working back from your essay's due date, set rough time limits for the different phases of the project. For an essay due November 22, you might create the following five-week schedule.

October 18	Decide on a topic and locate relevant sources
October 27	Read materials, take notes, and prepare an annotated bibliography
November 3	Locate additional information—conduct interviews and so on; update annotated bibliography
November 8	Write a first draft
November 15	Revise the draft
November 20	Edit, print, and proofread the essay
November 22	Submit the essay

You might find that your instructor requires you to write three drafts of your research essay rather than only two drafts. The research essay is usually longer and more complex than the other essays you write for this course. Learning how to effectively and correctly integrate sources, along with putting together a Works Cited page (if you are using MLA format) or a list of references (if you are using APA format), often requires additional drafting. If your instructor requires that you take this writing project through three drafts, you'll need to revise your schedule accordingly, probably adding an extra week to the suggested schedule above.

Conduct Primary Research

19.2 Conduct primary research—interviews and surveys.

Primary research falls into two categories: interviews and surveys.

Conduct Interviews

You may decide to conduct an information-gathering interview. Before you send your request for a personal interview, get feedback from your instructor on the effectiveness of your letter or e-mail message. Schedule enough interview time (30–60 minutes) to discuss your topic in depth. To record the interview, you must obtain permission from the interviewee beforehand. Also, ask in advance if you may quote the person directly.

Plan the interview carefully. First, determine what you want to accomplish: Do you want to get the interviewee's view on a controversial issue, or do you want to clear up confusion about a specific point? Then, well in advance, prepare a list of questions geared toward that goal. During the interview, remain flexible—follow up on interesting remarks even if they diverge somewhat from your original plan. (If you discover that your interviewee isn't as informed as you had hoped, graciously request the names of other people who might help you further.) Take accurate and complete notes (even if you're recording—equipment sometimes fails!). If certain comments seem especially quotable, make sure you get the statements down correctly. Finally, right after the interview ends, fill in any gaps in your notes. And of course, remember to thank the interviewee.

If a face-to-face interview isn't feasible, a phone interview often will provide the information you need. Contact the interviewee, explain the kind of help you would like, and see if the person is willing to schedule time to talk on the phone.

Another way to conduct an interview is by e-mail. You should describe the topic you're researching, explain your reasons for establishing contact, and list clearly and concisely the information you would like the interviewee to provide. It's also a good idea to give the date by which you hope the interviewee can get back to you.

Gather Information with Surveys

A survey helps you gather a good deal of information from a large number of people (*respondents*). Designing, administering, and interpreting a survey questionnaire are time-consuming tasks that demand considerable skill. So be sure to have someone knowledgeable about surveys evaluate both your questionnaire and its responses.

DEVELOP QUESTIONS Make your survey questions as clear and precise as possible. For example, if your goal is to determine the frequency of an occurrence, do not ask for vague responses such as "seldom," "often," and "occasionally." Instead, ask respondents to identify specific time periods: "weekly," "1–3 times a week," "4–6 times a week," and "daily."

Also, steer away from questions that favor one side of an issue or that restrict the range of responses. Consider the following survey questions:

> Should already overburdened college students be required to participate in a community service activity before they can graduate?
>
> Yes _____ No _____ Maybe _____

> In your opinion, how knowledgeable are college students about jobs in their majors?
>
> Knowledgeable _____ Not knowledgeable _____

Both of these questions need to be revised. The first assumes that students are "already overburdened" and biases respondents to reply negatively. To make the question more neutral, you must eliminate the prejudicial words. The second question asks respondents to answer in terms of a simple contrast: "Knowledgeable" or "Not knowledgeable." It ignores the likelihood that some respondents may wish to reply "Very knowledgeable," "Somewhat knowledgeable," and so on.

CHOOSE RESPONDENTS   Unless you can survey every member of your target group, you must poll a representative subgroup. By representative, we mean "having characteristics similar to the group as a whole." Imagine you're writing a research paper on unfair employment practices and you decide to poll students on campus about their job experiences. To gauge students' attitudes with accuracy, you'll have to hand out your survey in numerous places and on varied occasions on the campus. That way, your responses will be drawn from the whole spectrum of undergraduate backgrounds, majors, ages, and so forth.

To achieve a random sample, you must choose respondents by a scientific method. For example, to survey undergraduates on your campus, you would need a list of all enrolled students. From this list, you would pick names at a regular interval, perhaps every tenth student, and you would poll only those selected students. With this method, every enrolled student has the potential of being chosen as a respondent.

Often you'll use an informal method of collecting responses, such as handing your survey to passersby on campus or to people seated in classes, in student lounges, and so on. Or, if you're collecting information about the service at a particular facility, you might (with permission) place a short questionnaire where respondents can pick it up, fill it out, and return it to you. Also, online survey software such as *SurveyMonkey* makes it relatively easy to distribute a survey via e-mail and then to analyze the results.

Conduct Secondary Research

19.3 Conduct secondary research.

Even if your essay contains primary research, you are likely to get most of your information from secondary sources, such as books and periodicals, most of which you will find in your college library or through the library's online sources. See Figure 19.2 for information on the types of sources available.

You will probably find most of the print books you need to consult in your college or another library. Most college libraries contain several floors of bookshelves (called *stacks*), with fiction and nonfiction cataloged and arranged systematically. Sections are devoted to periodicals, microfilm and microfiche files, reference works, reserved books, government documents, rare books, and the like. Special collections may include, for example, an extensive music library or a rare book collection.

Don't wait until an essay is due to become familiar with your college library. It can be overwhelming to learn about the library and conduct research at the same time. Instead, early in the year, spend an hour or so at the library. Take an orientation tour, read any handouts that are provided, speak to the librarian, and experiment with the system. When you are ready to begin your search for secondary sources, talk with a librarian, who can explain to you the various types of sources available through your school's library and how to access them.

Find Books on Your Subject

In most college libraries, you will use a computerized catalog, available on a library computer or from your own computer, to locate books. A typical online catalog search is by author, title, or subject. If you're searching by author or title, you type into the search box the author's first and last names or the title. If you're searching by subject, you type in a key word or phrase describing your topic. You may have to try several key terms to discover where the catalog lists sources on your topic. Also be aware that many classic texts are available as free e-books online. Just make sure you access copies from a reliable source.

Find Periodicals on Your Subject

Periodicals are publications issued at regular or intermittent intervals throughout the year. There are three broad types of periodicals: general, scholarly, and serious (Figure 19.2). You may be able to use all three types as sources, or your instructor may limit you to one or two types. More than books, periodicals tend to contain information on the most

Figure 19.2 Research Sources

Source Material	Description	How to Locate It
Books	Background information and lengthy in-depth treatment of subjects	Library catalog, web searches for e-books
Scholarly journals	Articles containing the latest research results by experts in a field	Online library databases
Serious magazines	Articles with less depth than scholarly articles but with a broader perspective	Online library databases, library catalog
General magazines	Easy-to-read overviews of subjects with some background information	Online library databases, web searches, library catalog
Newspapers	Easy-to-read summaries and coverage of current developments in a field	Online library databases, web searches, library catalog
Government publications	Statistical and research studies conducted by governments and others	Library catalog and government websites
Multimedia	Videos, photos, reproductions of art, and so on	Library catalog, online library databases, Internet searches

recent discoveries, ideas, and trends in most fields. For many academic subjects, especially in the sciences, periodicals will be the main source of material for a research essay.

Libraries subscribe to a wide range of periodicals. Many periodicals come in print form, and most have, in addition, an electronic or online version; other periodicals appear only online. You will find print and sometimes electronic (for example, CD-ROM) versions of some publications in your library. Other publications can be accessed online through your library's system, either with the library's computers or with your own computer.

To identify specific articles on your subject, first consult periodical indexes, abstracts, bibliographies, or full-text databases. This may seem like a daunting task, but it doesn't have to be. Ask a librarian to assist you in finding and accessing the various databases and other sources you need to conduct your research.

Find Sources on the Internet

The web consists of millions of websites. Some feature text only; others contain illustrations and graphics; still others contain audio and video components. Although there's great variation in the content and design of websites, nearly all have a home page that provides the site's title, introductory descriptive material about the site, and a menu consisting of links to other pages on the site or to related websites.

Know the Advantages and Limitations of the Library and the Web

Because it's not subject to a central system of organization and because anyone can post material on it at any time, the web is in a state of constant flux. Also, the quality of information found online ranges from authoritative to speculative to fraudulent.

Both the library and the web are good starting points for research. Depending on your topic and its focus, one may serve this function better than the other. Here are some points to consider:

- The library is consistently organized. With some guidance from the catalog and the reference librarian, you can quickly locate materials that are relevant to your topic.

- Because the web doesn't have a centralized organizational structure, you are automatically—and somewhat haphazardly—exposed to a staggering array of material. If you're not sure how to focus your topic, browsing the web may help you narrow your topic by identifying directions you wouldn't have thought of on your own. Conversely, the sheer volume of material on your subject may leave you confused about how to proceed.

- Some sources in the library may be dated or even no longer accurate. By contrast, online material is often up to date because it can be posted on the web as soon as it's created. (See Learning Objective 19.5 for hints on evaluating the currency of electronic data.)

- The instantaneous nature of web postings can create problems. Library materials certainly aren't infallible, but most have gone through a process of editorial review before being published. They also have been chosen by knowledgeable librarians. This is often not the case with material on the web. It's a good idea not to rely solely on the web when you research your topic. (For more about evaluating the validity of material on the web, see the checklist in Learning Objective 19.5.)

Prepare an Annotated Bibliography

19.4 Prepare an annotated bibliography.

As you look up promising books, reference volumes, articles, and online material about your subject, prepare an annotated bibliography—a list of potential sources you locate with *annotations* (brief notes and comments) on the content of the sources and how you might use each one in your research essay. You will have the beginnings of such a list from the preliminary research you did at the beginning of the project. Keeping track of sources in an annotated bibliography means that you won't have to waste time later tracking down a source whose title you remember only vaguely. You'll also have annotations that remind you of the source's content and how you might use it later, when you begin writing your research essay.

Record Information About the Source

As you consult sources, make note of at least the following information in your annotated bibliography. If you are in doubt about additional bibliographic information given by a source, record it.

- For each print book, record the author, title, publisher, publication date, and library call number. For online books, record the author, title, and digital object identifier (DOI) if available. If the online book has no DOI, record the complete web address (URL).

- For each article, record the author, title, publication name, date, and page numbers as well as how it can be located in the library or electronically.

- For each website, record any author named, the title of the page, the name of the site, and either the DOI or the URL. MLA guidelines (eighth edition) recommend including the DOI (if it is available) rather than the URL because DOIs provide more reliable links to digital sources than URLs, which change frequently.

- For each potential source you list, make annotations that will help you remember the kind of information included in the source and ideas about how you might use it in your research essay. You can copy and paste quotations into the bibliography, but be sure to identify completely the source of the quotation. Also be sure to put quotation marks around any material that you copy and paste so that you do not end up committing unintentional plagiarism.

You need to read as much as you can about your subject. Consequently, in the early stages of working on your research essay, your annotated bibliography will contain more sources than you will eventually use in your final draft. For example, if your instructor requires you to include six to eight sources in your final draft, you might be asked to include ten to twelve possible sources in your annotated bibliography. You'll revise the annotated bibliography later, as your research project takes shape and you decide which sources to include in your final draft.

You might find it easiest to use a computer file for your annotated bibliography because you can often e-mail library catalog information and journal articles to yourself and copy and paste DOIs (or URLs, if you cannot locate DOIs) directly into the annotated bibliography. Doing so can help you avoid *transcription errors* (that is, typographical errors when you are recording the source information). A computer document can also be sorted and resorted alphabetically as you develop your list. (Check the Help feature on your word processing program for instructions on sorting.)

Here's an example of an annotated bibliography entry with a note about the content and a direct quotation that the student thought he might want to include in his research essay. The entry uses MLA format for a Works Cited entry:

> Cazzuffi, Alessandra, et al. "Case Study: Young Man with Anorexia Nervosa." *Journal of the Royal Society of Medicine Short Reports*, vol. 1, no. 5, 2010, p. 39. *SAGE*, doi:10.1258/shorts.2010.010051.

> This article presents a case study of a male with anorexia nervosa. It points out that while the disorder is less common among males than it is among females, the symptoms are usually more severe in men than they are in women.

> A quote from the article I might want to use when I discuss how males with anorexia nervosa often strive for perfection in every aspect of their lives:

> "His parents underlined 'perfectionism' as a core feature of his personality: he wants to be the best in everything he does and he always organizes and plans his life and his future" (39).

Notice that in the example annotated bibliography entry above, the student cited the source in MLA format. If the instructor had required students to use APA format, the citation would have looked like this:

> Cazzuffi, A., Manzato, E., Gualandi, M., Fabbian, F., & Scanelli, G. (2010). Case study: Young man with anorexia nervosa. *Journal of the Royal Society of Medicine Short Reports*, 1(5), 39. doi:10.1258/shorts.2010.010051.

Taking time during the early stages of the research process to follow MLA guidelines for works cited—or APA guidelines for a list of references—makes the workload lighter later in the research essay composing process. In addition, citing sources correctly in the annotated bibliography ensures that you have recorded all of the source information you'll need for your research project. For more information on using MLA and APA formats, see the next chapter.

Later in the research writing process, after you have critically analyzed potential sources, you'll likely need to make more extensive notes than the annotations included in your bibliography.

Critically Evaluate Sources

19.5 Critically evaluate your sources.

At this point you've formed a tentative thesis, identified promising sources, and started compiling an annotated bibliography. Your goal now is to find support for your thesis—and to pay close attention to material suggesting alternative viewpoints. Sifting through this conflicting information will enable you to refine your working thesis.

Keep your working thesis firmly in mind as you assess and react to what others say about your subject. Some authors will support your working thesis; others will prod you to consider opposing viewpoints. In either case, critically evaluating, synthesizing, and reacting to your sources helps you refine your position and develop a sound basis for your conclusions.

The success of your essay depends in large part on the evidence you provide. Evidence from sources, whether print or electronic, needs to be critically evaluated for relevance, timeliness, seriousness of approach, and objectivity.

Relevance

Titles can be misleading. To determine if a source is relevant for your essay, review it carefully. For a book, read the preface or introduction, skim the table of contents, and check the index to see whether the book is likely to contain information that's important to your topic. If the source is influential in the field, you may want to read the entire book for background and specific ideas. For an article, read the abstract of the article, if there is one. An **abstract** is a brief summary of the article's key conclusions; it is usually found near the beginning of the article. If no abstract is provided, read the first few paragraphs and skim the rest to determine if the article might be useful. For a website or other nonprint source, skim the site to see if it includes pertinent, reliable information that might help you write a stronger essay. When considering using information from a website, make certain that the site is reputable and that the information has been recently updated.

Timeliness

To some extent, the topic and the kind of research you're doing determine whether a work is outdated. If you're researching a historical topic such as the internment of Japanese Americans during World War II, you will most likely consult sources published in the 1940s and 1950s as well as more up-to-date sources. In contrast, if you're investigating a recent scientific development—cloning, for example—it would make sense to restrict your search to current material. For most college research, a source older than ten years is considered outdated unless it was the first to present key concepts in a field.

Seriousness of Approach

As you review a source, ask yourself if it is suitable for your purpose and your instructor's requirements. Articles from general periodicals (newspapers and widely read magazines such as *The New Yorker* and *The Atlantic*) and serious publications (such as *National Geographic* and *Scientific American*) may be sufficient to provide support in a personal essay. But an in-depth research essay in your major field of study will require material from scholarly journals and texts (for example, *American Journal of Public Health* and *Film Quarterly*).

Objectivity

As you examine your sources for possible bias, remember that a strong conclusion or opinion is not in itself a sign of bias. As long as a writer doesn't ignore opposing positions or distort evidence, he or she can't be considered biased. A biased source presents only those facts that fit the writer's predetermined conclusions. Such a source is often marked by emotionally charged language. Publications sponsored by special interest groups—a particular industry, religious association, advocacy group, or political party—are usually biased. Reading such materials familiarizes you with a specific point of view, but remember that contrary evidence has probably been ignored or skewed. The following checklist provides some questions to ask as you critically evaluate articles and books.

☑ Critically Evaluating Articles and Books: A Checklist

☐ If the work is scholarly, is the author well known in his or her field? Is the author affiliated with an accredited college or university? A nonscholarly author, such as a journalist, should have a reputation for objectivity and thoroughness.

☐ Is the publication reputable? If a scholarly publication is peer-reviewed, experts in the field have a chance to comment on the author's work before it is published. Nonscholarly publications such as newspapers and magazines should be well established and widely respected.

☐ Is the source recently published and up to date? Alternatively, is it a classic in its field? In the sciences and social sciences, recent publication is particularly critical.

☐ Is the material at an appropriate level—neither too scholarly nor too general—for your purpose and audience? Make sure you can understand and present the material for your readers.

☐ Does the information appear to be accurate, objectively presented, and complete? Statistics and other evidence should not be distorted or manipulated to make a point.

Special care must be taken to critically evaluate the worth of material found on the web. Electronic documents often seem to appear out of nowhere and can disappear without a trace. And anyone—from scholar to con artist—can create a webpage. How, then, do you know if an Internet source is credible? As you evaluate online sources, ask yourself the questions in the following checklist.

☑ Critically Evaluating Internet Materials: A Checklist

☐ Who is the author of the material? Does the author provide a résumé or biographical note? Do these credentials qualify the author to provide reliable information on the topic? Is there an e-mail address so you can request more information? The less you know about an author, the more suspicious you should be about using the data.

☐ Can you verify the information's accuracy? Does the author refer to studies or to other authors you can investigate? If the author doesn't cite other works or other points of view, the document may be opinionated or one-sided. In such cases, it's important to track down material addressing alternative points of view.

☐ Who sponsors the website? Check for an "About Us" link on the home page, which may tell you the site's sponsorship and goals. Many sites are established by organizations—businesses, agencies, lobby groups. If a sponsor pushes a single point of view, you should use the material with great caution. Make an extra effort to locate material addressing other sides of the issue.

☐ What does the site's Internet address (URL) tell you? A URL ending with *.com* indicates a commercial website, which is probably interested in selling a product or service. The URL extension *.edu* indicates an educational institution. Though educational institutions can be trustworthy, remember that students at a university can post documents using their institution's web address; such materials are not necessarily reliable. A URL that includes *.gov* identifies a government site. These sites can be valuable for statistical information and background material, but they may not include all points of view. Finally, *.org* in a URL usually points to a nonprofit organization. Nonprofits may support worthy causes, but they usually advocate a specific position and don't always provide counterarguments.

☐ Is the cited information up to date? Being on the Internet doesn't guarantee that information is current. To assess the timeliness of Internet materials, check at the top or bottom of the document for copyright date, publication date, posting date, or revision date. Those dates will help you determine whether the material is recent enough for your purposes.

☐ Is the information original or taken from another source? Is quoted material accurate? Some webpages may reproduce material from other sources without identifying them. Watch out for possible plagiarism. Nonoriginal material should be accurately quoted and acknowledged on the site.

Analyze and Synthesize Source Material

19.6 Analyze and synthesize source material.

As you read your sources and begin keeping track of what you find, you may not be able to judge immediately how helpful a source will be. At that time, you should probably take fairly detailed notes, in addition to the annotations you include in your bibliography. For these detailed notes, you'll need to open a separate file keyed to the annotated bibliography. Put the bibliographic entry at the beginning of the file and insert an identifier (for example, "p. 10") before each separate note. Make sure to use a filename that identifies the source. If quoted material covers several pages, indicate clearly where the page breaks occur in the source. That way, if you use only a portion of the material later, you will know its exact page number. You may also find it helpful to write a key word or phrase before the note. For example, in a paper on erosion, you might have notes labeled "Beach erosion" and "Mountain erosion." If you print your annotated bibliography and notes to work with them, print on only one side of the sheet to avoid confusion, and number the printed sheets to keep them in order.

As you continue working on your research project, you'll find that you are thinking more critically about the material you read, isolating information and ideas that are important to your thesis, and formulating questions about your topic. In other words, you will be *analyzing* your source material.

Analyzing Source Material

You should spend some time analyzing each source for its central ideas, main supporting points, and key details. As you read, keep asking yourself how the source's content meshes with your working thesis and with what you know about your subject. Does the source repeat only what you already know, or does it supply new information? If a source provides detailed support for important ideas or suggests a new angle on your subject, read carefully and take full notes. If the source refers to other sources, you might decide to consult them.

Make sure you have all necessary citation information for *every* source you consult. Then, as you read relevant sources, take plenty of notes to include in your annotated bibliography. Articles you have printed out can be highlighted and annotated with your comments. In addition, you may wish to photocopy selected book pages to annotate, or you may copy and paste material from online sources into a word processing document. However, you will also have to take handwritten or typewritten notes on some material. When you do so, make sure to put quotation marks around direct quotes. Annotating and note-taking will help you think through and respond to the source's ideas.

Your notes might include any of the following: facts, statistics, anecdotal accounts, expert opinion, case studies, surveys, reports, results of experiments, and analyses of photos, graphs, or other images. When you are recording data, check that you have copied the figures accurately. Also note how and by whom the statistics were gathered as well as where and when they were first reported.

Take down your source's interpretation of the statistics, but be sure to scrutinize the interpretation for any "spin" that distorts them. For example, if 80 percent of Americans think that violent crime is our number-one national problem, that doesn't mean that violent crime is our main problem; it simply means that 80 percent of the people *polled* think it is. And if a "majority" of people think that eliminating homelessness should be one of our top national priorities, it may be that a mere 51 percent—a bare majority—felt that way. In short, make sure the statistics mean what your sources say they mean. If you have any reason to suspect distortion, corroborate such figures elsewhere. Tracking down the original source of a statistic is the best way to ensure that numbers are being reported fairly.

Synthesizing Source Materials

As you go along, you may come across material that challenges your working thesis and forces you to think differently about your subject. Indeed, the more you learn, the more difficult it may be to state anything conclusively. This is a sign that you're *synthesizing* (integrating) and weighing all the evidence. In time, the confusion will lessen, and you'll emerge with a better understanding of your subject.

Suppose you find sources that take positions contrary to the one that you had previously considered credible. When you come across such conflicting material, you can be sure you've identified a pivotal issue within your topic. To decide which position is more valid, take good notes or carefully annotate your photocopies, electronic materials, and printed documents. Then evaluate the sources for bias. On this basis alone, you might discover serious flaws in one or several sources. Also compare the key points and supporting evidence in the sources. Where do they agree? Where do they disagree? Does one source argue against another's position, perhaps even discrediting some of the opposing view's evidence? The answers to these questions may well cause you to question the quality, completeness, or fairness of one or more sources.

To resolve such a conflict, you can also research your subject more fully. For example, if your conflicting sources are at the general or serious level, you should probably turn to more scholarly and authoritative sources to help determine which of the conflicting sources is more valid.

When you attempt to resolve discrepancies among sources, do not let your own bias come into play. Try not to favor one position over the other simply because it supports your working thesis. Remember, your goal is to arrive at the most well-founded position you can. In fact, researching a topic may lead you to change your original viewpoint. In this case, you shouldn't hesitate to revise your working thesis to match the evidence you've gathered.

☑ Analyzing and Synthesizing Source Material: A Checklist

- ☐ As you read sources, note central ideas, main supporting points, and key details.
- ☐ Make sure to record all bibliographic information carefully, identify any quotations, and copy statistical data accurately.
- ☐ Annotate and take full notes on sources that deal with ideas that are important to your topic or suggest a new angle on your subject.
- ☐ Examine statistics and other facts for any distortions.
- ☐ Carefully read material that causes you to take a different view of your subject. Keep an open mind and do additional research to confirm or change your thesis.

Use Quotation, Summary, and Paraphrase Without Plagiarizing

19.7 Use quotation, summary, and paraphrase without plagiarizing.

Your essay should contain your own ideas stated in your own words. To support your ideas, you can use evidence from sources in three ways—with direct quotations, summaries, and paraphrases. Knowing how and when to use each type is an important part of the research process.

Quotation

A **quotation** reproduces, word for word, that which is stated in a source. Although quoting can demonstrate the thoroughness with which you reviewed relevant sources, don't simply use one quotation after another without any intervening commentary or analysis. Doing so would mean you haven't evaluated and synthesized your sources sufficiently. Aim for one to three quotations from each major source. Consider using quotations in the following situations:

- If a source's ideas are unusual or controversial, include a representative quotation to show that you have accurately conveyed the source's viewpoint.

- Record a quotation if a source's wording is so eloquent or convincing that it would lose its power if you restated the material in your own words.

- Use a quotation if a source's ideas reinforce your own conclusions. If the source is a respected authority, the quotation will lend authority to your own ideas.

- In an analysis of a literary work, use quotations from the work to support your interpretations.

Remember to clearly identify quotes in your notes so that you don't confuse the quotation with your own comments when you begin drafting your paper. Record the author's statement exactly as it appears in the original work, right down to the punctuation. In addition, make sure to properly document the quotation. See the following chapter on how to correctly document quotations in MLA and APA formats.

Original Passage 1. The following is the entire text of Amendment I of the Constitution of the United States.

> Congress shall make no law respecting an establishment of religion, or prohibiting the free exercise thereof; or abridging the freedom of speech, or of the press; or the right of the people peaceably to assemble, and to petition the Government for a redress of grievances.

Original Passage 2. In this excerpt from *The Canon: A Whirligig Tour of the Beautiful Basics of Science*, by Natalie Angier, page 22, the author is discussing the subject of scientific reasoning.

Much of the reason for its success is founded on another fundamental of the scientific bent. Scientists accept, quite staunchly, that there is a reality capable of being understood, and understood in a way that can be shared with and agreed upon by others. We can call this "objective" reality if we like, as opposed to subjective reality, or opinion, or "whimsical set of predilections." The concept is deceptive, however, because it implies that the two are discrete entities with remarkably little in common.

Acceptable Use of Quotation. The following examples are acceptable uses of the preceding quotations. For a paper on society's perception of important freedoms, a student writer included a quotation (highlighted) from the Constitution.

The First Amendment of the Constitution of the United States delineates what were thought to be society's most cherished freedoms: "Congress shall make no law respecting an establishment of religion, or prohibiting the free exercise thereof; or abridging the freedom of speech, or of the press; or the right of the people peaceably to assemble, and to petition the Government for a redress of grievances."

In a paper on science education in schools, one student writer used a direct quotation (highlighted) from Angier's book:

In explaining scientific reasoning, Angier says, "Scientists accept, quite staunchly, that there is a reality capable of being understood, and understood in a way that can be shared with and agreed upon by others" (22).

Notice that both quotations are reproduced exactly as they appear in the source and are enclosed in quotation marks. The parenthetical reference to the page number in the second example is a necessary part of documenting the quotation. The first example requires no page number because quotations from well-known sources such as the Constitution and the Bible are sufficiently identified by their own numbering systems—in this case, the text's use of "First Amendment of the Constitution."

Incorrect Use of Quotation. Another student writer, attempting to provide some background on the scientific method, used the source material *incorrectly*.

To understand the scientific method, it is important to understand that scientists believe there is a reality capable of being understood (Angier 22).

The highlighted phrase "a reality capable of being understood," which consists of the source's exact words, should have quotations around it. Even though the source is identified correctly in the parenthetical reference, the lack of quotation marks constitutes **plagiarism**, the use of someone's words or ideas without proper acknowledgement.

Summary

A **summary** is a condensation of a larger work. You extract the essence of someone's ideas and restate it in your own words. The length of a summary depends on your topic and purpose, but generally a summary is much shorter than the work you are summarizing. For example, you may summarize the plot of a novel in a few short paragraphs, or you might summarize a reading from this book in a few sentences. You might choose to use a summary for the following reasons:

- To give a capsule presentation of the main ideas of a book or an article.
- If the relevant information is too long to be quoted in full.
- To give abbreviated information about elements such as plot, background, or history.
- To present an idea from a source without including all the supporting details.

To summarize a source, read the material; jot down or underline the main idea, main supporting points, and key details; and then restate the information in shortened form in your own words.

Your summary should follow the order of information in the original. Also be sure to treat any original wording as quotations in your summary. A caution: When summarizing, don't use the ellipsis (...) to signal that you have omitted some ideas. The ellipsis is used only when quoting.

Original Passage 3. This excerpt is from Sherzod Abdukadirov and Michael Marlow's "Government Intervention Will Not Solve Our Obesity Problem," published as a blog post in *U.S. News and World Report* on June 5, 2012.

> It is clear the United States is facing a rising obesity problem. But the challenge remains: We have yet to determine a successful way to tackle it. According to the National Center for Health Statistics, the prevalence of obesity among adults more than doubled from 13.4 percent in 1960 to 34.3 percent in 2008 (Ogden & Carroll, 2010). A new report released this month by the *American Journal of Preventive Medicine* predicts that by 2030, 42 percent of Americans will be obese and 11 percent will be severely obese, or 100 pounds overweight (Finkelstein et al., 2012, p. 563).
>
> Despite the myriad of studies showing American obesity is increasing, research does not clearly support that government can solve this complex problem. And yet, government solutions that provide information the public already knows—weight gain occurs when we eat too much and exercise too little— have been the focus to eliminate this epidemic.
>
> Not only is this method not solving the problem, we may actually be increasing the social stigma associated with weight gain. Rather than pursuing a one-size-fits-all solution, we need to push back against government intervention, and allow people to find the solution that best meets their needs.

Acceptable Use of Summary. The following summary was written by a student working on a paper related to obesity in the United States.

> In their blog post "Government Intervention Will Not Solve Our Obesity Problem," Abdukadirov and Marlow assert that while there is no doubt that obesity is a growing problem in the United States, government should not attempt to find a blanket solution that will supposedly work for everyone. Solutions to the problem of obesity must be determined by individuals and must be based on what works best for them.

The writer gives the gist of Abdukadirov and Marlow's argument in his own words. There is no parenthetical reference at the end because the reader has already referenced the authors as well as the title of the selection and there is no page number for the web source.

Incorrect Use of Summary. The student who wrote the following has incorrectly summarized ideas from the Abdukadirov and Marlow passage.

> Who are the obese? According to Abdukadirov and Marlow, they are the people who do not control the amount of food they consume and do not exercise regularly. Because they fail to understand what makes them obese, they do not know what to do about the problem.

The writer was so determined to put things her way that she added her own ideas and ended up distorting Abdukadirov and Marlow's meaning. For instance, note the way she emphasizes that obese individuals don't understand what causes them to gain weight. Abdukadirov and Marlow do just the opposite. They highlight the idea that although people understand the causes of weight gain, that understanding alone is not enough to help them control obesity.

Paraphrase

Unlike a summary, which condenses the original, a **paraphrase** recasts material by using roughly the same number of words and retaining the same level of detail as the original. The challenge with paraphrasing is to capture the information without using the material's original language. Paraphrasing is useful in these situations:

- If you want to include specific details from a source but you want to avoid using a long quotation or string of quotations.
- To interpret or explain material as you include it.
- To avoid injecting another person's style into your own writing.

One way to compose a paraphrase is to read the original passage and then set it aside while you draft your restatement. As you write, make sure to use appropriate synonyms and to vary the sentence structure from that of the original. Then compare the passages to make sure you have not used any of the original language unless you have enclosed it in quotation marks.

Acceptable Use of Paraphrase. In the following example, the student writer paraphrases the third paragraph of Abdukadirov and Marlow's original, fitting the restatement into her argument.

> Can we find a solution to our nation's obesity problem? Two leading researchers urge us to reject the idea that government should take charge of finding "a one-size-fits-all solution." They stress that this approach only makes the problem worse. Obesity is a complex issue that cannot be solved with a simple answer. Solutions to obesity must be determined on an individual basis (Abdukadirov and Marlow).

Note that the paraphrase is roughly the same length as the original. Apart from the single instance of original language, enclosed in quotation marks, the writer has not used phrases or even sentence structures from the original. Notice also that it is easy to see where the paraphrase starts and ends: The phrase "Two leading researchers" begins the paraphrase, and the parenthetical reference ends it. Because the text does not identify the source by name, the source's authors are included in the parenthetical reference.

Incorrect Use of Paraphrase.   When preparing the following paraphrase, the student stayed too close to the source and borrowed much of Abdukadirov and Marlow's language word for word (highlighted). Because the student did not enclose the original phrases in quotation marks, this paraphrase constitutes plagiarism, even though this student acknowledged the authors in the essay. The lack of quotation marks implies that the language is the student's when, in fact, it is Abdukadirov and Marlow's.

> Most Americans clearly understand that the United States is facing a rising obesity problem. Even so, we have yet to figure out how to tackle it. Many individuals are depending on our government to intervene and take charge of the issue, but research does not clearly support that government can solve this complex problem. We need to realize that it is time for us to push back against government intervention, and allow people to find the solution that works best for them.

As the following example shows, another student believed, erroneously, that if he changed a word here and there and jumped from one part of the original text to another, he'd be preparing an effective paraphrase. Note that the language is all Abdukadirov and Marlow's except for the words not highlighted, which are the student's.

> It is clear the United States is facing a rising obesity problem, but research does not clearly support that our government can solve this difficult problem. Rather than pursuing a one-size-fits-all solution, we need to resist government intervention, and allow individuals to find the solution that best meets their needs (Abdukadirov and Marlow).

The near-quotes in the two preceding examples are deceptive; the lack of quotation marks suggests that the language is the student's when actually it's substantially (but not exactly) Abdukadirov and Marlow's. Such near-quotes are considered plagiarism, even if, when writing the essay, the student supplies a parenthetical reference citing the source.

☑ Using Quotation, Summary, and Paraphrase: A Checklist

- ☐ For a quotation, give the statement exactly as it was originally written.
- ☐ Always accompany quotations with your own commentary or analysis.
- ☐ Don't string quotations together one after the other without intervening text.
- ☐ Avoid using too many quotations. One to three quotations from any major source is sufficient.

☐ For a summary, restate ideas from the source in your own words.

☐ Keep summaries much shorter than the original material.

☐ Make sure your summary does not distort the meaning or tone of the original.

☐ For a paraphrase, recast ideas with the same level of detail as the original.

☐ Make sure to use your own language in a paraphrase—finding appropriate synonyms and varying sentence structure from that of the original.

☐ Check that any original source language used in a summary or paraphrase is enclosed in quotation marks.

Avoiding Plagiarism

Plagiarism occurs when a writer borrows someone else's ideas, facts, or language but doesn't properly credit that source. Copyright law and the ethics of research require that you give credit to those whose words and ideas you borrow; that is, you must represent the source's words and ideas accurately and provide full documentation.

Sometimes, plagiarism is *intentional*. A writer understands that what she is doing is wrong. She knows that the ideas, facts, or language she included in her essay came from an outside source, but she wants to pass the material off as hers rather than give proper credit to that source. Certainly, students who submit a friend's essay as their own or use an essay from an Internet site are committing intentional plagiarism.

However, plagiarism can also be *unintentional*.

- Forgetting to use quotation marks around direct quotations is plagiarism.

- Inadvertently omitting a parenthetical reference or a works cited entry is plagiarism.

- Mistakenly including a source's language in your paraphrase or summary without giving credit is plagiarism.

The consequence—missing or faulty documentation—can undermine your credibility. For one thing, readers may suspect that you're hiding something if you fail to identify your sources clearly. Further, readers planning follow-up research of their own will be perturbed if they have trouble locating your sources. Finally, weak documentation makes it difficult for readers to distinguish your ideas from those of your sources.

You can avoid unintentional plagiarism by taking careful notes on sources you use and making sure you can identify, at every stage in the writing process, which words and ideas are your own and which come from another source.

Some writers may fall into the trap of using "patchwork writing"—that is, stringing together words from one or more sources—which can easily lead to plagiarism. In the first place, if you pile up quotations without adding your own ideas in your own language (or adding only a few words of your own here and there), readers will feel you haven't thought deeply about your subject and don't really have much to say. In addition, patchwork writing can lead to confusion: it's easy to omit quotation marks and forget where your writing ends and someone else's begins, and it's also easy to omit or confuse parenthetical references and works cited entries. Plagiarism can be the result.

In a college-level course, ignorance is no excuse for plagiarism. As a college student, you must understand how to avoid plagiarism because, whether it is intentional or unintentional, plagiarism can lead to failing a course or even academic suspension. This book, and, more specifically, the section of this book that you are reading right now, provides you with the information you need to avoid plagiarism. Closely reading the information and studying the examples on summarizing, paraphrasing, and quoting in this chapter will help you understand how to correctly incorporate information from outside sources into your writing.

To avoid plagiarizing, you must provide proper documentation in the following situations:

- When you include a word-for-word quotation from a source.

- When you paraphrase or summarize ideas or information from a source, unless that material is commonly known and accepted (whether or not you yourself were previously aware of it) or is a matter of historical or scientific record.

- When you combine a summary or paraphrase with a quotation.

One exception to formal documentation occurs in writing for the general public. For example, you may have noticed that although the authors of this book's essays, as well as newspaper and magazine writers, identify sources they have used, some of these writers don't use full documentation. Academic writers, though, must provide full documentation for all borrowed information.

Activities: Locating, Critically Evaluating, Analyzing and Synthesizing Research Sources

1. Use the computer catalog to answer the following questions:
   a. What are three books dealing with the subject of adoption? of urban violence? of genetically modified fruits and vegetables?
   b. What is the title of a book by Betty Friedan? by John Kenneth Galbraith?
   c. Who is the author of *The Invisible Man*? of *A Swiftly Tilting Planet*?

2. Prepare an annotated bibliography entry for each of the following books. Gather all the information necessary at the library so that you can write an accurate and complete entry that includes the author, the title, the library call number, a brief description of the book's content, and a note on how the book might be used as a source in a research essay:
   a. Barbara Tuchman, *Practicing History*
   b. L. Jacobs, *The Documentary Tradition*
   c. Margaret Mead, *Coming of Age in Samoa*

3. Using reference works available in your library, find the answers to the following questions:

   a. When was the Persian Gulf War fought?

   b. Who invented Kodachrome film, and when?

   c. What television show won the Emmy in 2015 for Outstanding Comedy Series?

4. Select one of the following limited topics. Then, using the appropriate periodical indexes and bibliographies, locate three periodicals that would be helpful in research-ing the topic. Examine each periodical to determine whether it is aimed at a general, serious, or scholarly audience.

   a. Drug abuse among health-care professionals

   b. Deforestation of the Amazon rain forest

   c. Differences between the 2009 novel *Brooklyn* by Irish author Colm Tóibín and the 2015 film based on the novel

5. Select one of the following limited topics. Then, using the Internet, locate at least three relevant articles on the topic: one from a general-interest magazine, one from a newspaper, and one from a serious or scholarly journal. Make a bibliography entry for each article, recording the author, title, publication name, date, and page numbers as well as how it can be located in the library or electronically.

   a. Ordaining women in U.S. churches

   b. Attempts to regulate Internet pornography

   c. The growing interest in painter David Hockney

Chapter 20
Writing the Research Essay

Learning Objectives

20.1 Create a refined thesis.

20.2 Revise your annotated bibliography and organize additional notes.

20.3 Create an outline for your research essay.

20.4 Write a first draft of your research essay.

20.5 Integrate sources into your writing.

20.6 Document sources to avoid plagiarism.

20.7 Create in-text references to your sources using MLA format.

20.8 Revise, edit, and proofread your first draft.

20.9 Prepare a works cited list in MLA format.

20.10 Prepare a works cited list in APA format.

20.11 Examine how research is used effectively in one student-authored selection.

A fter you finish recording information from your sources in your annotated bibliography and in any additional notes you've made, you're ready to begin the writing phase of the research project. Figure 20.1 illustrates the writing stage of the research essay.

Figure 20.1 The Research Essay: Writing Stage

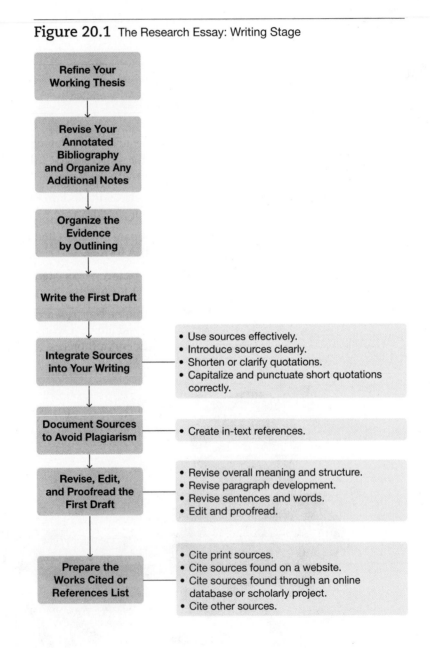

Refine Your Working Thesis

20.1 Create a refined thesis.

It's quite likely that your working thesis has evolved since you first started your research. Indeed, now that you're more informed about the topic, you may feel that your original thesis oversimplifies the issue. To refine your working thesis, begin by reading through your annotated bibliography and reviewing any additional notes you've made, using your research to adjust your ideas. Then revise your working thesis, keeping in mind the evidence you've gathered from your sources. This new thesis statement will serve as the starting point for your first draft. Remember, though—as you write the essay, new thoughts may emerge that will cause you to modify your thesis even further.

Revise Your Annotated Bibliography and Organize Any Additional Notes

20.2 Revise your annotated bibliography and organize additional notes.

With your refined thesis in mind, carefully review your annotated bibliography and any additional notes you've made on particular sources. If you come across sources listed on your annotated bibliography that don't work to support your thesis or that won't work well in your essay because they aren't relevant, timely, serious, or objective, delete them from the bibliography. You'll also need to remove additional notes you've made on inappropriate sources from your collection of notes. (Save these deleted annotations and extra notes in a separate file—in case you realize later that you can use some of the material.)

Next, sort your information by topic. Because the sources in your annotated bibliography are listed alphabetically by author—or by title if no author is listed—you'll need to create a new file in which you group your sources by topic. You should also create a new file in which you group by topic any additional notes you've made on particular sources.

At this point, you should consider which organizational approach (chronological, spatial, emphatic, simple-to-complex) will help you sequence your material. Also determine which specific pattern(s) of development your research essay will use. Arrange your topics to reflect the organizational pattern you have chosen.

Once you've arranged your annotations and additional notes according to the topic headings, arrange the information by subtopic. For example, annotations and additional notes about types of state programs might be copied and pasted under three subtopics: programs for the elderly, programs for preschool children, programs for the physically disabled. Next, using the patterns of development and organizational approaches you've chosen, order each set of subtopics to match the sequence in which you think you'll discuss those subtopics in your essay. This sorting will make your next step—preparing an outline—much easier.

Organize the Evidence by Outlining

20.3 Create an outline for your research essay.

Whether or not your instructor requires an outline, it's a good idea to prepare one before you begin writing the essay. Because an outline groups and sequences points, it provides a blueprint you can follow when writing. Outlining clarifies what your main ideas are, what your supporting evidence is, and how everything fits together. It reveals where your argument is well supported and where it is weak.

To design your outline, focus first on the essay's body. How can you best explain and support your thesis? For now, don't worry about your introduction or conclusion. As you prepare your outline, keep in mind the points listed in the following checklist.

☑ Outlining Research Evidence: A Checklist

- ☐ Base your outline on your organized notes.

- ☐ Ask yourself, "What are the main ideas that support my thesis?" These ideas are your main topic headings. Label them with Roman numerals (I, II, III, and so on) to indicate the order in which you plan to discuss them in the essay.

- ☐ Next, for each main idea, ask yourself, "What subtopics do I want to discuss?" Label these with capital letters (A, B, C) and group them under the main topic headings. Indent the subtopic entries under their respective main topics, listing them in the order you plan to discuss them.

- ☐ Now, for each subtopic, ask, "What are the supporting points for this item?" Label supporting points with Arabic numbers (1, 2, 3) and indent them under the appropriate subtopics. Finally, for each supporting point, ask yourself, "What specific details support this item?" Label specific details (facts, quotations, statistics, examples, expert opinion) with lowercase letters (a, b, c) and indent them under the appropriate supporting points. Use shorthand for details. For example, write, "Bittner quote here" instead of copying the entire quotation into your outline.

- ☐ Where appropriate, map out sections of the essay that will provide background information or define key terms.

Your first outline probably won't be a formal full-sentence outline; it's more likely to be a topic (or phrase) outline. A topic outline helps you clarify an essay's overall structure. A full-sentence outline or a combined topic and sentence outline is better suited to mapping out in detail the development of an essay's ideas. If you're preparing an outline that will be submitted with the essay, find out in advance which kind your instructor prefers.

Before you go any further, it's a good idea to get some feedback on your outline—from an instructor or a critical friend—to make sure others agree that your meaning and organization are logical and clear. Then, using your readers' reactions, make whatever changes are necessary.

Write the First Draft

20.4 Write a first draft of your research essay.

Once you've refined your working thesis, organized the material you gathered on your sources, and constructed an outline, you're ready to write your first draft. As with the early versions of an essay, don't worry at this stage about grammar, spelling, or style. Just try to get down as much of the essay's basic content and structure as you can.

As you write the first draft of your research essay, keep the following points discussed in mind.

☑ **Writing the First Draft of a Research Essay: A Checklist**

☐ As you write, use the material you've gathered on your sources along with your outline. Don't rely on your memory for the information you've gathered.

☐ Feel free to deviate from your outline if, as you write, you discover a more effective sequence, realize some material doesn't fit, or see new merit in previously discarded information.

☐ Include any quotations and summaries in the draft by copying and pasting material from your annotated bibliography or typing in material from your notes.

☐ To avoid plagiarism, identify the sources for all borrowed material in your draft.

☐ Use the third-person point of view throughout unless your instructor has indicated that you may use the first person when presenting primary research.

☐ Give your first draft and subsequent drafts different filenames: "Lotteries_draft1," "Lotteries_draft2," and so on.

If your instructor requires you to conduct primary research, remember that your primary purpose is to provide evidence for your thesis. Include only the material that furthers your goal. To preserve the draft's overall unity, you should also avoid the temptation to mass, without commentary, all your primary research in one section of the essay. Instead, insert the material where it supports the points you want to make. Sometimes instructors will ask you to devote one part of the essay to a detailed discussion of the process you used to conduct primary research—everything from your methodology to a detailed interpretation of your results. In such a case, before writing your draft, ask your instructor where you should cover your primary research. Perhaps it should be placed in a separate introductory section or in an appendix.

Integrate Sources into Your Writing

20.5 Integrate sources into your writing.

On the whole, your essay should be written in your own words. As you draft your essay, however, you will add evidence from sources to support your ideas. Depending on the source and the support you need, you may choose to use quotations, paraphrases, or summaries to present this evidence. Be mindful, however, that you must also correctly document the sources that you use. Specific documentation guidelines appear later in this chapter.

Using Sources Effectively

As you write individual paragraphs, take care to use *introductions, transitions,* and *conclusions* to tie each paragraph to those that precede and follow it. At a minimum, every paragraph should have a topic sentence. Use quotations sparingly, drawing on them only when they dramatically illustrate key points you want to make or when they lend authority to your own conclusions. Remember that a quotation, by itself, won't make your case for you. A string of quotations signals that you haven't sufficiently evaluated and distilled your sources.

To be effective, quotations, paraphrases, and summaries need to be seamlessly blended into your own writing. Successfully blending source material into your essay involves:

- Identifying the source with an appropriate introduction (known as an *attribution*).
- Quoting, paraphrasing, or summarizing the source material accurately.
- Providing a parenthetical reference to a Works Cited or References list (discussed in detail later in this chapter).
- Interpreting the material to show why it is important and explain how it supports your main points. Interpretive statements can come before or after the source material.

Your interpretive commentary is often precisely what's needed to blend the source material gracefully into your discussion.

Awkward Use of a Quotation

In the example paragraph that follows, the writer starts with a topic sentence. Note, though, that the quotation is dropped awkwardly into the text, without any transition or commentary.

> Studies of parenting styles are designed to control researcher bias. "Recent studies screen out researchers whose strongly held attitudes make objectivity difficult" (Layden 10).

Here is the example with the quotation blended nicely into discussion:

> Studies of parenting styles are designed to control research bias. As Layden has pointed out, "Recent studies screen out researchers whose strongly held attitudes make objectivity difficult" (10).

Effective Use of a Source

In the following example, the first sentence provides a transition into the paragraph. The second sentence—the topic sentence—expresses the writer's idea. The third sentence gives the evidence (source material) to support that idea: the attribution (<u>underlined</u>), a paraphrase of the source's words (**boldfaced**), the direct quotation (highlighted), and the parenthetical reference at the end. Notice how the source material (paraphrase and quotation) merges smoothly with the surrounding material:

> One problem with research into parenting styles has been the preconceived notions of researchers. The latest studies of parenting styles, however, are designed to control researcher bias. <u>The psychologist Marsha Layden, a harsh critic of earlier studies, acknowledges that</u> **most current investigations** "screen out researchers whose strongly held beliefs make objectivity difficult" (10).

In the next example, two plot summaries (highlighted) are used as evidence for the writer's main idea, expressed in the first sentence. Since the attributions (<u>underlined</u>) contain enough information for the source to be located in the Works Cited list, no parenthetical reference is needed.

> Literature has many examples of lovers who must overcome the societal obstacles that separate them. Some stories, for example, <u>Shakespeare's *Romeo and Juliet*</u>, end tragically. In that play, a feud between Romeo's family, the Montagues, and Juliet's, the Capulets, forces the young lovers to meet in secret. They eventually devise a way to be together, but the plan goes wrong and ends in their deaths. Many stories, however, end happily. In <u>Jane Austen's novel *Pride and Prejudice*</u>, class differences and mistaken beliefs are successfully worked out so that Elizabeth Bennet and her sister Jane can end up marrying the men they love.

Introducing a Source

Try to avoid such awkward constructions as these: "According to Sherzod Abdukadirov and Michael Marlow, they say that ..." and "In the blog post by Sherzod Abdukadirov and Michael Marlow, they argue that ..." Instead, follow these hints for writing smooth, graceful attributions.

IDENTIFYING THE SOURCE   An introduction to a source may specify the author's name, inform readers of an author's expertise, or refer to a source more generally. To call attention to an author who is prominent in the field, important to your argument, or referred to many times in your essay, you may give the author's full name and identifier at the first mention in the text. On subsequent mentions, give only the last name. Don't use personal titles such as *Mr.* or *Ms.* In the following two examples, language that identifies or explains the source is highlighted.

> Natalie Angier, a Pulitzer Prize–winning journalist who writes about science, says that....Angier goes on to explain....

> The leading researchers Sherzod Abdukadirov and Michael Marlow argue that.... As Abdukadirov and Marlow explain....

For other sources, use a more general attribution and include the source's name (highlighted below), along with any page number, in the *parenthetical citation.*

> One writer points out...(Angier 22).

> According to statistics, 42 percent...(Abdukadirov and Marlow).

As part of an introduction, you may mention the title of the book, article, or other source.

> In "Government Intervention Will Not Solve Our Obesity Problem," Abdukadirov and Marlow maintain that....

> According to the National Aeronautics and Space Administration (NASA), ...

When the author's name is provided in the text, don't repeat the name in the parenthetical reference.

> One psychologist who is a harsh critic of earlier studies acknowledges that most current investigations "screen out researchers whose strongly held beliefs make objectivity difficult" (Layden 10).

> The psychologist Marsha Layden acknowledges that...(10).

Using Variety in Attributions

Don't always place attributions at the beginning of the sentence; experiment by placing them in the middle or at the end:

> To begin to solve our nation's obesity problem, Abdukadirov and Marlow explain, we must "allow people to find the solution that best meets their needs."

> Close to half of Americans will be obese by 2030, according to statistics (Abdukadirov and Marlow).

Try not to use a predictable subject-verb sequence ("Abdukadirov and Marlow argue that..."; "Abdukadirov and Marlow explain that...") in all your attributions. Aim for variations like the following:

> The information compiled by Abdukadirov and Marlow shows...

> In Abdukadirov and Marlow's opinion, ...

> Abdukadirov and Marlow's study reveals that....

Rather than repeatedly using the verbs *says* or *writes* in your introductions, seek out more vigorous verbs, making sure the verbs you select are appropriate to the tone and content of the work from which you're quoting. Also, take care to use the verbs in present tense when quoting or summarizing a source ("Abdukadirov and Marlow report that..." rather than "Abdukadirov and Marlow reported that..."). The list that follows offers a variety of effective verbs for attributions.

acknowledges	compares	grants	questions	shows
adds	confirms	implies	reasons	speculates
admits	contends	insists	reports	states
argues	declares	maintains	responds	suggests
asserts	demonstrates	notes	reveals	wonders
believes	endorses	points out	says	writes

Shortening or Clarifying Quotations

To make the best use of quotations, you will often need to shorten or excerpt them. It is acceptable to omit parts of quotations as long as you do not change the wording or distort the meaning of the original.

QUOTING A SINGLE WORD, A PHRASE, OR PART OF A SENTENCE Put double quotation marks around a quoted element you are integrating into your own sentence. In the following examples, the quotations are highlighted.

> Angier says that to speak of "objective" and "subjective" realities is to imply that these are "discrete entities" (22).

> As we try to find a way to curb the rate of obesity in our country, we must keep in mind that "research does not clearly support that government can solve this complex problem," according to Abdukadirov and Marlow.

OMITTING MATERIAL IN THE MIDDLE OF THE ORIGINAL SENTENCE Insert three spaced periods, called an *ellipsis* (...), in place of the deleted words. Leave a space before the first period of the ellipsis and leave a space after the third period of the ellipsis before continuing with the quoted matter.

> "Rather than pursuing a one-size-fits-all solution, we need to ... allow people to find the solution that best meets their needs" (Abdukadirov and Marlow).

OMITTING MATERIAL AT THE END OF THE ORIGINAL SENTENCE If no parenthetical reference is needed, insert a period before the first ellipsis period and provide the closing quotation mark, as in the first example below. If a parenthetical reference is needed, use only the ellipsis and add the period after the parentheses.

> The First Amendment of the Constitution of the United States lays the foundation for the doctrine of free speech: "Congress shall make no law respecting an establishment of religion, or prohibiting the free exercise thereof; or abridging the freedom of speech, or of the press...."

> In discussing scientific reasoning, Angier states, "We can call this 'objective' reality if we like, as opposed to subjective reality..." (22).

OMITTING MATERIAL AT THE START OF A QUOTATION No ellipses are required. Simply place the quotation marks where you begin quoting directly. Capitalize the first word if the resulting quotation forms a complete sentence.

> "The United States is facing a rising obesity problem," a reality confirmed by leading researchers Sherzod Abdukadirov and Michael Marlow.

ADDING MATERIAL TO A QUOTATION If, for the sake of clarity or grammar, you need to add a word or short phrase to a quotation (for example, by changing a verb tense or replacing a vague pronoun with a noun), enclose your insertion in brackets:

> Moreover, Angier discredits the concept that "the two [objective and subjective reality] are discrete entities with remarkably little in common" (22).

Capitalizing and Punctuating Short Quotations

The way a short quotation is used in a sentence determines whether it begins or doesn't begin with a capital letter and whether it is or isn't preceded by a comma.

INTRODUCING A QUOTATION THAT CAN STAND ALONE AS A SENTENCE If a quotation can stand alone as a grammatical sentence, capitalize the quotation's first word. Also, precede the quotation with a comma:

> Abdukadirov and Marlow observe, "Despite the myriad of studies showing American obesity is increasing, research does not clearly support that government can solve this complex problem."

> According to Abdukadirov and Marlow, "Not only is this method not solving the problem, we may actually be increasing the social stigma associated with weight gain."

USING *THAT*, *WHICH*, OR *WHO* (STATED OR IMPLIED) If you use *that*, *which*, or *who* to blend a quotation into the structure of your own sentence, don't capitalize the quotation's first word and don't precede it with a comma.

> Abdukadirov and Marlow maintain that "research does not clearly support" government intervention.

> Angier describes scientists as firmly believing there is "a reality capable of being understood" (22).

Even if, as in the first example above, the material being quoted originally started with a capital letter, you still use lowercase when incorporating the quotation into your own sentence. Note that in the second example, the word *that* is implied (before the word *there*).

INTERRUPTING A FULL-SENTENCE QUOTATION WITH AN ATTRIBUTION Place commas on both sides of the attribution, and resume the quotation with a lowercase letter.

> "Rather than pursuing a one-size-fits-all solution," Abdukadirov and Marlow comment, "we need to push back against government intervention and allow people to find the solution that best meets their needs."

USING A QUOTATION WITH A QUOTED WORD OR PHRASE When a source you're quoting contains a quoted word or phrase, place single quotation marks around the quoted words.

> "We can call this 'objective' reality if we like, as opposed to subjective reality, or opinion, or 'whimsical set of predilections,'" Angier posits (22).

Note that the comma after *predilections* goes inside the single quotation mark.

PUNCTUATING WITH A QUESTION MARK OR AN EXCLAMATION POINT If the question mark or exclamation point is part of the quotation, place it inside the quotation marks. If the mark is part of the structure of the framing sentence, as in the second example below, place it outside the quotation marks and after any parenthetical reference.

> Discussing a child's epileptic attack, the psychoanalyst Erik Erikson asks, in *Childhood and Society*, "What was the 'psychic stimulus'?" (26).

> On the other hand, in what ways can society "allow people to find the solution that best meets their needs" (Abdukadirov and Marlow)?

Presenting Statistics

Citing statistics can be a successful strategy for supporting your ideas. Be careful, though, not to misinterpret the data or twist their significance, and remember to provide an attribution indicating the source. Also, be sure not to overwhelm readers with too many statistics; include only those that support your central points in compelling ways. Keep in mind, too, that statistics won't speak for themselves. You need to interpret them for readers, showing how the figures cited reinforce your key ideas.

INEFFECTIVE USE OF STATISTICS In an essay on the issue of obesity in the United States, one student writer presented the following statistics from Abdukadirov and Marlow:

> The authors report that 13.4 percent of adults were obese in 1960 and that 34.3 percent were obese in 2008, an increase of little more than 20 percentage points. They go on to state that reports indicate that "by 2030, 42 percent of Americans will be obese," an increase of less than 10 percentage points over a 22-year period.

Although the statistics that the student cited were those reported by Abdukadirov and Marlow, they were incomplete, and the omission of the additional statistics distorted the authors' intended meaning. The student's comment led readers to believe that obesity rates would not continue to rise at the drastic rate at which they had risen between 1960 and 2008. However, the student failed to point out that the statistics also stated that "by 2030 … 11 percent [would] be severely obese, or 100 pounds overweight."

EFFECTIVE USE OF STATISTICS Instead of distorting the statistics, the writer could have clearly presented them and could have clearly explained their significance, as follows:

> The authors cite figures from the National Center of Health Statistics that report that 13.4 percent of adults were obese in 1960, and that 34.3 percent were obese

in 2008, an increase of little more than 20 percentage points. Abdukadirov and Marlow go on to cite the predictions of a report published by the *American Journal of Preventive Medicine*, which states that reports indicate that "by 2030, 42 percent of Americans will be obese and 11 percent will be severely obese, or 100 pounds overweight." These figures clearly indicate that we can no longer simply tell people that they need to eat less and exercise more. We must understand the necessity of taking steps to help individuals figure out how to best deal with this serious issue.

☑ Integrating Sources into Your Writing: A Checklist

- ☐ Introduce an important or oft-used source by giving the author's full name and credentials at the first mention. Thereafter, refer to the author by last name only. Don't use personal titles such as *Mr.* or *Ms.*

- ☐ Use general introductions (*One researcher says...*) for less important sources.

- ☐ Vary the style of attributions by sometimes positioning them at the middle or end of a sentence, using different verbs, or blending quotations into your own sentences.

- ☐ Words may be deleted from a quotation as long as the author's original meaning isn't changed. Insert an ellipsis (...) in place of the deleted words. An ellipsis is not needed when material is omitted from the start of a quotation. Use a period plus an ellipsis when the end of a sentence is deleted.

- ☐ Use brackets to add clarifying information to quotations.

- ☐ If a quotation can stand alone as a grammatical sentence, capitalize its first word and precede it with a comma. If a quotation is blended into the structure of your own sentence, don't capitalize the quotation's first word and don't precede it with a comma. If an attribution interrupts a quotation, place commas before and after the attribution and resume the quotation with a lowercase letter.

- ☐ For a quotation within a quotation, use single quotation marks.

- ☐ Place question marks and exclamation points inside quotation marks only if they belong to the quotation.

- ☐ Limit statistics and explain them fully to convey essential information.

Document Sources to Avoid Plagiarism

20.6 Document sources to avoid plagiarism.

Copyright law and the ethics of research require that you give credit to those whose words and ideas you borrow; that is, you must provide full and accurate *documentation*. Missing documentation results in *plagiarism*—using someone's material without properly crediting the source. Faulty documentation undermines your credibility. The best way to guard against plagiarism is to take very careful notes and thoroughly check your essay and Works Cited or References list for errors.

What Needs to Be Documented?

In general, any material—written or visual—that you take from outside sources (such as books, periodicals, websites, any type of performance, speeches, and so on) must be documented. To avoid plagiarizing, you must provide documentation for the following:

- A direct (word-for-word) quotation from a source.
- A paraphrase or summary of ideas, facts, opinions, or information from a source.
- A reproduction of an image, such as a photograph, or a graphic from a source.
- Any combination of quotation, paraphrase, summary, and visuals.

What Does Not Need to Be Documented

Academic writers must provide full documentation for all borrowed information. However, an exception is made for *common knowledge*—information that is widely known and accepted (whether or not you yourself were previously aware of it) as a matter of record. Well-known historical, scientific, and geographical facts, in particular, are often common knowledge. To determine whether information is common knowledge, ask yourself:

- *Are people likely to know this information without looking it up?* For example, the fact that the United States shares international borders with Canada and Mexico is common knowledge.
- *Is the information easily found in many sources?* For example, the fact that Japan attacked Pearl Harbor on December 7, 1941, is common knowledge.
- *Can a general dictionary supply the information?* For example, the fact that dogs belong to the same family of mammals as wolves is common knowledge.
- *Is it a commonly accepted view?* For example, the fact that the separation of church and state is an important principle in U.S. politics is common knowledge.

Remember, though, that your instructor might ask you to document *all* the information you acquire during your research, regardless of whether it is common knowledge.

Creating In-Text References: MLA Format

20.7 Create in-text references to your sources using MLA format.

The following discussion focuses on the MLA—Modern Language Association— format for documenting borrowed material. The MLA format, based on the *MLA Handbook,* eighth edition, is used widely in the liberal arts. For a sample paper that uses MLA documentation, see the student essay at the end of this chapter.

Whenever you quote or summarize material in the body of your essay, you must (1) identify the source as it appears in the Works Cited list and (2) specify the page(s) in your source on which the material appears. For this information, the MLA documentation system uses the *parenthetical reference,* a brief note in parentheses inserted after a quotation, paraphrase, or summary. The parenthetical reference presents enough information so that readers can turn to the Works Cited list (discussed later in this chapter) at the end of the essay for complete documentation.

What to Provide Within the Parentheses

- Give the author's last name only, even when you cite the author for the first time. If there is no author, use a shortened version of the title or whatever element is given first in the Works Cited entry for the item.

- If you give the author's name in the text ("Bittman says that . . ."), do not repeat it in the parenthetical reference.

- Write the page number after the author's last name with no punctuation between. (If the source is only one page, only the author's name is needed.) If the material quoted, paraphrased, or summarized spans more than one page, give the full range of pages if it is available. Don't use the designation *p.* or *page.*

Where to Place the Parentheses

- Place the parenthetical reference at the end of the sentence or immediately after the borrowed material if necessary for clarity.

- Put any period after the parenthetical reference—unless that reference follows a long quotation that is set off from the text, in which case the reference comes after any final punctuation.

- Make sure the parenthetical reference appears after an ellipsis and bracket at the end of a quotation but before the final period.

In the examples that follow, the two parts of the reference—author's name or identifier and page number—are highlighted.

SINGLE SOURCE: PARENTHESES ONLY   In the following example, the parenthetical reference following the summary contains the author's name and the page number of the material summarized.

> According to a recent study, excessive video game play can lead to a variety of psychological issues (Young 356).

A complete parenthetical reference follows the quotations in the next example. Note that the comma in the quotation is not part of the original quotation. It has been added because the sentence grammar requires a comma.

> Leading researchers say that "it is important to be able to recognize the symptoms of online gaming addiction," but they add that signs of the addiction are often "masked by realistic and practical use of the Internet for home or work" (Young 360).

SINGLE SOURCE: PARENTHESES AND ATTRIBUTIONS   When the attribution gives the author's name, only the page number appears in the parenthetical reference. The attribution should make it clear where the quotation, summary, or paraphrase begins.

> Kimberly Young argues that excessive video game play can lead to serious psychological issues (356). In "Understanding Online Gaming Addiction and Treatment Issues for Adolescents," Young maintains that the dangers of video game addiction must be taken seriously (356).

> Young points out that "parents who try to put time limits on the game may find a child becomes angry, irrational, and even violent" (359), as many parents of avid gamers can attest.

Note that in the immediately preceding example, the parenthetical reference follows the quotation in the middle of the sentence; placing the reference at the end of the sentence would imply that the idea expressed by "as many parents of avid gamers can attest" is Young's.

MORE THAN ONE SOURCE BY THE SAME AUTHOR   When your essay includes references to more than one work by the same author, you must specify—either in the parenthetical reference or in the attribution—the particular work being cited. You do this by providing the title, as well as the author's name and the page(s). Here are examples from an essay in which two works by Jean Piaget were used.

> In *The Language and Thought of the Child,* Jean Piaget states that "discussion forms the basis for a logical point of view" (240).

> Piaget considers dialogue essential to the development of logical thinking (*Language* 240).

Notice that when you name a work in your text, the full title appears; when you give a title in the parenthetic citation, though, only the first few significant words appear. (However, don't use an ellipsis to indicate that words have been omitted from the title; the ellipsis is used only within quotations.) When name, title, and page number all appear in the parenthetical reference, a comma follows the author's name.

TWO AUTHORS   Supply both authors' last names either in the attribution or in parentheses.

> A classic book on writing, *The Elements of Style* is an "attempt to cut the vast tangle of English rhetoric down to size" (Strunk and White xi).

MORE THAN TWO AUTHORS   Either in the attribution or in parentheses, give the last name of the first author followed by *et al.* (which means "and others").

> Researchers have found that the relationship between childhood obesity rates and family income level differs somewhat by race (Freedman et al. 26).

TWO OR MORE AUTHORS WITH THE SAME LAST NAME   When you use two or more sources written by authors with the same last name, you must include (either in the attribution or in parentheses) each author's first name or initial(s). The following example is from a paper that cites sources for both Bill Clinton and Hillary Clinton.

Discussing the fears young people have today, Hillary Clinton asserts that children are more "aware" than adults of "the threats posed by global climate change, catastrophic environmental events, and the spread of deadly diseases that know no national boundaries" (xvi).

A SOURCE WITH NO AUTHOR For a source without a named author, use a shortened version of the title of the work or the name of the issuing organization, whichever you used to alphabetize the source on the Works Cited list. In the following example, the full title of the source is "Supreme Court of the United States." Because the source is an entry in an alphabetically arranged reference book, the parenthetical reference has no page number.

The U.S. Supreme Court is fundamentally an appeals court, responsible for "cases arising under the Constitution, laws, or treaties of the United States" among others ("Supreme Court").

INFORMATION FOUND IN TWO OR MORE SOURCES When you come across several sources who cite the same highly specialized information or who share the same controversial opinion, that material does need to be documented. In such a case, state the material in your own words. In the parenthetical reference list the sources, separated by semicolons, as they appear in the Works Cited list.

A number of educators agree that an overall feeling of competence—rather than innate intelligence—is a key factor in determining which students do well the first year in college (Greene 208; Jones 72; Smith 465).

If you use a quotation to express an idea that occurs in several sources, provide an attribution for the quoted source and, in the parentheses, give the source's page number followed by a note that other sources make the same point:

The educator Henry Schneider argues that "students with low self-esteem tend to disregard the academic success they achieve" (23; also pointed out in Rabb 401).

SOURCE WITHIN A SOURCE If you quote or summarize a *secondary source* (a source whose ideas come to you only through another source), you need to make this clear. The parenthetic documentation should indicate "as quoted in" with the abbreviation *qtd. in*:

According to Sherman, "Recycling has, in several communities, created unanticipated expenses" (qtd. in Pratt 3).

Sherman explains that recycling can be surprisingly costly (qtd. in Pratt 3).

If the material you're quoting includes a quotation, place single quotation marks around the secondary quotation:

Pratt believes that "recycling efforts will be successful if, as Sherman argues, 'communities launch effective public-education campaigns'" (3).

Note: Your Works Cited list should include the source you actually read ("Pratt") rather than the source you refer to secondhand ("Sherman").

A SOURCE WITH NO PAGE NUMBERS, SUCH AS A WEBSITE The parenthetic reference does not give a page number when no page number is available or when the item is an entry in an alphabetically arranged reference book, such as an encyclopedia.

EACH VOLUME OF A MULTIVOLUME SOURCE PAGED SEPARATELY Indicate the volume number—"3" in the following example—then the page number, with a colon between the two. Do not use *vol.* or *v.*

(Kahn 3: 246)

A NONPRINT SOURCE (TELEVISION SHOW, LECTURE, INTERVIEW) In a parenthetic citation, give only the item (title, speaker, person interviewed) you used to alphabetize the source on your Works Cited list. Or provide the identifying information in the attribution, thus eliminating the need for parenthetic information:

> The world that director James Cameron creates in the movie *Avatar* can be seen, in some ways, as an idealized version of Earth.

LONG (BLOCK) QUOTATIONS A quotation longer than four lines starts on a new line and is indented, throughout, one-half inch from the left margin and typed without quotation marks. Double-space the block quotation. Don't leave extra space above or below the quotation. Long quotations, always used sparingly, require a lead-in. A lead-in that isn't a full sentence is followed by a comma; a lead-in that is a full sentence (highlighted) is followed by a colon:

> Young describes how video game addicts use gaming:

> Gaming addicts use the online world as a psychological escape. The game becomes a safe means to cope with life's problems. It is a legal and inexpensive way to soothe troubling feelings and can quickly become a convenient way to instantly forget whatever stresses and pains they are experiencing. Like a drug addict or alcoholic who uses drugs or alcohol as a way to escape problems that they aren't able to deal with, gaming addicts use the game to avoid stressful situations and unpleasant feelings. (362)

Notice that the page number in parentheses appears *after* the period, not before as it would with a short quotation.

Revise, Edit, and Proofread the First Draft

20.8 Revise, edit, and proofread your first draft.

After completing your first draft, set the essay aside for a while. When you pick it up later, you'll have a fresh, more objective view of it. Then reread your entire draft to evaluate the essay's overall meaning and structure. Outlining the draft—without referring to the outline that guided the draft's preparation—is a helpful analytical tool.

Despite all your work, you may find that a main support point seems weak. Sometimes a review of your annotations and other notes—including those you didn't use for your draft—will uncover material that you can add to the essay. Other times, though, you may need to do additional research. Once you're confident that the essay's overall meaning and structure are strong, write your introduction and conclusion—if you haven't already done so.

 Evaluate your essay's paragraph development, consulting the writing process diagrams for each pattern of development for more tips on revising each pattern. As you work, pay special attention to the way you present evidence in the paragraphs.

Look closely at how you integrate borrowed material. Does your evidence consist of one quotation after another, or do you express borrowed ideas in your own words? Do you simply insert borrowed material without commentary, or do you interpret the material and show its relevance to the points you want to make? If you prepared the draft without providing many attributions, now is the time to supply them. Then refine your draft's words and sentences.

Finally, when you start editing and proofreading, allow enough time to verify the accuracy of quoted material. Check such material against your notes, and check your documentation against both your annotated bibliography and your Works Cited list, making sure that everything matches. When preparing the final copy of your essay, follow the sample research paper in this chapter as a model.

Prepare the Works Cited List: MLA Format

20.9 Prepare a works cited list in MLA format.

At this point, you need to assemble your essay's Works Cited list. This list will provide readers with full bibliographic information about the sources you cite in the essay. As a first step, refer to your annotated bibliography. This list will be a huge help to you if you took time to record each source in MLA format as you assembled your annotated bibliography. Make sure you've (1) removed the sources you did not use in your essay and (2) alphabetized the remaining entries by the authors' last names or, for those works with no author listed, by the title of the work.

General Instructions for the MLA Works Cited List

The instructions below and the sample entries that follow are for MLA style. If you don't spot an entry for the type of source you need to document, consult the most recent edition of the *MLA Handbook* for more comprehensive examples. You can also visit the MLA's help center online at https://style.mla.org. (See also the sample Works Cited list in the student research essay at the end of this chapter.)

- Include only those works you quote, paraphrase, summarize, or otherwise directly refer to in your essay.
- Start a new page, with the heading *Works Cited* centered, at the top, and place the list at the end of your essay.
- Double-space the entries in the list, and don't add extra space between entries.

- Start the first line of each new entry at the left margin; indent all subsequent lines in an entry five spaces (half an inch).

- Alphabetize by author's last name. Give the last name, then a comma, and then the first name and any initial. End with a period. For an entry with two authors, give both authors' names but reverse only the first name. List the names in the order given in the source. For a work with three or more authors, give only the first author's name followed by a comma and *et al.* (Latin for "and others"), not italicized.

- If an entry doesn't have an author, alphabetize it by the title. Disregard an initial *A, An,* or *The* in alphabetizing.

- Use italics as noted below.

- For dates in entries, use the following: *Jan., Feb., Mar., Apr., May, June, July, Aug., Sept., Oct., Nov., Dec.,* not italicized.

The *MLA Handbook* does not divide sources according to whether they are print, nonprint, books, journals, and so on. The *"MLA Handbook,* 8th edition, Summary for Authors and Editors" explains that the new edition shifts "from a focus on types of sources to a focus on the process of building citations.... MLA style is based on a series of basic principles and elements of citations that can be applied to a wide variety of source types and formats" (1).

The guidelines go on to explain:

> Works cited entries are based on a set of 'core elements.' These elements are listed [below] in the order in which they should appear. An element should be omitted from the entry if it's not relevant to the work being documented. Each element is followed by the punctuation mark shown [in the list that follows] unless it is the final element, which should end with a period (3).

1. **Author.**

    Author names are spelled out.

    For works by one author, include the author's last name, followed by a comma, and then the author's first name.

    For works by two authors, second author names are written first name, last name.

    For three or more authors, reverse the first name and follow with a comma and *et al.* (Note that "et al." should not be italicized in your Works Cited list or in-text citations.)

    For editors and other non-author creators, add labels and spell them out: editor, translator, creator, performer.

    Pseudonyms and online identities are spelled out like regular author names.

    For works published without an author name, begin the entry with the work's title.

    A period follows the name of the author(s).

2. **Title of source.**

    Italicize self-contained sources (books, journals, websites). Place quotation marks around parts of larger works (article titles, essays, poems).

    A period follows the title of the source.

3. **Title of container.**

    The "*MLA Handbook*, 8th Edition, Summary for Authors and Editors" includes the following information regarding its use of the term *container*:

    > "Container" is a new term in the MLA citation world. When the source being documented forms part of a larger whole, the larger whole can be thought of as a container that holds the source. The container is crucial to the identification of the source. The title of the container is normally italicized and is followed by a comma, since the information that comes next describes the container.

    > Container is a generic term, intended to capture any type of print or digital medium. A container may be a book, periodical, television series, website, comic book, and so forth.

    > A container can be nested in a larger container. A blog may be part of a network of blogs. A journal issue may be stored on a database like *JSTOR*. A book may be read on *Google Books*. (4–5)

    A comma follows the title of the container.

    (*Note*: When a container is nested in a larger container, each container should be documented with a period between the two containers.)

4. **Other contributors.**

    Examples include *translated by, adapted by, directed by, edited by, illustrated by, introduction by, narrated by, performance by, translated by, general editor*, and *guest editors.*
    A comma follows other contributors.

5. **Version.**

    If the source has been released in more than one form, identify the version you are citing.
    A comma follows the version.

6. **Number.**

    For journal volume and issue numbers, use the abbreviations *vol.* and *no.* Separate volume and issue numbers with a comma.
    A comma follows the number.

7. **Publisher.**

    Supply the publisher's name in full, omitting only words such as *Co.* or *Ltd.* However, use *UP* to abbreviate the names of university presses (as in *Columbia UP* and *U of California P*).
    A comma follows the name of the publisher.

8. **Publication date.**

    When there is more than one date for a source (for example, an online article that was also published in print), cite the date that is most relevant to your use of the source. If you accessed an article online that was also published in print, use the publication date of the online version of the article.
    A comma follows the publication date.

9. **Location.**

For print sources, use a page number (for example, *p.* 22) or page number range preceded by *pp.*

For online sources, include either the URL (Internet address) or, if available, the digital object identifier (DOI). If a source has a DOI, use it rather than the URL. The DOI is preferred because it is a more stable identifier.

If you are using an online source and no publication date is available, end your entry by listing the date on which you accessed the site. Use this format: *Accessed 17 Jan. 2017.*

(*Note*: The *MLA Handbook*, eighth edition, page 48, states that you can leave URLs out of your Works Cited list if your instructor prefers that they not be included.)

The following templates will help you compile the information you need for your MLA Works Cited list and format your entries correctly. Take note of the punctuation following each element, and use the same punctuation in your entries. Note that *Location* usually refers to page numbers in a print work and to a URL or DOI in an online source.

Print Source

Author.	Bollig, Chase.
Title of source.	"Is College Worth It? Arguing for Composition's Value with the Citizen-Worker."
Title of container,	*College Composition and Communication,*
Other contributors,	
Version,	
Number,	vol. 67, no. 2,
Publisher,	
Publication date,	2015,
Location.	pp. 150–72.

Online Source

Note that http:// and https:// are not included in URLs.

Author.	Affleck, John.
Title of source.	"Why We Watch Football Even Though We Know It's Deadly."
Title of container,	*Time,*
Other contributors,	
Version,	
Number,	
Publisher,	
Publication date,	5 Feb. 2016,
Location.	time.com/4210319/super-bowl-football-psychology.

Citation Examples

The following examples, as well as the list of Works Cited included in the sample essay later in this chapter, provide you with examples of how to correctly document sources in MLA format. For additional examples, consult the latest edition of the *MLA Handbook*.

ARTICLE IN A WEEKLY OR BIWEEKLY PRINT MAGAZINE
Rodrick, Stephen. "Who Poisoned Flint, Michigan?" *Rolling Stone,* 11 Feb. 2016, pp. 52+.

ARTICLE IN A MONTHLY OR BIMONTHLY PRINT MAGAZINE
Beinart, Peter. "America's Lurch to the Left." *The Atlantic,* Jan.-Feb. 2016, pp. 60–62.

ARTICLE IN A DAILY PRINT NEWSPAPER
Perez-Peña, Richard. "Benefits of College Degree in Recession Are Outlined." *The New York Times,* 10 Jan. 2013, p. A15.

EDITORIAL, LETTER TO THE EDITOR, OR REPLY TO A PRINT LETTER
Baldwin, William. "Sidelines: Defend Yourself against Tax Torture." Editorial. *Forbes,* 10 May 2010, p. 10.
Brooks, David. "A Question of Moral Radicalism." Letter to the Editor. *The New York Times,* 5 Feb. 2016, p. A27.

ARTICLE IN A PRINT SCHOLARLY JOURNAL   Regardless of how a journal is paginated, include *both* the volume number and the issue number (if available).
Bollig, Chase. "Is College Worth It? Arguing for Composition's Value with the Citizen-Worker." *College Composition and Communication,* vol. 67, no. 2, 2015, pp. 150–72.

PRINT ARTICLE WITH MORE THAN ONE AUTHOR   For a citation with two authors, see the first example. For a citation with more than two authors, see the second example. Notice that a comma follows the first author's name.
Benjamin, Ludy T., and David B. Baker. "Recapturing a Context for Psychology: The Role of History." *Perspectives on Psychological Science,* vol. 4, no.1, 2009, pp. 97–98.
Troubleyn, Liesbeth, et al. "Consumption Patterns and Living Conditions inside Het Steen, the Late Medieval Prison of Malines (Mechelen, Belgium)." *Journal of Archaeology in the Low Countries,* vol. 1, no. 2, 2009, pp. 5–47.

PRINT REVIEW OF A BOOK
Chiasson, Don. "Forms of Attention." Review of *Rain,* by Don Paterson. *The New Yorker,* 19 Apr. 2010, pp. 116–18.

PRINT OR ELECTRONIC BOOK BY ONE AUTHOR   According to MLA, a book is a book whether you read it in print or on an e-reader (such as a Kindle, Nook, or iPad).
Koretz, Daniel. *Measuring Up: What Educational Testing Really Tells Us.* Harvard UP, 2008.
Rigolosi, Steven. *The Outsmarting of Criminals.* Ransom Note Press, 2014.

PRINT OR ELECTRONIC BOOK BY TWO AUTHORS
Lewis, Robin, and Michael Dart. *The New Rules of Retail: Competing in the World's Toughest Marketplace.* Macmillan, 2010.

PRINT OR ELECTRONIC BOOK BY THREE OR MORE AUTHORS
Charlton, Colin, et al. *GenAdmin: Theorizing WPA Identities in the Twenty-First Century*. Parlor
    Press, 2011.

TWO OR MORE PRINT WORKS BY THE SAME AUTHOR   List each book separately.
Give the author's name in the first entry only; begin subsequent entries by the same
author with three hyphens followed by a period. Arrange the works alphabetically by title.
McChesney, Robert W. *Communication Revolution: Critical Junctures and the Future of Media*.
    New Press, 2007.
—. *The Political Economy of Media: Enduring Issues, Emerging Dilemmas*. Monthly Review, 2008.

PRINT REVISED EDITION   Indicate the edition (*rev. ed., 2nd ed., 3rd ed., 4th ed.*, and
so on) after the title.
Weiss, Thomas G., et al. *The United Nations and Changing World Politics*. 6th ed., Westview,
    2011.

PRINT BOOK WITH AN AUTHOR AND EDITOR OR TRANSLATOR   Use *Edited by*
or *Translated by* and then the name of the editor or translator.
Ferrante, Elena. *The Story of the Lost Child*. Translated by Ann Goldstein, Europa Editions,
    2015.

PRINT ANTHOLOGY OR COMPILATION OF WORKS BY DIFFERENT AUTHORS
Use *editor* or *editors*.
Coxwell-Teague, Deborah, and Ronald F. Lunsford, editors. *First-Year Composition: From
    Theory to Practice*. Parlor Press, 2014.

SECTION OF A PRINT ANTHOLOGY OR COMPILATION   Use *edited by* and the editors' names. Note that the entry gives the page numbers on which the selection appears.
Anson, Chris. "Writing, Language, and Literacy." *First-Year Composition: From Theory to
    Practice*, edited by Deborah Coxwell-Teague and Ronald F. Lunsford, Parlor Press,
    2014, pp. 3–26.

SECTION, POEM, OR CHAPTER IN A PRINT BOOK BY ONE AUTHOR
Corrigan, Maureen. "Rhapsody in Noir." *So We Read On*, Little, Brown, 2014, pp. 127–61.

ENTRY IN A REFERENCE WORK
"The Order of St. John." *Whitaker's 2016: An Almanack*. 148th ed., Bloomsbury, 2015, p. 104.

PRINT BOOK BY AN INSTITUTION (CORPORATE AUTHOR)   When a work's publisher and author are separate organizations, give both names, starting the entry with
the author.
    When an organization or institution is both publisher and author, begin the entry
with the title.
    When an entry starts with a government agency as the author, begin with the
name of the largest entity, followed by a comma, followed by smaller organizational
units within the agency, arranged from largest to smallest and separated by commas.
New York State, Committee on State Prisons. *Investigation of the New York State Prisons*. Arno
    Press, 1974.

Foreign Direct Investment, the Service Sector, and International Banking. Centre on Transnational Corporations, United Nations, 1987.

Great Britain, Ministry of Agriculture, Fisheries, and Food. *Our Countryside, the Future: A Fair Deal for Rural England.* Her Majesty's Stationery Office, 2000.

ONLINE NEWSPAPER OR MAGAZINE ARTICLE The second citation is to an online-only magazine.

Affleck, John. "Why We Watch Football Even Though We Know It's Deadly." *Time,* 5 Feb. 2016, time.com/4210319/super-bowl-football-psychology.

Norton, Ben. "Adopting Sustainable Energy Would Save Millions of Lives Each Year, U.N. Says." *Salon.com,* 26 Jan. 2016, www.salon.com/2016/01/26/adopting_sustainable_ energy_would_save_millions_of_lives_each_year_u_n_says.

Cieply, Michael. "Politics Invades Hollywood." *The New York Times,* 13 Mar. 2016, www.nytimes.com/2016/03/14/business/media/politics-invade-hollywood. html?emc=edit_th_20160314&nl=todaysheadlines&nlid=69810361.

ARTICLE IN AN ONLINE REFERENCE WORK

"Salem Witch Trials." *Encyclopaedia Britannica Online,* 2016, www.britannica.com/event/ Salem-witch-trials.

SCHOLARLY JOURNAL FOUND ON THE INTERNET Note that some articles published on the web do not give page numbers, as in the second example below. Also note that in the first example below, there are two containers listed separately, with a period following each one. Finally, note that there is no space after the colon in *doi:10.1002/icd.643.*

Ensor, Rosie, and Claire Hughes. "With a Little Help from My Friends: Maternal Social Support, via Parenting, Promotes Willingness to Share in Preschoolers Born to Young Mothers." *Infant and Child Development,* vol. 19, no. 2, 2010, pp. 127–221. *Wiley Online Library,* doi:10.1002/icd.643.

Njeng, Eric Sipyinyu. "Achebe, Conrad, and the Postcolonial Strain." *Comparative Literature and Culture,* vol. 10, no. 1, 2008, docs.lib.purdue.edu/clcweb/vol10/iss1/3.

PERSONAL AND PROFESSIONAL WEBSITES In the entry, *Uncle Tom's Cabin* is *not* italicized. Although it's a title that would ordinarily be italicized, because the rest of the website title is in italics, the book title is set off in regular type.

Railton, Stephen, editor. Uncle Tom's Cabin *and American Culture: A Multi-Media Archive,* Dept. of English, U of Virginia, 2007, utc.iath.virginia.edu.

BLOG

Waldman, Deane. "'Care' Has Deserted Managed Care." *The Huffington Post,* 26 June 2008, http://www.huffingtonpost.com/deane-waldman/care-has-deserted-managed_ b_109407.html.

PODCAST

Khalid, Asma. "New Asian-American SuperPAC Formed to Increase 'the Power of Our Vote.'" *It's All Politics: NPR Weekly News Roundup,* 14 Jan. 2016, www.npr. org/2016/01/14/463058466/new-asian-american-superpac-formed-to-increase-the-power-of-our-vote.

POSTINGS TO AN ONLINE GROUP

Das, Shyamal Kumar. "The Value of Pi." *The Math Forum @Drexel*, 7 Apr. 2015, mathforum. org/kb/thread.jspa?threadID=2690558.

E-BOOK

Austen, Jane. *Emma*. John Murray, 1815. *Project Gutenberg*, www.gutenberg.org/files/158/ 158-h/158-h.htm.

POSTING ON SOCIAL MEDIA

UN Refugee Agency. "Please share! We're rushing in aid as 66,000 #Congolese refugees stream into western #Uganda." *Twitter*, 15 July 2013, twitter.com/refugees/status/356871357339926530.

"Randy Pausch's Last Lecture." *YouTube*, 29 Mar. 2010, content.time.com/time/specials/ packages/article/0,28804, 1974961_1974925_1974724,00.html.

@persiankiwi. "We have report of large street battles in east & west of Tehran now - #Iranelection." *Twitter*, 23 June 2009, 11:15 a.m., twitter.com/persiankiwi/status/2298106072.

The third example above comes from the *MLA Handbook*, eighth edition, page 29. The handbook specifies that "a short untitled message, such as a tweet," should be identified "by reproducing its full text, without changes, in place of a title. Enclose the text in quotation marks."

SCHOLARLY JOURNAL FOUND IN AN ONLINE DATABASE   In the entry below there are two containers: *Phi Delta Kappan*, a professional magazine for educators; and *JSTOR*, an online database of journals and books. Issues of *Phi Delta Kappan* are nested in *JSTOR*. Each container is listed separately, with a period at the end of each one.

Rossen, Eric, and Katherine C. Cowan. "Improving Mental Health in Schools." *Phi Delta Kappan*,vol.96,no.4,Dec.2014–Feb.2015,pp.8–13.*JSTOR*,doi:10.1177/0031721714561438.

CD-ROM OR DVD-ROM

The Oxford English Dictionary, 2nd ed., version 4.0, edited by John Simpson, Oxford UP, 21 May 2009.

WORK OF ART EXPERIENCED FIRSTHAND IN A MUSEUM   The following example comes from the *MLA Handbook*, eighth edition, page 49.

Bearden, Romare. *The Train*. 1975, Museum of Modern Art, New York.

   The name of the city would be omitted if it were part of the place's name.

ARTIFACT EXPERIENCED FIRSTHAND IN AN ARCHIVE   The following example appears in the *MLA Handbook*, eighth edition, page 50. Note the inclusion of the number that the archive uses to identify the object.

Chaucer, Geoffrey. *The Canterbury Tales*. Circa 1400-10, British Library, London, Harley MS 7334.

SHORT STORY NESTED IN A DIGITAL LIBRARY   The following example comes from the *MLA Handbook*, eighth edition, page 35.

Poe, Edgar Allan. "The Masque of the Red Death." *The Complete Works of Edgar Allan Poe*, edited by James A. Harrison, vol. 4, Thomas Y. Crowell, 1902, pp. 250–58. *HathiTrust Digital Library*, babel.hathitrust.org/cgi/pt?id=coo.31924079574368;view=1up;seq=266.

ONLINE CARTOON OR COMIC STRIP

Sipress, David. "Anger Management Therapy." *The New Yorker,* 14 Mar. 2016, www
.newyorker.com/cartoons/daily-cartoon/monday-march-14th-anger-management.

Thompson, Dan. "Brevity." *GoComics.com,* 14 Mar. 2016, www.gocomics.com/brevity.

TELEVISION PROGRAM WATCHED ON TV

"Barcelona." *I'll Have What Phil's Having*, episode 5, PBS, 1 Nov. 2015.

TELEVISION PROGRAM WATCHED ONLINE   The following example comes from
the *MLA Handbook*, eighth edition, page 33.

"Under the Gun." *Pretty Little Liars*, season 4, episode 6, ABC Family, 16 July 2013. *Hulu*,
www.hulu.com/watch/511318.

SONG ON A CD

Dylan, Bob. "Visions of Johanna." *Blonde on Blonde*, 1966. Sony, 2004.
   The title of the CD is *Blonde on Blonde*.

FILM OR MOVIE

The Hurt Locker. Directed by Kathryn Bigelow, Voltage Pictures, 2008.

PERSONAL OR TELEPHONE INTERVIEW

Crittenden, Alicia. Telephone interview, 4 May 2016.

Strickland, Casey. Personal interview, 26 Jan. 2016.

LECTURE, SPEECH, ADDRESS, OR READING

Lunsford, Andrea. "What Is Literacy Today?" School of Journalism and Graphic Communication Guest Lecture, 11 Feb. 2016, Florida A&M University, Tallahassee.

E-MAIL MESSAGE   Start with the sender's name. The title is the subject line.

Young, Melinda. "Plans for Future Editions." Received by Kyler Johnston, 21 June 2016.

Prepare the References List: APA Format

20.10 Prepare a works cited list in APA format.

Researchers in the social sciences and in education use a citation format developed by
the American Psychological Association (APA) and explained in the *Publication Manual of
the American Psychological Association*. If you're writing an essay for a course in sociology,
psychology, anthropology, economics, or political science, your professor will probably
expect APA-style documentation. History, philosophy, and religion are sometimes considered humanities, sometimes social sciences, depending on your approach to the topic.

Parenthetic Citations in the Text

As in the MLA format, APA citations are enclosed in parentheses within the text and
provide the author's last name. The main differences between the two formats are these:

- The year of publication appears after the name.

- Page numbers appear after the year only when a source is quoted or when specific parts of a source are paraphrased or summarized. (A citation without a page
number refers to the source as a whole.)

- The abbreviation *p.* or *pp.* appears before any page number(s).

- A comma appears between the author's name and the year and between the year and the page number.

Here are examples of APA parenthetic citations:

> Education experts have observed that "as arts education funding dwindles in school systems, theatres of all sizes have assumed more and more of the burden of training young people and exposing them to the arts" (Cameron, 2004, p. 6).

If you use an attribution that gives the author's name, put the publication year (in parentheses) right after the author's name and put the page number at the end. The attribution is underlined in this example.

> <u>Leading food columnist and television personality Mark Bittman</u> (2014) argues that "we should make it a national priority to create two new programs, a research program to determine precisely what causes diet-related chronic illnesses ... and a program that will get this single, simple message across: Eat Real Food" (p. 1).

If a work has two authors, cite both, using *and* in a text attribution and an ampersand (&) in a parenthetic reference. For a work with three to five authors, name all authors in the first citation. In subsequent citations, name only the first author followed by *et al.* For a work with six or more authors, cite the first author followed by *et al.*

> In their classic book on writing, *The Elements of Style*, <u>William Strunk and E. B. White</u> (1918) "attempt to cut the vast tangle of English rhetoric down to size" (p. xi).

> Researchers have found that the relationship between childhood obesity rates and family income level differs somewhat by race (Blank, Freedman, May, & Sherry, 2013, p. 120).

General Instructions for the APA References List

A double-spaced alphabetical list of sources, titled *References*, appears at the end of a research essay using APA documentation style. The citations include much of the same information as MLA citations do, but they are formatted in different ways. Notice that the first four items in the following instructions are the same as for a Works Cited list.

- Include only those works you quote, paraphrase, summarize, or otherwise directly refer to in your essay.

- Start a new page, with the heading *References* centered, at the top, and place the list at the end of your essay.

- Double-space the entries in the list, and don't add extra space between entries.

- Start the first line of each new entry at the left margin; if an entry extends beyond one line, indent all subsequent lines five spaces (half an inch).

- Place the publication date in parentheses directly after the author's name and follow it with a period.

- For two or more works by the same author, arrange the works by publication date, giving the earliest first.

- For two or more works by the same author that are published in the same year, differentiate the dates with lowercase letters—(2016a), (2016b)—and alphabetize them by title.

- For an item with up to seven authors, give the last names and initials for all authors. Use an ampersand (&) instead of *and* before the last author. If there are more than seven, list the first six, add a comma and an ellipsis, and end with the name of the last author. Invert the names of all authors.

- Invert all author names, and use only initials for an author's first and middle names.

- For an article, capitalize only the first letter of the title (and subtitle) and any proper names. Do not enclose the title in quotation marks.

- For a book, capitalize only the first letter of the title (and subtitle) and any proper names. Italicize the title.

- For a journal, give the full title, in capital and lowercase letters, italicized.

- Abbreviate publishers' names but include the word *Books, Press,* or *University* when it is part of a publisher's name.

Here's the general order of information for an entry:

- Author or other creative individual
- Relevant dates
- Title of a shorter work
- Descriptive information
- Larger work or source of a shorter work
- Place of publication
- Publisher or distributor
- Relevant identifying numbers or letters
- Medium (format)

Citing Print Sources—Periodicals

For a periodical in print form, you'll need to consult (1) the page with the journal title and copyright information and (2) all pages on which the article appears.

BASIC APA FORMAT FOR A PRINTED PERIODICAL

Author's last name, author's initials. (date). Article title: Article subtitle. *Periodical Title,* volume (issue), pages.

- **Author.** See the guidelines on authors' names in "General Instructions for the APA References List." If the article is unsigned, begin with its title.

- **Date of publication.** Include the year, in parentheses, followed by a period. For newspapers and weekly magazines, include the year, followed by a comma, then the month and day.

- **Article title.** Give the article's complete title, with capitals for the first word of the main title and subtitle and any proper nouns. Do not put the title into quotation marks. End with a period.

- **Periodical title.** Supply the periodical's full name, in italics. Follow with a comma.

- **Volume and issue numbers.** For scholarly journals, give the volume number in italics. If the journal is paginated by issue, include the issue number in parentheses after the volume number with no intervening space. Do not italicize the issue number. Do not use the abbreviation *vol*. Follow with a comma.

- **Page numbers.** Give the page range (for example, 27–34). If the pages in an article aren't continuous, give all the page numbers separated by commas (for example, 67–68, 70, 72). End with a period. Do not use *p., pp., page*, or *pages* before the numbers, except when citing a newspaper article.

ARTICLE IN A WEEKLY OR BIWEEKLY PRINT MAGAZINE
Rodrick, S. (2015, February 11). Who poisoned Flint, Michigan? *Rolling Stone*, 1254, 52–57, 63.

ARTICLE IN A MONTHLY OR BIMONTHLY PRINT MAGAZINE
Beinart, P. (2016, January/February). America's lurch to the left. *Atlantic Monthly*, 60–62.

ARTICLE IN A DAILY PRINT NEWSPAPER   Include the abbreviation *p.* or *pp.* before the page number(s).
Perez-Pena, R. (2013, January 10). Benefits of college degree in recession are outlined. *The New York Times*, p. A15.

PRINT EDITORIAL, LETTER TO THE EDITOR, OR REPLY TO A LETTER   For an unsigned editorial, start with the title, and add the word *Editorial* in brackets, a period, and then the date.
Brooks, D. (2016, February 5). A question of moral radicalism [Editorial]. *The New York Times*, p. A27.
Seattle's homeless problem requires a regional response [Editorial]. (2016, January 30). *The Seattle Times*, p. D2.

ARTICLE IN A CONTINUOUSLY PAGINATED SCHOLARLY PRINT JOURNAL
Include a digital object identifier (DOI) at the end of your entry if one is available.
Morrison, G. Z. (2010). Two separate worlds: Students of color at a predominantly white university. *Journal of Black Studies*, 40, 987–1015. doi:10.1177/0021934708325408

ARTICLE IN A SCHOLARLY PRINT JOURNAL THAT PAGINATES EACH ISSUE SEPARATELY
Bollig, C. (2015). Is college worth it? Arguing for composition's value with the citizen-worker. *College Composition and Communication*, 67(2), 150–172.

PRINT ARTICLE BY MORE THAN ONE AUTHOR   Follow the format in the first example for a citation with up to seven authors. For a citation with more than seven authors, follow the format in the second example. (See the guidelines on authors' names in the "General Instructions for the APA References List.")

Seamon, M. J., Fass, J. A., Maniscalco-Feichtl, M., & Abu-Shraie, N. A. (2007). Medical marijuana and the developing role of the pharmacist. *American Journal of Health-System Pharmacy, 64*(10), 1037–1044.

Troubleyn, L., Kinnaer, F., Ervynck, A., Beeckmans, L., Caluwé, D., Cooremans, B.,...Wouters, W. (2009). Consumption patterns and living conditions inside Het Steen, the late medieval prison of Malines (Mechelen, Belgium). *Journal of Archaeology in the Low Countries, 1*(2), 5–47.

PRINT REVIEW OF A BOOK

Chiasson, D. (2010, April 19). Forms of attention [Review of the book *Rain,* by Don Paterson]. *The New Yorker,* 116–118.

Citing Print Sources—Books

For a book, you'll need to consult (1) the title page and (2) the copyright notice on the back of the title page. You will also need to know the specific page numbers of any material you are citing.

BASIC APA FORMAT FOR A PRINTED BOOK

Author's last name, Author's initials. (year). *Book title: Book subtitle.* City, State (or Country): Publisher.

- **Author.** See the guidelines on authors' names in "General Instructions for the APA References List."

- **Year of publication.** Supply the most recent year of copyright in parentheses, followed by a period. Don't use the year of the most recent printing.

- **Book title.** Give the complete book title in italics. If the book has a subtitle, separate it from the title with a colon and a single space. Capitalize only the first word of the main title and subtitle and any proper nouns. End the title with a period.

- **Place of publication.** Give the first city of publication listed on the title page. Unless the state is mentioned in the publisher's name (as in a university press), give the state also, using U.S. postal abbreviations. For cities outside the United States, spell out the city and country. Separate city and state or country with a comma. Follow with a colon and a space.

- **Publisher.** Shorten the publisher's name, giving only key words and omitting the terms like *Co., Publishers, Inc.* However, keep the words *University, Press,* and *Books* spelled out. (For example, write *Norton* for *W. W. Norton and Company* but spell out *University of Chicago Press.*) End with a period.

PRINT BOOK BY ONE AUTHOR

Koretz, D. (2008). *Measuring up: What educational testing really tells us.* Cambridge, MA: Harvard University Press.

MULTIPLE PRINT WORKS BY THE SAME AUTHOR Repeat the author's name with each entry, and list the entries by year of publication, from earliest to latest.

McChesney, R. W. (2007). *Communication revolution: Critical junctures and the future of media.* New York, NY: The New Press.

McChesney, R. W. (2008). *The political economy of media: Enduring issues, emerging dilemmas.* New York, NY: Monthly Review Press.

PRINT BOOK BY MULTIPLE AUTHORS

Yancey, K. B., Robertson, L., & Taczak, K. (2014). *Writing across contexts: Transfer, composition, and sites of writing.* Logan: Utah State University Press.

PRINT REVISED EDITION

Weiss, T. G., Forsythe, D. P., & Coate, R. A. (2011). *The United Nations and changing world politics* (6th ed.). Boulder, CO: Westview.

PRINT BOOK WITH AN AUTHOR AND EDITOR OR TRANSLATOR Use the abbreviations *Ed.* and *Trans.*

Ferrante, E. (2015). *The story of the lost child.* (A. Goldstein, Trans.). New York, NY: Europa Editions.

PRINT ANTHOLOGY OR COMPILATION OF WORKS BY DIFFERENT AUTHORS

Coxwell-Teague, D. & Lunsford, R. F. (Eds.). (2014). *First-year composition: From theory to practice.* Anderson, SC: Parlor Press.

PRINT SECTION OF AN ANTHOLOGY OR COMPILATION Give the inclusive page numbers, preceded by *pp.*, for the section you are citing.

Anson, C. (2014). Writing, language, and literacy. In D. Coxwell-Teague & R. F. Lunsford (Eds.), *First-year composition: From theory to practice* (pp. 3–26). Anderson, SC: Parlor Press.

SECTION, POEM, OR CHAPTER IN A PRINT BOOK BY ONE AUTHOR

Corrigan, M. (2014). Rhapsody in noir. In M. Corrigan, *So we read on* (pp. 127–161). New York, NY: Little, Brown and Company.

PRINT REFERENCE WORK

The Order of St. John. (2015). In *Whitaker's 2016: An almanack* (148th ed.) London, United Kingdom: Bloomsbury Publishing Company.

PRINT BOOK BY AN INSTITUTION (CORPORATE AUTHOR)

United Nations Department of Economic and Social Affairs. (2015). *Human development report 2015: Work for human development.* New York, NY: United Nations.

Citing Sources Found on a Website

Citations for websites require much of the same information used in citations for print sources. To this, add retrieval information—an Internet address (URL) or a DOI. The DOI, used primarily with scholarly materials, is a permanent, unique identifier for articles on the web. For an online newspaper, magazine, or similar publication, use the publication's home page URL. For difficult-to-find sites, include the entire URL. To construct a citation, you will need information from (1) the entire screen of the webpage you are citing, including the address bar, and (2) the home page of the website, if that is different from the page you are citing.

BASIC APA FORMATS FOR AN ONLINE SOURCE   Print publication information. doi:10.xxxx/xxxxxxxxxx

Author's last name, Author's initials. (date). Item title. *Website Title* (version or edition, if any). Retrieved from [URL]

- **Author's name.** Give the author's name, as for a print item.
- **Title of the selection.** Give the title of the selection, followed by a period. To cite an entire website, see "Source" below.
- **Date of publication.** Give the date of publication as for a print item. If the date is not available, use *n.d.* (for "no date").
- **Source.** Give the title of the website, as for a book or publication title.
- **Version or edition.** List any volume, issue, and page numbers as for a print edition. Or list any relevant version, edition, or report number in parentheses after the source, followed by a period.
- **Sponsor.** Give the sponsor or owner in the retrieval information if a URL is cited.
- **Medium.** Include the retrieval information. If a DOI is available, use *doi:* plus the number. Otherwise, use *Retrieved from* plus the site owner's name (if different from the source) and the URL of the source's home page. Do not end with a period.

ONLINE NEWSPAPER OR MAGAZINE ARTICLE   The third citation is to an online-only magazine.

Cieply, M. (2016, March 13). Politics invades Hollywood. *New York Times.* Retrieved from http://www.nytimes.com

Affleck, J. (2016, February 5). Why we watch football even though we know it's deadly. *Time.* Retrieved from http://www.time.com

Norton, B. (2016, January 26). Adopting sustainable energy would save millions of lives each year, U.N. says. *Salon.* Retrieved from http://www.salon.com

ONLINE REFERENCE WORK

Salem witch trials. 2016. In *Encyclopaedia Britannica Online.* Retrieved from http://www .britannica.com

SCHOLARLY JOURNAL FOUND ON THE INTERNET   For articles accessed from a website, follow the citation format for print articles and end with retrieval information. If a DOI is available, as in the first example, include it. Otherwise, include the URL of the site's home page, or use the URL of the actual page cited if finding the document would otherwise be difficult. No retrieval date is needed for documents that are in final (published) form and unlikely to change. Note that some articles published on the web do not give page numbers, as in the first example on the next page.

Ensor, R., & Hughes, C. (2010, March/April). With a little help from my friends: Maternal social support, via parenting, promotes willingness to share in preschoolers born to young mothers. *Infant and Child Development,* 19(2), 127–221. doi:10.1002 /icd.643

Njeng, E. S. (2008). Achebe, Conrad, and the postcolonial strain. *Comparative Literature and Culture,* 10(1). Retrieved from http://docs.lib.purdue.edu/clcweb /vol10/iss1/3

Qin, D. B. (2006). The role of gender in immigrant children's educational adaptation. *Current Issues in Comparative Education,* 9(1), 8–19. Retrieved from http://www.tc.edu/cice

PERSONAL AND PROFESSIONAL WEBSITES

Railton, S. (Ed.). (2009). Uncle Tom's Cabin & *American Culture: A Multi-Media Archive.* Department of English, University of Virginia. Retrieved from http://utc.iath .virginia.edu

BLOG

Waldman, D. (2008, June 26). "Care" has deserted managed care. *Huffington Post* [Web log post]. Retrieved from http://huffingtonpost.com

Winter, C. (2010, May 17). Re: Should you believe anything BP says? [Web log comment]. Retrieved from http://climateprogress.org/2010/05/17/bp-oil-spill-blame-bob-bea-60-minutes

PODCAST

Elving, R., & Rudin, K. [Eds.]. (2010, May 28). *It's all politics, May 27: NPR's weekly news roundup* [Audio podcast]. Retrieved from http://www.npr.org

POSTINGS TO AN ONLINE GROUP   Include an appropriate description (*Online forum comment; Electronic mailing list message;* and so on) in brackets.

Das, S. K. (2015, April 7). The value of Pi. [Online group comment]. Retrieved from http:// mathforum.org/kb/thread.jspa?threadID=2690558

E-BOOK ON IPAD, KINDLE, NOOK, OR ANOTHER DEVICE

Lagercrantz, D. (2015). *The girl in the spider's web*. [Kindle ed]. New York: Alfred A. Knopf.

POSTING ON SOCIAL MEDIA

United Nations Refugee Agency. (2013, July 15, 4:22 p.m.). Please share! We're rushing in aid as 66,000 #Congolese refugees stream into western #Uganda [Twitter post]. Retrieved from https//: twitter.com/UNRefugeeAgency

MoMA. (2013, July 10). Photo by Emilio Guerra. Retrieved from https://facebook.com/ MuseumofModernArt

Citing Sources Found Through an Online Database or Scholarly Project

Follow the format for "Citing Sources Found on a Website," but also specify the database or project. Do not include the URL or information about the library system used.

SCHOLARLY JOURNAL FOUND IN AN ONLINE DATABASE   If the database entry provides a DOI, include that in the citation. (See "Scholarly Journal Found on the Internet.") If there is no DOI, do not include the database name. Instead, find the home page of the journal and include its URL.

Rossen, E., & Cowan, K. C. (2014–2015). Improving mental health in schools. *Phi Delta Kappan* 96(4). Retrieved from http://www. littletonpublicschools.net/

BOOK FOUND IN AN ONLINE SCHOLARLY PROJECT Include the date the book appeared online and, when available, the book's original publication date.

Franklin, B. (1995). *The autobiography of Benjamin Franklin.* Retrieved from http://etext.lib .virginia.edu/toc/modeng/public/Fra2Aut.html (Original work published 1793)

Citing Other Common Sources

Include the medium through which you accessed the source, for example, *CD* for "compact disc" or *E-mail* for an e-mail message you received.

CD-ROM OR DVD-ROM

The Oxford English Dictionary. (2009). [CD-ROM]. Oxford, United Kingdom.

VISUAL ART The following formats are adapted from other APA citation formats. The first citation is to a work of art viewed in a book; the second, to a work viewed in person at a museum; the third, to a work viewed online.

Blake, W. (2001). *A vision of the Last Judgment* [Reproduction of a watercolor painting.] In *William Blake* (p. 68). New York, NY: Abrams.

Cole, T. (1836). *View from Mount Holyoke, Northampton, Massachusetts, after a thunderstorm— The Oxbow* [Oil on canvas]. The Metropolitan Museum of Art, New York, NY.

Cole, T. (1836). *View from Mount Holyoke, Northampton, Massachusetts, after a thunderstorm— The Oxbow* [Oil on canvas]. Retrieved from the Metropolitan Museum of Art at http://www.MetMuseum.org

CARTOON OR COMIC STRIP The following formats are adapted from other APA citation formats.

Sipress, D. (2016, March 14). Anger management therapy. [Cartoon]. *The New Yorker.* Retrieved from http://www.newyorker.com/cartoons

Thompson, D. (2016, March 14). Brevity. [Comic strip]. *GoComics.com.* Retrieved from http://www.gocomics.com/brevity

TELEVISION OR RADIO PROGRAM

Rosenthal, P. (Narrator). (2015, October 26). Barcelona (Episode 5). [Television series episode]. On *I'll have what Phil's having.* Tallahassee, FL: WFSU-TV (PBS).

MOVIE, RECORDING, CD, DVD, VIDEOTAPE, AUDIOTAPE, FILMSTRIP, OR SLIDE PROGRAM Include the original date of release in parentheses at the end of the citation. For motion pictures, include only the country of origin.

Bigelow, K. (Producer & Director). (2008). *The hurt locker* [Motion picture]. United States: Voltage Pictures.

Bigelow, K. (Producer & Director). (2010). *The hurt locker* [DVD]. Los Angeles, CA: Universal Studios Home Entertainment. (2008)

PERSONAL OR TELEPHONE INTERVIEW According to APA style, personal communications are not included in the References list. Instead, cite such communications only in the text. If your instructor asks for interviews to be documented in the References list, you may use the following format.

Crittenden, A. (2016, May 4). [Telephone interview].

Strickland, C. (2016, January 26). [Personal interview].

LECTURE, SPEECH, ADDRESS, OR READING

Lunsford, A. (2016, February 11). *What is literacy today?* Presented in the School of Journalism and Graphic Communication Lecture Series, Florida A&M University, Tallahassee, FL.

E-MAIL MESSAGE   See the comment under "Personal or Telephone Interview."

Mack, L. (2016, August 30). New developments in early childhood education [E-mail message].

Sample Student Research Essay MLA-Style Documentation

20.11 Examine how research is used effectively in one student-authored selection.

MLA-Style Documentation

The sample research essay that follows was written by Lydia Eileish Kelley for a composition class. In her essay, Lydia Eileish uses the MLA documentation system. (Following the full MLA paper, excerpts from the research essay are formatted in APA style.) To help you spot various types of sources, quotations, and attributions, we've annotated the essay. Our marginal comments also flag key elements, such as the essay's thesis statement, plan of development, and concluding summary.

As you read the essay, pay special attention to the way Lydia Eileish incorporates source material and uses it to support her own ideas.

Courtney 1

½"

1"

Lydia Eileish Kelley
Professor Sean Towey
ENC 2135, Section 67
2 Nov. 2015

1"

Double-space

Double-space

MMORPGs: Creating a Culture of Inclusion

In the early 1970s, a new type of fantasy game came to the forefront: the genre of interactive strategic war games, complete with goblins, elves, dungeons, and dragons. This new genre was given the title "role-playing games," or RPGs. By the time computers began to become more widely used in household settings, RPGs had branched off into an electronic medium. As early as 1978, text-based computer RPGs started appearing (Patrick). Once the Internet became available to more people, RPGs had to find a way to adapt to a younger, more tech-savvy audience, and thus the Massive-Multiplayer Online RPG was born. In the article "Relationship between Passion and Motivation for Gaming in Players of Massively Multiplayer Online Role-Playing Games," the authors define MMORPGS as "online games involving a computer-based simulated environment through which geographically separated individuals interact by means of virtual representations (avatars) and have the ability to use and create objects" (Fuster et al. 292). While many think of MMORPGs in a negative context, associating them with introverts who spend hours on end locked in their bedrooms, glued to their screens, depriving themselves of sleep, exercise, and proper nutrition, MMORPGs can have positive effects on those who play them in moderation.

Since these are online games, most if not all of the communication among members of the online role-play gaming community takes place in digital media and "brings together more than 22 million players worldwide" (Fuster et al. 292). Many games involve *grouping*, a term researcher Lee Sherlock defines as "a form of ad hoc collaboration between players that allows them to band together temporarily and work toward particular in-game objectives" (264).

1

2

Marginal annotations:

Double-space the heading.

Introduction

Common knowledge is not documented

Parenthetical reference for source having one author. No quotation marks needed because information from source is paraphrased. Author's name is included because it was not noted in the sentence. No page given because electronic text is unpaged

Attribution gives title of article

Parenthetical citation provides last name of first author and page number

Attribution gives name of author

Parenthetical citation provides page number only because author's name was included earlier in the sentence

Courtney 2

Players must make allies if they are to succeed in the game. To efficaciously "group," gamers often talk to one another in real time inside the games using chatting mechanisms, in-game messages that players can send to one another.

3   Recently, MMORPGs began using a type of virtual reality simulator called a MOO (Peterson 362), which stands for "Multi-User-Dungeon, Object Oriented" (Shah and Romine 238). This simulator greatly facilitates quick and efficient communication within the games. According to Mark Peterson, a college professor whose research focuses on digital media,

4   > In a MOO world, individual characters may utilize unique pseudonyms in order to undertake text chat, role play, and navigation, through the use of specific commands. More recently, accessibility was enhanced with the introduction of browser-based MOOs that utilize hypertext, and this development significantly increased opportunities to interact with a wider range of users. (362)

5   MOOs make it possible for a player to input a particular code, which results in the game producing an output, such as a command to another player. This makes communication among players faster and easier, which is crucial in situations in which the players must think and act swiftly. If the players were unable to warn, command, or give advice to others speedily, they would be less likely to win their battles.

6   Players also connect through another vital form of communication—online forums and discussion boards. On the *World of Warcraft* website, the tab entitled "Forums" leads to a page including 335 different discussion boards. This means that if a player needs to know something specific, he or she can find the answer if another community member has already asked the same question. Players can also ask a new question and wait for someone (or often multiple players) to answer. For example, the *World of Warcraft* community member Blinkbreezy asked the question, "New to mage pvp and I'm working for burst I've

Parenthetical citation for a work with two authors

Attribution leads to a long quotation and gives author's name and area of expertise. Attribution is followed by a comma because the lead-in is not a full sentence. If the lead-in is a full sentence, use a colon after the attribution. Parenthetical reference at end of sentence gives just the page number because the author is cited in the attribution

Long quotation indented half an inch from the left margin. Double-space the quotation, as you do the rest of the essay. Don't leave extra space above or below the quotation. Do not include quotation marks around a long quotation. At the end of the quotation, place appropriate closing punctuation such as a period or question mark. Include page number(s) in parentheses following the closing punctuation

No parenthetical citation needed because name of website is provided in the text

No parenthetical citation is needed because website's and author's name appear in text and electronic text is unpaged

Full sentence quotation is preceded by a comma and begins with a capital letter

been doing deep, comet, FB, Orb, 2 novas and ice Lance procs
on kill target. Should I bother deeping the kill target or just use
deep for CC?" Obviously, Blinkbreezy used jargon and grammatically incorrect language, but this practice of using seemingly unacceptable diction and syntax happens regularly because
most of the people within the MMORPG community, and in
particular the *World of Warcraft* subset of the community in this
case, know the terms used within the game. Players not familiar
with the jargon would not have the credibility to answer the
question. Unfortunately, because anybody can use these discussion forums, answers are sometimes irrelevant or indecipher-
able. Luckily for Blinkbreezy, the response to the posted question, though it also incorporated jargon, was understandable to
a well-versed *World of Warcraft* player and answered the question reasonably enough.

7   But how do people become experts and learn the lingo of
MMORPGs? Though individuals often learn by simply playing or hearing from others, sometimes gamers must turn to
handbooks to gain basic information before joining a game.
Traditionally, game developers published these in print, but
nowadays, it is more common to find the handbooks electronically published online. For instance, on the *World of Warcraft*
website, there is a tab entitled "Game Guide," which links to
several different articles about different features and characteristics of the game. In particular, there is a "Beginner's Guide,"
which helps new players discover many aspects of the game
from a simple description of MMORPGs to basics of the game's
plot and character types and more. These articles are written by
the game developers and help integrate all skill and knowledge
levels into *World of Warcraft*. This means that the makers of the
games built a culture of inclusion into MMORPGs. The developers want to make sure every player has some level of fairness
upon entering the game's universe. By making the handbooks
available free online, the developers grant anyone who plays
these games access to a myriad of information at all times,

Courtney 4

which means that no players must fend for themselves to find information. They are automatically given the chance to learn what they need to know in order to become the best player they can be.

In addition to making information easily available online, the developers of MMORPGs appeal to their prospective audience by creating engaging advertisements. The players of these games are often incredibly passionate about the worlds and characters within, and game developers use this passion to their advantage. Developers rely on dedicated players to be anxious to play the newest games and therefore market ads towards them to create enthusiasm for new games, find new followers, and ultimately, make a profit. Many of the ads for MMORPGs are found online, simply because the games are online, but they also appear in magazines, on television, and in movie theaters. On August 14, 2014, Blizzard Entertainment company (the producers of the *World of Warcraft* franchise) posted an ad on YouTube for an upcoming expansion set entitled "World of Warcraft: Warlords of Draenor Cinematic." This nearly five-minute video, like most *World of Warcraft* ads, begins with dramatic orchestral music and a glimpse of the company's logo in a shiny gold font. From the start, the advertisers want to get viewers in the mindset of *World of Warcraft* and associate the rest of the video with the producers of the game. The video then shows a sweep over a grungy, dark, fantasy landscape with the words "35 years ago" over the picture. The ad tries to appeal to its audience's pathos by engrossing viewers in a cinematic experience. By seeing the timeframe in the ad, viewers can assume that a story will be presented, which makes them curious and pulls them in. Over the course of the advertisement, the story of a feud among the orcs (a class in the game) leads to the killing of a powerful orc monster. Most of the video is combat, a central aspect of *World of Warcraft*'s gameplay. So by showing a battle and different combat strategies in the ad, advertisers attempt to get viewers excited about playing this fighting game, and of course, eventually buying it. The final image of the video shows the release date in shiny silver letters behind a black background, which sticks

8

Courtney 5

in the mind and helps viewers remember when they'll be able to purchase the game.

Since people often play MMORPGs alone, some criticize the games for leading players to become antisocial or unhealthy. In their journal article, "The Impact of Massively Multiplayer Online Role Playing Games (MMORPGs) on Psychological Wellbeing and the Role of Play Motivations and Problematic Use," Amy Kirby et al. explain that there is a negative correlation between time spent playing *World of Warcraft* and psychological wellbeing (45). While the authors' research shows that playing MMORPGs excessively can lead to negative side effects, there is no evidence to indicate that a healthy amount of game play cannot result in social benefits. Too much of almost anything can lead to health issues. If players were to moderate their gaming times, sticking to half an hour to an hour a day, they could make friends online while still having time to participate in other real-world activities. This self-management would not only allow players to maintain psychological wellbeing by being functional members of society, but would also elicit new friendships, which would be beneficial for all parties involved.

9

Another argument against MMORPGs is that because the games are competitive in nature, players become "self-involving" (Guegan et al. 349). Some studies found that MMORPG players think more highly of those within their own group, or guild, and often act rudely to those outside of their guilds (Guegan et al. 351). While there's no denying that game play does separate people to a certain extent, it also brings people together. Players form alliances and often real-life friendships (Ang et al. 168). This type of team building and interaction is very similar to what goes on in sports. The players are members of teams, and individuals come together for a common goal and for the simple fun of it. At the same time, rivalries arise and people begin to oppose those outside of their team or guild. But more importantly, players form friendships and learn how to work together to overcome challenges and reach their goals.

10

The world continues to grow increasingly digital. Instead of trying to fight this inevitable trend, people must learn new ways to

11

Attribution gives name of article and the first author's name because the article was written by three authors. Parenthetical reference at end of sentence gives page but not authors because authors are cited in the sentence

Courtney 6

effectively socialize online. With millions of people all over the
Earth having access to the Internet, the human race is now connected in a way that it has never been before. MMORPGs connect
people from many places and cultures and facilitate players learning about fellow human beings. Though the majority of interaction
happens within an online setting, real and meaningful relationships do come about as a result of MMORPGs. Individuals must
learn to interact effectively, not only face-to-face, but within digital
media as well. Massive Multiplayer Online Role Playing Games
can help make this happen.

Conclusion provides
a summary, makes
a final point, and
restates the thesis

Article by more than two authors in a scholarly journal obtained in an online database. Article's pages are consecutive. Citation includes DOI

Online forum comment to a website. Citation includes both the name of the website and the URL

Article by more than two authors in a scholarly journal

Article by more than two authors in a scholarly journal obtained in an online database

Article by more than two authors in a scholarly journal obtained in an online database

Online video clip

Article by a single author in a scholarly journal obtained in an online database

Book by two authors

Article by a single author in a scholarly journal obtained in an online database

Unsigned selection on a website. Because no date of publication or page numbers are provided on the website, date of access is included

Unsigned video clip with date of publication

Courtney 7

Works Cited

Ang, Chee Siang, et al. "A Model of Cognitive Loads in Massively Multiplayer Online Role Playing Games." *Interacting with Computers*, vol. 19, no. 2, 2007, pp. 167–79. ACMDS, doi:10.1016/j.intcom.2006.08.006.

Blinkbreezy. "Mage pvp question." Online forum comment. *World of Warcraft*, 11 Oct. 2015, us.battle.net/wow/en/forum/984270.

Fuster, Héctor, et al. "Relationship between Passion and Motivation for Gaming in Players of Massively Multiplayer Online Role-Playing Games." *Cyberpsychology, Behavior, and Social Networking*, vol. 17, no. 5, 2014, pp. 292–97.

Guegan, Jérôme, et al. "Why Are Online Games So Self-involving? A Social Identity Analysis of Massively Multiplayer Online Role-playing Games." *European Journal of Social Psychology*, vol. 45, no. 3, 2015, pp. 349–55. EBSCOhost, doi:10.1002/ejsp.2103.

Kirby, Amy, et al. "The Impact of Massively Multiplayer Online Role Playing Games (MMORPGs) on Psychological Wellbeing and the Role of Play Motivations and Problematic Use." *International Journal of Mental Health and Addiction*, vol. 12, no. 1, 2014, pp. 36–51. EBSCOhost, doi:10.1007/s11469-013-9467-9.

Patrick, Matthew. "Game Theory: Is the MMO Genre DYING?" *YouTube*, 26 Sept. 2015, www.youtube.com/watch?v=bgkoz5EZTok.

Peterson, Mark. "Learner Interaction in a Massively Multiplayer Online Role Playing Game (MMORPG): A Sociocultural Discourse Analysis." *RECALL*, vol. 24, no. 3, 2012, pp. 361–80. CJO, doi:http://dx.doi.org/10.1017/S0958344012000195.

Shah, Rawn, and Jim Romine. *Playing MUDS on the Internet*. Wiley, 1995.

Sherlock, Lee. "Genre, Activity, and Collaborative Work and Play in World of Warcraft: Places and Problems of Open Systems in Online Gaming." *Journal of Business and Technical Communication*, vol. 23, no. 3, 2009, pp. 263–93. SAGE, doi:10.1177/ 1050651909333150.

"What Is World of Warcraft?" *World of Warcraft*, us.battle.net/wow/en/game/guide. Accessed 31 Oct. 2015.

"World of Warcraft: Warlords of Draenor." *YouTube*, 14 Aug. 2014, www.youtube.com/ watch?v =TLzhlsEFcVQ.

COMMENTARY Lydia Eileish Kelley begins her introduction with background information about role-playing games (RPGs) and how they led to the creation of a more sophisticated type of game called massively multiplayer online role-playing games (MMORPGs). She cites an article from an academic journal that provides a definition of MMORPGs and points out that they enable "geographically separated individuals [to] interact by means of virtual representations (avatars) and have the ability to use and create objects." This quote focusing on positive aspects of MMORPGs leads to Lydia Eileish's thesis: "While many think of MMORPGs in a negative context, associating them with introverts who spend hours on end locked in their bedrooms, glued to their screens, depriving themselves of sleep, exercise, and proper nutrition, MMORPGs can have positive effects on those who play them in moderation." She makes clear to her readers that, in her essay, she will argue for the benefits of engaging in this type of game play.

By researching her subject thoroughly, Lydia Eileish was able to discover many reputable sources that addressed her topic. She sorted through this complex web of material and arrived at a logical structure that reinforces her thesis. In paragraphs 2–4 she explains how these games "bring together more than 22 million players worldwide," making it possible for players to make new friends, form groups, make allies, and communicate with one another not only while playing games but also in online discussion forums. Then, in paragraphs 5–6, she describes ways that game developers appeal to their audience by providing easily accessible tools such as handbooks to help players become more skillful and by producing engaging ads that describe new games that will soon be coming out. Lydia Eileish devotes paragraphs 7–8 to opposing views. She references a scholarly article that discusses the negative effects that playing MMORPGs can have on psychological health, but she then counters that argument with one of her own. She goes on to address another claim that MMORPGs can lead to players "think[ing] more highly of those within their own group," and she then counters that argument as well. Note, too, that the author writes in the present tense and uses the third-person point of view.

Beyond being clearly organized and maintaining a consistent point of view, the essay is unified and coherent. The author often uses transitions: "Players also" (4), "In addition to" (6). In other places, she asks a question (for example, at the beginning of the fifth paragraph) or uses a bridging sentence (for instance, at the beginning of the second, third, and seventh paragraphs). Moreover, the author provides clear attributions and parenthetical references so that readers know whose idea is being presented. Lydia Eileish has prepared a well-written, carefully documented essay.

APA-Style Documentation

To give you an idea of how a research essay in APA style would look, we've excerpted Lydia Eileish's research essay and reformatted those pages in APA style. APA papers may also require a title page and an abstract. The pages are numbered continuously, starting with the title page, and the References list starts on a new page.

MMORPGS   3

MMORPGs: Creating a Culture of Inclusion

In the early 1970s, a new type of fantasy game came to the forefront: the genre of interactive strategic war games, complete with goblins, elves, dungeons, and dragons. This new genre was given the title "role-playing games," or RPGs. By the time computers began to become more widely used in household settings, RPGs had branched off into an electronic medium. As early as 1978, text-based computer RPGs started appearing (Patrick, 2015). Once the Internet became available to more people, RPGs had to find a way to adapt to a younger, more tech-savvy audience, and thus the Massive-Multiplayer Online RPG was born. In the article "Relationship between Passion and Motivation for Gaming in Players of Massively Multiplayer Online Role-Playing Games," the authors define MMORPGS as "online games involving a computer-based simulated environment through which geographically separated individuals interact by means of virtual representations (avatars) and have the ability to use and create objects" (Fuster, Andrés, Xavier, & Vallerand, 2014, p. 292). While many think of MMORPGs in a negative context, associating them with introverts who spend hours on end locked in their bedrooms, glued to their screens, depriving themselves of sleep, exercise, and proper nutrition, MMORPGs can have positive effects on those who play them in moderation.

Since these are online games, most if not all of the communication among members of the online role-play gaming community takes place in digital media and "bring[s] together more than 22 million players worldwide" (Fuster et al., p. 292). Many games involve *grouping,* a term researcher Lee Sherlock (2009) defines as "a form of ad hoc collaboration between players that allows them to band together temporarily and work toward particular in-game objectives (p. 264). Players must make allies if they are to succeed in the game. To efficaciously "group," gamers often talk to one another in real time inside the games using chatting mechanisms, in-game messages that players can send to one another.

Margin annotations:

Because the author's name does not appear in the text, it is included in the parenthetical citation along with the year of publication. A comma appears between the author's name and the year

For a source with three to five authors, name all authors in the first citation

For a source with three to five authors, after the first citation, name only the first author followed by et al.

If you use an attribution that gives the author's name, put the publication year (in parentheses) right after the author's name.

Because the author's name and publication are included in the text, only the page number is included in the parenthetical citation

MMORPGS   10

References

Ang, C., S., Zaphiris, P., & Mahmood, S. (2007). A model of cognitive loads in massively multiplayer online role playing games. *Interacting with Computers* 19(2), 167–179. doi:10.1016/j.intcom. 2006.08.006

Fuster, H., Andrés, C., Xavier, C., & Vallerand, R. J. (2014). Relationship between passion and motivation for gaming in players of massively multiplayer online role-playing games. *Cyberpsychology, Behavior, and Social Networking*, 17(5): 292–297. doi:10.1089/cyber.2013.0349

Patrick, M. (2015, September 26). Game theory: Is the MMO genre dying?" *YouTube*. Retrieved from https://www. youtube.com/watch?v=bgkoz5EZTok

Shah, R., & Romine, J. (1995). *Playing MUDS on the Internet*. New York, NY: Wiley.

What is World of Warcraft? (n.d.). *World of Warcraft*. Retrieved from http://eu.battle.net/wow/en/game/ guide

Center "References" at the top of a new page and double-space to the first line. Start each entry flush left and indent subsequent lines 5 spaces. Double-space throughout.

Give the authors' last names and initials followed by the date. For three to seven authors, give the last names and initials for all authors. Use an ampersand (&) instead of and before the last author.

For journal, magazine, and newspaper articles, capitalize the first word of the title and subtitle and proper nouns. Use regular type.

For a journal, give the full title, in capital and lowercase letters, italicized.

For page numbers, do not use p., pp., page, or pages before the numbers, except when citing a newspaper article.

Place the date in parentheses right after the author's name.

For an online source, include the retrieval information. If a DOI is available, use "doi:" plus the number. Otherwise, use "Retrieved from" plus the site owner's name (if different from the source) and the URL of the source's home page. Do not end with a period.

For a book, capitalize only the first letter of the title (and subtitle) and any proper names. Italicize the title.

For two authors, use an ampersand (&) between names and invert the second author's name.

For place of publication, give the city and the state, using U.S. postal abbreviations.

When no author is provided, list source alphabetically by title.

When no date is provided, include (n.d.) in parentheses.

Activities: Writing the Research Essay

1. Imagine that you've just written a research essay exploring how parents can ease their children's passage through adolescence. Prepare a Works Cited list for the following sources, putting all information in the correct MLA format. When you are finished, reformat the list as a References list in APA style.

   a. "The Emotional Life of the Adolescent," a chapter in Ralph I. Lopez, M.D.'s *The Teen Health Book: A Parent's Guide to Adolescent Health and Well-Being.* The chapter runs from page 55 to page 70. The book was published by W.W. Norton & Company (New York, NY) in 2002.

   b. A radio broadcast in the series *Voices in the Family*, hosted by Dr. Daniel Gottlieb and produced by Laura Jackson. The broadcast, "Adolescents, TV, and Sex," aired on 27 September 2004, on WHYY-FM, Philadelphia.

   c. An article titled "Transmission of Values from Adolescents to Their Parents," by Martin Pinquart and Rainer K. Silbereisen. The article appeared on pages 83 to 100 in the Spring 2004 issue (volume 39, issue 153) of *Adolescence* (which paginates each issue separately).

   d. An unpaginated article, titled "Normal Adolescent Development," on the website *Adolescence Directory On-Line*, published by the Center for Adolescent Studies at Indiana University. The article appeared on 29 September 1998 and was accessed on 27 March 2007. The URL is <http://education.indiana.edu/cas/adol/development.html>.

2. Assume you're writing a research essay on obesity. You decide to incorporate into your essay points made by Mark Bittman in "What Causes Weight Gain" (page 438). To practice using attributions, parenthetic citations, and correct punctuation with quoted material, do the following:

   a. Choose a statement from the essay to quote. Then write one or more sentences that include the quotation, a specific attribution, and the appropriate parenthetic citation.

   b. Choose an idea to summarize from the essay. Then write one or more sentences that include the summary and the appropriate parenthetic documentation.

   c. Find a place in the essay where the author quotes an expert or experts. Use this quotation to write one or more sentences in which you:

      • First, quote the expert(s) and

      • Second, summarize the ideas of the expert(s).

   Each of the above should include the appropriate attribution and parenthetic citation.

Chapter 21
Writing About Literature

Learning Objectives

21.1 Identify the elements of literary works.

21.2 Critically read a literary work.

21.3 Write a literary analysis.

21.4 Analyze a student's literary analysis of a short story.

Your purpose in **literary analysis** is to share with readers some insights about an aspect of a poem, play, story, or novel. (For the sake of simplifying a complex subject, we discuss literary analysis as though it focuses on a single work. In practice, though, a literary analysis often examines two or more works.) In a literary analysis, your thesis and supporting evidence grow directly out of your reading of the text. Your job is to select the textual evidence that supports your thesis.

By examining both *what* the author says and *how* he or she expresses it, you increase your readers' understanding and appreciation of the work. Close textual analysis develops your ability to think critically and independently. Studying literature also strengthens your own writing. Finally, literary analysis is one way to learn more about yourself, others, and life in general.

Elements of Literary Works

21.1 Identify the elements of literary works.

Before you can analyze a literary text, you need to become familiar with literature's key elements.

Literary Terms

Alliteration: repetition of initial consonant sounds ("A *b*utterfly *b*looms").

Assonance: repetition of vowel sounds (like the "a" sounds in "m*a*d *a*s *a* h*a*tter").

Character: an individual within a poem, play, story, or novel.

Characterization: the way an author develops an individual in the work.

Climax: the most dramatic point in the action, usually near the end of a work and usually involving the resolution of conflict.

Conflict: a struggle between individuals, between an individual and some social or environmental force, or within an individual.

Figure of speech: a nonliteral comparison of dissimilar things. The most common figures of speech are **similes**, which use the word *like* or *as*; **metaphors**, which state or imply that one thing *is* another; and **personification**, which gives human attributes to something nonhuman.

Foreshadowing: hints, within the work, of events to come.

Image: a short, vivid description that creates a strong sensory impression.

Imagery: a combination of images.

Irony: a discrepancy or incongruity of some kind. *Verbal irony,* which is often tongue in cheek, involves a discrepancy between the literal words and what is actually meant ("Here's some news that will make you sad. You received the highest grade in the course"). If the ironic comment is designed to be hurtful or insulting, it qualifies as *sarcasm* ("Congratulations! You failed the final exam"). In *dramatic irony,* the discrepancy is between what the speaker says and what the author means or what the audience knows. The wider the gap between the speaker's words and what can be inferred about the author's attitudes and values, the more ironic the point of view.

Meter: a basic, fixed rhythm of accented and unaccented syllables that the lines of a particular poem follow.

Motif: a recurring word, phrase, image, figure of speech, or symbol that has particular significance.

Narrator or speaker: the individual in the work who relates the story. The narrator is *not* the same as the author.

Plot: the series of events that occurs within the work.

Point of view: the perspective from which a story is told. In the **first-person** (*I*) point of view, the narrator tells the story as he or she experienced it. The first-person narrator either participates in or observes the action. In the **third-person** point of view, the narrator tells the story the way someone else experienced it. The third-person narrator is not involved in the action. He or she may simply report outwardly observable behavior or events, enter the mind of only one character, or enter the minds of several characters. Such a third-person narrator may be *omniscient* (all knowing) or have only *limited knowledge* of characters and events.

Rhyme: a match between two or more words' final sounds.

Satire: ridicule (either harsh or gentle) of vice or folly with the purpose of developing awareness—even bringing about reform. Besides using wit, satire often employs irony to attack absurdity, injustice, and evil.

Setting: the time and place in which events unfold.

Sonnet: a fourteen-line, single-stanza poem following a strict pattern of meter and rhyme. The Italian, or *Petrarchan,* sonnet consists of two main parts: eight lines in the rhyme pattern *a b b a, a b b a,* followed by six lines in the pattern *c d c, c d c* or *c d e, c d e.* The English, or *Shakespearean,* sonnet consists of twelve lines in the rhyme scheme *a b a b, c d c d, e f e f,* followed by two rhymed lines *g g* (called a *couplet*). Traditionally, sonnets are love poems that involve some change in tone or outlook near the end.

Stanza: two or more lines of a poem that are grouped together. A stanza is preceded and followed by some blank space.

Structure: a work's form, as determined by plot construction, act and scene divisions, stanza and line breaks, repeated images, patterns of meter and rhyme, and other elements that create discernible patterns. (See also *image, meter, rhyme,* and *stanza.*)

Symbol: an object, place, characteristic, or phenomenon that suggests one or more things (usually abstract) in addition to itself (rain as mourning, a lost wedding ring as betrayal).

Theme: a work's controlling idea, the main issue the work addresses. Most literary analyses deal with theme, even if the analysis focuses on the methods by which that theme is conveyed.

How to Critically Read a Literary Work

21.2 Critically read a literary work.

Reading a literary work involves reading to form an impression, asking questions about the work, rereading and annotating, and modifying your annotations. After you've completed these steps, you can go on to write your literary analysis.

Read to Form a General Impression

The first step in analyzing a literary work is to read it through for an overall impression. Do you like the work? What does the writer seem to be saying? Do you have a strong reaction to the work? Why or why not?

Ask Questions About the Work

One way to focus your initial impressions is to ask yourself questions about the literary work. You could, for example, select from the following checklist those items that interest you the most or those that seem most relevant to the work you're analyzing.

☑ Analyzing a Literary Work: A Checklist

- ☐ What *themes* appear in the work? How do *structure, plot, characterization, imagery,* and other literary strategies reinforce the theme?

- ☐ What gives the work its *structure* or shape? Why might the author have chosen this form? If the work is a poem, how do *meter, rhyme, alliteration, assonance,* and *line breaks* emphasize key ideas? Where does the work divide into parts? What words and images are repeated? What patterns do they form?

- ☐ How is the *plot* developed? Where is there any *foreshadowing?* What are the points of greatest suspense? Which *conflicts* add tension? How are they resolved? Where does the *climax* occur? What does the *resolution* accomplish?

- ☐ What do the various *characters* represent? What motivates them? How is character revealed through dialogue, action, commentary, and physical description? In what ways do major characters change? What events and interactions bring about the changes?

- ☐ What is the relationship between *setting* and *action*? To what extent does setting mirror the characters' psychological states?

- ☐ Who is the *narrator*? Is the story told in the *first person* or the *third person*? Is the narrator omniscient or limited in his or her knowledge of characters and events? Is the narrator recalling the past or reporting events as they happen?

- ☐ What is the author's own *point of view*? What are the author's implied *values* and *attitudes*? Does the author show any biases? Is there any discrepancy between the author's values and attitudes and those of the narrator? To whom in the work does the author grant the most status and consideration?

- ☐ What about the work is *ironic* or surprising? Where is there a discrepancy between what is said and what is meant?

- ☐ What role do *figures of speech* play? What *metaphors*, if any, are sustained and developed?

☐ What functions as a *symbol*? How can you tell?

☐ What *flaws* do you find in the work? Which elements fail to contribute to thematic development? Where does the work lose impact because ideas are stated directly rather than implied?

Reread and Annotate

Begin a second, closer reading of the literary work. Look for answers to your questions. Underline striking words, images, and ideas. Draw connecting lines between related items. Jot down questions, answers, and comments in the margins. If you're reading something online, print it out and annotate the printed copy. We've marked the following poem, William Shakespeare's Sonnet 29, with sample annotations.

a	When, in disgrace with Fortune and men's eyes,	*Contrast between*
b	(I) all alone beweep (my) outcast state,	*unhappy self-absorption*
	useless	*("beweep") and*
a	And trouble deaf heaven with (my) bootless cries,	*thoughts of "sweet*
b	And look upon (myself) and curse (my) fate,	*love," between "outcast*
		state" and "scorn to
c	Wishing (me) like to one more rich in hope,	*change my state."*
	good looks-	
d Envy	Featur'd like him, like him with friends possess'd,	
	talent *knowledge*	
c	Desiring this man's art, and that man's scope,	
d	With what (I) most enjoy contented least;	
e	Yet in these thoughts (myself) almost despising ◄———	*Changes to increasing*
	by chance *(First time lover is mentioned.)*	*joy. Turns away from*
b	Haply I think on thee, and then my state,	*self-absorption.*
e	Like to the lark at break of day arising	
b	From sullen earth, sings hymns at heaven's gate;	
f	For thy sweet love rememb'red such wealth brings	*Joyous images. New*
	don't want to trade places	*beginning. Healing*
f	That then I scorn to change my state with kings.	*power of love.*

Modify Your Annotations

Your annotations will help you begin to clarify your thoughts about the work. Read the work again; make further annotations on anything that seems relevant and modify earlier annotations in light of your greater understanding of the work. At this point, you're ready to move on to writing the full literary analysis.

Write the Literary Analysis

21.3 Write a literary analysis.

When you prepare a literary analysis, the steps you follow are the same as those for writing an essay: prewrite; identify your thesis; support the thesis with evidence; organize the evidence; write the first draft; revise overall meaning, structure, and paragraph development; edit and proofread.

Prewrite

Early in the prewriting stage, you should take time to think about your purpose, audience, point of view, and tone. Your **purpose** is to share your insights about the work; you assume that your **audience** is composed of readers already familiar with the work.

As you write, you should adopt an objective, **third-person point of view**. Guard against veering off into first-person statements like "In my opinion" and "I feel that." The **tone** of a literary analysis is generally serious and straightforward. However, if your aim is to point out that an author's perspective is narrow or biased or that a work is artistically unworthy of high regard, your tone may also have a critical edge. Be careful, though, to concentrate on the textual evidence in support of your view; don't simply state your objections.

Prewriting actually begins when you annotate the work in light of several key questions you pose about it (see the "Analyzing a Literary Work" checklist earlier in this chapter). After refining your initial annotations, try to impose a tentative order on your annotations. List the most promising of these points on a separate sheet; then link these points to your annotations. For instance, you could simply list the annotations under the points they support. Or you can number each point and give relevant annotations the same number as that point. Another possibility is to color-code your annotations: Give each point a color; then underline or circle in the same color any annotation related to that point. Finally, prepare a scratch outline of the main points you plan to cover, inserting your annotations in the appropriate spots.

If you have trouble generating and focusing ideas in this way, you might *freewrite* a page or two on what you have highlighted in the literary text, *brainstorm* a list of ideas, or *map out* the work's overall structure. Mapping is especially helpful when analyzing a poem.

 If the work still puzzles you, it may be helpful to consult outside sources. Online encyclopedias, biographies of the author, and history books can clarify the context in which the work was written.

Identify Your Thesis

Formulate a **working thesis**. As in other kinds of writing, your thesis statement for a literary analysis should include both your *limited subject* (the literary work you'll analyze and what aspect of the work you'll focus on) and your *attitude* toward that subject (the claim you'll make about the work's themes, the author's methods, the author's attitudes, and so on).

Here are two effective thesis statements for literary analysis:

> In the poem "The Garden of Love," William Blake uses sound and imagery to depict what he considers the deadening effect of organized religion.

> The characters in the novel *Judgment Day* illustrate James Farrell's belief that psychology, not sociology, determines fate.

If your instructor asks you to include commentary from professional critics or other sources, try to formulate your thesis about the work *before* you read anyone else's interpretation. Then use others' opinions as added evidence in support of your thesis or as opposing viewpoints that you can counter.

THESIS STATEMENTS TO AVOID   Guard against a simplistic thesis. A statement like "The author shows that people are often hypocritical" doesn't say anything surprising and fails to convey a work's complexity. More likely, the author shares insights about the *nature* of hypocrisy, the *reasons* underlying it, the *forms* it can take, or its immediate and long-term *effects*.

An overly narrow thesis is equally misguided. You shouldn't, for example, sum up the theme of Hawthorne's *The Scarlet Letter* with the thesis "Hawthorne examines the intolerance of seventeenth-century Puritan New England." Hawthorne's novel probes the general, or universal, nature of communal intolerance. Puritan New England is simply the setting in which the work's themes are dramatized.

Also, make sure your thesis is about the work. Discussion of a particular social or political issue is relevant only if it sheds light on the work. If you feel a work has a strong feminist theme, it's fine to say so. It's a mistake, however, to stray to a nonliterary thesis such as "Feminism liberates both men and women."

A biographical thesis is just as inappropriate as a sociopolitical one. Point out the way a particular work embodies an author's prejudices or beliefs, but don't devise a thesis that passes judgment on the author's personal or psychological shortcomings ("Poe's neurotic attraction to inappropriate women is reflected in the poem 'To Helen'"). It's usually impossible to infer such personal flaws from the text alone.

Support the Thesis with Evidence

Once you've identified a working thesis, return to the text to make sure that nothing in the text contradicts your theory. Also, keeping your thesis in mind, search for previously overlooked **evidence** (*quotations* and *examples*) that develops your thesis. Consider, too, how *summaries* of portions of the work might support your interpretation.

If you don't find solid textual evidence for your thesis, either drop or modify it. Don't—in an effort to support your thesis—cook up possible relationships among characters, twist metaphors out of shape, or concoct elaborate patterns of symbolism. Be sure there's plentiful evidence in the work to support your interpretation.

Organize the Evidence

When it comes time to **organize your evidence**, look over your scratch list and evaluate the main points, textual evidence, and outside research it contains. Focusing on your thesis, decide which points to delete and which new ones to add. Then identify an effective sequence for your points. That done, check to see if you've placed textual evidence and outside research under the appropriate points. What you're aiming for is a solid, well-developed outline that will guide your writing of the first draft. When preparing your outline, remember that the patterns of development can help you sequence material:

Comparison-Contrast
In Mark Twain's *Huckleberry Finn,* what traits do the Duke and the Dauphin have in common? In what ways do the two characters differ?

Definition
How does Ralph Waldo Emerson define *forbearance* in his poem of that name?

Process Analysis
Discuss the stages by which Morgan Evans is transformed into a scholar in Emlyn Williams's play *The Corn Is Green.*

Notice that, in these assignments, certain words and phrases (*have in common; in what ways…differ; define;* and *discuss the stages*) signal which pattern would be particularly appropriate.

Write the First Draft

When preparing the draft, you should take into account the following four conventions of literary analysis.

USE THE PRESENT TENSE   The literary work continues to exist after its completion. Use of the past tense is appropriate only when you refer to a time earlier than that in which the narrator speaks.

IDENTIFY YOUR TEXT   Even if your only source is the literary work itself, some instructors may want you to identify it by author, title, and publication data in a formal Works Cited entry. For more about Works Cited entries, consult Chapter 20 of this text or the guidelines provided by your instructor.

USE PARENTHETIC REFERENCES   If you're writing about a very short literary work, your instructor may not require documentation. Usually, however, documentation is expected.

Fiction quotations are followed by the page number(s) in parentheses (89); poetry quotations, by the line number(s) (12–14); and drama quotations, by act, scene, and line numbers (2.1.34–37). The parenthetic reference goes right after the quotation, even if your own sentence continues. If you use sources other than the literary text itself, document these as you would quotations or borrowed ideas in a research essay.

QUOTE POETRY APPROPRIATELY   If you're writing about a short poem, it's a good idea to include the poem's entire text in your essay. When you need to quote fewer than four lines from a poem, you can enclose them in quotation marks and indicate each line break with a slash (/): "But at my back I always hear / Time's winged chariot hurrying near" (from Andrew Marvell's poem "To His Coy Mistress"). Verse quotations of four or more lines should be indented ten spaces from the left margin of your paper and should appear line for line, as in the original source.

Revise Overall Meaning, Structure, and Paragraph Development

After completing your first draft, you'll gain helpful advice by showing it to others. The following checklist will help you revise your literary analysis.

☑ **Revising a Literary Analysis: A Checklist**

Revise Overall Meaning and Structure

☐ What is the thesis of the analysis? According to the thesis, which elements of the work will be discussed? In what ways, if any, is the thesis simplistic or too narrow? In what ways, if any, does it introduce extraneous social, political, or biographical issues?

☐ What main points support the thesis? If any points stray from or contradict the thesis, what changes should be made?

☐ How well supported by textual evidence is the essay's thesis? What evidence, crucial to the thesis, needs more attention? What other interpretation, if any, seems better supported by the evidence?

☐ Which patterns of development help shape the analysis? How do these patterns support the thesis?

☐ What purpose does the analysis fulfill? Does it simply present a straightforward interpretation of some aspect of the work? Does it point out some flaw in the work? Does it try to convince readers to accept an unconventional interpretation?

☐ How well does the analysis suit an audience already familiar with the work? How well does it suit an audience that may or may not share the interpretation expressed?

☐ What tone does the analysis project? Is it too critical or too admiring? Where does the tone come across as insufficiently serious?

Revise Paragraph Development

☐ What method of organization underlies the sequence of paragraphs? How effective is the sequence?

☐ Which paragraphs lack sufficient or sufficiently developed textual evidence? Where does textual evidence fail to develop a paragraph's central point? What important evidence, if any, has been overlooked?

☐ Which paragraphs contain too much textual evidence? Which quotations are longer than necessary?

☐ Where could textual evidence in a paragraph be more smoothly incorporated into the analysis?

☐ If any of the paragraphs include outside research, how does this material strengthen the analysis? If any of the paragraphs consider alternative interpretations, are these opposing views refuted?

Revise Sentences and Words

☐ Which words and phrases wrongly suggest that there is only one correct interpretation of the work?

☐ What words give the false impression that it is possible to read an author's mind?

☐ Where does the analysis fail to maintain the present tense? Which uses of past tense aren't justified?

☐ Where is there inadequate or incorrect documentation?

☐ Where does language lapse into needless literary jargon?

☐ If poetry is quoted, where should slash marks indicate line breaks? Where should lines be indented?

Edit and Proofread

When editing and proofreading your literary analysis, you should proceed as you would with any other type of essay. Be sure to check textual quotations with special care. Make sure you quote correctly, use ellipses (…) appropriately, and follow punctuation and capitalization conventions.

Pulling It All Together

21.4 Analyze a student's literary analysis of a short story.

In this section, you will read a short story to form a general impression of it, and you will then analyze a student's literary analysis of the story.

Read to Form a General Impression

The following short story was written by Katherine Mansfield (1888–1923), a New Zealand short story writer best known for her short story collections, including *Bliss* (1920) and *The Garden Party* (1922), in which "Miss Brill" first appeared. Read the story and gather your first impressions. Then follow the suggestions after the story.

KATHERINE MANSFIELD

Miss Brill

Although it was so brilliantly fine—the blue sky powdered with gold and   1
great spots of light like white wine splashed over the Jardins Publiques[1]—Miss
Brill was glad that she had decided on her fur. The air was motionless, but when
you opened your mouth there was just a faint chill, like a chill from a glass of iced
water before you sip, and now and again a leaf came drifting—from nowhere,
from the sky. Miss Brill put up her hand and touched her fur. Dear little thing! It
was nice to feel it again. She had taken it out of its box that afternoon, shaken out

---

[1] A public park somewhere in France (editor's note).

the moth-powder, given it a good brush, and rubbed the life back into the dim little eyes. "What has been happening to me?" said the sad little eyes. Oh, how sweet it was to see them snap at her again from the red eiderdown[2]! But the nose, which was of some black composition, wasn't at all firm. It must have had a knock, somehow. Never mind—a little dab of black sealing-wax when the time came—when it was absolutely necessary. Little rogue! Yes, she really felt like that about it. Little rogue biting its tail just by her left ear. She could have taken it off and laid it on her lap and stroked it. She felt a tingling in her hands and arms, but that came from walking, she supposed. And when she breathed, something light and sad—no, not sad, exactly—something gentle seemed to move in her bosom.

There were a number of people out this afternoon, far more than last Sunday. And the band sounded louder and gayer. That was because the Season had begun. For although the band played all the year round on Sundays, out of season it was never the same. It was like someone playing with only the family to listen; it didn't care how it played if there weren't any strangers present. Wasn't the conductor wearing a new coat, too? She was sure it was new. He scraped with his foot and flapped his arms like a rooster about to crow, and the bandsmen sitting in the green rotunda blew out their cheeks and glared at the music. Now there came a little "flutey" bit—very pretty! —a little chain of bright drops. She was sure it would be repeated. It was; she lifted her head and smiled.   2

Only two people shared her "special" seat: a fine old man in a velvet coat, his hands clasped over a huge carved walking-stick, and a big old woman, sitting upright, with a roll of knitting on her embroidered apron. They did not speak. This was disappointing, for Miss Brill always looked forward to the conversation. She had become really quite expert, she thought, at listening as though she didn't listen, at sitting in other people's lives just for a minute while they talked round her.   3

She glanced, sideways, at the old couple. Perhaps they would go soon. Last Sunday, too, hadn't been as interesting as usual. An Englishman and his wife, he wearing a dreadful Panama hat and she button boots. And she'd gone on the whole time about how she ought to wear spectacles; she knew she needed them; but that it was no good getting any; they'd be sure to break and they'd never keep on. And he'd been so patient. He'd suggested everything—gold rims, the kind that curved round your ears, little pads inside the bridge. No, nothing would please her. "They'll always be sliding down my nose!" Miss Brill had wanted to shake her.   4

The old people sat on the bench, still as statues. Never mind, there was always the crowd to watch. To and fro, in front of the flower-beds and the band rotunda, the couples and groups paraded, stopped to talk, to greet, to buy a handful of flowers from the old beggar who had his tray fixed to the railings. Little children ran among them, swooping and laughing; little boys with big white silk bows under their chins, little girls, little French dolls, dressed up in velvet and lace. And sometimes a tiny staggerer came suddenly rocking into the open from under the trees, stopped, stared, as suddenly sat down "flop," until its small high-stepping mother, like a young hen, rushed scolding to its rescue. Other people sat on the benches and green chairs, but they were nearly always the same, Sunday after Sunday, and— Miss Brill had often noticed—there was something funny about nearly all of them.   5

---

[2] A soft quilt (editor's note).

They were odd, silent, nearly all old, and from the way they stared they looked as though they'd just come from dark little rooms or even—even cupboards!

Behind the rotunda the slender trees with yellow leaves down drooping, and through them just a line of sea, and beyond the blue sky with gold-veined clouds.   6

Tum-tum-tum tiddle-um! tiddle-um! tum tiddley-um tum ta! blew the band.   7

Two young girls in red came by and two young soldiers in blue met them, and they laughed and paired and went off arm-in-arm. Two peasant women with funny straw hats passed, gravely, leading beautiful smoke-coloured donkeys. A cold, pale nun hurried by. A beautiful woman came along and dropped her bunch of violets, and a little boy ran after to hand them to her, and she took them and threw them away as if they'd been poisoned. Dear me! Miss Brill didn't know whether to admire that or not! And now an ermine toque[3] and a gentleman in grey met just in front of her. He was tall, stiff, dignified, and she was wearing the ermine toque she'd bought when her hair was yellow. Now everything, her hair, her face, even her eyes, was the same colour as the shabby ermine, and her hand, in its cleaned glove, lifted to dab her lips, was a tiny yellowish paw. Oh, she was so pleased to see him—delighted! She rather thought they were going to meet that afternoon. She described where she'd been—everywhere, here, there, along by the sea. The day was so charming—didn't he agree? And wouldn't he, perhaps? But he shook his head, lighted a cigarette, slowly breathed a great deep puff into her face, and even while she was still talking and laughing, flicked the match away and walked on. The ermine toque was alone; she smiled more brightly than ever. But even the band seemed to know what she was feeling and played more softly, played tenderly, and the drum beat, "The Brute! The Brute!" over and over. What would she do? What was going to happen now? But as Miss Brill wondered, the ermine toque turned, raised her hand as though she'd seen someone else, much nicer, just over there, and pattered away. And the band changed again and played more quickly, more gayly than ever, and the old couple on Miss Brill's seat got up and marched away, and such a funny old man with long whiskers hobbled along in time to the music and was nearly knocked over by four girls walking abreast.   8

Oh, how fascinating it was! How she enjoyed it! How she loved sitting here, watching it all! It was like a play. It was exactly like a play. Who could believe the sky at the back wasn't painted? But it wasn't till a little brown dog trotted on solemn and then slowly trotted off, like a little "theatre" dog, a little dog that had been drugged, that Miss Brill discovered what it was that made it so exciting. They were all on the stage. They weren't only the audience, not only looking on; they were acting. Even she had a part and came every Sunday. No doubt somebody would have noticed if she hadn't been there; she was part of the performance after all. How strange she'd never thought of it like that before! And yet it explained why she made such a point of starting from home at just the same time each week—so as not to be late for the performance—and it also explained why she had quite a queer, shy feeling at telling her English pupils how she spent her Sunday afternoons. No wonder! Miss Brill nearly laughed out loud. She was on the stage. She thought of the old invalid gentleman to whom she   9

---

[3] A brimless, close-fitting fur hat (editor's note).

read the newspaper four afternoons a week while he slept in the garden. She had got quite used to the frail head on the cotton pillow, the hollowed eyes, the open mouth and the high pinched nose. If he'd been dead she mightn't have noticed for weeks; she wouldn't have minded. But suddenly he knew he was having the paper read to him by an actress! "An actress!" The old head lifted; two points of light quivered in the old eyes. "An actress—are ye?" And Miss Brill smoothed the newspaper as though it were the manuscript of her part and said gently; "Yes, I have been an actress for a long time."

The band had been having a rest. Now they started again. And what they 10 played was warm, sunny, yet there was just a faint chill—a something, what was it?—not sadness—no, not sadness—a something that made you want to sing. The tune lifted, lifted, the light shone; and it seemed to Miss Brill that in another moment all of them, all the whole company, would begin singing. The young ones, the laughing ones who were moving together, they would begin, and the men's voices, very resolute and brave, would join them. And then she too, she too, and the others on the benches—they would come in with a kind of accompaniment— something low, that scarcely rose or fell, something so beautiful—moving. And Miss Brill's eyes filled with tears and she looked smiling at all the other members of the company. Yes, we understand, we understand, she thought—though what they understood she didn't know.

Just at that moment a boy and girl came and sat down where the old couple 11 had been. They were beautifully dressed; they were in love. The hero and heroine, of course, just arrived from his father's yacht. And still soundlessly singing, still with that trembling smile, Miss Brill prepared to listen.

"No, not now," said the girl. "Not here, I can't." 12

"But why? Because of that stupid old thing at the end there?" asked the boy. 13 "Why does she come here at all—who wants her? Why doesn't she keep her silly old mug at home?"

"It's her fu-ur which is so funny," giggled the girl. "It's exactly like a fried 14 whiting[4]."

"Ah, be off with you!" said the boy in an angry whisper. Then: "Tell me, ma 15 petite chere—"

"No, not here," said the girl. "Not yet." 16

On her way home she usually bought a slice of honey-cake at the baker's. It 17 was her Sunday treat. Sometimes there was an almond in her slice, sometimes not. It made a great difference. If there was an almond it was like carrying home a tiny present—a surprise—something that might very well not have been there. She hurried on the almond Sundays and struck the match for the kettle in quite a dashing way.

But today she passed the baker's by, climbed the stairs, went into the little 18 dark room—her room like a cupboard—and sat down on the red eiderdown. She sat there for a long time. The box that the fur came out of was on the bed. She unclasped the necklet quickly; quickly, without looking, laid it inside. But when she put the lid on she thought she heard something crying.

---

[4] A small, slender type of fish (editor's note).

Ask Questions About the Work

Now that you've read Mansfield's story, consult the questions in the "Analyzing a Literary Work" checklist in this chapter so that you can devise your own set of questions to solidify your first impressions. Here are some questions you might consider:

1. What functions as a *symbol* in the story? How can you tell?

   Answer: The main character's fur and the box that houses the fur are symbols in the story. The fur symbolizes Miss Brill, who, like the fur, is worn and old. The box in which she keeps the fur represents both the place where the main character lives and her little world.

2. From what *point of view* is the story told? How does it relate to the story's meaning?

   Answer: The point of view is the third-person limited omniscient. It enables the author to show the discrepancy between what characters are thinking and what they are willing or able to communicate.

3. What *words* and *images* are repeated in the course of the story? How do these *motifs* reflect the story's theme?

   Answer: The words *young* and *old* appear a number of times. This repetition helps emphasize the contrast between the youthful, vibrant characters and the older, lonely characters who frequent the park on Sunday afternoons. *Funny* is another repeated word that evokes in the reader more pity than laughter. *Little* is a repeated word that gives the reader the sense of the limited scope of Miss Brill's life. The phrases "sad—no, not sad" and "not sadness—no, not sadness" emphasize how hard the main character is trying to remain optimistic and to see her life in a positive light.

Reread and Annotate

In light of the questions you develop, reread and annotate Mansfield's story. Then consider the following writing assignments.

1. Write an essay in which you defend the main character's need to eavesdrop on the conversations of others, including details from the story to support your claims.

2. Analyze how Mansfield develops the theme that it is important for individuals to find a way to create a meaningful existence out of their lives.

3. Write a literary analysis in which you discuss the aspects of Mansfield's story that continue to make it relevant today, close to a hundred years after it was first published.

Student Essay

Student Bella Clemmons decided to write in response to the third assignment. After using questions to focus her initial impressions, Bella organized her prewriting and began to draft her literary analysis. The final version of her analysis follows. As you read the essay, consider how well Bella incorporates details from the story to support her claims. Because the story was assigned in class and everyone used the same text, she didn't need to provide a bibliographic citation. Similarly, her instructor didn't require parenthetic documentation of quoted material because the story is so brief.

At Least for a While—Perhaps Forever
by Bella Clemmons

Introduction

While our world has changed dramatically since Katherine Mansfield's short story, "Miss Brill," was first published in 1922, it remains a timeless story to which readers of various ages and ethnicities, from different parts of the world, and with a wide variety of educational and social backgrounds can relate. Mansfield's emphasis on basic human needs for interacting socially, making meaning out of life, and being treated with respect are characteristics common to almost all individuals, and the author's focus on these characteristics makes for a story as applicable today as it was close to a century ago. 1

Thesis with plan of development

First supporting paragraph: focus on the need for social interaction

While some individuals need more social contact than others, human beings, in general, need to interact with others. The main character in Mansfield's story, Miss Brill, appears to have the company of only "her English pupils," the various individuals she encounters in the park on Sunday afternoons, and the old man to whom she reads the newspaper four afternoons a week while he sleeps. It appears that her closest "companion" is the fur she wraps around her neck each Sunday afternoon before she leaves for the park and then puts back in its little box when she returns home. As far as the reader can tell, Miss Brill has no real friends, but even so, she finds a way to spend time around others. 2

Second supporting paragraph: focus on the need to make meaning out of life

In addition to the human need for social interaction, the need to make meaning out of life is also emphasized in Mansfield's story. While many would consider Miss Brill's life a sad and lonely one, the main character manages to create a somewhat meaningful existence for herself. Miss Brill makes sure she has something to look forward to: spending her Sunday afternoons in the park each week—where she imagines herself as an actress playing a role in a weekly performance—followed by a stop at the baker's for a slice of honey cake—which just might, if she's very lucky, include an almond. 3

Third supporting paragraph: focus on the need for respect

A third human need that Mansfield addresses in her story is the need for respect. The lack of respect shown Miss Brill by the young couple who refer to her as a "stupid old thing" and make fun of her cherished fur, saying that it looks like a "fried whiting," crushes Miss Brill's spirit so much that she no longer has any desire to stop at the baker's for her Sunday treat on her way home from the park. 4

Conclusion

The young couple's mean-spirited comments take the joy out of Miss Brill's life, at least for a while—perhaps forever.

Miss Brill is a character who will long be remembered by many   5
readers because she is someone they know, someone they are afraid they might become—or both. It is difficult to imagine a time when readers will no longer be able to relate to Mansfield's rich story.

Commentary

Note that Bella states her *thesis* in the opening paragraph: "Mansfield's emphasis on basic human needs for interacting socially, making meaning out of life, and being treated with respect are characteristics common to almost all individuals, and the author's focus on these characteristics makes for a story as applicable today as it was close to a century ago." The thesis makes clear to readers that the essay will focus on the aspects of Mansfield's story that make it relevant today. It also announces the essay's *plan of development*. Bella will discuss the need for social interaction, then the need for making meaning out of life, and then the need for being treated with respect, with one paragraph devoted to each of these elements. In the body of the analysis, Bella backs up her thesis with *textual evidence* in the form of summaries and quotations. The quotations are no longer than is necessary to support her points. In the concluding paragraph, Bella reinforces her thesis by pointing out the relevance of the story's theme to the reader's own life.

Writing Assignment on "Miss Brill"

Having seen what one student did with "Miss Brill," look back at the first and second writing assignments under the heading "Reread and Annotate" and select one for your own analysis of Mansfield's story. Then, in light of the assignment you select, read the story again, making any adjustments in your annotations. Next, organize your pre-writing annotations into a scratch list, identify a working thesis, and organize your ideas into an outline. That done, write your first draft. Before submitting your analysis, take time to revise, edit, and proofread it carefully.

Additional Selections and Writing Assignments

The two selections that follow—a poem by Robert Frost and a short story by Kate Chopin—will give you further practice in analyzing literary texts. No matter which selection you decide to write about, the guidelines in this chapter should help you approach the literary analysis with confidence.

ROBERT FROST

Best known for his poetry about New England life, Robert Frost (1874–1963) was born in San Francisco and moved to Massachusetts in 1885. His first two collections of poetry, *A Boy's Will*

(1913) and *North of Boston* (1914), were published in England, where he went after failing to be published in the United States. These collections—and the distinctly American voice shaping them—eventually won Frost recognition back home, where he returned to publish *Mountain Interval* (1916), a volume containing some of his most recognized poems. Frost received four Pulitzer Prizes and presented the poem "The Gift Outright" at President John F. Kennedy's inauguration in 1961. The following poem first appeared in *Mountain Interval*. The title alludes to the words of Shakespeare's Macbeth on receiving news that his queen is dead: "Out, out, brief candle! / Life's but a walking shadow, a poor player / That struts and frets his hour upon the stage / And then is heard no more. It is a tale / Told by an idiot, full of sound and fury, / Signifying nothing" (*Macbeth* 5.5.23–28).

"Out, Out—"

The buzz-saw snarled and rattled in the yard
And made dust and dropped stove-length sticks of wood,
Sweet-scented stuff when the breeze drew across it.
And from there those that lifted eyes could count
Five mountain ranges one behind the other   5
Under the sunset far into Vermont.
And the saw snarled and rattled, snarled and rattled,
As it ran light, or had to bear a load.
And nothing happened: day was all but done.
Call it a day, I wish they might have said   10
To please the boy by giving him the half hour
That a boy counts so much when saved from work.
His sister stood beside them in her apron
To tell them "Supper." At the word, the saw,
As if to prove saws knew what supper meant,   15
Leaped out at the boy's hand, or seemed to leap—
He must have given the hand. However it was,
Neither refused the meeting. But the hand!
The boy's first outcry was a rueful laugh,
As he swung toward them holding up the hand   20
Half in appeal, but half as if to keep
The life from spilling. Then the boy saw all—
Since he was old enough to know, big boy
Doing a man's work, though a child at heart—
He saw all spoiled. "Don't let him cut my hand off—   25
The doctor, when he comes. Don't let him, sister!"
So. But the hand was gone already.
The doctor put him in the dark of ether.
He lay and puffed his lips out with his breath.
And then—the watcher at his pulse took fright.   30
No one believed. They listened at his heart.
Little—less—nothing—and that ended it.
No more to build on there. And they, since they
Were not the one dead, turned to their affairs.

Writing Assignments on "Out, Out—"

1. Because it tells a story, "Out, Out—" can be described as a narrative poem. Discuss the poem's various narrative elements, including its setting, plot, characters, conflict, climax, and resolution. Analyze how these narrative elements work to convey the poem's main theme.

2. Despite the poem's concise language, Frost manages to provide clear descriptions of the boy and the men in the timber mill and what each of them represents. Looking closely at how Frost depicts the boy and the men—known as *they* in the poem—write an essay analyzing the different views of human nature that Frost conveys.

3. The buzz-saw plays a central role in Frost's poem—to such an extent that it can be considered a character in its own right. Analyze the ways in which the buzz-saw is characterized in the poem. Be sure to discuss what commentary Frost might be making about the relationship between people and their objects of labor in his depiction of the buzz-saw.

KATE CHOPIN

Fiction writer Kate Chopin (1851–1904) is best known for her novel *The Awakening* (1899). When first published, the novel shocked readers with its frank sensuality and the independent spirit of its female protagonist. The following story, first published in *Vogue* in 1894, shows a similar defiance of socially prescribed expectations and norms.

The Story of an Hour

Knowing that Mrs. Mallard was afflicted with heart trouble, great care was taken to break to her as gently as possible the news of her husband's death. 1

It was her sister Josephine who told her, in broken sentences, veiled hints that revealed in half concealing. Her husband's friend Richards was there, too, near her. It was he who had been in the newspaper office when intelligence of the railroad disaster was received, with Brently Mallard's name leading the list of "killed." He had only taken the time to assure himself of its truth by a second telegram, and had hastened to forestall any less careful, less tender friend in bearing the sad message. 2

She did not hear the story as many women have heard the same, with a paralyzed inability to accept its significance. She wept at once, with sudden, wild abandonment, in her sister's arms. When the storm of grief had spent itself she went away to her room alone. She would have no one follow her. 3

There stood, facing the open window, a comfortable, roomy armchair. Into this she sank, pressed down by a physical exhaustion that haunted her body and seemed to reach into her soul. 4

She could see in the open square before her house the tops of trees that were all aquiver with the new spring life. The delicious breath of rain was in the air. In the street below a peddler was crying his wares. The notes of a distant song which someone was singing reached her faintly, and countless sparrows were twittering in the eaves. 5

There were patches of blue sky showing here and there through the clouds   6
that had met and piled one above the other in the west facing her window.

She sat with her head thrown back upon the cushion of the chair, quite mo-   7
tionless, except when a sob came up into her throat and shook her, as a child who
has cried itself to sleep continues to sob in its dreams.

She was young, with a fair, calm face, whose lines bespoke repression and   8
even a certain strength. But now there was a dull stare in her eyes, whose gaze was
fixed away off yonder on one of those patches of blue sky. It was not a glance of
reflection, but rather indicated a suspension of intelligent thought.

There was something coming to her and she was waiting for it, fearfully. What   9
was it? She did not know, it was too subtle and elusive to name. But she felt it,
creeping out of the sky, reaching toward her through the sounds, the scents, the
color that filled the air.

Now her bosom rose and fell tumultuously. She was beginning to recognize   10
this thing that was approaching to possess her, and she was striving to beat it back
with her will—as powerless as her two white slender hands would have been.

When she abandoned herself a little whispered word escaped her slightly   11
parted lips. She said it over and over under her breath: "Free, free, free!" The va-
cant stare and the look of terror that had followed it went from her eyes. They
stayed keen and bright. Her pulses beat fast, and the coursing blood warmed and
relaxed every inch of her body.

She did not stop to ask if it were not a monstrous joy that held her. A clear and   12
exalted perception enabled her to dismiss the suggestion as trivial.

She knew that she would weep again when she saw the kind, tender hands   13
folded in death; the face that had never looked save with love upon her, fixed and
gray and dead. But she saw beyond that bitter moment a long procession of years
to come that would belong to her absolutely. And she opened and spread her arms
out to them in welcome.

There would be no one to live for during those coming years; she would live   14
for herself. There would be no powerful will bending her in that blind persistence
with which men and women believe they have a right to impose a private will
upon a fellow creature. A kind intention or a cruel intention made the act seem no
less a crime as she looked upon it in that brief moment of illumination.

And yet she had loved him—sometimes. Often she had not. What did it mat-   15
ter! What could love, the unsolved mystery, count for in face of this possession
of self-assertion which she suddenly recognized as the strongest impulse of her
being.

"Free! Body and soul free!" she kept whispering.   16

Josephine was kneeling before the closed door with her lips to the keyhole,   17
imploring for admission. "Louise, open the door! I beg; open the door—you will
make yourself ill. What are you doing, Louise? For heaven's sake open the door."

"Go away. I am not making myself ill." No; she was drinking in a very elixir of   18
life through that open window.

Her fancy was running riot along those days ahead of her. Spring days, and   19
summer days, and all sorts of days that would be her own. She breathed a quick
prayer that life might be long. It was only yesterday she had thought with a shud-
der that life might be long.

She arose at length and opened the door to her sister's importunities. There 20
was a feverish triumph in her eyes, and she carried herself unwittingly like a god-
dess of Victory. She clasped her sister's waist, and together they descended the
stairs. Richards stood waiting for them at the bottom.

Some one was opening the front door with a latchkey. It was Brently Mallard 21
who entered, a little travel-stained, composedly carrying his gripsack and um-
brella. He had been far from the scene of the accident, and did not even know
there had been one. He stood amazed at Josephine's piercing cry; at Richards'
quick motion to screen him from the view of his wife.

But Richards was too late.   22

When the doctors came they said she had died of heart disease—of joy 23
that kills.

Writing Assignments on "The Story of an Hour"

1. Show how Chopin uses imagery and descriptive detail to contrast the rich possibilities for which Mrs. Mallard yearns with the drab reality of her everyday life.

2. Argue that "The Story of an Hour" dramatizes the theme that domesticity saps
   a woman's spirit and physical strength.

3. Does Chopin's characterization of Mrs. Mallard justify the story's unexpected and
   ironic climax? Explain your response.

Chapter 22
Writing Essay Exams

Learning Objectives

22.1 Identify the three forms that written answers can take on an essay exam.

22.2 Prepare for an essay exam.

22.3 Use test-taking strategies during an essay exam.

If you have trouble writing essays at home, the idea of preparing for an **essay exam** may throw you into a panic. How, you may wonder, can you show what you know under such pressure?

Instructors give essay exams to test your understanding of the subject—and to stimulate you to interpret course material in perceptive ways. They realize that the writing done under time pressure won't result in a masterpiece. However, they *do* expect reasonably complete essay answers, with focused, developed, and coherent responses.

Three Forms of Written Answers on Essay Exams

22.1 Identify the three forms that written answers can take on an essay exam.

All essay exams have one thing in common: They all require writing. However, the amount of writing may vary. Some questions require an answer as short as one or two sentences, while other questions require you to write a full, several-paragraph essay.

Short Answers

One kind of question calls for a **short answer** of only a few sentences. Such questions often ask you to identify (or define) a term *and* explain its importance. Be prepared to write one to three full sentences.

Here are two examples of short-answer questions and their answers (in italics) for an exam in modern art history.

Directions: Identify and explain the significance of the following:

1. **"Concerning the Spiritual in Art":** This is an essay written by Wassily Kandinsky in 1912 to justify the abstract painting style he used. Showing Matisse's influence, the essay maintains that pure forms and basic colors convey reality more accurately than true-to-life depictions.

2. **The Eiffel Tower Series:** Done around 1910 by Robert Delaunay, this is a series of paintings having the Eiffel Tower as the subject. Delaunay used a cubist approach, analyzing surface, space, and intersecting planes.

Paragraph-Length Answers

Questions requiring a **paragraph-length answer** may signal—directly or indirectly—the length of response expected. A successful answer should address the question as completely yet as concisely as possible. Beginning with a strong topic sentence will help you focus your response.

Following is a paragraph-length answer to a question on a political science exam:

[*Question*] Discuss the meaning of the term *interest group* and comment briefly on the role such groups play in the governing of democratic societies.

[*Answer*] An interest group is an informal type of political organization; its goal is to influence government policy and see legislation enacted that favors its members. An interest group differs from a political party; the interest group doesn't want to control the government or have an actual share in governing (the whole purpose of a political party). Interest groups are considered informal because they are not officially part of the governing process. Still, they exert tremendous power. Democratic governments constantly respond to interest groups by passing new laws and policies. Some examples of interest groups are institutions (the military, the Catholic Church), associations (the American Medical Association, Mothers Against Drunk Driving), and nonassociational groups (car owners, television viewers).

Essay-Length Answers

You will frequently be asked to write an **essay-length answer** as part of a longer examination. Here is a typical essay question from an exam in an introductory course in linguistics. A response to this question appears under the heading "Sample Essay Answer" later in this chapter.

> Account for the differences in American and British English by describing at least three major influences that affected the way this country's settlers spoke English. Give as many examples as you can of words derived from these influences.

How to Prepare for Essay Exams

22.2 Prepare for an essay exam.

Spaced study throughout the semester gives you a sense of the *why* of the subject, not just the *who, what, where,* and *when*. Try to avoid cramming whenever possible. It prevents you from gaining a clear overview of a course and a real understanding of a course's main issues. As you prepare for an essay exam, follow the guidelines listed here.

☑ **Preparing for an Essay Exam: A Checklist**

- ☐ In light of the main concepts covered in the course, identify key issues that the exam might logically address.

- ☐ With these issues in mind, design several possible essay exam questions.

- ☐ Draft an answer for each anticipated question.

- ☐ Commit to memory any facts, quotations, data, lists of reasons, and so forth that you would include in your answers.

Taking Essay Exams

22.3 Use test-taking strategies during an essay exam.

To maximize your grades on essay exams, use the following suggestions.

Survey the Entire Test

Look over the entire written-answer section of a test before working on any part of it. Note which sections are worth the highest point value, and plan to spend the longest time on those sections. Follow the test's directions regarding the length of the response. When "a brief paragraph" is all that is required, don't launch into a full-scale essay.

Understand the Essay Question

Examine each question carefully to determine its slant or emphasis. Most essay questions ask you to focus on a specific issue or to bring together material from different parts of the course.

Many questions use **key directional words** that suggest an answer developed according to a particular pattern of development:

Key Directional Words	Pattern of Development
Provide details about	Description
Give the history of, Trace the development of	Narration
Explain, List, Provide examples of	Illustration
Analyze the parts of, Discuss the types of	Division-classification
Analyze, Explain how, Show how	Process analysis
Discuss advantages and disadvantages of, Show similarities and differences between	Comparison-contrast
Account for, Analyze, Discuss the consequences of, Explain the reasons for, Explain why, Show the influence of	Cause-effect
Clarify, Explain the meaning of, Identify	Definition
Argue, Defend, Evaluate, Justify, Show the failings or merits of, Support	Argumentation-persuasion

Write the Essay

The steps in the writing process are the same whether you compose an essay at home or prepare an essay response in a classroom test situation. The main difference is that during a test the process is streamlined and timed.

PREWRITE Prewriting begins when you analyze the essay question and determine your essay's basic approach. Underline key directional terms, circle crucial words, and put numbers next to points that you should cover.

Make notes for an answer. Jot down main points as well as facts and examples. Try brainstorming, freewriting, mapping, or another prewriting technique to get yourself going.

What to Avoid. You won't have time to generate pages of notes, so try using words and phrases. Also, don't spend time analyzing your audience (you know it's your instructor) or choosing a tone (exams require a serious, analytic approach).

IDENTIFY YOUR THESIS   Answers to essay questions should have a **thesis**. Often, the thesis is a statement answering the exam question. For example, in response to a question asking you to "Discuss the origins of apartheid," your thesis might begin, "The South African law of 'separateness,' or apartheid, originated in 1948, a result of a series of factors that . . . ." On essay exams, thesis statements are somewhat informal. They state the *subject* of the essay but not the writer's *attitude* toward the subject. In a test-taking situation, less-structured thesis statements are acceptable.

SUPPORT THE THESIS WITH EVIDENCE   In the prewriting stage, you jotted down material needed to answer the question. At this point, you should review the **evidence** quickly to make sure it's *adequate*. Also, check that support for your thesis is *unified, specific, accurate,* and *representative*.

ORGANIZE THE EVIDENCE   Before you start writing, devise some kind of **outline**. You may simply sequence your prewriting jottings by placing numbers or letters beside them. Or you can quickly translate the jottings into a brief, informal outline.

Go back and review the essay question one more time. If the question has two or three parts, your outline should tackle each one in turn.

Focus again on the question's key *directional words*. If the question asks you to discuss similarities and differences, your outline should draw on one of the two basic *comparison-contrast* formats. Because many exam questions call for more than one task (for example, you may be asked both to *define* a theory and to *argue* its merits), you should make sure your outline reflects the appropriate patterns of development.

Many outlines use an *emphatic* approach to organize material. However, when discussing historical or developmental issues, you often structure material *chronologically*. In some fields (art history, for example) you may choose a *spatial* approach—for instance, if you describe a work of art. Quickly assess the situation to determine which approach would work best, and keep it in mind as you sequence the points in your outline.

What to Avoid.   Don't prepare a formal or many-leveled outline; you'll waste valuable time. A phrase outline with two levels of support should be sufficient.

WRITE THE DRAFT   Generally, you won't have time to write a formal introduction, so it's fine to begin the essay with your thesis, perhaps followed by a *plan of development*. Write as many paragraphs as you need to show that you have command of the concepts and facts taught in the course. Refer to your outline as you write, but if inspiration strikes, feel free to add material or deal with a point in a different order.

As you draft your response, you shouldn't feel hesitant about crossing out material. *Do* make these changes, but make them neatly.

When preparing the draft, remember that you'll be graded in part on how *specific, accurate,* and *representative* your evidence is. Make sure, too, that your response is *unified.* Stay focused on the question. Using topic sentences to structure your paragraphs will help you stay on track.

Your instructor will need transitions and other markers to understand how your points connect to one another. Try to show how your ideas relate by using *signal devices*.

As you near the end of the essay, check the original question. Have you covered everything? Does the question call for a final judgment or evaluative comment? If so, provide it. Also, if you have time, you may want to close with a brief, one- or two-sentence summary.

What to Avoid.   Your first and only draft should be the one written on the exam booklet or paper. Don't cast your answer as one long paragraph spanning three pages. If you've outlined your ideas, you'll have a clear idea where paragraph breaks should occur. Finally, don't cram your response with everything you know about the subject. Give focused, intelligent responses.

REVISE, EDIT, AND PROOFREAD   If you've budgeted your time, you should have a few minutes left to review your essay answer. Above all, read your response to be sure it answers the question fully. Make any changes that will improve the answer. If something is in the wrong place, use an arrow and a brief note to indicate where it should go. Instructors will accept insertions and deletions. Use the standard editing marks such as the caret (^) to indicate additions and other changes.

As you reread, check grammar and spelling. Obvious grammatical errors and spelling mistakes may affect your grade. If spelling is a problem for you, request permission to have your dictionary at hand.

Sample Essay Answer

① Maritime pidgin (Portug. influ.)

② African pidgin (Slaves comm. with each other and with owners)

③ Native American pidgin (words for native plants and animals)

The following essay was written by Andrew Kahan in response to this take-home exam question:

> Account for the differences in American and British English by describing at least three major influences that affected the way this country's settlers spoke English. Give as many examples as you can of words derived from these influences.

Andrew started by underlining the question's key words. Then he listed in the margin the main points and some of the supporting evidence he planned to include in his answer. That done, he formulated a thesis and began writing his essay. The handwritten annotations reflect the changes Andrew made when he refined his answer before handing in his exam.

American English diverged from British English because those who settled the New World had contact with people that those back in England generally did not. As a result of *this* contact, several pidgin languages developed. A pidgin language, which has its own grammar and vocabulary, comes about when the speakers of two or more unrelated languages communicate ~~for a while~~ over a period of time. Maritime pidgin, African pidgin, and Indian pidgin were three influences that helped shape American English.

By the time the New World began to be settled, sailors and sea merchants *all* of the European nations had traveled widely. A maritime pidgin thus ~~immerged~~ *emerged* that enabled diverse groups to communicate.* Since Portugal controlled the seas around the time the colonies were settled, maritime pidgin was largely influenced by the Portuguese. Such Portuguese-derived words as "cavort," "palaver," and "savvy" first entered American English in this way.

and trade with each other

The New World's trade with Africa also ~~effec~~ affected American English. The slave trade, in particular, took American sailors and merchants all over the African continent. Since the traders mixed up slaves of many tribes to prevent them from becoming unified, the Africans had to rely on *their own* pidgin to communicate with each other. Moreover, slave owners relied on this African-based pidgin to communicate with their slaves**. Since slaves tended to be settled in the heavily populated American coastal areas, elements of the African pidgin readily worked their way into the language of the New World. Words and phrases derived from African pidgins include "caboodle" and "kick the bucket." Other African-based words include "buckaroo" and "goobers," plus words known only in the Deep South, like "cooter" for turtle. African-based slang terms and constructions ("uptight," "put-on," and "hip," meaning "cool" or "in") continue to enter mainstream English from Black English even today.

Another *important* influence on American English, in the nation's early days, was contact with Native American cultures. As settlers moved inland from coastal areas, they confronted different indigenous peoples, and new pidgins grew up, melding English and Native American terms. In particular, many words for places, plants, and animals have Native American roots: "squash," "raccoon," and "skunk" are just a few. Another possible effect of Native American languages on American English may be the tendency to form noun-noun compounds ("apple butter" and "shade tree"). While such constructions do occur in British English, they are *much* more frequent in American English.

British and American English differ because the latter has been shaped by contact with European languages like Portuguese as well as by contact with non-European languages—especially those spoken by Africans and Native Americans.

**until they mastered English.*

COMMENTARY Alert to such phrases as *account for* and *influences that affected* in the question, Andrew wrote an essay that describes three *causes* for the divergence of American English from British English. The three causes are organized roughly chronologically, beginning with the influence of maritime exploration, moving to the effect of contact with African culture, and concluding with the influence of Native Americans.

Although the essay is developed mainly through a description of causes, other patterns of development come into play. The first paragraph *defines* the term *pidgin,* whereas the second, third, and fourth paragraphs draw on *process analysis;* they describe how pidgins developed as well as how they affected the language spoken by early settlers. Finally, the essay includes numerous *examples,* as the exam question requested. Andrew's response shows a solid knowledge of the material taught in the course and demonstrates his ability to organize the material into a clear, coherent statement.

Activity: Writing Essay Exams

In preparation for an exam with essay questions, devise four possible essay questions on the material in one of your courses. For each, do some quick prewriting, determine a thesis, and jot down an outline. Then, for one of the questions, write a full essay answer, giving yourself a time limit of fifteen to twenty-five minutes, whatever is appropriate for the question. Don't forget to edit and proofread your answer.

A Concise Handbook
Sentence Faults

Fragments

A **sentence** satisfies two conditions: (1) it has a subject and a verb, and (2) it can stand alone as a complete thought. Although a **fragment** is punctuated like a full sentence, it doesn't satisfy these two requirements. There are two kinds of fragments: phrase fragments and dependent clause fragments.

Phrase Fragments

If you punctuate a phrase as if it were a sentence, the result is a **phrase fragment**. Following are five kinds of phrase fragments and ways to correct such fragments.

Noun Phrase Fragment

I was afraid of my wrestling coach. *A harsh and sarcastic man.* He was never satisfied with my performance.

Added-Detail Phrase Fragment

Many people have difficulty getting up in the morning. *Especially on Mondays after a hectic weekend.* They wish they had one more day to relax.

Prepositional Phrase Fragment

After a long day at work. I drove to the bank that opened last week. *On the corner of Holly Avenue and Red Oak Lane. Next to the discount supermarket.*

Present Participle, Past Participle, or Infinitive Phrase Fragment

Waiting [present participle] *to buy tickets for the concert.* The crowd stood quietly in line. No one cared that the box office would be closed until the morning.

The children presented the social worker with a present. *Wrapped* [past participle] *in gold aluminum foil.*

After years of negotiating, several nations signed a treaty. *To ban* [infinitive] *the sale of ivory in their countries.*

Missing-Subject Phrase Fragment

Every weekend, the fraternities sponsored a joint open-house party. *And blared music all night long.* Not surprisingly, neighbors became furious.

frag

HOW TO CORRECT PHRASE FRAGMENTS

There are four strategies for eliminating phrase fragments from your writing. When using these strategies, you may need to reword sentences slightly to maintain smoothness.

1. Attach the fragment to the preceding or following sentence, changing punctuation and capitalization as needed.   When attaching a phrase fragment to the *beginning of a preceding sentence,* place a comma between the fragment and the start of the original sentence:

Fragment	Environmentalists predict a drought this summer. *In spite of heavy spring rains.* Everyone hopes the predictions are wrong.
Correct	In spite of heavy spring rains, environmentalists predict a drought this summer. Everyone hopes the predictions are wrong.

To attach a phrase fragment to the *end of a preceding sentence,* change the period at the end of the preceding sentence to a comma and change the first letter of the fragment to lowercase:

Fragment	I spent several hours in the college's Career Services Office. *Trying to find an interesting summer job.* Nothing looked promising.
Correct	I spent several hours in the college's Career Services Office, trying to find an interesting summer job. Nothing looked promising.

To attach a phrase fragment to the *beginning of a full sentence that follows it,* change the period at the end of the fragment to a comma and make the capital letter at the start of the full sentence lowercase:

Fragment	*Overwhelmed by school pressures and family demands.* She decided to postpone her education. That was a mistake.
Correct	Overwhelmed by school pressures and family demands, she decided to postpone her education. That was a mistake.

2. Insert the fragment into the preceding or following sentence, adding commas as needed:

Fragment	The tests were easy. *Especially the essay questions.* We felt confident that we had done well.
Correct	The tests, especially the essay questions, were easy. We felt confident that we had done well. [fragment inserted into preceding sentence]
Fragment	*A robust girl who loved physical activity from the time she was a baby.* My sister qualified for the Olympics when she was seventeen.
Correct	My sister, a robust girl who loved physical activity from the time she was a baby, qualified for the Olympics when she was seventeen. [fragment inserted into following sentence]

3. Attach the fragment to a newly created sentence:

Fragment	Although I proudly call it mine, my apartment does have some problems. *For example, very little heat in the winter.*
Correct	Although I proudly call it mine, my apartment does have some problems. For example, *it has* very little heat in the winter.

4. Supply the missing subject:

Fragment	Although they argued frequently, my grandparents doted on each other. *And held hands wherever they went.*
Correct	Although they argued frequently, my grandparents doted on each other. *They* held hands wherever they went.

or

Correct	Although they argued frequently, my grandparents doted on each other *and* held hands wherever they went.

Dependent Clause Fragments

Unlike phrases, which lack either a subject or a full verb, **clauses** contain both a subject and a full verb. Clauses may be **independent** (expressing a complete thought and able to stand alone as a sentence) or **dependent** (not expressing a complete thought and therefore not able to stand alone). A dependent clause (often called a **subordinate clause**) begins with a word that signals the clause's reliance on something more for completion. Such introductory words may take the form of **subordinating conjunctions** or **relative pronouns**:

Subordinating Conjunctions

after	once	even though	when
although	since	if	while
as	so that	in order that	
because	unless	until	

Relative Pronouns

that	which	whoever	whomever
what	who	whom	whose

Dependent clauses introduced by relative pronouns are often referred to as *relative clauses.*

If you punctuate a dependent clause as though it were a complete sentence, the result is a **dependent clause fragment** (identified by italics in the example):

Fragment	*Because my parents wanted to be with their children at bedtime.* They arranged to leave their late-shift jobs a few minutes early.

HOW TO CORRECT DEPENDENT CLAUSE FRAGMENTS

There are two main ways to correct dependent clause fragments. When using the strategies, you may need to reword sentences slightly to maintain smoothness.

1. Connect the fragment to the preceding or following full sentence, adding a comma if needed:

Fragment   I thought both my car and I would be demolished. *When the motorcycle hit me from behind.*

Correct   When the motorcycle hit me from behind, I thought both my car and I would be demolished. [fragment attached, with a comma, to beginning of preceding sentence]

or

Correct   I thought both my car and I would be demolished when the motorcycle hit me from behind. [fragment attached, without a comma, to end of preceding sentence]

Fragment   *Although the clean-up crews tried to scrub the oil-coated rocks thoroughly.* Many birds nesting on the rocky shore are bound to die.

Correct   Although the clean-up crews tried to scrub the oil-coated rocks thoroughly, many birds nesting on the rocky shore are bound to die. [fragment attached, with a comma, to beginning of following sentence]

or

Correct   Many birds nesting on the rocky shore are bound to die, although the clean-up crews tried to scrub the oil-coated rocks thoroughly. [fragment attached, with a comma, to end of following sentence]

Guidelines for Using Commas with Dependent Clauses

- If a dependent clause with a subordinating conjunction (like *when* or *although*) precedes the full sentence, the dependent clause is followed by a comma.
- If a dependent clause follows the full sentence, it isn't preceded by a comma.
- The exception is dependent clauses beginning with such words as *although* and *though*—words that show contrast. When such clauses follow a full sentence, they are preceded by a comma.

When connecting a relative clause to a full sentence, you set off the *relative clause* with a comma if the clause is **nonrestrictive** (that is, if it is *not essential* to the sentence's meaning):

Fragment   As a child, I went to the mountains with my parents. *Who never relaxed long enough to enjoy the lazy times there.*

Correct   As a child, I went to the mountains with my parents, who never relaxed long enough to enjoy the lazy times there.

Note that in the corrected version there's a comma between the independent and relative clauses because the relative clause (*who never relaxed long enough to enjoy the lazy times there*) is nonrestrictive. In other words, it isn't needed to identify the writer's parents.

Take a look, though, at the following:

Fragment   As a child, I went to the mountains with the family. *Who lived next door.*

Correct   As a child, I went to the mountains with the family who lived next door.

In this case, the relative clause (*who lived next door*) is needed to identify which family is being referred to. That is, the clause is **restrictive** (*essential*) and therefore is *not* set off with a comma.

When a relative clause beginning with *that* is attached to a nearby sentence, no comma is used between the relative and independent clauses:

Fragment	My uncle got down on his hands and knees to rake away the dry leaves. *That he felt spoiled the beauty of his flower beds.*
Correct	My uncle got down on his hands and knees to rake away the dry leaves that he felt spoiled the beauty of his flower beds.

2. Remove or replace the dependent clause's first word:

Fragment	The typical family-run farm is up for sale these days. *Because few small farmers can compete with agricultural conglomerates.*
Correct	The typical family-run farm is up for sale these days. Few small farmers can compete with agricultural conglomerates.

Comma Splices and Run-on Sentences

A **comma splice** is an error that occurs when a comma is used to join, or splice together, two complete thoughts, even though a comma alone is not strong enough to connect the two independent clauses. A **run-on**, or **fused**, **sentence** is an error that occurs when two sentences are connected, or run together, without any punctuation to indicate where the first sentence ends and the second begins.

cs

r-o

Three Common Pitfalls

Following are three situations that often lead to comma splices or run-on sentences and ways to correct these sentence errors.

1. When the second sentence starts with a personal or demonstrative pronoun: The following are **personal pronouns:** *I, you, he, she, it, we,* and *they. This, that, these,* and *those* are **demonstrative pronouns**.

Comma Splice	The college's computerized billing system needs to be overhauled, *it billed more than a dozen students twice for tuition.*
Run-on	Lobsters are cannibalistic and will feed on each other *this is one reason they are difficult to raise in captivity.*

2. When the second sentence starts with a transition: Some common **transitions** include the words *finally, next, second,* and *then.*

Comma Splice	You start by buttering the baking dish, *next you pour in milk and mix it well with the butter.*
Run-on	The dentist studied my X rays *then she let out an ominous sigh.*

3. **When two sentences are connected by a transitional adverb:** **These are some of the most common transitional adverbs:**

Transitional Adverbs

accordingly	furthermore	meanwhile	still
also	however	moreover	therefore
anyway	indeed	nevertheless	thus
besides	instead	nonetheless	
consequently	likewise	otherwise	

Comma Splice	We figured the movie tickets would cost about five dollars, *however, we forgot to calculate the cost of all the junk food we would eat.*
Run-on	Fish in a backyard pond will thrive simply by eating the bugs, larvae, and algae in the pond *nevertheless, many people enjoy feeding fish by hand.*

HOW TO CORRECT COMMA SPLICES AND RUN-ON SENTENCES

There are four strategies for eliminating comma splices and run-on sentences from your writing.

1. **Place a period, question mark, or exclamation point at the end of the first sentence and capitalize the first letter of the second sentence:**

Comma Splice	Our team played badly, *we deserved to lose by the wide margin we did.*
Correct	Our team played badly. We deserved to lose by the wide margin we did.
Run-on	Which computer do experts recommend for the average college student *which system do experts consider most all-purpose?* They seldom agree.
Correct	Which computer do experts recommend for the average college student? Which system do experts consider most all-purpose? They seldom agree.

2. **Use a semicolon (;) to mark where the first sentence ends and the second begins:**

Comma Splice	In the eighteenth century, beauty marks were considered fashionable, *people even glued black paper dots to their faces.*
Correct	In the eighteenth century, beauty marks were considered fashionable; people even glued black paper dots to their faces.
Run-on	Many men use hairstyling products, facial scrubs, and cologne *however, most draw the line at powder and eye makeup.*
Correct	Many men use hairstyling products, facial scrubs, and cologne; however, most draw the line at powder and eye makeup.

Note that when the second sentence starts with a transitional adverb (such as *however* in the last corrected sentence above), a *comma* is placed *after* the transition.

3. **Turn one of the sentences into a dependent clause:**

Comma Splice	The camping grounds have no electricity, *however, people flock there anyway.*
Correct	*Although* the camping grounds have no electricity, people flock there anyway.
Run-on	The highway was impassable *it had snowed all night and most of the morning.*
Correct	The highway was impassable *because* it had snowed all night and most of the morning.

4. **Keep or add a comma at the end of the first sentence, but follow the comma with a coordinating conjunction.**   The following words are **coordinating conjunctions**: *and, but, for, nor, or, so, yet.*

Comma Splice	Well-prepared and confident, I expected the exam to be easy, *it turned out to be a harrowing experience.*
Correct	Well-prepared and confident, I expected the exam to be easy, but it turned out to be a harrowing experience.
Run-on	Last election we campaigned enthusiastically *this year we expect to be equally involved.*
Correct	Last election we campaigned enthusiastically, *and* this year we expect to be equally involved.

Faulty Parallelism

Words in a pair or in a series should be placed in parallel (matching) grammatical structures. If they're not, the result is **faulty parallelism**:

Faulty Parallelism	After the exam, we were *exhausted, hungry,* and *experienced depression.*

In the preceding sentence, three items make up the series. However, the first two items are adjectives (*exhausted* and *hungry*), whereas the last one is a verb plus a noun (*experienced depression*).

Words that follow correlative conjunctions (*either...or, neither...nor, both...and, not only...but also*) should also be parallel:

Faulty Parallelism	Every road into the city is either *jammed* or *is closed* for repairs.

Here, *either* is followed by an adjective (*jammed*), but *or* is followed by a verb (*is*).

HOW TO CORRECT FAULTY PARALLELISM

To correct faulty parallelism, place words in a pair or in a series in the same grammatical structure:

Faulty Parallelism	*After the car baked in the sun for hours, the steering wheel was hot, the seats were sticky, and there was stuffiness in the air.*
Correct	After the car baked in the sun for hours, the steering wheel was hot, the seats were sticky, and the air was stuffy.
or	
Correct	After the car baked in the sun for hours, the steering wheel was hot, the seats sticky, and the air stuffy.
Faulty Parallelism	*Parents are either too permissive or they are too strict.*
Correct	Parents are either too permissive or too strict.
or	
Correct	Parents either are too permissive or are too strict.
or	
Correct	Either parents are too permissive, or they are too strict.

Verbs

Problems with Subject-Verb Agreement

S-V
agr

A **verb** should match its subject in number. If the subject is singular (one person, place, or thing), the verb should have a singular form. If the subject is plural (two or more persons, places, or things), the verb should have a plural form.

HOW TO CORRECT FAULTY SUBJECT-VERB AGREEMENT

To deal with each of the following six problems, you must determine the *verb's subject* and make sure the *verb agrees with it*, rather than with some other word in the sentence.

1. When there are two or more subjects: When the word *and* joins two or more subjects in a sentence, use a plural verb.

Correct	A beautiful maple *and* a straggly oak *flank* [not *flanks*] the building.

However, when the word *or* joins the subjects, use a singular verb:

Correct	A maple *or* an oak *offers* [not *offer*] good shade in the summer.

2. When the subject and verb are separated by a prepositional phrase: Be sure to match the verb to its subject—not to a word in a prepositional phrase that comes between the subject and the verb.

Correct

> *One* of the desserts *was* [not *were*] too sweet even for me.
>
> To pass inspection, the *plumbing* in all the apartments *needs* [not *need*] to be repaired.

3. When the words *either...or* or *neither...nor* connect subjects: When *either...or* or *neither...nor* link two subjects, use the verb form (singular or plural) that agrees with the subject *closer* to the verb.

Correct

> *Neither* the students *nor* the *professor likes* [not *like*] the textbook.
>
> *Neither* the professor *nor* the *students like* [not *likes*] the textbook.

4. When the subject is an indefinite pronoun: Some **indefinite pronouns** (such as *anyone, anything, each, either, every, everyone, everybody, everything, neither,* and *nobody*) take a *singular verb*—whether they act as a pronoun subject (as in the first sentence that follows) or as an adjective in front of a noun subject (as in the second sentence).

Correct

> *Neither* of the libraries *was* [not *were*] open.
>
> *Neither* library *was* [not *were*] open.

Other indefinite pronouns (such as *all, any, most, none,* and *some*) take a *singular or a plural verb,* depending on whether they refer to one thing or to a number of things. In the following sentence, *some* refers to a single tutoring session, so the verb is singular:

Correct   The student reported that only *some* of her tutoring *session was* helpful.

In this next sentence, however, *some* refers to multiple sessions, so the verb is plural:

Correct   The student reported that only *some* of her tutoring *sessions were* helpful.

5. When there is a group subject: When the subject of a sentence refers to a group acting in unison, or as a unit, use a singular verb.

Correct   The debate *club* is [not *are*] on a winning streak.

However, when the subject is a group whose members are acting individually, rather than as a unit, use a plural verb:

Correct   The *debate club argue* [not *argues*] among themselves constantly.

If, in this case, the plural verb sounds awkward, reword the sentence so that the group's individual members are referred to directly:

Correct   The debate club *members argue* among themselves constantly.

6. When the verb comes before the subject: Words such as *here, there, how, what, when, where, which, who,* and *why,* as well as *prepositional phrases,* often invert normal sentence order, causing the verb to precede the subject. In such cases, look ahead for the subject and make sure it and the verb agree in number.

Correct

> There *is* [not *are*] always a long *line* of students at the library's duplicating machine.
> What *are* [not *is*] the *reasons* for consumers' complaints about the car?
> Near the lifeguard station, looking for us everywhere, *were* [not *was*] our *parents.*

Problems with Verb Tense

vt

A **verb's tense** indicates the time—*past, present,* or *future*—of an event. Here we show how to correct two common problems with verb tense: (1) inappropriate shifts in tense, and (2) faulty use of past tense.

HOW TO CORRECT INAPPROPRIATE SHIFTS IN VERB TENSE
The sentence that follows switches from the past tense (*bought*) to the present (*breaks*), even though both events took place in the same (past) period of time. To avoid such inappropriate shifts, *use the same verb tense to relate all events occurring in the same time period*:

Inappropriate Tense Shift	The township *bought* a powerful new lawn mower, which *breaks* down after two weeks.
Correct	The township *bought* a powerful new lawn mower, which *broke* down after two weeks.

When writing, decide which verb tense will be most effective; then use that tense throughout—unless you need to change tenses to indicate a different time period.

Much of the writing you do in college will use the past tense:

> Changes in the tax law *created* chaos for accounting firms.

However, when writing about literature, you generally use the present tense:

> Mark Twain *examines* the conflict between humane impulses and society's prejudices.

HOW TO CORRECT FAULTY USE OF PAST TENSE
The following sentence uses the **simple past tense** (*finished, burst*) for both verbs, even though one event ("the plane finished rolling down the runway") *preceded* the other (the plane "burst into flames"). To distinguish one past event from an earlier one, use the **past perfect tense** ("*had* washed," "*had* gone," "*had* finished") for the earlier event:

| Faulty Past Tense | The plane already *finished* rolling down the runway when it *burst* into flames. |
| Correct | The plane *had* already *finished* [past perfect] rolling down the runway when it *burst* [simple past] into flames. |

Pronouns

Problems with Pronoun Use

Pronouns are words that take the place of nouns (persons, places, things, and concepts). As the following sentences show, pronouns keep you from repeating words unnecessarily:

> After I fertilized the plant, *it* began to flourish. [*it* takes the place of *plant*]

> When the students went to register *their* complaint, *they* were told to come back later. [*their* and *they* replace *students*]

When using pronouns, you need to be careful not to run into problems with case, agreement, and reference.

Pronoun Case

A pronoun's correct form, or **case**, depends on the way the pronoun is used in the sentence. A pronoun acting as a *subject* requires the **nominative case**. One acting as a *direct object* (receiving a verb's action), an *indirect object* (indicating to or for whom the action is performed), or an *object of a preposition* (following a preposition such as *at, near,* or *to*) requires the **objective case**. A pronoun indicating *possession* takes the **possessive case**.

Nominative Case	Objective Case	Possessive Case	
I	me	my	mine
we	us	our	ours
you	you	your	yours
he	him	his	his
she	her	her	hers
it	it	its	its
they	them	their	theirs
who	whom	whose	

HOW TO CORRECT FAULTY PRONOUN CASE

To correct any of these five problems, *determine whether the pronoun is used as object or subject; then put the pronoun in the appropriate case.*

1. Pronoun pairs or a pronoun and a noun: Use the nominative case when two pronouns act as subjects.

Correct   *He* and *I* [not *Him* and *me*] are different ages, but we have several traits in common.

Also use the nominative case when a pronoun and noun serve as subjects:

Correct   *She* [not *Her*] and *several transfer students* enrolled in the new course.

     Use the objective case when a pronoun pair acts as direct object, indirect object, or object of a preposition:

Correct (Direct Objects)   My parents sent *her* [not *she*] and *me* [not *I*] to the store to buy decorations.

Correct (Indirect Objects)   The committee presented *him* [not *he*] and *me* [not *I*] with the award.

Similarly, use the objective case when a pronoun and noun function as direct object, indirect object, or object of a preposition:

Correct (Object of Preposition)   The doctor gave the pills to the three other patients and *me* [not *I*].

     A hint: When a pronoun is paired with another pronoun or with a noun and you're not sure which case to use, imagine the sentence with only one pronoun. For example, perhaps you wonder whether it's correct to write, "The student senate commended my roommates and *I* for our actions." "The student senate commended *I*" doesn't sound right, so you know *me* is the correct form.

2. A pronoun-noun pair acting together as subject or object: If a pronoun-noun pair acts as the subject, use the nominative case.

Correct   *We* [not *Us*] *dorm residents* plan to protest the ruling.

If the pronoun-noun pair serves as an object, use the objective case:

Correct   The dropout rate among *us* [not *we*] *commuting students* is high.

3. Pronouns following forms of the verb *to be*:   In formal English, use the nominative case in constructions like the following.

Correct

It is *I* [not *me*].   This is *she* [not *her*].

In such constructions, the objective case (*me* and *her*, for example) is so common that the formally correct nominative case may sound strange. However, before using the more colloquial objective case, check with your instructor to make sure such informality will be acceptable.

4. Pronouns following the comparative *than*: Comparisons using the word *than* tend to imply, rather than state directly, the sentence's final word (placed in brackets in the following sentence).

> The other employees are more willing to negotiate *than we* [are].

To determine the appropriate case for the pronoun in a sentence with a *than* comparison, simply add the implied word. For example, maybe you're not sure whether *we* or *us* is correct in the preceding sentence. As soon as you supply the implied word (*are*), it becomes clear that *we*, not *us*, is correct.

5. *Who* and *whom*: When, as in the first example that follows, a pronoun acts as the subject of a sentence or clause, use *who* (the nominative case). When, as in the second example, the pronoun acts as the object of a verb or preposition, use *whom* (the objective case). You can test whether *who* or *whom* is correct by answering the question stated or implied in the *who/whom* portion of the sentence. The pronoun that answers *who/whom* will reveal which case to use.

> "*Who/Whom* did you meet at the jazz festival"? → "I met *him* at the festival." → Since *him* is the objective case, use *whom*.

> "The employees want to know *who/whom* will supervise the project." → "*She* will supervise the project." → Since *she* is the nominative case, use *who*.

Pronoun Agreement

A pronoun must **agree in number** with its **antecedent**—the noun or pronoun it replaces or refers to. If the antecedent is singular, the pronoun must be singular. If the antecedent is plural, the pronoun must be plural.

HOW TO CORRECT FAULTY PRONOUN AGREEMENT
To deal with these four problems, either *change the pronoun so it agrees in number and person with its antecedent* or *change the noun to agree with the pronoun you have used*.

1. Compound subject: A compound subject (two or more nouns joined by *and*) requires plural pronouns.

Correct	Both the oak *tree* and the rose *bush* had trouble regaining *their* strength after the storm.

However, when the nouns are joined by *or* or *nor*, whichever noun is closer to the verb determines whether the pronoun should be singular or plural:

Faulty Pronoun Agreement	Neither the oak tree nor the rose *bushes* regained *its* strength after the storm.
Correct	Neither the oak tree nor the rose *bushes* regained *their* strength after the storm.
Correct	Neither the rose bushes nor the oak *tree* regained *its* strength after the storm.

2. Collective nouns: Collective nouns represent a collection of people or things. Some examples are *company, university, team,* and *committee.* If the collective noun refers to a group or entity that acts as one unit, use the singular pronoun.

Faulty Pronoun Agreement	The *band* showed *their* appreciation by playing several encores.
Correct	The *band* showed *its* appreciation by playing several encores.

If, in this case, the singular pronoun form sounds awkward, simply make the antecedent plural. Then use the plural pronoun:

Correct   The band *members* showed *their* appreciation by playing several encores.

When the collective noun refers to members of a group who act individually, use a plural pronoun:

Correct   *The band* disagreed among *themselves* about the songs to be played.

3. Indefinite pronouns: Here is a list of singular indefinite pronouns.

Indefinite Pronoun	Possessive Form		Reflexive Form
anybody	his, her	his, hers	himself, herself
everybody	his, her	his, hers	himself, herself
nobody	his, her	his, hers	himself, herself
somebody	his, her	his, hers	himself, herself
anyone	his, her	his, hers	himself, herself
everyone	his, her	his, hers	himself, herself
no one	his, her	his, hers	himself, herself
someone	his, her	his, hers	himself, herself
either	his, her	his, hers	himself, herself
neither	his, her	his, hers	himself, herself
each	his, her	his, hers	himself, herself
one	one's		oneself

In everyday speech, we often use plural pronouns (*their* and *themselves*) because such pronouns cause us to picture more than one person. For example, we may say, "*Everyone* should bring *their* own computer disks." In formal writing, though, these indefinite pronouns are considered singular and thus take singular pronouns:

Correct
  Each of the buildings had *its* [not *their*] lobby redecorated.
  Neither of the ballerinas was pleased with *her* [not *their*] performance.

Using the singular form with indefinite pronouns may mean that you find yourself in the awkward situation of having to choose between *his* or *her* or between *himself* and *herself*. As a result, you may end up writing sentences that exclude either males or females: "Everybody in the mall seemed lost in *his* own thoughts." (Surely some of the shoppers were female.) To avoid this problem, you may make the antecedent plural and use the plural pronoun:

> The *shoppers* in the mall seemed lost in *their* own thoughts.

4. A shift in person: Within a sentence, pronouns shouldn't disrupt pronoun-antecedent agreement by shifting person (point of view).

Faulty Pronoun Agreement
> To drop a course, *students* [third person] should go to the registrar's office, where *you* [second person] obtain a course-change card.

Such shifts are most often from the third or first person to the second person (*you*). In the preceding example, *you* should be *they*.

Pronoun Reference

Besides agreeing with its antecedent in number and person, a pronoun must have a *clear antecedent*. A sentence that lacks clear **pronoun reference** is vague and ambiguous.

pro
ref

HOW TO CORRECT UNCLEAR PRONOUN REFERENCE
To make sure that each pronoun has an unmistakable antecedent, use the four strategies that follow.

1. Leave no ambiguity about the noun to which a pronoun refers:

Unclear Antecedent	The newcomer battled the longtime champion for the tennis prize. In the end, she won. [Who won? The newcomer or the longtime champion?]
Correct	The newcomer battled the longtime champion for the tennis prize. In the end, *the newcomer* won.

2. Replace a pronoun that lacks an antecedent with the appropriate noun:

Omitted Antecedent	In his talk on child abuse, the caseworker pointed out the number of *them* mistreated by daycare employees. [*Them* is meant to refer to *children*, but this word doesn't appear in the sentence.]
Correct	In his talk on child abuse, the caseworker pointed out the number of *children* mistreated by daycare employees.

3. Make sure a pronoun doesn't refer to the possessive form of a noun or to an adjective:

Omitted Antecedent	In *journalists' articles,* they often quote unidentified sources. [*They* refers to *journalists,* which is in the possessive case.]
Correct	*Journalists* often quote unidentified sources in *their* articles.

4. **Place pronouns near their antecedents:**

Unclear Antecedent	The *dancers*, performing almost daily, traveled by bus and train. The trip spanned several states. *They* returned exhausted and out of debt.
Correct	Performing almost daily, traveling by bus and train on a trip that spanned several states, the *dancers* returned exhausted. *They* were also out of debt.

Modifiers

Problems with Modification
Misplaced and Ambiguous Modifiers

A **modifier** is a word or group of words that describes something else. Sometimes sentences are written in such a way that modifiers are **misplaced** or **ambiguous**. Here are examples of misplaced and ambiguous modifiers:

Misplaced Modifier	Television stations carried the story of the disastrous fire *in every part of the nation*. [The fire was in every part of the nation?]
Ambiguous Modifier	Singers who don't warm up *gradually* lose their voices. [What does the sentence mean: that singers who don't warm up will lose their voices gradually or that singers who don't gradually warm up will lose their voices?]

HOW TO CORRECT MISPLACED OR AMBIGUOUS MODIFIERS
Here are two strategies for correcting misplaced or ambiguous modifiers.

1. **Place the modifier next to the word(s) it describes:**

Misplaced Modifier	We scanned the menu *with hungry eyes*. [The menu had hungry eyes?]
Correct	With hungry eyes, we scanned the menu.
Misplaced Modifier	They *only* studied a few minutes for the exam. [Doesn't the word *only* describe *a few minutes*, not *studied?*]
Correct	They studied *only* a few minutes for the exam.

2. **Rewrite the sentence to eliminate ambiguity:**

Ambiguous Modifier	Giving money *frequently* relieves people's guilt about living well.

Writing the sentence this way could mean *either* that the frequent giving of money relieves guilt *or* that giving money relieves guilt frequently. Moving the modifier to the front of the sentence conveys the first meaning.

mm

Frequently, giving money relieves people's guilt about living well.

The second meaning, however, can be conveyed only by rewriting the sentence:

Giving money *on a frequent basis* relieves people's guilt about living well.

Dangling Modifiers

An introductory modifier must modify the subject of the sentence. If it doesn't, the result is a **dangling modifier**. Here's an example of a dangling modifier:

Dangling Modifier   *Driving along the highway,* the blinding sun obscured our view of the oncoming car. [The sentence says that the sun was driving along the highway.]

dg1

HOW TO CORRECT DANGLING MODIFIERS

To eliminate a dangling modifier, you may *rewrite the sentence by adding to the modifying phrase the word being described* (as in the first corrected example that follows). Or you may *rewrite the sentence so that the word being modified becomes the sentence's subject* (as in the second corrected example):

Dangling Modifier   *While relaxing in my backyard hammock,* a neighbor's basketball hit me on the head. [The basketball was relaxing in the backyard?]

Correct   While *I* was relaxing in my backyard hammock, a neighbor's basketball hit me on the head.

or

Correct   While relaxing in my backyard hammock, *I* was hit on the head by my neighbor's basketball.

Punctuation

p

Correct **punctuation** is no trivial matter. Notice how a single comma alters the meaning of this sentence:

Their uncle would be the only visitor they feared.

Their uncle would be the only visitor, they feared.

The first sentence suggests that the uncle's visit is a source of anxiety; the second sentence suggests that the uncle is, unfortunately, the only person to pay a visit. So choose your punctuation carefully. Skillful punctuation helps you get your message across; careless punctuation can undermine your credibility and spoil an otherwise effective piece of writing.

Period (.)

The most frequent misuse of the **period** is at the end of a *fragment*—a word or group of words that doesn't constitute a full sentence, only part of one. The correct uses of the period are outlined here.

1. At the end of full statements: A period correctly completes any full sentence not worded as a question or exclamation.

> The campus senators asked when the college administrators would approve the new plan.

Although the preceding sentence reports that a question was asked, the sentence itself is a statement. For this reason, it ends with a period, not with a question mark.

2. With some abbreviations: A period is also used to indicate a shortened form of a word–that is, an abbreviation.

> Prof. (Professor)   Dec. (December)   p.m.   (*post meridiem,* Latin phrase meaning "after noon")

When an abbreviation ends a sentence, only one period is needed at the sentence's close:

> They didn't place the order until 3 a.m.

Some abbreviations, though, have no period at all. These include the abbreviated titles of organizations and government agencies, as well as the official U.S. Postal Service abbreviations for state names:

> FDA (Food and Drug Administration)   ME (Maine)

In addition, it is becoming increasingly acceptable to omit the periods in frequently used abbreviations—for example, *mph* (miles per hour). If you're in doubt whether to include a period in an abbreviation, consult a recent dictionary. Many dictionaries have a separate section that lists abbreviations.

3. In decimal numbers: A period precedes the fractional portion of a decimal number.

> 5.38 (five and thirty-eight hundredths)

Because money is counted according to the decimal system, a period occurs between dollars and cents:

> $10.35

Question Mark (?)

1. At the end of direct questions: Just as a period concludes a statement, a **question mark** concludes a question.

> The panelists debated the question "Should drugs be legalized?"

> Did the consultants name their report "The Recycling Crisis"**?**

Notice that in the first example above, the actual question occurs only within the quotation marks. Therefore, the question mark is placed *before* the final quotation marks (and no final period is necessary). In the second example, though, the whole sentence is a question, so the question mark goes *after* the final quotation marks.

2. In parentheses, following an item of questionable accuracy: Whenever you're unable to confirm the accuracy of a name, date, or other item, indicate your uncertainty by following the item with a question mark enclosed in parentheses.

> The fraud, begun in 1977 **(?)**, was discovered only this year.

Exclamation Point (!)

At the end of emphatic sentences: An **exclamation point** is placed at the end of a sentence to indicate strong emotion.

> That's the worst meal I've ever eaten!

Use exclamation points sparingly; otherwise, they lose their effectiveness.

Comma (,)

The **comma** is so frequent in writing that mastering its use is essential. By dividing a sentence into its parts, commas clarify meaning. Compare the following:

> As soon as we had won the contest was declared illegal.

> As soon as we had won, the contest was declared illegal.

The comma shows the reader where to pause to make sense of the sentence. The following rules discuss the correct use of the comma.

1. Between sentences joined by a coordinating conjunction: When joining two complete sentences with a coordinating conjunction (*and, but, for, nor, or, so, yet*), place a comma *before* the coordinating conjunction.

> My father loves dining out, *but* he is fussy about food.

It's permissible to omit the comma, though, if the two complete sentences are very short:

> They lied *yet* they won the case.

☑ Two Cautions

☐ Don't use a comma when the coordinating conjunction serves as the link between two verbs or nouns of equal weight.

Incorrect   We *visit* the boardwalk, *and picnic* on the beach every summer. [you should delete the comma between the verbs]

☐ Don't use a comma when a coordinating conjunction links words or phrases that cannot stand alone as sentences:

Incorrect   Many people believe that herbal teas are medicinal, *and that drinking them will cure disease.* [delete the comma]

---

2. Between items in a series: Use a comma to separate *three or more* items in a series.

It was a long, lonely, frightening drive to the cabin.

Notice that in the preceding example a comma appears before the last item in the series, whether or not this last item is preceded by *and* or *or*. (Although journalists and popular writers often omit the last comma in a series, the inclusion of a comma is expected in most other writing.)

However, if each item in the series is joined by *and* or *or,* do not place commas between them:

We didn't applaud *or* support *or* encourage the protesters.

3. Between adjectives of equal weight: A comma can substitute for the word *and* between adjectives of *equal weight* that describe the same noun.

Collecting exotic, colorful plants is one of my grandparents' hobbies.

In this sentence, the adjectives *exotic* and *colorful* contribute equally to the description of the noun *plants.* To test whether two adjectives have equal weight, reverse them or imagine the word *and* between them. If the sentence sounds fine, the adjectives have equal weight; thus, there should be a comma between them.

☑ Caution

☐ Don't use a comma between adjectives of *unequal weight*:

Incorrect   We bought a new, American-made stereo.

☐ The fact that the stereo is *American-made* has more weight than the fact that it is *new.* Moreover, the sentence would sound strange if the adjectives were reversed or if *and* appeared between them. For these reasons, there should be no comma between *new* and *American-made.*

---

4. Setting off nonrestrictive word groups: When a word, phrase, or clause describes a noun but isn't crucial for identifying that noun, it is *set off* from the rest of the sentence with a comma. Such a word or group of words is considered **nonrestrictive**, or **nonessential**.

The professor asked the class to read Twain's *Pudd'nhead Wilson,* a novel both droll and dark.

Because *Pudd'nhead Wilson* identifies the novel sufficiently, the phrase *a novel both droll and dark* is nonrestrictive and, thus, set off with a comma. If the nonrestrictive phrase appears midsentence, it is preceded and followed by commas:

The professor asked the class to read Twain's *Pudd'nhead Wilson,* a novel both droll and dark, by the end of the week.

In the next sentence, however, the book's title is *not set off by a comma* because the word group making up the title is **restrictive**, or **essential**; that is, it is needed for identification (Twain wrote more than one novel):

The professor asked the class to read Twain's droll and dark novel *Pudd'nhead Wilson.*

5. Setting off words that precede the main body of the sentence: When introductory material precedes the sentence's main subject and verb, such material is usually followed by a comma.

Yes, I'll be happy to read the report.   *Like most children,* my little sister loves animals.

If, however, the introductory material is very brief, you may often omit the comma:

Surely everyone has an urge to see exotic places.

6. Setting off words that follow the main body of the sentence: Material attached to the end of a sentence—after the main subject and verb—is preceded by a comma.

Many people think a walk is a waste of time, *like napping or daydreaming.*

7. Setting off interrupting words and phrases: Some words and phrases inserted into the body of a sentence can be removed without significant loss of meaning. Such *interrupting* elements are preceded and followed by commas when they occur midsentence.

I told him, *when he mentioned the accident,* my version of what had happened.

The snowfall was heavy; classes, *however,* were held as usual.

☑ **Caution**

☐ Note that a *pair of commas* must be used to set off interrupting words or phrases that occur midsentence. A single comma is *not* enough to set off interrupting elements:

Incorrect   The high school reunion, scheduled for Memorial Day weekend should be well attended. [comma needed after *weekend*]

Incorrect   The autumn day was surprisingly warm; we therefore, decided to go on a picnic. [comma needed before *therefore*]

☐ In the last sentence, the transitional adverb *therefore* should be flanked by commas because it occurs *within* an independent clause. But when a transitional adverb comes *between* two independent clauses, it is preceded by a semicolon and followed by a comma.

---

8. Setting off words in direct address: Use a comma before and/or after the name of a person or group being addressed directly:

Ladies and gentlemen, the meeting is about to begin.

9. Between a short quotation and the phrase that indicates the quotation's source: Use a comma between a short quotation and a reference to its source or speaker:

My roommate remarked, "You remind me of a hungry bulldog."

10. Between the elements of a date or place: Use a comma to separate the non-numerical portions of a mailing address, as well as the numbers in a date:

> The witness testified that the package was delivered to 102 Glendale Road, Kirkwood, New Jersey 08043, on January 23, 2014.

Also, place a comma after the year if the date appears before the end of the sentence:

> They were married on June 28, 1974, in New York City.

When you reverse the day and month in a date or give only the month and year or the month and day, do not use commas. Also, don't put a comma between a state and a ZIP code:

February 14, 2018	14 February 2018	February 2018
New York, NY 10022		

Semicolon (;)

1. Between independent clauses closely related in meaning: You may connect two independent clauses with a **semicolon** rather than writing them as separate sentences. When you do, though, the clauses should be closely related in meaning. They might, for example, *reinforce* each other.

> Making spaghetti sauce is easy; most people can do it after only a few tries.

Or the clauses might *contrast* with each other:

> Many homebuyers harbor suspicious feelings about the real estate industry; most realtors, however, are honest and law-abiding.

Use of the semicolon is especially common when the *clauses* are *short*:

> Smile when you are introduced; nod or bow slightly to acknowledge applause; wait for silence; pause a second; then begin your speech.

You may also use a semicolon (instead of a period) between independent clauses linked by *transitions* (like *then* and *next*) or by *transitional adverbs* (such as *moreover* and *however*):

> We continually lost track of our sales; *finally,* a friend showed us a good accounting system.

Note that when the second independent clause starts with a transitional expression, a comma is placed *after* the transition. However, if a comma is placed *before* the transition, an error called a *comma splice* results.

2. Between items in a series, when any of the items contains a comma: When individual items in a series have internal commas, another form of punctuation is needed to signal clearly where one item ends and another begins. For this purpose, use the semicolon.

After dinner, we had to choose between seeing a movie classic, like *Casablanca, Rear Window,* or *It's a Wonderful Life*; playing Clue, Scrabble, or Monopoly; or working out.

3. Before coordinating conjunctions used to join independent clauses, when any of the clauses contains a comma: Ordinarily, independent clauses joined by a coordinating conjunction (*and, but, for, nor, or, so, yet*) have a comma, not a semicolon, between them. However, when any such clause has internal commas, a semicolon is needed between the clauses.

> The mist settled in the valley, hiding the fields, the foliage, and the farms; and the pleasant road became a menace.

Colon (:)

1. To introduce an illustrative statement or list of examples: Use a colon to introduce lengthy illustrative material—either a full statement or a number of examples—whenever that material is preceded by a full sentence.

> In the spring, the city has a special magic: Street musicians, jugglers, and ethnic festivals enthrall tourists and residents alike.

As the first example shows, when the material following the colon can stand alone as a complete sentence, it begins with a capital letter (*Street*). Otherwise, the material after the colon starts with a lowercase letter (*my*).

2. To introduce a long quotation: Use a colon when a complete sentence introduces a long quotation (five or more lines) that is set off in block (indented) form without quotation marks.

> The witness to the accident told the police:
>
> I was walking to my car in the parking lot when I glanced over at the other side of the street. I saw the traffic light turn yellow, and a silver convertible started to slow down. Just then, a red station wagon came racing down the street. When the convertible stopped for the light, the station wagon kept going—right into the convertible's rear fender.

3. After the opening of a business letter: Follow the opening of a business letter with a colon.

> Dear Ms. Goldwin:

Use a comma, however, in the salutation of a personal letter.

> Dear Gina,

4. Between parts of certain conventional notations: A number of standard notations include colons. One example is time notation, with hours and minutes separated by a colon.

> 4:52 p.m.

In a ratio, a colon substitutes for the word *to*:

> By a ratio of 3:2, Americans prefer Glocko cleanser.

In a reference to the Bible, the colon separates chapter and verse numbers:

> Genesis 2:14

Titles and subtitles (of books, journal articles, short stories, works of art, films, and so on) are also separated by a colon:

> *Election Handbook: A Participant's Guide*

Quotation Marks (" ")

1. Direct quotations: A *direct quotation* reproduces exactly the wording, punctuation, and spelling of the source. It is also enclosed in *double* **quotation marks**.

> "Youngsters in elementary school should learn the importance of budgeting money," the psychologist said.

A quotation within a quotation is enclosed in *single* (' ') *quotation marks*.

> The psychologist said, "It was gratifying when my children told me, 'We're glad you taught us how to spend money sensibly.'"

☑ Caution

Indirect Quotations

☐ *Indirect quotations*—those referred to or paraphrased rather than reproduced word for word—*don't* get quotation marks:

> **Correct**   The psychologist said that even young children should be taught how to manage money wisely.

☐ In the preceding sentence, the word *that* is used to introduce an indirect quotation. There is *no comma* before or after *that* in this case.

Use a comma between a short quotation and an identifying phrase like *they commented* or *he said*. Such phrases may be placed before, after, or within the quotation:

> *She argued,* "They won't reject the plan."

> "They won't reject the plan," *she argued,* "if they understand its purpose."

When, as in the last example, the identifier interrupts the quotation midsentence, commas flank both sides of the identifier. But if the identifier comes between two quoted sentences, it is followed by a period:

> "They won't reject the plan," *she argued.* "They understand its purpose."

☑ **Caution**

More on Punctuating Direct Quotations:

☐ Place a period or comma *inside* the closing quotation marks:

Correct "You know what you meant to say," the instructor remarked, "but the reader doesn't."

☐ Place a colon or semicolon *outside* the closing quotation marks:

Correct The article stated, "Rice is the major foodstuff of all Asian peoples"; in particular, the Japanese eat ten times more rice than Americans.

☐ Place question marks and exclamation points according to their context. If a quotation is itself a question or exclamation, the question mark or exclamation point goes *inside* the closing quotation marks. No other end punctuation is used:

Correct

"Who's responsible for this decision?" the chief executive demanded.
Each department head responded, "Not me!"

☐ No comma is used when an identifying phrase follows a quoted question or exclamation. If the entire sentence, not just the quotation, is a question or an exclamation, the question or exclamation mark goes *outside* the quotation marks, at the end of the entire sentence:

Correct

Who taught you to ask for things by saying "Gimme"?

☐ Use no punctuation other than quotation marks when a quotation is blended (with or without the word *that*) into the rest of a sentence:

Correct

People who believe that "rules are made to be broken" only substitute their own rules.

Capitalization in Direct Quotations

☐ Start a quotation with a capital letter if it is a full sentence:

Correct

The author admitted, "The classy-sounding pseudonym was a marketing strategy."

☐ Start a quotation with a lowercase letter if it is not a complete sentence, or if it is blended (with or without the word *that*) into the rest of your sentence:

Correct

Using a "classy-sounding pseudonym" was, the author admitted, "a marketing strategy."

---

2. Titles of short works: Put quotation marks around the titles of short works—book chapters, poems, stories, articles, editorials, essays, individual episodes of a television or radio program—that are part of a larger work or series.

Kenneth Koch's poem "Mending Sump" parodies Robert Frost's "Mending Wall."

Titles of longer works are italicized.

3. Calling attention to a word's use: To focus attention on a particular word or term, you may enclose it in quotation marks.

> People frequently say "between" when they should say "among."

4. Quotation marks also enclose words being used humorously or ironically:

> To celebrate their victory, the team members indulged in such "adult" behavior as pouring champagne over one another's heads.

Ellipsis (…)

An **ellipsis**, consisting of three spaced periods (…), indicates that *words have been omitted from quoted material*. To use the ellipsis correctly, follow the guidelines presented here.

1. When to use the ellipsis: You may use an ellipsis to shorten a quotation, as long as you don't distort its meaning.

Original

> The judge commented, "It won't surprise you to learn that this has been the most disturbing and the most draining case I have tried in all my years on the bench."

With Ellipsis

> The judge commented, "It won't surprise you to learn that this has been the most disturbing…case I have tried in all my years on the bench."

When you drop words from the end of a sentence or omit an entire sentence, the period that ends the sentence appears in its usual place, followed by the three spaced periods that signal the omission:

> The judge commented, "It won't surprise you to learn that this has been the most disturbing and the most draining case I have tried…."

Notice that in this case, there is no space between the last word in the sentence and the sentence's period.

2. When *not* to use the ellipsis: When you omit words from the beginning of a quotation, do not use an ellipsis; just begin your quotation at the point you've selected.

> The judge commented, "This has been the most disturbing and the most draining case I have tried in all my years on the bench."

Apostrophe (')

1. In place of omitted letters: In standard contractions, an **apostrophe** replaces any omitted letters.

> can't, don't, I'm, it's, she's, we've

Apostrophes also replace any letters dropped for the purpose of reproducing casual speech or slang:

> "Keep singin' an' marchin'!" he shouted.

2. **To indicate possession:**   To show the possessive form of most *singular nouns,* add *'s:*

> The singer**'s** debut was a disaster. The boss**'s** office was small and poorly lit.

For *plural nouns* ending in *s,* add only an apostrophe to show possession:

> Students**'** grades improved after computer-assisted instruction.

Plural nouns that do *not* end in *s* need both an apostrophe and an *s* to show possession:

> The children**'s** school was set on fire.

To show *joint possession* (two or more owners of the same thing), make only the last noun possessive:

> Lubin and Wachinsky**'s** firm handled the defense.

To show *individual possession* of more than one thing, make each noun possessive:

> The girl**'s** and the boy**'s** parents urged them to date other people.

☑ **Caution**

☐ The possessive forms of personal pronouns do *not* include an apostrophe. Here are the correct forms:

mine, yours, his, hers, its, ours, theirs

☐ Note that *its* (*without* an apostrophe) is the *possessive* form of *it*:

Correct

The theater closed *its* [not *it's*] doors last week.

☐ The word *it's* means "it is" or "it has" (the apostrophe takes the place of the omitted letters):

Correct

It's [meaning "it is"] cold today.

It's [meaning "it has"] been a difficult time for us.

☐ Similarly, *whose* (*without* an apostrophe) is the possessive form of *who*:

Correct

Whose [not *who's*] coat is on the table?

☐ The word *who's* means "who is" or "who has" (the apostrophe takes the place of the omitted letters):

Correct

We wonder *who's* [meaning "who is"] going to take her place.

They want to know *who's* [meaning "who has"] been tabulating the results.

Amounts (of time, money, weight, and so on) should be written in possessive form when appropriate:

> Employees can accumulate a maximum of a month's sick leave.

3. To indicate some plurals: When a letter, symbol, or word treated as a word is made plural, an apostrophe often precedes the final *s*.

> I got mostly *C*'s in my first semester of college.

> He uses too many *and*'s to connect one thought to another.

However, common abbreviations such as *DVR*, *ESP*, and *SAT* don't take the apostrophe in the plural:

> The local television station reported that residents sighted three *UFO*s last summer.

When you refer to a decade, you may omit the apostrophe:

> The 1960s were turbulent and exciting.

An apostrophe is required only to replace omitted numerals that indicate the century:

> The '60s were turbulent and exciting.

☑ Caution

☐ Don't use an apostrophe when forming the simple plural of a noun:

Incorrect The plant's (or plants') need to be watered. [delete apostrophe]
Correct The plants need to be watered.

☐ Don't use an apostrophe when forming the third-person singular form of the verb:

Incorrect The television blare's all day in many homes.
Correct The television blares all day in many homes.

Parentheses ( )

Parentheses enclose subordinate but related ideas, facts, or comments—items that would unnecessarily interrupt the sentence if set off by commas. A parenthetic remark may be located anywhere in a sentence except at the beginning, but it should immediately follow the item to which it refers. The presence of parentheses does not otherwise affect a sentence's punctuation. Here are some guidelines to follow when using parentheses.

1. A parenthetic sentence between two other sentences or at the end of a paragraph: If you place a parenthetic sentence between two other sentences or at the end of a paragraph, simply write the parenthetic sentence as you normally would; then enclose it in parentheses. The sentence in parentheses should begin with a capital letter and end with a period or other end punctuation.

> Writing home from summer camp is a chore most youngsters avoid. (Some camps have children write home once a week.) Most parents, though, eagerly await letters from their kids.

2. At the end of a sentence: Material that extends or illustrates a sentence should be inserted in parentheses at the end of the sentence *before* the closing period. Such parenthetic material shouldn't start with a capital letter. Also, the parenthetic material doesn't have its own period.

> It is a cruel irony that everything I am allergic to is wonderful (like chocolate, roses, and dogs).

3. A parenthetic sentence inside another sentence: When parenthetic material that can stand alone as a full statement occurs within another sentence, the parenthetic material should *not* begin with a capital letter or end with a period.

> Watering a garden the right way (yes, there's a wrong way) is important.

If, however, the parenthetic material is a question, do end it with a question mark:

> Watering a garden the right way (you didn't think there was a wrong way?) is important.

4. After a word that would be followed by a comma: When you insert a parenthetic comment after a word that would otherwise be followed by a comma, move the comma to the end of the parenthetic element.

Original	Without sufficient water, the trees started to lose their leaves in July.
Parenthetic	Without sufficient water (only half an inch the whole month), the trees started to lose their leaves in July.

5. Enclosing numbers or letters assigned to items in a series: Use parentheses to enclose the numbers or letters assigned to items in a series. The items in a series are followed by commas.

> Before making a drastic change in your life, you should (1) discuss it with friends, (2) seek the advice of people who have had a similar change, and (3) determine whether a less dramatic change would be sufficient.

6. Enclosing inserted dates and organizations' abbreviations: When you add information such as dates and abbreviations to an otherwise complete sentence, enclose this information in parentheses.

> Frank Lloyd Wright (1869–1959) was one of America's foremost architects.

Brackets [ ]

1. To clarify a quotation: When, for the purpose of clarification or correction, you insert your own words into a quotation, enclose them within **brackets**.

> "Research done at that laboratory [Sci-Tech] is suspect," the physician testified.

Use parentheses, not brackets, to insert a comment within your *own* sentence or paragraph.

2. To signal a linguistic irregularity within a quotation: Quotations sometimes contain linguistic irregularities—such as colloquialisms or errors in spelling, grammar, or usage. In such cases, you may want to follow the irregularity with the Latin term *sic* in brackets, thus indicating that the questionable word or expression appears exactly as used by the quoted writer or speaker.

> "None of the tenents [sic] complained about the building," the landlord wrote in a letter to the housing authority.

Note: When omitting words from a quotation, you should insert an ellipsis enclosed within brackets to indicate that *you*, rather than the original author, are inserting the ellipsis.

Hyphen (-)

A **hyphen** consists of one short line (and should not be confused with the dash).

1. To break a word: A word that is too long to fit at the end of a typed line may be divided between two syllables, with a hyphen indicating the break. (Check the dictionary if you're uncertain where the syllables begin and end.)

> Once a clear contest between good and evil, between right and wrong, television wrestling now features stereotype-defying and ambiguous protagonists.

Most word-processing programs automatically either break long words at the end of lines or move them to the next line (called "word wrapping").

2. To combine words into an adjective or noun: When you combine two or more words to form a new adjective or noun, use hyphens between the original words.

> The question is whether this country should maintain first-strike capability.

The only exception is a compound adjective that contains an adverb ending in *ly*. In this case, don't place a hyphen after the *ly*:

> The poorly constructed DVD player jammed within the week.

In a series of hyphenated compound adjectives or nouns all having the same final word, write that word only at the end of the series:

> First-, second-, and third-year students must take one semester of gym.

3. Between a combined number and word: Hyphenate a numeral combined with a word:

> The new car has a 2.6-liter engine.

4. After certain prefixes: Compound words beginning with *self* or *ex* take a hyphen after the prefix.

> My ex-roommate is self-employed as a computer consultant.

Words that without the hyphen would be misread as other words also take a hyphen.

> A growing number of young professionals live in co-ops.

5. To write certain numbers: Use a hyphen when writing most numbers composed of two words.

> The zoning ordinance outlines twenty-one restrictions.

Note, however, that two-word numbers such as *one hundred* and *two thousand* don't take a hyphen.

A hyphen is required when a fraction is used as a compound modifier:

> The class was almost one-half empty.

Dash (—)

A **dash** (—) is composed of two (or three) typed hyphens (- or —). Don't leave a space between the hyphens or between the words that precede or follow the dash. Many word processing programs will automatically convert two or three typed hyphens into a dash.

To highlight a thought or idea: A dash signals an *added* or *interrupting thought* and, unlike parentheses, highlights that thought. When the added thought occurs at the sentence's end, it is preceded by a single dash.

> The package finally arrived—badly damaged.

When the added thought occurs midsentence, it receives two dashes, one before the added thought and another after:

> The ambassador—after serving for more than two decades—suddenly resigned her post.

Mechanics

Capitalization

Always capitalize the pronoun *I* and the first word of a sentence. Following are other **capitalization** guidelines.

1. Proper names: Whether they appear in noun, adjective, or possessive form, proper names are always capitalized. **Proper names** include the following: names of individuals; countries, states, regions, and cities; political, racial, and religious groups; languages; institutions and organizations; days, months, and holidays; historical periods; product brand names; fully specified academic degrees (Master of Science in Chemistry); and particular academic courses. Here are some examples:

> *Representative O'Dwyer,* a *Democrat from the Midwest,* introduced several bills in *Congress* last *March.*

All *Buddhists* are vegetarians.

Do not capitalize the names of ideologies and philosophies, such as *communism* and *idealism* (unless the name is derived from that of an individual—for example, *Marxism*). Similarly, avoid capitalizing compass directions, unless the direction serves as the name of a region (the *West,* the *Northeast*) or is attached to the name of a conti-nent, country, or city (*North America, South Angola, West Philadelphia*).

Finally, don't capitalize the following: seasons; animal breeds (unless part of the name is derived from that of a place—such as *French poodle* and *Labrador retriever*); types of academic degrees (*bachelor's, master's, doctorate*); or academic subjects and areas (*sociology, mathematics*), unless they're part of a course title or department name (*Sociology 101, Mathematics Department*). Here are some more examples:

On one side of the Continental Divide, rivers flow *east;* on the other, they flow *west.*

In San Francisco, there is little temperature variation between *spring* and *summer.*

2. Titles of literary and other artistic works: When writing a title, capitalize the first word and all other words, except articles (*a, an, the*), conjunctions (*and, but*), and prepo-sitions (*on, to*) of fewer than five letters.

In *The Structure of Scientific Revolutions,* Thomas Kuhn discusses the way the sci-entific establishment resists innovation. However, Anna Stahl disputes Kuhn's argument in *The Controversy over Scientific Conservatism.*

3. Official and personal titles: Capitalize official and personal titles when they pre-cede a name or are used in place of the name of a specific person:

Only *Reverend* Zager could stretch a sermon to an hour and a half.

Weeks before Father's Day, the stores start featuring gifts for *Dad.*

Do not capitalize such titles otherwise:

The *reverend* encouraged the congregation to donate food and clothing to the poor.

His *dad* writes for the local paper.

Italics

ital

The following guidelines explain when to use **italics** (*slanted type*). Underlining is an acceptable substitute for italics when you are writing by hand.

1. Titles of individual works: Italicize the titles of works that are published individually—not as part of a magazine, anthology, or other collection. Such works are often lengthy—entire books, magazines, journals, newspapers, movies, television programs, musical recordings, plays, and so on. They may, however, also be works of visual art, such as paintings and sculptures. Here are some examples:

When I was a child, my favorite book was *At the Back of the North Wind.*

The movie critic panned *Friday the 13th, Part 83.*

However, titles of certain historical documents and major religious writings, such as the books of the Bible, are neither italicized nor enclosed in quotation marks, but important words begin with a capital letter:

Bhagavad Gita	the Koran	Exodus and Leviticus
the book of Genesis	Bill of Rights	Old Testament
the Bible	U.S. Constitution	Monroe Doctrine

2. Foreign terms: Foreign words not fully incorporated into mainstream English should be italicized.

> Before protesters knew what was happening, the legislation was a *fait accompli*.

3. For emphasis: Italicize words you wish to stress, but do so sparingly because too many italicized words actually weaken emphasis.

> The campaign staff will *never* allow the candidate to appear in an open forum.

4. Letters and numbers referred to as words: Italicize letters or numbers when they function as words.

> In the local high school, teachers give *A*'s and *B*'s only to outstanding students.

5. Calling attention to a word's use: To call attention to the way a word is being used, you may italicize it.

> Why use *conflagration* when a simple word like *fire* will do?

6. Vehicles of transportation: Italicize the names of ships, planes, trains, and space-craft.

> A design flaw led to the explosion of the space shuttle *Challenger*.

Numbers

num

1. When to use words: Generally, *words* instead of numerals are used for numbers that can be written out in *one* or *two words*. When written out, numbers between 21 and 99 (except round numbers) are hyphenated (*twenty-one; ninety-nine*). If the number requires *three or more words*, use *numerals*; a hyphenated number counts as one word. Also use words for any number that occurs at the start of a sentence.

> The store manager came up with *three* fresh ideas for attracting more customers.

> *Two hundred forty-eight* people were on the hijacked plane.

You may prefer to rephrase a sentence that begins with a long number, so that you can use numerals instead of words:

> The hijacked plane had *248* people on board.

2. When to use numerals: Numerals are generally used to indicate measurements.

> The office was approximately *10 feet, 8 inches* wide.

Dates, times, addresses, page numbers, decimals, and percentages are also usually given as numerals. When a date includes the day as well as the month and year, give only the numeral to identify the day (for example, write *March 4*, not *March 4th*; *May 2*, not *May 2nd*):

> The builder claims that the wood delivered on *August 3, 2013,* was defective.

Use numerals when a time reference contains *a.m.* or *p.m.* or specifies the minutes as well as the hour:

> We set the alarm for *5 a.m.* and left the house by *5:45*.

However, use words with *o'clock*:

> My roommate has trouble getting up before *eleven o'clock* in the morning.

In addresses, the house or building number is always given in numerals:

> Last weekend, I visited my childhood home at *80 Manemet Road*.

For a numbered street, use numerals unless the number is less than ten or the building and street numbers would be written next to each other—a potential source of confusion:

> The shelter moved from 890 East 47th Street to *56 Second Avenue*.

Always give page numbers as numerals. It's also standard to give percentages and decimal amounts in numerals:

> Sales increased *5%* last year.

> More than *2.5 million* boxes of oat bran were sold last year.

Abbreviations

ab

1. Personal and professional titles: The **abbreviations** for some personal titles appear *before* the person's name.

> *Dr.* Tony Michelin   *Ms.* Carla Schim

> Others come *after*:

> Houston J. Marshall, *Esq.*   Nora Rubin, *MD*

Professional titles such as *Professor, Senator,* and *Governor* may be abbreviated only before a full name:

> Prof. Eleanor Cross   Rep. George M. Dolby

2. Common terms and organizations: Use the standard initials for common terms and widely known organizations.

> DVR   FBI   NATO   CIA   URL   ESP   AT&T

Notice that these abbreviations do not include periods.

The first time you refer to a less familiar organization, give its full name, followed by the abbreviation in parentheses. Thereafter, you may refer to the organization with only the abbreviation. If the organization uses an ampersand (&) for *and* or abbreviations for terms such as *Incorporated* (Inc.) and *Company* (Co.), you may use them as well.

3. Time: Use the Latin abbreviations *a.m.* (*ante meridiem*) and *p.m.* (*post meridiem*) for time of day.

> They started work at *4 a.m.* and got home at *6:15 p.m.*

Use numerals with the abbreviations *AD* (*anno Domini*—"in the year of the Lord"), *BC* ("before Christ"), *CE* (the common era), and *BCE* (before the common era), unless you refer to centuries rather than specific years. In that case, write out the century before the abbreviation:

> The pottery was made around *AD 56,* but the tools date back to the *third century BC.*

Note that the year precedes *BC* (*684 BC*) but follows *AD* (*AD 2016*).

4. Latin terms: If you use the Latin abbreviations *i.e.* ("that is") and *e.g.* ("for example"), remember that they should be followed by a comma and used parenthetically.

> Employees are enthusiastic about recent trends in the business world (**e.g.,** the establishment of on-site daycare programs and fitness centers).

Whenever possible, however, replace these abbreviations with their English equivalents. In addition, try to avoid *etc.* ("and so on") by citing all examples you have in mind instead of leaving them up to the reader's imagination.

5. Names of regions: Except in addresses, don't abbreviate geographic regions.

> With a student rail pass, you can tour *Great Britain* [not *G.B.*] at discount rates.

Exceptions to this rule include *Washington, D.C.* and *U.S.* when it is used as a modifier (*U.S. policy,* for example).

In addresses, states' names are abbreviated according to the postal designations—with two capital letters and no periods:

> NY   RI   NJ

6. Units of measure: Don't abbreviate common units of measure.

> The bedroom was *15 feet, 9 1/2 inches* wide.

However, do abbreviate such technical units of measure as millimeters (*mm*) and revolutions per minute (*rpm*).

Acknowledgments

Adams, Charlene. "Professors Open Up About the Benefits of a College Degree" from *The Penn* newspaper. Reprinted by permission of the Student Cooperative Association, Inc.

Ahmed, Leila. "Reinventing the Veil." Reprinted by permission of the author.

Angier, Natalie. *The Canon: A Whirligig Tour of the Beautiful Basics of Science*. Houghton Mifflin Harcourt, 2008.

Appleton, Josie. "The Body Piercing Project" from *Spike Magazine*, 9 July 2003. Used by permission of Spiked US, Inc.

Barry, Lynda. "The Sanctuary of School" from the *New York Times*, January 5, 1992. Copyright © 1992 by Lynda Barry. All rights reserved. Used with permission.

Clemmons, Bella. "At Least for a While—Perhaps Forever."

Clinton, Hillary Rodham. "Remarks to the United Nations Fourth World Conference on Women Plenary Session." Courtesy of William J. Clinton Presidential Library.

Dunn, Laura Rose. "Letters from Dad." Used by permission.

Fletcher, Olivia. "'Tweet, Tweedle-lee-dee' (118 Characters Left)." Reproduced by permission of the author.

Fraser, Laura. "The Inner Corset" from *Losing It: America's Obsession with Weight and the Industry That Feeds on It*. Copyright 1997 by Laura Fraser. Used by permission of the author.

Garibaldi, Garry. "How The Schools Shortchange Boys" from *City Journal*, Summer 2006. Copyright 2006 The Manhattan Institute. Used with permission from *City Journal*.

Gispert, Catherine. "The Benchers, the Nappers, the Jellyfish, and the Musicians." Reproduced by permission of the author.

Grandin, Temple. "Seeing in Beautiful, Precise Pictures" by Temple Grandin. Copyright © 2006 by Temple Grandin. From the book *This I Believe: The Personal Philosophies of Remarkable Men and Women*, edited by Jay Allison and Dan Gediman. Copyright © 2006 by This I Believe, Inc. Reprinted by permission of Henry Holt and Company, LLC. All rights reserved.

Gumm, Lydia. "It's About Time, Augusta." Reproduced by permission of the author.

Horton, Alex. "On Getting By" from *Army of Dude* blog. Used by permission of the author.

Hymowitz, Kay S. "Tweens: Ten Going on Sixteen" from *City Journal*, Autumn 1998. Copyright 1998 The Manhattan Institute. Used by permission from *City Journal*.

Kelley, Lydia Eileish. "MMORPGs: Creating a Culture of Inclusion." Reproduced by permission of the author.

Kimmel, Michael S. "A War Against Boys" from *Dissent Magazine*. 2006. © Michael Kimmel, 2006. Used by permission of the author. All rights reserved.

Lorde, Audre. "The Fourth of July from Zami: A New Spelling of My Name" published by Crossing Press. Copyright © 1982, 2006 by Audre Lorde. Used herewith by permission of the Charlotte Sheedy Literary Agency.

Marlow, Michael and Sherzod Abdukadirov. "Government Intervention Will Not Solve Our Obesity Problem" from *U.S. News and World Report*, June 5, 2012. Used by permission of *U.S. News and World Report*.

McDonald, Cherokee Paul. "A View from the Bridge." © 1989 by Cherokee Paul Mcdonald. Used by permission of the author. First published in the *Florida Sun-Sentinel*. All rights reserved.

Mosley, Jared. "Don't Write Poetry—Be a Poet." Reproduced by permission of the author.

Nadell, Judith, Langan, John, Comodromos, Eliza A. *The Longman Reader*, 11th Ed., © 2016, pp. 71–73, 86–88. Reprinted and Electronically reproduced by permission of Pearson Education, Inc., New York, NY.

Norman, Blake. "Buying a Cross-Country Mountain Bike." Reproduced by permission of the author.

Quinlan, Anna. "Driving to the Funeral." Copyright 2007 by Anna Quindlen. First appeared in *Newsweek*, June 11, 2007. Used by permission of International Creative Management.

Rego, Caroline. "The Fine Art of Complaining." © Caroline Rego by Permission of Beth Johnson.

Riverbend. "Bloggers without Borders . . ." (October 22, 2007) from *Baghdad Burning* blog, http://riverbendblog.blogspot.com. Reprinted by permission of The Permissions Company, Inc., on behalf of The Feminist Press at the City University of New York, www.feministpress.org. All rights reserved.

Rosen, Larry. "Our Obsessive Relationship with Technology." Reproduced by permission of the author.

Shaw, Jane S. "Nature in the Suburbs," Heritage Foundation Background Paper 1724, February 18, 2004. Copyright © 2004. Used with permission.

Sherry, Mary. "In Praise of the 'F' Word" from *My Turn, Newsweek*, May 6, 1991. Used by permission of the author.

Suárez, Mario. From *Chicano Sketches: Short Stories by Mario Suárez* by Mario Suárez. © 2004 The Arizona Board of Regents. Reprinted by permission of the University of Arizona Press.

Sutherland, Amy. "What Shamu Taught Me About a Happy Marriage" from the *New York Times*, June 25, 2006. Used by permission of Amy K. Sutherland.

Tan, Amy. "Mother Tongue." Copyright © 1990 by Amy Tan. First appeared in *The Threepenny Review*. Reprinted by permission of the author and the Sandra Dijkstra Literary Agency.

Wasserstrom, Jeffrey, N. "A Mickey Mouse Approach to Globalization: Global icons can have very different local meanings." Used by Permission of the Yale Center for the Study of Globalization.

Young, Kimberly. "Understanding online gaming addiction and treatment issues for adolescents." *American Journal of Family Therapy*, 37(5), 355–372. 2009.

Zinsser, William. "College Pressures." Copyright © 1979 by William K. Zinsser. Reprinted by permission of the author. Originally appeared in *Blair & Ketchum's Country Journal*, Vol. VI, No. 4, April 1979.

Zwieg, Erica. "Party with a Purpose." Reproduced by permission of the author.

Photo Credits

Index